Psalms Volume II

THE CROSSWAY CLASSIC COMMENTARIES

Volume II

Psalms

by
Charles Spurgeon

Series Editors
Alister McGrath and J. I. Packer

CROSSWAY BOOKS
WHEATON, ILLINOIS

Psalms Volume II

Published by Crossway
1300 Crescent Street
Wheaton, Illinois 60187

Art Direction: Mark Schramm

First printing, 1993

Printed in the UK by 4edge Limited

ISBN-13: 978-0-89107-740-4
ISBN-10: 0-89107-740-5
PDF ISBN: 978-1-4335-3215-3
Mobipocket ISBN: 978-1-4335-3216-0
ePub ISBN: 978-1-4335-3217-7

Library of Congress Cataloging-in-Publication Data
Spurgeon, C. H. (Charles Haddon), 1834–1892.
    Psalms / by Charles H. Spurgeon.
        p.   cm. — (Crossway classic commentaries)
    ISBN 13: 978-0-89107-740-4
    ISBN 10: 0-89107-739-1 (v. 1). — ISBN 0-89107-740-5 (v. 2).
    1. Bible. O.T. Psalms—Commentaries. I. Bible. O.T. Psalms. English.
Authorized. 1993. II. Title. III. Series.
BS1430.3.S685   1993
223'.207—dc20   93–25952

Crossway is a publishing ministry of Good News Publishers.

CH		23	22	21	20	19	18	17	16	15	14	13
22	21	20	19	18	17	16	15	14	13	12	11	10

Contents of Volume II

Series Preface

The purpose of the Crossway Classic Commentaries is to make some of the most valuable commentaries on the books of the Bible, by some of the greatest Bible teachers and theologians in the last five hundred years, available to a new generation. These books will help today's readers learn truth, wisdom, and devotion from such authors as J. C. Ryle, Martin Luther, John Calvin, J. B. Lightfoot, John Owen, Charles Spurgeon, Charles Hodge, and Matthew Henry.

We do not apologize for the age of some of the items chosen. In the realm of practical exposition promoting godliness, the old is often better than the new. Spiritual vision and authority, based on an accurate handling of the biblical text, are the qualities that have been primarily sought in deciding what to include.

So far as is possible, everything is tailored to the needs and enrichment of thoughtful readers — lay Christians, students, and those in the ministry. The originals, some of which were written at a high technical level, have been abridged as needed, simplified stylistically, and unburdened of foreign words. However, the intention of this series is never to change any thoughts of the original authors, but to faithfully convey them in an understandable fashion.

The publishers are grateful to Dr. Alister McGrath of Wycliffe Hall, Oxford, Dr. J. I. Packer of Regent College, Vancouver, and Watermark of Norfolk, England, for the work of selecting and editing that now brings this project to fruition.

The Publishers
Crossway Books
Wheaton, Illinois

Introduction

In C. H. Spurgeon's own day he was not thought of as a scholarly man. Because he was a popular preacher, fulfilling a marvelous evangelistic and nurturing ministry to ordinary people; because his writings, too, were addressed to ordinary people rather than academics; because he was a Dissenter, belonging to a minority culture in Anglican-dominated England; because the stereotype of a Dissenter was of an uncultured boor, whose forthrightness betokened crudity of mind; because Spurgeon himself had never attended a university or theological college; and because he resisted supposedly enlightened and progressive trends (the acceptance of Darwinism and the fallibility of the Bible; the denial of a penal atonement and the eternal punishment of the lost), he was often dismissed, even by admirers of his preaching, as a brash upstart for challenging the wisdom of the learned and as a myopic dinosaur for proffering the old paths.

Yet he was a bookworm from childhood, and a diligent student all his life. He was an amazingly rapid reader, with a photographic memory, virtually total recall, and as he put it "a shelf in my mind" for storing every fact with a view to its future use. Each week he would work his way through a number of books—major treatments of scientific, historical, and philosophical questions. He had 30,000 volumes of every kind (save fiction) in his personal library, and claimed to know the contents of them all. The stereotypes of Spurgeon as a brash ignoramus cannot be sustained either from his lifestyle or from his words. His limpid, thought-laden rhetoric came from a shrewd, mature, extremely well-stocked mind.

Is his exposition of the Psalms then a scholarly work? James Stalker, a Scottish scholar-preacher who was Spurgeon's younger contemporary, spoke to that question as follows:

> For many years it has been my wont, week after week . . . to read over his commentary on the Psalms along with the best and most learned commentaries in existence. . . . That is the best test, and the severest test. . . . Mr. Spurgeon stands the test well. Not only do you everywhere feel the presence of a vigorous and vigilant mind, and a heart in thorough sympathy with the spirit of the Psalms; but . . . I have often been perfectly astonished to observe how, without any parade of learning, he shows himself to be thoroughly acquainted with the results of the most advanced scholarship; and the truth is that there is scarcely a point in the Psalms of real importance—scarcely a point on which scholarship can give us anything of real importance—as to which there are not sufficient hints to the intelligent reader in Mr. Spurgeon's work.

High praise? Definitely! Just praise? I think so. And the devotional, worshipful tone of Spurgeon's exposition give us something that "the best and most learned commentaries" do not always provide. Spurgeon on the Psalms has indeed classic status. I trust you will enjoy this second volume of it.

J. I. PACKER

Preface

by
C. H. Spurgeon

The delightful study of the Psalms has yielded me boundless profit and ever-growing pleasure; common gratitude constrains me to communicate to others a portion of the benefit, with the prayer that it may induce them to search further for themselves. That I have nothing better of my own to offer upon this peerless book is to me matter of deepest regret; that I have anything whatever to present is subject for devout gratitude to the Lord of grace. I have done my best, but, conscious of many defects, I heartily wish I could have done better.

The exposition here given is my own. I consulted a few authors before penning it, to aid me in interpretation and arouse my thoughts; but, still I can claim originality for my comments, at least so I honestly think. Whether they are better or worse for that, I know not; at least I know I have sought heavenly guidance while writing them, and therefore I look for a blessing on the printing of them.

In commenting upon some of them, I have been overwhelmed with awe, and said with Jacob, "How dreadful is this place, it is none other than the house of God." Especially was this the case with Psalm 51; I postponed expounding it week after week, feeling more and more my inability for the work. Often I sat down to it, and rose up again without having penned a line. It is a bush burning with fire yet not consumed, and out of it a voice seemed to cry to me, "Draw not nigh hither, put off thy shoes from off thy feet." The psalm is very human, its cries and sobs are of one born of woman; but it is freighted with an inspiration all divine, as if the great Father were putting words into his child's mouth. Such a psalm may be wept over, absorbed into the soul, and exhaled again in devotion; but, commented on – ah! where is he who having attempted it can do other than blush at his defeat?

More and more is the conviction forced upon my heart that every man must traverse the territory of the Psalms himself if he would know what a goodly land they are. They flow with milk and honey, but not to strangers; they are only fertile to lovers of their hills and vales. None but the Holy Spirit can give a man the key to the Treasury of David; and even he gives it rather to experience than to study. Happy he who for himself knows the secret of the Psalms.

Some of them are specially notable, and have, therefore, been expounded and preached upon on all hands, but others remain almost untrodden ground in sacred literature. Where one author writes upon a portion of Scripture, all write, while other passages remain almost untouched. When I have found one sermon upon a passage, it has generally been easy to collect a score upon the same; preachers evidently run so much in ruts that they leave a large portion of the Scriptures without exposition. As most of the commentators upon the Psalms proceed in their work they become slovenly, and appear to write hurriedly and think superficially, either because they grow weary of their huge enterprise, or else because they have said their best things already. The lazy practice of referring to a parallel passage in a former psalm is continually carried out by commentators; or, what is rather worse, the writers fall into the habit of repeating, with scarce a variation of language, that which they have said before.

Our greatest trouble is occasioned by the fact that the expounders are not impartial, but spend all their love, or at least their energies, upon favorite portions of the sacred volume, passing by other passages with scarcely a remark, as if all Scripture were not equally inspired. Why should so much be written upon Psalm 116 and so little upon 118? Here and there is a passage everybody seems to have written or spoken upon, but having passed through these few frequented places we have had to travel along an untrodden road. Of many a text we have had to sigh, "Few there be that find it." We are writing of the Psalms, the best read portion of the Old Testament, and therefore the fact is the more singular. We have thousands of writers, of one kind or another, but they go in flocks, like sheep, traversing only the same texts and passages. For want of a conscientious effort to expound the whole of Scripture, much of it lies as little considered as if it had never been written for our instruction.

I have been bewildered in the expanse of Psalm 119. Its dimensions and its depth alike overcame me. It spread itself out before me like a vast, rolling prairie, to which I could see no bound, and this alone created a feeling of dismay. It expanse was unbroken by a bluff or headland, and hence it threatened a monotonous task, although the fear has not been realized. This marvelous poem seemed to me a great sea of holy teaching, moving, in its many verses, wave upon wave; altogether without an island of special and remarkable statement to break it up. I confess I hesitated much to launch upon it. Other psalms have been mere lakes, but this is the main ocean. It is a continent of sacred thought, every inch of which is fertile as the garden of the Lord: it is an amazing level of abundance, a mighty stretch of harvest fields. I have now crossed the great plain for myself, but not without persevering, and, I will add, pleasurable, toil. Several great authors have traversed this region and left their tracks behind them, and so far the journey has been all the easier for me; but yet to me and to my helpers it has been no mean feat of patient authorship and research. This great psalm is a book in itself: instead of being one among many psalms, it is worthy to be set forth by itself as a poem of surpassing excellence. Those who have never studied it may pronounce it commonplace, and complain of its repetitions; but to the thoughtful student it is like the great deep, full, so as never to be measured; and varied, so as never to weary the eye. Its depth is as great as its length; it is mystery, not set forth as mystery, but concealed beneath the simplest statements; may I say that it is experience allowed to prattle, to preach, to praise, and to pray like a child-prophet in his own father's house?

We have desired to complete this work at our best, and not to allow the close of it to exhibit signs of fatigue and decline. We have often sat down to write our comment upon a psalm, and have risen from the task because we did not feel at home at it. It is of no use compelling the mind; its productions in such a case are like forced fruits, disappointing and devoid of flavor. We like to write after the manner of John Bunyan, who said, "As I pulled, it came," and we prefer that the pulling should be as gentle as possible. So it has happened that we have lingered for months over a psalm, feeling quite unfit to enter upon it. The grand cosmos of Psalm 104 was not to be dismissed in a few days; even now, after laying our best efforts at its feet, we feel dissatisfied with the poor result. However, we have done our best, and have grappled honestly with all hard places. It must be more useful to give hints for the interpretation of passages which have been neglected than merely to present our readers with what they could easily have found for themselves. Reflecting upon this, we thank God and take courage.

We cannot but express our sense of the superficiality of the best and most laborious of comments when compared with the bottomless depths of the sacred Word, nor can we refrain from uttering our growing conviction that the Scriptures possess a verbal as well as a plenary inspiration; indeed, we are quite unable to see how they could have the one without the other. So much of the meaning dwells in the turn of an expression, the tense of a verb, or the number of a noun that we believe in the inspiration of the words themselves; certainly the words are the things *written,* and the only things that can be written – for the refined spirit of a passage is not the creature of pen and ink. "It is written" must of necessity apply to words, for only words are written. Those words which the Holy Spirit teaches are, however, by no means to be regarded as mere words, for besides their office of conserving the inner meaning, as the shell preserves the mystic germ within the egg, they are themselves spirit and life. From all of them we gather quickening, and they breathe fire into our souls.

May the enlightening Spirit rest upon all students of the Psalms, and grant them to see far more deeply into the hidden meaning of these sacred hymns than we have been enabled to do. We rise from our perusal of each holy passage abashed at our own short-sightedness, and almost overwhelmed at our temerity in having desired to undertake such a work. May he who accepteth us according to what a man hath, and not according to what he hath not, bless our unworthy labors to his own glory, for Christ's sake.

I trust that the Holy Spirit has been with me in writing these expositions, and therefore I expect that he will bless them both to the conversion of the unrenewed and to the edification of believers. The writing of this book has been a means of grace to my own heart; I have enjoyed for myself what I have prepared for my readers. The Book of Psalms has been a royal banquet to me, and in feasting upon its contents I have seemed to eat angels' food. It is no wonder that old writers should call it the school of patience, the soul's soliloquies, the little Bible, the anatomy of conscience, the rose garden, the pearl island, and the like. It is the Paradise of devotion, the Holy Land of poesy, the heart of Scripture, the map of experience, and the tongue of saints. Does it not say just what we wished to say? Are not its prayers and praises exactly such as our hearts delight in?

It is to be feared that the Psalms are by no means so prized as in earlier ages of the Church. Even Councils of the Church have decreed that none should hold ecclesiastical office unless they knew the whole psalter by heart. These sacred hymns express all modes of holy feeling; they are fit both for childhood and old age: they furnish maxims for the entrance of life, and serve as watchwords at the gates of death. The Book of Psalms instructs us in the use of wings as well as words: it sets us both mounting and singing. Often have I ceased my commenting upon the text, that I might rise with the psalm, and gaze upon visions of God. If I may only hope that these volumes will be as useful to other hearts in the readings as to mine in the writing, I shall be well rewarded by the prospect.

In these busy days, it would be greatly to the spiritual profit of Christians if they were more familiar with the Book of Psalms, in which they would find a complete armory for life's battles, and a perfect supply for life's needs. Here we have both delight and usefulness, consolation and instruction. For every condition there is a psalm, suitable and elevating. The Book supplies the babe in grace with penitent cries, and the perfected saint with triumphant songs. Its breadth of experience stretches from the jaws of hell to the gate of heaven.

We hope that when the author sleeps with his fathers, the libraries of his brethren will remain enriched, and other minds will be assisted in setting forth the infinite fullness of this incomparable portion of the Word of God.

C. H. SPURGEON
(1834–1892)

Expositions

Psalm 86

1. Bow down thine ear, O Lord, hear me. When our prayers are lowly by reason of our humility, or feeble by reason of our sickness, or without wing by reason of our despondency, the Lord will bow down to them. Faith, when she has the loftiest name of God on her tongue, and calls him Jehovah, yet dares to ask from him the most tender and condescending acts of love. Great as he is he loves his children to be bold with him. **For I am poor and needy.** Our distress is a forcible reason for our being heard by the Lord God, merciful, and gracious, for misery is ever the master argument with mercy. Such reasoning as this would never be adopted by a proud man. Of all despicable sinners those are the worst who use the language of spiritual poverty while they think themselves to be rich and increased in goods.

2. Preserve my soul. Let my life be safe from my enemies, and my spiritual nature be secure from their temptations. **For I am holy.** I am set apart for holy uses; therefore do not let thine enemies commit a sacrilege by injuring or defiling me: I am clear of the crimes laid to my charge, and in that sense innocent; therefore, I beseech thee, do not allow me to suffer from unjust charges; and I am gentle towards others, therefore deal mercifully with me as I have dealt with my fellow-men. Any of these renderings may explain the text; perhaps all together will expound it best. It is not self-righteous in good people to plead their innocence as a reason for escaping from the results of sins wrongfully ascribed to them; penitents do not bedaub themselves with mire for the love of it, or make themselves out to be worse than they are. To plead guilty to offenses we have never committed is as great a lie as the denial of our real faults. **O thou my God, save thy servant that trusteth in thee.** Lest anyone should suppose that David trusted in his own holiness he immediately declared his trust in the Lord, and begged to be saved as one who was not holy in the sense of being perfect, but was even yet in need of the very elements of salvation. How sweet is the title **my God** when joined to the other, **thy servant**; and how sweet is the hope that on this ground we shall be saved. Note how David's poor **I am** (or rather the **I** repeated without the) appeals to the great I AM with sacred boldness engendered by necessity, aided by the faith which removes mountains.

3. Be merciful to me, O Lord. The best people need mercy, and appeal to mercy. **For I cry unto thee daily.** Is there not a promise that importunity will prevail? He who prays every day, and all the day, for so the word may mean, may rest assured that the Lord will hear him. If we cried sometimes to man, or other false confidences, we might expect to be referred to them in the hour of our calamity, but if in all former times we have looked to the Lord alone, we may be sure that he will not desert us now.

4. Rejoice the soul of thy servant. Make my heart glad, for I count it my

1

honor to call myself thy servant, and I reckon thy favor to be all the wages I could desire. I look for all my happiness in thee only, and therefore **unto thee, O Lord, do I lift up my soul.** Thou art as the brazen serpent to my sick nature, and I lift up my soul's eye to thee that I may live. I know that the nearer I am to thee the greater is my joy; therefore be pleased to draw me nearer while I am laboring to draw near. It needs a strong shoulder at the wheel when a heart sticks in the miry clay of despondency; but the Lord will take the will for the deed, and come in with a hand of almighty grace to raise his poor servant out of the earth and up to heaven.

5. For thou, Lord, art good, and ready to forgive. Good at giving and forgiving; supplying us with *his* good, and removing *our* evil. Some men who would be considered good are so self-exaltingly indignant at the injuries done them by others that they cannot forgive; but the better a being is, the more willing he is to forgive, and the best and highest of all is ever ready to blot out the transgressions of his creatures. **And plenteous in mercy unto all them that call upon thee.** God does not dispense his mercy from a store so impoverished as to give out altogether, but his goodness flows abundantly. In two places in this psalm David almost quotes word for word the passage in Exodus 34:6.

6. Give ear, O LORD, unto my prayer. Even the glory which his spirit had beheld did not withdraw him from his prayer, but rather urged him to be more fervent in it; hence he implores the Lord to hear his requests. Note the expression **the voice of my supplications,** as if they were not all voice but were partly inarticulate noise, yet amid much that was superfluous there really was an inner meaning which was the heart's intention. This he would have the Lord sift out from the chaff, and hear amid the mingled din. May our soul's intent always give our prayers a live core of meaning.

7. A pious resolve backed by a judicious reason. It is useless to cry to those who cannot or will not hear. Our experience confirms us in the belief that Jehovah the living God really does aid those who call upon him, and therefore we pray because we really find it to be a practical and effectual means of obtaining help from God in the hour of need. There can be no reason for praying if there be no expectation of the Lord's answering.

8. Among the gods there is none like unto thee, O Lord. There are gods by delegated office, such as kings and magistrates, but they are as nothing in the presence of Jehovah; there are also gods by the nomination of superstition, but these are vanity itself, and cannot be compared with the living and true God. **Neither are there any works like unto thy works.** What have the false gods ever made or unmade? What miracles have they wrought?

9. All nations whom thou hast made, and these include all mankind, since they all come of the first Adam, thy creature, and their lives are all distinct creations of thine omnipotence. All these **shall come** with penitent hearts, in thine own way, to thine own self, **and worship before thee, O Lord.** Because thou art

2

thus above all gods, people will at last discover thy greatness, and will render thee the worship which is thy due. This was David's reason for resorting to the Lord in trouble. It makes us content to be in the minority today, when we are sure that the majority will be with us tomorrow. David was not a believer in the theory that the world will grow worse and worse, and that the dispensation will wind up with general darkness and idolatry. We look for a day when the dwellers in all lands worship thee alone, O God, **and shall glorify thy name.**

10. **For thou art great.** It is only in the Divine Being that either greatness or goodness exists absolutely, and essentially. To be great and not good might lead to tyranny in the King, and for him to be good and not great might involve countless calamities. **And doest wondrous things.** Being good, he is said to be ready to forgive; being great, he works wonders; we may blend the two, for there is no wonder so wonderful as the pardon of our transgressions. Even the commonest daisy is a marvel, and a pebble enshrines wisdom. Only to fools is anything which God has made uninteresting. Note that the verb **doest** is in the present: the Lord is doing wondrous things, they are transpiring before our eyes. Look upon the bursting buds of spring or the maturing fruits of autumn, gaze on the sky or skim the sea, mark the results of providence and the victories of grace. **Thou art God alone.** Our God is not to be worshiped as one among many good and true beings, but as God alone; his gospel is not to be preached as one of several saving systems, but as the sole way of salvation.

11. **Teach me thy way, O Lord.** Instruct me thus at all times, but teach me now especially since I am in trouble and perplexity. Show me the way which thy wisdom and mercy have prepared for my escape. Not *my* way give me, but **thy** way teach me; I would follow thee and not be willfull. **I will walk in thy truth.** When taught I will practice what I know; truth will not be a mere doctrine or sentiment to me, but a matter of daily life.

Unite my heart to fear thy name. Having taught me one way, give me one heart to walk therein, for too often I feel two natures contending. God who created the bands of our nature can draw them together, tighten, strengthen, and fasten them, and so we shall be powerful for good, but not otherwise.

12. **I will praise thee, O Lord my God, with all my heart.** Praise should never be rendered with less than all our heart, and soul, and strength, or it will be both unreal and unacceptable. This is the second time in the psalm that David calls the Lord **my God**; the first time he was in an agony of prayer (verse 2), and now he is in an ecstasy of praise. If anything can make a man pray and praise, it is the knowledge that the Lord is his God. **And I will glorify thy name for evermore.** God has never done blessing us; let us never have done blessing him.

13. **For great is thy mercy toward me.** Personal experience is ever the master singer. Whatever thou art to others, to me thy mercy is most notable. **And thou hast delivered my soul from the lowest hell.** David had been kept by God, for his enemies would have done more than send him to hell had they been able.

His sense of sin also made him feel as if the most overwhelming destruction would have been his portion had not grace prevented. There are some alive now who can use this language unfeignedly, and he who pens these lines most humbly confesses that he is one. Left to myself to indulge my passions, to rush onward with my natural vehemence, what a candidate for the lowest abyss should I have made myself by this time.

The psalmist here again touches a bold and joyful note, but soon he exchanges it for the mournful song.

14. O God, the proud are risen against me. His walk with God was as smoke to their eyes, and therefore they determined to destroy him. **And the assemblies of violent men have sought after my soul.** They hunted in packs, with keen scent, and eager foot. **And have not set thee before them.** They would not have molested the servant if they had cared for the Master. Those who fear not God are not afraid to commit violent and cruel acts.

15. But thou, O Lord. What a contrast! We get away from the blusterings of proud but puny people to the glory and goodness of the Lord. **Art a God full of compassion, and gracious, long-suffering, and plenteous in mercy and truth.** A truly glorious doxology, mainly from Exodus 34:6. Here is compassion for the weak and sorrowing, grace for the undeserving, long-suffering for the provoking, mercy for the guilty, and truth for the tried. Are we sorrowful? We find the Lord full of compassion. Are we contending with temptation? His grace comes to our aid. Do we err? He is patient with us. Have we sinned? He is plenteous in mercy. Are we resting on his promise? He will fulfill it with abundant truth.

16. O turn unto me. One turn of God's face will turn all our darkness into day. **And have mercy upon me.** That is all he asks, for he is lowly in heart; that is all he wants, for mercy answers all a sinner's needs. **Give thy strength unto thy servant.** Gird me with it that I may serve thee; guard me with it that I may not be overcome. When the Lord gives us his own strength we are sufficient for all emergencies, and have no cause to fear any adversaries. **And save the son of thine handmaid.** As the sons of slaves were their master's property by their birth, so he gloried in being the son of a woman who herself belonged to the Lord. What others might think a degrading illustration he uses with delight, to show how intensely he loved the Lord's service.

17. Show me a token for good. Let me be assured of thy mercy by being delivered out of trouble. **That they which hate me may see it, and be ashamed.** What bodes good to me will make them quail and blush. Disappointed and defeated, the foes of the good man would feel ashamed of what they had designed. **Because thou, LORD, hast helped me, and comforted me.** God does nothing by halves; those whom he helps he also consoles, and so makes them not merely safe but joyful. Lord, deal thus with us evermore; so shall we glorify thee.

Psalm 87

1. His foundation is in the holy mountains. The psalm begins abruptly: the poet's heart was full, and it gained a vent on a sudden. Sudden passion is evil, but bursts of holy joy are most precious. God has chosen to found his earthly temple upon the mountains. The church, which is the mystical Jerusalem, is founded not on the sand of carnal policy, nor in the morass of human kingdoms, but on Jehovah's Godhead. The church is the chief of all his works.

2. The gates are put for the city itself. The love of God is greatest to his own elect nation. God delights in the prayers and praises of Christian families and individuals, but he has a special eye to the assemblies of the faithful. The great festivals, when the crowds surrounded the temple gates, were fair in the Lord's eyes, and this should lead each separate believer to identify with the church of God; where the Lord reveals his love the most, there should each believer most delight to be found.

3. Glorious things are spoken of thee, O city of God. This is true of Jerusalem. It is yet more true of the church. We may glory in her without being braggarts; she has a luster which none can rival. Never let thy praises cease, O bride of Christ, in whom the Lord himself has placed his delight, calling you by that pearl of names, Hephzibah – "for my delight is in her." The years to come will unveil your beauties to the astonished eyes of all peoples. **Selah.** With the prospect of a world converted, and the most implacable foes transformed into friends, it was fitting that the psalmist should pause.

4. I will make mention of Rahab and Babylon to them that know me. Zion's old foes are new-born and have become her friends, worshiping in the temple of her God. Some consider that these are the words of God himself, and should be rendered, "I will mention Rahab and Babylon as knowing me," but we feel content with our common version, and attribute the words to the psalmist himself, who anticipates the conversion of the two great rival nations and speaks of it with exultation. **Behold Philistia, and Tyre, with Ethiopia.** These also are to bow before the Lord. **This man was born there.** That is, this nation has been born into Zion, regenerated into the church of God. The new births of nations it is at once a great blessing and a great wonder.

Many understand the sense of these verses to be that all people are proud of their native country, and so also is the citizen of Zion. The passage is not so clear that anyone should become dogmatic as to its meaning, but we prefer the interpretation given above.

5. And of Zion, it shall be said, This and that man was born in her. Not as nations only, but one by one, as individuals, the citizens of the New Jerusalem will be counted, and their names publicly declared. The individual will not be lost in the mass, but each one will be of high account. The original, by using the noblest word for man, intimates that many remarkable men will be born

5

in the church, and indeed everyone who is renewed in the image of Christ is an eminent personage, while there are some who, even to the dim eyes of the world, shine with a luster of character which cannot but be admitted to be unusual and admirable. **And the highest himself shall establish her.** When the numbers of the faithful are increased by the new birth, the Lord proves himself to be higher than all those who are against us.

6. At the great census which the Lord himself takes, he will number the nations without exception. Jehovah's census of his chosen will differ much from ours; he will count many whom we should have disowned, and he will leave out many whom we should have reckoned. Let us pray for the adoption and regeneration which will secure us a place among the heaven-born.

7. In vision the psalmist sees the citizens of Zion rejoicing at some sacred festival, and marching in triumphant procession with vocal and instrumental music. **As well the singers as the players on instruments shall be there.** Where God is there must be joy, and where the church is increased by numerous conversions the joy becomes exuberant and finds out ways of displaying itself. **All my springs are in thee.** Did the poet mean that henceforth he would find all his joys in Zion, or that to the Lord he would look for all inspiration? The last is the truest doctrine. The Lord who founded the church is the eternal source of all our supplies.

Psalm 88

1. O LORD God of my salvation. This is a hopeful title by which to address the Lord, and it has about it the only ray of comfortable light which shines throughout the psalm. The writer has salvation, he is sure of that, and God is the sole author of it. While a person can see God as his Saviour, it is not altogether midnight with him. **I have cried day and night before thee.** His distress had not blown out the sparks of his prayer, but quickened them till they burned perpetually like a furnace at full blast. His prayer was personal; it was intensely earnest, so that it was correctly described as a cry, such as children utter to move the pity of their parents; and it was unceasing – neither the business of the day nor the weariness of the night had silenced it; surely such intreaties could not be in vain. It is a good thing that sickness will not let us rest if we spend our restlessness in prayer. Evil is transformed to good when it drives us to prayer. **Before thee** is a remarkable intimation that the psalmist's cries had an aim and a direction towards the Lord, and were not the mere clamors of nature, but the groanings of a gracious heart towards Jehovah, the God of salvation.

2. Let my prayer come before thee. Admit it to an audience; let it speak with thee. Though it be *my* prayer, and therefore very imperfect, yet deny it not *thy* gracious consideration. **Incline thine ear unto my cry.** There may be obstacles which impede the upward flight of our prayers – let us intreat the Lord to remove them; and there may also be offenses which prevent the Lord from giving favorable regard to our requests – let us implore him to put these out of the way.

3. For my soul is full of troubles. Trouble in the soul is the soul of trouble. **And my life draweth nigh unto the grave.** All his life was going, spiritual, mental, bodily. Some of us can enter into this experience, for many a time have we traversed this valley of death-shade, and dwelt in it by the month together. Really to die and be with Christ will be a gala day's enjoyment compared with our misery when a worse than physical death has cast its dreadful shadow over us. Are good people ever permitted to suffer thus? Indeed they are; and some of them are even all their lifetime subject to bondage. O Lord, let none of thy mourners imagine that a strange thing has happened unto him, but rejoice as he sees the footprints of brethren who have trodden this desert before.

4. I am counted with them that go down into the pit. My weakness is so great that both by myself and others I am considered as good as dead. If those about me have not ordered my coffin they have at least conversed about my sepulchre, discussed my estate, and reckoned their share of it. **I am as a man that hath no strength.** My constitution is broken up; I can scarce crawl about my sick room, my mind is even weaker than my body, and my faith weakest of all. The sons and daughters of sorrow will need but little explanation of these sentences; they are to such tried ones as household words.

5. Free among the dead. Unbound from all that links a person with life, a freeman of the city of the sepulchre, I seem no more one of earth's drudges. **Like the slain that lie in the grave, whom thou rememberest no more.** He felt as if he were as utterly forgotten as those whose carcasses are left to rot on the battlefield. It is all very well for those who are in robust health and full of spirits to blame those whose lives are sicklied o'er with the pale cast of melancholy, but the evil is as real as a gaping wound, and all the more hard to bear because it lies so much in the region of the soul that to the inexperienced it appears to be a mere matter of fancy and diseased imagination. Never ridicule the nervous and hypochondriacal; their pain is real; though much of the evil lies in the imagination, it is not imaginary. **And they are cut off from thy hand.** He mourned that the hand of the Lord had gone out against him, and that he was divided from the great author of his life. Men's blows are trifles, but God's smitings are terrible to a gracious heart.

6. What a collection of forcible metaphors, each one expressive of the utmost grief. The flesh can bear only a certain number of wounds and no more, but the soul can bleed in ten thousand ways, and die over and over again each hour. It is grievous to the good man to see the Lord whom he loves laying him in the sepulchre of despondency; evil from so good a hand seems evil

7

indeed, and yet if faith could but be allowed to speak she would remind the depressed spirit that it is better to fall into the hand of the Lord than into the hands of man, and moreover she would tell the despondent heart that God never placed a Joseph in a pit without drawing him up again to fill a throne: that he never caused a horror of great darkness to fall upon an Abraham without revealing his covenant to him. Alas, when under deep depression the mind forgets all this; it is only conscious of its unutterable misery. It is an unspeakable consolation that our Lord Jesus knows this experience, right well, having, with the exception of the sin, felt it all and more than all in Gethsemane when he was exceedingly sorrowful even unto death.

7. **Thy wrath lieth hard upon me.** Dreadful plight this, the worst in which a man can be found. Joy or peace, or even numbness of indifference, there can be none to one who is loaded with this most tremendous of burdens. **And thou hast afflicted me with all thy waves,** or "all thy breakers." He pictures God's wrath as breaking over him like those waves of the sea which swell, and rage, and dash with fury upon the shore. It appeared impossible for him to suffer more; he had exhausted the methods of adversity and endured *all* its waves. So have we imagined, and yet it is not really quite so bad. God has other and more terrible waves which, if he chose to let them forth, would sweep us into the infernal abyss, whence hope has long since been banished. **Selah.** There was need to rest. Even lamentation must have its pauses.

8. **Thou hast put away mine acquaintance far from me.** If ever we need friends it is in the dreary hour of despondency and the weary time of bodily sickness. **Thou hast made me an abomination unto them.** They turned from him as though he had become loathsome and contaminating, and this because of something which the Lord had done to him; therefore, he brings his complaint to the prime mover in his trouble. **I am shut up, and I cannot come forth.** He was a prisoner in his room, and felt like a condemned criminal in his cell. When God shuts friends out, and shuts us in to pine away alone, it is no wonder if we water our couch with tears.

9. **Mine eye mourneth by reason of affliction.** Tears in showers are a blessing, and work our good; but in floods they become destructive and injurious. **LORD, I have called daily upon thee.** He prayed still, though no answer came to dry his eyes. Nothing can make a true believer cease praying; it is a part of his nature, and pray he must. **I have stretched out my hands unto thee.** As a little child stretches out its hands to its mother while it cries.

10. **Wilt thou show wonders to the dead?** While I live thou canst in me display the glories of thy grace, but when I have passed into the unknown land, how canst thou illustrate in me thy love? **Shall the dead arise and praise thee?** True, the souls of departed saints render glory to God, but the dejected psalmist's thoughts do not mount to heaven but survey the gloomy grave: he stays on this side of eternity, where in the grave he sees no wonders and hears no

songs. **Selah**. At the mouth of the tomb he sits down to meditate, and then returns to his theme.

11. Shall thy lovingkindness be declared in the grave? The dead know nothing, and therefore can declare nothing. **Or thy faithfulness in destruction?** If the Lord let his servant die before the divine promise was fulfilled, it would be quite impossible for his faithfulness to be proclaimed. The poet is dealing with this life only; if a believer were deserted and permitted to die in despair, there could come no voice from his grave to inform mankind that the Lord had rectified his wrongs and relieved him of his trials.

12. Shall thy wonders be known in the dark? If not here permitted to prove the goodness of Jehovah, how could the singer do so in the land of darkness and deathshade? **And thy righteousness in the land of forgetfulness?** Where memory and love are lost, what witness to the divine holiness can be borne? If the believer dies unblessed, how will God's honor be preserved?

13. But unto thee have I cried, O Lord. I have continued to pray for help to thee, even though thou hast so long delayed to answer. A true-born child of God may be known by his continuing to cry; a hypocrite is great at a spurt, but the genuine believer holds on till he wins his suit. **And in the morning shall my prayer prevent thee.** He intended to begin to pray before the sun was up. If the Lord is pleased to delay, he has a right to do as he wills, but we must not therefore become tardy in supplication.

14. Lord, why castest thou off my soul? Hast thou not aforetime chosen me? Can thy beloveds become thy cast-offs? **Why hidest thou thy face from me?** Wilt thou not so much as look upon me? Canst thou not afford me a solitary smile? We may put these questions to the Lord. It is not undue familiarity, but holy boldness. It may help us to remove the evil which provokes the Lord to jealousy, if we seriously beg him to show us wherefore he contends with us. He cannot act towards us in other than a right and gracious manner; therefore for every stroke of his rod there is a sufficient reason in the judgment of his loving heart; let us try to learn that reason and profit by it.

15. I am afflicted and ready to die from my youth up. His affliction had now lasted so long that he could hardly remember when it commenced. There are holy men and women whose lives are a long apprenticeship to patience, and these deserve our sympathy and our reverence – for since the Saviour became the acquaintance of grief, sorrow has become honorable in believers' eyes.

While I suffer thy terrors I am distracted. God's terrors had become more overwhelming and had driven the man to despair. He could not judge and weigh his own condition in a calm and rational manner. Sickness alone will thus distract the mind; and when a sense of divine anger is added thereto, it is not to be wondered at if reason finds it hard to hold the reins. How near akin to madness the soul-depression sometimes may be, it is not our province to decide; but we speak what we do know when we say that a featherweight

9

might be sufficient to turn the scale at times. You who yet retain your reason, thank God that the devil himself cannot add that feather while the Lord stands by to adjust all things.

16. Thy fierce wrath goeth over us. No punitive anger ever falls upon the saved one, for Jesus shields him from it all; but a father's anger may fall upon his dearest child, because he loves it. **Thy terrors have cut me off.** They have made me feel like a leper separated from the congregation of thy people. Blessed be God, this is the sufferer's idea and not the very truth, for the Lord will neither cast off nor cut off his people.

17. They came round about me daily like water. Such is the permeating power of spiritual distress, there is no shutting it out. **They compassed me about together.** He was like the deer in the hunt, when the dogs are all around and at his throat. And yet he was a man greatly beloved of heaven!

18. Lover and friend hast thou put far from me. Even when they are near me bodily, they are so unable to swim with me in such deep waters that they stand like people far away on the shore while I am buffeted with the billows; alas, the dearest lover of all is afraid of such a distracted one. The Lord Jesus knew the meaning of this when in his passion. Lonely sorrow falls to the lot of not a few; let them not repine, but enter herein into close communion with that dearest lover and friend who is never far from his tried ones. **And mine acquaintance into darkness,** or better still, "my acquaintance is darkness." I am familiar only with sadness; all else has vanished. I am a child crying alone in the dark. Will the Heavenly Father leave his child there?

We have not attempted to interpret this psalm concerning our Lord, but we fully believe that where the members are, the Head is to be seen preeminently.

Psalm 89

1. I will sing of the mercies of the LORD forever. Whatever we may observe about us or experience in our own persons, we ought still to praise God for his mercies, since they most certainly remain the same, whether we can perceive them or not. We are not only to believe the Lord's goodness, but to rejoice in it evermore. We have not one, but many **mercies** to rejoice in, and should therefore multiply the expressions of our thankfulness. It is *Jehovah* who deigns to deal out to us our daily benefits; he blesses it with eternal mercies – let us sing unto him **forever. With my mouth will I make known thy faithfulness to all generations.** The mouth has a warmer manner than the pen, but the pen's speech lives longest, and is heard farther and wider. Note that in this second sentence he speaks of **faithfulness.** The grace of an unfaithful God would be a poor subject for music, but unchangeable love and immutable promises demand everlasting songs. In times of trouble it is the divine faithfulness which the soul hangs upon. It will also be always desirable to make it known, for people are too apt to forget it, or to doubt it, when hard times press upon them. Skeptics are so ready to repeat old doubts and invent new ones that believers should be equally prompt to bring forth evidences both old and new.

2. For I have said, Mercy shall be built up forever. He was certain that upon a sure foundation the Lord intended to pile up a glorious palace of goodness – a house of refuge for all people, wherein the Son of David should forever be glorified as the dispenser of heavenly grace. **Thy faithfulness shalt thou establish in the very heavens.** God's faithfulness is no thing of earth, for here nothing is firm; come what will, mercy and faithfulness are built up by "the eternal Builder," and his own nature is the guarantee for their perpetuity. This is to be called to mind whenever the church is in trouble, or our spirits bowed.

3. I have made a covenant with my chosen, I have sworn unto David my servant. This was the ground of the psalmist's confidence in God's mercy and truth (2 Samuel 7). David was the Lord's elect, and with him a covenant was made which ran along in his seed until it received fulfillment in "the Son of David." In Christ there is a covenant established with all the Lord's **chosen**, and they are by grace led to be the Lord's "servants," and then are ordained kings and priests by Christ Jesus.

4. Thy seed will I establish forever. David must always have a seed, and truly in Jesus this is fulfilled beyond his hopes. **And build up thy throne to all generations.** David's dynasty never decays. Jesus is a king as well as a progenitor, and his throne is ever being built up – his kingdom comes – his power extends.

Thus runs the covenant; and when the church declines, it is ours to plead it before the ever-faithful God. The more gracious Christians are, the more will they be moved to jealousy by the sad estate of the Redeemer's cause, and the more will they argue the case with the great Covenant-maker. **Selah.** Let each syllable of the covenant ring in your ears; and then lift up the heart and proceed with the sacred poet to tell forth the praises of the Lord.

5. And the heavens shall praise thy wonders, O LORD. Looking down upon what God had done, and was about to do, in connection with his covenant of grace, all heaven would be filled with adoring wonder. **Thy faithfulness also in the congregation of the saints.** By which is probably intended the holy ones on earth. Saints above see most clearly into the heights and depths of divine love, therefore they praise its wonders; and saints below, being conscious of their many sins and multiplied provocations of the Lord, admire his faithfulness.

6. For who in the heaven can be compared unto the LORD? Therefore all heaven worships him, seeing none can equal him. **Who among the sons of the mighty can be likened unto the LORD?** Therefore the assemblies of the saints on earth adore him, seeing none rival him.

7. God is greatly to be feared in the assembly of his saints. The holiest tremble in the presence of the thrice Holy One. Perfect love casts out the fear which

11

has torment, and works that other fear which is akin to joy unutterable. How reverent should our worship be! Sin is akin to presumptuous boldness, but holiness is sister to holy fear. **And to be had in reverence of all them that are about him.** The nearer they are the more they adore. God's children are those who most earnestly pray, "hallowed be thy name." Irreverence is rebellion. Thoughts of the covenant of grace tend to create a deeper awe of God, and the more his glories are seen by us, the more humbly we prostrate ourselves before his majesty.

8. O LORD God of hosts, who is a strong Lord like unto thee? Or, "Jehovah, God of Hosts, who is like thee, Mighty Jah?" Here we have the name which displays his self-existence, the title which denotes his dominion over all his creatures, and an adjective which sets forth the power with which he exercises his sovereignty. Yet this great and terrible God has entered into covenant with men! Who would not reverence him with deepest love? **Or to thy faithfulness round about thee.** He dwells in faithfulness; it is said to be the girdle of the loins of his only-begotten Son, who is the express image of his person. People often fail in truth because their power is limited, and then they find it easier to break their word than to keep it; but the strong Jehovah is equal to all his engagements, and will assuredly keep them. Unrivaled might and unparalleled truth are wedded in the character of Jehovah.

9. Thou rulest the raging of the sea. Always, even in the hour of ocean's maddest fury, the Lord controls it. **When the waves thereof arise, thou stillest them.** So did the Lord's Anointed calm the storms of Galilee, for he is Lord of all; so also does the great Ruler of Providence evermore govern the fickle wills of people, and quiet their tumults. As a mother stills her babe to sleep, so that Lord calms the fury of the sea, the anger of people, the tempest of adversity, the despair of the soul, and the rage of hell.

10. Thou hast broken Rahab in pieces as one that is slain. Egypt was Israel's ancient foe, and its overthrow was a theme to which devout minds constantly reverted. We, too, have seen our Rahab broken, our sins o'erthrown, and we cannot but unite in praise to the Lord. **Thou hast scattered thine enemies with thy strong arm.** Thy strength has strewn thy foes dead upon the plain, or compelled them to flee. Proud Rahab was utterly broken and scattered.

11. The heavens are thine, the earth also is thine. All things are alike God's – rebellious earth as well as adoring heaven. Let us not despair of the kingdom of truth; the Lord has not abdicated the throne of earth or handed it over to the sway of Satan. **As for the world and the fullness thereof, thou hast founded them.** The habitable and cultivated earth, with all its produce, owns the Lord to be both its Creator and Sustainer, builder and upholder.

12. The north and the south thou hast created them. Opposite poles agree that Jehovah fashioned them. **Tabor and Hermon shall rejoice in thy name** – that is, east and west are equally formed by thee, and therefore give thee praise.

13. Thou hast a mighty arm. Omnipotence is thine in smiting or uplifting; **strong is thy hand** – thy power to create and grasp is beyond conception great; **and high is thy right hand** – thy skill is incomparable, thy favor ennobling, thy working glorious.

14. Justice and judgment are the habitation of thy throne. They are the basis of the divine government, the sphere within which his sovereignty moves. God as a sovereign is never unjust or unwise. He is too holy to be unrighteous, too wise to be mistaken; this is constant matter for joy to the upright in heart. **Mercy and truth shall go before thy face.** They are the harbingers and heralds of the Lord; he calls these to the front to deal with guilty and doubting people; he makes them, in the person of the Lord Jesus, to be his ambassadors, and so poor, guilty people are enabled to endure the presence of their righteous Lord.

15. Blessed is the people that know the joyful sound. They are a blessed people who partake of God's bounty, and know how to exult in his favor. The covenant promises have also a sound beyond measure precious, and they are highly favored who understand their meaning and recognize their own personal interest in them. **They shall walk, O LORD, in the light of thy countenance.** For them it is joy enough that Jehovah is favorable to them. If we give God our ear and hear the joyful sound, he will show us his face and make us glad. When the Lord smiles on us we live without grief as to our souls.

16. In thy name shall they rejoice all the day. To the soul which, in Christ Jesus, has entered into covenant with God, every attribute is a fountain of delight. We can rejoice without physical comforts; the Lord is an all-sufficient source of joy. **And in thy righteousness shall they be exalted.** By the Lord's righteous dealings the saints are uplifted in due time, however great the oppression and the depression from which they may have suffered. If God were unjust, or regarded us as being without righteousness, we must be filled with misery; but as neither of these things are so, we are exalted indeed.

17. For thou art the glory of their strength. He is our beauty and glory when we are strong in him, as well as our comfort and sustenance when we tremble because of conscious weakness in ourselves. No one whom the Lord makes strong may dare to glory in themselves, but must ascribe all honor to the Lord alone. **And in thy favor our horn shall be exalted.** By the use of the word **our** the psalmist identifies himself with the blessed people, and this indicates how much sweeter it is to sing in the first person than concerning others. The horn was an eastern ornament, worn by men and women, and by the uplifting of this the wearer showed himself to be in good spirits, and in a confident frame of mind: we wear no such outward vanities, but our inward soul is adorned and made bravely triumphant when the favor of God is felt by us. Worldly people need outward prosperity to make them lift up their heads, but the saints find more than enough encouragement in the secret love of God.

18. For the LORD is our defense. He is our ultimate Defender and Shield. **And**

13

the Holy One of Israel is our king. Kings are called the shields of nations, and the God of Israel is both our Ruler and our Defense. Another sense may be that Israel's defender and king was of the Lord, belonging to him and sent by him. The title **the Holy One of Israel** is especially delightful to the renewed heart. God is holiness itself, the only being who can be called **the Holy One.** He who is holy cannot break his promises, or act unjustly concerning his oath and covenant. Moreover, he is **the Holy One *of Israel,*** ours forever and ever.

19. **Then thou spakest in vision to thy holy one.** The holy one here meant may be either David or Nathan the prophet, but most probably the latter, for it was to him that the word of the Lord came by night (2 Samuel 7:4–5). God condescends to employ his gracious ministers to be the means of communication between himself and his favored ones. **I have lain help upon one that is mighty.** The Lord has made David a mighty man of valor, and now he covenants to make him the helper and defender of the Jewish state. In a far fuller sense the Lord Jesus is essentially and immeasurably mighty, and on him the salvation of his people rests by divine appointment. **I have exalted one chosen out of the people.** David was God's elect, elect out of the people, as one of themselves, and elect to the highest position in the state. In his extraction, election, and exaltation, he was a type of the Lord Jesus. Whom God exalts let us exalt.

20. **I have found David my servant.** David was discovered by the Lord among the sheepfolds and recognized as a man of gracious spirit, full of faith and courage, and therefore fit to be leader in Israel. **With my holy oil have I anointed him.** By the hand of Samuel, David was anointed to be king long before he ascended the throne. The verse must also be expounded of the Prince Emmanuel; he became the servant of the Lord for our sakes; upon him rested the Spirit without measure. Jesus is also the Lord's Christ, or anointed. The oil with which he is anointed is the Spirit of holiness.

21. **With whom my hand shall be established,** or, "with whom my hand shall ever be present." The almightiness of God abides permanently with Jesus as Redeemer and Ruler of his people. **Mine arm also shall strengthen him.** The fullness of divine power will attend him. This promise ought to be urged in prayer before the Lord, for the great lack of the church at this time is power.

22. **The enemy shall not exact upon him.** He will not be vexed and persecuted as a helpless debtor by an extortionate creditor. **Nor the son of wickedness afflict him.** Graceless people will no longer make his life a burden. David had striven to act justly towards Saul, because he was the Lord's anointed, yet Saul persecuted him relentlessly. The covenant, therefore, engaged that his life of hardship and oppression should come to an end forever; it did so in David's own person, and more remarkably still in the life of Solomon, his son. Who does not in all this see a type of the Lord Jesus, who though he was once seized for our debts, and also evilly treated by the ungodly, is now so exalted that he can never be exacted upon any more.

23. And I will beat down his foes before his face – crushing them and their plans. God himself thus fights the battles of his Son, and effectually overturns his foes. **And plague them that hate him,** or "smite his haters." May none of us learn the terror of this threatening, which is surely being fulfilled upon all those unbelievers who have rejected the Son of God, and died in the hardness of their hearts. The prophecy is also having another fulfilment in the overthrow of systems of error, and the vexation caused to their promoters.

24. But my faithfulness and my mercy shall be with him. To David and his descendants, God was gracious and faithful, and though through their sin the literal kingdom lost all its glory and the dynasty became obscure, yet the line remained unbroken and more than all its former glory was restored in Jesus. **And in my name shall his horn be exalted.** The fullest exaltation of the horn of Jesus is yet to come in that millennial period which is hastening on.

25. I will set his hand also in the sea, and his right hand in the rivers. He shall reach far beyond the little rivers which stand for boundaries in Palestine. His power is to be given him of the Lord, and is to be abiding; so we understand the words **I will set.** The verse has in it a voice of good cheer concerning sailors, and all dwellers on the waters; the hand of Jesus is over them.

26. He shall cry unto me, Thou art my father. David's descendants would be a praying race, and so in the main they were, and when they were not they smarted for it. The Lord Jesus was preeminent in prayer, and his favorite mode of address was "Father." **My God** – so our Lord called his Father when upon the cross. **And the rock of my salvation.** It was to his Father that he turned in Gethsemane, and to him he committed his spirit in death. To say to God **Thou art my father** is more than learning and talent can teach us; the new birth is essential to this.

27. Also I will make him my firstborn. Among the kings the descendants of David were to be most favored, but in Jesus we see this in the highest degree verified, for he has preeminence in all things, and is **higher than the kings of the earth.** Kings are honored when they honor him, and those who honor him are kings! In the millennial glory it will be seen what the covenant stores up for the once despised Son of David, but even now faith sees him exalted as King of kings and Lord of lords. Jesus is no servant of princes, nor would he have his bride, the church, degrade herself by bowing before kings.

28. My mercy will I keep for him for evermore. The kings of David's line needed mercy, and mercy prevented their house from utterly perishing until the Son of Mary came. He needs no mercy for himself, but he is a representative man, and the mercy of God is required for those who are in him. **And my covenant shall stand fast with him.** With Jesus the covenant is ratified by blood of sacrifice and by oath of God; it cannot be canceled or altered. The covenant of grace is *sure* to all the descendants, because it stands **fast with him** with whom we are indissolubly united.

29. His seed also will I make to endure forever. David's seed lives on in the Lord Jesus, and the seed of Jesus in believers. Saints are a race that neither death nor hell can kill. **And his throne as the days of heaven.** Jesus reigns on, and will reign till the skies shall fall; when the heavens pass away, and the elements melt with fervent heat, his throne will stand. Some commentators talk of conditions, but we fail to see any; the promises are as absolute as they can possibly be, and if any conditions as to the conduct of the favored individuals can be conceived, they are disposed of in the succeeding verses.

30. It was possible, terribly possible, that David's posterity might wander from the Lord; indeed they did so, but what then? Was the mercy of God to pass away from David's descendants? Far from it. So, too, the descendants of the Son of David are apt to start aside, but are they therefore cast away? Not a single word gives liberty for such an idea, but the very reverse.

31. If they break my statutes, and keep not my commandments. The dreadful if is suggested again, and the sad case is stated in other forms. But if it should be so, what then? Death and rejection? Ah, no. Blessed be God, no! Legalism will import its ifs, but the Lord slays the ifs as fast as they rise. Eternal shalls and wills make glorious havoc among the ifs and buts.

32. Then will I visit their transgression with the rod. Not with the sword, not with death and destruction, but still with a painful rod. Saints must smart if they sin; God will see to that. He hates sin too much and he loves his saints too well not to chasten **their iniquity with stripes,** which are either many or few in proportion as the heart is properly affected by them.

33. Nevertheless my lovingkindness will I not utterly take from him. O glorious fear-killing sentence! This crowns the covenant with exceeding glory. Mercy may seem to depart from the Lord's chosen, but it will never altogether do so. Jesus still enjoys the divine favor, and therefore under the most trying circumstances the Lord's lovingkindness to each one of his chosen will endure the strain. If the covenant be made void by our sins it would have been void long ere this. God may leave his people, and they may thereby suffer much, but utterly and altogether he never can remove his love from them; for that would be to cast a reflection upon his own truth, and this he will never allow, for he adds **nor suffer my faithfulness to fail.** Humankind fails in all points, but God in none. To be faithful is one of the eternal characteristics of God.

34. My covenant will I not break. It is his own covenant. He devised it, drew up the draft of it, and voluntarily entered into it; he therefore thinks much of it. **Nor alter the thing that is gone out of my lips.** Alterations and afterthoughts belong to short-sighted human beings who meet with unexpected events which operate upon them to change their minds, but the Lord who sees everything from the beginning has no such reason for shifting his ground. He is besides immutable in his nature and designs, and cannot change in heart, and therefore not in promise. It is evident he takes pleasure in that most ancient and solemn contract. If it were conceivable that he had repented of it, he would not be found dwelling upon it, and repeating it with renewed emphasis.

35. Because he could swear by no greater he swore by himself, and by that especial attribute which is his highest glory. God here pledges the essence of his nature. He does as good as say that if ceases to be true to his covenant he will have forfeited his holy character.

36. His seed shall endure forever. David's line in the person of Jesus is an endless one, and the race of Jesus, as represented in successive generations of believers, shows no sign of failure. No power, human or Satanic, can break the Christian succession; as saints die others will rise up to fill their places, so that till the last day, the day of doom, Jesus will have a seed to serve him. **And his throne as the sun before me.** In our Lord Jesus the dynasty of David remains upon the throne. Jesus has never abdicated, nor gone into banishment. He reigns, and must reign so long as the sun continues to shine upon the earth. We are the seed who must endure forever, and we are protected and ennobled by that King whose royalties are to last forever.

37. It shall be established for ever as the moon. The kingdom may wax and wane to mortal eyes, but it will still abide as long as the moon walks in her silver beauty. **And as a faithful witness in heaven.** The most stable part of the universe is selected as a type of Messiah's kingdom, and both sun and moon are made to be symbols of its long endurance. Whatever else there is in the sky which faithfully witnesses to the unbending course of nature is also called upon to be a sign of the Lord's truth. When heaven and earth witness, and the Lord himself swears, there remains no excuse for doubting, and faith joyfully reposes in confident expectation.

38. But thou hast cast off and abhorred. The Lord had promised not to cast off the seed of David, and yet it looked as if he had done so, and that too in the most angry manner, as if he loathed the person of the king. God's actions may appear to us to be the reverse of his promises, and then our best course is to come before him in prayer and put the matter before him just as it strikes our apprehension. We are allowed to do this, for this holy and inspired man did so unrebuked, but we must do it humbly and in faith. **Thou hast been wroth with thine anointed.** He deserved the wrath, doubtless, but the psalmist's point is that this appeared to him to conflict with the gracious covenant. He puts the matter plainly, and makes bold with the Lord, and the Lord loves to have his servants so do; it shows that they believe his engagements to be matters of fact.

39. Thou hast made void the covenant of thy servant. The dispensations of providence looked as if there had been a disannulling of the sacred compact, though indeed it was not so. **Thou hast profaned his crown by casting it to the ground.** The king had been subject to such sorrow and shame that his diadem had been as it were taken from his head, dashed on the earth, and rolled in the mire. He was a theocratic monarch, and the Lord, who gave him his crown, took it from him and treated it with contempt – at least so it seemed. In these sad days also we may utter the same plaint, for Jesus is not acknowledged in many of the churches.

40. Thou hast broken down all his hedges. He was no longer sheltered from the slanderous assaults of contemptuous tongues; the awe which should guard the royal name had ceased to separate him from his fellows. The royal family had been like a vine within an enclosure, but the wall was now laid low, and the vine was unprotected. It is sorrowfully true that in many places the enclosures of the church have been destroyed, the line of demarcation between the church and the world has almost vanished, and godless people fill the sacred offices. **Thou hast brought his strongholds to ruin.** The forts of the kingdom were in the possession of the enemy and were dismantled; the defenses of the kingdom were overthrown. Thus has it happened that precious truths which were the bulwarks of the church have been assailed by heresy, and the citadels of sound doctrine have been abandoned to the foe.

41. All that pass by the way spoil him. Woe is the day when every petty reasoner has an argument against religion, and men in their cups are fluent with objections against the Gospel of Jesus. Although Jesus on the cross is nothing to them, and they pass him by without inquiring into what he has done for them, they can loiter as long as you will, if there be but the hope of driving another nail into his hands. **He is a reproach to his neighbors.** David's successors had neighbors who were a reproach to good fellowship, because they were so ready to reproach their neighbor. The people of God, who follow the Lord fully, are subject to a thousand reproaches, and some of them of the most bitter kind. These reproaches are really the reproach of Christ, and at bottom are meant for him.

42. Thou hast set up the right hand of his adversaries. Thou hast done it, **thou,** who hast sworn to give him help and victory; thou hast, instead thereof, sided by his enemies, and lent them thy strength, so that they have gained the supremacy. **Thou hast made all his enemies to rejoice.** They are boasting over him, and are glorying in his defeat, and this is done by thyself. O God, how is this? Where is the covenant? Hast thou forgotten thine own pledges and promises?

43. Also turned the edge of his sword. When he goes to war he is as unsuccessful as though his sword refused to cut, and gave way like a sword of lead. His weapons fail him. **And hast not made him to stand in the battle.** His heart fails him as well as his sword – he wavers, he falls. At this present the church has few swords of true Jerusalem metal; her sons are pliable, her ministers yield to pressure. We need men whose edge cannot be turned, firm for truth, keen against error, sharp towards sin. Charity towards heresy is the fashionable vice, and indifference to all truth, under the name of liberal-mindedness, is the crowning virtue of the age.

44. Thou hast made his glory to cease. The brightness of his reign and the prosperity of his house are gone, his fame is tarnished, his honor disgraced. **And cast his throne down to the ground.** He has lost his power to govern at home or to conquer abroad. This happened to kings of David's line, and, more grievous to tell, it is happening in these days to the visible kingdom of the Lord Jesus. The glory has departed, and the Gospel throne of Jesus is hidden from our eyes!

45. The days of his youth hast thou shortened. The time of the king's energy was brief; he grew feeble before his time. **Thou hast covered him with shame.** Shame was heaped upon him because of his premature decay and his failure in arms. In this our day we have to bemoan the lack of vigor in religion. Let us plead with the righteous Judge of all the earth to fulfill his word wherein he has promised that those who wait upon him shall renew their strength. **Selah.** The interceding poet takes breath amid his lament, and then turns from describing the sorrows of the kingdom to pleading with the Lord.

46. How long, Lord? The appeal is to Jehovah, and the argument is the length of the affliction endured. Chastisement with a rod is not a lengthened matter; therefore he appeals to God to cut short the time of tribulation. **Wilt thou hide thyself forever?** Hast thou not promised to appear for thy servant – wilt thou then forever forsake him? **Shall thy wrath burn like fire?** Wilt thou burn up the throne which thou hast sworn to perpetuate? Thus would we intreat the Lord to remember the cause of Christ in these days. Will truth die out, and saints exist no more? Surely he must interpose soon, for, if he do not, true religion will be utterly consumed, as it were, with fire.

47. Remember how short my time is. If thine anger burn on it will outlast this mortal life, and then there will be no time for thy mercy to restore me. Some expositors ascribe these words, and all the preceding verses, to the state of the Lord Jesus in the days of his humiliation, and this gives an instructive meaning; but we prefer to continue our reference all through to the church, which is the seed of the Lord Jesus, as the succeeding kings were the seed of David. We, having transgressed, are made to feel the rod, but we pray the Lord not to continue his stripes lest our whole life be passed in misery. **Wherefore hast thou made all men in vain?** If the Lord do not shine upon his work we live for nothing – we count it no longer life if his cause does not prosper. Creation is a blot, providence an error, and our own existence a hell, if the faithfulness of God can fail and his covenant of grace can be dissolved. If the Gospel system can be disproved, nothing remains for us which can render existence worth the having.

48. What man is he that liveth, and shall not see death? All must die. None of our race can answer to the question here propounded except in the negative; there is none that can claim to elude the arrows of death. **Shall he deliver his soul from the hand of the grave?** Since we must all die, do not make this life all wretchedness, O Lord. Let us not be so deserted of thee in this brief span that we are unable to testify to thy faithfulness. **Selah.** Here we rest again, and proceed to further pleadings.

49. We may remind the Lord of his former love to his church, his former favor to ourselves. Then may we plead his oath, and beg him to remember that he has sworn to bless his chosen; and we may wrestle hard also, by urging upon him his own character, and laying hold upon his inviolable truth.

50. Remember, Lord, the reproach of thy servants. By their great troubles they were made a mock of by ungodly people, and hence the Lord's pity is intreated. **How I do bear in my bosom the reproach of all the mighty people.** The psalmist felt as if all the reproaches which vexed his nation were centered in himself; reproach upon the saints and their cause ought to burden us. Our grief at the griefs of the Lord's people may be pleaded in prayer.

There is one interpretation of this verse which must not be passed over; the original is, "Remember my bearing in my bosom all the many nations," and this may be understood as a pleading of the church that the Lord would remember her because she was yet to be the mother of many nations, according to the prophecy of Psalm 77. She was as it were ready to give birth to nations, but how could they be born if she herself died in the meanwhile? The church is the hope of the world; should she expire, the nations would never come to the birth of regeneration.

51. Wherewith thine enemies have reproached, O LORD. Here is another forcible point; the scoffers are the Lord's enemies as well as ours, and their reproach falls upon him as well as upon us. **Wherefore they have reproached the footsteps of thine anointed.** Not only watching his words and actions, but even his harmless steps. Neither Christ nor his church can please the world; whichever way we turn scoffers will rail. Does this verse refer to the delays of the Messiah, those long-expected footfalls which as yet are unheard?

52. Blessed be the LORD for evermore. He ends where he began. Let us bless God before we pray, and while we pray, and when we have done praying, for he always deserves it of us. If we cannot understand him, we will not distrust him. When his ways are beyond our judgment we will not be so foolish as to judge; yet we shall do so if we consider his dealings to be unkind or unfaithful. He is, he must be, he shall be forever our blessed God. **Amen, and Amen.** So be it, Lord; we wish it over and over again. Be thou blessed evermore.

Psalm 90

1. LORD, thou hast been our dwelling place in all generations. We must consider the whole psalm as written for the tribes in the desert, and then we shall see the primary meaning of each verse. Moses, in effect, says – wanderers though we be in the howling wilderness, yet we find a home in thee, even as our forefathers did when they came out of Ur and dwelt in tents among the Canaanites. To the saints the Lord Jehovah, the self-existent God, stands instead of mansion: he shelters, comforts, protects, preserves, and cherishes all his own. It is wise to draw from the Lord's eternal condescensions reasons for expecting present and future mercies, as the psalmist did in the next psalm wherein he describes the safety of those who dwell in God.

2. **Before the mountains were brought forth.** Mountains to him are young things whose birth was but yesterday. **Or ever thou hadst formed the earth and the world.** Earth was born but the other day, and her solid land was delivered from the Flood but a short while ago. **Even from everlasting to everlasting, thou art God,** or, "thou art, O God." God was, when nothing else was. He was God when the earth was not a world but a chaos. If God himself were of yesterday, he would not be a suitable refuge for mortals. The eternal existence of God is here mentioned to set forth, by contrast, the brevity of human life.

3. **Thou hast turned man to destruction,** or, "to dust." The human body is resolved into its elements, as though it had been ground to powder. **And sayest, Return, ye children of men,** that is, return to the dust out of which you were taken. Human frailty is thus forcibly set forth; God creates us out of the dust, and back to the dust we go at the word of our Creator. Observe how the action of God is recognized: man is not said to die because of the decree of fate, or the action of inevitable law, but the Lord is made the agent of all.

4. **For a thousand years in thy sight are but as yesterday when it is past.** A thousand years! How much may be crowded into it – the rise and fall of empires, the glory and obliteration of dynasties, countless events, all important to household and individual. Yet this period is to the Lord as nothing. In comparison with eternity, the most lengthened reaches of time are mere points; there is, in fact, no possible comparison between them. **And as a watch in the night,** a time which is no sooner come than gone.

5. **Thou carriest them away as with a flood.** As when a torrent bears all before it, so does the Lord bear away by death the succeeding generations. **They are as a sleep.** Not only are our plans like a sleep, but we ourselves are such. **In the morning they are like grass which groweth up.** As grass is green in the morning and hay at night, so people are changed from health to corruption in a few hours.

6. **In the morning it flourisheth, and groweth up.** The grass has a golden hour, as man in his youth has a heyday of flowery glory. **In the evening it is cut down, and withereth.** Natural decay would put an end both to us and the grass; few, however, experience the full result of age, for death comes with his scythe.

7. This mortality is not accidental, neither was it inevitable in the original of our nature, but sin has provoked the Lord to anger, and therefore thus we die. **For we are consumed by thine anger.** This is the scythe which mows and the scorching heat which withers. This was specially the case in reference to the people in the wilderness. As well might grass grow in an oven as people

flourish when the Lord is angry with them. **And by thy wrath are we troubled,** or terror-stricken. A sense of divine anger confounded them, so that they lived as people who knew that they were doomed. This is true of us in a measure, but not altogether, for now that immortality and life are brought to light by the Gospel, death has changed its aspect, and, to believers in Jesus, it is no more a judicial execution. Anger and wrath are the sting of death, and in these believers have no share; love and mercy now conduct us to glory by way of the tomb. It is not seemly to read these words at a Christian's funeral without words of explanation, and a distinct endeavor to show how little they belong to believers in Jesus. To apply an ode written by the leader of the legal dispensation under circumstances of particular judgment, in reference to a people under penal censure, to those who fall asleep in Jesus seems to be the height of blundering. We may learn much from it, but we ought not to misapply it by taking to ourselves, as the beloved of the Lord, that which was chiefly true of those to whom God had sworn in his wrath that they should not enter into his rest. When, however, a soul is under conviction of sin, the language of this psalm is highly appropriate to his case, and will naturally suggest itself to the distracted mind. No fire consumes like God's anger, and no anguish so troubles the heart as his wrath.

8. Thou hast set our iniquities before thee. Sin seen by God must work death; it is only by the covering blood of atonement that life comes to any of us. When God was overthrowing the tribes in the wilderness he had their iniquities before him, and therefore dealt with them in severity. He could not have their iniquities before him and not smite them. **Our secret sins in the light of thy countenance.** There are no secrets before God. If by his countenance is here meant his love and favor, it is not possible for the heinousness of sin to be more clearly manifested than when it is seen to involve ingratitude to one so infinitely good and kind. Rebellion in the light of justice is black, but in the light of love it is devilish. How can we grieve so good a God? The children of Israel had been brought out of Egypt with a high hand, fed in the wilderness with a liberal hand, and guided with a tender hand, and their sins were especially atrocious. We, too, having been redeemed by the blood of Jesus, and saved by abounding grace, will be verily guilty if we forsake the Lord. What manner of persons ought we to be? How ought we to pray for cleansing from secret faults?

It is to us a wellspring of delights to remember that our sins, as believers, are now cast behind the Lord's back, and will never be brought to light again: therefore we live, because, the guilt being removed, the death-penalty is removed also.

9. For all our days are passed away in thy wrath. Justice shortened the days of rebellious Israel; each halting place became a graveyard; they marked their march by the tombs they left behind them. Because of the penal sentence their days were dried up, and their lives wasted away. **We spend our years as a tale that is told.** Not their days only, but their **years** flew by them, rapid and idle as a gossip's story. Sin had cast a shadow over all things, and made the lives of the dying wanderers both vain and brief. The first sentence is not intended for believers to quote, as though it applied to themselves, for our days are all passed amid the lovingkindness of the Lord. Neither is the life of gracious people unsubstantial as a story-teller's tale; they live in Jesus, they have the divine Spirit within them; the simile only holds good if we consider that our lives are illustrations of heavenly goodness, parables of divine wisdom. Happy are we whose lives are such tales.

10. The days of our years are threescore years and ten. It is nothing when contrasted with eternity. Yet is life long enough for virtue and piety, and all too long for vice and blasphemy. Moses here in the original writes in a disconnected manner, as if he would set forth the utter insignificance of hurried human existence. His words may be rendered, "The days of our years! In them seventy years"; as much as to say, "The days of our years? What about them? Are they worth mentioning? The account is utterly insignificant; their full tale is but seventy." **And if by reason of strength they be fourscore years, yet is their strength labor and sorrow.** The strength of old age, its very prime and pride, is a weariness and sorrow; what must its weakness be? Yet mellowed by hallowed experience, and solaced by immortal hopes, the latter days of aged Christians are not so much to be pitied as envied. The mortal fades to make room for the immortal; the old man falls asleep to wake up in the region of perennial youth. **For it is soon cut off, and we fly away.** The chain is snapped, and the eagle mounts to its native air above the clouds. Moses mourned for people as he thus sang; and well he might, as all his comrades fell at his side. His words are more nearly rendered, "He drives us fast and we fly away." As the quails were blown along by the strong west wind, so are people hurried before the tempests of death. To us, however, as believers, the winds are favorable. Who wishes it otherwise? Wherefore should we linger here? What has this poor world to offer us that we should tarry on its shores? This is not our rest. Let the Lord's winds drive fast if so he ordains, for they waft us the more swiftly to himself.

11. Who knoweth thine anger? Moses saw people dying all around him: he lived among funerals, and was overwhelmed at the terrible results of the divine displeasure. He felt that none could measure the might of the Lord's wrath. **Even according to thy fear, so is thy wrath.** Good people dread that wrath beyond conception, but they never ascribe too much terror to it: bad people are dreadfully convulsed when they awake to a sense of it, for it is a fearful thing to fall into the hands of an angry God. Who is able to stand against this justly angry God? Be it ours to submit ourselves as dying sinners to this eternal God, who can, even at this moment, command us to the dust, and thence to hell.

12. So teach us to number our days. Instruct us to set store by time, mourning for that time past wherein we have wrought the will of the flesh, using diligently the time present, which is the accepted hour and the day of salvation, and reckoning the time which lies in the future to be too uncertain to allow us safely to delay any gracious work or prayer. **That we may apply our hearts unto wisdom.** People are led by reflections upon the brevity of time to give their earnest attention to eternal things; they become humble as they look into the grave. But this is only the case when the Lord himself is the teacher; he alone can teach to real and lasting profit. We have not enough time at our disposal to justify us in misspending a single quarter of an hour. Neither are we sure of enough of life to justify us in procrastinating for a moment.

13. Return, O LORD, how long? Come in mercy to us again. Do not leave us to perish. As sin drives God from us, so repentance cries to the Lord to return to us. When people are under chastisement they are allowed to expostulate, and ask, **how long?** Our fault in these times is not too great boldness with God, but too much backwardness in pleading with him. **And let it repent thee concerning thy servants.** They had rebelled, but they had not utterly forsaken the Lord; they owned their obligations to obey his will, and pleaded them as a reason for pity. Will a man not spare his own servants? Though God smote Israel, yet they were his people, and he had never disowned them; therefore is he intreated to deal favorably with them.

14. O satisfy us with thy mercy. He who has but the heart to pray need never be without pleas in prayer. The only satisfying food for the Lord's people is the favor of God. Our day is short, and the night hastens on. O give us in the early morning of our days to be satisfied with thy favor, that all through our little day we may be happy. **That we may rejoice and be glad all our days.** Being filled with divine love, their brief life on earth would become a joyful festival, and would continue so as long as it lasted. When the Lord refreshes us with his presence, our joy is such that no one can take it from us. Apprehensions of speedy death are not able to distress those who enjoy the present favor of God; though they know that the night is coming they see nothing to fear in it.

15. None can gladden the heart as thou canst, O Lord; therefore as thou hast made us sad be pleased to make us glad. The prayer is original, childlike, and full of meaning; it is moreover based upon a great principle in providential goodness, by which the Lord puts the good over against the evil. Great trial enables us to bear great joy, and may be regarded as the herald of extraordinary grace. Small lives are small throughout; and great histories are great both in sorrow and happiness. Where there are high hills there are also deep valleys. If we have fierce afflictions we may look for overflowing delights, and our faith may boldly ask for them. God who is great in justice when he chastens will not be little in mercy when he blesses; he will be great all through. Let us appeal to him with unstaggering faith.

16. Let thy work appear unto thy servants. See how he dwells upon that word **servants**. It is as far as the law can do, and Moses goes to the full length permitted him; henceforth Jesus calls us not servants but friends, and if we are wise we shall make full use of our wider liberty. Moses asks for displays of divine power and providence conspicuously wrought, that all the people might be cheered thereby. **And thy glory unto their children.** While their sons were growing up around them, they desired to see some outshinings of the promised glory gleaming upon them. We are content with the work if our children may but see the glory which will result from it: we sow joyfully if they may reap.

17. And let the beauty of the LORD our God be upon us. Even upon us who must not see thy glory in the land of Canaan; it will suffice us if in our characters the holiness of God is reflected, and if over all our camp the lovely excellencies of our God cast a sacred beauty. Sanctification should be the daily object of our petitions. **And establish thou the work of our hands upon us; yea, the work of our hands establish thou it.** Let what we do be done in truth, and last when we are in the grave; may the work of the present generation minister permanently to the building up of the nation. We come and go, but the Lord's work abides. We are content to die, so long as Jesus lives and his kingdom grows.

Psalm 91

1. He that dwelleth in the secret place of the Most High. The blessings here promised are not for all believers, but for those who live in close fellowship with God. Every child of God looks towards the inner sanctuary and the mercy-seat, yet all do not *dwell* in the most holy place; they run to it at times, and enjoy occasional appraoches, but they do not habitually reside in the mysterious presence. Those who through rich grace obtain unusual and continuous communion with God, so as to abide in Christ and Christ in them, become possesors of rare and special benefits, which are missed by those who follow afar off, and grieve the Holy Spirit of God. Into the secrt place those only come who know the love of God in Christ Jesus, andf those only *dwell* there to whom to live is Christ. To them the veil is rent, and the awful glory of the Most High is apparent: these, like Simeon, have the Holy Spirit upon them, and like Anna they depart not from the temple; of them it is truly said that their conversation is in heaven. Special grace like theirs brings with it special immunity. Outer court worshipers little know what belongs to the inner sanctuary, or surely they would press on until the place of nearness and divine familiarity became theirs. Those who are the Lord's constant guests will find that he will never let any be injured within his gates.

Shall abide under the shadow of the Almighty. The omnipotent Lord will shield all those who dwell with him; they will remain under his care as guests under the protection of their host. This protection is constant – they **abide** under it, and it is all-sufficient, for it is **the shadow of** *the* **Almighty**, whose omnipotence will surely screen them from all attack. The more closely we cling to our Almighty Father, the more confident may we be.

2. **I will say of the Lord, he is my refuge and my fortress.** To take up a general truth and make it our own by personal faith is the highest wisdom. Those who believe should also speak – **I will** *say* – for such bold avowals honor God and lead others to seek the same confidence. Let others say what they will, be it ours to say of the Lord, "He is our **refuge**." But what we say we must prove by our actions; we must fly to the Lord for shelter, and not to an arm of flesh. Let us, when we are secure in the Lord, rejoice that our position is unassailable, for he is our **fortress** as well as our refuge. Walls cannot keep out the pestilence, but the Lord can.

As if it were not enough to call the Lord his refuge and fortress, he adds, **My God! in him will I trust.** Now he can say no more; **my God** means all, and more than all, than the heart can conceive by way of security. It was most meet that he should say, **in him will I trust,** since to deny faith to such a one were willfull wickedness and wanton insult. He who dwells in an impregnable fortress naturally trusts in it; and will not he who dwells in God feel himself well at ease, and repose his soul in safety?

3. **Surely he shall deliver thee from the snare of the fowler.** Assuredly no subtle plot will succeed against one who has the eyes of God watching for his defense. We are foolish and weak as poor little birds, and are very apt to be lured to our destruction by cunning foes, but if we dwell near to God, he will see to it that the most skillfull deceiver will not entrap us. **And from the noisome pestilence.** He who is a Spirit can protect us from evil spirits; he who is mysterious can rescue us from mysterious dangers; he who is immortal can redeem us from mortal sickness. There is a deadly pestilence of error; we are safe from that if we dwell in communion with the God of truth. There is a fatal pestilence of sin; we shall not be infected by it if we abide with the thrice Holy One. There is also a pestilence of disease, and even from that calamity our faith shall win immunity if it be of that high order which abides in God, walks on in calm serenity, and ventures all things for duty's sake. It is not of all believers that the psalmist sings, but only of those who dwell in the secret place of the Most High. Too many among us are weak in faith, and in fact place more reliance in a phial or a globule than in the Lord and giver of life, and if we die of pestilence as others die it is because we acted like others. The great mercy is that in such a case our deaths are blessed, and we are forever with the Lord. Pestilence to the saints will not be noisome but the messenger of heaven.

4. **He shall cover thee with his feathers, and under his wings shalt thou trust.** As a hen covers her chickens, so does the Lord protect the souls which dwell in him; let us cower down beneath him for comfort and for safety. **His truth** – his

true promise, and his faithfulness to his promise – **shall be thy shield and buckler.** Double armor has he who relies upon the Lord. He bears a shield and wears an all-surrounding coat of mail – such is the force of the word "buckler." We will wear no other ornament; his truth will still be our shield and buckler.

5. Thou shalt not be afraid for the terror by night. Night is when our fears turn the sweet season of repose into one of dread, and though angels are abroad and fill our chambers, we dream of demons and dire visitants from hell. Blessed is that communion with God which renders us impervious to midnight frights, and horrors born of darkness. Not to be afraid is in itself an unspeakable blessing, since for every suffering which we endure from real injury we are tormented by a thousand griefs which arise from fear only. The shadow of the Almighty removes all gloom from the shadow of night. **Nor for the arrow that flieth by day.** That arrow is not made which can destroy the righteous, for the Lord has said, "No weapon that is formed against thee shall prosper." In times of great danger those who have made the Lord their refuge, and therefore have refused to use the carnal weapon, have been singularly preserved; the annals of the Quakers bear good evidence to this; yet probably the main thought is that from the cowardly attacks of crafty malice those who walk by faith will be protected, from cunning heresies they will be preserved, and in sudden temptations they will be secured from harm. Day has its perils as well as night, and we shall be their victims unless we find both shield and buckler in our God.

6. Nor for the pestilence that walketh in darkness. It is shrouded in mystery as to its cause and cure, yet those who dwell in God are not afraid of it. They shall not be afraid of the plagues which in darkness walk, **nor for the destruction that wasteth at noonday.** Famine may starve, or bloody war devour, earthquake may overturn and tempest may smite, but amid all, the person who has sought the mercy-seat and is sheltered beneath the wings which overshadow it will abide in perfect peace. God's peace is not a thing of times and seasons; it does not rise and set with the sun, nor does it depend upon the healthiness of the atmosphere or the security of the country. Upon the child of the Lord's own heart pestilence has no destroying power, and calamity no wasting influence: pestilence walks in darkness, but he dwells in light; destruction wastes at noonday, but upon him another sun has risen whose beams bring restoration. Remember that the voice which says "thou shalt not fear" is that of God himself, who hereby pledges his word for the safety of those who abide under his shadow, and not for their safety only but for their serenity.

7. A thousand shall fall at thy side, and ten thousand at thy right hand. Terribly may the plague rage among people; yet such as this psalm speaks of survive the scythe of death. **It shall not come nigh thee.** It will be so near as to be at your side, and yet not near enough to touch you. How true is this of the plague of moral evil, or heresy, and of backsliding. Whole nations are infected, yet the person who communes with God is not affected by the contagion. The church is wasted, the very life of religion decays, but in the same place and time, in fellowship with God, the believer renews his youth, and his soul knows no sickness. In a measure this is also true of physical evil; the Lord still puts a difference between Israel and Egypt in the day of his plagues.

8. The sight will reveal both the justice and the mercy of God; in them that perish the severity of God will be manifest, and in the believer's escape the richness of divine goodness will be apparent. Joshua and Caleb verified this promise. The Puritan preachers during the plague of London must have been much impressed with this verse as they came out of their hiding-places to proclaim mercy and judgment to the dissolute age which was so sorely visited with the pest. Let us but watch providence, and we shall find ourselves living in a school where examples of the ultimate reward of sin are very plentiful. One case may not be judged alone lest we misjudge, but instances of divine visitation will be plentiful in the memory of any attentive observer of people and things; from all these put together we may fairly draw conclusions, and we shall soon perceive that there is after all a moral ruler over humankind, who sooner or later rewards the ungodly with due punishment.

9–10. The psalmist in these verses assures people who dwell in God that they will be secure. Though faith claims no merit of its own, yet the Lord rewards it wherever he sees it. He who makes God his refuge will find him a refuge; he who dwells in God will find his dwelling protected. We must *make* the Lord our habitation by choosing him for our trust and rest, and then we shall receive immunity from harm. The **dwelling** here intended by the original was only a tent, yet the frail covering would prove to be a sufficient shelter from harm of all sorts. It matters little whether our abode be a hut or a palace if the soul has made the Most High its habitation. Get into God and you dwell in all good, and ill is banished far away. It is not because we are perfect or highly esteemed among people that we can hope for shelter in the day of evil, but because our refuge is the Eternal God. It is impossible that any ill should happen to those who are beloved of the Lord; the most crushing calamities can only shorten their journey and hasten them to their reward. They are secure where others are in peril; they live where others die.

11. For he shall give his angels charge over thee. Not one guardian angel, as some fondly dream, but all the angels are here alluded to. **To keep thee in all thy ways.** To be a bodyguard, a garrison to the body, soul, and spirit of the saint. **In all thy ways** is yet no limit to the heart which is right with God. It is not the way of the believer to go out of his way. He keeps in his way, and then the angels keep him. How angels thus keep us we cannot tell. Whether they repel demons, counteract spiritual plots, or even ward off the subtler physical forces of disease, we do not know. Perhaps we shall one day stand amazed at the multiplied services which the unseen bands have rendered to us.

12. They, that is God's own angels, will cheerfully become our servitors.

They shall bear thee up in their hands; as nurses carry little children, with careful love, so will those glorious spirits bear each individual believer. **Lest thou dash thy foot against a stone.** Even minor ills they ward off. If we cannot have the way smoothed it answers every purpose if we have angels to bear us up in their hands. Since the greatest ills may arise out of little accidents, it shows the wisdom of the Lord that from the smaller evils we are protected.

13. Thou shalt tread upon the lion and adder. Over force and fraud shalt thou march victoriously; bold opponents and treacherous adversaries will alike be trodden down. **The young lion and the dragon shalt thou trample under feet.** The strongest foe in power, and the most mysterious in cunning, will be conquered by the child of God. To those who dwell in God the most evil forces become harmless; they wear a charmed life, and defy the deadliest ills. Their feet come into contact with the worst of foes; even Satan himself nibbles at their heel, but in Christ Jesus they have the assured hope of bruising Satan under their feet shortly.

14. Here we have the Lord himself speaking of his own chosen one. **Because he hath set his love upon me, therefore will I deliver him.** Not because he deserves to be thus kept, but because with all his imperfections he does love his God; therefore not the angels of God only, but the God of angels himself will come to his rescue in all perilous times. When the heart is enamored of the Lord, all taken up with him, and intensely attached to him, the Lord will recognize the sacred flame, and preserve the one who bears it in his bosom. It is love – love set upon God – which is the distinguishing mark of those whom the Lord secures from ill. **I will set him on high, because he hath known my name.** The man has known the attributes of God so as to trust in him, and then by experience has arrived at a yet deeper knowledge; this will be regarded by the Lord as a pledge of his grace, and he will set the owner of it above danger or fear. None abide in intimate fellowship with God unless they possess a warm affection towards God, and an intelligent trust in him. If we climb on high it may be dangerous, but if God sets us there it is glorious.

15. He shall call upon me, and I will answer him. He will need to pray, he will be led to pray aright, and the answer will surely come. Saints are first called *of* God, and then they call **upon** God; such calls as theirs always obtain answers. Not without prayer will the blessing come to the most favored, but by means of prayer they will receive all good things. **I will be with him in trouble,** or, "I *am* with him in trouble." Heirs of heaven are conscious of a special divine presence in times of severe trial. God is always near in sympathy and in power to help his tried ones. **I will deliver him, and honor him.** The man honors God, and God honors him. Believers are not delivered or preserved in a way which lowers them, and makes them feel themselves degraded; far from it, the Lord's salvation bestows honor upon those it delivers. God first gives us conquering grace, and then rewards us for it.

29

16. With long life will I satisfy him. The man described in this psalm fills out the measure of his days, and whether he dies young or old he is quite satisfied with life, and is content to leave it. **And show him my salvation.** The full sight of divine grace shall be his closing vision. Not with destruction before him black as night, but with salvation bright as noonday smiling upon him he shall enter into his rest.

Psalm 92

1. It is a good thing to give thanks unto the LORD, or JEHOVAH. It is good ethically, for it is the Lord's right; it is good emotionally, for it is pleasant to the heart; it is good practically, for it leads others to render the same homage. To give thanks to God is but a small return for the great benefits wherewith he daily loads us; yet as he by his Spirit calls it a good thing, we must not despise it, or neglect it. We thank people when they oblige us; how much more ought we to bless the Lord when he benefits us. Devout praise is always good; it is never out of season, never superfluous, but it is especially suitable to the Sabbath; a Sabbath without thanksgiving is a Sabbath profaned. **And to sing praises unto thy name, O most High.** It is good to give thanks in the form of vocal song. Nature itself teaches us thus to express our gratitude to God; do not the birds sing, and the brooks warble as they flow? To give our gratitude a tongue is wise. Silent worship is sweet, but vocal worship is sweeter.

2. To show forth thy lovingkindness in the morning. The day should begin with praise: no hour is too early for holy song. We leave unpleasant tasks as long as we can, but our hearts are so engrossed with the adoration of God that we would rise early to attend to it. **And thy faithfulness every night.** No hour is too late for praise; the end of the day must not be the end of gratitude. Evening is the time for retrospect, memory is busy with the experience of the day; hence the appropriate theme for song is the divine **faithfulness,** of which another day has furnished fresh evidences. **Every night,** clouded or clear, moonlit or dark, calm or tempestuous, is alike suitable for a song upon the faithfulness of God, since in all seasons, and under all circumstances, it abides the same, and is the mainstay of the believer's consolation.

3. Upon an instrument of ten strings. With the fullest range of music, uttering before God with the full compass of melody the richest emotions of his soul. **And upon the psaltery,** thus giving variety to praise: the psalmist felt that every sweet-sounding instrument should be consecrated to God. George Herbert and Martin Luther aided their private devotions by instrumental music; and whatever may have been the differences of opinion in the Christian church, as to the performance of instrumental music in public, we have met with no objection to its personal and private use. **Upon the harp with a solemn sound,** or upon "meditation with a harp"; as much as to say, my meditative soul is, after all, the best instrument, and the harp's dulcet tones come in to aid my thoughts. It is, however, much to be feared that attention to the mere mechanism of music, noting keys and strings, measures and quarter notes, has carried many away from the spiritual harmony which is the soul and essence of praise. Fine music without devotion is but a splendid garment upon a corpse.

4. For thou, Lord, hast made me glad through thy work. It was natural for the psalmist to sing, because he was glad, and to sing unto the Lord, because his gladness was caused by a contemplation of the divine work. If we consider either creation or providence, we shall find overflowing reasons for joy; but when we come to review the work of redemption, gladness knows no bounds. **I will triumph in the works of thy hands.** I cannot help it, I must rejoice in the Lord, even as one who has won the victory and has divided great spoil. In the first sentence of this verse he expresses the unity of God's **work,** and in the second the variety of his **works**; in both there is reason for gladness and triumph.

5. O LORD, how great are thy works! He is lost in wonder. Great for number, extent, and glory and design are all the creations of the Infinite One. **And thy thoughts are very deep.** The Lord's plans are as profound as his doings are vast. Some people think but cannot work, and others are mere drudges working without thought; in the Eternal the conception and the execution go together. Providence is inexhaustible, and the divine decrees which originate it are inscrutable. Redemption is grand beyond conception, and the thoughts of love which planned it are infinite. Human beings are superficial, God is deep. We stand by the fathomless sea of divine wisdom, and exclaim with holy awe, "Oh the depth!"

6. In this and the following verses the effect of the psalm is heightened by contrast. Alas, the character described here is no uncommon one. The boorish or boarish man, for such is almost the very Hebrew word, sees nothing in nature, and if it be pointed out to him, his foolish mind will not comprehend it. The unbelieving heart does not know; and with all its parade of intellect, it does not understand. O God, how sorrowful a thing it is that people whom thou hast so largely gifted, and made in thine own image, should so brutify themselves that they will neither see nor understand what thou hast made so clear.

7. When the wicked spring as the grass, in abundance, and apparent strength, hastening on their progress like verdant plants, which come to perfection in a day, **and when all the workers of iniquity do flourish,** flowering in their prime and pride, their pomp and their prosperity; **it is that they shall be destroyed for ever.** They flower for a short space to wither without end. Greatness and glory are to them but the prelude of their overthrow. Little does their opposition matter; the Lord reigns on as if they had never blasphemed him. The Most High is unaffected by the fleeting mortals who dare oppose him: they will soon vanish forever from among the living. But as for the wicked – how can our minds endure the contemplation of their doom **for ever?** Destruction **for ever** is a portion far too terrible for the mind to realize. Eye hath not seen, nor ear heard, the full terror of the wrath to come!

8. This is the middle verse of the psalm, and the great fact which this Sabbath song is meant to illustrate. God is at once the highest and most enduring of all beings. Others rise to fall, but he is the Most High to eternity. The ungodly are destroyed forever, and God is most high forever; evil is cast down, and the Holy One reigns supreme eternally.

9. For, lo, thine enemies, O LORD. It is a wonder full of instruction and warning, observe it; **for, lo, thine enemies shall perish,** they shall be known no more. In that the thing is spoken twice it is confirmed by the Lord; it shall surely be, and that speedily. **All the workers of iniquity shall be scattered.** Their forces will be dispersed, their hopes broken and themselves driven hither and thither like chaff before the tempest. They will not have the courage to remain in arms, nor the unity to abide in confederacy. Terrible as this fact is, no true-hearted person would wish to have it otherwise. Treason against the great Monarch of the universe ought not to go unpunished; such wanton wickedness richly merits the severest doom.

10. But my horn shalt thou exalt like the horn of an unicorn. The believer rejoices that he will not be allowed to perish, but will be strengthened and enabled to triumph over his enemies, by the divine aid. The unicorn may have been some gigantic ox or buffalo now unknown, and perhaps extinct – among the ancients it was the favorite symbol of unconquerable power; the psalmist adopts it as his emblem. Faith takes delight in foreseeing the mercy of the Lord, and sings of what he will do as well as of what he has done. **I shall be anointed with fresh oil.** Strengthening will be attended with refreshment and honor. As guests were anointed at feasts with perfumed unguents, so shall the saints be cheered and delighted by fresh outpourings of divine grace; and for this reason they will not pass away like the wicked. Observe the contrast between the happiness of the brutish people and the joy of the righteous: the brutish grow with a sort of vegetable vigor of their own, but the righteous are dealt with by the Lord himself, and all the good which they receive comes directly from his own right hand, and so is doubly precious in their esteem. The psalmist speaks in the first person, and it should be a matter of prayer with the reader that he may be enabled to do the same.

11. Mine eye also shall see my desire on mine enemies. The words **my desire,** inserted by the translators, had far better have been left out. He does not say what he should see concerning his enemies; he leaves that blank, and we have no right to fill in the vacant space with words which look vindictive. He would see that which would be for God's glory, and that which would be eminently right and just. **And mine ears shall hear my desire of the wicked that rise up against me.** Here, again, the words **my desire** are not inspired, and are a needless and perhaps a false interpretation. The good man is quite silent as to what he expected to hear; he knew that what he heard would vindicate his faith in his God, and he was content to leave his cruel foes in God's hands, without an expression concerning his own desire one way or the other. It is always best to leave Scripture as we find it. The broken sense of inspiration is better let alone than pieced out with additions of a translator's own invention; it is like repairing pure gold with tinsel, or a mosaic of gems with painted wood. The holy psalmist had seen the beginning of the ungodly, and expected to see their end; he felt sure that God would right all wrongs, and clear his Providence from the charge of favoring the unjust; this confidence he here expresses, and sits down contentedly to wait the issues of the future.

12. The song now contrasts the condition of the righteous with that of the graceless. The wicked "spring as the grass," but **the righteous shall flourish like the palm tree,** whose growth may not be so rapid, but whose endurance for centuries is in fine contrast with the transitory verdure of the meadow. When we see a noble palm standing erect, sending all its strength upward in one bold column, and growing amid the dearth and drought of the desert, we have a fine picture of the godly person, who in uprightness aims alone at the glory of God, and, independent of outward circumstances, is made by divine grace to live and thrive where all things else perish. The text tells us not only what the righteous is, but what he will be; come what may, the good person will flourish, and flourish after the noblest manner. **He shall grow like a cedar in Lebanon.** This is another noble and long-lived tree. On the summit of the mountain, unsheltered from the blast, the cedar waves its mighty branches in perpetual verdure, and so the truly godly person under all adversities retains joy of soul, and continues to make progress in the divine life. Grass, which makes hay for oxen, is a good enough emblem of the unregenerate; but cedars, which build the temple of the Lord, are none too excellent to set forth the heirs of heaven.

13. Those that be planted in the house of the LORD shall flourish in the courts of our God. In the courtyards of oriental houses trees were planted, and being thoroughly screened, they would be likely to bring forth their fruit to perfection in trying seasons; in the same way, those who by grace are brought into communion with the Lord will be likened to trees planted in the Lord's house, and will find it food to their souls. No heart has so much joy as that which abides in the Lord Jesus. If someone abides in Christ, he brings forth much fruit. Those who are rooted to the world do not flourish; those who send forth their roots into the marshes of frivolous pleasure cannot be in a vigorous condition; but those who dwell in habitual fellowship with God will come to full growth, rich in grace, happy in experience, mighty in influence, honored and honorable. No tree grows in God's garden self-sown; once planted of the Lord, we shall never be rooted up, but in his courts we shall take root downward, and bring forth fruit upward to his glory forever.

14. They shall still bring forth fruit in old age. Nature decays but grace thrives. Fruit, as far as nature is concerned, belongs to days of vigor; but in the garden of grace, when plants are weak in themselves, they become strong in the Lord, and abound in fruit acceptable with God. Happy are they who can sing this Sabbath psalm, enjoying the rest which breathes through every verse of it; no fear as to the future can distress them, for their evil days, when the strong man faileth, are the subject of a gracious promise, and therefore they await them with quiet expectancy. Aged believers possess a ripe experience, and by their mellow tempers and sweet testimonies they feed many. Even if bedridden, they bear the fruit of patience; if poor and obscure, their lowly and contented spirit becomes the admiration of those who know how to appreciate modest worth. Grace does not leave the saint when the keepers of the house do tremble; the promise is still sure though the eyes can no longer read it; the bread of heaven is fed upon when the grinders fail; and the voice of the Spirit in the soul is still melodious when the daughters of music are brought low. Blessed be the Lord for this! Because even to hoary hairs he is the I AM, who made his people; he therefore bears and carries them.

They shall be fat and flourishing. God does not pinch his poor servants, and diminish their consolations when their infirmities grow upon them; rather does he see to it that they renew their strength, for their mouths will be satisfied with his own good things.

15. This mercy to the aged proves the faithfulness of their God, and leads them **to show that the LORD is upright,** by their cheerful testimony to his ceaseless goodness. We do not serve a Master who will run back from his promise. Every aged Christian is a letter of commendation to the immutable fidelity of Jehovah. **He is my rock, and there is no unrighteousness in him.** Here is the psalmist's own seal and sign manual: still was he building upon his God, and still was the Lord a firm foundation for his trust. He has tried us, but he has never allowed us to be tempted above what we are able to bear; he has delayed our reward, but he has never been unrighteous to forget our work of faith and labor of love. He is a friend without fault, a helper without fail. Whatever he may do with us, he is always in the right.

Psalm 93

1. The LORD reigneth, Jehovah reigns. Whatever opposition may arise, his throne is unmoved; he has reigned, does reign, and will reign forever and ever. In the verse before us it would seem as if the Lord had for a while appeared to vacate the throne, but on a sudden he puts on his regal apparel and ascends his lofty seat, while his happy people proclaim him with new joy. **He is clothed**

with majesty. Not with emblems of majesty, but with majesty itself: everything which surrounds him is majestic. Happy are those among whom the Lord appears in all the glory of his grace, conquering their enemies, and subduing all things unto himself; then indeed is he seen to be clothed with majesty.

The LORD is clothed with strength. He is always strong, but sometimes he displays his power in a special manner, and may therefore be said to be clothed with it. May the Lord appear in his church, in our day, in manifest majesty and might, saving sinners, slaying errors, and honoring his own name. **Wherewith he hath girded himself.** As men gird up their loins for running or working, so the Lord appears in the eyes of his people to be preparing for action, girt with his omnipotence. Strength always dwells in the Lord Jehovah, but he hides his power full often, until, in answer to his children's cries, he puts on strength, assumes the throne, and defends his own. It should be a constant theme for prayer that in our day the reign of the Lord may be conspicuous, and his power displayed in his church and on her behalf. "Thy kingdom come" should be our daily prayer: that the Lord Jesus does actually reign should be our daily praise.

The world also is stablished, that it cannot be moved. Society would be the football of the basest of mankind if God did not establish it, and even the globe itself would fly through space, like thistle-down across the common, if the Lord did not hold it in its appointed orbit. That there is any stability, either in the world or in the church, is the Lord's doings, and he is to be adored for it. Atheism is the mother of anarchy; the reigning power of God exhibited in true religion is the only security for the human commonwealth. A belief in God is the foundation and corner-stone of a well-ordered state.

2. Thy throne is established of old. Though thou mayest just now appear in more conspicuous sovereignty, yet thine is no upstart sovereignty: in the most ancient times thy dominion was secure; indeed, before time was, thy throne was set up. **Thou art from everlasting.** The Lord himself is eternal. Let the believer rejoice that the government under which he dwells has an immortal ruler at its head, has existed from all eternity, and will flourish when all created things have forever passed away. Vain are the rebellions of mortals; the kingdom of God is not shaken.

3. The floods have lifted up, O LORD. People have raged like angry waves of the sea, but vain has been their tumult. Observe that the psalmist turns to the Lord when he sees the billows foam, and hears the breakers roar; he does not waste his breath by talking to the waves, or to violent men; but like Hezekiah he spreads the blasphemies of the wicked before the Lord. **The floods have lifted up their voice; the floods lift up their waves.** These repetitions are needed for the sake both of the poetry and the music, but they also suggest the frequency and the violence of wicked assaults upon the government of God, and the repeated defeats which they sustain. Sometimes people are furious in words – they lift up their **voice,** and at other times they rise to acts of violence – they lift up their **waves**; but the Lord has control over them in either case.

4. The LORD on high is mightier than the noise of many waters. The utmost of their power is to him but a sound and he can readily master it; therefore he calls it a **noise** by way of contempt. When people combine to overthrow the kingdom of Jesus, the Lord thinks no more of it than of so much noise upon the sea-beach. **Yea, than the mighty waves of the sea.** When the storm raises Atlantic billows, and drives them on with terrific force, the Lord is still able to restrain them, and so also when impious men are haughty and full of rage the Lord is able to subdue them and overrule their malice. Kings or mobs, emperors or savages, all are in the Lord's hands, and he can forbid their touching a hair of the heads of his saints.

5. They testimonies are very sure. As the rocks remain unmoved amid the tumult of the sea, so does divine truth resist all the currents of human opinion and the storms of human controversy; they are not only sure, but **very sure.** Our faith is grounded upon the eternal truth of the Most High. **Holiness becometh thine house, O LORD, for ever.** The teaching and the character of God are both unaltered. God has not admitted evil to dwell with him; he will not tolerate it in his house; he is eternally its enemy, and is forever the sworn friend of holiness. The church must remain unchanged, and forever be holiness unto the Lord. "Jehovah reigns" is the first words and the main doctrine of the psalm, and holiness is the final result: a due esteem for the great King will lead us to adopt a behavior becoming his royal presence. Divine sovereignty both confirms the promises as sure testimonies, and enforces the precepts as seemly and becoming in the presence of so great a Lord.

The whole psalm is most impressive, and is calculated to comfort the distressed, confirm the timorous, and assist the devout. O thou who art so great and gracious a King, reign over us forever!

Psalm 94

1. O LORD God, to whom vengeance belongeth; O God, to whom vengeance belongeth, show thyself: or, "God of retributions, Jehovah, God of retributions, shine forth!" A very natural prayer when innocence is trampled down, and wickedness exalted on high. If the execution of justice be a right thing – and who can deny the fact? – then it must be a very proper thing to desire it; not out of private revenge, in which case one would hardly dare to appeal to God, but out of sympathy with right, and pity for those who are made wrongfully to suffer. Who can see a nation enslaved, or even an individual downtrodden, without crying to the Lord to arise and vindicate the righteous cause? The toleration of injustice is here attributed to the Lord's being hidden, and it is implied that the bare sight of him will suffice to alarm the tyrants into ceasing their oppressions. God has but to show himself, and the good cause wins the day. *He* comes, he sees, he conquers! In these evil days we need a display of his power, for the ancient enemies of God and man are again struggling for the mastery, and if they gain it, woe unto the saints of God.

2. **Lift up thyself, thou judge of the earth.** Ascend thy judgment-seat and be acknowledged as the ruler of people: and, moreover, raise thyself as men do who are about to strike with all their might; for the abounding sin of mankind requires a heavy blow from thy hand. **Render a reward to the proud;** give them measure for measure, blow for blow. Let them know that thou art far more above them than they can be above the meanest of their fellow-men.

3. **LORD, how long shall the wicked, how long shall the wicked triumph?** Shall wrong forever rule? Are slavery, robbery, tyranny never to cease? Since there is certainly a just God in heaven, armed with almighty power, surely there must be sooner or later an end to the ascendancy of evil, innocence must one day find a defender. This **how long?** of the text is the bitter plaint of all the righteous in all ages, and expresses wonder caused by that great enigma of providence, the existence and predominance of evil. In due time God will publish his reply, but the full end is not yet.

4. **How long shall they utter and speak hard things?** The ungodly are not content with deeds of injustice, but they add hard speeches, boasting, threatening, and insulting over the saints. Will the Lord forever endure this? Will he leave his own children much longer to be the prey of their enemies? Words often wound more than swords; they are as hard to the heart as stones to the flesh; and these are poured forth by the ungodly in redundance, for such is the force of the word translated **utter**; and they use them so commonly that they become their common speech (they **utter and speak** them) – will this always be endured? **And all the workers of iniquity boast themselves?** They even talk to themselves, and of themselves, in arrogance of spirit, as if they were doing some good deed when they crush the poor and needy, and spit their spite on gracious men. It is the nature of workers of iniquity to boast, just as it is a characteristic of good men to be humble.

5. **They break in pieces thy people, O LORD,** grinding them with oppression, crushing them with contempt. Yet the people they break in pieces are God's own people, and they are persecuted because they are so; this is a strong plea for the divine interposition. **And afflict thine heritage,** causing them sorrowful humiliation and deep depression of heart. The term **thine heritage** marks out the election of the saints, God's peculiar interest and delight in them, his covenant relation, of long standing, to them and their fathers; this also is a storehouse of arguments with their faithful God. Will he not defend his own?

6. They deal most arrogantly with those who are the most evident objects

of compassion. The law of God especially commends these poor ones to the kindness of good people, and it is particular wickedness which singles them out to be the victims not only of fraud but of murder. As surely as there is a God in heaven, he will visit those who perpetrate such crimes; though he bear long with them, he will yet take vengeance, and that speedily.

7. Yet they say, the LORD shall not see. When people believe that the eyes of God are dim, there is no reason to wonder that they give full license to their brutal passions. **Neither shall the God of Jacob regard it.** How dare the ungodly assert that he will not notice the wrongs done to God's people? There is no limit to the proud profanity of the proud; reason itself cannot restrain them; they have broken through the bounds of common sense. Jacob's God heard him at the brook Jabbok; Jacob's God led him and kept him all his life long, and said concerning him and his family, "Touch not mine anointed, and do my prophets no harm"; and yet these brutish ones profess to believe that he neither sees nor regards the injuries wrought upon the elect people! Surely in such unbelievers is fulfilled the saying of the wise, that those whom the Lord means to destroy he leaves to the madness of their corrupt hearts.

8. Understand, ye brutish among the people. They said that God did not *note,* and now, using the same word in the original, the psalmist calls on the wicked to *note,* and have regard to the truth. They thought themselves to be wise, and indeed the only people of wit in the world, but he calls them "boars among the people." When a man has done with God, he has done with his manhood, and has fallen to the level of the ox and the ass, indeed beneath them, for "the ox knoweth his owner, and the ass his master's crib." Instead of being humbled in the presence of scientific infidels, we ought to pity them. **And ye fools, when will ye be wise?** Have you no relics of reason left? No shreds of sense?

9. He that planted the ear, shall he not hear? He made you hear; can he not himself hear? Unanswerable question! It overwhelms the skeptic, and covers him with confusion. **He that formed the eye, shall he not see?** He gives us vision; is it conceivable that he has no sight himself? If there be a God, he must be a personal intelligent being, and no limit can be set to his knowledge.

10. He that chastiseth the heathen, shall not he correct? He reproves whole nations; can he not reprove individuals? The question which follows is equally full of force, and is asked with a degree of warmth which checks the speaker, and causes the inquiry to remain incomplete. It begins, **He that teacheth man knowledge,** and then it comes to a pause, which the translators have supplied with the word, **shall not he know?** But no such words are in the original, where the sentence comes to an abrupt end, as if the inference were too natural to need to be stated, and the writer had lost patience with the brutish men with whom he had argued. The earnest believer often feels as if he could say, "Go to, you are not worth arguing with!" Human knowledge comes from God. Science in its first principles was taught to our progenitor

Adam, and all after advances have been due to divine aid; does not the author and revealer of all knowledge himself know?

11. Whether people admit or deny that God knows, one thing is here declared, namely, that **The LORD knoweth the thoughts of man, that they are vanity.** Not their words alone are heard, and their works seen, but he reads the secret motions of their minds, for men themselves are not hard to be discerned of him; before his glance they themselves are but vanity. It is in the Lord's esteem no great matter to know the thoughts of such transparent pieces of vanity as mankind are; he sums them up in a moment as poor vain things. This is the sense of the original, but that given in the Authorized Version is also true – the thoughts, the best part, the most spiritual portion of human nature, even these are vanity itself, and nothing better. And yet such a creature as this boasts, plays at monarch, tyrannizes over his fellow worms, and defies his God! Madness is mingled with human vanity, like smoke with the fog, to make it fouler but not more substantial than it would have been alone.

How foolish are those who think God does not know their actions, when the truth is that their vain thoughts are all perceived by him! How absurd to make nothing of God when in fact we ourselves are as nothing in his sight.

12. Blessed is the man whom thou chastenest, O LORD. The psalmist's mind is growing quiet. He no longer complains to God or argues with people, for his faith perceives that with the most afflicted believer all is well. Though he may not feel blessed while smarting under the rod of chastisement, yet blessed he is; he is precious in God's sight, or the Lord would not take the trouble to correct him. The psalmist calls the chastened one a **man** in the best sense, using the Hebrew word which implies strength. He is a man, indeed, who is under the teaching and training of the Lord. **And teacheth him out of thy law.** The book and the rod, the law and the chastening, go together, and are made doubly useful by being found in connection. The blessing of God belongs far rather to those who suffer under the divine hand than to those who make others suffer. The afflicted believer is under tuition, he is in training for something higher and better, and all that he meets with is working out his highest good.

13. The chastening hand and instructive book are sanctified to us, so that we learn to rest in the Lord. We see that his end is our everlasting benefit, and therefore abide quiet under all trying providences and bitter persecutions, waiting our time. The Mighty Hunter is preparing the pit for the brutish ones; they are prowling about at this time, and tearing the sheep, but they will soon be captured and destroyed; therefore the people of the Lord learn to rest in days of adversity, and tarry the leisure of their God.

14. For the LORD will not cast off his people. He may cast them down, but he never can cast them off. The Lord will not withdraw his love, **neither will he forsake his inheritance.** For a time he may leave his own with the design of benefiting them, yet never can he utterly destroy them.

15. But judgment shall return unto righteousness. The great Judge will come, the reign of righteousness will commence, the course of affairs will yet be turned into the right channel, and then all the godly will rejoice. The chariot of right will be drawn in triumph through our streets, **and all the upright in heart shall follow it,** as in gladsome procession. The government of the world has been for a while in the hands of those who have used it for the basest and most vicious ends; but the cry of prayer will bring back righteousness to the throne, and then every upright heart will have its portion of joy.

16. Notwithstanding the psalmist's persuasion that all would be well eventually he could not at the time perceive anyone who would stand side by side with him in opposing evil. This also is a bitter trial, and a sore evil under the sun; yet it has its purpose, for it drives the heart still more completely to the Lord, compelling it to rest alone in him. If we could find friends elsewhere, it may be our God would not be so dear to us; but when, after calling upon heaven and earth to help, we meet with no succor but such as comes from the eternal arm, we are led to prize our God, and rest upon him with undivided trust. Never is the soul safer or more at rest than when, all other helpers failing, she leans upon the Lord alone. The verse before us is an appropriate cry, now that the church sees error invading her on all sides, while faithful ministers are few, and fewer still are bold enough to **stand up** and defy the enemies of truth. A false charity has enfeebled most of the valiant men of Israel. Our grand consolation is that the God of Knox and Luther is yet with us, and in due time will call out his chosen champions.

17. Without Jehovah's help the psalmist declares that he would have died outright, and gone into the silent land, where no more testimonies can be borne for the living God. Or he may mean that he would not have had a word to speak against his enemies, but would have been wrapped in speechless shame. Blessed be God, we are not left to that condition yet, for the Almighty Lord is still the helper of those who look to him. Our inmost soul is bowed down when we see the victories of the Lord's enemies – we cannot brook it, we cover our mouths in confusion; but he will yet arise and avenge his own cause, therefore have we hope.

18. When I said, My foot slippeth – is slipping even now: I perceived my danger, and cried out in horror, and then, at the very moment of my extremity, came the needed help. **Thy mercy, O Lord, held me up.** Often enough is this the case: we feel our weakness, and see our danger, and in fear and trembling we cry out. At such times nothing can help us but **mercy**; we can make no appeal to any fancied merit, for we feel that it is our inbred sin which makes our feet so ready to fail us; our joy is that mercy endures forever, and is always at hand to pluck us out of the danger, and hold us up.

19. In the multitude of my thoughts within me. When I am tossed to and fro with various reasonings, distractions, questionings, and forebodings, I will fly to my true rest, for **thy comforts delight my soul.** From my sinful thoughts, my vain thoughts, my sorrowful thoughts, my griefs, my cares, my conflicts, I will hasten to the Lord; he has divine **comforts,** and these will not only console but actually **delight** me. How sweet are the comforts of the Spirit! Who can muse upon eternal love, immutable purposes, covenant promises, finished redemption, the risen Saviour, his union with his people, the coming glory, and such like themes, without feeling his heart leaping with joy? The little world within is, like the great world without, full of confusion and strife; but when Jesus enters it, and whispers, "Peace be unto you," there is a calm.

20. Shall the throne of iniquity have fellowship with thee? God enters into no alliance with unjust authority; he gives no sanction to unrighteous legislation. **Which frameth mischief by a law?** They legalize robbery and violence, and then plead that it is the law of the land; and so indeed it may be, but it is a wickedness for all that. No injustice can be permanent, for God will not set his seal upon it, nor have any fellowship with it, and therefore down it must come, and happy will be the day which sees it fall.

21. They gather themselves together against the soul of the righteous. So many are there of them that they crowd their assemblies, and carry their hard measures with enthusiasm; they are the popular party, and are eager to put down the saints. **And condemn the innocent blood.** They are great at slander and false accusation, nor do they stick at murder; no crime is too great for them, if only they can trample on the servants of the Lord. This description is historically true in reference to persecuting times. The dominant sect has the law on its side, and boasts that it is the national church; but the law which establishes and endows one religion rather than another is radically an injustice.

22. Let the wicked gather as they may, the psalmist is not afraid, but sweetly sings. Firm as a rock is Jehovah's love, and there do we go for shelter.

23. The natural result of oppression is the destruction of the despot; his own iniquities crush him ere long. **He shall bring upon them their own iniquity, and shall cut them off in their own wickedness.** While the stolen bread is in their mouths wrath slays them. God himself conspicuously visits them, and reveals his own power in their overthrow. **Yea, the LORD our God shall cut them off.**

Here, then, the matter ends; faith reads the present in the light of the future, and ends her song without a trembling note.

Psalm 95

1. O come, let us sing unto the LORD. We love him, we admire him, we reverence him; let us express our feelings with the choicest sounds, using our noblest faculty for its noblest end. It is well thus to urge others to magnify the Lord, but we must be careful to set a worthy example ourselves, so that we may be able not only to cry **Come,** but also to add *let us* **sing,** because we are singing ourselves. It is to be feared that very much even of religious singing is not unto the Lord, but unto the ear of the congregation: above all things we must in our service of song take care that all we offer is with the heart's sincerest and most fervent intent directed towards the Lord himself. **Let us make a joyful noise to the rock of our salvation.** With holy enthusiasm let us sing, making a sound which indicates our earnestness; with abounding joy let us lift up our voices, actuated by that happy and peaceful spirit which trustful love is sure to foster. The author of this song had in his mind's eye the rock, the tabernacle, the Red Sea, and the mountains of Sinai, and he alludes to them all in this first part of his hymn. God is our abiding, immutable, and mighty rock, and in him we find deliverance and safety; therefore it becomes us to praise him with heart and with voice from day to day; and especially should we delight to do this when we assemble as his people for public worship.

2. Let us come before his presence with thanksgiving. Here is probably a reference to the special presence of God in the Holy of Holies above the mercy-seat, and also to the glory which shone forth out of the cloud which rested above the tabernacle. Everywhere God is present, but there is a special presence of grace and glory into which us should never come without the profoundest reverence. We may make bold to come before the immediate presence of the Lord – for the voice of the Holy Spirit in this psalm invites us, and when we do draw near to him we should remember his great goodness to us and cheerfully confess it. Our worship should have reference to the past as well as to the future; if we do not bless the Lord for what we have already received, how can we reasonably look for more. We are permitted to bring our petitions, and therefore we are in honor bound to bring our thanksgivings. **And make a joyful noise unto him with psalms.** We should shout as exaltingly as those do who triumph in war, and as solemnly as those whose utterance is a psalm. It is not always easy to unite enthusiasm with reverence, and it is a frequent fault to destroy one of these qualities while straining after the other. The perfection of singing is that which unites joy with gravity, exultation with humility, fervency with sobriety. The invitation given in the first verse is thus repeated in the second with the addition of directions, which indicate more fully the intent of the writer. One can imagine David in earnest tones persuading his people to go up with him to the worship of Jehovah with sound of harp and hymn, and holy delight. The gladsomeness of his exhortation is noteworthy. The noise is to be **joyful;** this quality he insists upon twice. It is to be feared that this is too much overlooked in ordinary services; people are so impressed with the idea that they ought to be serious that they put on the aspect of misery, and quite forget that joy is as much a characteristic of true worship as solemnity itself.

3. No doubt the surrounding nations imagined Jehovah to be a merely local deity, the god of a small nation, and therefore one of the inferior deities; the psalmist utterly repudiates such an idea. Idolaters tolerated gods many and lords many, giving to each a certain measure of respect; the monotheism of the Jews was not content with this concession; it rightly claimed for Jehovah the chief place, and the supreme power. This verse and the following supply some of the reasons for worship, drawn from the being, greatness, and sovereign dominion of the Lord.

4. In his hand are the deep places of the earth. He is the God of the valleys and the hills, the caverns, and the peaks. Far down where miners sink their shafts, deeper yet where lie the secret oceans by which springs are fed, and deepest of all in the unknown abyss where the huge central fires of earth rage, there Jehovah's power is felt, and all things are under the dominion of his hand. When Israel drank of the crystal fount which welled up from the great deep, below the smitten rock, the people knew that in the Lord's hands were the deep places of the earth. **The strength of the hills is his also.** When Sinai was issuing smoke the tribes learned that Jehovah was God of the hills as well as of the valleys. Everywhere and at all times is this true. Strength is the main thought which strikes the mind when gazing on those vast ramparts of cliff which front the raging sea, or peer into the azure sky, piercing the clouds, but it is to the devout mind the strength of God; hints of Omnipotence are given by those stern rocks which brave the fury of the elements, and like walls of brass defy the assaults of nature in her wildest rage.

5. The sea is his. This was seen to be true at the Red Sea when the waters saw their God, and obediently stood aside to open a pathway for his people. It was not Egypt's sea though it washed her shores. The Lord on high reigned supreme over the flood, as King forever and ever. So is it with the broad ocean; Neptune is but a phantom, the Lord is God of ocean. **And he made it.** Hence his right and sovereignty.

And his hands formed the dry land. As the potter molds his clay, so did Jehovah with his hands fashion the habitable parts of the earth. Count it all as the floor of a temple where the footprints of the present Deity are visible before your eyes if you do but care to see.

6. Here the exhortation to worship is renewed and backed with a motive which, to Israel of old, and to Christians now, is especially powerful; for both the Israel after the flesh and the Israel of faith may be described as the people of his pasture, and by both he is called "our God." **O come, let us worship and bow down.** The adoration is to be humble. The "joyful noise" is to be accompanied with lowliest reverence. We are to worship in such style that the bowing indicates that we count ourselves as nothing in the presence of the all-glorious Lord. **Let us kneel before the LORD our maker.** Posture is not everything – prayer is heard when knees cannot bend – but it is seemly that an adoring heart should show its awe by prostrating the body, and bending the knee.

7. For he is our God. Here is the master reason for worship. Jehovah has entered into covenant with *us*, and from all the world beside has shown us to be his own elect. Happy is the person who can sincerely believe that this sentence is true in reference to himself. **And we are the people of his pasture, and the sheep of his hand.** As he belongs to us, so do we belong to him. And we are his as the people whom he daily feeds and protects. Our pastures are not ours, but his; we draw all our supplies from his stores. We are his, just as sheep belong to the shepherd, and his hand is our rule, our guidance, our government, our succor, our source of supply. Israel was led through the desert, and we are led through this life by "that great Shepherd of the sheep." Can we refuse to worship and bow down when we clearly see that this God is our God forever and ever, and will be our guide, even unto death?

But what is this warning which follows? The favored nation grew deaf to their Lord's command, and proved not to be truly his sheep, of whom it is written, "My sheep hear my voice"; will this turn out to be our character also? God forbid. **Today if ye will hear his voice.** Dreadful **if.** Many would not hear; they put off the claims of love, and provoked their God. **Today,** in the hour of grace, in the day of mercy, we are tried as to whether we have an ear for the voice of our Creator. Nothing is said of tomorrow; he presses for immediate attention; for our own sakes he asks instantaneous obedience.

8. Harden not your heart. We cannot soften our hearts, but we can harden them, and the consequences will be fatal. **As in the provocation, and as in the day of temptation in the wilderness** (or, "like Meribah, like the day of Massah in the wilderness"). Be not willfully, wantonly, repeatedly, obstinately rebellious. Let the example of that unhappy generation serve as a beacon; do not repeat the offenses which have already more than enough provoked the Lord.

9. When your fathers tempted me. As far as they could do so they tempted God to change his usual way, and to do their sinful bidding. God's way is perfect, and when we would have him alter it to please us, we are guilty of tempting him; and the fact that we do so in vain, while it magnifies the Lord's holiness, by no means excuses our guilt. We are in most danger of this sin in times of need, for then it is that we are apt to fall into unbelief, and to demand a change in those arrangements of providence which are the transcript of perfect holiness and infinite wisdom. **Proved me.** They put the Lord to needless tests, demanding new miracles, fresh interpositions, and renewed tokens of his presence. Are we not prone to demand specialities, with the alternative secretly offered in our hearts, that if they do not come at our bidding we will disbelieve? True, the Lord is very condescending, and frequently grants us marvelous evidences of his power, but we ought not to require them. If we were forever testing the love of our wife or husband, and remained unconvinced after years of faithfulness, we should wear out the utmost human patience. Friendship only flourishes in the atmosphere of confidence; shall the

Lord God, true and immutable, be day after day suspected by his own people? Will not this provoke him to anger? **And saw my work.** They tested him again and again, though each time his work was conclusive evidence of his faithfulness. We must forever be seeing, or we waver in our believing.

10. Forty years long was I grieved with this generation. The impression upon the divine mind is most vivid; he sees them before him now, and calls them *this generation*. He does not leave his prophets to upbraid the sin, but himself utters the complaint and declares that he was grieved, nauseated, and disgusted. It is no small thing which can grieve our long-suffering God to the extent which the Hebrew word here indicates, and if we reflect a moment we shall see the abundant provocation here given; for no one who values his veracity can endure to be suspected, mistrusted, and belied, when there is no ground for it. Which shall we most wonder at, the cruel insolence of mankind or the tender patience of the Lord? **And said, It is a people that do err in their heart, and they have not known my ways.** Their heart was obstinately and constantly at fault; it was not their head which erred, but their very heart was perverse: love, which appealed to their affections, could not convert them. The heart is the mainspring of the man, and if it be not in order, the entire nature is thrown out of gear. If sin were only skin-deep, it might be a slight matter; but since it has defiled the soul, the case is bad indeed. Wanderers in body, they were also wanderers in heart. Are we better than they? Are we not quite as apt to misinterpret the dealings of the Lord? Many treat unbelief as a minor fault, even rather as an infirmity than a crime, but the Lord thinketh not so.

11. There can be no rest to an unbelieving heart. If man and miracles could not satisfy Israel, neither would they have been content with the land which flowed with milk and honey. Solemn warning this to all who leave the way of faith for paths of petulant grumbling and mistrust. The rebels of old could not enter in because of unbelief; "let us therefore fear, lest, a promise being left us of entering into his rest, any of us should even seem to come short of it."

One blessed inference from this psalm must not be forgotten. It is clear that there is a rest of God, and that some must enter into it. The unbelievers could not enter, but "we which have believed do enter into rest." Let us enjoy it, and praise the Lord for it forever. While we do so, let us "come into his presence with thanksgiving, and make a joyful noise unto him with psalms."

Psalm 96

1. O sing unto the LORD a new song. New joys are filling human hearts, for the glad tidings of blessing to all people are proclaimed; therefore let them sing a new song. Angels inaugurated the new dispensation with new songs, and shall not we take up the strain? Unto the one only God all music is to be dedicated.

Mourning is over, and the time of the singing of hearts has come. People are made new creatures, and their song is new also.

Sing unto the LORD, all the earth. National jealousies are dead; a Jew invites the Gentiles to adore, and joins with them. All the earth Jehovah made, and all the earth must sing to him. Nor people alone, but the earth itself is to praise its Maker. Made subject to vanity for a while by a sad necessity, the creation itself also is to be delivered from the bondage of corruption, and brought into the glorious liberty of the children of God, so that sea and forest, field and flood, are to be joyful before the Lord.

2. Sing unto the LORD, bless his name. Thrice is the name of the Lord repeated, and not without meaning. Is it not unto the Three-One Lord that the enlightened nations will sing? Unitarianism is the religion of units; it is too cold to warm the world to worship; the sacred fire of adoration only burns with vehement flame where the Trinity is believed in and beloved. In other ways beside singing, the blessed Lord is to be blessed. His name, his fame, his character, his revealed word and will are to be delighted in, and remembered with perpetual thanksgiving. We may well bless him who so divinely blesses us. **Show forth his salvation from day to day.** The Gospel is the clearest revelation of himself; salvation outshines creation and providence. Let us proclaim the glad tidings, and do so continually, never ceasing the blissful testimony. Each day brings us deeper experience of our saving God, each day shows us anew how deeply we need his salvation, each day reveals the power of the Gospel, each day the Spirit strives with the sons of men; therefore, never pausing, be it ours to tell out the glorious message of free grace. Let those do this who know for themselves what **his** salvation means.

3. Declare his glory among the heathen. His salvation is his glory, the word of the Gospel glorifies him; and this should be published far and wide, till the remotest nations of the earth have known it. Too often the name of the Lord Jesus has been dishonored among the heathen by the vices and cruelties of those who call themselves Christians; may this fact excite true believers to greater diligence in causing the Gospel to be proclaimed as with a trumpet in all quarters of the habitable globe. **His wonders among all people.** The Gospel is a mass of wonders, its history is full of wonders, and it is in itself far more marvelous than miracles themselves. In his Son the Lord has displayed wonders of love, wisdom, grace, and power. All nations need to hear of God's marvelous works; and if a really living, self-denying church would solemnly resolve that right speedily they all shall hear thereof. The tribes which are dying out are not to be excluded from Gospel teaching. None are too degraded, none too cultured, none too savage, and none too refined.

4. For the LORD is great and greatly to be praised. Nothing mean or narrow can be found in him or his acts; in all things he is infinite. Praise should be proportionate to its object; therefore let it be infinite when rendered unto the Lord.

All the honor rendered unto him should be given in largeness of heart, with the utmost zeal for his glory. **He is to be feared above all gods.** Dread of other gods is mere superstition; awe of the Lord is pure religion. Holy fear is the beginning of the graces, and yet it is the accompaniment of their highest range.

5. For all the gods of the nations are idols. Mere images of wood and stone, vanities, nothings. **But the LORD made the heavens.** The reality of his Godhead is proved by his works. The idol gods have no existence, but our God is the author of all existences; they are mere earthly vanities, while he is not only heavenly, but made the heavens.

6. Honor and majesty are before him. People can but mimic these things; their pompous pageants are but the pretense of greatness. In the presence of Jehovah real glory and sovereignty abide. **Strength and beauty are in his sanctuary.** In him are combined all that is mighty and lovely, powerful and resplendent. In Chronicles we read strength and **gladness**; and the two renderings do not disagree in sense. Not in outward show or parade of costly robes does the glory of God consist; such things are tricks of state with which the ignorant are dazzled; holiness, justice, wisdom, grace, these are the splendors of Jehovah's courts.

7. The first six verses commenced with an exhortation to sing, three times repeated, with the name of the Lord thrice mentioned; here we meet with the expression **Give unto the LORD,** used in the same triple manner. The invocation of the sweet singer is still addressed to all mankind, to whom he speaks as **Ye kindreds of the people.** Divided into tribes and families, we are called in our courses and order to appear before him and ascribe to him all honor. Family worship is especially pleasing unto him who is the God of all the families of Israel. **Give unto the LORD glory and strength;** that is to say, recognize the glory and power of Jehovah, and ascribe them unto him in your solemn hymns. Great nations, who count yourselves both famous and mighty, cease your boastings! Monarchs, who are styled imperial and powerful, humble yourselves in the dust before the only Potentate. Glory and strength are nowhere to be found save with the Lord; all others possess but the semblance thereof.

8. Give unto the LORD glory due unto his name. However much of zealous homage we may offer to him, we cannot give him more than his due. If we cannot bring in the full revenue which he justly claims, at least let us not fail from want of honest endeavor. **Bring an offering, and come into his courts.** Atonement for sin having been made, it only remains to bring thank-offerings, and let not these be forgotten. When assembling for public worship we should make a point of bringing with us a contribution to his cause, according to that ancient word, "None of you shall appear before me empty." The time will come when from all ranks and all nations the Lord will receive gifts when they gather together for his worship.

9. O worship the LORD in the beauty of holiness. This is the only beauty which he cares for in our public services, and it is one for which no other can compensate. Beauty of architecture and apparel he does not regard; moral and spiritual beauty is that in which his soul delighteth. Worship must not be rendered to God in a slovenly, sinful, superficial manner; we must be reverent, sincere, earnest, and pure in heart both in our prayers and praises. **Fear before him, all the earth.** "Tremble" is the word in the original, and it expresses the profoundest awe, just as the word "worship" does, which would be more accurately translated by "bow down." Even the bodily frame would be moved to trembling and prostration if people were thoroughly conscious of the power and glory of Jehovah. The sight of the King in his beauty caused no alarm to John in Patmos, and yet it made him fall at his feet as dead.

10. Say among the heathen that the LORD reigneth. This is the gladdest news which can be carried to them – the Lord Jehovah, in the person of his Son, has assumed the throne, and taken to himself his great power. Tell this out among the heathen, and let the heathen themselves, being converted, repeat the same rejoicingly. **The world also shall be established that it shall not be moved.** A settled government is essential to national prosperity; the reign of the God of truth and righteousness will promote this to the highest degree. Sin has shaken the world; the reign of Jesus will set it fast again upon sure foundations. **He shall judge the people righteously.** Iniquity makes the dynasties of tyrants fall; equity causes the throne of Jesus to stand. He will impartially rule over Jew and Gentile, prince and peasant.

11. Let the heaven rejoice, and let the earth be glad. Above and below let the joy be manifested. Let the angels who have stood in amazement at the wickedness of men now rejoice over their repentance and restoration to favor, and let men themselves express their pleasure in seeing their true prince set upon his throne. **Let the sea roar, and the fulness thereof.** Let it be no more a troubled sea; let all its teeming life express the utmost joy because the Lord reigneth even in the depth of the sea. In common with the rest of the creation, the sea has groaned and travailed until now.

12. Let the field be joyful, and all that is therein. Let the cultivated plains praise the Lord. Peace enables their owners to plow and sow and reap, without fear of the rapine of invaders, and therefore in glad notes they applaud him whose empire is peace. Both men, and creatures that graze the plain, and the crops themselves are represented as swelling the praises of Jehovah. **Then shall all the trees of the wood rejoice.** He does not say, let them rejoice, but they **shall** do so. Perhaps the psalmist was thinking of the birds.

13. Before the LORD: for he cometh. Even now he is near; his advent should, therefore, be the cause of immediate rejoicing: already are we in his presence; let us worship him with delight. **For he cometh to judge the earth,** to rule it with discretion; not to tax it, and control it by force, as kings often do, but to preside as magistrates do whose business it is to see justice carried out between people. All the world will be under the jurisdiction of this great Judge, and before his bar all will be summoned to appear. At this moment he is on the road, and the hour of his coming draweth nigh. **He shall judge the world with righteousness.** His essential rectitude will determine all causes and cases; there will be no bribery and corruption there, neither can error or failure be found in his decisions. **And the people with his truth,** or rather "the nations in faithfulness." Honesty, veracity, integrity will rule upon his judgment-seat. No nation will be favored there, and none be made to suffer through prejudice. The black man will be tried by the same law as his white master; the aboriginal will have justice executed for him against his civilized exterminator.

In closing, let us ourselves join in the song. Since the whole universe is to be clothed with smiles, shall not we be glad?

Psalm 97

1. The Lord reigneth. This is the watchword of the psalm – Jehovah reigns. It is also the essence of the Gospel proclamation, and the foundation of the Gospel kingdom. Jesus has come, and all power is given unto him in heaven and in earth; therefore people are bidden to yield him their obedient faith. Saints draw comfort from these words, and only rebels cavil at them. **Let the earth rejoice,** for there is cause for joy. Other reigns have produced injustice, oppression, bloodshed, terror; the reign of the infinitely gracious Jehovah is the hope of mankind, and when they all yield to it the race will have its paradise restored. To every willing subject Jesus brings untold blessings. **Let the multitude of isles be glad thereof.** To the ancient Israelites all places beyond the seas were isles, and the phrase is equivalent to all lands which are reached by ships. It is remarkable, however, that upon actual islands some of the greatest victories of the Cross have been achieved.

2. Clouds and darkness are round about him. So the Lord revealed himself at Sinai; so must he ever surround his essential Deity when he shows himself to us, or his excessive glory would destroy us. There must be a veiling of his infinite splendor if anything is to be seen by finite beings. It is often thus with the Lord in providence; when working out designs of unmingled love he conceals the purpose of his grace that it may be the more clearly discovered at the end. Around the history of his church dark clouds of persecution hover, and an awful gloom at times settles down; still the Lord is there; and though people for a while see not the bright light in the clouds, it bursts forth in due season to the confusion of the adversaries of the Gospel. This passage should teach us the impertinence of attempting to pry into the essence of the Godhead, the vanity of all endeavors to understand the mystery of the Trinity in Unity, the arrogance of arraigning the Most High before the bar of human reason, the folly of dictating to the Eternal One the manner in which he should proceed.

Righteousness and judgment are the habitation of his throne.. There he abides; he never departs from strict justice and right, his throne is fixed upon the rock of eternal holiness. Righteousness is his immutable attribute, and judgment marks his every act.

3. A fire goeth before him. Like an advance guard clearing the way. So was it at Sinai; so must it be: the very Being of God is power, consuming all opposition; omnipotence is a devouring flame which **burneth up his enemies round about.** God is long-suffering, but when he comes forth to judgment he will make short work with the unrighteous; they will be as chaff before the flame. Reading this verse in reference to the coming of Jesus, and the descent of the Spirit, we are reminded of the tongues of fire, and of the power which attended the Gospel, so that all opposition was speedily overcome. Even now where the Gospel is preached in faith, and in the power of the Spirit, it burns its own way, irresistibly destroying falsehood, superstition, unbelief, sin, indifference, and hardness of heart.

4. His lightnings enlightened the world. In times of tempest the whole of nature is lighted up. Jesus in the Gospel lights up the earth with such a blaze of truth and grace as was never seen or even imagined before. **The earth saw, and trembled.** In God's presence the solid earth quakes; astonished by his glory it is convulsed with fear. To the advent of our Lord and the setting up of his kingdom among mankind these words are also most applicable; nothing ever caused such a shaking and commotion as the proclamation of the Gospel. When the Holy Spirit rested upon his servants their course was like that of a mighty storm, the truth flashed with the force and speed of a thunderbolt, and philosophers and priests, princes and people were utterly confounded, and altogether powerless to withstand it. It will be so again. Faith even now sets the world on fire, and rocks the nations to and fro.

5. The hills melted like wax at the presence of the LORD. Inanimate nature knows its Creator, and worships him in its own fashion. States and kingdoms which stand out upon the world like mountains are utterly dissolved when he decrees their end. Systems as ancient and firmly rooted as the hills pass away when he does but look upon them. **At the presence of the Lord of the whole earth.** His power is everywhere felt. People cannot move the hills, with difficulty do they climb them, with incredible toil do they pierce their way through their fastnesses, but it is not so with the Lord: his presence makes a clear pathway, obstacles disappear by his mere presence, for power goes forth from him with a word or a glance. Oh for the presence of the Lord after this sort with his church at this hour! It is our one and only need. With it the mountains of difficulty would flee away, and all obstacles would disappear.

In the little world of our nature the presence of Jesus in reigning power is as a fire to consume our lusts and melt our souls to obedience. Sometimes we doubt the present of the Lord within, for he is concealed with clouds, but we are again assured that he is within us when his light shines in and fills us with holy fear, while at the same time the warmth of grace softens us to penitence, resignation and obedience, as wax becomes soft in the presence of fire.

6. The heavens declare his righteousness. It is as conspicuous as if written across the skies. It is the manner of the inspired poets to picture the whole creation as in sympathy with the glory of God, and indeed it is not *mere* poetry, for a great truth underlies it; the whole creation has been made to groan through human sin, and it is yet to share in the joy of his restoration. **And all the people see his glory.** The glorious Gospel became so well known and widely promulgated that it seemed to be proclaimed by every star, and published by the very skies themselves; therefore all races of men became acquainted with it, and were made to see the exceeding glory of the face of God which is resplendent therein. May it come to pass ere long that, by a revival of the old missionary ardor, the glad tidings may yet be carried to every tribe of Adam's race, and once again all flesh may see the glory of Jehovah. It must be so; therefore let us rejoice before the Lord.

7. Confounded be all they that serve graven images, that boast themselves of idols. They will be so; shame will cover their faces; they will blush to think of their former besotted boastings. **Worship him, all ye gods.** Bow down yourselves, you fancied gods. If the false gods are thus bidden to worship the coming Lord, how much more will they adore him who are godlike creatures in heaven, that is, the angelic spirits? Paul quotes this passage as the voice of God to angels when he sent his Son into the world. All powers are bound to recognize the chief power; since they derive their only rightful authority from the Lord, they should be careful to acknowledge his superiority at all times by the most reverent adoration.

8. Zion heard, and was glad. While the heathen are confounded the people of God are made to triumph, for they love to see their God exalted. **And the daughters of Judah rejoiced.** In the first ages of Christianity the believing Israel rejoiced to see Christ's kingdom victorious among the heathen, and even yet, though for a little while turning aside, the daughters of Judah will sympathize in the widespread reign of Jehovah their God, through the Gospel of his Son.

9. For thou, LORD, are high above all the earth. And therefore do we rejoice to see the idols abolished and to see all mankind bending at thy throne. **Thou art exalted far above all gods.** As much as all is exalted above nothing, and perfection above folly. Jehovah is not alone high over Judea, but over all the earth; nor is he exalted over mankind only, but over everything that can be called god: the days are on their way when everyone will discern this truth, and will render unto the Lord the glory which is due alone to him.

10. Ye that love the LORD, hate evil. For he hates it; his presence shakes it out of its place. We cannot love God without hating that which he hates. We are not only to avoid evil, and to refuse to countenance it, but we must be in arms against it, and bear towards it a hearty indignation. **He preserveth the souls of his saints.** The saints are the safe ones: they have been saved and will be saved. God keeps those who keep his law. Those who love the Lord will see his love manifested to them in their preservation from their enemies, and as they keep far from evil so shall evil be kept far from them. **He delivereth them out of the hand of the wicked.** It is not consistent with the glory of his name to give over to the power of his foes those whom his grace has made his friends. He may leave the bodies of his persecuted saints in the hand of the wicked, but not their souls; these are very dear to him, and he preserves them safe in his bosom. This foretells for the church a season of battling with the powers of darkness, but the Lord will preserve it and bring it forth to the light.

11. **Light is sown for the righteous.** All along their pathway it is strewn. Their night is almost over, their day is coming, the morning already advancing with rosy steps is sowing the earth with orient pearls. The full harvest of delight is not yet ours, but it is sown for us; it is springing; it will yet appear in fullness. This is only for those who are right before the Lord in his own righteousness; for all others the blackness of darkness is reserved. **And gladness for the upright in heart.** Gladness is not only for one righteous man in the singular, but for the whole company of the upright. In the furrows of integrity lie the seeds of happiness, which will develop into a harvest of bliss. The Gospel of Jesus, wherever it goes, sows the whole earth with joy for believers, for these are the people who are righteous before the Lord.

12. **Rejoice in the LORD, ye righteous.** The psalmist had bidden the earth rejoice, and here he turns to the excellent of the earth and bids them lead the song. If all others fail to praise the Lord, the godly must not. To them God is especially revealed; by them he should be specially adored. **And give thanks at the remembrance of his holiness** – which is the harmony of all his attributes, the superlative wholeness of his character. This is a terror to the wicked, and a cause of thankfulness to the gracious. To remember that Jehovah is holy is becoming in those who dwell in his courts, to give thanks in his presence. In reference to the triumphs of the Gospel, this text teaches us to rejoice greatly in its purifying effect; it is the death of sin and the life of virtue. God will fill the world with holiness, and so with happiness; therefore let us glory in his holy name, world without end. Amen.

Psalm 98

1. **O sing unto the LORD a new song; for he hath done marvelous things.** We had a new song before (Psalm 96) because the Lord was coming, but now we have

another new song because he has come, and seen and conquered. Jesus, our King, has lived a marvelous life, died a marvelous death, risen by a marvelous resurrection, and ascended marvelously into heaven. By his divine power he has sent forth the Holy Spirit doing marvels, and by that sacred energy his disciples have also wrought marvelous things and astonished all the earth. Idols have fallen, superstitions have withered, systems of error have fled, and empires of cruelty have perished. For all this he deserves the highest praise. His acts have proved his Deity: Jesus is Jehovah, and therefore we sing unto him as the LORD. **His right hand, and his holy arm, hath gotten him the victory;** not by the aid of others, but by his own unweaponed hand his marvelous conquests have been achieved. Sin, death, and hell fell beneath his solitary prowess, and the idols and the errors of mankind have been overthrown and smitten by his hand alone. The victories of Jesus among us are all the more wonderful because they are accomplished by means to all appearance most inadequate; they are due not to physical but to moral power – the energy of goodness, justice, truth; in a word, to the power of his **holy** arm. His holy influence has been the sole cause of success. Jesus never stoops to use policy, or brute force; his unsullied perfections secure to him a real and lasting victory over all the powers of evil.

2. **The LORD hath made known his salvation** – by the coming of Jesus and by the outpouring of the Holy Spirit, by whose power the gospel was preached among the Gentiles. The Lord is to be praised not only for effecting human salvation, but also for making it known, for we would never have discovered it for ourselves. In every case it is a divine revelation to the mind and heart. In God's own light his light is seen. He must reveal his Son in us, or we shall be unable to discern him. **His righteousness hath he openly showed in the sight of the heathen.** This word **righteousness** is the favorite word of the apostle of the Gentiles; he loves to dwell on the Lord's method of making people righteous, and vindicating his own justice by the atoning blood. What was hidden in the types is "openly showed" in the Gospel.

3. **He hath remembered his mercy and his truth toward the house of Israel.** To them Jesus came in the flesh, and to them was the Gospel first preached; and though they counted themselves unworthy of eternal life, yet the covenant was not broken, for the true Israelites were called into fellowship and still remain so. **All the ends of the earth have seen the salvation of our God.** Not to Abraham's physical descendants alone, but to the elect among all nations, has grace been given; therefore, let the whole church of God sing unto him a new song. It was no small blessing, or little miracle, that throughout all lands the Gospel should be published in so short a time, with such singular success and such abiding results. Pentecost deserves a new song as well as the Passion and the Resurrection; let our hearts exult as we remember it. *Our God,* our own forever blessed God, has been honored by those who once bowed down

before dumb idols; his salvation has not only been heard of but seen among all people; it has been experienced as well as explained; his Son is the actual Redeemer of a multitude out of all nations.

4–6. In these three verses we are taught how to praise the Lord.

4. Make a joyful noise unto the LORD, all the earth. Every tongue must applaud, and that with the vigor which joy of the heart alone can arouse to action. If ever people shout for joy it should be when the Lord comes among them in the proclamation of his Gospel reign. **Make a loud noise, and rejoice, and sing praise;** or "Burst forth, and sing, and play." Let every form of exultation be used, every kind of music pressed into the service. There is no fear of our being too hearty in magnifying the God of our salvation; only we must take care that the song comes from the heart, otherwise the music is nothing but a noise in his ears, whether it be caused by human throats, or organ pipes, or far-resounding trumpets. Loud let our hearts ring out the honors of our conquering Saviour; with all our might let us extol the Lord who has vanquished all our enemies, and led our captivity captive. He will do this best who is most in love with Jesus.

5. Sing unto the LORD with the harp. Skill in music should not be desecrated to the world's evil mirth; it should aid the private devotions of the saint. God's praises should be performed in the best possible manner, but their sweetness mainly lies in spiritual qualities. The concords of faith and repentance, the harmonies of obedience and love are true music in the ear of the Most High. **With the harp.** The repetition of the word is highly poetical, and shows that the daintiest expressions of poetry are none too rich for the praise of God. All repetitions are not vain repetitions; in sacred song there should be graceful repeats; they render the sense emphatic, and help to fire the soul; even preachers go not amiss when they dwell on a word and sound it out again and again, till dull ears feel its emphasis. **And the voice of a psalm,** or with "a musical voice," as distinguished from common speech. Our voice has in it many modulations; there is the voice of conversation, the voice of complaint, the voice of pleading, the voice of command, and there ought to be with each of us the voice of a psalm.

6. With trumpets and sound of cornet make a joyful noise. God's worship should be heartily loud. The far resounding trump and horn well symbolize the power which should be put forth in praise. **Before the LORD, the King.** On coronation days, and when beloved monarchs ride abroad, the people shout and the trumpets sound till the walls ring again. Let but the reigning power of Jesus be felt in the soul and we shall cast aside that shill mutter, downed by the pealing organ, which is now so commonly the substitute for earnest congregational singing.

7. Let the sea roar, and the fulness thereof. Even its thunders will not be too grand for such a theme. Handel, in some of his sublime choruses, would have been glad of its aid to express his lofty conceptions. **The world, and they that dwell therein.** The land should be in harmony with the ocean. Its mountains and plains, cities and villages, should prolong the voice of jubilee which welcomes the Lord of all. Nothing can be more sublime than this verse; yet no song is equal to the majesty of the theme when Jehovah, the King, is to be extolled.

8. **Let the floods clap their hands.** The rolling rivers, the tidal estuaries, the roaring cataracts, are here summoned to pay their homage, and to clap their hands, as men do when they greet their sovereign with acclamation. **Let the hills be joyful together,** or in concert with the floods. Silent as are the mighty mountains, let them forget themselves, and burst forth into a sublime uproariousness of mirth.

9. **Before the LORD; for he cometh to judge the earth.** Stiller music such as made the stars twinkle with their soft kind eyes suited his first coming at Bethlehem, but his second advent calls for trumpets, for he is a judge; and for all earth's acclamations, for he has put on his royal splendor. The rule of Christ is the joy of nature. All things bless his throne, yea, and the very coming of it. **With righteousness shall he judge the world, and the people with equity.** This is the joy of it. If ever there was a thing to rejoice in upon this poor earth, it is the coming of such a deliverer, the ascension to the universal throne of such a governor.

Psalm 99

1. **The LORD reigneth.** One of the most joyous utterances which ever leaped from mortal lip. The overthrow of the reign of evil and the setting up of Jehovah's kingdom of goodness, justice, and truth is worthy to be hymned again and again. **Let the people tremble.** Let the chosen people feel a solemn yet joyful awe, which will thrill their whole humanity. Saints quiver with devout emotion, and sinners quiver with terror when the rule of Jehovah is fully perceived and felt. It is not a light or trifling matter; it is a truth which, above all other, should stir the depths of our nature. **He sitteth between the cherubims.** In sublime glory, yet in nearness, Jehovah revealed himself above the mercy-seat, whereon stood the likeness of those flaming ones who gaze upon his glory and forever cry, "Holy, Holy, Holy, Lord God of hosts." The Lord reigning on that throne of grace which is sprinkled with atoning blood, and veiled with the covering wings of mediatorial love, is above all other revelations wonderful, and fitted to excite emotion among all mankind; hence it is added, **Let the earth be moved.** Not merely "the people," but the whole earth should feel a movement of adoring awe when it is known that on the mercy-seat God sits as universal monarch. The pomp of heaven surrounds him, and is symbolized by the outstretched wings of the waiting cherubs.

2. The Lord is great in Zion. Of old the temple's sacred hill was the center of the worship of the great King, and the place where his grandeur was most clearly beheld; his church is now his favored palace, where his greatness is displayed, acknowledged, and adored. **And he is high above all the people**; towering above their highest thoughts and loftiest conceptions. If Israel delighted in Saul because he was head and shoulders above the people, how much more should we exult in our God and King, who is as high above us as the heavens are above the earth.

3. Let them praise thy great and terrible name. Let all the dwellers in Zion and all the nations upon the earth praise the Lord, or "acknowledge thankfully" the goodness of his divine nature, albeit that there is so much in it which must inspire their awe. Under the most terrible aspect the Lord is still to be praised. The terrible Avenger is to be praised, as well as the loving Redeemer. Against this the sympathy of man's evil heart with sin rebels; it cries out for an effeminate God in whom pity has strangled justice. The well-instructed servants of Jehovah praise him in all the aspects of his character, whether terrible or tender. Grace streaming from the mercy-seat can alone work in us this admirable frame of mind. **For it is holy,** or "He is holy." In him is no fault, excess or deficiency, error or iniquity. He is wholly excellent, and is therefore called holy.

4. The king's strength also loveth judgment. God is the king, the mercy-seat is his throne, and the scepter which he sways is holy like himself. His power never exerts itself tyrannically; he is a sovereign, and his authority is absolute in his government, but his might delights in right, his force is used for just purposes only. People in these days are constantly arraigning the Lord's government, and setting up to judge whether he does right or not; but saintly people in the olden times were of another mind; they were sure that what the Lord did was just, and instead of calling him to account they humbly submitted themselves to his will. **Thou dost establish equity.** Not even for the sake of mercy does the Lord remove or injure the equity of his moral government; both in providence and in grace he is careful to conserve the immaculate parity of his justice. The Lord our God demolishes every system of injustice, and right alone is made to stand. **Thou executest judgment and righteousness in Jacob.** The laws are carried out; the executive is as righteous as the legislative. Herein let all the oppressed, indeed all who love that which is right, find large occasion for praise. The annals of most human governments have been written in the tears of the donwtrodden, and the curses of the oppressed; the chronicles of the Lord's kingdom are of another sort; truth shines in each line, goodness in every syllable, and justice in every letter.

5. Exalt yet the Lord our God. If no others adore him, let his own people render to him the most ardent worship. Infinite condescension makes him stoop to be called *our* **God,** and truth and faithfulness bind him to maintain that covenant relationship; and surely we, to whom by grace he so lovingly gives himself, should exalt him with all our hearts. He shines upon us from under the veiling wings of cherubim, and above the seat of mercy; therefore let us come and **worship at his footstool.** When he reveals himself in Christ Jesus, as our reconciled God, who allows us to approach even to his throne, it becomes us to unite earnestness and humility, joy and adoration. **For he is holy.** Holiness is the harmony of all the virtues. The Lord has not one glorious attribute alone, or in excess, but all glories are in him as a whole. His power is not his choicest jewel, nor his sovereignty, but his holiness.

6. **Moses and Aaron among his priests, and Samuel among them that call upon his name.** Though not ordained to the typical priesthood, Moses was a true priest. God has ever had a priesthood beside and above that of the law. The three holy men here mentioned all stood in his courts, and saw his holiness, each one after his own order. Moses saw the Lord in flaming fire revealing his perfect law, Aaron often watched the sacred fire devour the sin-offering, and Samuel witnessed the judgment of the Lord on Eli's house, because of the error of his way. These each one stood in the gap when the wrath of God broke forth, because his holiness had been insulted; and acting as intercessors, they screened the nation from the great and terrible God, who otherwise would in a dreadful manner have executed judgment in Jacob. Let these men, or such as these, lead us in our worship, and let us approach the Lord at the mercy-seat as they did, for he is as accessible to us as to them. They made it their life's business to call upon him in prayer, and by so doing brought down innumerable blessings upon themselves and others. Does not the Lord call us also to come up into the mount with Moses, and to enter the most holy place with Aaron? Do we not hear him call us by our name as he did Samuel? And do we not answer, "Speak, Lord, for thy servant heareth"? **They called upon the Lord, and he answered them.** Being a holy God he was true to his promises, and hearkened to them from off the mercy-seat. Here is reason for praise, for answers to the petitions of some are proofs of God's readiness to hear others. These three men asked large things, they pleaded for a whole nation, and they stayed great plagues and turned away fiery wrath; who would not exercise himself in adoring so great and merciful a God?

7. **He spake unto them in the cloudy pillar.** Responses came to Moses and Aaron out of that glorious overshadowing cloud, and though Samuel saw it not, yet to him also came the mystic voice. People have had converse with God; let us therefore speak to God in return. He has told us things to come; let us in return confess the sins which are past. He has revealed his mind to us; let us then pour out our hearts before him. **They kept his testimonies.** When others turned aside they were faithful; in their hearts they laid up his word, and in their lives they obeyed it. When he spoke to them they observed his will, and therefore when they spoke to him he yielded to their desires. This keeping of the divine testimonies is a virtue all too rare in these our days; people run after

their own views and opinions, and make light of the truth of God; hence it is that they fail in prayer. May the good Lord bring back his people to reverence his word, and then will he also have respect unto the voice of their cry. **And the ordinance that he gave them.** His practical precept they observed as well as his doctrinal instruction. A light estimate of inspired dogma is sure to end in neglect of moral virtues. Lord, if thou wilt make us mighty with thee in prayer, we shall also be kept faithful before thee in the service which thou hast laid upon us.

8. **Thou answeredst them, O LORD our God.** A sweet title and a cheering fact. **Thou wast a God that forgavest them, though thou tookest vengeance of their inventions.** He forgave the sinners, but he slew their sins. The passage refers to the nation which was spared through the intercession of these three holy men, but yet was severely chastened for its transgressions. In answer to the cry of Moses the tribes lived on, but the then existing generation could not enter Canaan; Aaron's golden calf was broken, though the fire of the Lord did not consume the people; and Israel smarted under the harsh government of Saul, though at Samuel's request its grumbling against the theocratic rule of their fathers' God was not visited with pestilence or famine. So to forgive sin as at the same time to express abhorrence of it is the special glory of God, and is best seen in the atonement of our Lord Jesus. Are you a believer? Then paternal discipline will be laid upon you if your walk be not close with God.

9. **Exalt the LORD our God.** A second time the delightful title of Jehovah our God is used, and it is quickly followed by a third. The psalm is Trinitarian in its whole structure. In each of his sacred persons the Lord is the God of his people; the Father is ours, the Son is ours, and the Holy Spirit is ours; let us exalt him with all our ransomed powers. **And worship at his holy hill.** Where he appoints his temple let us resort. No spot of ground is now fenced about as especially holy, or to be regarded as more sacred than another; yet his visible church is his chosen hill, and there would we be found, numbered with his people, and unite with them in worship. **For the LORD our God is holy.** Again this devout description is repeated, and made the climax of the song. Oh for hearts made pure within, so that we may rightly perceive and worthily praise the infinite perfection of the Triune Lord.

Psalm 100

1. This is a repetition of Psalm 98:4. The original word signifies a glad shout, such as loyal subjects give when their king appears among them. Our happy God should be worshiped by a happy people; a cheerful spirit is in keeping with his nature, his acts, and the gratitude which we should cherish for his mercies. In every land Jehovah's goodness is seen; therefore in every land

should he be praised. Never will the world be in its proper condition until with one unanimous shout it adores the only God.

2. Serve the LORD with gladness. He is our Lord, and therefore he is to be served; he is our gracious Lord, and therefore to be served with joy. **Come before his presence with singing.** We ought in worship to realize the presence of God, and by an effort of the mind to approach him. This is an act which must to every rightly instructed heart be one of great solemnity, but at the same time it must not be performed in the servility of fear, and therefore we come before him with psalms and hymns. Singing, as it is a joyful, and at the same time a devout, exercise, should be a constant form of approach to God.

3. Know that the LORD he is God. Our worship must be intelligent. We ought to know whom we worship and why. Only those who practically recognize his Godhead are at all likely to offer acceptable praise. **It is he that hath made us, and not we ourselves.** Some men call themselves "self-made men," and they adore their supposed creators; but Christians recognize the origin of their being and their well-being, and take no honor to themselves either for being, or for being what they are. Neither in our first or second creation dare we put so much as a finger upon the glory, for it is the sole right and property of the Almighty. To disclaim honor for ourselves is as necessary a part of true reverence as to ascribe glory to the Lord. For our part, we find it far more easy to believe that the Lord made us than that we were developed by a long chain of natural selections from floating atoms which fashioned themselves. **We are his people, and the sheep of his pasture.** It is our honor to have been chosen from all the world besides to be **his** own people, and our privilege to be therefore guided by his wisdom, tended by his care, and fed by his bounty. Sheep gather around their shepherd and look up to him; in the same manner let us gather around the great Shepherd of mankind. The avowal of our relation to God is in itself praise; when we recount his goodness we are rendering to him the best adoration. Our songs require none of the inventions of fictions; the bare facts are enough; the simple narration of the mercies of the Lord is more astonishing than the productions of imagination. That we are the sheep of his pasture is a plain truth, and at the same time the very essence of poetry.

4. Enter into his gates with thanksgiving. To the occurrence of the word **thanksgiving** in this place the psalm probably owes its title. In all our public service the rendering of thanks must abound; it is like the incense of the temple, which filled the whole house with smoke. Expiatory sacrifices are ended, but those of gratitude will never be out of date. So long as we are receivers of mercy we must be givers of thanks. Mercy permits us to enter his gates; let us praise that mercy. **And unto his courts with praise.** The innermost court is now open to believers, and we enter into that which is within the veil; it is incumbent upon us that we acknowledge the high privilege by our songs. **Be thankful unto him.** Let the praises be in your heart as well as on your tongue, and let it all be for him to whom it all belongs. **And bless his name.** He blessed you; bless him in return. Bless his name, his character, his person. Whatever he does, be sure that you bless him for it: bless him when he takes away as well as when he gives; bless him as long as you live, under all circumstances; bless him in all his attributes, from whatever point of view you consider him.

5. For the LORD is good. This sums up his character and contains a mass of reasons for praise. He is good, gracious, kind, bountiful, loving. Whoever does not praise the good is not good himself. **His mercy is everlasting.** God is not mere justice, stern and cold: he has compassion, and wills not the sinner's death. Towards his own people mercy is still more conspicuously displayed. Everlasting mercy is a glorious theme for sacred song. **And his truth endureth to all generations.** He has entered into covenant with his people, and he will never revoke it. Our heart leaps for joy as we bow before One who has never broken his word or changed his purpose. Resting on his sure word, we feel that joy which is here commanded, and in the strength of it we come into his presence even now, and speak good of his name.

Psalm 101

1. I will sing of mercy and judgment. He would extol both the love and the severity which the Lord had mingled in his experience; he would admire the justice and the goodness of the Lord. Such a song would fitly lead up to godly resolutions as to his own conduct, for that which we admire in our superiors we naturally endeavor to imitate. Mercy and judgment would temper the administration of David, because he had adoringly perceived them in the dispensations of his God. Everything in God's dealing with us may fittingly become the theme of song, and we have not viewed it aright until we feel we can sing about it. We ought as much to bless the Lord for the judgment with which he chastens our sin as for the mercy with which he forgives it. **Unto thee, O LORD, will I sing.** The mercy or the judgment must hold a very subordinate place in our memory, and the Lord alone must be hymned by our heart.

2. I will behave myself wisely in a perfect way. To be holy is to be wise; a perfect way is a wise way. David's resolve was excellent, but his practice did not fully tally with it. Householders, employers, and especially ministers should pray for both wisdom and holiness, for they will need them both. **O when wilt thou come unto me?** He feels the need not merely of divine help, but also of the divine presence, that so he may be instructed, and sanctified, and made fit for the discharge of his high vocation. If God be with us we shall neither err in judgment nor transgress in character; his presence brings us both wisdom and holiness; away from God we are away from safety. Good people are so aware of infirmity that they cry for help from God, so full of prayer that they cry at all seasons, so intense in their desires that they cry with sighs and groanings which cannot be uttered. **I will walk within my house with a perfect heart.** Piety must begin at home. Notice that these words are a part of a song, and that there is no music like the harmony of a gracious life, no psalm so sweet as the daily practice of holiness. What we are at home, that we are indeed.

3. I will set no wicked thing before mine eyes. I will neither delight in it, aim at it, or endure it. If I have wickedness brought before me by others I will turn away from it. The psalmist is very sweeping – *no* **wicked thing**; not only shall it not dwell in his heart, but not even before his eyes. **I hate the work of them that turn aside.** He did not view it with indifference, but with utter scorn and abhorrence. Hatred of sin is a good sentinel for the door of virtue. David would pay no secret service money; he loathed the practices of people who deviate from righteousness. It is greatly to be deplored that in after years he did not keep himself clear in this matter in every case, though in the main he did. How much we all need divine keeping! We are no more perfect than David; indeed we fall far short of him in many things; and, like him, we shall need to write a psalm of penitence very soon after our psalm of good resolution. **It shall not cleave to me.** I will disown their ways, I will not imitate their policy; like dirt it may fall upon me, but I will wash it off, and never rest till I am rid of it. Sin, like pitch, is very apt to stick. In the course of our family history crooked things will turn up, for we are all imperfect, and some of those around us are far from being what they should be; it must, therefore, be one great object of our care to disentangle ourselves. This cannot be done unless the Lord both comes to us, and abides with us evermore.

4. A froward heart shall depart from me. He would neither be crooked in heart himself, nor employ people of evil character in his house. We cannot turn out of our family all whose hearts are evil, but we can keep them out of our confidence, and let them see that we do not approve of their ways. **I will not know a wicked person.** If I know him to be wicked, I will not know him any further, and with his evil I will have no communion. "To know" in Scripture means more than mere perception; it includes fellowship.

5. Whoso privily slandereth his neighbor, him will I cut off. He had known so bitterly the miseries caused by slanderers that he intended to deal severely with such vipers when he came into power, not to revenge his own neighbor but to prevent others from suffering as he had done. **Him that hath an high look and a proud heart will not I suffer.** Proud, domineering, supercilious gentlemen, who look down upon the poor as though they were so many worms crawling in the earth beneath their feet, the psalmist could not bear. He resolved that none should be great in his palace but those who had more grace and more sense than to indulge in such abominable vanity. Proud men are generally hard, and therefore very unfit for office.

6. Mine eyes shall be upon the faithful of the land, that they may dwell with me. He would seek them out, engage their services, take care of them and promote them to honor. Those who are not faithful to God will not be likely to be faithful to men; if we are faithful ourselves, we shall not care to have those about us who cannot speak the truth or fulfill their promises; we shall not be satisfied until all the members of our family are upright in character. **He that walketh in a perfect way, he shall serve me.** Employers are to a great degree responsible for their servants, and it is customary to blame a master if he retains in his service people of notorious character. Even irreligious people have the sense to perceive the value of Christian servants, and surely their own Christian brethren ought not to have a lower appreciation of them.

7. He that worketh deceit shall not dwell within my house. Deceit among most Orientals is reckoned to be a virtue, and is only censured when it is not sufficiently cunning, and therefore comes to be found out; it is therefore all the more remarkable that David should have so determinedly set his face against it. **He that telleth lies shall not tarry in my sight.** Grace makes people truthful, and creates in them an utter horror of everything approaching to falsehood. If David would not have a liar in his sight, much less will the Lord.

8. I will early destroy all the wicked of the land. At the very outset of his government he would promptly deal out justice to the worthless; he would make them leave their wickedness or feel the lash of the law. Undue leniency to the bad is unkindness to the good. When our Lord comes in judgment, this verse will be fulfilled on a large scale; till then he bids people leave their sins and find pardon. Under the Gospel we also are bidden to suffer long, and to be kind, even to the unthankful and the evil; but the office of the magistrate is of another kind, and he must have a sterner eye to justice than would be proper in private people. **That I may cut off all wicked doers from the city of the LORD.** Jerusalem was to be a holy city. Judgment must begin at the house of God. How pure ought the church to be, and how diligently should all those who hold office therein labor to keep out and chase out people of unclean lives. Honorable offices involve serious responsibilities; to trifle with them will bring our own souls into guilt, and injure beyond calculation the souls of others. Lord, come to us, that we may walk before thee with perfect hearts.

Psalm 102

1. Hear my prayer, O LORD. Or, "O Jehovah." Sincere suppliants are not content with praying for praying's sake; they desire really to reach the ear and heart of the great God. It is a great relief in time of distress to acquaint others with our trouble, but it the sweetest solace of all to have God himself as a sympathizing listener to our plaint. **And let my cry come unto thee.** When sorrow rises to such a height that words become too weak a medium of expression, and prayer is intensified into a cry, then the heart is even more urgent to have audience with the Lord.

2. Hide not thy face from me in the day when I am in trouble. Reserve thy frowns for other times when I can bear them better, if, indeed, I can ever bear them; but now in my heavy distress, favor me with looks of compassion. **Incline thine ear unto me.** Bow thy greatness to my weakness. If because of sin thy face is turned away, at least let me have a side view of thee; lend me thine ear if I may not see thine eye. Turn thyself to me again if my sin has turned thee away. **In the day when I call answer me speedily.** Because the case is urgent, and my soul little able to wait. We may ask to have answers to prayer as soon as possible, but we may not complain of the Lord if he should think it more wise to delay. If it be important that the deliverance should arrive at once, we are quite right in making an early time a point of our intreaty, for God is as willing to grant us a favor now as tomorrow. When answers come upon the heels of our prayers they are all the more encouraging.

In these two verses the psalmist has gathered up a variety of expressions all to the same effect; in them all he intreats an audience and answer of the Lord, and the whole may be regarded as a preface to the prayer which follows.

3. For my days are consumed like smoke. My grief has made life unsubstantial to me. To the unhappy, life seems to be surrounded by so much that is darkening, defiling, blinding, and depressing that, sitting down in despair, they compare themselves to people wandering in a dense fog, and themselves little better than pillars of smoke. When our days have neither light nor fire of energy in them, but become as a smoking flax which dies out ignobly in darkness, then have we cause enough to appeal to the Lord that he would not utterly quench us. **And my bones are burned as an hearth.** His soul was ready to be blown away as smoke, and his body seemed likely to remain as the bare hearth when the last comforting ember is quenched. How often has our piety appeared to us to be in this condition! We have had to question its reality, and fear that it never was anything more than smoke; we have had the most convincing evidence of its weakness, for we could not derive even the smallest comfort from it, any more than a chilled traveler can derive from the cold hearth on which a fire had burned long ago. Soul-trouble experienced in our own heart will help us to interpret the language here employed; and church-troubles may help us also, if unhappily we have been called to endure them. The psalmist was moved to grief by a view of national calamities, and these so wrought upon his patriotic soul that he was wasted with anxiety, his spirits were dried up, and his very life was ready to expire. There is hope for any country while true hearts are ready to die for it.

4. My heart is smitten, like a plant parched by the fierce heat of a tropical sun, **and withered like grass,** which dries up when once the scythe has laid it low.

So that I forget to eat my bread, or, "because I forget to eat my bread." Grief often destroys the appetite, and the neglect of food tends further to injure the constitution and create a yet deeper sinking of spirit. A heart parched with intense grief often refuses consolation for itself and nourishment for the bodily frame, and descends at a doubly rapid rate into weakness and despondency.

5. It will be a very long time before the distresses of the church of God make some Christians shrivel in anatomy, but this good man was so moved with sympathy for Zion's ills that he was wasted down to skin and bone.

6. I am like a pelican of the wilderness, a mournful and even hideous object, the very image of desolation. **I am like an owl of the desert;** loving solitude, moping among ruins, hooting discordantly. The two birds were commonly used as emblems of gloom and wretchedness. Should we not also lament when the ways of Zion mourn and her strength languishes? Were there more of this holy sorrow we should soon see the Lord returning to build up his church. It is a terrible thing to see people flocking like vultures to devour a decaying church, when they ought to be lamenting among her ruins like the owl.

7. I keep a solitary vigil as the lone sentry of my nation; my fellows are too selfish, too careless to care for the beloved land. The psalmist compared himself to a bird when it has lost its mate or its young, or is for some other reason made to mope alone in a solitary place. Probably he did not refer to the cheerful sparrow of our own land, but if he did, the illustration would not be out of place, for the sparrow is happy in company, and if it were alone, the sole one of its species in the neighborhood, there can be little doubt that it would become very miserable. He who has felt himself to be so weak and inconsiderable as to have no more power over his times than a sparrow over a city has also, when bowed down with despondency concerning the evils of the age, sat himself down in utter wretchedness to lament the ills which he could not heal. Christians of an earnest, watchful kind often find themselves among those who have no sympathy with them; even in the church they look in vain for kindred spirits.

8. Mine enemies reproach me all the day. Their rage was unrelenting and unceasing, and vented itself in taunts and insults; the psalmist's patriotism and his griefs were both made the subjects of their sport. Pointing to the sad estate of his people they would ask him, "Where is your God?" and exult over him because their false gods were in the ascendant. **And they that are mad against me are sworn against me.** They were so furious that they bound themselves by oath to destroy him, and used his name as their usual execration, a word to curse by, the synonym of abhorrence and contempt.

9. For I have eaten ashes like bread. He had so frequently cast ashes upon his head in token of mourning that they had mixed with his ordinary food. He forgot to eat, and then the fit changed and he ate with such a hunger that even ashes were devoured. Grief has strange moods. **And mingled my drink with**

weeping. This is a telling description of all-saturating, all-embittering sadness – and this was the portion of one of the best of men, and that for no fault of his own, but because of his love to the Lord's people. If we, too, are called to mourn, let us not be amazed by the fiery trial as though some strange thing had happened unto us.

10. A sense of the divine wrath which had been manifested in the overthrow of the chosen nation and their sad captivity led the psalmist into the greatest distress. He felt like a sere leaf caught up by a hurricane and carried right away, or the spray of the sea which is dashed upwards that it may be scattered and dissolved. Our translation gives the idea of a vessel uplifted in order that it may be dashed to the earth with all the greater violence. The first interpretation which we have given is, however, more fully in accordance with the original, and sets forth the utter helplessness which the writer felt, and the sense of overpowering terror which bore him along in a rush of tumultuous grief which he could not withstand.

11. My days are like a shadow that declineth. A shadow is unsubstantial enough; how feeble a thing must a declining shadow be? **And I am withered like grass.** There are times when through depression of spirit a man feels as if all life were gone from him, and existence had become merely a breathing death. Heartbreak has a marvelously withering influence over our entire system; our flesh at its best is but as grass, and when it is wounded with sharp sorrows its beauty fades, and it becomes a shriveled, dried, uncomely thing.

12. Now the writer's mind is turned away from his personal and relative troubles to the true source of all consolation, namely, the Lord himself, and his gracious purposes towards his own people. **But thou, O Lord, shalt endure forever.** I perish, but thou wilt not; my nation has become almost extinct, but thou art altogether unchanged. The original has the word "sit" – "thou, Jehovah, to eternity shalt sit" – that is to say, thou reignest on; thy throne is still secure even when thy chosen city lies in ruins, and thy peculiar people are carried into captivity. The sovereignty of God in all things is an unfailing ground for consolation; he rules and reigns whatever happens, and therefore all is well. **And thy remembrance unto all generations.** People will forget me, but the constant tokens of thy presence will keep the race of man in mind of thee from age to age. What God is now he always will be, that which our forefathers told us of the Lord we find to be true at this present time, and what our experience enables us to record will be confirmed by our children and their children's children. All things else are vanishing like smoke, and withering like grass, but over all the one eternal, immutable light shines on, and will shine on when all these shadows have declined into nothingness.

13. Thou shalt arise, and have mercy upon Zion. He firmly believed and boldly prophesied that apparent inaction on God's part would turn to effective working. Others might remain sluggish in the matter, but the Lord would most surely bestir himself. Zion had been chosen of old, highly favored, gloriously inhabited, and wondrously preserved, and therefore by the memory of her past mercies it was certain that mercy would again be showed to her. God will not always leave his church in a low condition; he may for a while make her see her nakedness and poverty apart from himself, but in love he must return to her, and stand up in her defense, to work her welfare. **For the time to favor her, yea, the set time, is come.** When the time came for the walls to rise stone by stone, no Tobiah or Sanballat could stay the work, for the Lord himself had arisen, and who can restrain the hand of the Almighty? When God's own time is come, neither Rome, nor the devil, nor persecutors, nor atheists, can prevent the kingdom of Christ from extending its bounds. It is God's work to do it – he must **arise**; he will do it, but he has his own appointed season; and meanwhile we must, with holy anxiety and believing expectation, wait upon him.

14. They delight in her so greatly that even her rubbish is dear to them. It was a good omen for Jerusalem when the captives began to feel a homesickness, and began to sigh after her. To the church of God no token can be more full of hope than to see the members thereof deeply interested in all that concerns her; no prosperity is likely to rest upon a church when carelessness about ordinances, enterprises, and services is manifest; but when even the least and lowest matter connected with the Lord's work is carefully attended to, we may be sure that the set time to favor Zion is come. The poorest church member, the most grievous backslider, the most ignorant convert, should be precious in our sight, because forming a part, although possibly a very feeble part, of the new Jerusalem.

15. So the heathen shall fear the name of the Lord. Mercy within the church is soon perceived by those without. When a candle is lit in the house, it shines through the window. When Zion rejoices in her God, the heathen begin to reverence his name, for they hear of the wonders of his power, and are impressed thereby. **And all the kings of the earth thy glory.** The restoration of Jerusalem was a marvel among the princes who heard of it, and its ultimate resurrection in days yet to come will be one of the prodigies of history. Oh that we might see in our day such a revival of religion that our senators and princes might be compelled to pay homage to the Lord, and own his glorious grace. This cannot be till the saints are better edified, and more fully builded together for an habitation of God though the Spirit.

16. As kings display their skill and power and wealth in the erection of their capitals, so would the Lord reveal the splendor of his attributes in the restoration of Zion, and so will he now glorify himself in the edification of his church. Never is the Lord more honorable in the eyes of his saints than when he prospers the church. To add converts to her, to train these for holy service, to instruct, illuminate, and sanctify the brotherhood, to bind all together in the bonds of Christian love, and to fill the whole body with the energy of the Holy Spirit – this is to build up Zion. Other builders do but puff her up, and their wood, hay, and stubble come to an end almost as rapidly as it was heaped together; but what the Lord builds is surely and well done, and redounds to his glory.

17. He will regard the prayer of the destitute. Only the poorest of the people were left to sigh and cry among the ruins of the beloved city, yet the prayers of the captives and the forlorn offscourings of the land would be heard of the Lord, who in mercy listens most readily to the cry of the greatest need. **And not despise their prayer.** When great kings are building their palaces it is not reasonable to expect them to turn aside and listen to every beggar who pleads with them; yet when the Lord builds up Zion, he will incline his ear to hear, his heart to consider, and his hand to help. It is worthwhile to be destitute to be thus assured of the divine regard.

18. This shall be written for the generation to come. A note shall be made of it, for there will be destitute ones in future generations. Registers of divine kindness ought to be made and preserved: we write down in history the calamities of nations; how much rather should we set up memorials of the Lord's lovingkindnesses! Those who have in their own souls endured spiritual destitution, and have been delivered out of it, cannot forget it; they are bound to tell others of it, and especially to instruct their children in the goodness of the Lord. **And the people which shall be created shall praise the Lord.** The rebuilding of Jerusalem would be a fact in history for which the Lord would be praised from age to age. Revivals of religion not only cause great joy to those who are immediately concerned in them, but they give encouragement and delight to the people of God long after, and are indeed perpetual incentives to adoration throughout the church of God. This verse teaches us that we ought to have an eye to posterity, and especially should we endeavor to perpetuate the memory of God's love to his church and to his poor people, so that young people as they grow up may know that the Lord God of their fathers is good and full of compassion. Sad as the psalmist was when he wrote the dreary portions of this complaint, he was not so absorbed in his own sorrow as to forget the claims of coming generations; this, indeed, is a clear proof that he was not without hope for his people, for he who is making arrangement for the good of a future generation has not yet despaired of his nation. The praise of God should be the great object of all that we do, and to secure him glory both from the present and the future is the noblest aim of intelligent beings.

19–20. For he hath looked down from the height of his sanctuary, or "leaned from the high place of his holiness." **From heaven did the Lord behold the earth.** The Lord does not look upon mankind to note the doings of their nobles, but **to hear the groaning of the prisoner; to loose those that are appointed to death.** The groans of those in prison are very horrible to hear, yet God bends to hear them: those who are bound for death are usually ill company, yet Jehovah deigns to stoop from his greatness to relieve their extreme distress and break their chains. This he does by providential rescues, by restoring health to the dying, and by finding food for the famishing; and spiritually this deed of grace is accomplished by sovereign grace, which delivers us by pardon from the sentence of sin, and by the sweetness of the promise from the deadly despair which a sense of sin had created within us. Well may those of us praise the Lord who were once the children of death, but are now brought into the glorious liberty of the children of God. The Jews in captivity were in Haman's time appointed to death, but their God found a way of escape for them, and they joyfully kept the feast of Purim in memorial thereof; let all souls that have been set free from the crafty malice of the old dragon magnify the Lord of infinite compassion.

21. Great mercy displayed to those greatly in need of it is the plainest method of revealing the attributes of the Most High. Actions speak louder than words; deeds of grace are a revelation even more impressive than the most tender promises. Jerusalem restored, the church re-edified, desponding souls encouraged, and all other manifestations of Jehovah's power to bless, are so many manifestations and proclamations put up upon the walls of Zion to publish the character and glory of the great God. Every day's experience should be to us a daily dispatch from the headquarters of grace. We are bound to inform our fellow Christians of all this, making them helpers in our praise, as they hear of the goodness which we have experienced.

22. The great work of restoring ruined Zion is to be spoken of in those golden ages when the heathen nations are converted unto God. Happy will be the day when all nations unite in the sole worship of Jehovah; then will shouts of exulting praise ascend to heaven in honor of him who loosed the captives, delivered the condemned, raised up the desolations of ages, and made out of stone and rubbish a temple for his worship.

23. He weakened my strength in the way. The psalmist's sorrow had cast down his spirit, and even caused weakness in his bodily frame, so that he was like a pilgrim who limped along the road, and was ready to lie down and die. **He shortened my days.** Though he had bright hope for Jerusalem, he feared that he should have departed this life long before those visions had become realities; he felt that he was pining away and would be a short-lived man. Perhaps this may be our lot, and it will materially help us to be content with it, if we are persuaded that the grandest of all interests is safe, and the good old cause secure in the hands of the Lord.

24. I said, O my God, take me not away in the midst of my days. He betook himself to prayer. What better remedy is there for heart-sickness and depression? We may lawfully ask for recovery from sickness and may hope to be heard. Good people should not dread death, but they are not forbidden to love life: for many reasons the person who has the best hope of heaven may nevertheless think it desirable to continue here a little longer, for the sake of family, work, the church of God, and even the glory of God itself. Some read the passage, "Take me not up," let me not ascend like disappearing smoke, do not whirl me away like Elijah in a chariot of fire, for as yet I have only seen half my days, and that a sorrowful half; give me life till the blustering morning has softened into a bright afternoon of happier existence. **Thy years are throughout all generations.** Thou livest, Lord; let me live also. A fullness of existence is with thee; let me partake therein. Note the contrast between himself pining and ready to expire, and his God living on in the fullness of strength forever and ever; this contrast is full of consolatory power to the one whose heart is stayed upon the Lord. Blessed be his name, he faileth not, and, therefore our hope will not fail us, neither will we despair for ourselves or for his church.

25. Of old hast thou laid the foundation of the earth. Creation is no new work of God, and therefore to "create Jerusalem a praise in the earth" will not be difficult to him. We can neither continue our own existence nor give being to others; but the Lord not only is, but he is the Maker of all things that are; hence, when our affairs are at the very lowest ebb we are not at all despairing, because the Almighty and Eternal Lord can yet restore us. **And the heavens are the work of thine hands.** Thou canst therefore not merely lay the foundations of Zion, but complete its roof. When a great labor is to be performed it is eminently reassuring to contemplate the power of him who has undertaken to accomplish it; and when our own strength is exhausted it is supremely cheering to see the unfailing energy which is still engaged on our behalf.

26. They shall perish, but thou shalt endure. The power which made them will dissolve them, as the city of thy love was destroyed at thy command; yet neither the ruined city nor the ruined earth can make a change in thee, reverse thy purpose, or diminish thy glory. Thou standest when all things fall. **Yea, all of them shall wax old like a garment; as a vesture shalt thou change them, and they shall be changed.** Time impairs all things. The visible creation, which is like the garment of the invisible God, is waxing old and wearing out, and our great King is not so poor that he must always wear the same robes; he will ere long fold up the worlds and put them aside as worn-out vestures, and he will array himself in a new heaven and a new earth wherein dwelleth righteousness. How readily will all this be done. As in the creation, so in the restoration, omnipotence will work its way without hindrance.

27. But thou art the same, or, "thou art he." As a man remains the same when he has changed his clothing, so is the Lord evermore the unchanging One, though his works in creation may be changed, and the operations of his providence may vary. When heaven and earth flee away from the dread presence of the great Judge, he will be unaltered by the terrible confusion, and the world in conflagration will effect no change in him; even so, the psalmist remembered that when Israel was vanquished, her capital destroyed, and her temple leveled with the ground, her God remained the same self-existent, all-sufficient being, and would restore his people, just as he will restore the heavens and the earth, bestowing at the same time a new glory never known before. **And thy years shall have no end.** God lives on; no decay can happen to him, or destruction overtake him. What a joy is this! We may lose our dearest earthly friends, but not our heavenly Friend. Men's days are often suddenly cut short, and at the longest they are few, but the years of the right hand of the Most High cannot be counted, for they have neither first nor last, beginning nor end. O my soul, rejoice in the Lord always, since he is always the same.

28. The children of thy servants shall continue. The psalmist had early in the psalm looked forward to a future generation, and here he speaks with confidence that such a race would arise and be preserved and blessed of God. Some read it as a prayer: "Let the sons of thy servants abide." Any way, it is full of good cheer to us; we may plead for the Lord's favor to our offspring, and we may expect that the cause of God and truth will revive in future generations. Let us hope that those who are to succeed us will not be so stubborn, unbelieving and erring as we have been. If the church has been brought low by the lukewarmness of the present race, let us intreat the Lord to raise up a better order of people, whose zeal and obedience will win and hold a long prosperity. May our own children be among the better generation who continue in the Lord's ways, obedient to the end. **And their seed shall be established before thee.** God does not neglect the children of his servants. It is the rule that Abraham's Isaac should be the Lord's, that Isaac's Jacob should be beloved of the Most High, and that Jacob's Joseph should find favor in the sight of God. Grace is not hereditary, yet God loves to be served by the same family time out of mind. Here is Zion's hope: her offspring will restore her former glories. We may, therefore, not only for our own sakes but also out of love to the church of God, daily pray that our sons and daughters may be saved, and kept by divine grace even unto the end – established before the Lord.

We have thus passed through the cloud, and in the next psalm we shall bask in the sunshine. Such is the checkered experience of the believer. Paul in Romans 7 cries and groans, and then in Romans 8 rejoices and leaps for joy; and so we now advance to the dancing of Psalm 103, blessing the Lord that "though weeping may endure for a night, joy cometh in the morning."

Psalm 103

1. Bless the LORD, O my soul. Soul music is the very soul of music. The psalmist strikes the best key-note when he begins with stirring up his inmost self to magnify the Lord. He soliloquizes, holds self-communion and exhorts himself as though he felt that dullness would all too soon steal over his faculties, as, indeed, it will over us all, unless we are diligently on the watch. Jehovah is worthy to be praised by us in that highest style of adoration which is intended by the term **bless.** Our very life and essential self should be engrossed with this delightful service, and each one of us should arouse his own heart to the engagement. **And all that is within me, bless his holy name.** Many are our faculties, emotions, and capacities, but God has given them all to us, and they ought all to join in chorus to his praise. Half-hearted, ill-conceived, unintelligent praises are not such as we should render to our loving Lord. If the law of justice demanded all our heart and soul and mind for the Creator, much more may the law of gratitude put in a comprehensive claim for the homage of our whole being to the God of grace. The psalmist dwells upon the **holy** name of God, as if his holiness were dearest to him; or, perhaps, because the holiness or wholeness of God was to his mind the grandest motive for rendering to him the homage of his nature in its holiness. By the **name** we understand the revealed character of God, and assuredly those songs which are suggested, not by our fallible reasoning and imperfect observation, but by unerring inspiration, should more than any others arouse all our consecrated powers.

2. **Bless the LORD, O my soul.** We need again and again to bestir ourselves when we are about to worship God, for it would be shameful to offer him anything less than the utmost our souls can render. These first verses are a tuning of the harp, a screwing up of the loosened strings that not a note may fail in the sacred harmony. **And forget not all his benefits.** Not so much as one of the divine dealings should be forgotten; they are all subjects for praise. Memory is very treacherous about the best things; by a strange perversity, engendered by the fall, it treasures up the refuse of the past and permits priceless treasures to lie neglected; it is tenacious of grievances and holds benefits all too loosely. Observe that he calls **all** that is within him to remember **all** the Lord's benefits. God's all cannot be praised with less than our all. Let us read our diaries and see if there be not choice favors recorded there for which we have rendered no grateful return.

3. **Who forgiveth all thine iniquities.** Here David begins his list of blessings received, which he rehearses as themes and arguments for praise. He selects a few of the choicest pearls from the casket of divine love, threads them on the string of memory, and hangs them about the neck of gratitude. Pardoned sin is, in our experience, one of the choicest boons of grace, one of the earliest gifts of mercy, in fact the needful preparation for all that follows it. Till iniquity is forgiven, healing, redemption, and satisfaction are unknown blessings. Forgiveness is first in the order of our spiritual experience, and in some respects first in value. The pardon granted is a present one – **forgiveth**; it is continual, for he still **forgiveth**; it is divine, for God gives it; it is far-reaching, for it removes **all** our sins; it takes in omissions as well as commissions; and it is

most effectual, for it is as real as the healing, and the rest of the mercies with which it is placed. **Who healeth all thy diseases.** When the cause is gone, namely, iniquity, the effect ceases. Sicknesses of body and soul came into the world by sin, and as sin is eradicated, diseases bodily, mental, and spiritual will vanish, till "the inhabitant shall no more say, I am sick." Many-sided is the character of our Heavenly Father, for, having forgiven as a judge, he then cures as a physician. He is all things to us, as our needs call for him, and our infirmities do but reveal him in new characters. God gives efficacy to medicine for the body, and his grace sanctifies the soul. Spiritually we are daily under his care, and he visits us, as the surgeon does his patient, "healing" still (for that is the exact word) each malady as it arises. No disease of our soul baffles his skill; he goes on healing **all**, and he will do so till the last trace of taint has gone from our nature. The two **alls** of this verse are further reasons for **all** that is within us praising the Lord.

The two blessings of this verse the psalmist was personally enjoying; he sang not of others but of himself, or rather of his Lord, who was daily forgiving and healing him. He must have known that it was so, or he could not have sung of it. He had no doubt about it, he felt in his soul that it was so, and, therefore, he bade his pardoned and restored soul bless the Lord with all its might.

4. Who redeemeth thy life from destruction. By purchase and by power the Lord redeems us from the spiritual death into which we had fallen, and from the eternal death which would have been its consequence. Had not the death penalty of sin been removed, our forgiveness and healing would have been incomplete portions of salvation, fragments only, and but of small value, but the removal of the guilt and power of sin is fitly attended by the reversal of the sentence of death which had been passed upon us. Glory be to our great Substitute, who delivered us from going down into the pit, by giving himself to be our ransom. Redemption will ever constitute one of the sweetest notes in the believer's grateful song. **Who crowneth thee with lovingkindness and tender mercies.** Our Lord does nothing by halves; he will not stay his hand till he has gone to the uttermost with his people. Cleansing, healing, redemption are not enough; he must make them kings and crown them. The princes of God's family do not earn the crown, for it is mercy, not of merit; they feel their own unworthiness of it, therefore he deals with tenderness; but he is resolved to bless them, and, therefore, he is always surrounding their brows with coronets of mercy and compassion. Our sin deprived us of all our honors, but he who removed the sentence of death by redeeming us from destruction restores to us more than all our former honors by crowning us anew.

5. Who satisfieth thy mouth with good things, or rather, "filling with good thy soul." No one is ever filled to satisfaction but a believer, and only God himself can satisfy even him. Many a worldling is satiated, but not one is satisfied. God satisfies our very soul, our noblest part, our ornament and glory; and of consequence he satisfies our mouth, however hungry and craving it might otherwise be. Soul-satisfaction loudly calls for soul-praise, and when the mouth is filled with good it is bound to speak good of him who filled it. Our good Lord bestows really **good things**, not idle pleasures; and these he is always giving; shall we not be still praising him? **So that thy youth is renewed like the eagle's.** Renewal of strength was granted to the psalmist so that he grew young again. Our version refers to the annual molting of the eagle, after which it looks fresh and young, but the original does not appear to allude to any such fact of natural history, but simply to describe the diseased one as so healed and strengthened that he became as full of energy as the bird which is strongest of the feathered race, most fearless, most majestic, and most soaring. He who sat moping with the owl in the last psalm here flies on high with the eagle: the Lord works marvelous changes in us, and we learn by such experiences to bless his holy name. To grow from a sparrow to an eagle, and leave the wilderness of the pelican to mount among the stars, is enough to make anyone bless the Lord.

Thus is the endless chain of grace complete. Sin is forgiven, its power subdued, and its penalty averted; then we are honored, supplied, and our very nature renovated, till we are as new-born children in the household of God. O Lord, we must bless thee, and we will; as thou dost withhold nothing from us, so we would not keep back from thy praise one solitary power of our nature, but with all our heart and soul and strength praise thy holy name.

6. Our own personal obligations must not absorb our song; we must also magnify the Lord for his goodness to others. He does not leave the poor and needy to perish at the hands of their enemies, but interposes on their behalf, for he is the executor of the poor and the executioner of the cruel. When his people were in Egypt he heard their groanings and brought them forth, but he overthrew Pharaoh in the Red Sea. Man's injustice will receive retribution at the hand of God. Mercy to his saints demands vengeance on their persecutors, and he will repay it. No blood of martyrs will be shed in vain; no groans of confessors in prison will be left without inquisition being made concerning them. **All** wrongs shall be righted, all the oppressed avenged. God will make the tyrant bite the dust; often he visits the haughty persecutor even in this life, so that "the Lord is known by the judgments which he executeth."

7. He made known his ways unto Moses. Moses was made to see the manner in which the Lord deals with people; he saw this in each of the three periods of his life, in the court, in retirement, and at the head of the tribes of Israel. To him the Lord gave specially clear manifestations of his dispensations and modes of ruling among mankind, granting to him to see more of God than had before been seen by mortals, while he communed with him upon the mount. **His acts unto the children of Israel.** They saw less than Moses, for they beheld the deeds of God without understanding his method therein; yet this was much, very much, and might have been more if they had not been so perverse. It is a great act of sovereign grace and condescending love when the Lord reveals himself to any people, and they ought to appreciate the distinguished favor shown to them. We, as believers in Jesus, know the Lord's **ways** of covenant grace, and we have by experience been made to see his **acts** of mercy towards us; how heartily ought we to praise our divine teacher, the Holy Spirit, who has made these things known to us, for had it not been for him we should have continued in darkness unto this day.

Observe how prominent is the personality of God in all this gracious teaching – *He* **made known.** He did not leave Moses to discover the truth for himself, but became his instructor. What should we ever know if he did not make it known? If Moses needed the Lord to make him known, how much more do we who are so much inferior to the great lawgiver?

8. The LORD is merciful and gracious. Those with whom he deals are sinners. However much he favors them they are guilty and need mercy at his hands; nor is he slow to show compassion on their lost estate, or reluctant by his grace to lift them out of it. Mercy pardons sin, grace bestows favor; in both the Lord abounds. This is that way of his which he made known to Moses (Exodus 34:6), and in that way he will abide as long as the age of grace lasts. **Slow to anger.** He can be angry, and can deal out righteous indignation upon the guilty, but it is his strange work; he lingers long, with loving pauses, tarrying by the way to give space for repentance and opportunity for accepting his mercy. Thus deals he with the greatest sinners, and with his own children much more so: towards them his anger is short-lived and never reaches into eternity, and when it is shown in fatherly chastisements he does not afflict willingly, and soon pities their sorrows. From this we should learn to be ourselves slow to anger; if the Lord is long-suffering under our great provocations how much more ought we to endure the errors of our brethren! **And plenteous in mercy.** Rich in it, quick in it, overflowing with it; and so had he need to be or we should soon be consumed. Above the mountains of our sins the floods of his mercy rise. All the world tastes of his sparing mercy; those who hear the Gospel partake of his inviting mercy; the saints live by his saving mercy, are preserved by his upholding mercy, are cheered by his consoling mercy, and will enter heaven through his infinite and everlasting mercy. Let grace abounding be our hourly song in the house of our pilgrimage.

9. He will not always chide. He will sometimes, for he cannot endure that his people should harbor sin in their hearts, but not forever will he chasten them; as soon as they turn to him and forsake their evil ways he will end the quarrel. He might find constant cause for striving with us, for we have always something in us which is contrary to his holy mind, but he refrains himself lest our spirits should fail before him. It will be profitable for any one of us who may be at this time out of conscious fellowship with the Lord, to inquire at his hands the reason for his anger. When his children turn from their sins he soon turns from his wrath. **Neither will he keep his anger forever.** He bears no grudges. The Lord would not have his people harbor resentments, and in his own course of action he sets them a grand example. When the Lord has chastened his child he has done with his anger: he is not punishing as a judge, but acting as a father, and therefore after a few blows he ends the matter, and presses his beloved one to his bosom as if nothing had happened; or if the offense lies too deep in the offender's nature to be thus overcome, he continues to correct, but he never ceases to love, and he does not let his anger with his people pass into the next world, but receives his erring child into his glory.

10. We ought to praise the Lord for what he has not done as well as for what he has wrought for us; even the negative side deserves our adoring gratitude. We have never suffered as we deserved to suffer. Every power of our being might have been rent with anguish, instead of which we are all in the enjoyment of comparative happiness, and many of us are exceedingly favored with inward joy; let all that is within us bless his holy name.

11. Boundless in extent towards his chosen is the mercy of the Lord; it is no more to be measured than the height of heaven or the heaven of heavens. "Like the height of the heaven" is the original language, which implies other points of comparison besides extent, and suggests sublimity, grandeur, and glory. As the lofty heavens canopy the earth, water it with dews and rains, enlighten it with sun, moon, and stars, and look down upon it with unceasing watchfulness, so the Lord's mercy from above covers all his chosen, enriches them, embraces them, and stands forever as their dwelling-place. The idea of our version is a very noble one, for who shall tell how exceeding great is the height of heaven? All this mercy is for **them that fear him**; there must be a humble, hearty reverence of his authority, or we cannot taste of his grace. Godly fear is one of the first products of the divine life in us; it is the beginning of wisdom, yet it fully ensures to its possessor all the benefits of divine mercy, and is indeed here and elsewhere employed to set forth the whole of true religion. Many a true child of God is full of filial fear, and yet at the same time stands trembling as to his acceptance with God; this trembling is groundless, but it is infinitely to be preferred to that baseborn presumption which incites people to boast of their adoption and consequent security when all the while they are in the gall of bitterness. Those who are presuming upon the infinite extent of divine mercy should here be led to consider that although it is wide as the horizon and high as the stars, yet it is only meant for them that fear the Lord.

12. Sin is removed from us by a miracle of love! If sin be removed so far, then we may be sure that the scent, the trace, the very memory of it must be entirely gone. There is no fear of its ever being brought back again. Our sins are gone; Jesus has borne them away. Glorify the Lord for this richest of blessings. The Lord alone could remove sin at all, and he has done it in a Godlike fashion, making a final sweep of all our transgressions.

13. To those who truly reverence his holy name, the Lord is a Father and acts as such. These he pities, for in the very best of people the Lord sees much to pity, and when they are at their best state they still need his compassion. This should check every propensity to pride, though at the same time it should yield us the richest comfort. Father feel for their children, especially when they are in pain; they would like to suffer in their stead, their sighs and groans cut them to the quick: thus sensitive towards us is our Heavenly Father. His pity never fails to flow, and we never cease to need it.

14. For he knoweth our frame. He knows how we are made, for he made us. Our make and build, our constitution and temperament, our prevailing infirmity and most besetting temptation he well perceives, for he searches our inmost nature. **He remembereth that we are dust.** Made of dust, dust still, and ready to return to dust. We too often forget that we are dust, and try our minds and bodies unduly by excessive mental and bodily exertion; we are also too little mindful of the infirmities of others, and impose upon them burdens grievous to be borne; but our Heavenly Father never overloads us, and never fails to give us strength equal to our lot.

15. As for man, his days are as grass. He lives on the grass and lives like the grass. Corn is but educated grass, and man, who feeds on it, partakes of its nature. The grass lives, grows, flowers, falls beneath the scythe, dries up, and is removed from the field; read this sentence over again, and you will find it the history of man. **As a flower of the field, so he flourisheth.** He has a beauty and a comeliness just as the meadows have, but alas, how short-lived! A large congregation always reminds us of a meadow bright with many hues, and the comparison becomes sadly true when we reflect that as the grass and its goodliness soon pass away, just so will those we gaze upon, and all their visible beauty. Happy are they who, born from above, have in them an incorruptible seed which lives and abides forever.

16. For the wind passeth over it, and it is gone. Only a little wind is needed, not even a scythe is demanded, for the flower is so frail. A puff of foul air fails not to lay low the healthiest son of man. **And the place thereof shall know it no more.** The flower blooms no more. It may have a successor, but as for itself its leaves are scattered, and its perfume will never again sweeten the evening air. Man also dies and is gone from his old haunts, his dear home, and his daily labors, never to return. As far as this world is concerned, he is as though he had never been; all things continue in their courses as though they missed him not, so little a figure does he make in the affairs of nature. True, there are enduring memories, and an existence of another kind coeval with eternity, but these belong not to our flesh, which is but grass, but to a higher life, in which we rise to close fellowship with the Eternal.

17. But the mercy of the LORD is from everlasting to everlasting upon them that

fear him. Blessed **but!** How vast the contrast between the fading flower and the everlasting God! How wonderful that his mercy should link our frailty with his eternity, and make us everlasting too! From old eternity the Lord viewed his people as objects of mercy, and as such chose them to become partakers of his grace; the doctrine of eternal election is most delightful to those who have light to see it and love wherewith to accept it. The **to everlasting** is equally precious. Never will those who fear Jehovah find that either their sins or their needs have exhausted the great deep of his grace. The main question is, "Do we **fear him?**" If we are lifting up to heaven the eye of filial fear, the gaze of paternal love is never removed from us, and it never will be, world without end. **And his righteousness unto children's children.** Mercy to those with whom the Lord makes a covenant is guaranteed by **righteousness**; it is because he is just that he never revokes a promise, or fails to fulfill it. Our believing children and their descendants forever will find the word of the Lord the same; to them will he display his grace and bless them just as he has blessed us. For our descendants let us sing as well as pray.

18. Children of the righteous are not, however, promised the Lord's mercy without stipulation. The parents must be obedient and the children too. Those who run off to any other confidence than the finished work of Jesus are not among those who obey this precept; those with whom the covenant is really made stand firm to it, and having begun in the Spirit, they do not seek to be made perfect in the flesh. The truly godly keep the Lord's commands carefully – they **remember**; they observe them practically – **to do them**; moreover they do not pick and choose, but remember **his commandments** as such, without exalting one above another as their own pleasure or convenience may dictate. May our offspring be a thoughtful, careful, observant race, eager to know the will of the Lord, and prompt to follow it fully; then will his mercy enrich and honor them from generation to generation.

This verse also suggests praise, for who would wish the Lord to smile on those who will not regard his way? From the manner in which some people unguardedly preach the covenant, one might infer that God would bless a certain set of people however they might live, and however they might neglect his laws. But the word teaches not so. The covenant is not legal, but it is holy. Its general aim is the sanctifying of a people unto God, zealous for good works.

19. The LORD has prepared his throne in the heavens. Here is a grand burst of song produced by a view of the boundless power, and glorious sovereignty of Jehovah. His throne is "fixed," for that is the word; about his government there is no alarm, disorder, perturbation, surprises or catastrophes. His matchless sovereignty is the pledge of our security, the pillar upon which our confidence may safely lean.

And his kingdom ruleth over all. Over the whole universe he stretches his scepter. He now reigns universally; he always has done so, and he always will.

To us the world may seem rent with anarchy, but he brings order out of confusion. A clear view of his ever active, and everywhere supreme, providence is one of the most delightful of spiritual gifts; he who has it cannot do otherwise than bless the Lord with all his soul.

Thus has the sweet singer hymned the varied attributes of the Lord as seen in nature, grace, and providence, and now he gathers up all his energies for one final outburst of adoration, in which he would have all unite, since all are subjects of the great King.

20. Bless the LORD, ye his angels, that excel in strength. They see in nearer vision the glory which we would adore. To them is given an exceeding might of intellect, and voice, and force which they delight to use in sacred services for him; let them now turn all their strength into that solemn song which we would send up to the third heaven. **That do his commandments, hearkening unto the voice of his word.** We are bidden to do these commandments, and alas we fail; let those unfallen spirits, whose bliss it is never to have transgressed, give to the Lord the glory of their holiness. They hearken for yet more commands, obeying as much by reverent listening as by energetic action, and in this they teach us how the heavenly will should evermore be done.

21. Bless ye the LORD, all ye his hosts. To whatever race of creatures you may belong, you are all his troops, and he is the general of all your armies. All creatures should unite in praising their Creator, after the best of their ability. **Ye ministers of his, that do his pleasure.** In whatever way you serve him, bless him as you serve. The psalmist would have every servant in the Lord's palace unite with him, and all at once sing out the praises of the Lord. We have attached a new sense to the word **ministers** in these latter days, and so narrowed it down to those who serve in word and doctrine. Yet no true minister would wish to alter it, for we are above all bound to be the Lord's servants, and we would, beyond all other ministering intelligences or forces, desire to bless the glorious Lord.

22. Bless the LORD, all his works in all places of his dominion. Here is a trinity of blessing for the thrice blessed God, and each one of the three blessings is an enlargement upon that which went before. This is the most comprehensive of all, for what can be a wider call than to all in all places? See how finite humans can awaken unbounded praise! Redeemed man is the voice of nature, the priest in the temple of creation, the leader in the worship of the universe. Oh that all the Lord's works on earth were delivered from the vanity to which they were made subject, and brought into the glorious liberty of the children of God: the time is hastening on and will most surely come; then will all the Lord's works bless him indeed. The immutable promise is ripening; the sure mercy is on its way. Hasten ye winged hours!

Bless the LORD, O my soul. He closes on his key-note. He cannot be content to call on others without taking his own part; nor because others sing more loudly and perfectly will he be content to be set aside. O my soul, come home to thyself and to thy God, and let the little world within thee keep time and tune to the spheres which are ringing out Jehovah's praise. O infinitely blessed Lord, favor us with this highest blessing of being forever and ever wholly engrossed in blessing thee.

Psalm 104

1. Bless the LORD, O my soul. This psalm begins and ends like Psalm 103, and it could not do better: when the model is perfect it deserves to exist in duplicate. It is idle to stir up others to praise if we are ungratefully silent ourselves. **O LORD my God, thou art very great.** This ascription has in it a remarkable blending of the boldness of faith and the awe of holy fear: the psalmist calls the infinite Jehovah **my God,** and at the same time, prostrate in amazement at the divine greatness, he cries out in utter astonishment, **Thou art very great.** God was great on Sinai, yet the opening words of his law were, "I am the Lord thy God"; his greatness is no reason why faith should not put in her claim, and call him all her own. The declaration of Jehovah's greatness here given would have been very much in place at the end of the psalm, for it is a natural inference and deduction from a survey of the universe: its position at the very commencement of the poem is an indication that the whole psalm was well considered and digested in the mind before it was actually put into words; only on this supposition can we account for the emotion preceding the contemplation. Observe also that the wonder expressed does not refer to the creation and its greatness, but to Jehovah himself. It is not "the universe is very great!" but "Thou art very great." Many stay at the creature, and so become idolatrous in spirit; to pass onward to the Creator himself is true wisdom. **Thou art clothed with honor and majesty.** Thou thyself art not to be seen, but thy works, which may be called thy garments, are full of beauties and marvels which redound to thine honor. Garments both conceal and reveal a person, and so do the creatures of God. The Lord is seen in his works as worthy of **honor** for his skill, his goodness, and his power, and as claiming **majesty,** for he has fashioned all things in sovereignty, doing as he wills, and asking no one's permit. He must be blind indeed who does not see that nature is the work of a king. His **majesty** is, however, always so displayed as to reflect **honor** uppon his whole character; he does as he wills, but he wills only that which is thrice holy, like himself. The very robes of the unseen Spirit teach us this, and it is ours to recognize it with humble adoration.

2. Who coverest thyself with light as with a garment: wrapping the light about him as a monarch puts on his robe. The conception is sublime, but it makes us feel how altogether inconceivable the personal glory of the Lord must be; if light itself is but his garment and veil, what must be the blazing splendor of his own essential being! **Who stretchest out the heavens like a curtain** – within which he might swell. Light was created on the first day and the firmament upon the second, so that they fitly follow each other in this verse. Oriental princes put on their glorious apparel and then sit in state within curtains, and the Lord is spoken of under that image; but how far above all comprehension the figure must be lifted, since the robe is essential light, to which suns and moons owe their brightness, and the curtain is the azure sky studded with stars for gems.

3. Who layeth the beams of his chambers in the waters. His lofty halls are framed with the waters which are above the firmament. The upper rooms of God's great house, the secret stories far above our ken, the palatial chambers wherein he resides, are based upon the floods which form the upper ocean. We are not to interpret literally where the language is poetical – it would be simple absurdity to do so. **Who maketh the clouds his chariot.** When he comes forth from his secret pavilion it is thus he makes his royal progress. "His chariots of wrath the deep thunder-clouds form," and his chariot of mercy drops plenty as it traverses the celestial road. **Who walketh** or rather, "goes" **upon the wings of the wind.** With the clouds for a carriage, and the winds for winged steeds, the great King hastens on his movements whether for mercy or for judgment. Thus we have the idea of a king still further elaborated – his lofty palace, his chariot, and his coursers are before us; but what a palace must we imagine, whose beams are of crystal, and whose base is consolidated vapor!

4. Who maketh his angels spirits, or "winds," for the word means either. Angels are pure spirits, though they are permitted to assume visible form when God desires us to see them. God is a spirit, and he is waited upon by spirits in his royal courts. Angels are like winds for mystery, force, and invisibility, and no doubt the winds themselves are often the angels or messengers of God. **His ministers a flaming fire.** Here, too, we may choose which we will of two meanings: God's ministers or servants he makes to be as swift, potent, and terrible as fire, and on the other hand he makes fire, that devouring element, to be his minister flaming forth upon his errands. That the passage refers to angels is clear from Hebrews 1:7; and it was most proper to mention them here in connection with light and the heavens, and immediately after the robes and palace of the great King.

5. Who laid the foundations of the earth. Thus the commencement of creation is described, in almost the very words employed by the Lord himself in Job 38:4. **That it should not be removed for ever.** The language is, of course, poetical, but the fact is none the less wonderful: the earth is so placed in space that it remains as stable as if it were a fixture.

6. Thou coveredst it with the deep as with a garment. The new-born earth was wrapped in aqueous swaddling bands. Before humans appeared, the proud waters ruled the whole earth, **the waters stood above the mountains,** no dry land was visible, vapor as from a steaming cauldron covered all. Geologists inform us of this as a discovery, but the Holy Spirit had revealed the fact long before. The passage before us shows us the Creator commencing his work, and laying the foundation for future order and beauty: to think of this reverently will fill us with adoration; to conceive of it grossly and carnally would be highly blasphemous.

7. When the waters and vapors covered all, the Lord had but to speak and they disappeared at once. As though they had been intelligent agents the waves hurried to their appointed deeps and left the land to itself; then the mountains lifted up their heads, the high lands rose from the main, and at length continents and islands, slopes and plains were left to form the habitable earth. The voice of the Lord effected this great marvel.

8. The vanquished waters are henceforth obedient. **They go up by the mountains,** climbing in the form of clouds even to the summits of the Alps. **They go down by the valleys unto the place which thou hast founded for them**: they are as willing to descend in rain and brooks and torrents as they were eager to ascend in mists. The loyalty of the mighty waters to the laws of their God is most notable; the fierce flood, the boisterous rapid, the tremendous torrent, are only forms of that gentle dew which trembles on the tiny blade of grass, and in those ruder shapes they are equally obedient to the laws which their Maker has impressed upon them.

9. The bound has once been passed, but it shall never be so again. The deluge was caused by the suspension of the divine mandate which held the floods in check: they knew their old supremacy, and hastened to reassert it, but now the covenant promise forever prevents a return of that carnival of waters, that revolt of the waves.

10. This is a beautiful part of the Lord's arrangement of the subject waters: they find vents through which they leap into liberty where their presence will be beneficial in the highest degree.

11. **They give drink to every beast of the field.** Who else would water them if the Lord did not? They are his cattle, and therefore he leads them forth to watering. Not one of them is forgotten of him. **The wild asses quench their thirst.** The good Lord gives them enough and to spare. They know their Master's crib. Though bit or bridle of man they will not brook, and we denounce them as unteachable, they learn of the Lord, and know better far than man where flows the cooling crystal of which they must drink or die. They are only asses, and wild, yet our Heavenly Father cares for them. Will he not also care for us?

12. How refreshing are these words! What happy memories they arouse of splashing waterfalls and entangled boughs, where the merry din of the falling and rushing water form a sort of solid background of music, and the sweet

tuneful notes of the birds are the brighter and more flashing lights in the harmony.

13. He watereth the hills. As the mountains are too high to be watered by rivers and brooks, the Lord himself refreshes them from those waters above the firmament which the poet had in a former verse described as the upper chambers of heaven. **The earth is satisfied with the fruit of thy works.** The result of the divine working is fullness everywhere, the soil is saturated with rain, the seed germinates, the beasts drink, and the birds sing – nothing is left unsupplied. So, too, is it in the new creation; he giveth more grace, he fills his people with good, and makes them all confess, "of his fullness have all we received and grace for grace."

14. He causeth the grass to grow for the cattle, and herb for the service of man. Grass grows as well as herbs, for cattle must be fed as well as humans. **That he may bring forth food out of the earth.** Both grass for cattle and corn for humans are food brought forth out of the earth, and they are signs that is was God's design that the very dust beneath our feet, which seems better adapted to bury us than to sustain us, should actually be transformed into the staff of life. The more we think of this the more wonderful it will appear. How great is that God who from among the sepulchres finds the support of life, and out of the ground which was cursed brings forth the blessings of corn and wine and oil.

15. And wine that maketh glad the heart of man. By the aid of genial showers the earth produces not merely necessaries but luxuries, that which furnishes a feast as well that which makes a meal. Oh that we were wise enough to know how to use this gladdening product of the vine; but, alas, we full often turn it to ill account, and debase ourselves therewith. Of this we must ourselves bear the blame; he deserves to be miserable who turns even blessings into curses. **And oil to make his face to shine.** The easterns use oil more than we do, and probably are wiser in this respect than we are: they delight in anointings with perfumed oils, and regard the shining of the face as a choice emblem of joy. God is to be praised for all the products of the soil, not one of which could come to us were it not that he causeth it to grow. **And bread which strengtheneth man's heart.** Men have more courage after they are fed: many a depressed spirit has been comforted by a good substantial meal. We ought to bless God for strength of heart as well as force of limb, since if we possess them they are both the bounties of his kindness.

16. The watering of the hills not only produces the grass and the cultivated herbs, but also the nobler species of vegetation, which comes not within the range of human culture. **The trees of the LORD** – the greatest, noblest, and most royal of trees; those too which are unowned of mankind, and untouched by our hand. **Are full of sap,** or are full, well supplied, richly watered, so that they become, as the cedars, full of resin, flowing with life, and verdant all the year round. **The cedars of Lebanon, which he hath planted.** They grow where none ever thought of planting them, where for ages they were unobserved, and where at this moment they are too gigantic for man to prune them. Planted by grace, and owing all to our Heavenly Father's care, we may defy the hurricane, and laugh at the drought, for none that trust in him shall be left unwatered.

17. So far from being in need, these trees of God afford shelter to others; birds small and great make their nests in the branches. Thus what they receive from the great Lord they endeavor to return to his weaker creatures. How one thing fits into another in this fair creation, each link drawing on its fellow: the rains water the fir trees, and the fir trees become the happy home of birds; thus do the thunder clouds build the sparrow's house, and the descending rain sustains the basis of the stork's nest. Has the reader ever walked through a forest of great trees and felt the awe which strikes the heart in nature's sublime cathedral? Then you will remember feeling that each bird was holy, since it dwelt amid such sacred solitude. Those who cannot see or hear of God except in Gothic edifices, amid the swell of organs, and the voices of a surpliced choir will not be able to enter into the feeling which makes the simple, unsophisticated soul hear "the voice of the Lord God walking among the trees."

18. All places teem with life. We call our cities populous, but are not the forests and the high hills more densely populated with life? See how goats, and storks, and conies, and sparrows each contribute a verse to the psalm of nature; have we not also our canticles to sing unto the Lord? Little though we may be in the scale of importance, yet let us fill our sphere, and so honor the Lord who made us with a purpose.

19. The appointed rule of the great lights is now the theme for praise. The moon is mentioned first, because in the Jewish day the night leads the way. **He appointed the moon for seasons.** By the waxing and waning of the moon the year is divided into months, and weeks, and by this means the exact dates of the holy days were arranged. Thus the lamp of night is made to be of service to mankind, and in fixing the period of religious assemblies (as it did among the Jews) it enters into connection with his noblest being. Never let us regard the moon's motions as the inevitable result of inanimate impersonal law, but as the appointment of our God. **The sun knoweth his going down.** In finely poetic imagery the sun is represented as knowing when to retire from sight, and sink below the horizon.

20. Thou makest darkness, and it is night. Drawing down the blinds for us, he prepares our bedchamber that we may sleep. Were there no darkness we should sigh for it, since we should find repose so much more difficult if the weary day were never calmed into night. Let us see God's hand in the veiling of the sun, and never fear either natural or providential darkness, since both are of the Lord's own making. **Wherein all the beasts of the forest do creep forth.** Why should not the wild beast have his hour as well as man? He has a service to perform; should he not also have his food? Darkness is fitter for beasts than man; and those people are most brutish who love darkness rather than light. When the darkness of ignorance broods over a nation, then all sorts of superstitions, cruelties, and vices abound; the Gospel, like the sunrising, soon clears the world of the open ravages of these monsters, and they seek more congenial abodes. We see here the value of true light, for we may be sure that where there is night there will also be wild beasts to kill and to devour.

21. This is the poetic interpretation of a roar. To whom do the lions roar? Certainly not to their prey, for the terrible sound tends to alarm their victims, and drive them away. They after their own fashion express their desires for food, and the expression of desire is a kind of prayer. Out of this fact comes the devout thought of the wild beast's appealing to its Maker for food. But neither with lions nor men will the seeking of prayer suffice; there must be practical seeking too, and the lions are well aware of it. What they have in their own language asked for they go forth to seek, being in this thing far wiser than many people who offer formal prayers not half so earnest as those of the young lions, and then neglect the means in the use of which the object of their petitions might be gained. The lions roar and seek; too many are liars before God, and roar but never seek.

22. The sun ariseth. Every evening has its morning to make the day. Were it not that we have seen the sun rise so often we should think it the greatest of miracles, and the most amazing of blessings. **They gather themselves together, and lay them down in their dens.** Thus they are out of man's way, and he seldom encounters them unless he desires to do so. The forest's warriors retire to their quarters when the morning's drum is heard, finding in the recesses of their dens a darkness suitable for their slumbers; there they lay them down and digest their food, for God has allotted even to them their portion of rest and enjoyment. There was one who in this respect was poorer than lions and foxes, for he had not where to lay his head: all were provided for except their incarnate Provider. Blessed Lord, thou hast stooped beneath the conditions of the brutes to lift up worse than brutish men!

23. Man goeth forth. It is his turn now, and the sunrise has made things ready for him. His warm couch he forsakes and the comforts of home, to find his daily food; this work is good for him, both keeping him out of mischief and exercising his faculties. **Unto his work and to his labor until the evening.** He goes not forth to sport but to work, not to loiter but to labor; at least, this is the lot of the best part of mankind. We are made for work and ought to work, and should never grumble that so it is appointed.

24. O LORD, how manifold are thy works. They are not only many for number but manifold for variety. Mineral, vegetable, animal – what a range of works is suggested by these three names! The kingdom of grace contains as manifold and as great works as that of nature, but the chosen of the Lord alone discern them. **In wisdom hast thou made them all,** or "wrought" them all. They are all his works, wrought by his own power, and they all display his wisdom. **The earth is full of thy riches.** It is not a poor-house, but a palace; not a hungry ruin, but a well-filled store-house. The Creator has not set his creatures down in a dwelling-place where the table is bare, and the buttery empty; he has filled the earth with food; and not with bare necessaries only, but with **riches.**

25. So is this great and wide sea. He gives an instance of the immense number and variety of Jehovah's works by pointing to the sea. "Look," says he, "at yonder ocean, stretching itself on both hands and embracing so many lands; it too swarms with animal life, and in its deeps lie treasure beyond all counting." The heathen made the sea a different province form the land, and gave the command thereof to Neptune, but we know of a surety that Jehovah rules the waves. **Wherein are things creeping innumerable, both small and great beasts**; read "moving things and animals small and great," and you have the true sense. The number of minute forms of animal life is indeed beyond all reckoning: when a single phosphorescent wave may bear millions of protozoa, and around a fragment of rock armies of microscopic beings may gather, we renounce all idea of applying arithmetic to such a case. The sea in many regions appears to be all alive, as if every drop were a world. Truly, O Lord, thou makest the sea to be as rich in the works of thy hands as the land itself.

26. There go the ships. So that ocean is not altogether deserted of mankind. It is the highway of nations, and unites, rather than divides, distant lands. **There is that leviathan, whom thou hast made to play therein.** The huge whale turns the sea into his recreation ground, and frolics as God designed that he should do. The thought of this amazing creature caused the psalmist to adore the mighty Creator who created him, formed him for his place and made him happy in it.

27. These wait all upon thee. They come around thee as fowls around the farmer's door at the time for feeding, and look up with expectation. Men or marmots, eagles or ants, whales or minnows, they alike rely upon thy care. **That thou mayest give them their meat in due season**; that is to say, when they need it and when it is ready for them. God has a time for all things, and does not feed his creatures by fits and starts; he gives them daily bread, and a quantity proportioned to their needs. This is all that any of us should expect; if even the brute creatures are content with a sufficiency we ought not to be more greedy than they.

28. That thou givest them they gather. God gives it, but they must gather it. We often forget that animals and birds in their free life have to work to obtain food just as we do; and yet it is true with them as with us that our Heavenly Father feeds all. **Thou openest thine hand, they are filled with good.** Here is divine liberality filling the needy creatures till they want no more: and here is divine omnipotence feeding a world by simply opening its hand.

29. Thou hidest thy face, they are troubled. So dependent are all living things upon God's smile that a groan fills them with terror, as though convulsed with anguish. This is so in the natural world, and certainly not less so in the spiritual: saints when the Lord hides his face are in terrible perplexity. **Thou takest away their breath, they die, and return to their dust.** The breath appears to be a trifling matter, and the air an impalpable substance of but small importance; yet, once withdrawn, the body loses all vitality, and crumbles back to the earth from which it was originally taken. All animals come under this law, and even the dwellers in the sea are not exempt from it. Thus dependent is all nature upon the will of the Eternal. Note here that death is caused by the act of God – *thou takest* **away their breath**; we are immortal till he bids us die, and so are even the little sparrows, who fall not to the ground without our Father.

30. The loss of their breath destroys them, and by Jehovah's breath a new race is created. The works of the Lord are majestically simple, and are performed with royal ease – a breath creates, and its withdrawal destroys. If we read the word **spirit** as we have it in our version, it is also instructive, for we see the divine Spirit going forth to create life in nature just as we see him in the realms of grace.

31. The glory of the LORD shall endure for ever. His works may pass away, but not his glory. Were it only for what he has already done, the Lord deserves to be praised without ceasing. His personal being and character ensure that he would be glorious even were all the creatures dead. **The LORD shall rejoice in his works.** He did so at the first, when he rested on the seventh day, and saw that everything was very good; he does so still in a measure where beauty and purity in nature still survive the Fall, and he will do do yet more fully when the earth is renovated, and the trail of the serpent is cleansed from the globe. The poet finds his heart gladdened by beholding the works of the Lord, and he feels that the Creator himself must have felt unspeakable delight in exercising so much wisdom, goodness, and power.

32. He looketh on the earth, and it trembleth. The Lord who has graciously displayed his power in acts and works of goodness might, if he had seen fit, have overwhelmed us with the terrors of destruction, for even at a glance of his eye the solid earth rocks with fear. **He toucheth the hills, and they smoke.** Sinai was altogether in smoke when the Lord descended upon it. It was but a touch, but it sufficed to make the mountain dissolve in flame. Even our God is a consuming fire. Woe unto those who shall provoke him to frown upon them; they shall perish at the touch of his hand.

33. I will sing unto the LORD as long as I live, or, literally, "in my lives." Here and hereafter the psalmist would praise the Lord, for the theme remains forever fresh and new. **I will sing praise to my God while I have my being.** A resolve both happy for himself and glorifying to the Lord. Note the sweet title – **my God.** We never sing so well as when we know that we have an interest in the good things of which we sing, and a relationship to the God whom we praise.

34. My meditation of him shall be sweet. Sweet both to him and to me. I shall be delighted thus to survey his works and think of his person, and he will graciously accept my notes of praise. Meditation is the soul of religion. We ought, therefore, both for our own food and for the Lord's honor to be much occupied with meditation, and that meditation should chiefly dwell upon the Lord himself: it should be **meditation of him.** For want of it much communion is lost and much happiness is missed. **I will be glad in the Lord.** To the meditative mind every thought of God is full of joy. Each one of the divine attributes is a well-spring of delight now that in Christ Jesus we are reconciled to God.

35. Let the sinners be consumed out of the earth, and let the wicked be no more. They are the only blot upon creation. In holy indignation the psalmist would rid the world of beings so base as not to love their gracious Creator, so blind as to rebel against their Benefactor. The Christian way of putting it will be to ask that grace may turn sinners into saints, and win the wicked to the ways of truth. **Bless thou the Lord, O my soul.** Here is the end of the matter – whatever sinners may do, do thou, my soul, stand to thy colors, and be true to thy calling. O ye saints, **Praise ye the Lord.** Let your hearts cry, "Hallelujah" – for that is the word in the Hebrew. Let it close the psalm; for what more remains to be said or written? Hallelujah. **Praise ye the Lord.**

Psalm 105

1. O give thanks unto the Lord. Jehovah is the author of all our benefits; therefore let him have all our gratitude. **Call upon his name,** or call him by his name; proclaim his titles and fill the world with his renown. **Make known his deeds among the people,** or among the nations. Let the heathen hear of our God, that they may forsake their idols and learn to worship him.

2. Sing unto him. Bring your best thoughts and express them in the best language to the sweetest sounds. Take care that your singing is **unto him,** and not merely for the sake of the music or to delight the ears of others. **Talk ye of all his wondrous works.** People love to speak of marvels, and others are generally glad to hear of surprising things; surely the believer in the living God has before him the most amazing series of wonders ever heard of or imagined; his themes are inexhaustible, and they are such as should hold people spellbound.

3. Glory ye in his holy name. Make it a matter of joy that you have such a God. His character and attributes are such as will never make you blush to call him your God. **Let the heart of them rejoice that seek the Lord.** If they have not yet found him so fully as they desire, yet even to be enabled to seek such a God is cause for gladness. To worship the Lord and seek his kingdom and righteousness is the way to happiness; indeed there is no other. Even seekers find bliss in the name of Jesus, but as for the finders, we may say with the poet:

And those who find thee find a bliss
Nor tongue nor pen can show;
The love of Jesus what it is
None but his loved ones know.

4. Seek the LORD and his strength. Put yourselves under his protection. Regard him not as a puny God but look unto his omnipotence, and seek to know the power of his grace. We all need strength; let us look to the strong place, let us look to the Almighty Jehovah for it. **Seek his face evermore.** Seek, seek, seek, we have the word three times, and though the words differ in the Hebrew, the sense is the same. It must be a blessed thing to **seek,** or we should not be thus stirred up to do so. To seek his face is to desire his presence, his smile, his favor consciously enjoyed. First we seek **him,** then **his strength,** and then **his face**; from the personal reverence, we pass on to the imparted power, and then to the conscious favor. This seeking must never cease – the more we know, the more we must seek to know.

5. Remember his marvelous works that he hath done. Memory is never better employed than upon such topics. Alas, we are far more ready to recollect foolish and evil things than to retain in our minds the glorious deeds of Jehovah. **His wonders, and the judgment of his mouth** – these also should be had in memory. The judgments of his mouth are as memorable as the marvels of his hand.

6. O ye seed of Abraham his servant, ye children of Jacob his chosen. Should all the world forget, you are bound to remember. Your father Abraham saw his wonders and judgments upon Sodom, and upon the kings who came from far, and Jacob also saw the Lord's marvelous works in visiting the nations with famine, yet providing for his chosen a choice inheritance in a goodly land; therefore let the children praise their father's God. The Israelites were the Lord's elect nation, and they were bound to imitate their progenitor, who was the Lord's faithful servant and walked before him in holy faith: the seed of Abraham should not be unbelieving, nor should the children of so true a servant become rebels. As we read this pointed appeal to the chosen seed we should recognize the special claims which the Lord has upon ourselves, since we too have been favored above all others. Election is not a couch for ease, but an argument for sevenfold diligence. If God has set his choice upon us, let us aim to be choice people.

7. He is the LORD our God. Blessed be his name. Jehovah condescends to be **our** God. This sentence contains a greater wealth of meaning than all the eloquence of orators can compass, and there is more joy in it than in all the sonnets of them that make merry. **His judgments are in all the earth,** or "in all the land," for the whole of the country was instructed by his law, ruled by his statutes, and protected by his authority. What a joy that God is never absent from us; his judgments are in all the places in which we dwell.

8. He hath remembered his covenant for ever. Here is the basis of all his dealings with his people: he had entered into covenant with them in their father Abraham, and to this covenant he remained faithful. The exhortation to remember (in verse 5) receives great force from the fact that God has remembered. If the Lord has his promise in memory surely we ought not to forget the wonderful manner in which he keeps it. To us it should be matter for deepest joy that never has the Lord been unmindful of his covenant engagements, nor will he be so world without end. Oh that we were as mindful of them as he is. **The word which he commanded to a thousand generations.** This is only an amplification of the former statement, and serves to set before us the immutable fidelity of the Lord during the changing human generations. His promise is here said to be **commanded,** or vested with all the authority of a law. It is a proclamation from a sovereign, whose laws will stand fast though heaven and earth pass away. Therefore let us give thanks unto the Lord and talk of all his wondrous works, so wonderful for their faithfulness and truth.

9. Which covenant he made with Abraham. When the victims were divided and the burning lamp passed between the pieces (Genesis 15), then the Lord made, or ratified, the covenant with the patriarch. This was a solemn deed, performed not without blood, and the cutting in pieces of the sacrifice: it points us to the greater covenant which in Christ Jesus is signed, sealed, and ratified, that it may stand fast forever and ever. **And his oath unto Isaac.** Isaac did not in vision see the solemn making of the covenant, but the Lord renewed unto him his oath (Genesis 26:2–5). This was enough for him, and must have established his faith in the Most High. We have the privilege of seeing in our Lord Jesus both the sacrificial seal, and the eternal oath of God, by which every promise of the covenant is made yea and amen to all the chosen seed.

10. And confirmed the same unto Jacob for a law. Jacob in his wondrous dream (Genesis 28:10–15) received a pledge that the Lord's mode of procedure with him would be in accordance with covenant relations: for said Jehovah, "I will not leave thee till I have done that which I have spoken to thee of." Thus, if we may so speak with all reverence, the covenant became a law unto the Lord himself by which he bound himself to act. Oh matchless condescension, that the most free and sovereign Lord should put himself under covenant bonds to his chosen, and make a law for himself, though he is above all law. **And to Israel for an everlasting covenant.** When he changed Jacob's name he did not change his covenant, but "he blessed him there" (Genesis 32:29), and it was with the old blessing, according to the unchangeable word of abiding grace.

11–12. Saying, Unto thee will I give the land of Canaan, the lot of your inheritance. This repetition of the great covenant promise is recorded in Genesis 35:9–12 in connection with the change of Jacob's name, and very soon after that slaughter of the Shechemites, which had put the patriarch into such great alarm and caused him to use language almost identical with that of the next verse. **When they were but a few men in number; yea, very few, and strangers in it.** Jacob said to Simeon and Levi, "Ye have troubled me to make me to stink among the inhabitants of the land, among the Canaanites and the Perizzites: and I being few in number, they shall gather themselves together against me, and slay me, and I shall be destroyed, and my house." Thus the fears of the man of God declared themselves, and they were reasonable if we look only at the circumstances in which he was placed, but they are soon seen to be groundless when we remember that the covenant promise, which guaranteed the possession of the land, necessarily implied the preservation of the race to whom the promise was made. We often fear where no fear is.

13. Migrating as the patriarchs did from the region of one tribe to the country of another they were singularly preserved. The little wandering family might have been off root and branch had not a special mandate been issued from the throne for their protection. It was not the gentleness of their neighbors which screened them; they were hedged about by the mysterious guardianship of heaven. Whether in Egypt, or in Philistia, or in Canaan, the heirs of the promises, dwelling in their tents, were always secure.

14. He suffered no man to do them wrong. Men cannot wrong us unless he lets them do so; the greatest must wait his permission before they can place a finger upon us. The wicked would devour us if they could, but they cannot even cheat us of a farthing without divine sufferance. **Yea, he reproved kings for their sakes.** Pharaoh and Abimelech must both be made to respect the singular strangers who had come to sojourn in their land; the greatest kings are very second-rate persons with God in comparison with his chosen servants.

15. Saying, touch not mine anointed, and do my prophets no harm. Abraham and his descendants were in the midst of the world a generation of priests anointed to present sacrifice unto the Most High God; since to them the oracles were committed, they were also the prophets of mankind; and they were kings too – a royal priesthood; hence they had received a threefold anointing. Their holy office surrounded them with a sacredness which rendered it sacrilege to molest them. The Lord was pleased to impress the wild tribes of Canaan with a respectful awe of the pious strangers who had come to abide with them, so that they came not near them to do them ill. The words here mentioned may not have been actually spoken, but the impression of awe which fell upon the nations is thus poetically described. God will not have those touched who have been set apart unto himself. He calls them his own, saying, **Mine anointed**; he declares that he has **anointed** them to be prophets, priests, and kings unto himself, and yet again he claims them as *his* prophets – **Do *my prophets* no harm.** All through the many years in which the three great fathers dwelt in Canaan no one was able to injure them: they were not able to defend themselves by force of arms, but the eternal God was their refuge.

16–23. The presence of God having remained with his chosen ones while they sojourned in Canaan, it did not desert them when they were called to go down into Egypt. They did not go there of their own choice, but under divine direction, and hence the Lord prepared their way and prospered them until he saw fit to conduct them again to the land of promise.

16. Moreover he called for a famine upon the land. He had only to call for it as a man calls for his servant, and it came at once. How grateful ought we to be that he does not often call in that terrible servant of his, so meager and gaunt and grim, so pitiless to the women and the children, so bitter to the strong men, who utterly fail before it. **He brake the whole staff of bread.** Our feeble life cannot stand without its staff – if bread fail us, we fall. To God it is as easy to make a famine as to break a staff. He could make that famine universal, too, so that all countries should be in like case: then would the race of man fall indeed, and its staff would be broken forever. There is this sweet comfort in the matter, that the Lord has wise ends to serve even by famine: he meant his people to go down into Egypt, and the scarcity of food was his method of leading them there, for "they heard that there was corn in Egypt."

17. He sent a man before them, even Joseph. He was the advance guard and pioneer for the whole clan. His brethren sold him, but God sent him. Where the hand of the wicked is visible God's hand may be invisibly at work, over-ruling their malice. No one was more of **a man,** or more fit to lead the clan than Joseph: an interpreter of dreams was wanted, and his brethren had said of him, "Behold, this dreamer cometh." **Who was sold for a servant,** or rather for a slave. Joseph's journey into Egypt was not so costly as Jonah's voyage when he paid his own fare: his free passage was provided by the Midianites, who also secured his introduction to a great officer of state by handing him over as a slave. His way to a position in which he could feed his family lay through the pit, the slaver's caravan, the slave market and the prison, and who will deny but what it was the right way, the surest way, the wisest way, and perhaps the shortest way. Yet assuredly it seemed not so. Were we to send a man on such an errand we would furnish him with money – Joseph goes as a pauper; we would clothe him with authority – Joseph goes as a slave; we would leave him at full liberty – Joseph is a bondman; yet money would have been of little use when corn was so dear, authority would have been irritating rather than influential with Pharaoh, and freedom might not have thrown Joseph into connection with Pharaoh's captain and his other servants, and so the knowledge of his skill in interpretation might not have reached the monarch's ear. God's way is *the* way. Our Lord's path to his mediatorial throne ran by the cross of Calvary; our road to glory runs by the rivers of grief.

18. Whose feet they hurt with fetters. From this we learn a little more of Joseph's sufferings than we find in the book of Genesis: inspiration had not ceased, and David was as accurate an historian as Moses, for the same Spirit guided his pen. **He was laid in iron,** or "into iron came his soul." The prayer book version, "the iron entered into his soul," is ungrammatical, but probably expresses much the same truth. His fetters hurt his mind as well as his body.

19. Until the time that his word came. God has his times, and his children must wait till his **until** is fulfilled. Joseph was tried as in a furnace, until the Lord's assaying work was fully accomplished. The word of the chief butler was nothing; he had to wait until God's word came, and meanwhile **the word of the Lord tried him.** He believed the promise, but his faith was sorely exercised. A delayed blessing tests people, and proves their metal, whether their faith is of that precious kind which can endure the fire. Of many a choice promise we may say with Daniel, "the thing was true, but the time appointed was long."

20. The king sent and loosed him. He was thrust into the roundhouse by an officer, but he was released by the monarch himself. **Even the ruler of the people, and let him go free.** The tide had turned, so that Egypt's haughty potentate gave him a call from the prison to the palace. He had interpreted the dreams of captives, himself a captive; he must now interpret for a ruler and become a ruler himself. When God means to enlarge his prisoners, kings become his turnkeys.

21. He made him lord of his house. Reserving no power, but saying, "only in the throne will I be greater than thou." The servitor of slaves becomes lord over nobles. How soon the Lord lifteth his chosen from the dunghill to set them among princes. **And ruler of all his substance.** He empowered him to manage the storing of the seven plenteous harvests, and to dispense the provisions in the coming days of scarcity. All the treasures of Egypt were under his lock and key; indeed the granaries of the world were sealed or opened at his bidding. Thus was he in the best conceivable position for preserving alive the house of Israel with whom the covenant was made. As our Lord was himself secured in Egypt from Herod's enmity, so, ages before, the redeemed race found an equally available shelter, in the hour of need.

22. To bind his princes at his pleasure. He who was bound obtains authority to bind. He is no longer kept in prison, but keeps all prisons, and casts into them the greatest nobles when justice demands it. **And teach his senators wisdom.** The heads of the various peoples, the elders of the nations, learned from him the science of government, the art of providing for the people. Joseph was a great instructor in political economy, and we doubt not that he mingled with it the purest morals, the most upright jurisprudence, and something of that divine wisdom without which the most able senators remain in darkness.

23. Israel also came into Egypt. The aged patriarch came, and with him that increasing company which bore his name. He was hard to bring there. Perhaps nothing short of the hope of seeing Joseph could have drawn him to take so long a journey from the tombs of his forefathers; but the divine will was accomplished and the church of God was removed into an enemy's country, where for a while it was nourished. **And Jacob sojourned in the land of Ham.**

Shem the blessed came to lodge awhile with Ham the accursed. God so willed it for a time, and therefore it was safe and right; still it was only a sojourn, not a settlement. The fairest Goshen in Egypt was not the covenant blessing, neither did the Lord mean his people to think it so; even so to us "earth is our lodge" but only our lodge, for heaven is our home.

Thus the song rehearsed the removals of the Lord's people, and was a most fit accompaniment to the upbearing of the ark, as the priests carried it into the city of David, where the Lord had appointed it a resting-place.

24. And he increased his people greatly. In Goshen they seem to have increased rapidly from the first, and this excited the fears of the Egyptians, so that they tried to retard their increase by oppression, but the Lord continued to bless them. **And made them stronger than their enemies.** Both in physical strength and in numbers they threatened to become the more powerful race. Nor was this growth of the nation impeded by tyrannical measures, but the very reverse took place, thus giving an early instance of what has since become a proverb in the church – "the more they oppressed them the more they multiplied." It is idle to contend either with God or his people.

25. He turned their heart to hate his people. It was his goodness to Israel which called forth the ill-will of the Egyptian court, and so far the Lord caused it, and moreover he made use of this feeling to lead on to the discomfort of his people, and so to their readiness to leave the land to which they had evidently become greatly attached. Thus far but no further did the Lord turn the hearts of the Egyptians. God cannot in any sense be the author of sin so far as to be morally responsible for its existence, but it often happens through the evil which is inherent in human nature that the acts of the Lord arouse the ill-feelings of ungodly people. Is the sun to be blamed because while it softens wax it hardens clay? Hatred is often allied with cunning, and so in the case of the Egyptians, they began **to deal subtilely with his servants.** They treated them in a fraudulent manner, they reduced them to bondage by their exactions, they secretly concerted the destruction of their male children, and at length openly ordained that cruel measure, and all with the view of checking their increase, lest in time of war they should side with invaders in order to obtain their liberty. Surely the depths of Satanic policy were here reached, but vain was the cunning of man against the chosen seed.

26. When the oppression was at the worst, Moses came. For the second time we have here the expression **he sent**; he who sent Joseph sent also Moses and his eloquent brother. The Lord had the men in readiness, and all he had to do was to commission them and thrust them forward.

27. The miracles which were wrought by Moses were the Lord's, not his own: hence they are here called *his signs,* as being the marks of Jehovah's presence and power.

28. He sent darkness, and made it dark. It was no natural or common darkness; it was beyond all precedent and out of the range of ordinary events. It was a horrible palpable obscurity which people felt clinging about them as though it were a robe of death. It was a total darkness, a darkness which lasted three days, a darkness in which no one dared to stir. **And they rebelled not against his word.** Moses and Aaron did as they were bidden, and during the darkness the Egyptians were so cowed that even when it cleared away they were anxious for Israel to be gone, and had it not been for the pride of Pharaoh they would have rejoiced to speed them on their journey there and then.

29. The plague was not a mere coloring of the water with red earth, as some suppose, but the river was offensive and fatal to the fish.

30. **Their land brought forth frogs in abundance.** If fish could not live frogs might; indeed they multiplied both on land and in the water till they swarmed beyond all count. **In the chambers of their kings.** They penetrated the choicest rooms of the palace, and were found upon the couches of state.

31. **He spake.** See the power of the divine word. He had only to say it and it was done: **and there came divers sorts of flies.** Insects of various annoying kinds came up in infinite hordes, a mixture of biting, stinging, buzzing gnats, mosquitoes, flies, beetles, and other vermin such as make people's flesh their prey, the place of deposit for their eggs, and the seat of particular torments. **And lice in all their coasts.** These unutterably loathsome forms of life were as the dust of the ground, and covered their persons, their garments, and all they ate. Nothing is too small to master man when God commands it to assail him.

32. **He gave them hail for rain.** They seldom had rain, but now the showers assumed the form of heavy, destructive hailstorms, and being accompanied with a hurricane and thunderstorm, they were overwhelming, terrible, and destructive. **And flaming fire in their land.** The lightning was particularly vivid, and seemed to run along upon the ground, or fall in fiery flakes. Thus all the fruit of the trees and the harvests of the fields were either broken to pieces or burned on the spot, and universal fear bowed the hearts of men to the dust. No phenomena are more appalling to most people than those which attend a thunderstorm; even the most audacious blasphemers quail when the dread artillery of heaven opens fire upon the earth.

33. **He smote their vines also and their fig trees.** So that all hope of gathering their best fruits was gone, and the trees were injured for future bearing. All the crops were destroyed, and these are mentioned as being the more prominent forms of their produce, used by them both at festivals and in common meals. **And brake the trees of their coasts.** From end to end of Egypt the trees were battered and broken by the terrible hailstorm. God is in earnest when he deals with proud spirits; he will either end them or mend them.

34–35. **He spake, and the locusts came, and caterpillars, and that without number.** One word from the Captain and the armies leaped forward. The expression is very striking, and sets forth the immediate result of the divine word. The caterpillar is called "the licker," because it seems to lick up every green thing as in a moment. Perhaps the caterpillar here meant is still the locust in another form. That locusts swarm in countless armies is a fact of ordinary observation, and the case would be worse on this occasion. We have ourselves ridden for miles through armies of locusts, and we have seen with our own eyes how completely they devour every green thing. The description is not strained when we read, **And did eat up all the herbs in their land, and devoured the fruit of their ground.** Nothing escapes these ravenous creatures; they even climb the trees to reach any remnant of foliage which may survive. Commissioned as these were by God, we may be sure they would do their work thoroughly, and leave behind them nothing but a desolate wilderness.

36. Now came the master blow. The Lord spoke before, but now he smites; before he only smote vines, but now he strikes men themselves. The glory of the household dies in a single night, the prime and pick of the nation are cut off, the flower of the troops, the heirs of the rich, and the hopes of the poor all die at midnight. Now the target was struck in the center; there was no confronting this plague. Pharaoh feels it as much as the woman-slave at the mill; he had smitten Israel, the Lord's firstborn, and the Lord repaid him to his face. What a cry went up throughout the land of Egypt when every house wailed its firstborn at the dead of night! O Jehovah, thou didst triumph in that hour, and with an outstretched arm didst thou deliver thy people.

37. He brought them forth also with silver and gold. This they asked of the Egyptians, perhaps even demanded, and well they might, for they had been robbed and spoiled for many a day, and it was not meet that they should go forth empty-handed. Glad were the Egyptians to hand over their jewels to propitiate a people who had such a terrible friend above; they needed no undue pressure, they feared them too much to deny them their requests. **And there was not one feeble person among their tribes** – a great marvel indeed. The number of their army was very great and yet there was not one in hospital, not one carried in an ambulance, or limping in the rear.

38. Egypt was glad when they departed, which would not have been the case had the gold and silver been borrowed by the Israelites, for men do not like to see borrowers carry their goods into a far country. What a change from the time when the sons of Jacob were the drudges of the land, the offscouring of all things, the brickmakers whose toil was only requited by the lash or the stick. Now they were reverenced as prophets and priests; **for the fear of them fell upon them,** the people proceeded to a superstitious terror of them. Thus with cheers and good wishes their former taskmasters sent them on their way: Pharaoh was foiled and the chosen people were once more on the move, journeying to the place which the Lord had given to them by a covenant of salt.

39. He spread a cloud for a covering. Never people were so favored. What would not travelers in the desert now give for such a canopy? The sun could not scorch them with its burning ray; their whole camp was screened like a king in his pavilion. Nothing seemed to be too good for God to give his chosen nation. **And fire to give light in the night.** While cities were swathed in darkness, their town of tents enjoyed light.

40. The people asked. But how badly, how wickedly! And yet his grace forgave the sin of their grumbling and heard its meaning: or perhaps we may consider that while the multitude grumbled there were a few who were really gracious people, who prayed, and therefore the blessing came. **He brought quails, and satisfied them with the bread of heaven.** He gave them what they asked amiss as well as what was good for them, mingling judgment with goodness, for their discipline. The quails were more a curse than a blessing in the end, because of their greed and lust, but in themselves they were a particular indulgence, and favor: it was their own fault that the dainty meat brought death with it. As for the manna it was unmingled good to them, and really satisfied them, which the quails never did. It was bread *from* heaven, and the bread **of** heaven, sent *by* heaven; it was a pity that they were not led to look up to heaven whence it came, and fear and love the God who out of heaven rained it upon them. Thus they were housed beneath the Lord's canopy and fed with food from his own table; never people were so lodged and boarded. O house of Israel, praise ye the Lord.

41. He opened the rock, and the waters gushed out. With Moses' rod and his own word he cleft the rock in the desert, and forth leaped abundant floods for their drinking where they had feared to die of thirst. From most unlikely sources the all-sufficient God can supply his people's needs; hard rocks become springing fountains at the Lord's command. **They ran in the dry places like a river,** so that those at a distance from the rock could stoop down and refresh themselves, and the stream flowed on, so that in future journeyings they were supplied.

42. Here is the secret reason for all this grace. The covenant and he for whose sake it was made are ever on the heart of the Most High. He remembered his people because he remembered his covenant.

43. Up from the wilderness he led them, rejoicing over them himself and making them rejoice too. They were *his* people, *his* chosen, and hence in them he rejoiced, and upon them he showered his favors, that they might rejoice in him as their God, and their portion.

44. And gave them the lands of the heathen. He drove out the Canaanites and allotted the lands to the tribes. They were called on to fight, but the Lord wrought so wonderfully that the conquest was not effected by their bow or spear – the Lord **gave** them the land. **And they inherited the labor of the people;** they dwelt in houses which they had not built, and gathered fruit from vines and olives which they had not planted.

45. That they might observe his statutes, and keep his laws. The chosen nation was to be the conservator of truth, the examplar of morality, the pattern of devotion: everything was so ordered as to place them in advantageous circumstances for fulfilling this trust. Theirs was a high calling and a glorious election. It involved great responsibilities, but it was in itself a distinguished blessing, and one for which the nation was bound to give thanks. Most justly then did the music close with the jubilant but solemn shout of Hallelujah. **Praise ye the Lord.** If this history did not make Israel praise God, what would?

Psalm 106

1. Praise ye the LORD. Hallelujah. Praise Jah. This song is for the assembled people, and they are all exhorted to join in praise to Jehovah. It is not meet for a few to praise and the rest to be silent, but all should join. If David were present in churches where quartets and choirs carry on all the singing, he would turn to the congregation and say, **Praise ye the LORD.** Our meditation dwells upon human sin; but on all occasions and in all occupations it is seasonable and profitable to praise the Lord. **O give thanks unto the LORD; for he is good.** To us needy creatures the goodness of God is the first attribute which excites praise, and that praise takes the form of gratitude. **For his mercy endureth for ever.** Goodness towards sinners assumes the form of mercy; mercy should therefore be a leading note in our song. Since people cease not to be sinful, it is a great blessing that Jehovah ceases not to be merciful. From age to age the Lord deals graciously with his church, and to every individual in it is he is constant and faithful in his grace forevermore. In a short space we have here two arguments for praise, **for he is good: for his mercy endureth for ever.** These two arguments are themselves praises. The very best language of adoration is that which adoringly in the plainest words sets forth the simple truth with regard to our great Lord. No rhetorical flourishes or poetical hyperboles are needed; the bare facts are sublime poetry, and the narration of them with reverence is the sense of adoration. This first verse is the text of all that which follows; we are now to see how from generation to generation the mercy of God endured to his chosen people.

2. Who can utter the mighty acts of the LORD? What human or angelic tongue can duly describe the great displays of divine power? **Who can show forth all his praise?** To declare his works is the same things as to praise him, for his own doings are his best commendation.

3. Since the Lord is so good and so worthy to be praised, it must be for our happiness to obey him. **Blessed are they that keep judgment, and he that doeth righteousness at all times.** Multiplied are the blessednesses which must descend upon that one rare person who at all times follows that which is right. Holiness is happiness. The way of right is the way of peace. Hence the story which follows is in sad contrast with the happiness here depicted, because the way of Israel was not that of judgment and righteousness, but that of folly and iniquity.

4. Remember me, O LORD, with the favor which thou bearest unto thy people. Insignificant as I am, do not forget me. Think of me with kindness, just as thou thinkest of thine own elect. I cannot ask more, nor would I seek less. Treat me as the least of thy saints are treated and I am content. The sentence before us is a sweet prayer, at once humble and aspiring, submissive and expansive; it might be used by a dying thief or a living apostle; let us use it now.

O visit me with thy salvation. Bring it home to me. Come to my house and to my heart, and give me the salvation which thou hast prepared, and art alone able to bestow. We sometimes hear of someone dying by the visitation of God, but here is one who knows that he can only *live* by the visitation of God. Jesus said of Zacchaeus, "This day is salvation come to this house," and that was the case, because he himself had come there. There is no salvation apart from the Lord, and he must visit us with it or we shall never obtain it.

5. That I may see the good of thy chosen. His desire for the divine favor was excited by the hope that he might participate in all the good things which flow to the people of God through their election. The Father has blessed us with all spiritual blessings in Christ Jesus, according as he has chosen us in him, and in these precious gifts we desire to share through the saving visitation of the Lord. No other good do we wish to see, perceive, and apprehend, but that which is the peculiar treasure of the saints. **That I may rejoice in the gladness of thy nation.** The psalmist, having sought his portion in the good of the chosen, now also begs to be a partaker in their joy: for of all the nations under heaven the Lord's true people are the happiest. **That I may glory with thine inheritance.** He would have a part and lot in their honor as well as their joy. He was willing to find glory where saints find it, namely, in being reproached for truth's sake. To serve the Lord and endure shame for his sake is the glory of the saints below: Lord, let me rejoice to bear my part.

These introductory thanksgivings and supplications, though they occur first in the psalm, are doubtless the result of the contemplations which succeed them, and may be viewed not only as the preface, but also as the moral of the whole sacred song.

6. We have sinned with our fathers. Here begins a long and particular confession. Confession of sin is the readiest way to secure an answer to the prayer of verse 4; God visits with his salvation the soul which acknowledges its need of a Saviour. People may be said to have sinned with their fathers when they imitate them, when they follow the same objects, and make their own lives to be mere continuations of the follies of their sires. Moreover, Israel was but one nation in all time, and the confession which follows sets forth the national rather than the personal sin of the Lord's people. They enjoyed national privileges, and therefore they shared in national guilt. **We have committed iniquity, we have done wickedly.** Thus is the confession repeated three times, in token of the sincerity and heartiness of it. Sins of omission, commission, and rebellion we ought to acknowledge under distinct heads, that we may show a due sense of the number and heinousness of our offenses.

7. **Our fathers understood not thy wonders in Egypt.** The Israelites saw the miraculous plagues and ignorantly wondered at them: their designs of love, their deep moral and spiritual lessons, and their revelation of the divine power and justice they were unable to perceive. A long sojourn among idolaters had blunted the perceptions of the chosen family, and cruel slavery had ground them down into mental sluggishness. **They remembered not the multitude of thy mercies.** The sin of the understanding leads on to the sin of the memory. What is not understood will soon be forgotten. People feel little interest in preserving husks; if they knew nothing of the inner kernel they will take no care of the shells. **But provoked him at the sea, even at the Red sea.** To fall out at starting was a bad sign. Those who did not begin well can hardly be expected to end well. Israel is not quite out of Egypt, and yet she begins to provoke the Lord by doubting his power to deliver, and questioning his faithfulness to his promise.

8. When he could find no other reason for his mercy he found it in his own glory, and seized the opportunity to display his power. This respect unto his own honor ever leads him to deeds of mercy, and hence we may well rejoice that he is a jealous God.

9. **He rebuked the Red sea also, and it was dried up.** A word did it. The sea heard his voice and obeyed. How many rebukes of God are lost upon us! **So he led them through the depths, as through the wilderness.** As if it had been the dry floor of the desert the tribes passed over the bottom of the gulf; nor was their passage venturesome, for he bade them go; nor dangerous, for he led them. We also have under divine protection passed through many trials and afflictions, and with the Lord as our guide we have experienced no fear and endured no perils.

10. **And he saved them from the hand of them that hated them.** Pharaoh was drowned, and the power of Egypt so crippled that throughout the forty years' wanderings of Israel they were never threatened by their old masters. **And redeemed them from the hand of the enemy.** This was a redemption by power, and one of the most instructive types of the redemption of the Lord's people from sin and hell by the power which works in them.

11. What he begins he carries through to the end. This, again, made Israel's sin the greater, because they saw the thoroughness of the divine justice, and the perfection of the divine faithfulness. In the covering of their enemies we have a type of the pardon of our sins; they are sunk as in the sea, never to rise again; and, blessed be the Lord, there is "not one of them left."

12. Then believed they his words. That is to say, they believed the promise when they saw it fulfilled, but not till then. This is mentioned, not to their credit, but to their shame. Those who do not believe the Lord's word till they see it performed are not believers at all. Who would not believe when the fact stares them in the face? The Egyptians would have done as much as this. **They sang his praise.** How could they do otherwise? Their song was very excellent, and is the type of the song of heaven: but sweet as it was, it was quite as short, and when it was ended they fell to grumbling. Between Israel singing and Israel sinning there was scarce a step. Their song was good while it lasted, but it was no sooner begun than over.

13. They soon forgat his works. They seemed in a hurry to get the Lord's mercies out of their memories; they hasted to be ungrateful. **They waited not for his counsel,** neither waiting for the word of command or promise; eager to have their own way, and prone to trust in themselves. This is a common fault in the Lord's family to this day; we are long in learning to wait *for* the Lord, and *upon* the Lord. With him is counsel and strength, but we are vain enough to look for these to ourselves, and therefore we grievously err.

14. But lusted exceedingly in the wilderness. Though they would not wait for God's will, they are hot to have their own. When the most suitable and pleasant food was found in abundance, it did not please them long, but they grew dainty and sniffed at angel's food, and must needs have flesh to eat, which was unhealthy diet for that warm climate, and for their easy life. This desire of theirs they dwelt upon till it became a mania with them, and, like a wild horse, carried away its rider. For a meal of meat they were ready to curse their God and renounce the land which floweth with milk and honey. What a wonder that the Lord did not take them at their word! It is plain that they vexed him greatly – **And tempted God in the desert.** In the place where they were absolutely dependent upon him and were every day fed by his direct provision, they had the presumption to provoke their God.

15. And he gave them their request. Prayer may be answered in anger and denied in love. That God gives a man his desire is no proof that he is the object of divine favor; everything depends upon what that desire is. **But sent leanness into their soul.** Ah, that but! It embittered all. The meat was poison to them when it came without a blessing; whatever it might do in fattening the body, it was poor stuff when it made the soul lean. If we must know scantiness, may God grant it may not be scantiness of soul: yet this is a common attendant upon worldly prosperity.

16. They envied Moses also in the camp. Though to him as the Lord's chosen instrument they owed everything they grudged him the authority which it was needful that he should exercise for their good. Some were more openly rebellious than others, and became leaders of the mutiny, but a spirit of dissatisfaction was general, and therefore the whole nation is charged with it.

Who can hope to escape envy when the meekest of men was subject to it? **And Aaron the saint of the Lord.** By divine choice Aaron was set apart to be holiness unto the Lord, and instead of thanking God that he had favored them with a high priest by whose intercession their prayers would be presented, they railed at the divine election, and quarreled with the man who was to offer sacrifice for them. Thus neither church nor state was ordered aright for them; they would snatch from Moses his scepter, and from Aaron his miter. It is the mark of bad men that they are envious of the good, and spiteful against their best benefactors.

17. Korah is not mentioned, for mercy was extended to his household, though he himself perished. The earth could no longer bear up under the weight of these rebels and ingrates: God's patience was exhausted when they began to assail his servants, for his children are very dear to him. Moses had opened the sea for their deliverance, and now that they provoke him, the earth opens for their destruction.

18. The Levites who were with Korah perished by fire, which was a most fitting death for those who intruded into the priesthood, and so offered strange fire. God has more than one arrow in his quiver; the fire can consume those whom the earthquake spares. These terrible things in righteousness are mentioned here to show the obstinacy of the people in continuing to rebel against the Lord. Terrors were as much lost upon them as mercies had been; they could neither be drawn nor driven.

19. They made a calf in Horeb. In the very place where they had solemnly pledged themselves to obey the Lord they broke the second, if not the first, of his commandments, and set up the Egyptian symbol of the ox, and bowed before it. The ox image is here sarcastically called **a calf;** idols are worthy of no respect, scorn is never more legitimately used than when it is poured upon all attempts to set forth the Invisible God. The Israelites were foolish indeed when they thought they saw the slightest divine glory in a bull, indeed in the mere image of a bull. To believe that the image of a bull could be the image of God must need great credulity. **And worshiped the molten image.** Before it they paid divine honors, and said, "These be thy gods, O Israel." This was sheer madness. After the same fashion the Ritualists must set up their symbols and multiply them exceedingly. Spiritual worship they seem unable to apprehend; their worship is sensuous to the highest degree, and appeals to eye, and ear, and nose.

20. They said that they only meant to worship the one God under a fitting and suggestive similitude by which his great power would be set forth to the multitude; but in very deed they had given up the true God, whom it had been their glory to adore, and had set up a rival to him, not a representation of him; for how should he be likened to a bullock? The psalmist is very contemptuous, and justly so: irreverence towards idols is an indirect reverence to God.

False gods, attempts to represent the true God, and indeed all material things which are worshiped are so much filth upon the face of the earth. God abhors them, and so should we.

21–22. They forgat God their saviour. Remembering the calf involved forgetting God. He had commanded them to make no image, and in daring to disobey they forgot his commands. **Which had done great things in Egypt.** God in Egypt had overcome all the idols, and yet they so far forgot him as to liken him to them. Could an ox work miracles? Could a golden calf cast plagues upon Israel's enemies? They were brutish to set up such a wretched mockery of deity, after having seen what the true God could really achieve. **Wondrous works in the land of Ham, and terrible things by the Red sea.** They saw several ranges of miracles, the Lord did not stint them as to the evidence of his eternal power and Godhead, and yet they could not rest content with worshiping him in his appointed way, but must have an elaborate ritual after the old Egyptian fashion, and a manifest object of worship to assist them in adoring Jehovah.

23. Therefore he said that he would destroy them. The threatening of destruction came at last. For the first wilderness sin he chastened them, sending leanness into their soul; for the second he weeded out the offenders, the flame burned up the wicked; for the third he threatened to destroy them; for the fourth he lifted up his hand and almost came to blows (verse 26); for the fifth he actually smote them, "and the plague brake in upon them"; and so the punishment increased with their perseverance in sin. This is worth noting, and it should serve as a warning to the man who goeth on in his iniquities. God tries words before he comes to blows – **he *said* that he would destroy them** – but his words are not to be trifled with, for he means them, and has power to make them good. **Had not Moses his chosen stood before him in the breach.** Like a bold warrior who defends the wall when there is an opening for the adversary and destruction is rushing upon the city, Moses stopped the way of avenging justice with his prayers. Moses had great power with God. He was an eminent type of our Lord, who is called, as Moses here is styled, "mine *elect*, in whom my soul delighteth." As the Elect Redeemer interposed between the Lord and a sinful world, so did Moses stand between the Lord and his offending people. The story as told by Moses himself is full of interest and instruction, and tends greatly to magnify the goodness of the Lord, who thus suffered himself to be turned from the fierceness of his anger.

With disinterested affection, and generous renunciation of privileges, the great lawgiver interceded with the Lord **to turn away his wrath, lest he should destroy them.** Behold the power of a righteous man's intercession. Mighty as was the sin of Israel to provoke vengeance, prayer was mightier in turning it away. How diligently ought we to plead with the Lord for this guilty world, and especially for his own backsliding people!

24. Yea, they despised the pleasant land. They spoke lightly of it, though it was the joy of all lands: they did not think it worth the trouble of seeking and conquering; they even spoke of Egypt, the land of their iron bondage, as though they preferred it to Canaan, the land which floweth with milk and honey. It is an ill sign with a Christian when he begins to think lightly of heaven and heavenly things; it indicates a perverted mind, and it is, moreover, a high offense to the Lord to despise that which he esteems so highly that he in infinite love reserves it for his own chosen. **They believed not his word.** This is the root of sin. If we do not believe the Lord's word, we shall think lightly of his promised gifts.

25. But murmured in their tents. From unbelief to murmuring is a short and natural step; they even fell to weeping when they had the best ground for rejoicing. Grumbling is a great sin and not a mere weakness; it contains within itself unbelief, pride, rebellion, and a whole host of sins. It is a home sin, and is generally practiced by complainers **in their tents;** but it is just as evil there as in the streets, and will be quite as grievous to the Lord. **And hearkened not unto the voice of the LORD.** Making a din with their own voices, they refused attention to their best Friend. Murmurers are bad hearers.

26–27. Therefore he lifted up his hand against them, to overthrow them in the wilderness. He swore in his wrath that they should not enter into his rest; he commenced his work of judgment upon them, and they began to die. Only let God lift his hand against a man and his day has come; he galls terribly whom Jehovah overthrows. **To overthrow their seed also among the nations, and to scatter them in the lands.** Foreseeing that their descendants would reproduce their sins, he solemnly declared that he would give them over to captivity and the sword.

28. They joined themselves also unto Baal-peor. Ritualism led on to the adoration of false gods. If we choose a false way of worship we shall, ere long, choose to worship a false god. This abomination of the Moabites was an idol in whose worship women gave up their bodies to the most shameless lust. Think of the people of a holy God coming down to this. **And ate the sacrifices of the dead.** In the orgies with which the Baalites celebrated their detestable worship Israel joined, partaking even in their sacrifices as earnest inner-court worshipers, though the gods were but dead idols.

29. Open licentiousness and avowed idolatry were too gross to be winked at. This time the offenses clamored for judgment, and the judgment came at once. Twenty-four thousand people fell before a sudden and deadly disease which threatened to run through the whole camp. Their new sins brought on them a disease new to their tribes. Their vices were a moral pest, and they were visited with a bodily pest: so the Lord meets like with like.

30. God has his champions left in the worst times, and they will stand up when the time comes for them to come forth to battle. His righteous indignation moved him to a quick execution of two open offenders. His honest spirit could not endure that lewdness should be publicly practiced at a time when a fast had been proclaimed. Such daring defiance of God and of all law he could not brook, and so with his sharp javelin he transfixed the two guilty ones in the very act. It was a holy passion which inflamed him, and no enmity to either of the persons whom he slew.

31. Down to the moment when this psalm was penned the house of Phinehas was honored in Israel. His faith had performed a valorous deed, and his righteousness was testified of the Lord, and honored by the continuance of his family in the priesthood. He was impelled by motives so pure that what would otherwise have been a deed of blood was justified in the sight of God; indeed, thus was made *the* evidence that Phinehas was righteous. No personal ambition, or private revenge, or selfish passion, or even fanatical bigotry, inspired the man of God; but zeal for God, indignation at open filthiness, and true patriotism urged him on.

Once again we have cause to note the mercy of God that even when his warrant was out, and actual execution was proceeding, he stayed his hand at the suit of one man, finding, as it were, an apology for his grace when justice seemed to demand immediate vengeance.

32. They angered him also at the waters of strife. Will they never have done? The scene changes, but the sin continues. Aforetime they had mutinied about water when prayer would soon have turned the desert into a standing pool, but now they do it again after their former experience of the divine goodness. This made the sin a double, indeed a sevenfold offense, and caused the anger of the Lord to be the more intense. **So that it went ill with Moses for their sakes.** Moses was at last wearied out, and began to grow angry with them, and utterly hopeless of their ever improving; can we wonder at it, for he was man and not God? After forty years bearing with them the meek man's temper gave way, and he called them rebels, and showed unhallowed anger; and therefore he was not permitted to enter the land which he desired to inherit. Truly, he had a sight of the goodly country from the top of Pisgah, but entrance was denied him, and thus it went ill with him. It was **their** sin which angered him, but *he* had to bear the consequences; however clear it may be that others are more guilty than ourselves, we should always remember that this will not screen *us,* but every man must bear his own burden.

33. It seems a small sin compared with that of others, but then it was the sin of Moses, the Lord's chosen servant, who had seen and known so much of the Lord, and therefore it could not be passed by. He did not speak blasphemously, or falsely, but only hastily and without care; but this is a serious fault in a lawgiver, and especially in one who speaks for God. This passage is to our mind one of the most terrible in the Bible. Truly we serve a jealous God. Yet he is not a hard master, or austere; we must not think so, but we must the rather be jealous of ourselves, and watch that we live the more carefully, and speak the more advisedly, because we serve such a Lord. We ought also to be very careful how we treat the ministers of the Gospel, lest by provoking their spirit we should drive them into any unseemly behavior which should bring upon them the chastisement of the Lord. Little do a grumbling, quarrelsome people dream of the perils in which they involve their pastors by their untoward behavior.

34. They were commissioned to act as executioners upon races condemned for their unnatural crimes, and through sloth, cowardice, or sinful complacency they sheathed the sword too soon, very much to their own danger and disquietude. It is a great evil with believers that they are not zealous for the total destruction of all sin within and without. The measure of our destruction of sin is not to be our inclination, or the habit of others, but the Lord's command. We have no warrant for dealing leniently with any sin.

35. It was not the wilderness which caused Israel's sins; they were just as disobedient when settled in the land of promise. They found evil company, and delighted in it. Those whom they should have destroyed they made their friends. Having enough faults of their own, they were yet ready to go to school to the filthy Canaanites, and educate themselves still more in iniquity. None can tell what evil has come of the folly of worldly conformity.

36. And they served their idols: which were a snare unto them. They were fascinated by the charms of idolatry, though it brings misery upon its votaries. A man cannot serve sin without being ensnared by it.

37–38. Yea, they sacrificed their sons and daughters unto devils. This was being snared indeed; they were spell-bound by the cruel superstition, and were carried so far as even to become murderers of their own children, in honor of the most detestable deities, which were rather devils than gods. **And shed innocent blood.** The poor little ones whom they put to death in sacrifice had not been partakers of their sin, and God looked with the utmost indignation upon the murder of the innocent. **Even the blood of their sons and of their daughters, whom they sacrificed unto the idols of Canaan.** Who knows how far evil will go? It drove men to be unnatural as well as ungodly. Had they but thought for a moment, they must have seen that a deity who could be pleased with the blood of babes spilt by their own parents could not be a deity at all, but must be a demon, worthy to be detested and not adored. How could they prefer such service to that of Jehovah? **And the land was polluted with blood.** The promised land, the holy land, which was the glory of all lands, for God was there, was defiled with the reeking gore of innocent babes, and by the blood-red hands of their parents, who slew them in order to pay homage to devils.

39. Not only the land but the inhabitants of it were polluted. They broke the marriage bond between them and the Lord, and fell into spiritual adultery. The language is strong, but the offense could not be fitly described in less forcible words.

40—41. Therefore was the wrath of the Lord kindled against his people, insomuch that he abhorred his own inheritance. Not that even then he broke his covenant or utterly cast off his offending people, but he felt the deepest indignation, and even looked upon them with abhorrence. How far the divine wrath can burn against those whom he yet loves in his heart it is hard to say, but certainly Israel pushed the experiment to the extreme. **And he gave them into the hand of the heathen.** This was the manifestation of his abhorrence. He gave them a taste of the result of sin; they spared the heathen, mixed with them and imitated them, and soon they had to smart from them, for hordes of invaders were let loose upon them to spoil them at their pleasure. People make rods for their own backs. **And they that hated them ruled over them.** And who could wonder? Sin never creates true love. They joined the heathen in their wickedness, and they did not win their hearts, but rather provoked their contempt. If we mix with people of the world they will soon become our masters and our tyrants, and we cannot want worse.

42. Their enemies also oppressed them. This was according to their nature; an Israelite always fares ill at the hands of the heathen. Leniency to Canaan turned out to be cruelty to themselves. **And they were into subjection under their hand.** They were bowed down by laborious bondage, and made to lie low under tyranny. God can make our enemies to be rods in his hands to flog us back to our best Friend.

43. Many times did he deliver them. By reading the book of Judges we shall see how truthful is this sentence: again and again their foes were routed, and they were set free again, only to return with vigor to their former evil ways. **But they provoked him with their counsel.** With deliberation they agreed to transgress anew; self-will was their counselor, and they followed it to their own destruction. **And were brought low for their iniquity.** Worse and worse were the evils brought upon them, lower and lower they fell in sin, and consequently in sorrow. In dens and caves of the earth they hid themselves; they were deprived of all warlike weapons, and were utterly despised by their conquerors; they were rather a race of serfs than of free men until the Lord in mercy raised them up again.

The lesson to ourselves, as God's people, is to walk humbly and carefully before the Lord, and above all to keep ourselves from idols. May grace be given to us to keep the separated path, and remain undefiled.

44. Notwithstanding all these provoking rebellions and detestable enormities the Lord still heard their prayer and pitied them. This is very wonderful, very Godlike. One would have thought that the Lord would have shut out their prayer, seeing they had shut their ears against his admonitions; but no, he had a father's heart, and a sight of their sorrows touched his soul, the sound of their cries overcame his heart, and he looked upon them with compassion.

45. And he remembered for them his covenant. The covenant is the sure foundation of mercy, and when the whole fabric of outward grace manifested in the saints lies in ruins we see the fundamental basis of love which is never moved, and upon it the Lord proceeds to build again a new structure of grace. Covenant mercy is sure as the throne of God. **And repented according to the multitude of his mercies.** He did not carry out the destruction which he had commenced. Speaking after the manner of men he changed his mind, and did not leave them to their enemies to be utterly cut off, because he saw that his covenant would in such a case have been broken.

46. Having the hearts of all men in his hands he produced compassion even in heathen hearts.

47. This is the closing prayer, arranged by prophecy for those who would in future time be captives, and suitable for all who before David's days had been driven from home by the tyranny of Saul, or who had remained in exile after the various scatterings by famine and distress which had happened in the iron age of the judges. **Save us, O LORD our God.** The mention of the covenant encouraged the afflicted to intreat him to interpose on their behalf and rescue them. **And gather us from among the heathen.** Weary now of the ungodly and their ways, they long to be brought into their own separated country, where they might again enjoy the means of grace, enter into holy fellowship with their brethren, escape from contaminating examples, and be free to wait upon the Lord. How often do true believers nowadays long to be removed from ungodly households, where their souls are vexed with the conversation of the wicked. **To give thanks unto thy holy name, and to triumph in thy praise.** Weaned from idols, they desire to make mention of Jehovah's name alone, and to ascribe their mercies to his ever-abiding faithfulness and love. The Lord had often saved them for his holy name's sake, and therefore they feel that when again restored they would render all their gratitude to that saving name; it would be their glory to praise Jehovah and none else.

48. Blessed be the LORD God of Israel from everlasting to everlasting. Has not his mercy endured forever, and should not his praise be of like duration? **And let all the people say, Amen.** They have all been spared by his grace; let them all join in the adoration with loud unanimous voice. Yet should a nation thus magnify him, indeed should all the nations past and present unite in the solemn acclaim, it would fall far short of his deserts. O for the happy day when all flesh will see the glory of God, and proclaim his praise. **Praise ye the LORD.**

Psalm 107

1. O give thanks unto the LORD, for he is good. It is all we can give him, and the least we can give; therefore let us diligently render to him our thanksgiving.

The psalmist is in earnest in the exhortation, hence the use of the interjection **O** to intensify his words: let us be at all times thoroughly fervent in the praises of the Lord, both with our lips and with our lives, by thanksgiving and thanks-living. Jehovah, for that is the name here used, is not to be worshiped with groans and cries, but with thanks, for he is good; and these thanks should be heartily rendered, for his is no common goodness: he is good by nature, and essence, and proven to be good in all the acts of his eternity. Compared with him there is none good, no, not one: but he is essentially, perpetually, superlatively, infinitely good. We are the perpetual partakers of his goodness, and therefore ought above all his creatures to magnify his name. Our praise should be increased by the fact that the divine goodness is not a transient thing, but in the attribute of mercy abides forever the same, **for his mercy endureth for ever.** The word **endureth** has been properly supplied by the translators, but yet it somewhat restricts the sense, which will be better seen if we read it, **for his mercy for ever.** That mercy had no beginning, and will never know an end. Our sin required that goodness should display itself to us in the form of mercy, and it has done so, and will do so evermore; let us not be slack in praising the goodness which thus adapts itself to our fallen nature.

2. **Let the redeemed of the LORD say so.** Whatever others may think or say, the redeemed have overwhelming reasons for declaring the goodness of the Lord. Theirs is a special redemption, and for it they ought to render special praise. The Redeemer is so glorious, the ransom price so immense, and the redemption so complete that they are under sevenfold obligations to give thanks unto the Lord, and to exhort others to do so. Let them not only feel so but **say so**; let them both sing and bid their fellows sing. **Whom he hath redeemed from the hand of the enemy.** Snatched by superior power away from fierce oppressions, they are bound above all men to adore the Lord, their Liberator. Theirs is a divine redemption; **he hath redeemed** them, and no one else has done it.

3. **And gathered them out of the lands, from the east, and from the west, from the north and from the south.** Gathering follows upon redeeming. The captives of old were restored to their own land from every quarter of the earth, and even from beyond the sea; for the word translated **south** is really "the sea." No matter what divides, the Lord will gather his own into one body, and first on earth by "one Lord, one faith, and one baptism," and then in heaven by one common bliss they will be known to be the one people of the One God.

4. **They wandered in the wilderness.** They **wandered,** for the track was lost, no vestige of a road remained; worse still, they wandered **in a wilderness,** where all around was burning sand. They were lost in the worst possible place, even as the sinner is who is lost in sin; they wandered up and down in vain searches and researches as a sinner does when he is awakened and sees his lost estate; but it ended in nothing, for they still continued in the wilderness, though they had hoped to escape from it. **In a solitary way.** No human dwelling was near,

and no other company of travelers passed within hail. Solitude is a great intensifier of misery. The loneliness of a desert has a most depressing influence upon the person who is lost in the boundless waste. The traveler's way in the wilderness is a **waste** way, and when he leaves even that poor, barren trail to get utterly beyond the path of man, he is in a wretched light indeed. A soul without sympathy is on the borders of hell: a solitary way is the way of despair. **They found no city to dwell in.** How could they? There was none. Israel in the wilderness abode under canvas, and enjoyed none of the comforts of settled life; wanderers in the Sahara find no town or village. People when under distress of soul find nothing to rest upon, no comfort and no peace; their efforts after salvation are many, weary, and disappointing, and the dread solitude of their hearts fills them with dire distress.

5. **Hungry and thirsty, their soul fainted in them.** The spirits sink when the bodily frame becomes exhausted by long privations. Who can keep his courage up when he is ready to fall to the ground at every step through utter exhaustion? The supply of food is all eaten, the water is spent in the bottles, and there are neither fields nor streams in the desert; the heart therefore sinks in dire despair. Such is the condition of an awakened conscience before it knows the Lord Jesus; it is full of unsatisfied cravings, painful needs, and heavy fears. It is utterly spent and without strength, and there is nothing in the whole creation which can minister to its refreshment.

6. **Then they cried unto the Lord in their trouble.** Not till they were in extremities did they pray, but the mercy is that they prayed **then,** and prayed in the right manner, with a **cry,** and to the right person, **unto the Lord.** Nothing else remained for them to do; they could not help themselves, or find help in others, and therefore they cried to God. If hunger brings us to our knees it is more useful to us than feasting; if thirst drives us to the fountain it is better than the deepest draughts of worldly joy; and if fainting leads to crying it is better than the strength of the mighty. **And he delivered them out of their distresses.** Deliverance follows prayer most surely. The cry must have been very feeble, for they were faint, and their faith was as weak as their cry; but yet they were heard, and heard at once. A little delay would have been their death; but there was none, for the Lord was ready to save them.

7. **And he led them forth by the right way.** There are many wrong ways, but only one right one, and into this none can lead us but God himself. When the Lord is leader the way is sure to be right; we never need question that. Forth from the pathless mazes of the desert he conducted the lost ones; he found the way, made the way, and enabled them to walk along it, faint and hungry as they were. **That they might go to a city of habitation.** The end was worthy of the way: he did not lead them from one desert to another, but he gave the wanderers an abode, the weary ones a place of rest. *They* found no city to dwell in, but *he* found one readily enough. What *we* can do and what *God* can do are two

very different things. What a difference it made to them to leave their solitude for a city, their trackless path for well-frequented streets, and their faintness of heart for the refreshment of a home! Far greater are the changes which divine love works in the condition of sinners when God answers their prayers and brings them to Jesus. Shall not the Lord be magnified for such special mercies? Can we who have enjoyed them sit down in ungrateful silence?

8. Oh that men would praise the LORD for his goodness. Men are not mentioned here in the original, but the word is fitly supplied by the translators; the psalmist would have all things in existence magnify Jehovah's name. Surely **men** will do this without being exhorted to it when the deliverance is fresh in their memories. They must be horrible ingrates who will not honor such a deliverer for so happy a rescue from the most cruel death. It is well that the redeemed should be stirred up to bless the Lord again and again, for preserved life deserves life-long thankfulness. Even those who have not encountered the like peril, and obtained the like deliverance, should bless the Lord in sympathy with their fellows, sharing their joy. **And for his wonderful works to the children of men.** These favors are bestowed upon *our* race, upon children of the family to which we belong, and therefore we ought to join in the praise. The children of men are so insignificant, so feeble, and so undeserving, that it is a great wonder that the Lord should do anything for them; but he is not content with doing little works, he puts forth his wisdom, power, and love to perform marvels on the behalf of those who seek him.

9. For he satisfieth the longing soul. This is the summary of the lost traveler's experience. He who in a natural sense has been rescued from perishing in a howling wilderness ought to bless the Lord who brings him again to eat bread among men. The spiritual sense is, however, the more rich in instruction. The Lord sets us longing and then completely satisfies us. That longing leads us into solitude, separation, thirst, faintness and self-despair, and all these conduct us to prayer, faith, divine guidance, satisfying of the soul's thirst, and rest: the good hand of the Lord is to be seen in the whole process and in the divine result. **And filleth the hungry soul with goodness.** As for thirst he gives satisfaction, so for hunger he supplies filling. In both cases the need is more than met, there is an abundance in the supply which is well worthy of notice: the Lord does nothing in a stingy fashion; satisfying and filling are his especial modes of treating his guests. Nor does he fill the hungry with common fare, but with **goodness** itself. It is not so much good, as the essence of goodness which he bestows on needy suppliants.

10. Such as sit in darkness and in the shadow of death. The cell is dark of itself, and the fear of execution casts a still denser gloom over the prison. Such is the cruelty of man to man that tens of thousands have been made to linger in places only fit to be tombs; unhealthy, suffocating, filthy sepulchres, where they have sickened and died of broken hearts. Meanwhile the dread of sudden death has been the most hideous part of the punishment; the prisoners have felt as if the chill shade of death himself froze them to the very marrow. The state of a soul under conviction of sin is forcibly symbolized by such a condition; people in that state cannot see the promises which would yield them comfort, they sit still in the inactivity of despair, they fear the approach of judgment, and are thereby as much distressed as if they were at death's door. **Being bound in affliction and iron.** Many prisoners have been thus doubly fettered in heart and hand. In a spiritual sense affliction frequently attends conviction of sin, and then the double grief causes a double bondage. O you who are made free by Christ Jesus, remember those who are in bonds.

11. **Because they rebelled against the words of God.** This was the general cause of bondage among the ancient people of God; they were given over to their adversaries because they were not loyal to the Lord. God's words are not to be trifled with, and those who venture on such rebellion will bring themselves into bondage. **And condemned the counsel of the Most High.** They thought that they knew better than the Judge of all the earth, and therefore they left his ways and walked in their own. When men do not follow the divine counsel they give the most practical proof of their contempt for it. There is too much contending of the divine counsel, even among Christians, and hence so few of them know the liberty wherewith Christ makes us free.

12. **Therefore he brought down their heart with labor.** In eastern prisons men are frequently made to labor like beasts of the field. As they have no liberty, so they have no rest. God has methods of abating the loftiness of rebellious looks: the cell and the mill make even giants tremble. **They fell down, and there was none to help.** Stumbling on in the dark beneath their weary task, they at last fell prone upon the ground, but no one came to pity them or to lift them up. Their fall might be fatal for aught that any one cared about them; their misery was unseen, or, if observed, no one could interfere between them and their tyrant masters. In such a wretched plight the rebellious Israelite became more lowly in mind, and thought more tenderly of his God and of his offenses against him. When a soul finds all its efforts at self-salvation prove abortive, and feels that it is now utterly without strength, then the Lord is at work hiding pride from man and preparing the afflicted one to receive his mercy.

13. **Then they cried unto the LORD in their trouble.** Not a prayer till then. While there was any to help below they would not look above. No cries till their hearts were brought down and their hopes were all dead – *then they cried,* but not before. So many a one offers what he calls prayer when he is in good case and thinks well of himself, but in very deed the only real cry to God is that which is forced out of him by a sense of utter helplessness and misery. We pray best when we are fallen on our faces in painful helplessness. **And he saved them out of their distresses.** Speedily and willingly he sent relief. He who saved people in the open wilderness can also save in the close prison; bolts and bars

cannot shut him out, nor long shut in his redeemed ones.

14. He brought them out of darkness and the shadow of death. The Lord in providence fetches out prisoners from their cells and bids them breathe the fresh air again, and then he takes off their fetters and gives liberty to their aching limbs. So also he frees people from care and trouble, and especially from the misery and slavery of sin. The Lord's deliverances are of the most complete and triumphant kind; he neither leaves the soul in darkness nor in bonds, nor does he permit the powers of evil again to enthral the liberated captive. What he does is done forever.

15. The sight of such goodness makes a right-minded person long to see the Lord duly honored for his amazing mercy. When dungeon doors fly open, and chains are snapped, who can refuse to adore the goodness of the Lord?

16. This verse belongs to that which precedes it, and sums up the mercy experienced by captives. The Lord breaks the strongest gates and bars when the time comes to set free his prisoners; and spiritually the Lord Jesus has broken the most powerful of spiritual bonds and made us free indeed.

17. Many sicknesses are the direct result of foolish acts. Thoughtless and lustful people by drunkenness, gluttony, and the indulgence of their passions fill their bodies with diseases of the worst kind. Sin is at the bottom of all sorrow, but some sorrows are the immediate results of wickedness.

18. Their soul abhorreth all manner of meat. Appetite departs from men when they are sick. **And they draw near unto the gates of death.** From want of food, and from the destructive power of their malady, they slide gradually down till they lie at the door of the grave; neither does the skill of the physician suffice to stay their downward progress. Thus it is with souls afflicted with a sense of sin; they cannot find comfort in the choicest promises, but turn away with loathing even from the Gospel, so that they gradually decay into the grave of despair. The mercy is that though near the gates of death they are not yet inside the sepulchre.

19. Then they cry unto the LORD in their trouble. They join the praying legion at last. Saul also is among the prophets. The fool lays aside his jester's robe in prospect of the shroud, and gets to his knees. What a cure for the soul sickness of body is often made to be by the Lord's grace! **And he saveth them out of their distresses.** Prayer is as effectual on a sick-bed as in the wilderness or in prison; it may be tried in all places and circumstances with certain result.

20. He sent his word and healed them. Man is not healed by medicine alone, but by the word which proceeds out of the mouth of God. A word will do it, a word has done it thousands of times. **And delivered them from their destructions.** They escape though dangers had surrounded them, dangers many and deadly. The word of the Lord has a great delivering power; he has but to speak and the armies of death fall in an instant. Sin-sick souls should remember the power of the Word, and be much in hearing it and meditating upon it.

Spiritually considered, these verses describe a sin-sick soul: foolish but yet aroused to a sense of guilt, it refuses comfort from any and every quarter, and a lethargy of despair utterly paralyzes it. To its own apprehension nothing remains but utter destruction in many forms: the gates of death stand open before it, and it is, in its own apprehension, hurried in that direction. Then is the soul driven to cry in the bitterness of its grief unto the Lord, and Christ, the eternal Word, comes with healing power in the direst extremity, saving to the uttermost.

21. It is marvelous that people can be restored from sickness and yet refuse to bless the Lord. It would seem impossible that they should forget such great mercy, for we should expect to see both themselves and the friends to whom they are restored uniting in a lifelong act of thanksgiving. When a spiritual cure is wrought by the great Physician, praise is one of the surest signs of renewed health.

22. And let them sacrifice the sacrifices of thanksgiving. In such a case let there be gifts and oblations as well as works. Let the good Physician have his fee of gratitude. **And declare his works with rejoicing.** Such things are worth telling, for the personal declaration honors God, relieves ourselves, comforts others, and puts everyone in possession of facts concerning the divine goodness which they will not be able to ignore.

23. They that go down to the sea in ships. Navigation was so little practiced among the Israelites that mariners were invested with a high degree of mystery, and their craft was looked upon as one of singular daring and peril. Tales of the sea thrilled all hearts with awe, and he who had been to Ophir or to Tarshish and had returned alive was looked upon as a man of renown, an ancient mariner to be listened to with reverent attention. **That do business in great waters.** If they had not business to do, they would never have ventured on the ocean, for we never read in the Scriptures of anyone taking pleasure on the sea: so averse was the Israelitish mind to seafaring, that we do not hear of even Solomon himself keeping a pleasure boat.

24. These see the works of the LORD. Beyond the dwellers on the land they see the Lord's greatest works, or at least such as stayers at home judge to be so when they hear the report thereof. Instead of the ocean proving to be a watery wilderness, it is full of God's creatures, and if we were to attempt to escape from his presence by flying to the uttermost parts of it, we should only rush into Jehovah's arms, and find ourselves in the very center of his workshop. **And his wonders in the deep.** They see wonders in it and on it. It is in itself a wonder and it swarms with wonders. Seamen, because they have fewer objects around them, are more observant of those they have than landsmen are, and hence they are said to **see** the wonders in the deep. At the same time, the ocean really does contain many of the more striking of God's creatures, and it is the scene of many of the more tremendous of the physical phenomena by which the power and majesty of the Lord are revealed among us. The chief wonders alluded to by the psalmist are a sudden storm and the calm which follows it.

All believers have not the same deep experience; but for wise ends, that they may do business for him, the Lord sends some of his saints to the sea of soul-trouble, and there they see, as others do not, the wonder of divine grace.

25. For he commandeth: his word is enough for anything; he has but to will it and a tempest rages. **And raiseth the stormy wind.** It seemed to lie asleep before, but it knows its Master's bidding, and is up at once in all its fury. **Which lifteth up the waves thereof.** The glassy surface of the sea is broken, and myriads of white heads appear and rage and toss themselves to and fro as the wind blows upon them.

Thus it needs but a word from God and the soul is in troubled waters, tossed to and fro with a thousand afflictions. Doubts, fears, terrors, anxieties lift their heads like so many angry waves, when once the Lord allows the storm-winds to beat upon us.

26. They mount up to the heaven. Borne aloft on the crest of the wave, the sailors and their vessels appear to climb the skies, but it is only for a moment, for very soon in the trough of the sea **they go down again to the depths.** As if their vessel were but a sea bird, the mariners are tossed. **Their soul is melted because of trouble.** Weary, wet, dispirited, hopeless of escape, their heart is turned to water, and they seem to have no manhood left. Those who have been on the spiritual deep in one of the great storms which occasionally agitate the soul know what this verse means. Some of us have weathered many such an internal hurricane, and have indeed seen the Lord's wondrous works.

27. They reel to and fro, and stagger like a drunken man. The violent motion of the vessel prevents their keeping their legs, and their fears drive them out of all power to use their brains, and therefore they look like intoxicated men. **And are at their wit's end.** What more can they do? They have used every expedient known to navigation, but the ship is so strained and beaten about that they know not how to keep her afloat. Here too the spiritual mariner's log agrees with that of the sailor on the sea. We have staggered frightfully! We knew not what to do, and could have done nothing if we had known it. We were as men distracted, and felt as if destruction itself would be better than our horrible state of suspense. As for wit and wisdom, they were clean washed out of us.

28. Then they cry unto the LORD in their trouble. Though at their wit's end, they had wit enough to pray; their heart was melted, and it ran out in cries for help. This was well and ended well, for it is written, **And he brought them out of their distresses.** Prayer is good in a storm. We may pray staggering and reeling, and when we are at our wit's end. God will hear us amid the thunder and answer us. He brought their distresses upon the mariners, and therefore they did well to turn to him for the removal of them; nor did they look in vain.

29. He maketh the storm a calm. He reveals his power in the sudden and marvelous transformations which occur at his bidding. He commanded the storm and now he ordains a calm: God is in all natural phenomena, and we do well to recognize his working. **So that the waves thereof are still.** They bow in silence at his feet. When God makes peace it is peace indeed, the peace of God which passes all understanding.

30. Then are they glad because they be quiet. No one can appreciate this verse unless he has been in a storm at sea. **So he bringeth them unto their desired haven.** The rougher the voyage, the more the mariners long for port, and heaven becomes more and more "a desired haven" as our trials multiply. By storms and by favorable breezes, through tempest and fair weather, the great Pilot and Ruler of the sea brings mariners to port, and his people to heaven. Our heavenly haven will ring with shouts of grateful joy when once we reach its blessed shore.

31. Let the sea sound forth Jehovah's praises because of his delivering grace. As the sailor touches the shore let him lift the solemn hymn to heaven, and let others who see him rescued from the jaws of death unite in his thanksgiving.

32. Let them exalt him also in the congregation of the people. Thanks for such mercies should be given in public in the place where people congregate for worship. **And praise him in the assembly of the elders.** The praise should be presented with great solemnity in the presence of men of years, experience, and influence. High and weighty service should be rendered for great and distinguished favors, and therefore let the sacrifice be presented with due decorum and with grave seriousness. When a heart has been in great spiritual storms and has at last found peace, there will follow as a duty and a privilege the acknowledgment of the Lord's mercy before his people, and it is well that this should be done in the presence of those who hold office in the church, and who from their riper years are better able to appreciate the testimony.

33. When the Lord deals with rebellious people he can soon deprive them of those blessings of which they feel most assured: their rivers and perennial springs they look upon as certain never to be taken from them, but the Lord at a word can deprive them even of these.

34. A fruitful land into barrenness. This has been done in many instances, and notably in the case of the psalmist's own country, which was once the glory of all lands and is now almost a desert. **For the wickedness of them that dwell therein.** Sin is at the bottom of sorrow. If we have not the salt of holiness we shall soon receive the salt of barrenness, for the text in the Hebrew is "a fruitful land into saltness." If we will not yield the Lord a harvest of obedience he may forbid the soil to yield us a harvest of bread, and what then? Let not saints who are now useful run the risk of enduring the loss of their services, but let them be watchful that all things may go well with them.

35. He turneth the wilderness into a standing water. With another turn of his hand he more than restores that which in judgment he took away. He does his work of mercy on a royal scale, for a deep lake is seen where before there was only a sandy waste. It is not by natural laws, working by some innate force, that this wonder is wrought, but by himself. **And dry ground into watersprings.** Continuance, abundance, and perpetual freshness are all implied in **watersprings,** and these are created where all was dry. This wonder of mercy is the precise reversal of the deed of judgment, and wrought by the selfsame hand. Even thus in the church, and in each individual saint, the mercy of the Lord soon works wonderful changes where restoring and renewing grace begin their benign work.

36. And there he maketh the hungry to dwell, where none could dwell before. They will appreciate the change and prize his grace; as the barrenness of the land caused their hungers, so will its fertility banish it forever, and they will settle down a happy and thankful people to bless God for every handful of corn which the land yields to them. **That they may prepare a city for habitation.** When the earth is watered and men cultivate it, cities spring up and teem with inhabitants; when grace abounds where sin formerly reigned, hearts find peace and dwell in God's love as in a strong city.

37. Men work when God works. His blessing encourages the sower, cheers the planter, and rewards the laborer. Not only necessaries but luxuries are enjoyed, wine as well as corn, when the heavens are caused to yield the needed rain to fill the watercourses. Divine visitations bring great spiritual riches, foster varied works of faith and labors of love, and cause every good fruit to abound to our comfort and to God's praise. When God sends the blessing it does not supersede, but encourages and develops human exertion. Paul plants, Apollos waters, and God gives the increase.

38. God's blessing is everything. It not only makes people happy, but it makes people themselves, by causing them to be multiplied upon the earth. Oh that nations in the day of their prosperity would but own the gracious hand of God, for it is to his blessing that they owe their all.

39. As they change in character, so do their circumstances alter. Under the old dispensation, this was very clearly to be observed; Israel's ups and downs were the direct consequences of her sins and repentances. Trials are of various kinds; here we have three words for affliction, and there are numbers more: God has many rods and we have many smarts, and all because we have many sins. Nations and churches soon diminish in number when they are diminished in grace.

40–41. In these two verses we see how the Lord at will turns the wheel of providence. Paying no respect to man's imaginary grandeur, he puts princes down and makes them wander in banishment as they had made their captives wander when they drove them from land to land: at the same time, having ever a tender regard for the poor and needy, the Lord delivers the distressed and sets them in a position of comfort and happiness. This is to be seen upon the roll of history again and again, and in spiritual experience we remark its counterpart: the self-sufficient are made to despise themselves and search in vain for help in the wilderness of their nature, while poor convicted souls are added to the Lord's family and dwell in safety as the sheep of his fold.

42. The righteous shall see it, and rejoice. Divine providence brings joy to God's true people; they see the hand of the Lord in all things, and delight to study the ways of his justice and of his grace. **And all iniquity shall stop her mouth.** What can she say? God's providence is often so conclusive in its arguments of fact that there is no replying or questioning. It is not long that the impudence of ungodliness can be quiet, but when God's judgments are abroad it is driven to hold its tongue.

43. Those who notice providences will never be long without a providence to notice. It is wise to observe what the Lord does, for he is wonderful in counsel; has given us eyes to see with, and it is foolish to close them when there is most to observe; but we must observe wisely, otherwise we may soon confuse ourselves and others with hasty reflections upon the dealings of the Lord. In a thousand ways the lovingkindness of the Lord is shown, and if we will but prudently watch, we shall come to a better understanding of it. To understand the delightful attribute of lovingkindness is an attainment as pleasant as it is profitable: those who are proficient scholars in this art will be among the sweetest singers to the glory of Jehovah.

Psalm 108

1. O God, my heart is fixed. Though I have many wars to disturb me, and many cares to toss me to and fro, yet I am settled in one mind and cannot be driven from it. My heart has taken hold and abides in one resolve. Thy grace has overcome the fickleness of nature, and I am now in a resolute and determined frame of mind. **I will sing and give praise.** Both with voice and music will I extol thee – "I will sing and play," as some read it. Even though I have to shout in the battle I will also sing in my soul, and if my fingers must be engaged with the bow, yet shall they also touch the ten-stringed instrument and show forth thy praise. **Even with my glory** – with my intellect, my tongue, my poetic faculty, my musical skill, or whatever else causes me to be renowned, and confers honor upon me. It is my glory to be able to speak and not be a dumb animal, therefore my voice will show forth thy praise; it is my glory to know God and not to be a heathen, and therefore my instructed intellect will adore thee.

2. Awake, psaltery and harp. As if he could not be content with voice alone, but must use the well-tuned strings, and communicate to them something of his own liveliness. Strings are wonderful things when some people play upon them; they seem to become sympathetic and incorporated with the minstrel, as if his very soul were imparted to them and thrilled through them. Only when a thoroughly enraptured soul speaks in the instrument can music be acceptable with God. **I myself will awake early.** I will call up the dawn. The best and brightest hours of the day will find me heartily aroused to bless my God. In all worship this should be the personal resolve of each worshiper.

3. I will praise thee, O LORD, among the people. Whoever may come to hear me, devout or profane, believer or heathen, civilized or barbarian, I will not cease my music. Happy man, to have thus made his choice to be the Lord's musician; he retains his office as the Poet Laureate of the kingdom of heaven, and will retain it till the crack of doom. **And I will sing praises unto thee among the nations.** This is written, not only to complete the parallelism of the verse, but to reaffirm his fixed resolve. He would march to battle praising Jehovah, and when he had conquered he would make the captured cities ring with Jehovah's praises. He would carry his religion with him wherever he pushed his conquests, and the vanquished should not hear the praises of David, but the glories of the Lord of Hosts. Nations and peoples would soon know the Gospel of Jesus if every Christian traveler were as intensely devout as the psalmist.

4. For thy mercy is great above the heavens, and therefore there must be no limit of time, or place, or people, when that mercy is to be extolled. As the heavens overarch the whole earth, and from above mercy pours down upon people, so shalt thou be praised everywhere beneath the sky. **And thy truth reacheth unto the clouds.** As far as we can see we behold thy truth and faithfulness, and there is much beyond which lies shrouded in cloud, but we are sure that it is all mercy, though it be far above and out of our sight. Therefore shall the song be lifted high and the psalm shall peal forth without stint of far-resounding music. Here is ample space for the loudest chorus, and a subject which deserves thunders of praise.

5. Let thy praise be according to the greatness of thy mercy. Ah, if we were to measure our devotion thus, with what ardor should we sing! We long for the time when God will be universally worshiped, and his glory in the Gospel will be everywhere made known. This is a truly missionary prayer. David had none of the exclusiveness of the modern Jew, or the narrow-heartedness of some nominal Christians. For God's sake, that his glory might be everywhere revealed, he longed to see heaven and earth full of the divine praise. Amen.

6–12. Now prayer follows upon praise, and derives strength of faith and holy boldness therefrom. It is frequently best to begin worship with a hymn, and then to bring forth our vials full of odors after the harps have commenced their sweeter sounds.

6. Let my prayer avail for all the beloved ones. Sometimes a nation seems to hang upon the petitions of one man. With what ardor should such a one pour out his soul! David does so here. It is easy praying for the Lord's beloved, for we feel sure of a favorable answer, since the Lord's heart is already set upon doing them good: yet it is solemn work to plead when we feel that the condition of a whole beloved nation depends upon what the Lord means to do with us whom he has placed in a representative position. David felt that the case demanded the **right hand** of God – his wisest, speediest, and most efficient interposition, and he feels sure of obtaining it for himself, since his cause involved the safety of the chosen people. When our suit is not a selfish one, but is bound up with the cause of God, we may be very bold about it.

7. **God hath spoken in his holiness.** Aforetime the Lord had made large promises to David, and these his holiness had guaranteed. The divine attributes were pledged to give the son of Jesse great blessings; there was no fear that the covenant God would run back from his plighted word. **I will rejoice.** If God has spoken we may well be glad: the very fact of a divine revelation is a joy. If the Lord had meant to destroy us he would not have spoken to us as he has done. But what God has spoken is a still further reason for gladness, for he has declared "the sure mercies of David," and promised to establish his descendants upon his throne, and to subdue all his enemies. David greatly rejoiced after the Lord had spoken to him by the mouth of Nathan. He sat before the Lord in a wonder of joy. See 1 Chronicles 17, and note that in the next chapter David began to act vigorously against his enemies, just as in this psalm he vows to do. **I will divide Shechem.** Home conquests come first. Foes must be dislodged from Israel's territory, and lands properly settled and managed. **And mete out the valley of Succoth.** On the other side of Jordan as well as on this the land must be put in order, and secured against all wandering marauders. Some rejoicing leads to inaction, but not that which is grounded upon a lively faith in the promise of God. See how David prays, as if he had the blessing already, and could share it among his men: this comes of having sung so heartily unto the Lord his helper. See how he resolves on action, like a man whose prayers are only a part of his life and vital portions of his action.

8. **Gilead is mine.** Thankful hearts dwell upon the gifts which the Lord has given them, and think it no task to mention them one by one. **Manasseh is mine.** I have it already, and it is to me the token and assurance that the rest of the promised heritage will also come into my possession in due time. If we gratefully acknowledge what we have we shall be in better heart for obtaining that which as yet we have not received. He who gives us Gilead and Manasseh will not fail to put the rest of the promised territory into our hands. **Ephraim also is the strength of mine hand.** This tribe furnished David with more than twenty thousand "mighty men of valor, famous throughout the house of their fathers": the faithful loyalty of this band was, no doubt, a proof that the rest of the tribe were with him, and so he regarded them as the helmet of the state, the guard of his royal crown. **Judah is my lawgiver.** There had he seated the government and chief courts of justice. No other tribe could lawfully govern

but Judah: till Shiloh came the divine decree fixed the legal power in that state. To us also there is no lawgiver but our Lord who sprang out of Judah; and whenever Rome, or Canterbury, or any other power attempts to set up laws and ordinances for the church, we have but one reply – "Judah is my lawgiver." Thus the royal psalmist rejoiced because his own land had been cleansed of intruders, and a regular government had been set up, and guarded by an ample force, and in all this he found encouragement to plead for victory over his foreign foes. Even thus do we plead with the Lord that as in one land and another Christ's holy Gospel has been set up and maintained, so also in other lands the power of his scepter of grace may be owned till the whole earth bows before him, and the Edom of Antichrist will be crushed beneath his feet.

9. Moab is my washpot. This nation had shown no friendly spirit to the Israelites, but had continually viewed them as a detested rival; therefore they were to be subdued and made subject to David's throne. He claims by faith the victory, and regards his powerful enemy with contempt. Nor was he disappointed, for "the Moabites became David's servants and brought him gifts" (2 Samuel 8:2). As people wash their feet after a long journey, and so are revived, so vanquished difficulties serve to refresh us: we use Moab for a washpot. **Over Edom will I cast out my shoe.** It will be as the floor upon which the bather throws his sandals; it will lie beneath his foot, subject to his will and altogether his own. Edom was proud, but David throws his slipper at it; its capital was high, but he casts his sandal over it; it was strong, but he hurls his shoe at it as a pledge of battle. He had not entered yet into its rock-built fortresses, but since the Lord was with him he felt sure that he would do so. Under the leadership of the Almighty, he felt so secure of conquering even fierce Edom itself that he looks upon it as a mere slave, over which he could exult with impunity. We ought never to fear those who are defending the wrong side, for since God is not with them their wisdom is folly, their strength is weakness, and their glory is their shame. We think too much of God's foes and talk of them with too much respect. **Over Philistia will I triumph.** David had done so in his youth, and he is all the more sure of doing it again. We read that "David smote the Philistines and subdued them" (2 Samuel 8:1), just as he had smitten Edom and filled it with his garrison. The enemies with whom we battled in our youth are yet alive, and we shall have more brushes with them before we die, but, blessed be God, we are by no means dismayed at the prospect, for we expect to triumph over them even more easily than aforetime.

10. Faith leads on to strong desire for the realization of the promise, and hence the practical question, **Who will bring me into the strong city? who will lead me into Edom?** The difficulty is plainly perceived. Petra is strong and hard to enter: the psalmist warrior knows that he cannot enter the city by his own power, and he therefore asks who is to help him. He asks of the right person, even of his Lord, who has all men at his beck, and can say to this man, "show my servant the road," and he will show it, or to this band, "cut your way into the rock city," and they will assuredly do it. Of Edom it is written by Obadiah, "The pride of thine heart hath deceived thee, thou that dwellest in the clefts of the rock, whose habitation is high; that saith in his heart, who shall bring me down to the ground? Though thou exalt thyself as the eagle, and though thou set thy nest among the stars, thence will I bring thee down, saith the Lord." David looked for his conquest to Jehovah's infinite power, and he looked not in vain.

11. Wilt not thou, O God, who hast cast us off? This is grand faith which can trust the Lord even when he seems to have cast us off. Some can barely trust him when he pampers them, and yet David relied upon him when Israel seemed under a cloud and the Lord had hidden his face. **And wilt not thou, O God, go forth with our hosts?** Canst thou forever leave thy people to be overthrown by thine enemies? The sweet singer is sure that Edom will be captured, because he cannot and will not believe that God will refrain from going forth with the armies of his chosen people. When we ask ourselves, "Who will be the means of our obtaining a promised blessing?" we need not be discouraged if we perceive no secondary agent, for we may then fall back upon the great Promiser himself, and believe that he himself will perform his word unto us. If no one else will lead us into Edom, the Lord himself will do it, if he had promised it. Or if there must be visible instruments he will use **our hosts,** feeble as they are. We need not that any new agency should be created; God can strengthen our present hosts and enable them to do all that is needed.

12. This prayer has often fallen from the lips of people who have been utterly disappointed by their fellows, and it has also been poured out unto the Lord in the presence of some gigantic labor in which mortal power is evidently of no avail. We ought to pray with all the more confidence in God when our confidence in man is altogether gone.

13. God's help will inspire us to help ourselves. Faith is neither a coward nor a sluggard: she knows that God is with her, and therefore she does valiantly. **Through God** is our secret support; from that source we draw all our courage, wisdom, and strength. **We shall do valiantly.** This is the public outflow from that secret source: our inward and spiritual faith proves itself by outward and valorous deeds. **He shall tread down our enemies.** They will fall before him, and as they lie prostrate he will march over them, and all the hosts of his people with him. This is a prophecy. It was fulfilled to David, but it remains true to the Son of David and all who are on his side. The church will yet arouse herself to praise her God with all her heart, and then with songs and hosannas she will advance to the great battle; her foes will be overthrown and utterly crushed by the power of her God, and the Lord's glory will be above all the earth. Send it in our time, we beseech thee, O Lord.

Psalm 109

1. Hold not thy peace. Mine enemies speak; be thou pleased to speak too. Break thy solemn silence, and silence those who slander me. It is the cry of a man whose confidence in God is deep, and whose communion with him is very close and bold. Note that he only asks the Lord to speak: a word from God is all a believer needs. **O God of my praise.** Thou whom my whole soul praises, be pleased to protect my honor and guard my praise. "My heart is fixed," said he in the former psalm; "I will sing and give praise," and now he appeals to the God whom he had praised. If we take care of God's honor he will take care of ours.

2. For the mouth of the wicked and the mouth of the deceitful are opened against me. Wicked people must say wicked things, and these we have reason to dread; but in addition they utter false and deceitful things, and these are worst of all. There is no knowing what may come out of mouths which are at once lewd and lying. **They have spoken against me with a lying tongue.** Lying tongues cannot lie still. Bad tongues are not content to vilify bad men, but choose the most gracious of saints to be the objects of their attacks.

3. They compassed me about also with words of hatred. Turn which way he would, they hedged him in with falsehood, misrepresentation, accusation, and scorn. Whispers, sneers, insinuations, satires, and open charges filled his ear with a perpetual buzz, and all for no reason, but sheer hate.

4. For my love they are my adversaries. They hate me because I love them. One of our poets says of the Lord Jesus, "Found guilty of excess of love." Surely it was his only fault. Our Lord might have used all the language of this complaint most emphatically – they hated him without a cause and returned him hatred for love. What a smart this is to the soul, to be hated in proportion to the gratitude which it deserved, hated by those it loved, and hated because of its love. This was a cruel case, and the sensitive mind of the psalmist writhed under it. **But I give myself unto prayer.** He did nothing else but pray. He became prayer as they became malice.

5. Evil for good is devil-like. This is Satan's line of action, and his children upon earth follow it greedily: it is cruel, and wounds to the quick.

Thus we see the harmless and innocent man upon his knees pouring out his lamentation: we are now to observe him rising from the mercy-seat, inspired with prophetic energy, and pouring forth upon his foes the forewarnings of their doom. We shall hear him speak like a judge clothed with stern severity, or like the angel of doom robed in vengeance, or as the naked sword of justice when she bares her arm for execution. When the Judge of all threatens to punish tyrannical cruelty and falsehearted treachery, virtue gives her assent and consent. Amen, so let it be, saith every just man in his inmost soul.

6. Set thou a wicked man over him. What worse punishment could a man have? The proud man cannot endure the proud, nor the oppressor brook the rule of another like himself. The righteous in their patience find the rule of the wicked a sore bondage; but those who are full of resentful passions, and haughty aspirations, are slaves indeed when men of their own class have the whip hand of them. For Herod to be ruled by another Herod would be wretchedness enough, and yet what retribution could be more just? What unrighteous man can complain if he finds himself governed by one of like character? What can the wicked expect but that their rulers should be like themselves? **And let Satan stand at his right hand.** Should not like come to like? Should not the father of lies stand near his children?? Who is a better right-hand friend for an adversary of the righteous than the great adversary himself? The curse is an awful one, but it is most natural that it should come to pass: those who serve Satan may expect to have his company, his assistance, his temptations, and at last his doom.

7. When he shall be judged, let him be condemned. He judged and condemned others in the vilest manner, he suffered not the innocent to escape; and it would be a great shame if in his time of trial, being really guilty, he should be allowed to go free. **And let his prayer become sin.** It is sin already; let it be so treated. To the injured it must seem terrible that the black-hearted villain should nevertheless pretend to pray, and very naturally do they beg that he may not be heard, but that his pleadings may be regarded as an addition to his guilt. He has devoured the widow's house, and yet he prays. He has put Naboth to death by false accusation and taken possession of his vineyard, and then he presents prayers to the Almighty. "Because that he remembered not to show mercy," he will himself be forgotten by the God of grace, and his bitter cries for deliverance will be regarded as mockeries of heaven.

8. Let his days be few. Who would desire a persecuting tyrant to live long? As well might we wish length of days to a mad dog. **And let another take his office.** Perhaps a better man may come; at any rate it is time a change were tried. So used were the Jews to look upon these verses and the doom of traitors of cruel and deceitful mind, that Peter saw at once in the speedy death of Judas a fulfillment of this sentence, and a reason for the appointment of a successor who should take his place of oversight. A bad man does not make an office bad: another may use with benefit that which he perverted to ill uses.

9. This would inevitably be the case when the man died, but the psalmist uses the words in an emphatic sense; he would have his widow "a widow indeed," and his children so friendless as to be orphaned in the bitterest sense. He sees the result of the bad man's decease, and includes it in the punishment. The tyrant's sword makes many children fatherless.

10. Let his children be continually vagabonds, and beg. May they have neither house nor home, settlement nor substance; and while they thus wander and beg may it ever be on their memory that their father's house lies in ruins – **let them seek their bread also out of their desolate places.** It has often been so: a race of tyrants has become a generation of beggars. Misused power and abused wealth have earned the family name universal detestation, and secured to the family character an entail of baseness. Justice herself would award no such doom except upon the supposition that the sin descended with the blood; but supreme providence which in the end is pure justice has written many a page of history in which the imprecation of this verse has been literally verified.

We confess that as we read some of these verses we have need of all our faith and reverence to accept them as the voice of inspiration; but the exercise is good for the soul, for it educates our sense of ignorance, and tests our teachableness. Yes, divine Spirit, we can and do believe that even these dread words from which we shrink have a meaning consistent with the attributes of the Judge of all the earth, though his name is Love. How this may be we shall know hereafter.

11. Let the extortioner catch all that he hath. A doom indeed. Those who have once fallen into the hands of the usurer can tell you what this means: it were better to be a fly in the web of a spider. In the most subtle, worrying, and sweeping manner the extortioner takes away, piece by piece, his victim's estate, till not a fraction remains to form a pittance for old age. **And let the strangers spoil his labor** – so that his kindred may have none of it. What with hard creditors and pilfering strangers the estate must soon vanish! Extortion drawing one way, and spoliation the other, a known moneylender and an unknown robber both at work, the man's substance would soon disappear, and rightly so, for it was gathered by shameless means. This too has been frequently seen. Wealth amassed by oppression has seldom lasted to the third generation.

12. Let there be none to extend mercy unto him. He had no mercy, but on the contrary he crushed down all who appealed to him. Loath to smite him with his own weapon, stern justice can do no otherwise; she lifts her scales and sees that this, too, must be in the sentence. **Neither let there be any to favor his fatherless children.** We are staggered to find the children included in the father's sentence, and yet as a mater of fact children do suffer for their father's sins, and as long as the affairs of this life are ordered as they are, it must be so. So involved are the interests of the race that it is quite impossible in all respects to view the father and the child apart.

13. Both from existence and from memory let them pass away till none know that such a vile brood ever existed. It would be undesirable that the sons of the utterly villainous and bloodthirsty should rise to honor, and if they did they would only revive the memory of their father's sins.

14. This verse is, perhaps, the most terrible of all, but yet as a matter of fact children do procure punishment upon their parents' sins, and are often themselves the means of such punishment. A bad son brings to mind his father's bad points of character; people say, "Ah, he is like the old man. He takes after his father." A mother's sins also will be sure to be called to mind if her daughter becomes grossly wicked. "Ah," they will say, "there is little wonder, when you consider what her mother was." These are matters of everyday occurrence. We cannot, however, pretend to explain the righteousness of this malediction, though we fully believe in it. We leave it till our Heavenly Father is pleased to give us further instruction. Yet, as a man's faults are often learned from his parents, it is not unjust that his consequent crimes should recoil upon him.

15. Again, he wishes that his father's sins may follow up the transgressor and assist to fill the measure of his own iniquities, so that for the whole accumulated load the family may be smitten with utter extinction. A king might justly wish for such an end to fall upon an incorrigible brood of rebels; and of persecutors, continuing in the same mind, the saints might well pray for their extinction; but the passage is dark, and we must leave it so. It must be right or it would not be here, but how we cannot see. Why should we expect to understand all things? Perhaps it is more for our benefit to exercise humility, and reverently worship God over a hard text, than it would be to comprehend all mysteries.

16. Because that he remembered not to show mercy. Because he had no memory to show mercy the Judge of all will have a strong memory of his sins. So little mercy had he ever shown that he had forgotten how to do it; he was without common humanity, devoid of compassion, and therefore only worthy to be dealt with after the bare rule of justice. **But persecuted the poor and needy man.** He looked on poor men as a nuisance upon the earth, he ground their faces, oppressed them in their wages, and treated them as the mire of the streets. Should he not be punished, and in his turn laid low? All who know him are indignant at his brutalities, and will glory to see him overthrown. **That he might even slay the broken in heart.** He had malice in his heart towards one who was already sufficiently sorrowful, whom it was a superfluity of malignity to attack. Yet no grief excited sympathy in him, no poverty ever moved him to relent.

17. As he loved cursing, so let it come unto him. Retaliation, not for private revenge, but as a measure of public justice, is demanded by the psalmist and deserved by the crime. Surely the malicious man cannot complain if he is judged by his own rule, and has his corn measured with his own bushel. Let him have what he loved. **As he delighted not in blessing, so let it be far from him.** He felt no joy in anyone's good, nor would he lift a hand to do another a service, but rather did he frown and fret when another prospered or mirth was heard under his window; what, then, can we wish him? Blessing was wasted on him; he hated those who gently sought to lead him to a better mind; even the blessings of providence he received with grumbling and repinings; he wished for famine to raise the price of his corn, and for war to increase his trade. Evil was good to him, and good he counted evil. To invoke blessings on such a man would be to participate in his wickedness; therefore let blessing be far from him, so long as he continues what he now is.

18–19. He was so openly in the habit of wishing ill to others that he seemed to wear robes of cursing; therefore let ill be as his raiment girded and belted about him; let it enter as water into his bowels, and search the very marrow of his bones like a penetrating oil. It is but common justice that he should receive a return for his malice, and receive it in kind, too.

20. This is the summing up of the entire imprecation, and fixes it upon the persons who had so maliciously assailed the inoffensive man of God. David was a man of gentle mold, and remarkably free from the spirit of revenge, and therefore we may here conceive him to be speaking as a judge or as a representative man, in whose person great principles needed to be vindicated and great injuries redressed.

Thousands of God's people are perplexed with this psalm, and we fear we have contributed very little towards their enlightenment. What then? Is it not good for us sometimes to be made to feel that we are not yet able to understand all the Word and mind of God? A thorough bewilderment, so long as it does not stagger our faith, may be useful to us by confounding our pride, arousing our faculties, and leading us to cry, "What I know not, teach me."

21. But do thou for me, O God the Lord, for thy name's sake. How eagerly he turns from his enemies to his God! He sets the great Thou in opposition to all his adversaries, and you see at once that his heart is at rest. He leaves himself in the Lord's hands, dictating nothing, but quite content so long as his God will but undertake for him. His plea is not his own merit, but the **name.** The saints have always felt this to be their most mighty plea. God himself has performed his grandest deeds of grace for the honor of his name, and his people know that this is the most potent argument with him. What the Lord himself has guarded with sacred jealousy we should reverence with our whole hearts and rely upon without distrust. **Because thy mercy is good, deliver thou me.** Not because I am good, but because thy mercy is good: see how the saints fetch their pleadings in prayer from the Lord himself. God's mercy is the star to which the Lord's people turn their eye when they are tossed with tempest and not comforted, for the special bounty and goodness of that mercy have a charm for weary hearts.

22. For I am poor and needy. When he does plead anything about himself he urges not his riches or his merits, but his poverty and his necessities: this is Gospel supplication, such as only the Spirit of God can indite upon the heart. **And my heart is wounded within me.** The Lord has always a tender regard to broken-hearted ones, and such the psalmist had become: the undeserved cruelty, the baseness, the slander of his remorseless enemies had pierced him to the soul, and this sad condition he pleads as a reason for speedy help.

23. I am gone like the shadow when it declineth. I am a mere shadow, a shadow at the vanishing point, when it stretches far, but is almost lost in the universal gloom of evening which settles over all, and so obliterates the shadows cast by the setting sun. Lord, there is next to nothing left of me; wilt thou not come in before I am quite gone? **I am tossed up and down as the locust,** which is the sport of the winds, and must go up or down as the breeze carries it. The psalmist felt as powerless in his distress as a poor insect, which a child may toss up and down at its pleasure.

24. My knees are weak through fasting; either religious fasting, to which he resorted in the dire extremity of his grief, or else through loss of appetite occasioned by distress of mind. **And my flesh faileth of fatness.** He was wasted to a skeleton, and as his body was emaciated, so was his soul bereft of comfort: he was pining away, and all the while his enemies saw it and laughed at his distress. How pathetically he states his case; this is one of the truest forms of prayer, the setting forth of our sorrow before the Lord. Weak knees are strong with God, and failing flesh has great power in leading.

25. I became also a reproach unto them. They made him the theme of ridicule, the butt of their ribald jests: his emaciation by fasting made him a tempting subject for their caricatures and lampoons. **When they looked upon me they shook their heads.** Words were not sufficient expression of their scorn, so they resorted to gestures which were meant both to show their derision and to irritate his mind. Though these things break no bones, yet they do worse, for they break and bruise far tenderer parts of us. Many a person who could have answered a malicious speech, and so have relieved his mind, has felt keenly a sneer, a putting out of the tongue, or some other sign of contempt. Those, too, who are exhausted by such fasting and wasting as the last verse describes are generally in a state of morbid sensibility, and therefore feel more acutely the unkindness of others. What they would smile at during happier seasons becomes intolerable when they are in a highly nervous condition.

26. Help me, O LORD my God. Laying hold of Jehovah by the appropriating word **my,** he implores his aid both to help him to bear his heavy load and to enable him to rise superior to it. He has described his own weakness, and the strength and fury of his foes, and by these two arguments he urges his appeal with double force. This is a very rich, short, and suitable prayer for believers in any situation of peril, difficulty, or sorrow. **O save me according to thy mercy.** As thy mercy is, so let thy salvation be. The measure is a great one, for the mercy of God is without bound. When man has no mercy it is comforting to fall back upon God's mercy. Justice to the wicked is often mercy to the righteous, and because God is merciful he will save his people by overthrowing their adversaries.

27. That they may know that this is thy hand. Ungodly people will not see God's hand in anything if they can help it, and when they see good people delivered into their power they become more confirmed than ever in their atheism, but all in good time God will arise and so effectually punish their malice and rescue the object of their spite that they will be compelled to say like the Egyptian magicians, "this is the finger of God." **That thou, LORD, hast done it.** There will be no mistaking the author of so thorough a vindication, so complete a turning of the tables.

28. Let them curse, but bless thou, or, "they will curse and thou wilt bless." Their cursing will then be of such little consequence that it will not matter a straw. One blessing from the Lord will take the poison out of ten thousand curses of men. **When they arise, let them be ashamed.** They lift up themselves to deal out another blow, to utter another falsehood, and to watch for its injurious effects upon their victim, but they see their own defeat and are filled with shame. **But let thy servant rejoice.** Not merely as a man protected and rescued, but as God's servant in whom his master's goodness and glory are displayed when he is saved from his foes. It ought to be our greatest joy that the Lord is honored in our experience; the mercy itself ought not so much to rejoice us as the glory which is thereby brought to him who so graciously bestows it.

29. Let mine adversaries be clothed with shame. It is a prophecy as well as a wish, and may we read both in the indicative and the imperative. Where sin is the underclothing, shame will soon be the outer vesture. He who would clothe good people with contempt will himself be clothed with dishonor. **And let them cover themselves with their own confusion, as with a mantle.** Let their confusion be broad enough to wrap them all over from head to foot; let them bind it about them and hide themselves in it, as being utterly afraid to be seen.

30. I will greatly praise the LORD with my mouth. Enthusiastically, abundantly, and loudly will he extol the righteous Lord, who redeemed him from all evil; and that not only in his own chamber or among his own family, but in the most public manner. **Yea, I will praise him among the multitude.** Remarkable and public providences demand public recognition, for otherwise men of the world will judge us to be ungrateful. We do not praise God to be heard of men, but as a natural sense of justice leads everyone to expect to hear a befriended person speak well of his benefactor, we therefore have regard to such natural and just expectations, and endeavor to make our praises as public as the benefit we have received.

31. For he shall stand at the right hand of the poor. God will not be absent when his people are on their trial; he will hold a brief for them and stand in court as their advocate, prepared to plead on their behalf. How different is this from the doom of the ungodly who has Satan at his right hand (verse 6). **To save him from those that condemn his soul.** The court only met as a matter of form. The malicious had made up their minds as to the verdict: they judged him guilty, for their hate condemned him; they pronounced sentence of damnation upon the very soul of their victim. But what mattered it? The great King was in court, and their sentence was turned against themselves. Nothing can more sweetly sustain the heart of a slandered believer than the firm conviction that God is near all who are wronged, and is sure to work out their salvation.

O Lord, save us from the severe trial of slander: deal in thy righteousness with all those who spitefully assail the characters of holy people, and cause all who are smarting under calumny and reproach to come forth unsullied from the affliction, just as did thine only-begotten Son. Amen.

Psalm 110

1. The LORD said unto my Lord – Jehovah said unto my Adonai: David in spirit heard the solemn voice of Jehovah speaking to the Messiah from of old. What wonderful fellowship there has been between the Father and the Son! From this secret and intimate communion spring the covenant of grace and all its marvelous arrangements. All the great acts of grace are brought into actual being by the word of God; had he not spoken, there had been no manifestation of Deity to us; but in the beginning was the Word, and from of old there was mysterious fellowship between the Father and his Son Jesus Christ concerning his people and the great contest on their behalf between himself and the powers of evil.

Though David was a firm believer in the unity of the Godhead, he yet spiritually discerns the two persons, distinguishes between them, and perceives that in the second he has an especial interest, for he calls him **my Lord**. This was an anticipation of the exclamation of Thomas, "My Lord and my God," and it expresses the psalmist's reverence, his obedience, his believing appropriation, and his joy in Christ. It is well to have clear views of the mutual relations of the persons of the blessed Trinity; indeed, the knowledge of these truths is essential for our comfort and growth in grace. There is a clear distinction in the divine persons, since one speaks to another; yet the Godhead is one.

Sit thou at my right hand, until I make thine enemies thy footstool. Away from the shame and suffering of his earthly life, Jehovah calls Adonai, our Lord, to the repose and honors of his celestial seat. His work is done, and he may sit; it is well done, and he may sit at his right hand; it will have grand results, and he may therefore quietly wait to see the complete victory which is certain to follow. The glorious Jehovah thus addresses the Christ as our Saviour; for, says David, he said **unto my Lord**. Jesus is placed in the seat of power, dominion, and dignity, and is to sit there by divine appointment while Jehovah fights for him, and lays every rebel beneath his feet.

2. The LORD shall send the rod of thy strength out of Zion. It is in and through the church that for the present the power of the Messiah is known. Jehovah has given to Jesus all authority in the midst of his people, whom he rules with his royal scepter, and this power goes forth with divine energy from the church for the ingathering of the elect, and the subduing of all evil. We need to pray for the sending out of the rod of divine strength. It was by his rod that Moses smote the Egyptians, and wrought wonders for Israel, and whenever the Lord Jesus sends forth the rod of his strength our spiritual enemies are overcome. O God of eternal might, let the strength of our Lord Jesus be more clearly seen, and let the nations see it as coming forth out of the midst of thy feeble people. **Rule thou in the midst of thine enemies,** as he does whenever his mighty scepter of grace is stretched forth to renew and save them. Moses' rod brought water out of the flinty rock, and the Gospel of Jesus soon causes repentance to flow in rivers from the once hardened heart of man. Or the text may mean that though the church is situated in the midst of a hostile world, yet it exerts a great influence, it continues to manifest inward majesty, and is after all the ruling power among the nations because the shout of a King is in her midst. Jesus, however hated by people, is still the King of kings. Jesus, it appears from this text, is not inactive while he sits at Jehovah's right hand, but in his own way proves the abiding nature of his kingdom both *in* Zion and *from* Zion, both among his friends and his foes. We look for the clearer manifestation of his almighty power in the latter days; but even in these waiting times we rejoice that to the Lord all power is given in heaven and on earth.

3. In consequence of the sending forth of the rod of strength, namely, the power of the Gospel, out of Zion, converts will come forward in great numbers to enlist under the banner of the Priest-King. Given to him of old, they are his people, and when his power is revealed, these hasten with cheerfulness to own his sway, appearing at the Gospel call as it were spontaneously, just as the dew comes forth in the morning. This metaphor is further enlarged upon, for as the dew has a sparkling beauty, so these willing armies of converts have a holy excellence and charm about them; and as the dew is the lively emblem of freshness, so are these converts full of vivacity and youthful vigor, and the church is refreshed by them and made to flourish exceedingly. Let but the Gospel be preached with divine unction, and the chosen of the Lord respond to it like troops in the day of the mustering of armies; they come in shining uniforms of holiness, and for number, freshness, beauty, and purity, they are as the dewdrops which come mysteriously from the morning's womb.

4. We have now reached the heart of the psalm, which is also the very center and soul of our faith. Our Lord Jesus is a Priest-King by the ancient oath of Jehovah: "he glorified not himself to be made a high priest," but was ordained thereunto from of old, and was called of God a high priest after the order of Melchizedek. It must be a solemn and a sure matter which leads the Eternal to swear, and with him an oath fixes and settles the decree forever; but in this case, as if to make assurance a thousand times sure, it is added, **and will not repent.** It is done, and done forever and ever; Jesus is sworn in to be the priest of his people, and he must abide so even to the end, because his commission is sealed by the unchanging oath of the immutable Jehovah. If his priesthood could be revoked, and his authority removed, it would be the end of all our security; the oath of God establishes our Lord both in his priesthood and in his throne. It is the Lord who has constituted him a priest forever; he has done it by oath; that oath is without repentance, is taking effect now, and will stand throughout all ages: hence our security in him is beyond all question.

The declaration runs in the present tense as being the only time with the Lord, and comprehending all other times. **Thou art,** that is, thou wast and art, and art to come, in all ages a priestly King. The order of Melchizedek's priesthood was the most ancient and primitive, the most free from ritual and ceremony, the most natural and simple, and at the same time the most honorable. That ancient patriarch was the father of his people, and at the same time ruled and taught them; he swayed both the scepter and the censer, reigned in righteousness, and offered sacrifice before the Lord. There has never arisen another like to him since his days, for whenever the kings of Judah attempted to seize the sacerdotal office they were driven back to their confusion: God would have no king-priest save his Son. Melchizedek's office was exceptional: none preceded or succeeded him; he comes upon the page of history mysteriously; no pedigree is given, no date of birth, or mention of death; he blesses Abraham, receives tithe, and vanishes from the scene amid honors which show that he was greater than the founder of the chosen nation. He is seen but once, and that once suffices. Aaron and his descendants came and went; their imperfect sacrifice contained for many generations, because it had no finality in it, and could never make the comers thereunto perfect. Our Lord Jesus, like Melchizedek, stands forth before us as a priest of divine ordaining; he was not made a priest by fleshly birth, as the sons of Aaron; he mentions neither father, mother, nor descent, as his right to the sacred office; he stands upon his personal merits, by himself alone; as no man came before him in his work, so none can follow after; his order begins and ends in his own person, and in himself it is eternal, "having neither beginning of days nor end of years." The King-Priest has been here and left his blessing upon the believing seed, and now he sits in glory in his complete character, atoning for us by the merit of his blood, and exercising all power on our behalf.

5–7. The last verses of this psalm we understand to refer to the future victories of the Priest-King. He will not forever sit waiting, but will come into the fight to end the weary war by his own victorious presence. He will lead the final charge in person; his own right hand and his holy arm will get him the victory.

5. Now that he has come into the field of action, the infinite Jehovah comes with him as the strength of his right hand. Eternal power attends the coming of the Lord, and earthly power dies before it as though smitten through with a sword. In the last days all the kingdoms of the earth will meet with swift and overwhelming ruin. What are kings when they dare oppose the Son of God? A single stroke will suffice for their destruction.

6. He shall judge among the heathen, or, among the nations. All nations will feel his power, and either yield to it joyfully or be crushed before it. **He shall fill the places with the dead bodies.** In the terrible battles of his Gospel all opponents will fall till the field of fight is heaped high with the slain. This need not be understood literally, but as a poetical description of the overthrow of all rebellious powers and the defeat of all unholy principles. Yet should kings oppose the Lord with weapons of war, the result would be their overwhelming defeat and the entire destruction of their forces. Read in connection with this prophecy Revelation 19:17–21. Terrible things in righteousness will be seen ere the history of this world comes to an end. **He shall wound the heads over many countries.** He will strike at the greatest powers which resist him, and wound not merely common people, but those who rule and reign. If the nations will not have Christ for their Head, they will find their political heads to be powerless to protect them. Or the passage may be read, "he has smitten the head over the wide earth." The monarch of the greatest nation will not escape the sword of the Lord; nor shall that dread spiritual prince who rules over the children of disobedience be able to escape without a deadly wound.

7. He shall drink of the brook in the way. So swiftly will he march to conquest that he will not stay for refreshment, but drink as he hastens on. Like Gideon's men that lapped, he will throw his heart into the fray and cut it short in righteousness, because a short work will the Lord make in the earth. **Therefore shall he lift up the head.** His own head will be lifted high in victory, and his people, in him, will be upraised also. When he passed this way before, he was burdened and had stern work laid upon him; but in his second advent he will win an easy victory; aforetime he was the man of sorrows, but when he comes a second time his head will be lifted in triumph. Let his saints rejoice with him. "Lift up your heads, for your redemption draweth nigh." In the latter days we look for terrible conflicts and a final victory. Long has Jesus borne with our rebellious race, but at length he will rise to end the warfare of long-suffering, by the blows of justice. O King-Priest, we who are, in a minor degree, king-priests too are full of gladness because thou reignest even now, and will come ere long to establish thine empire forever.

Psalm 111

1. Praise ye the LORD, or, "Hallelujah!" All ye his saints unite in adoring Jehovah, who worketh so gloriously. Do it now, do it always: do it heartily, do it unanimously, do it eternally. Even if others refuse, take care that you have always a song for your God. Put away all doubt, question, grumbling, and rebellion, and give yourselves up to the praising of Jehovah, both with your lips and in your lives. **I will praise the LORD with my whole heart.** The sweet singer commences the song, for his heart is all on flame: whether others will follow him or not, he will at once begin and long continue. What we preach we should practice. The best way to enforce an exhortation is to set an example; but we must let that example be of the best kind, or we may lead others to do the work in a limping manner. David brought nothing less than his whole heart to the duty; all his love went out towards God, and all his zeal, his skill, and his ardor went with it. Jehovah the one and undivided God cannot be acceptably praised with a divided heart, neither should we attempt so to dishonor him; for our whole heart is little enough for his glory, and there can be no reason why it should not all be lifted up in his praise. All his works are praiseworthy, and therefore all our nature should adore him. **In the assembly of the upright, and in the congregation** – whether with few or with many he would pour forth his whole heart and soul in praise, and whether the company was made up of select spirits or of the general mass of the people he would continue in the same exercise. For the choicest society there can be no better engagement than praise, and for the general assembly nothing can be more fitting. For the church and for the congregation, for the family or the community, for the private chamber of pious friendship, or the great hall of popular meeting, the praise of the Lord is suitable; and at the very least the true heart should sing hallelujah in any and every place.

2. **The works of the LORD are great.** In design, in size, in number, in excellence, all the works of the Lord are great. Even the little things of God are great. In some point of view or other each one of the productions of his power, or the deeds of his wisdom, will appear to be great to the wise in heart. **Sought out of all them that have pleasure therein.** Those who love their Maker delight in his handiworks; they perceive that there is more in them than appears upon the surface, and therefore they bend their minds to study and understand them. The devout naturalist ransacks nature, the earnest student of history pries into hidden facts and dark stories, and the man of God digs unto the mines of Scripture, and unearths each grain of its golden truth. God's works are worthy of our researches, they yield us instruction and pleasure wonderfully blended, and they grow upon reflection, appearing to be far greater after investigation than before. Men's works are noble from a distance; God's works are great when sought out. Delitzsch reads the passage, "Worthy of being sought after in all their purposes," and this also is a grand truth, for the end and design which God has in all that he makes or does is equally admirable with the work.

3. **His work is honorable and glorious.** His one special work, the salvation of his people, is here mentioned as distinguished from his many other **works**. It is deservedly the theme of the highest praise, and compels those who understand it to ascribe all honor and glory unto the Lord. Its conception, its sure

foundations, its gracious purpose, its wise arrangements, its gift of Jesus as Redeemer, its application of redemption by the Holy Spirit in regeneration and sanctification, and all else which make up the one glorious whole, all redound to the infinite honor of him who contrived and carried out so astounding a method of salvation. No other work can be compared with it: it honors both the Saviour and the saved, and while it brings glory to God it also brings us to glory. There is no salvation like that which God has wrought for his people. **And his righteousness endureth for ever.** In the work of grace righteousness is not forgotten, nor deprived of its glory; rather, it is honored in the eyes of the intelligent universe. The bearing of guilt by our great Substitute proved that not even to effect the purposes of grace would the Lord forget his righteousness; no future strain upon his justice can ever be equal to that which it has already sustained in the bruising of his dear Son; it must henceforth assuredly endure forever. Moreover, the righteousness of God in the whole plan can never now be suspected of failure, for all that it requires is enduring the vengeance due, and in rendering perfect obedience to the law.

4. He hath made his wonderful works to be remembered. He meant them to remain in the recollection of his people, and they do so: partly because they are in themselves memorable, and because also he has taken care to record them by the pen of inspiration, and has written them upon the hearts of his people by his Holy Spirit. By the ordinances of the Mosaic law, the coming out of Egypt, the sojourn in the wilderness, and other memorabilia of Israel's history were constantly brought before the minds of the people, and their children were by such means instructed in the wonders which God had wrought in old time. Deeds such as God has wrought are not to be admired for an hour and then forgotten; they are meant to be perpetual signs and instructive tokens to all coming generations; and especially are they designed to confirm the faith of his people in the divine love, and to make them know that **the Lord is gracious and full of compassion.** They need not fear to trust his grace for the future, for they remember it in the past. Grace is as conspicuous as righteousness in the great work of God; a fullness of tender love is seen in all that he has done. He treats his people with great consideration for their weakness, having the same pity for them as a father has towards his children.

5. He hath given meat unto them that fear him. Or "spoil," as some read it, for the Lord's people both in coming out of Egypt and at other times have been enriched from their enemies. Not only in the wilderness with manna, but everywhere else by his providence he has supplied the necessities of his believing people. Somewhere or other they have had food convenient for them, and that in times of great scarcity. As for spiritual meat, that has been plentifully furnished them in Christ Jesus; they have been fed with the finest of the wheat, and made to feast on royal dainties. His word is as nourishing to the soul as bread to the body, and there is such an abundance of it that no heir of heaven will ever be famished. Truly the fear of the Lord is wisdom, since it secures to us all that we need for soul and body. **He will ever be mindful of his covenant.** He could not let his people lack meat, because he was in covenant with them, and they can never want in the future, for he will continue to act upon the terms of that covenant. No promise of the Lord will fall to the ground, nor will any part of the great compact of eternal love be revoked or allowed to sink into oblivion. The covenant of grace is the plan of the great work which the Lord works out for his people, and it will never be departed from: the Lord has set his hand and seal to it, his glory and honor are involved in it, his very name hangs upon it, and he will not even in the least jot or tittle cease to be mindful of it. Of this the feeding of his people is the pledge: he would not so continually supply their needs if he meant after all to destroy them. Upon this most blessed earnest let us settle our minds; let us rest in the faithfulness of the Lord, and praise him with all our hearts every time that we eat bread or feed upon his word.

6. He hath showed his people the power of his works. They have seen what he is able to do and what force he is prepared to put forth on their behalf. This power Israel saw in physical works, and we in spiritual wonders, for we behold the matchless energy of the Holy Spirit and feel it in our own souls. We may well turn this verse into a prayer and ask to see more and more the power of the Lord at work among us in these latter days. O Lord, let us now see how mightily thou canst work in the saving of sinners and in preserving and delivering thine own people. **That he may give them the heritage of the heathen.** He put forth all his power to drive out the Canaanites and bring in his people. Even thus may it please his infinite wisdom to give to his church the heathen for her inheritance in the name of Jesus. Nothing but great power can effect this, but it will surely be accomplished in due season.

7. The works of his hands are verity and judgment. Truth and justice are conspicuous in all that Jehovah does. Nothing like artifice or crooked policy can ever be seen in his proceedings; he acts faithfully and righteously towards his people, and with justice and impartiality to all mankind. This also should lead us to praise him, since it is of the utmost advantage to us to live under a sovereign whose laws, decrees, acts, and deeds are the essence of truth and justice. **All his commandments are sure.** All that he has appointed or decreed will surely stand, and his precepts which he has proclaimed will be found worthy of our obedience, for surely they are founded in justice and meant for our lasting good. He is no fickle despot, commanding one thing one day and another another, but his commands remain absolutely unaltered, their necessity equally unquestionable, their excellence permanently proven, and their reward eternally secure. Take the word **commandments** to relate either to his decrees or his precepts, and we have in each case an important sense; but it seems more in accordance with the connection to take the first sense and consider the words to refer to the ordinances or decrees of the great King.

8. They stand fast for ever and ever. That is to say, his purposes, commands, and courses of action. The Lord is not swayed by transient motives, or moved by the circumstances of the hour; immutable principles rule in the courts of Jehovah, and he pursues his eternal purposes without the shadow of a turning. We take up a purpose for a while and then exchange it for another, but he is of one mind, and none can turn him. Much of this lasting character arises out of the fact which is next mentioned, namely, that they **are done in truth and uprightness.** Nothing stands but that which is upright. Falsehood soon vanishes, for it is a mere show, but truth has salt in it which preserves it from decay. God always acts according to the glorious principles of truth and integrity, and hence there is no need of alteration or revocation; his works will endure to the end of time.

9. He sent redemption unto his people. When they were in Egypt he sent not only a deliverer, but an actual deliverance; not only a redeemer, but complete redemption. He has done the like spiritually for all his people, having first by blood purchased them out of the hand of the enemy, and then by power rescued them from the bondage of their sins. Redemption we can sing of as an accomplished act: it has been wrought for us, sent to us, and enjoyed by us, and we are in very deed the Lord's redeemed. **He hath commanded his covenant for ever.** His divine decree has made the covenant of his grace a settled and eternal institution: redemption by blood proves that the covenant cannot be altered, for it ratifies and establishes it beyond all recall. This, too, is reason for the loudest praise. Redemption is a fit theme for the heartiest music, and when it is seen to be connected with gracious engagements from which the Lord's truth cannot swerve, it becomes a subject fitted to arouse the soul to an ecstasy of gratitude. **Holy and reverend is his name.** The whole name or character of God is worthy of profoundest awe, for it is perfect and complete, whole or holy. It ought not to be spoken without solemn thought, and never heard without profound homage. Even those who know him best rejoice with trembling before him. How good men can endure to be called "reverend" we know not. Being unable to discover any reason why our fellow-men should reverence *us*, we half suspect that in other men there is not very much which can entitle them to be called reverend.

10. The fear of the LORD is the beginning of wisdom. It is its first principle, but it is also its head and chief attainment. The word **beginning** in Scripture sometimes means the chief; and true religion is at once the first element of wisdom, and its chief fruit. To know God so as to walk aright before him is the greatest of all the applied sciences. Holy reverence of God leads us to praise him, and this is the point which the psalm drives at, for it is a wise act on the part of a creature towards his Creator. **A good understanding have all they that do his commandments.** Obedience to God proves that our judgment is sound.

Does not reason itself claim obedience for the Lord of all? Practical godliness is the test of wisdom. People may know and be very orthodox, they may talk and be very eloquent, they may speculate and be very profound; but the best proof of their intelligence must be found in their actually doing the will of the Lord. The former part of the psalm taught us the doctrine of God's nature and character, by describing his works; the second part supplies the practical lesson by drawing the inference that to worship and obey him is the dictate of true wisdom. **His praise endureth for ever.** The praises of God will never cease, because his works will always excite adoration, and it will always be the wisdom of men to extol their glorious Lord. Some regard this sentence as referring to those who fear the Lord – their praise will endure forever; and indeed it is true that those who lead obedient lives will obtain honor of the Lord, and commendations which will abide forever. A word of approbation from the mouth of God will be an honor which will outshine all the decorations which kings and emperors can bestow.

Psalm 112

1. Praise ye the LORD. This exhortation is never given too often; the Lord always deserves praise, we ought always to render it, we are frequently forgetful of it, and it is always well to be stirred up to it. The exhortation is addressed to all thoughtful people who observe the way of life of those who fear the Lord. If there be any virtue, if there be any praise, the Lord should have all the glory of it, for we are his workmanship. **Blessed is the man that feareth the LORD.** "The fear of the LORD is the beginning of wisdom" (Psalm 111:10); this man, therefore, has begun to be wise, and wisdom has brought him present happiness, and secured him eternal felicity. Jehovah is so great that he is to be feared and had in reverence of all them that are round about him, and he is at the same time so infinitely good that the fear is sweetened into filial love, and becomes a delightful emotion, by no means engendering bondage. **That delighteth greatly in his commandments.** This man not only studies the divine precepts and endeavors to observe them, but rejoices to do so: holiness is his happiness, devotion is his delight, truth is his treasure. He rejoices in the precepts of godliness; indeed he rejoices **greatly** in them. We have known hypocrites to rejoice in the doctrines, but never in the commandments. Ungodly people may in some measure obey the commandments out of fear, but only a gracious person will observe them with delight.

2. His soul shall be mighty upon earth; that is to say, successive generations of God-fearing people will have dominion. The true seed of the righteous are those who follow them in their virtues, just as believers are the seed of Abraham, because they imitate his faith; and these are the real heroes of their era, the truly great; their lives are sublime, and their power upon their age is far greater than at first sight appears. If the promise must be regarded as alluding to natural descendants, it must be understood as a general statement rather than a promise made to every individual, for the children of the godly are not all prosperous, nor all famous. Nevertheless, he who fears God and leads a holy life is, as a rule, doing the best he can for the future advancement of his house; no inheritance is equal to that of an unblemished name, no legacy can excel the benediction of a saint; and, taking matters for all in all, the children of the righteous man commence life with greater advantage than others, and are more likely to succeed in it, in the best and highest sense. **The generation of the upright shall be blessed.** The race of sincere, devout, righteous people is kept up from age to age, and ever abides under the blessing of God. The godly may be persecuted, but they will not be forsaken; human curses cannot deprive them of the blessing of God, for the words of Balaam are true, "He hath blessed, and I cannot reverse it." Their children also are under the special care of heaven, and as a rule it will be found that they inherit the divine blessing. To fear God and walk uprightly is a higher nobility than birth can bestow.

3. **Wealth and riches shall be in his house.** Understood literally this is rather a promise of the old covenant than of the new, for many of the best of the people of God are very poor; yet it has been found true that uprightness is the road to success, and all other things being equal the honest person is the rising person. Many are kept poor through knavery and profligacy; but godliness has the promise of the life that now is. If we understand the passage spiritually it is abundantly true. What wealth can equal that of the love of God? What riches can rival a contented heart? It matters nothing that the roof is thatched, and the floor is of cold stone: the heart which is cheered with the favor of heaven is "rich to all the intents of bliss." **And his righteousness endureth for ever.** Often when gold comes in the Gospel goes out; but it is not so with the blessed person. Prosperity does not destroy holiness of life, or humility of heart. The godly character stands the test of examination, overcomes the temptations of wealth, survives the assaults of slander, outlives the afflictions of time, and endures the trial of the last great day. The righteousness of a true saint endureth forever, because it springs from the same root as the righteousness of God, and is indeed the reflection of it. So long as the Lord abides righteous, he will maintain by his grace the righteousness of his people. They will hold on their way, and wax stronger and stronger. There is also another righteousness which belong to the Lord's chosen, which is sure to endure forever, namely the imputed righteousness of the Lord Jesus, which is called "everlasting righteousness," belonging as it does to the Son of God himself.

4. **Unto the upright there ariseth light in the darkness.** He does not lean to injustice in order to ease himself, but like a pillar stands erect, and he will be found so standing when the ungodly, who are as a collapsing wall, lie in ruins.

He will have his days of darkness, he may be sick and poor; his former riches may take wings and fly away, while even his righteousness may be cruelly suspect; thus the clouds may lower around him, but his gloom will not last forever; the Lord will bring him light in due season, for as surely as a good man's sun goes down it will rise again. If the darkness be caused by repression of spirit, the Holy Spirit will comfort him; if by pecuniary loss or personal bereavement, the presence of Christ will be his solace; and if by human cruelty and malignity, the sympathy of his Lord will be his support. **He is gracious, and full of compassion, and righteous.** This is spoken of God in Psalm 111:4, and now the same words are used of his servant; thus we are taught that when God makes someone upright, he makes that person like himself. We are at best but humble copies of the great original; still we are copies, and because we are so we praise the Lord, who has created us anew in Christ Jesus.

5. He showeth favor, and lendeth. Having passed beyond stern integrity into open-handed benevolence he looks kindly upon all around him, and finding himself in circumstances which enable him to spare a little of his wealth he lends judiciously where a loan will be of permanent service. Providence has made him able to lend, and grace makes him willing to lend. He is not a borrower, for God has lifted him above that necessity; neither is he a hoarder, for his new nature saves him from that temptation; but he wisely uses the talents committed to him. **He will guide his affairs with discretion.** Those who neglect their worldly business must not plead religion as an excuse, for when a man is truly upright he exercises great care in managing his accounts, in order that he may remain so. True religion is sanctified common sense. Attention to the things of heaven does not necessitate the neglect of the affairs of earth; on the contrary, he who has learned how to transact business with God ought to be best able to do business with men. The children of this world often are in their generation wiser than the children of light, but there is no reason why this proverb should continue to be true.

6. Surely he shall not be moved for ever. God has rooted and established him so that neither men nor devils will sweep him from his place. His prosperity will be permanent, and not like that of the gambler and the cheat, whose gains are evanescent; his reputation will be bright and lustrous from year to year, for it is not a mere pretense; his home will be permanent, and he will not need to wander from place to place as a bird that wanders from her nest; and even his memory will be abiding, for a good person is not soon forgotten, and **the righteous shall be in everlasting remembrance.** They are of a most ancient family, and not mushrooms of an hour, and their grand old stock will be found flourishing when all the proud houses of the ungodly have faded into nothing. The righteous are worth remembering, their actions are of the kind which record themselves, and God himself takes charge of their memorials. None of us like being forgotten, yet the only way to avoid it is to be righteous before God.

7. He shall not be afraid of evil tidings. He will have no dread that evil tidings will come, and he will not be alarmed when they do come. Rumors and reports he despises; prophecies of evil he ridicules; verified information of distress he bears with equanimity, resigning everything into the hands of God. **His heart is fixed, trusting in the LORD.** He is neither fickle nor cowardly; when he is undecided as to his course he is still fixed in heart: he may change his plan, but not the purpose of his soul. His heart being fixed in solid reliance upon God, a change in his circumstances but slightly affects him; faith has made him firm and steadfast, and therefore if the worst should come to the worst, he would remain quiet and patient, waiting for the salvation of God.

8. His heart is established. His love to God is deep and true, his confidence in God is firm and unmoved; his courage has a firm foundation, and is supported by omnipotence. He has become settled by experience, and confirmed by years. He is not a rolling stone, but a pillar in the house of the Lord. **He shall not be afraid.** He is ready to face any adversary – a holy heart gives a brave face. **Until he see his desire upon his enemies.** All through the conflict, even till he seizes the victory, he is devoid of fear. When the battle wavers, and the result seems doubtful, he nevertheless believes in God, and is a stranger to dismay. Grace makes him desire his enemies' good: though nature leads him to wish to see justice done to his cause, he does not desire for those who injure him anything by way of private revenge.

9. He hath dispersed, he hath given to the poor. What he received, he distributed, and distributed to those who most needed it. He was God's reservoir, and forth from his abundance flowed streams of liberality to supply the needy. If this be one of the marks of a man who fears the Lord, there are some who are strangely destitute of it. They are great at gathering, but very slow at dispersing; they enjoy the blessedness of receiving, but seldom taste the greater joy of giving. "It is more blessed to give than to receive" – perhaps they think that the blessing of receiving is enough for them. **His righteousness endureth for ever.** His liberality has salted his righteousness, proved its reality, and secured its perpetuity. This is the second time that we have this sentence applied to the godly man, and it must be understood as resulting from the enduring mercy of the Lord. The character of a righteous man is not spasmodic; he is not generous by fits and starts, nor upright in a few points only; his actions flow from settled, sure, and fixed convictions, and therefore his integrity is maintained when others fail. He is not turned about by companions, nor affected by the customs of society; he is resolute, determined, and immovable. **His horn shall be exalted with honor.** God will honor him, and even the wicked will feel an unconscious reverence of him. Let it be observed, in summing up the qualities of the God-fearing man, that he is described not merely as righteous, but as one bearing the character to which Paul refers as "a good man." Kindness, benevolence, and generosity are essential to the perfect character; to be strictly just is not good enough, for God is love, and we must act upon those same principles of grace which reign in the heart of God. The promises of prosperity are to souls who have proved their fitness to be stewards of the Lord by the right way in which they use their substance.

10. This verse sets forth very forcibly the contrast between the righteous and the ungodly, thus making the blessedness of the godly appear all the more remarkable. Usually we see the blessing and the curse set one over against the other, to invest both with the greater solemnity. **The wicked shall see it, and be grieved.** The ungodly will first see the example of the saints to their own condemnation, and will at last behold the happiness of the godly to the increase of their eternal misery. The child of wrath will fret and fume, but will not be able to prevent it, for God's blessing is sure and effectual. **He shall gnash with his teeth.** Being very wrathful, and exceedingly envious, he would grind the righteous between his teeth; but as he cannot do that, he grinds his teeth against each other. **And melt away.** The heat of his passion will melt him like wax, and the sun of God's providence will dissolve him like snow, and at the last the fire of divine vengeance will consume him as the fat of rams. How horrible must that life be which like the snail melts as it proceeds, leaving a slimy trail behind. Those who are grieved at goodness deserve to be worn away by such an abominable sorrow. **The desire of the wicked shall perish.** He shall not achieve his purpose; he will die a disappointed man. By wickedness he hoped to accomplish his purpose – that very wickedness will be his defeat. While the righteous will endure forever, and their memory will be always green, the ungodly and his name will rot from off the face of the earth.

Psalm 113

1. Praise ye the LORD, or Hallelujah, praise to Jah, Jehovah. Praise is an essential offering at all the solemn feasts of the people of God. Prayer is the myrrh, and praise is the frankincense, and both of these must be presented unto the Lord. How can we pray for mercy for the future if we do not bless God for his love in the past? The Lord hath wrought all good things for us; let us therefore adore him. All other praise is to be excluded; the entire devotion of the soul must be poured out unto Jehovah only. **Praise, O ye servants of the LORD.** You above all, for you are bound to do so by your calling and profession. If God's own servants do not praise him, who will? You are a people near to him, and should be heartiest in your loving gratitude. While they were slaves of Pharaoh, the Israelites uttered groans and sighs by reason of their hard bondage; but now that they had become servants of the Lord, they were to express themselves in songs of joy. His service is perfect freedom, and those who fully enter into it discover in that service a thousand reasons for adoration. They are

141

sure to praise God best who serve him best; indeed, service is praise. **Praise the name of the LORD.** Extol his revealed character, magnify every sacred attribute, exult in all his doings, and reverence the very name by which he is called. The name of Jehovah is thrice used in this verse, and may by us who understand the doctrine of the Trinity in Unity be regarded as a thinly-veiled allusion to that holy mystery. Let Father, Son, and Holy Spirit all be praised as the one, only, living, and true God.

2. **Blessed be the name of the LORD.** While praising him aloud, the people were also to **bless** him in the silence of their hearts, wishing glory to his name, success to his cause, and triumph to his truth. By mentioning **the name,** the psalmist would teach us to bless each of the attributes of the Most High, which are as it were the letters of his name; not quarreling with his justice or his severity, nor servilely dreading his power, but accepting him as we find him revealed in the inspired Word and by his own acts, and loving him and praising him as such. **From this time forth.** If we have never praised him before, let us begin now. As the Passover stood at the beginning of the year it was well to commence the new year with blessing him who wrought deliverance for his people. Every solemn feast had its own happy associations, and might be regarded as a fresh starting-place for adoration. Are there not reasons why the reader should make the present day the opening of a year of praise? When the Lord says, "From this time will I bless you," we ought to reply, "Blessed be the name of the Lord from this time forth."

And for evermore. Eternally. The psalmist could not have intended that the divine praise should cease at a future date however remote. "Forevermore" in reference to the praise of God must signify endless duration: are we wrong in believing that it bears the same meaning when it refers to gloomier themes? Can our hearts ever cease to praise the name of the Lord? Can we imagine a period in which the praises of Israel shall no more surround the throne of the Divine Majesty? Impossible. Forever, and more than "for ever" if more can be, let him be magnified.

3. From early morn till eve the ceaseless hymn should rise unto Jehovah's throne, and from east to west over the whole round earth pure worship should be rendered unto his glory. So ought it to be; and blessed be God, we are not without faith that so it shall be. We trust that ere the world's dread evening comes, the glorious name of the Lord will be proclaimed among all nations, and all people will call him blessed.

4. **The LORD is high above all nations.** Though the Gentiles knew him not, yet was Jehovah their ruler: their false gods were no gods, and their kings were puppets in his hands. The Lord is high above all the learning, judgment, and imagination of heathen sages, and far beyond the pomp and might of the monarchs of the nations. Like the great arch of the firmament, the presence of the Lord spans all the lands where dwell the varied tribes, for his providence

is universal: this may well excite our confidence and praise. **And his glory above the heavens** – higher than the loftiest part of creation; the clouds are the dust of his feet, and sun, moon, and stars twinkle far below his throne. His glory cannot be set forth by the whole visible universe, nor even by the solemn pomp of angelic armies; it is above all conception and imagination, for he is God – infinite. Let us above all adore him who is above all.

5. Who is like unto the LORD our God? The challenge will never be answered. None can be compared with him for an instant; Israel's God is without parallel; our own God in covenant stands alone, and none can be likened unto him. Even those whom he has made like himself in some respects are not like him in Godhead, for his divine attributes are many of them incommunicable and inimitable. None of the metaphors and figures by which the Lord is set forth in the Scriptures can give us a complete idea of him: his full resemblance is borne by nothing in earth or in heaven. Only in Jesus is the Godhead seen, but he unhesitatingly declared, "he that hath seen me hath seen the Father." **Who dwelleth on high.** In the height of his abode none can be like him. His throne, his whole character, his person, his being, everything about him, is lofty, and infinitely majestic, so that none can be likened unto him. His serene mind abides in the most elevated condition; he is never dishonored, nor does he stoop from the pure holiness and absolute perfection of his character.

6. He dwells so far on high that even to observe heavenly things he must humble himself. He must stoop to view the skies, and bow to see what angels do. What, then, must be his condescension, seeing that he observes the humblest of his servants upon earth, and makes them sing for joy like Mary when she said, "Thou hast regarded the low estate of thine handmaiden." How wonderful are those words of Isaiah, "For thus saith the high and lofty One that inhabiteth eternity, whose name is Holy; I dwell in the high and holy place, with him also that is of a contrite and humble spirit, to revive the spirit of the humble, and to revive the heart of the contrite ones."

7. He raiseth up the poor out of the dust. This is an instance of his gracious stoop of love: he frequently lifts the lowest of mankind out of their poverty and degradation, and places them in positions of power and honor. His good Spirit is continually visiting the down-trodden, giving beauty for ashes to those who are cast down, and elevating the hearts of his mourners till they shout for joy. These upliftings of grace are here ascribed directly to the divine hand, and truly those who have experienced them will not doubt the fact that it is the Lord alone who brings his people up from the dust of sorrow and death. When no hand but his can help he interposes, and the work is done. It is worthwhile to be cast down to be so divinely raised from the dust. **And lifteth the needy out of the dunghill,** whereon they lay like worthless refuse, cast off and cast out, left as they thought to rot into destruction, and to be everlastingly forgotten. How great a stoop from the height of his throne to a dunghill!

How wonderful that power which occupies itself in lifting up beggars, all befouled with the filthiness in which they lay! For he lifts them **out of** the dunghill, not disdaining to search them out from amidst the base things of the earth that he may by their means bring to nought the great ones, and pour contempt upon all human glorying. Almighty were the arms which lifted us up, which are still lifting us, and will lift us into the perfection of heaven itself.

8. That he may set him with princes. The Lord does nothing by halves: when he raises people from the dust he is not content till he places them among the peers of his kingdom. We are made kings and priests unto God, and we shall reign forever and ever. Instead of poverty, he gives us the wealth of princes; and instead of dishonor, he gives us a more exalted rank than that of the great ones of the earth. **Even with the princes of his people.** All his people are princes, and so the text teaches us that God places needy souls whom he favors among the princes of princes. He often enables those who have been most despairing to rise to the greatest heights of spirituality and gracious attainment, for those who once were last will be first. The Lord poureth contempt upon princes; but as for those who are in the dust and on the dunghill, he looks upon them with compassion, acts towards them in grace, and in their case displays the riches of his glory by Christ Jesus. Those who have experienced such amazing favor should sing continual hallelujahs to the God of their salvation.

9. The strong desire of the easterns to have children caused the birth of offspring to be hailed as the choicest of favors, while barrenness was regarded as a curse; hence this verse is placed last as if to crown the whole, and to serve as the climax to the story of God's mercy. The glorious Lord displays his condescending grace in regarding those who are despised on account of their barrenness, whether it be of body or of soul. Sarah, Rachel, the wife of Manoah, Hannah, Elizabeth, and others were all instances of the miraculous power of God in literally fulfilling the statement of the psalmist. We marvel greatly at the Lord who dwells on high, that he has deigned to visit such poor worthless things. Like Hannah we have said, "There is none holy as the Lord; for there is none beside thee: neither is there any rock like our God."

Praise ye the Lord. The psalm is a circle, ending where it began, praising the Lord. May our life-psalm bless the Lord, whose mercies never cease. Let us praise him in youth, and all along our years of strength; and when we bow in the ripeness of abundant age, let us still praise the Lord, who does not cast off his old servants.

Psalm 114

1. When Israel went out of Egypt. The song begins with a burst, as if the poetic fury could not be restrained, but overleaped all bounds. The soul elevated and filled with a sense of divine glory cannot wait to fashion a preface, but springs at once into the middle of its theme. Israel emphatically came out of Egypt, out of the population among whom they had been scattered, from under the yoke of bondage, and from under the personal grasp of the king who had made the people into national slaves. Israel came out with a high hand and a stretched-out arm, defying all the power of the empire, and making the whole of Egypt to travail with sore anguish, as the chosen nation was, as it were, born out of its midst. **The house of Jacob from a people of strange language.** They had gone down into Egypt as a single family – "the house of Jacob" – and, though they had multiplied greatly, they were still so united, and were so fully regarded by God as a single unit, that they are rightly spoken of as the house of Jacob. They were as one in their willingness to leave Goshen; numerous as they were, not a single individual stayed behind. Unanimity is a pleasing token of the divine presence, and one of its sweetest fruits.

2. The pronoun **his** comes in where we should have looked for the name of God; but the poet is so full of thought concerning the Lord that he forgets to mention his name. From the mention of Judah and Israel certain critics have inferred that this psalm must have been written after the division of the two kingdoms; but this is only another instance of the extremely slender basis upon which an hypothesis is often built up. Before the formation of the two kingdoms David had said, "Go number Israel and Judah," and this was common parlance, for Uriah the Hittite said, "The ark, and Israel, and Judah abide in tents"; so nothing can be inferred from the use of the two names. The meaning of the passage is that the whole people at the coming out of Egypt were separated unto the Lord to be a peculiar people, a nation of priests whose motto should be "Holiness unto the Lord." Judah was the Lord's "holy thing," set apart for his special use. The nation was especially Jehovah's dominion, for it was governed by a theocracy in which God alone was King. It was his domain in a sense in which the rest of the world was outside his kingdom. These were the young days of Israel, the time of her espousals, when she went after the Lord into the wilderness, her God leading the way with signs and miracles. The whole people were the shrine of Deity, and their camp was one great temple. What a change there must have been for the godly amongst them from the idolatries and blasphemies of the Egyptians to the holy worship and righteous rule of the great King in Jeshurun. They lived in a world of wonders, where God was seen in the wondrous bread they ate and in the water they drank, as well as in the solemn worship of his holy place. When the Lord is manifestly present in a church, and his gracious rule obediently owned, what a golden age has come, and what honorable privileges his people enjoy! May it be so among us.

3. **The sea saw it, and fled;** or rather, "The sea saw and fled" – it saw God and all his people following his lead, and it was struck with awe and fled away. A

bold figure! The Red Sea mirrored the hosts which had come down to its shore, and reflected the cloud which towered high over all, as the symbol of the presence of the Lord: never had such a scene been imaged upon the surface of the Red Sea, or any other sea, before. It could not endure the unusual and astounding sight, and fleeing to the right and to the left, opened a passage for the elect people. A like miracle happened at the end of the great march of Israel, for **Jordan was driven back.** This was a swiftly-flowing river, pouring itself down a steep decline, and it was not merely divided, but its current was driven back so that the rapid torrent, contrary to nature, flowed uphill. This was God's work: the poet does not sing of the suspension of natural laws, or of a singular phenomenon not readily to be explained; but to him the presence of God with his people is everything, and in his lofty song he tells how the river was driven back because the Lord was there. In this case poetry is nothing but the literal fact, and the fiction lies on the side of the atheistic critics who will suggest any explanation of the miracle rather than admit that the Lord made bare his holy arm in the eyes of all his people. The division of the sea and the drying up of the river are placed together though forty years intervened, because they were the opening and closing scenes of one great event. We may thus unite by faith our new birth and our departure out of the world into the promised inheritance, for the God who led us out of the Egypt of our bondage under sin will also conduct us through the Jordan of death out of our wilderness wanderings in the desert of this tried and changeful life. It is all one and the same deliverance, and the beginning ensures the end.

4. At the coming of the Lord to Mount Sinai, the hills moved; either leaping for joy in the presence of their Creator like young lambs, or, if you will, springing from their places in affright at the terrible majesty of Jehovah, and flying like a flock of sheep when alarmed. Men fear the mountains, but the mountains tremble before the Lord. Sheep and lambs move lightly in the meadows; but the hills, which we are wont to call eternal, were as readily made to move as the most active creatures.

5. What ailed thee, O sea? Were you terribly afraid? Did your strength fail you? Did your very heart dry up? **That thou fleddest?** You were neighbor to the power of Pharaoh, but you never feared his hosts; stormy wind could never prevail against you so as to divide you in two; but when the way of the Lord was in your great waters you were seized with affright, and became a fugitive from before him. **Thou Jordan, that thou wast driven back?** Your fountains had not dried up, neither had a chasm opened to engulf you! The near approach of Israel and her God sufficed to make you retrace your steps. What ails all our enemies that they fly when the Lord is on our side? What ails hell itself that it is utterly routed when Jesus lifts up a standard against it?

6. What ailed you that you were thus moved? There is but one reply: the majesty of God made you leap. A gracious mind will chide human nature for its strange insensibility, when the sea and the river, the mountains and the hills, are all sensitive to the presence of God. Man is endowed with reason and intelligence, and yet sees unmoved that which the material creation beholds with fear. God has come nearer to us than ever he did to Sinai, or to Jordan, for he has assumed our nature, and yet the mass of mankind are neither driven back from their sins nor moved in the paths of obedience.

7. Tremble, thou earth, at the presence of the Lord, at the presence of the God of Jacob. Or "from before the Lord, the Adonai, the Master and King." Very fitly does the psalm call upon all nature again to feel a holy awe because its Ruler is still in its midst.

8. Which turned the rock into a standing water, causing a lake to stand at its foot, making the wilderness a pool: so abundant was the supply of water from the rock that it remained like water in a reservoir. **The flint into a fountain of waters,** which flowed freely in streams, following the tribes in their devious marches. Behold what God can do! It seemed impossible that the flinty rock should become a fountain; but he speaks, and it is done.

Our deliverance from under the yoke of sin is strikingly typified in the going up of Israel from Egypt, and so also was the victory of our Lord over the powers of death and hell. The Exodus should therefore be earnestly remembered by Christian hearts. Did not Moses on the mount of transfiguration speak to our Lord of "the exodus" which he would shortly accomplish at Jerusalem? And is it not written of the hosts above that they sing the song of Moses the servant of God, and of the Lamb? Do we not ourselves expect another coming of the Lord, when before his face heaven and earth will flee away and there will be no more sea? We join then with the singers around the Passover table and make their Hallel ours, for we too have been led out of bondage and guided like a flock through a desert land, wherein the Lord supplies our wants with heavenly manna and water from the Rock of Ages.

Psalm 115

1. It will be well to remember that this psalm was sung at the Passover, and therefore it bears relationship to the deliverance from Egypt. The burden of it seems to be a prayer that the living God, who had been so glorious at the Red Sea and at the Jordan, should again for his own name's sake display the wonders of his power. **Not unto us, O LORD, but unto thy name give the glory.** The people undoubtedly wished for relief from the contemptuous insults of idolaters, but their main desire was that Jehovah himself should no longer be the object of heathen insults. The saddest part of all their trouble was that their God was no longer feared and dreaded by their adversaries. When Israel marched into Canaan, a terror was upon all the people round about, because of Jehovah, the mighty God; but this dread the nations had shaken off since there had been of late no remarkable display of miraculous power. Therefore Israel cried unto her God that he would again make bare his arm as in the day when he cut Rahab and wounded the dragon. The prayer is evidently tinctured with a consciousness of unworthiness; because of their past unfaithfulness they hardly dared to appeal to the covenant, and to ask blessings for themselves, but they fell back upon the honor of the Lord their God – an old style of argument which their great lawgiver, Moses, had used with such effect when he pleaded, "Wherefore should the Egyptians speak, and say, For mischief did he bring them out, to slay them in the mountains, and to consume them from the face of the earth? Turn from thy fierce wrath, and repent of this evil against thy people." Joshua also used the like argument when he said, "What wilt thou do unto thy great name?" In such manner also let us pray when no other plea is available because of our sense of sin; for the Lord is always jealous of his honor, and will work for his name's sake when no other motive will move him.

The repetition of the words **Not unto us** would seem to indicate a very serious desire to renounce any glory which they might at any time have proudly appropriated to themselves, and it also sets forth the vehemence of their wish that God would at any cost to them magnify his own name. They loathed the idea of seeking their own glory, and rejected the thought with the utmost detestation, again and again disclaiming any self-glorifying motive in their supplications. **For thy mercy, and for thy truth's sake.** These attributes seemed most in jeopardy. How could the heathen think Jehovah to be a merciful God if he gave his people over to the hands of their enemies? How could they believe him to be faithful and true if, after all his solemn covenant engagements, he utterly rejected his chosen nation? God is very jealous of the two glorious attributes of grace and truth, and the plea that these may not be dishonored has great weight with him. In these times, when the first victories of the Gospel are only remembered as histories of a dim and distant past, skeptics are apt to boast that the Gospel has lost its youthful strength, and they even presume to cast a slur upon the name of God himself. We may therefore rightly entreat the divine interposition that the apparent blot may be removed from his escutcheon, and that his own word may shine forth gloriously as in the days of old. We may not desire the triumph of our opinions, for our own sakes, or for the honor of a sect, but we may confidently pray for the triumph of truth, that God himself may be honored.

2. Wherefore should the heathen say, Where is now their God? Or, more literally, "Where, pray, is their God?" Why should the nations be allowed with a sneer of contempt to question the existence, and mercy, and faithfulness of Jehovah? They are always ready to blaspheme; we may well pray that they may not derive a reason for so doing from the course of providence, or the decline of the church. When they see the godly down-trodden while they themselves live at ease, and act the part of persecutors, they are very apt to speak as if they had triumphed over God himself, or as if he had altogether left the field of action and deserted his saints. When the prayers and tears of the godly seem to be unregarded, and their miseries are rather increased than assuaged, then do the wicked multiply their taunts and jeers, and even argue that their own wretched irreligion is better than the faith of Christians, because for the present their condition is so much preferable to that of the afflicted saints. And, truly, this is the very sting of the trials of God's chosen when they see the veracity of the Lord questioned, and the name of God profaned because of their sufferings. If they could hope that some good result would come out of all this they would endure it with patience; but as they are unable to perceive any desirable result consequent thereon, they inquire with holy anxiety, "Wherefore should the heathen be permitted to speak thus?" It is a question to which it would be hard to reply, and yet no doubt there is an answer. Sometimes the nations are permitted thus to blaspheme in order that they may fill up the measure of their iniquity, and in order that the subsequent interposition of God may be rendered the more illustrious in contrast with their profane blessings. Do they say, "Where is now their God?" They will know by-and-by, for it is written, "I will ease me of mine adversaries"; they will know it also when the righteous "shine forth as the sun in the kingdom of their Father." Do they say, "Where is the promise of his coming?" That coming will be speedy and terrible to them. In our own case, by our own lukewarmness and the neglect of faithful Gospel preaching, we have permitted the uprise and spread of modern doubt, and we are bound to confess it with deep sorrow of soul; yet we may not therefore lose heart, but may still plead with God to save his own truth and grace from the contempt of the world. Our honor and the honor of the church are small barriers, but the glory of God is the jewel of the universe, of which all else is but the setting; and we may come to the Lord and plead his jealousy for his name, being well assured that he will not let that name be dishonored. Let us by extraordinary intercession prevail upon him to interpose, by giving to his Gospel such a triumphant vindication as shall utterly silence the perverse opposition of the ungodly.

3. But our God is in the heavens – where he should be; above the reach of mortal sneers, overhearing all the vain janglings of people, but looking down with silent scorn upon the makers of the babel. Supreme above all opposing powers, the Lord reigns upon a throne high and lifted up. Incomprehensible in essence, he rises above the loftiest thought of the wise; absolute in will and infinite in power, he is superior to the limitations which belong to earth and time. This God is *our* God, and we are not ashamed to own him, albeit he may not work miracles at the beck and call of every vainglorious boaster who may choose to challenge him.

He hath done whatsoever he hath pleased. Up till this moment his decrees have been fulfilled, and his eternal purposes accomplished; he has not been asleep, nor oblivious of human affairs; he has worked, and he has worked effectually; none have been able to thwart, nor even so much as to hinder him. However distasteful to his enemies, the Lord has accomplished all his good pleasure without difficulty; even when his adversaries raved and raged against him they have been compelled to carry out his designs against their will.

4. Their idols are silver and gold, mere dead inert matter; at the best only made of precious metals, but that metal quite as powerless as the commonest wood or clay. The value of the idol shows the folly of the maker in wasting his substance, but certainly does not increase the power of the image, since there is no more life in silver and gold than in brass or iron. **The work of men's hands.** Inasmuch as the maker is always greater than the thing that he has made, these idols are less to be honored than the artificers, who fashioned them. How irrational that people should adore that which is less than themselves! Our God is a spirit, and his hands made the heavens and the earth: well may we worship him, and we need not be disturbed at the sneering question of those who are so proud as to refuse to adore the living God, and yet bow their knees before images of their own carving. We may make an application of all this to the times in which we are now living. The god of modern thought is the creation of the thinker himself, evolved out of his own consciousness, or fashioned according to his own notion of what a god should be. Now, it is evident that such a being is no god. It is impossible that there should be a god at all except the God of revelation. A god who can be fashioned by our own thoughts is no more a god than the image manufactured or produced by our own hands. The true God must of necessity be his own revealer.

5. They have mouths, but they speak not. The idols cannot utter even the faintest sound; they cannot communicate with their worshipers; they can neither promise nor threaten, command nor console, explain the past nor prophesy the future. **Eyes have they, but they see not.** They cannot tell who their worshipers may be or what they offer. He must be very blind who worships a blind god; we *pity* a blind man; it is strange to *worship* a blind image.

6. They have ears, but they hear not. The psalmist might have pointed to the monstrous ears with which some heathen deities are disfigured – truly they *have* ears, but no prayer can ever be heard by them. How can gold and silver hear, and how can a rational being address petitions to one who cannot even hear his words? **Noses have they, but they smell not.** The psalmist seems to heap together these sentences with something of the grim sardonic spirit of Elijah when he said, "Cry aloud: for he is a god; either he is talking, or he is pursuing, or he is on a journey, or peradventure he sleepeth, and must be awaked." In sacred scorn he mocks at those who burn spices and fill their temples with clouds of smoke offered to an image who nose cannot perceive the perfume.

7. They have hands, but they handle not. They cannot receive that which is handed to them, they cannot grasp the scepter of power of the sword of vengeance, they can neither distribute benefits nor dispense judgments, and the most trifling act they are utterly unable to perform. An infant's hand excels them in power. **Feet have they, but they walk not.** They must be lifted into their places or they would never reach their shrines; they must be fastened in their shrines or they would fall; they must be carried or they could never move; they cannot come to the rescue of their friends, nor escape the iconoclasm of their foes. The meanest insect has more power of locomotion than the greatest heathen god. **Neither speak they through their throat.** They cannot even reach so far as the guttural noise of the lowest order of beasts. Their priests asserted that the images of the gods upon special occasions uttered hollow sounds, but it was a mere pretense, or a crafty artifice.

8. They that make them are like unto them. Those who make such things for worship are as stupid, senseless, and irrational as the figures they construct. So far as any spiritual life, thought, and judgment are concerned, they are rather the images of men than rational beings. The censure is by no means too severe. **So is every one that trusteth in them.** Those who have sunk so low as to be capable of confiding in idols have reached the extreme of folly, and are worthy of as much contempt as their detestable deities.

The god of modern thought exceedingly resembles the deities described in this psalm. Pantheism is wondrously akin to polytheism, and yet differs very little from atheism. The god manufactured by our great thinkers is a mere abstraction; he has no eternal purposes, he does not interpose on the behalf of his people, he cares but very little as to how much man sins, for he has given to the initiated "a larger hope" by which the most incorrigible are to be restored. He is what the last set of critics chooses to make him, he has said what they choose to say, and he will do what they please to prescribe. Let this creed and its devotees alone, and they will work out their own refutation, for as now their god is fashioned like themselves, they will by degrees fashion themselves like their god; and when the principles of justice, law, and order have all been effectually sapped we may possibly witness in some form of socialism a repetition of the evils which have in former ages befallen nations which have refused the living God, and set up gods of their own.

9. O Israel, trust thou in the LORD. Whatever others do, let the elect of heaven keep fast to the God who chose them. Jehovah is the God of Jacob; let his children prove their loyalty to their God by their confidence in him. Whatever our trouble may be, and however fierce the blasphemous language of our enemies, let us not fear nor falter, but confidently rest in him who is able to vindicate his own honor, and protect his own servants. **He is their help and their shield.** He is the friend of his servants, both actively and passively, giving them both aid in labor and defense in danger. In the use of the pronoun **their,**

the psalmist may have spoken to himself in a sort of soliloquy: he had given the exhortation to trust in Jehovah, and then he whispers to himself, "They may well do so, for he is at all times the strength and security of his servants."

10. O house of Aaron, trust in the LORD. You who are nearest to him, trust him most; your very calling is connected with his truth and is meant to declare his glory; therefore never entertain a doubt concerning him, but lead the way in holy confidence. The priests were the leaders, teachers, and exemplars of the people, and above all others they should place an unreserved reliance upon Israel's God. The psalmist is glad to add that they did so, for he says, **He is their help and their shield.** It is good to exhort those to faith who have faith. We may stir up pure minds by way of remembrance, and exhort people to trust because we know they are trusting already.

11. The next verse is of the same tenor – **Ye that fear the LORD, trust in the LORD.** Whether belonging to Israel, or to the house of Aaron, or not, all those who reverence Jehovah are permitted and commanded to confide in him. **He is their help and their shield.** He does aid and protect all those who worship him in filial fear, to whatever nation they may belong. No doubt these repeated exhortations were rendered necessary by the trying condition in which the children of Israel were found: the sneers of the adversary would assail all the people; they would most bitterly be felt by the priests and ministers, and those who were secret proselytes would groan in secret under the contempt forced upon their religion and their God. All this would be very staggering to faith, and therefore they were bidden again and again to trust in Jehovah.

12. The LORD hath been mindful of us, or "Jehovah hath remembered us." His past mercies prove that we are on his heart, and though for the present he may afflict us, yet he does not forget us. We have not to put him in remembrance as though he found it hard to recollect his children, but he hath remembered us and therefore he will in future deal well with us. **He will bless us.** The word **us** is supplied by the translators, and is superfluous; the passage should run, "He will bless; he will bless the house of Israel; he will bless the house of Aaron." The repetition of the word **bless** adds great effect to the passage. The Lord has many blessings, each one worthy to be remembered. Where he has once bestowed his favor he continues it; his blessing delights to visit the same house very often and to abide where it has once lodged. Blessing does not impoverish the Lord: he has multiplied his mercies in the past, and he will pour them forth thick and threefold in the future. He will have a general blessing for all who fear him, a special blessing for the whole house of Israel, and a double blessing for the sons of Aaron. It is his nature to bless, it is his prerogative to bless, it is his glory to bless, it is his delight to bless; he has promised to bless, and therefore be sure of this, that he will bless without ceasing.

13. So long as a man fears the Lord it matters nothing whether he be prince or peasant, patriarch or pauper – God will assuredly bless him. He supplies the want of every living thing, from the leviathan of the sea to the insect upon a leaf, and he will let none of the godly be forgotten, however small their abilities, or mean their position. This is a sweet cordial for those who are little in faith, and own themselves to be babes in the family of grace. There is the same blessing for the least as for the greatest; if anything, the **small** will be first; for as the necessity is more pressing, the supply will be more speedy.

14. Just as in Egypt he multiplied the people exceedingly, so will he increase the number of his saints upon the earth; not only will the faithful be blessed with converts, and so with a spiritual seed; but those who are their spiritual children will become fruitful also, and thus the multitude of the elect will be accomplished; God will increase the people, and will increase the joy. Even to the end of the ages the race of true believers will be continued, and will growingly multiply in number and in power. The first blessing upon mankind was, "Be fruitful, and multiply, and replenish the earth"; and it is this blessing which God now pronounces upon them that fear him. Despite the idols of philosophy and sacramentarianism, the truth will gather its disciples, and fill the land with its defenders.

15. This is another form of the blessing of Melchizedek; upon us through our great Melchizedek this same benediction rests. It is an omnipotent blessing, conveying to us all that an almighty God can do, whether in heaven or on earth. This fullness is infinite, and the consolation which it brings is unfailing; he that made heaven and earth can give us all things while we dwell below, and bring us safely to his palace above. Happy are the people upon whom such a blessing rests; their portion is infinitely above that of those whose only hope lies in a piece of gilded wood, or an image of sculptured stone.

16. The heaven, even the heavens, are the LORD's. There he specially reigns, and manifests his greatness and his glory: **but the earth hath he given to the children of men.** He has left the world during the present dispensation in a great measure under the power and will of men, so that things are not here below in the same perfect order as the things which are above. It is true that the Lord rules over all things by his providence, but yet he allows and permits men to break his laws and persecute his people for the time being, and to set up their dumb idols in opposition to him. The free agency which he gave to his creatures necessitated that in some degree he should restrain his power and let the children of men follow their own devices; yet nevertheless, since he has not vacated heaven, he is still master of earth, and can at any time gather up all the reins into his own hands. Perhaps, however, the passage is meant to have another meaning, namely, that God will increase his people, because he has given the earth to them, and intends that they shall fill it. Man was constituted originally God's vicegerent over the world, and though as yet we see not all things put under him, we see Jesus exalted on high, and in him the children of men will receive a loftier dominion even on earth than as yet they have known.

PSALMS, VOLUME II

"The meek shall inherit the earth; and shall delight themselves in the abundance of peace"; and our Lord Jesus will reign amongst his ancients gloriously. All this will reflect the exceeding glory of him who reveals himself personally in heaven, and in the mystical body of Christ below. The earth belongs to the sons of God, and we are bound to subdue it for our Lord Jesus, for he must reign. The Lord has given him the heathen for his inheritance, and the uttermost parts of the earth for his possession.

17. The dead praise not the LORD – so far as this world is concerned. They cannot unite in the psalms and hymns and spiritual songs with which the church delights to adore her Lord. The preacher cannot magnify the Lord from his coffin, nor the Christian worker further manifest the power of divine grace by daily activity while he lies in the grave. **Neither any that go down into silence.** The tomb sends forth no voice; from moldering bones and flesh-consuming worms there arises no sound of Gospel ministry nor of gracious song. One by one the singers in the consecrated choir of saints steal away from us, and we miss their music. Thank God, they have gone above to swell the harmonies of the skies, but as far as we are concerned, we have need to sing all the more earnestly because so many songsters have left our choirs.

18. But we will bless the LORD from this time forth and for evermore. We who are still living will take care that the praises of God will not fail. Our afflictions and depressions of spirit will not cause us to suspend our praises; neither shall old age nor even death itself cause us to cease from the occupation. The spiritually dead cannot praise God, but the life within us constrains us to do so. The ungodly may abide in silence, but we will lift up our voices to the praise of Jehovah. Even though for a time he may work no miracle, and we may see no special interposition of his power, yet on the strength of what he has done in ages past we will continue to laud his name "until the day break," when he will once more gladden the faces of his children. The present time is auspicious for commencing a life of praise, since today he bids us hear his voice of mercy. **From this time forth** is the suggestion of wisdom, for this duty ought not to be delayed; and it is the dictate of gratitude. Once begin praising God and we have entered upon an endless service. Even eternity cannot exhaust the reasons why God should be glorified. **Praise the LORD,** or Hallelujah. Though the dead cannot, and the wicked will not, and the careless do not praise God, yet we will shout "Hallelujah" forever.

Psalm 116

1. I love the LORD. A blessed declaration: every believer ought to be able to declare it without the slightest hesitation. It was required under the law, but

154

was never produced in the human heart except by the grace of God, and upon Gospel principles. It is a great thing to say it, for the sweetest of all graces and the surest of all evidences of salvation is love. It is great goodness on the part of God that he condescends to be loved by such poor creatures as we are, and it is a sure proof that he has been at work in our heart when we can say, "Thou knowest all things, thou knowest that I love thee." **Because he hath heard my voice and my supplications.** The psalmist not only knows that he loves God, but he knows why he does so. When love can justify itself with a reason, it is deep, strong, and abiding. They say that love is blind; but when we love God our affection has its eyes open and can sustain itself with the most rigid logic. We have reason, superabundant reason, for loving the Lord; and so because in this case principle and passion go together, they make up an admirable state of mind. David's reason for his love was the love of God in hearing his prayers. The psalmist had used his **voice** in prayer, and the habit of doing so is exceedingly helpful to devotion. If we can pray aloud without being over-heard it is well to do so. Sometimes, however, when the psalmist had lifted up his voice, his utterance had been so broken and painful that he scarcely dared to call it prayer; words failed him, he could only produce a groaning sound, but the Lord heard his moaning voice. At other times his prayers were more regular and better framed: these he calls **supplications.** David had praised as best he could, and when one form of devotion failed him he tried another. He had gone to the Lord again and again, hence he uses the plural and says **my supplications;** but as often as he had gone, so often had he been welcome. Jehovah had heard, that is to say, accepted, and answered both his broken cries and his more composed and orderly supplications; hence he loved God with all his heart. Answered prayers are silken bonds which bind poor hearts to God. When someone's prayers are answered, love is the natural result. According to Alexander, both verbs may be translated in the present, and the text may run thus: "I love because Jehovah hears my voice, my supplications." This also is true in the case of every pleading believer. Continual love flows out of daily answers to prayer.

2. **Because he hath inclined his ear unto me.** The figure seems to be that of a tender physician or loving friend leaning over a sick man whose voice is faint and scarcely audible, so as to catch every accent and whisper. When our prayer is very feeble, so that we ourselves can scarcely hear it, and question whether we do pray or not, yet God bows a listening ear, and regards our sup-plications. **Therefore will I call upon him as long as I live,** or, "in my days." Throughout all the days of my life I will address my prayer to God alone, and to him I will unceasingly pray. It is always wise to go where we are welcome and are well treated. The word **call** may imply praise as well as prayer: calling upon the name of the Lord is an expressive name for adoration of all kinds. When prayer is heard in our feebleness, and answered in the strength and

greatness of God, we are strengthened in the habit of prayer, and confirmed in the resolve to make ceaseless intercession. We should not thank a beggar who informed us that because we had granted his request he would never cease to beg of us, and yet doubtless it is acceptable to God that his petitioners should form the resolution to continue in prayer: this shows the greatness of his goodness, and the abundance of his patience. In all days let us pray and praise the Ancient of Days. He promises that as our days our strength shall be; let us resolve that as our days our devotion shall be.

3. The psalmist now goes on to describe his condition at the time when he prayed unto God. **The sorrows of death compassed me.** As hunters surround a stag with dogs and men, so was David enclosed in a ring of deadly griefs. The bands of sorrow, weakness, and terror with which death is accustomed to bind men ere he drags them away to their long captivity were all around him. These things had come close to home, for he adds, **and the pains of hell gat hold upon me.** Horrors such as those which torment the lost seized me. He means those pangs which belong to death. **I found trouble and sorrow.** Trouble was around me, and sorrow within me.

4. Then I called upon the name of the LORD. Prayer is never out of season; he prayed **then,** when things were at their worst. When the good man could not run to God, he **called** to him. In his extremity his faith came to the front: it was useless to call on man, and it may have seemed almost as useless to appeal to the Lord; but yet he did with his whole soul invoke all the attributes which make up the sacred name of Jehovah, and thus he proved the truth of his confidence. We can some of us remember certain very special times of trial of which we can now say, "*then* called I upon the name of the Lord." The psalmist appealed to the Lord's mercy, truth, power and faithfulness, and this was his prayer – **O LORD, I beseech thee, deliver my soul.** This form of petition is short, comprehensive, to the point, humble, and earnest. Real trouble produces real prayer. Here we have no multiplicity of words, and no fine arrangement of sentences; everything is simple and natural; there is not a redundant syllable, and yet there is not one lacking.

5. Gracious is the LORD, and righteous. In hearing prayer the grace and righteousness of Jehovah are both conspicuous. It is a great favor to hear a sinner's prayer, and yet since the Lord has promised to do so, he is not unrighteous to forget his promise and disregard the cries of his people. At the cross we see how gracious is the Lord and righteous. **Yea, our God is merciful,** or compassionate. See how the attribute of righteousness seems to stand between two guards of love: gracious, **righteous,** merciful.

6. The LORD preserveth the simple. Those who have a great deal of wit may take care of themselves. Those who have no worldly craft and subtlety and guile, but simply trust in God, and do the right, may depend upon it that God's care will be over them. The worldly-wise with all their prudence will be taken in their own craftiness, but those who walk in their integrity with single-minded truthfulness before God will be protected against the wiles of their enemies, and enabled to outlive their foes. Though the saints are like sheep in the midst of wolves, and comparatively defenseless, yet there are more sheep in the world than wolves, and it is highly probable that the sheep will feed in safety when not a single wolf is left: even so the meek will inherit the earth when the wicked are no more. **I was brought low, and he helped me.** Simple though I was, the Lord did not pass me by. Though reduced in circumstances, slandered, depressed, and sick, the Lord helped me. There are many ways in which the child of God may be brought low, but the help of God is as various as the need of his people. There are thousands who can say, "*I* was brought low, and he helped *me.*" This should be said to the praise of his grace, and for the comforting of others who may pass through the like ordeal. Note how David after stating the general doctrine proves and illustrates it from his own experience.

7. **Return unto thy rest, O my soul.** He calls the rest still his own, and feels full liberty to return to it. What a mercy it is that even if our soul has left its rest for a while we can tell it: "It is thy rest still." The psalmist had evidently been somewhat disturbed in his mind, his troubles had ruffled his spirit; but now with a sense of answered prayer upon him he quiets his soul. He had rested before, for he knew the blessed repose of faith, and therefore he returns to the God who had been the refuge of his soul in former days. Even as a bird flies to its nest, so does his soul fly to his God. Whenever a child of God even for a moment loses his peace of mind, he should be concerned to find it again, not by seeking it in the world or in his own experience, but in the Lord alone. When the believer prays, and the Lord inclines his ear, the road to the old rest is before him. **For the LORD hath dealt bountifully with thee.** You have served a good God, and built upon a sure foundation; come back to him who in former days condescended to enrich you by his love. God lays his fullness open to us, and of that fullness have all we received. Let us come back to him who has treated us with such exceeding kindness. More arguments follow.

8. The triune God has given us a trinity of deliverances: our life has been spared from the grave, our heart has been uplifted from its griefs, and our course in life has been preserved from dishonor. We ought not to be satisfied unless we are conscious of all three of these deliverances. If our soul has been saved from death, why do we weep? And if our tears have been wiped away, can we endure to fall again into sin? Let us not rest unless with steady feet we pursue the path of the upright, escaping every snare and shunning every stumbling block. Salvation, joy, and holiness must go together.

9. This is the psalmist's second resolution, to live as in the sight of God in the midst of the sons of men. By a man's walk is understood his way of life: some live only as in the sight of their fellow-men, having regard to human

judgment and opinion; but the truly gracious consider the presence of God. The life of faith, hope, holy fear, and true holiness is produced by a sense of living and walking before the Lord, and he who has been favored with divine deliverances in answer to prayer finds his own experience the best reason for a holy life, and the best assistance to his endeavors. We know that God in a special manner is nigh unto his people: what manner of persons ought we to be in all holy conversation and godliness?

10. I believed, therefore have I spoken. I could not have spoken thus if it had not been for my faith: I should never have spoken unto God in prayer, nor have been able now to speak to my fellow-men in testimony if it had not been that faith kept me alive, and brought me a deliverance, whereof I have good reason to boast. Concerning the things of God no man should speak unless he believes; the speech of the waverer is mischievous, but the tongue of the believer is profitable; the most powerful speech which has ever been uttered by human lip has emanated from a heart fully persuaded of the truth of God. **I was greatly afflicted.** There was no mistake about that; the affliction was as terrible as could be, and since I have been delivered from it, I am sure that the deliverance is no fanatical delusion, but a self-evident fact; therefore I am the more resolved to speak to the honor of God. Though greatly afflicted, the psalmist had not ceased to believe: his faith was tried but not destroyed.

11. I said in my haste, all men are liars. All men will prove to be liars if we unduly trust in them; some from want of truthfulness, and others from want of power. But it is clear that the psalmist did not justify his own language, but considered it as the ebullition of a hasty temper. He had no right to distrust all men, for many of them are honest, truthful, and conscientious; there are faithful friends and loyal adherents yet alive; and if sometimes they disappoint us, we ought not to call them liars for failing when the failure arises entirely from want of power, and not from lack of will. Under great affliction our temptation will be to form hasty judgments of our fellow-men, and knowing this to be the case we ought carefully to watch our spirit, and to keep the door of our lips. The psalmist had believed, and therefore he spoke; he had doubted, and therefore he spoke in haste. He believed, and therefore he rightly prayed to God; he disbelieved, and therefore he wrongfully accused mankind. Speaking in haste is generally followed by bitter repentance. It is much better to be quiet when our spirit is disturbed and hasty, for it is so much easier to say than to unsay.

12. He wisely leaves off fretting about man's falsehood and his own ill humor, and directs himself to his God. It is of little use to be harping on the string of man's imperfection and deceitfulness; it is infinitely better to praise the perfection and faithfulness of God. The question of the verse is a very proper one: the Lord has rendered so much mercy to us that we ought to look about us, and look within us, and see what can be done by us to manifest our gratitude. We ought not only to do what is plainly before us, but also with holy ingenuity to search out various ways by which we may render fresh praises unto our God. Each person should have his own particular mode of expressing gratitude.

13. I will take the cup of salvation. To take the cup of salvation was in itself an act of worship, and it was accompanied with other forms of adoration; hence the psalmist says, **and call upon the name of the LORD.** He means that he will utter blessings and thanksgivings and prayers, and then drink of the cup which the Lord had filled with his saving grace. What a cup is this! Upon the table of infinite love stands the cup full of blessing; it is ours by faith to take it in our hand, make it our own, and partake of it, and then with joyful hearts to laud and magnify the gracious One who has filled it for our sakes. We can do this figuratively at the sacramental table; we can do it spiritually every time we grasp the golden chalice of the covenant, realizing the fullness of blessing which it contains, and by faith receiving its contents into our inmost soul.

14. The psalmist has already stated his third resolution, to devote himself to the worship of God evermore, and here he commences the performance of that resolve. The vows which he had made in anguish he now determines to fulfill. He does so at once, and publicly. Good resolutions cannot be carried out too speedily; vows become debts, and debts should be paid. We need not be afraid of having witnesses to the fulfilling of holy vows, for this will show that we are not ashamed of our Lord, and it may be a great benefit to those who look on and hear us publicly sounding forth the praises of our prayer-hearing God. Secret disciples, be encouraged to come into the light and own your Redeemer! If, indeed, you have been saved, come forward and declare it in his own appointed way.

15. He did not let the psalmist die. This seems to indicate that the song was meant to remind Jewish families of the mercies received by any one of the household, supposing him to have been sore sick and to have been restored to health, for the Lord values the lives of his saints, and often spares them where others perish. They will not die prematurely. The death-beds of saints are very precious to all believers, who delight to treasure up the last words of the departed, but they are most of all precious to the Lord himself, who views the triumphant deaths of his gracious ones with sacred delight. If we have walked before him in the land of the living, we need not fear to die before him when the hour of our departure is at hand.

16. The man of God in paying his vows rededicates himself unto God; the offering which he brings is himself. **I am thy servant, and the son of thine hand-maid,** a servant born of a servant and so born a servant, and doubly thine. Oh that children of godly parents would thus judge; but, alas, there are many who are the sons of the Lord's handmaids but are not themselves his servants. They give sad proof that grace does not run in the blood. **Thou hast loosed my bonds**

– freedom from bondage binds me to thy service. He who is loosed from the bonds of sin, death, and hell should rejoice to wear the easy yoke of the great Deliverer. It ought to create rapture in our souls if we are able to call Jesus Master, and are acknowledged by him as his servants.

17. I will offer to thee the sacrifice of thanksgiving. Being thy servant, I am bound to sacrifice to thee, and having received spiritual blessings at thy hands I will bring the thanksgiving of my heart. **And will call upon the name of the LORD** – that is to say, I will bow before thee reverently, lift up my heart in love to thee, think upon thy character, and adore thee as thou dost reveal thyself.

18. A good thing is worth saying twice. He thus stirs himself up to greater heartiness, earnestness, and diligence in keeping his vow – really paying it at the very moment that he is declaring his resolution to do so. The mercy came in secret, but the praise is rendered in public; the company was, however, select; he did not cast his pearls before swine but delivered his testimony before those who could understand and appreciate it.

19. In the courts of the LORD's house. In the proper place, where God had ordained that he should be worshiped. See how he is stirred up at the remembrance of the house of the Lord, and must speak of the holy city with a note of joyful exclamation – **In the midst of thee, O Jerusalem.** There would he pay his last vows, in the abode of fellowship, in the very heart of Judea. There is nothing like witnessing for Jesus where the report will be carried into a thousand homes. God's praise is not to be confined to a closet, nor his name to be whispered in holes and corners, as if we were afraid that men should hear us. We should lift up heart and voice unto the Lord, and invite others to join with us in adoring him, saying, **Praise ye the LORD,** or Hallelujah. This was a very fit conclusion of a song to be sung when all the people were gathered together at Jerusalem to keep the feast. When we worship the Lord we ought with great care to select the words of prayer and praise, and not to trust to the opening of a hymn-book, or to the unconsidered extemporizing of the moment. Let all things be done decently and in order, and let all things begin and end with Hallelujah.

Psalm 117

1. O praise the LORD, all ye nations. This is an exhortation to the Gentiles to glorify Jehovah, and a clear proof that the Old Testament spirit differed widely from that narrow and contracted national bigotry with which the Jews of our Lord's day became so inveterately diseased. The nations could not be expected to join in the praise of Jehovah unless they were also to be partakers of the benefits which Israel enjoyed; and hence the psalm was an intimation to Israel that the grace and mercy of their God were not confined to one nation, but would in happier days be extended to all the race, as Moses had prophesied when he said, "Rejoice, O ye nations, his people" (Deuteronomy 22:43), for so the Hebrew has it. The nations were to be his people. He would call them a people that were not a people, and her beloved that was not beloved. Individuals have already been gathered out of every kindred and people and tongue by the preaching of the Gospel, and these are but the advance-guard of a number which no one can number who will come ere long to worship the all-glorious One. **Praise him, all ye people.** Having done it once, do it again, and still more fervently, daily increasing in the reverence and zeal with which you extol the Most High. The multitude of the common folk will bless the Lord. Under the Gospel dispensation we worship the God of Abraham; the God of the whole earth shall he be called.

2. **For his merciful kindness is great toward us.** By which is meant not only his great love towards the Jewish people, but towards the whole family of man. The Lord is kind to us as his creatures, and merciful to us as sinners, hence his merciful kindness to us as sinful creatures. This mercy has been very great, or powerful. We can all join in this grateful acknowledgment, and in the praise which is therefore due. **And the truth of the LORD endureth for ever.** He has kept his covenant promise that in the seed of Abraham should all nations of the earth be blessed, and he will eternally keep every single promise of that covenant to all those who put their trust in him. This should be a cause of constant and grateful praise, wherefore the psalm concludes as it began, with another Hallelujah, **Praise ye the LORD.**

Psalm 118

1. **O give thanks unto the LORD.** The grateful hero feels that he cannot himself alone sufficiently express his thankfulness, and therefore he calls in the aid of others. The whole nation was involved in David's triumphal accession, and therefore it was right that they should unite in his adoring song of praise. The thanks were to be rendered unto Jehovah alone, and not to the patience or valor of the hero himself. It is always well to trace our mercies to him who bestows them, and if we cannot give him anything else, let us at any rate given him our thanks. We must not stop at the agent, but rise to the first cause and render all our praises **unto the LORD** himself. Have we been of a forgetful or grumbling spirit? Let the text speak to our hearts: "Cease your complainings, turn from all self-glorification, and give thanks unto the Lord." **For he is good.** Therefore he is always to be praised whether we are receiving anything from him or not. Those who only praise God because he *does* them good should rise to a higher note and give thanks to him because he *is* good. When we ourselves are conscious that we are far from being good, we should only the more

reverently bless him that he is good. It is not only that he was good, and will be good, but he *is* good, let his providence be what it may. Therefore let us even at this present moment, though the skies be dark with clouds, yet give thanks unto his name.

Because his mercy endureth for ever. Mercy is a great part of his goodness, and one which more concerns us than any other, for we are sinners and have need of his mercy. Angels may say that he is good, but they need not his mercy and cannot therefore take an equal delight in it; inanimate creation declares that he is good, but it cannot feel his mercy, for it has never transgressed; but man, deeply guilty and graciously forgiven, beholds mercy as the very focus and center of the goodness of the Lord. The endurance of the divine mercy is a special subject for song: notwithstanding our sins, our trials, our fears, his mercy **endureth for ever.** The best of earthly joys pass away, and even the world itself grows old and hastens to decay, but there is no change in the mercy of God; he was faithful to our forefathers, he is merciful to us, and he will be gracious to our children and our children's children.

2. God had made a covenant with their forefathers, a covenant of mercy and love, and to that covenant he was faithful evermore. Israel sinned in Egypt, provoked the Lord in the wilderness, went astray again and again under the judges, and transgressed at all times; and yet the Lord continued to regard them as his people, to favor them with his oracles, and to forgive their sins. He speedily ceased from the chastisements which they so richly deserved, because he had favor towards them. He put his rod away the moment they repented, because his heart was full of compassion. David's success was mercy to Israel, as well as mercy to himself. If Israel does not sing when the Son of David ascends the throne, the very stones will cry out.

3. The sons of Aaron were specially set apart to come nearest to God, and it was only because of his mercy that they were enabled to live in the presence of the thrice holy Jehovah, who is a consuming fire. Every time the morning and evening lamb were sacrificed, the priests saw the continual mercy of the Lord, and in all the holy vessels of the sanctuary, and all its services from hour to hour, they had renewed witness of the goodness of the Most High. When the high priest went into the holy place and came forth accepted, he might, above all people, sing of the eternal mercy. If this psalm refers to David, the priests had special reason for thankfulness on his coming to the throne, for Saul had made a great slaughter among them, and had at various times interfered with their sacred office. A man had now come to the throne who for their Master's sake would esteem them, give them their dues, and preserve them safe from all harm. Our Lord Jesus, having made all his people priests unto God, may well call upon them in that capacity to magnify the everlasting mercy of the Most High.

4. If there were any who did not belong to Israel but had a holy fear and lowly reverence of God, the psalmist calls upon them to unite with him in his thanksgiving, and to do it especially on the occasion of his exaltation to the throne; and this is no more than they would cheerfully agree to do, since every good person in the world is benefited when a true servant of God is placed in a position of honor and influence. In the three exhortations, to Israel, to the house of Aaron, and to them that fear the Lord, there is a repetition of the exhortation to **say, that his mercy endureth for ever.** We are not only to believe, but to declare the goodness of God. Specially is it our joy to speak out to the honor and glory of God when we think upon the exaltation of his dear Son. Notice carefully the word **now.** There is no time like the present for telling out the praises of God. The present exaltation of the Son of David now demands from all who are the subjects of his kingdom continual songs of thanksgiving to him who has set him on high in the midst of Zion. **Now** with us should mean always. When would it be right to cease from praising God, whose mercy never ceases?

5. I called upon the LORD in distress, or, "out of anguish I invoked Jah." Nothing was left him but prayer, his agony was too great for aught beside; but having the heart and the privilege to pray he possessed all things. Prayers which come out of distress generally come out of the heart, and therefore they go to the heart of God. Prayer may be bitter in the offering, but it will be sweet in the answering. The man of God had called upon the Lord when he was not in distress, and therefore he found it natural and easy to call upon him when he was in distress. He worshiped, he praised, he prayed: for all this is included in calling upon God, even when he was in a straitened condition. Some read the original "a narrow gorge"; and therefore it was the more joy to him when he could say, **the LORD answered me, and set me in a large place.** In God's case hearing means answering, hence the translators rightly put **the LORD answered me,** though the original word is "heard." Many of us can join with the psalmist in the declarations of this verse: deep was our distress on account of sin, and we were shut up as in a prison under the law, but in answer to the prayer of faith we obtained the liberty of full justification wherewith Christ makes men free, and we are free indeed. It was the Lord who did it, and unto his name we ascribe all the glory; we had no merits, no strength, no wisdom; all we could do was to call upon him, and even that was his gift; but the mercy which is to eternity came to our rescue, and we were brought out of bondage, and made to delight in the length and breadth of a boundless inheritance. All things are ours, all times are ours, all places are ours, for God himself is ours; we have earth to lodge in and heaven to dwell in – what larger place can be imagined? We need all Israel, the whole house of Aaron, and all them that fear the Lord, to assist us in the expression of our gratitude.

6. The LORD is on my side, or, he is "for me." Once his justice was against me, but now he is my reconciled God, and engaged on my behalf. The psalmist naturally rejoiced in the divine help; everyone turned against him, but God was his defender and advocate, accomplishing the divine purposes of his grace. The expression may also be translated "to me" – that is to say, Jehovah belongs to me, and is mine. What infinite wealth is here! If we do not magnify the Lord we are of all men most brutish. **I will not fear.** He does not say that he would not suffer, but that he would not fear: the favor of God infinitely outweighed the hatred of men; therefore setting the one against the other he felt that he had no reason to be afraid. He was calm and confident, though surrounded with enemies, and so may all believers be, for thus they honor God. **What can man do unto me?** He can do nothing more than God permits; at the very uttermost he can only kill the body, but he has no more that he can do. God having purposed to set his servant upon the throne, the whole race of mankind can do nothing to thwart the divine decree: the settled purpose of Jehovah's heart could not be turned aside, nor its accomplishment delayed, by the most rancorous hostility of the most powerful of men.

7. The LORD taketh my part with them that help me. Jehovah condescended to be in alliance with the good man and his comrades; his God was not content to look on, but he took part in the struggle. What a consolatory fact it is that the Lord takes our part, and that when he raises up friends for us he does not leave them to fight for us alone, but he himself as our chief defender deigns to come into the battle and wage war on our behalf. We are not to think little of the generous friends who rally around us; but still our great dependence and our grand confidence must be fixed upon the Lord alone. When our gracious Jehovah is pleased to support and strengthen those who aid us, they become substantial helpers to us.

Therefore shall I see my desires upon them that hate me. The words **my desire** are added by the translators; the psalmist said, "I shall look upon my haters; I shall look them in the face, I shall make them cease from their contempt, I shall myself look down upon them instead of their looking down upon me. I shall see their defeat, I shall see the end of them." Our Lord Jesus does at this moment look down upon his adversaries.

8. God is infinitely more able to help, and more likely to help, than man, and therefore prudence suggests that we put our confidence in him above all others. It is also morally better to do so, for it is the duty of the creature to trust in the Creator. God deserves to be trusted, and to place our reliance upon another rather than himself is a direct insult to his faithfulness. We can never be sure of our ground if we rely upon mortal man, but we are always secure in the hands of our God. To trust in man tends to make us mean, crouching, dependent; but confidence in God elevates, produces a sacred quietness of spirit, and sanctifies the soul. In many cases the human object of our trust fails from want of ability, generosity, affection, or memory; but the Lord does for us exceeding abundantly above all that we ask or even think. This verse is written out of the experience of many who have first of all found the broken reeds of the creature break under them, and have afterwards joyfully found the Lord a solid pillar sustaining all their weight.

9. The princes' word should be unquestionable. They are noblest in rank and mightiest in power, and yet as a rule princes are not one whit more reliable than the rest of mankind. In many troubles they cannot help us to the least degree; for instance, in sickness, bereavement, or death; neither can they assist us one jot in reference to our eternal state. The favor of princes is notoriously fickle. He who puts his confidence in God, the great King, is thereby made mentally and spiritually stronger, and rises to the highest dignity of manhood; in fact, the more he trusts the more is he free, but the fawning sycophant of greatness is meaner than the dirt he treads upon.

10. All nations compassed me about. The hero of the psalm, while he had no earthly friend upon whom he could thoroughly rely, was surrounded by innumerable enemies, who heartily hated him. He was hemmed in by his adversaries, and scarce could find a loophole of escape. As if by common consent all sorts of people set themselves against him, and yet he was more than a match for them all, because he was trusting in the name of the Lord. Therefore does he joyfully accept the battle, and grasp the victory, crying, **but in the name of the LORD will I destroy them,** or "cut them in pieces." They thought to destroy *him*, but he was sure of destroying *them*; they meant to blot out his name, but he expected to render not only his own name but the name of the Lord his God more illustrious in human hearts. He recognized his own individuality, and asserted it: he did not sit still supinely and leave the work to be done by God by some mysterious means; but he resolved with his own trusty sword to set about the enterprise, and so become in God's hand the instrument of his own deliverance: *I* **will destroy them.** He does not speak of merely escaping from them like a bird out of the snare of the fowler, but he vows that he will carry the war into his enemies' ranks, and overthrow them so thoroughly that there should be no fear of their rising up a second time.

11. They compassed me about; yea, they compassed me about. They made a double ring; they not only talked of doing so, but they actually shut him up and enclosed him. His heart had vividly recalled his position of peril at the time, and now he delights to call it again to mind in order that he may the more ardently adore the mercy which made him strong in the hour of conflict, so that he broke through a troop, and swept a host to destruction. **But in the name of the LORD will I destroy them.** I will subdue them, get them under my feet, and break their power in pieces. He is as certain about the destruction of his enemies as he was assured of their having compassed him about. It is grand to hear a man speak in this fashion when it is not boasting, but the calm declaration of his heartfelt trust in God.

12. They compassed me about like bees. They seemed to be everywhere, like a swarm of bees, attacking him at every point; nimbly flying from place to place, stinging him meanwhile, and inflicting grievous pain. They threatened at first to baffle him: what weapon could he use against them? They were so numerous, so inveterate; so insignificant and yet so capable of inflicting agony. He was in an evil case, but even there faith availed. All-powerful faith adapts itself to all circumstances; it can cast out devils, and it can drive out bees. **They are quenched as the fire of thorns.** Their fierce attack soon came to an end; like thorns which blaze with fierce crackling and abundant flame, but die out in a handful of ashes very speedily, so did the nations which surrounded our hero soon cease their clamor and come to an inglorious end. He had no need to crush the bees, for like crackling thorns they died out of themselves. For a third time he adds, **for in the name of the LORD will I destroy them,** or "cut them down," as people cut down thorns with a scythe.

What wonders have been wrought in the name of the Lord! It is the battle-cry of faith before which its adversaries fly apace. The name of the Lord is the only weapon which never fails in the day of battle; he who knows how to use it may chase a thousand with his single arm. Alas, we too often go to work and to conflict in our own name. Let us take care never to venture into the presence of the foe without first of all arming ourselves with this impenetrable mail. If we knew this name better, and trusted it more, our life would be more fruitful and sublime.

13. Thou hast thrust sore at me. "Thrusting, thou hast thrust at me." The enemy is described as concentrating all his power into the thrusts which he gave to the man of God. Wounds had been given and received, and these smarted much, and were exceeding sore. This is true of many a tried child of God who has been wounded by Satan, by the world, by temptation, by affliction; the sword has entered into his bones, and left its mark. **That I might fall.** This was the object of the thrusting: to throw him down, to make him depart from his integrity, and lose his confidence in God. If our adversaries can dishonor us, and God in us, their victory will be complete. **But the LORD helped me;** a blessed **but.** This is the saving clause. Other helpers were unable to chase away the angry nations, much less to destroy all the noxious swarms; but when the Lord came to the rescue the hero's single arm was strong enough to vanquish all his adversaries. How sweetly can many of us repeat in the retrospect of our past tribulations this delightful sentence, "But the Lord helped *me.*" I was assailed by innumerable doubts and fears, but the Lord helped me; my natural unbelief was terribly inflamed by the insinuations of Satan, but the Lord helped me; multiplied trials were rendered more intense by the cruel assaults of men, and I knew not what to do, but the Lord helped me.

14. The LORD is my strength and song, my strength while I was in the conflict, my song now that it is ended; my strength against the strong, and my song over their defeat. He is far from boasting of his own valor; he ascribes his victory to its real source; he has no song concerning his own exploits, but all his paeans are unto the Lord whose right hand and holy arm had given him the victory. **And is become my salvation.** The poet-warrior knew that he was saved, and he not only ascribed that salvation unto God, but he declared God himself to be his salvation. It is an all-comprehending expression, signifying that from beginning to end, in the whole and in the details of it, he owed his deliverance entirely to the Lord. Thus can all the Lord's redeemed say, "Salvation is of the Lord." We cannot endure any doctrine which puts the crown upon the wrong head and defrauds the glorious King of praise. God sometimes gives a secret strength to his people, and yet they question their own salvation, and cannot therefore sing of it. Many are, no doubt, truly saved, but at times have so little strength that they are ready to faint, and therefore they cannot sing: when strength is imparted and salvation is realized, then the song is clear and full.

15. **The voice of rejoicing and salvation is in the tabernacles of the righteous.** They sympathized in the delight of their leader and they abode in their tents in peace, rejoicing that one had been raised up who, in the name of the Lord, would protect them from their adversaries. The families of believers are happy, and they should take pains to give their happiness a voice by their family devotion. The dwelling-place of the saved should be the temple of praise. The struggling hero knew that the voice of woe and lamentation was heard in the tents of his adversaries, for they had suffered severe defeat at his hands; but he was delighted by the remembrance that the nation for whom he had struggled would rejoice from one end of the land to the other at the deliverance which God had wrought by his means. That hero of heroes, the conquering Saviour, gives to all the families of his people abundant reasons for incessant song now that he has led captivity captive and ascended up on high. Let none of us be silent in our households: if we have salvation let us have joy, and if we have joy let us give it a tongue wherewith it may magnify the Lord. If we hearken carefully to the music which comes from Israel's tents, we shall catch a stanza to this effect, **the right hand of the LORD doeth valiantly.** Jehovah had manifested his strength, given victory to his chosen champion, and overthrown all the armies of the foe.

16. **The right hand of the LORD is exalted,** lifted up to smite the foe, or extolled and magnified in the eyes of his people. It is the Lord's **right** hand, the hand of his skill, the hand of his greatest power, the hand which is accustomed to defend his saints. When that is lifted up, it lifts up all who trust in him, and it casts down all who resist him. **The right hand of the LORD doeth valiantly.** The psalmist speaks in triplets, for he is praising the triune God, his heart is warm and he loves to dwell upon the note; he is not content with the praise he has rendered; he endeavors to utter it each time more fervently and more jubilantly than before. He had dwelt upon the sentence, "they compassed me about," for his peril from encircling armies was fully realized; and now he

167

dwells upon the valor of Jehovah's right hand, for he has as vivid a sense of the presence and majesty of the Lord. How seldom is this the case: the Lord's mercy is forgotten and only the trial is remembered.

17. I shall not die, but live. His enemies hoped that he would die, and perhaps he himself feared he would perish at their hand; the news of his death may have been spread among his people, for the tongue of rumor is ever ready with ill news, the false intelligence would naturally cause great sorrow and despondency, but he proclaims himself as yet alive and as confident that he will not fall by the hand of the destroyer. Perhaps he had been sick, and brought to death's door, but he had a presentiment that the sickness was not unto death, but to the glory of God. At any rate, he knew that he would not so die as to give victory to the enemies of God; for the honor of God and the good of his people were both wrapped up in his continued success. Feeling that he would live, he devoted himself to the noblest of purposes: he resolved to bear witness to the divine faithfulness, **and declare the works of the LORD.** He determined to recount the works of Jah; and he does so in this psalm, wherein he dwells with love and admiration upon the splendor of Jehovah's prowess in the midst of the fight. While there is a testimony for God to be borne by us to anyone, it is certain that we shall not be hurried from the land of the living. The Lord's prophets will live on in the midst of famine, and war, and plague, and persecution, till they have uttered all the words of their prophecy; his priests will stand at the altar unharmed till their last sacrifice has been presented.

18. The LORD hath chastened me sore. This is faith's version of the former passage, "Thou hast thrust sore at me," for the attacks of the enemy are chastisements from the hand of God. The devil tormented Job for his own purposes, but in reality the sorrows of the patriarch were chastisements from the Lord. "Chastening, Jah has chastened me," says our poet: as much as to say that the Lord had smitten him very severely, and made him sorrowfully to know the full weight of his rod. The Lord frequently appears to save his heaviest blows for his best-beloved ones; if any one affliction be more painful than another it falls to the lot of those whom he most distinguishes in his service. The gardener prunes his best roses with most care. Chastisement is sent to keep successful saints humble, to make them tender towards others, and to enable them to bear the high honors which their heavenly Friend puts upon them. **But he hath not given me over unto death.** This verse, like verse 13, concludes with a blessed **but,** which constitutes a saving clause. The psalmist felt as if he had been beaten within an inch of his life, but yet death did not actually ensue. There is always a merciful limit to the scourging of the children of God. Forty stripes save one were all that an Israelite might receive, and the Lord will never allow that one, that killing stroke, to fall upon his children. Their pains are for their instruction, not for their destruction. By these things the ungodly die, but gracious Hezekiah could say, "By these things men live, and in all these things is the life of my spirit." No, blessed be the name of God, he may chastise us, but he will not condemn us. He does not give us over unto death at any time, and we may be quite sure that he has not done so while he condescends to chasten us, for if he intended our final rejection he would not take the pains to place us under his fatherly discipline. It may seem hard to be under the afflicting rod, but it would be a far more dreadful thing if the Lord were to say, "He is given unto idols, let him alone."

The hero, restored to health, and rescued from the dangers of battle, now lifts up his own song unto the Lord, and asks all Israel, led on by the goodly fellowship of the priests, to assist him in chanting a joyful Te Deum.

19. Open to me the gates of righteousness. The grateful champion, having reached the entrance of the temple, asks for admission in set form, as if he felt that he could only approach the hallowed shrine by divine permission, and wished only to enter in the appointed manner. The temple of God was meant for the righteous to enter and offer the sacrifice of righteousness; hence the gates are called the gates of righteousness. Righteous deeds were done within its walls, and righteous teachings sounded forth from its courts. The phrase "the gate" is sometimes used to signify power or empire; the entrance to the temple was the gate of righteousness, the palace of the Great King, who is in all things just. **I will go into them, and I will praise the LORD.** Only let the gates be opened, and the willing worshiper will enter; and he will enter in the right spirit, for the best of purposes, that he may render homage unto the Most High. Alas, there are multitudes who do not care whether the gates of God's house are opened or not; and although they know that they are opened wide they never care to enter, neither does the thought of praising God so much as cross their minds. The time will come for them when they will find the gates of heaven shut against them, for those gates are the gates of righteousness through which there will by no means enter anything that defiles. Our champion might have praised the Lord in secret, and doubtless he did so; but he was not content without going up to the assembly, there to register his thanksgivings. Those who neglect public worship generally neglect all worship; those who praise God within their own gates are among the readiest to praise him within his temple gates. Our hero had also in all probability been sore sick, and therefore like Hezekiah he says, "The Lord was ready to save me: therefore we will sing my songs to the stringed instruments all the days of my life in the house of the Lord." Public praise for public mercies is every way most appropriate, most acceptable to God, and most profitable to others.

20. This gate of the LORD, into which the righteous shall enter. The psalmist loves the house of God so well that he admires the very gate thereof, and pauses beneath its arch to express his affection for it. He loved it because it was the gate of the Lord, the gate of righteousness, and so many godly people had already entered it, and in all future ages such people will continue to pass through it. If the gate of the Lord's house on earth is so pleasant to us, how greatly shall we rejoice when we pass that gate of pearl, to which none but the righteous will ever approach, but through which all the just will in due time enter to eternal felicity. The Lord Jesus has passed that way, and not only set the gate wide open, but secured an entrance for all who are made righteous in his righteousness: all the righteous must and shall enter there, whoever may oppose them. Under another aspect our Lord is himself that gate, and through him, as the new and living Way, all the righteous delight to approach the Lord. Whenever we draw near to praise the Lord we must come by this gate.

21. Having entered, the champion exclaims, **I will praise thee,** not "I will praise the Lord," for now he vividly realizes the divine presence, and addresses himself directly to Jehovah, whom his faith discerns. How well it is in all our songs of praise to let the heart have direct and distinct communion with God himself! The psalmist's song was personal praise too: *I will praise thee;* resolute praise, spontaneous praise, and continuous praise. **For thou hast heard me, and art become my salvation.** He praises God by mentioning his favors, weaving his song out of the divine goodness which he had experienced. In these words he gives the reason for his praise – his answered prayer, and the deliverance which he had received in consequence. How fondly he dwells upon the personal interposition of God! *Thou* **hast heard me.** How heartily he ascribes the whole of his victory over his enemies to God: *Thou* **art become my salvation.** It is well to go directly to God himself, and not to stay even in his mercy, or in the acts of his grace. Answered prayers bring God very near to us; realized salvation enables us to realize the immediate presence of God. Considering the extreme distress through which the worshiper had passed, it is not at all wonderful that he should feel full of gratitude at the great salvation God had wrought for him, and should at his first entrance into the temple lift up his voice in thankful praise for personal favors so great, so needful, so perfect.

22–27. This passage would appear to be a mixture of the expressions of the people and of the hero himself.

22. Here the people magnify God for bringing his chosen servant to the honorable office which had been allotted him by divine decree. A wise king and valiant leader is a stone by which the national fabric is built up. David had been rejected by those in authority, but God had placed him in a position of the highest honor and the greatest usefulness, making him the chief cornerstone of the state. In the case of many others whose early life has been spent in conflict, the Lord has been pleased to accomplish his divine purposes in like manner; but to none is this text so applicable as to the Lord Jesus himself; he is the living stone, the tried stone, elect, precious, which God himself appointed from of old. The Jewish builders – scribe, priest, Pharisee, and

Herodian – rejected him with disdain. They could see no excellence in him that they should build upon him; he could not be made to fit in with their ideal of a national church; he was a stone of another quarry from themselves, and not after their mind nor according to their taste; therefore they cast him away and poured contempt upon him, as Peter said: "This is the stone which was set at nought of you builders." They reckoned him as nothing, though he is Lord of all. In raising him from the dead the Lord God exalted him to be the Head of his church. Since then he has joined the two walls of Jews and Gentiles into one stately temple, and is seen to be the binding cornerstone, making both one.

Jesus in all things has the preeminence; he is the principal stone of the whole house of God. Still the builders refuse him: even to this day the professional teachers of the Gospel are far too apt to fly to any and every new philosophy sooner than maintain the simple Gospel, which is the essence of Christ. Nevertheless, he holds his true position amongst his people, and the foolish builders will see to their utter confusion that his truth will be exalted over all.

23. This is the LORD's doing. The exalted position of Christ in his church is not the work of man, and does not depend for its continuation upon any builders or ministers; God himself has wrought the exaltation of our Lord Jesus. Considering the opposition which comes from the wisdom, the power, and the authority of this world, it is manifest that if the kingdom of Christ be indeed set up and maintained in the world it must be by supernatural power. Every hour in which the true church subsists is a prolonged miracle. This staggers the adversary, for he cannot understand what it is which baffles him: of the Holy Spirit he knows nothing. **It is marvelous in our eyes.** We actually see it; it is not in our thoughts and hopes and prayers alone, but the astonishing work is actually before our eyes. Jesus reigns, his power is felt, and we perceive that it is so. Faith sees our great Master, far above all principality, and power, and might, and dominion, and every name that is named, not only in this world, but also in that which is to come; she sees and marvels. It never ceases to astonish us, as we see, even here below, God by means of weakness defeating power, by the simplicity of his word baffling the craft of men, and by the invisible influence of his Spirit exalting his Son in human hearts in the teeth of open and determined opposition. It is indeed "marvelous in our eyes," as all God's works must be if we care to study them. In the Hebrew the passage reads, "It is wonderfully done": not only is the exaltation of Jesus itself wonderful, but the way in which its is brought about is marvelous: it is wonderfully done. The more we study the history of Christ and his church, the more fully shall we agree with this declaration.

24. This is the day which the LORD hath made. A new era has commenced. The day of David's enthronement was the beginning of better times for Israel; and in a far higher sense the day of our Lord's resurrection is a new day of

God's own making, for it is the dawn of a blessed dispensation. No doubt the Israelitish nation celebrated the victory of its champion with a day of feasting, music and song; and surely it is but meet that we should reverently keep the feast of the triumph of the Son of David. We observe the Lord's day as henceforth our true Sabbath, a day made and ordained of God, for the perpetual remembrance of the achievements of our Redeemer. We by no means wish to confine the reference of the passage to the Sabbath, for the whole Gospel day is the day of God's making, and its blessings come to us through our Lord's being placed as the head of the corner. **We will rejoice and be glad in it.** We will rejoice in heart and be glad in face, rejoice in secret and be glad in public, for we have more than a double reason for being glad in the Lord. We ought to be specially joyous on the Sabbath. Beholding the Lord Jesus as all in all in the assemblies of his people, we are bound to overflow with joy. Is it not written, "Then were the disciples glad when they saw the Lord"? When the King makes the house of prayer to be a banqueting house, and we have grace to enjoy fellowship with him, both in his sufferings and in his triumphs, we feel an intense delight, and we are glad to express it with the rest of his people.

25. **Save now, I beseech thee, O LORD.** Hosanna! God save our king! Let David reign! Or as we who live in these latter days interpret it, Let the Son of David live forever; let his saving help go forth throughout all nations. We plead also for ourselves, that the Lord would save us, deliver us, and continue to sanctify us. This we ask with great earnestness, beseeching it of Jehovah. Prayer should always be an intreating and beseeching. **O LORD, I beseech thee, send now prosperity.** Let the church be built up: through the salvation of sinners may the number of the saints be increased; through the preservation of saints may the church be strengthened, continued, beautified, perfected. Our Lord Jesus himself pleads for the salvation and prosperity of his chosen; as our Intercessor before the throne he asks that the Heavenly Father would save and keep those who were of old committed to his charge, and cause them to be one through the indwelling Spirit. Strange though it may seem, he who cries for salvation is already in a measure saved. None can so truly cry, "Save, I beseech thee," as those who have already participated in salvation; and the most prosperous church is that which most imploringly seeks prosperity. It may seem strange that, returning from victory, flushed with triumph, the hero should still ask for salvation; but so it is, and it could not be otherwise. When all our Saviour's work and warfare were ended, his intercession became even more prominently a feature of his life; after he had conquered all his foes he made intercession for the transgressors. What is true of him is true of his church also, for whenever she obtains the largest measure of spiritual blessing she is then most inclined to plead for more. She never pants so eagerly for prosperity as when she sees the Lord's doings in her midst, and marvels at them.

26. **Blessed is he that cometh in the name of the LORD.** The champion had

done everything "in the name of the Lord": in that name he had routed all his adversaries, and had risen to the throne, and in that name he had now entered the temple to pay his vows. We know who it is that cometh in the name of the Lord beyond all others. For his sake everybody is blessed to us who comes in the name of the Lord; we welcome all such to our hearts and our homes; but chiefly, and beyond all others, we welcome *himself* when he deigns to enter in and sup with us and we with him. Perhaps this sentence is intended to be the benediction of the priests upon the valiant servant of the Lord, and if so, it is appropriately added, **We have blessed you out of the house of the LORD.** The priests, whose business it was to bless the people, in a sevenfold degree blessed the people's deliverer, the one chosen out of the people whom the Lord has exalted. All those whose high privilege it is to dwell in the house of the Lord forever, because they are made priests unto God in Christ Jesus, can truly say that they bless the Christ who has made them what they are, and placed them where they are. Whenever we feel ourselves at home with God, and feel the spirit of adoption, the first thought of our hearts should be to bless the elder Brother, through whom the privilege of sonship has descended to such unworthy ones.

27. God is the LORD, which hath showed us light, or "God is Jehovah," the only living and true God. The words may also be rendered, "Mighty is Jehovah." Only the power of God could have brought us such light and joy as spring from the work of our Champion and King. With the light of knowledge has come the light of joy, for we are delivered from the powers of darkness and translated into the kingdom of God's dear Son. Let us do our best to magnify the great Father of lights from whom our present blessedness has descended. **Bind the sacrifice with cords, even unto the horns of the altar.** Some think that by this we are taught that the king offered so many sacrifices that the whole area of the court was filled, and the sacrifices were bound even up to the altar; but we are included to keep to our own version, and to believe that sometimes restive bullocks were bound to the altar before they were slain. The word rendered **cords** carries with it the idea of wreaths and boughs, so that it was not a cord of hard, rough rope, but a decorated band; just as in our case, though we are bound to the altar of God, it is with the cords of love and the bands of a man, and not by a compulsion which destroys the freedom of the will. The sacrifice which we would present in honor of the victories of our Lord Jesus Christ is the living sacrifice of our spirit, soul, and body. We bring ourselves to his altar, and desire to offer him all that we have and are. There remains a tendency in our nature to start aside from this; it is not fond of the sacrificial knife. In the warmth of our love we come willingly to the altar, but we need constraining power to keep us there. We are bound to the doctrine of atonement; we are bound to Christ himself, who is both altar and sacrifice; we desire to be more bound to him than ever.

28–29. Now comes the closing song of the champion, and of each one of his admirers.

28. Thou art my God, and I will praise thee. My mighty God who hath done this mighty and marvelous thing. Thou shalt be mine, and all the praise my soul is capable of shall be poured forth at thy feet. **Thou art my God, I will exalt thee.** Thou hast exalted me, and as far as my praises can do it, I will exalt thy name. However dull and cold I may sometimes feel myself, I will rouse my nature, and determine that as long as I have any being that being will be spent to thy praise. Forever thou art my God, and forever I will give thee thanks.

9. The psalm concludes as it began, making a complete circle of joyful adoration. We can well suppose that the notes at the close of the loud hallelujah were more swift, more sweet, more loud than at the beginning. Israel, the house of Aaron, and all that feared the Lord joined in one common hymn, and the people went every one to his own home, quietly and happily musing upon the goodness of the Lord, whose mercy fills eternity.

Psalm 119

The Psalm is alphabetical. Eight stanzas commence with one letter, and then another eight with the next letter, and so the whole psalm proceeds through the twenty-two letters of the Hebrew alphabet. This sacred ode is a little Bible, the Scriptures condensed, rewritten in holy emotions and actions. Blessed are they who can read and understand these saintly aphorisms; they will find golden apples and come to reckon that this psalm, like the whole Scripture which it praises, is a pearl island, or, better still, a garden of sweet flowers.

1–8. These first eight verses are taken up with a contemplation of the blessedness which comes through keeping the statutes of the Lord. The subject is treated in a devout manner rather than in a didactic style. Heart-fellowship with God is enjoyed through a love of that word which is God's way of communing with the soul by his Holy Spirit. Prayer and praise and all sorts of devotional acts and feelings gleam through the verses like beams of sunlight through an olive grove. You are not only instructed, but influenced to holy emotion, and helped to express the same.

Lovers of God's holy words are blessed, because they are preserved from defilement (verse 1), because they are made practically holy (verses 2–3), and are led to follow after God sincerely and intensely (verse 2). This holy walking must be desirable because God commands it (verse 4); therefore the pious soul prays for it (verse 5), and feels that its comfort and courage must depend upon obtaining it (verse 6). In the prospect of answered prayer, indeed while prayer is being answered, the heart is full of thankfulness (verse 7), and is fixed in solemn resolve not to miss the blessing if the Lord will give enabling grace (verse 8).

The changes are rung upon the words "way," "keep," and "walk." Yet there is no tautology, neither is the same thought repeated, though to the careless reader it may seem so.

The change from statements about others and about the Lord to more personal dealing with God begins in the third verse, and becomes more clear as we advance, till in the later verses the communion becomes most intense and soul moving. Oh that every reader may feel the glow.

1. Blessed. The psalmist is so enraptured with the Word of God that he regards it as the highest ideal of blessedness to be conformed to it. He has gazed on the beauties of the perfect law, and, as if this verse were the sum and outcome of all his emotions, he exclaims, "Blessed is the man whose life is the practical transcript of the will of God." True religion is not cold and dry; it has its exclamations and raptures. We not only judge the keeping of God's law to be a wise and proper thing, but we are warmly enamored of its holiness, and cry out in adoring wonder, "Blessed are the undefiled!" – meaning thereby that we eagerly desire to become such ourselves, and wish for no greater happiness than to be perfectly holy.

This first verse is not only a preface to the whole psalm, but it may also be regarded as the text upon which the rest is a discourse. It is similar to the benediction of Psalm 1, which is set in the forefront of the entire book: there is a likeness between this Psalm 119 and the psalter, and this is one point of it, that it begins with a benediction. In this, too, we see some foreshadowings of the Son of David, who began his great sermon as David began his great psalm. When we cannot bestow blessings, we can show the way of obtaining them, and even if we do not yet possess them ourselves, it may be profitable to contemplate them, that our desires may be excited, and our souls moved to seek after them.

As David thus begins his psalm, so should young men begin their lives, so should new converts commence their life of faith, so should all Christians begin every day. Holiness is happiness, and it is our wisdom first to seek the kingdom of God and his righteousness. Mankind began with being blessed in innocence, and if our fallen race is ever to be blessed again, it must find it where it lost it at the beginning, in conformity to the command of the Lord.

The undefiled in the way. They are in the way, the right way, the way of the Lord, and they keep that way, walking with holy carefulness and washing their feet daily, lest they be found spotted by the flesh. They enjoy great blessedness in their own souls; indeed, they have a foretaste of heaven where the blessedness lies much in being absolutely undefiled; and could they continue utterly and altogether without defilement, doubtless they would have the days of heaven upon the earth. Outward evil would little hurt us if we were entirely rid of the evil of sin, an attainment which with the best of us lies still in the region of desire, and is not yet fully reached, though we have so clear a view of it that we see it to be blessedness itself; and therefore we eagerly press towards it.

David speaks of a high degree of blessedness; for some are in the way, and are true servants of God, but they are as yet faulty in many ways and bring defilement upon themselves. Others who walk in the light more fully, and maintain closer communion with God, are enabled to keep themselves unspotted from the world, and these enjoy far more peace and joy than their less watchful brethren. Doubtless, the more complete our sanctification the more intense our blessedness. Christ is our way, and we are not only alive in Christ, but we are to live in Christ; the sorrow is that we bespatter his holy way with our selfishness, self-exaltation, willfullness, and carnality, and so we miss a great measure of the blessedness which is in him as our way. A believer who errs is still saved, but the joy of his salvation is not experienced by him; he is rescued but not enriched, greatly borne with, but not greatly blessed.

How easily may defilement come upon us even in our holy things, even **in the way.** We may even come from public or private worship with defilement upon the conscience gathered when we were on our knees. There was no floor to the tabernacle but the desert sand, and hence the priests at the altar were under frequent necessity to wash their feet, and by the kind foresight of their God the laver stood ready for their cleansing, just as for us our Lord Jesus still stands ready to wash our feet, that we may be clean every whit.

Who walk in the law of the LORD. In them is found habitual holiness. Their walk, their common everyday life, is obedience unto the Lord. They live by rule, that rule the command of the Lord God. To them religion is nothing out of the way, it is their everyday walk: it molds their common actions as well as their special devotions. Whoever walks in God's law walks in God's company, and must be blessed. The holy life is a steady progress, a quiet advance, a lasting continuance. Good people are never idle, but are still walking onward to their desired end. They are not hurried, and worried, and flurried, and they are not in perplexity as to how to conduct themselves, for they have a perfect rule, which they are happy to walk by. The law of the Lord is not irksome to them; it does not appear to them to be an impossible law, theoretically admirable but practically absurd, but they walk by it and in it. They do not consult it now and then as a sort of rectifier of their wanderings, but they use it as a chart for their daily sailing, a map of the road for their life-journey. Nor do they ever regret that they have entered upon the path of obedience, else they would leave it, and that without difficulty, for a thousand temptations offer them opportunity to return; their continued walk in the law of the Lord is their best testimony to the blessedness of such a condition of life. The psalmist had tried it, and wrote it down as a fact which defied all denial. Rough may be the way, stern the rule, hard the discipline, but a heaped-up blessedness is still found in godly living, for which we bless the Lord.

We have in this verse blessed people who enjoy five blessed things: a blessed way, blessed purity, a blessed law, given by a blessed Lord, and a blessed walk therein; to which we may add the blessed testimony of the Holy Spirit given in this very passage that they are in very deed the blessed of the Lord. The blessedness which is thus set before us we must aim at, but we must not think to obtain it without earnest effort.

2. Blessed are they that keep his testimonies. They are doubly blessed whose outward life is supported by an inward zeal for God's glory. Blessedness is ascribed to those who treasure up the testimonies of the Lord: in which is implied that they search the Scriptures, that they come to an understanding of them, that they love them, and then that they continue in the practice of them. We must first get a thing before we can keep it. We cannot keep in the heart that which we have not heartily embraced by the affections. God's Word is his witness or testimony to grand and important truths which concern himself and our relation to him: this we should desire to know; knowing it, we should believe it; believing it, we should love it; and loving it, we should hold it fast against all comers. There is a doctrinal keeping of the Word when we are ready to die for its defense, and a practical keeping of it when we actually live under its power. If we keep God's testimonies they will keep us right in opinion, comfortable in spirit, holy in conversation, and hopeful in expectation. The designed effect does not come through a temporary seizure of them, but by a persevering keeping of them.

And that seek him with the whole heart. Those who keep the Lord's testimonies are sure to seek after himself. If his Word is precious we may be sure that he himself is still more so. Personal dealing with a personal God is the longing of all those who have allowed the Word of the Lord to have its full effect upon them. If we once really know the power of the Gospel we must seek the God of the Gospel. See the growth which these sentences indicate: first, in the way, then walking in it, then finding and keeping the treasure of faith, and to crown all, seeking after the Lord of the way himself. Note also that the further a soul advances in grace the more spiritual and divine are its longings: an outward walk does not content the gracious soul, nor even the treasured testimonies; it reaches out in due time after God himself, and when it in a measure finds him, still yearns for more of him, and seeks him still.

Seeking after God signifies a desire to commune with him more closely, to follow him more fully, to enter into more perfect union with his mind and will, to promote his glory, and to realize completely all that he is to holy hearts. The blessed man has God already, and for this reason he seeks him. This may seem a contradiction; it is only a paradox.

That which the psalmist admires in this verse he claims in the tenth, where he says, "With my whole heart have I sought thee." It is well when admiration of a virtue leads to the attainment of it. Those who do not believe in the blessedness of seeking the Lord will not be likely to arouse their hearts to the pursuit, but he who calls another blessed because of the grace which he sees in him is on the way to gaining the same grace for himself.

3. They also do no iniquity. Blessed indeed would those people be of whom this could be asserted without reserve and without explanation: we shall have reached the region of pure blessedness when we altogether cease from sin. Those who follow the Word of God do no iniquity; the rule is perfect, and if it be constantly followed no fault will arise. Life, to the outward observer, at any rate, lies much in doing, and he who in his doings never swerves from equity, both towards God and man, has hit upon the way of perfection, and we may be sure that his heart is right. No one can claim to be absolutely without sin, and yet we trust there are many who do not designedly, willfully, knowingly, and continuously do anything that is wicked, ungodly, or unjust. Grace keeps the life righteous as to act even when the Christian has to bemoan the transgressions of the heart. Judged as we should be judged by our fellows, according to such just rules as people make for people, the true people of God do no iniquity: they are honest, upright, and chaste, and touching justice and morality they are blameless. Therefore are they happy.

They walk in his ways. They attend not only to the great main highway of the law, but to the smaller paths of the particular precepts. As they will perpetrate no sin of commission, so do they labor to be free from every sin of omission. It is not enough to them to be blameless; they wish also to be actively righteous. The surest way to abstain from evil is to be fully occupied in doing good. This verse describes believers as they exist among us: although they have their faults and infirmities, yet they hate evil, and will not permit themselves to do it; they love the ways of truth, right and true godliness, and habitually they walk therein. They do not claim to be absolutely perfect except in their desires, and there they are pure indeed, for they pant to be kept from all sin, and to be led into all holiness.

4. God's precepts require *careful* obedience: there is no keeping them by accident. Some give to God a careless service, a sort of hit or miss obedience, but the Lord has not commanded such service, nor will he accept it. His law demands the love of all our heart, soul, mind, and strength. We are also called to *zealous* obedience. We are to keep the precepts abundantly: the vessels of obedience should be filled to the brim, and the command carried out to the full of its meaning. As a man diligent in business arouses himself to do as much trade as he can, so must we be eager to serve the Lord as much as possible. Nor must we spare pains to do so, for a diligent obedience will also be *laborious and self-denying*. Those who are diligent in business rise up early and sit up late, and deny themselves much of comfort and repose. They are not soon tired, or if they are they persevere. So should we serve the Lord.

Some are diligent in superstition and will-worship; be it ours to be diligent in keeping God's precepts. God has not commanded us to be diligent in *making* precepts, but in *keeping* them. Some bind yokes upon their own necks, and make bonds and rules for others, but the wise course is to be satisfied with the rules of holy Scripture.

The psalmist began with the third person; he is now coming near home, and has already reached the first person plural, according to our version; we shall soon hear him crying out personally and for himself. As the heart glows with love to holiness, we long to have a personal interest in it.

5. Divine commands should direct us in the subject of our prayers. We cannot of ourselves keep God's statutes as he would have them kept, and yet we long to do so: what resort have we but prayer? We must ask the Lord to work in us, or we shall never work out his commandments. This verse is a sigh of regret because the psalmist feels that he has not kept the precepts diligently; it is a cry of weakness appealing for help to one who can aid, it is a request of bewilderment from one who has lost his way and would be directed in it, and it is a petition of faith from one who loves God and trusts in him for grace.

Our ways are by nature opposed to the way of God, and must be turned by the Lord's direction in another direction from that which they originally take or they will lead us down to destruction. God can direct the mind and will without violating our free agency, and he will do so in answer to prayer; in fact, he has begun the work already in those who are heartily praying after the fashion of this verse.

The sigh of the text is really a prayer, though it does not exactly take that form. Desires and longings are of the essence of supplication, and it little matters what shape they take. **O that** is as acceptable a prayer as "Our Father."

One would hardly have expected a prayer for direction; rather should we have looked for a petition for enabling. Can we not direct ourselves? The psalmist herein confesses that even for the smallest part of his duty he felt unable without grace. He longed for the Lord to influence his will, as well as to strengthen his hands.

6. Then shall I not be ashamed. He had known shame, and here he rejoices in the prospect of being freed from it. Sin brings shame, and when sin is gone, the reason for being ashamed is banished. What a deliverance this is, for to some people death is preferable to shame! **When I have respect unto all thy commandments.** When he respects God he will respect himself and be respected. Whenever we err we prepare ourselves for confusion of face and sinking of heart.

Many suffer from excessive diffidence, and this verse suggests a cure. An abiding sense of duty will make us bold: we shall be afraid to be afraid. No shame in the presence of other people will hinder us when the fear of God has taken full possession of our minds. David promises himself no immunity from shame till he has carefully paid homage to all the precepts. Mind that word **all,** and leave not one command out of your respect. Partial obedience still leaves us liable to be called to account for those commands which we have neglected. To a poor sinner who is buried in despair, it may seem a very unlikely thing that he should ever be delivered from shame. Let him read these words: "Then shall I not be ashamed." David is not dreaming, nor picturing an impossible case. Be assured that the Holy Spirit can renew in you the image of God.

7. I will praise thee. From prayer to praise is never a long or difficult journey. Be sure that he who prays for holiness will one day praise for happiness. Shame having vanished, silence is broken, and the formerly silent person declares, "I will praise thee." He cannot but promise praise while he seeks sanctification. Mark how well he knows upon what head to set the crown: **I will praise *thee*.** He would himself be praiseworthy, but he counts God alone worthy of praise. By the sorrow and shame of sin he measures his obligations to the Lord who would teach him the art of living so that he should clean escape from his former misery.

With uprightness of heart. His heart would be upright if the Lord would teach him, and then it should praise its teacher. There is such a thing as false and feigned praise, and this the Lord abhors; but there is no music like that which comes from a pure soul which stands in its integrity. Heart praise is required, uprightness in that heart, and teaching to make the heart upright. An upright heart is sure to bless the Lord, for grateful adoration is a part of its uprightness.

When I shall have learned thy righteous judgments. We must learn to praise, learn that we may praise, and praise when we have learned. If we are ever to learn, the Lord must teach us, and especially upon such a subject as his judgments, for they are a great deep. While these are passing before our eyes, and we are learning from them, we ought to praise God, for the original is not "when I have learned" but "in my learning." While yet I am a scholar I will be a chorister.

8. I will keep thy statutes. A calm resolve. "I will praise" should be coupled with "I will keep." This firm resolve is by no means boastful, for it is followed by a humble prayer for divine help, **O forsake me not utterly.** Feeling his own incapacity, he trembles lest he should be left to himself, and this fear is increased by the horror which he has of falling into sin. The **I will keep** sounds rightly enough now that the humble cry is heard with it. This is a happy amalgam: resolution and dependence. We meet with those who to all appearance humbly pray, but there is no force of character, no decision in them, and consequently the pleading of the closet is not embodied in the life: on the other hand, we meet with abundance of resolve with an entire absence of dependence upon God, and this makes as poor a character as the former.

This prayer is one which is certain to be heard, for assuredly it must be highly pleasing to God to see a man set upon obeying his will, and therefore it must be most agreeable to him to be present with such a person, and to help him in his endeavors. How can he forsake one who does not forsake his law?

The special dread which tinges this prayer with a somber hue is the fear of utter forsaking. But the Lord never has utterly forsaken his servants, and he never will, blessed be his name. If we long to keep his statutes he will keep us; his grace will keep us keeping his law.

There is rather a descent from the mount of benediction with which the first verse begins to the almost wail of this eighth verse; yet this is spiritually a growth, for from admiration of goodness we have come to a burning longing after God and communion with him, and an intense horror lest it should not be enjoyed.

9. Wherewithal shall a young man cleanse his way? How will he become and remain practically holy? He is but a young man, full of hot passions, and poor in knowledge and experience; how will he get right, and keep right? Never was there a more important question for any man; alas, his way is already unclean by actual sin which he has already committed, and he himself has within his nature a tendency towards that which defiles. Here, then, is the difficulty, first of beginning aright, next of being always able to know and choose the right, and of continuing in the right till perfection is ultimately reached. Let him not think that he knows the road to easy victory, nor dream that he can keep himself by his own wisdom; he will do well to follow the psalmist, and become an earnest inquirer asking how he may cleanse his way. Let him become a practical disciple of the holy God, who alone can teach him how to overcome the world, the flesh, and the devil, that trinity of defilers by whom many a hopeful life has been spoiled. He is young and unaccustomed to the road; let him not be ashamed often to inquire his way of him who is so ready and so able to instruct him in it.

Our **way** is a subject which concerns us deeply, but it is not to be answered by unaided reason, nor, when answered, can the directions be carried out by unsupported human power.

By taking heed thereto according to thy word. Young man, the Bible must be your chart, and you must exercise great watchfulness that your way may be according to its directions. You must take heed to your daily life as well as study your Bible, and you must study your Bible that you may take heed to your daily life. To obey the Lord and walk uprightly will need all our heart and soul and mind.

Yet the **word** is absolutely necessary, for otherwise care will darken into morbid anxiety, and conscientiousness may become superstition. It is not enough to desire to be right; for ignorance may make us think that we are doing God service when we are provoking him, and the fact of our ignorance will not reverse the character of our action, however much it may mitigate its criminality. Let each person, young or old, who desires to be holy have a holy watchfulness in his heart, and keep the Holy Bible before his open eye. There he will find every turn of the road marked down, every slough and miry place pointed out, with the way to go through unsoiled; and there, too, he will find light for his darkness, comfort for his weariness, and company for his loneliness, so that by its help he will reach the benediction of the first verse of the psalm, which suggested the psalmist's inquiry, and awakened his desires.

Note how the first section of eight verses has for its first verse, "Blessed are the undefiled in the way," and the second section runs parallel to it, with the question, "Wherewithal shall a young man cleanse his way?" The blessedness which is set before us in a conditional promise should be practically sought for in the way appointed. The Lord says, "For this will I be inquired of by the house of Israel to do it for them."

10. With my whole heart have I sought thee. His heart had gone after God himself: he had not only desired to obey his laws, but to commune with his person. The surest mode of cleansing the way of our life is to seek after God himself, and to endeavor to abide in fellowship with him. Up to the good hour in which he was speaking to his Lord, the psalmist had been an eager seeker after the Lord, and if faint, he was still pursuing. Had he not sought the Lord he would never have been so anxious to cleanse his way. He so powerfully feels the presence of his God that he speaks to him, and prays to him as to one who is near. A true heart cannot long live without fellowship with God. His petition is founded on life's purpose: he is seeking the Lord, and he prays the Lord to prevent his going astray in or from his search. It is by obedience that we follow after God, hence the prayer, **O let me not wander from thy commandments**; for if we leave the ways of God's appointment we certainly shall not find the God who appointed them. The more our whole heart is set upon holiness, the more do we dread falling into sin; we are not so much fearful of deliberate transgression as of inadvertent wandering.

Two things may be very like and yet altogether different: saints are "strangers" (verse 19), but they are not wanderers: they are passing through an enemy's country, but their route is direct; they are seeking their Lord while they traverse this foreign land. Their way is hidden from people; but yet they have not lost their way.

The man of God exerts himself, but does not trust himself: his heart is in his walking with God; but he knows that even his whole strength is not enough to keep him right unless his King is his keeper; hence the prayer, **O let me not wander.**

Where verse 2 pronounces that man blessed who seeks the Lord with his whole heart, the present verse claims the blessing by pleading the character: **With my whole heart have I sought thee.**

11. When a godly person sues for a favor from God he should carefully use every means for obtaining it, and accordingly, as the psalmist had asked to be preserved from wandering, he here shows us the holy precaution which he had taken to prevent his falling into sin. **Thy word have I hid in mine heart.** All that he had of the Word written, and all that had been revealed to him by the voice of God – all, without exception, he had stored away in his affections. He did not wear a text *on* his heart as a charm, but he hid it *in* his heart as a rule. We must mind that what we believe is truly God's Word; that being done, we must hide or treasure it each man for himself; and we must see that this is done, not as a mere feat of the memory, but as the joyful act of the affections.

That I might not sin against thee. Here was the object aimed at. Sinning "against God" is the believer's view of moral evil; other people care only when they offend against people. God's Word is the best preventive against offending God, for it tells us his mind and will, and tends to bring our spirit into conformity with the divine Spirit. No cure for sin in the life is equal to the Word in the seat of life, which is the heart. There is no hiding from sin unless we hide the truth in our souls.

A very pleasant variety of meaning is obtained by laying stress upon the words "thy" and "thee." He speaks *to* God, he loves the Word because it is *God's* Word, and he hates sin because it is sin against *God* himself. If he vexed others, he minded not so long as he did not offend his God. If we would not cause God displeasure we must treasure up his own Word.

The parallelism between the second octave and the first is still continued. Verse 3 speaks of doing no iniquity, while this verse treats of the method of not sinning. This can only be through heart-piety founded on the Scriptures.

12. Blessed art thou, O LORD. These are words of adoration arising out of an intense admiration of the divine character, which the writer is humbly aiming to imitate. No sooner is the Word in the heart than a desire arises to mark and learn it. When food is eaten, the next thing is to digest it; and when the Word is received into the soul the first prayer is, Lord, teach me its meaning. **Teach me thy statutes;** for thus only can I learn the way to be blessed. We need to be disciples or learners – **teach me** – but what an honor to have God himself for a teacher! The Lord put the desire in David's heart when the sacred Word was hidden there, and so we may be sure that he was not too bold in expressing it. The King who ordained the statutes knows best their meaning, and as they are the outcome of his own nature he can best inspire us with their spirit.

13. The taught one of verse 12 is here a teacher himself. What we learn in secret we are to proclaim upon the housetops. What the Lord has revealed it would be shameful for us to conceal. It is a great comfort to a Christian in time of trouble when in looking back upon his past life he can claim to have done his duty by the Word of God. If we have had such regard to that which comes out of God's mouth that we have published it far and wide, we may rest assured that God will respect the prayers which come out of our mouths.

It will be an effectual method of cleansing a young man's way if he addicts himself continually to preaching the Gospel. He cannot go far wrong in judgment whose whole soul is occupied in setting forth the judgments of the Lord. By teaching we learn; by training the tongue to holy speech we master the whole body; by familiarity with the divine procedure we are made to delight in righteousness; and thus in a threefold manner our way is cleansed by our proclaiming the way of the Lord.

14. I have rejoiced in the way of thy testimonies. Delight in the Word of God is a sure proof that it has taken effect upon the heart, and so is cleansing the life. The Way was as dear to David as the Truth and the Life. If he did make a selection, he chose the most practical first. **As much as in all riches.** David knew the riches that come of sovereignty, and which grow out of conquest; he valued the wealth which proceeds from labor, or is gotten by inheritance: he knew **all riches.**

15. I will meditate in thy precepts. He who has an inward delight in anything will not long withdraw his mind from it. No spiritual exercise is more profitable to the soul than that of devout meditation; why are many of us so exceeding slack in it? The preceptory part of God's Word was David's special subject of meditation, and this was the more natural because the question was still upon his mind as to how a young man should cleanse his way. Practical godliness is vital godliness.

And have respect unto thy ways. That is to say, I will think much about them so as to know what thy ways are; and next, I will think much of them so as to have thy ways in great reverence and high esteem.

Note how the verses grow more *inward* as they proceed: from the speech of verse 13 we advanced to the manifested joy of verse 14, and now we come to the secret meditation of the happy spirit. The richest graces are those which dwell deepest.

16. I will delight myself in thy statutes. In this verse delight follows meditation, of which it is the true flower and outgrowth. When we have no other solace, but are quite alone, it will be a glad thing for the heart to turn upon itself and sweetly whisper, **I will delight myself.** But there is no delighting ourselves with anything below that which God intended to be the soul's eternal satisfaction. The statute-book is intended to be the joy of every loyal subject.

I will not forget thy word. Men do not readily forget that which they have treasured up, that which they have meditated upon (verse 15), and that which they have often spoken of (verse 13). Yet since we have treacherous memories it is well to bind them well with the knotted cord of **I will not forget.**

This verse is molded upon verse 8: the changes are rung on the same words, but the meaning is quite different. The same thought is never given over again in this psalm. Something in the position of each verse affects its meaning, so that even where its words are almost identical with those of another the sense is delightfully varied.

17–24. In this section the trials of the way appear to be manifest to the psalmist's mind, and he prays accordingly for the help which will meet his case. As in the last eight verses he prayed as a youth newly come into the world, so here he pleads as a servant and a pilgrim, who growingly finds himself to be a stranger in an enemy's country. His appeal is to God alone, and his prayer is specially direct and personal. He speaks with the Lord as a man speaks with his friend.

17. Deal bountifully with thy servant. He takes pleasure in owning his duty to God, and counts it the joy of his heart to be in the service of his God. Out of his condition he makes a plea: let my wage be according to thy goodness, and not according to my merit. Reward me according to the largeness of thy liberality, and not according to the scantiness of my service. The hired servants of our Father have all of them bread enough and to spare, and he will not leave one of his household to perish with hunger. If the Lord will only treat us as he treats the least of his servants we may be well content, for all his true servants are sons, princes of the blood, heirs of life eternal.

That I may live. Without abundant mercy he could not live. It takes great grace to keep a saint alive. Only the Lord can keep us in being, and it is mighty grace which preserves to us the life which we have forfeited by our sin. It is right to desire to live, it is meet to pray to live, it is just to ascribe long life to the favor of God. Spiritual life, without which this natural life is mere existence, is also to be sought of the Lord's bounty, for it is the noblest work of divine grace, and in it the bounty of God is gloriously displayed. The Lord's servants cannot serve him in their own strength, for they cannot even live unless his grace abounds towards them.

And keep thy word. This should be the rule, the object, and the joy of our life. We may not wish to live and sin; but we may pray to live and keep God's Word. Being is a poor thing if it be not well-being. Life is only worth keeping while we can keep God's Word; indeed, there is no life in the highest sense apart from holiness.

The prayer of this verse shows that it is only through divine bounty or grace that we can live as faithful servants of God, and manifest obedience to his commands. If we give God service it must be because he gives us grace. We work *for* him because he works *in* us. Thus we may make a chain out of the opening verses of the three first octaves of this psalm: verse 1 blesses the holy man, verse 9 asks how we can attain to such holiness, and verse 17 traces such holiness to its secret source, and shows us how to seek the blessing. The more we prize holiness and earnestly strive after it, the more will we be driven towards God for help therein, for we will plainly perceive that our own strength is insufficient.

18. Open thou mine eyes. This is a part of the bountiful dealing which he has asked for. It is far better to have the eyes opened than to be placed in the midst of the noblest prospects and remain blind to their beauty. **That I may**

behold wondrous things out of thy law. Some people can perceive no wonders in the Gospel, but David felt that God had laid up great bounties in his Word, and he begs for power to perceive, appreciate, and enjoy the same. We need not so much that God should give us more benefits, as the ability to see what he has given.

The prayer implies a conscious darkness, a dimness of spiritual vision, a powerlessness to remove that defect, and a full assurance that God can remove it. It shows also that the writer knew that there were vast treasures in the Word which he had not yet fully seen, marvels which he had not yet beheld, mysteries which he had scarcely believed. The Scriptures teem with marvels, yet what are these to closed eyes? And who can open their own eyes, since we are born blind? Scripture needs opening, but not one half so much as our eyes do. What perfect precepts, what precious promises, what priceless privileges are neglected by us because we wander among them like blind people among the beauties of nature, and they are to us as a landscape shrouded in darkness!

The psalmist had a measure of spiritual perception, or he would never have known that there were wondrous things to be seen, nor would he have prayed, **open thou mine eyes**; but what he had seen made him long for a clearer and wider sight. This longing proved the genuineness of what he possessed, for it is a test mark of the true knowledge of God that it causes its possessor to thirst for deeper knowledge.

David's prayer in this verse is a good sequel to verse 10, which corresponds to it in position in its octave: there he said, "O let me not wander," and who is so apt to wander as a blind person? There, too, he declared, "with my whole heart have I sought thee," and hence the desire to see the object of his search.

19. I am a stranger in the earth. This is meant for a plea. By divine command people are bound to be kind to strangers, and what God commands in others he will exemplify in himself. The psalmist was a stranger for God's sake, else he had been as much at home as worldlings are: he was not a stranger to God, but a stranger to the world, a banished man so long as he was out of heaven. Therefore he pleads, **Hide not thy commandments from me.** If these are gone, what have I else? Since nothing around me is mine, what can I do if I lose thy Word? Since none around me know or care to know the way to thyself, what shall I do if I fail to see thy commands, by which alone I can guide my steps to the land where thou dwellest? David implies that God's commands were his solace in exile: they reminded him of home, and showed him the way thither, and therefore he begged that they might never be hidden from him, by his being unable either to understand them or to obey them. This prayer is a supplement to "open thou mine eyes," and as the one prays to see, the other deprecates the negative of seeing, namely, the command being hidden. We do well to look at both sides of the blessing we are seeking, and to plead for it from every point of view.

20. God's **judgments** are his decisions upon points which else had been in dispute. Every precept is a judgment of the highest court upon a point of action, an infallible and immutable decision upon a moral or spiritual question. True godliness lies very much in desires. A high value of the Lord's commandment leads to a pressing desire to know and to do it, and this so weighs upon the soul that it is ready to break in pieces under the crush of its own longings. We may well pray for such longings. **Longing** is the soul of praying, and when the soul longs till it breaks, it cannot be long before the blessing will be granted. The most intimate communion between the soul and its God is carried on by the process described in the text. God reveals his will, and our heart longs to be conformed thereto. God judges, and our heart rejoices in the verdict. Note well that our desire after the mind of God should be constant – **at all times.** Desires which can be put off and on like our garments are at best but mere wishes, and possibly they are hardly true enough to be called by that name – they are temporary emotions born of excitement, and doomed to die when the heat which created them has cooled down.

Remark how this fourth of the third eight chimes with the fourth of the fourth eight. **My soul breaketh**; "my soul melteth."

21. Thou hast rebuked the proud that are cursed. This is one of God's judgments: he is sure to deal out a terrible portion to people of lofty looks. Nobody blesses the proud, and they soon become a burden to themselves. In itself, pride is a plague and torment. Even if no curse came from the law of God, there seems to be a law of nature that the proud should be unhappy. This led David to abhor pride; he dreaded the rebuke of God and the curse of the law. The proud sinners of his day were his enemies, and he felt happy that God was in the quarrel as well as he.

Which do err from thy commandments. Only humble hearts are obedient, for they alone will yield to rule and government. The looks of the proud are too high to mark their own feet and keep the Lord's way. Pride lies at the root of all sin. God rebukes pride even when the multitudes pay homage to it, for he sees in it rebellion against his own majesty, and the seeds of yet further rebellions. People talk of an honest pride; but if they were candid they would see that it is of all sins the least honest, and the least becoming in a creature, and especially in a fallen creature: yet so little of the proud know their own true condition that they censure the godly, and express contempt for them, as may be seen in the next verse. We may well be of good comfort under the rebukes of the ungodly since their power to hurt us is destroyed by the Lord himself.

In the fifth of the former octave the psalmist wrote, "I have desired all the judgments of thy mouth," and here he continues in the same strain, giving a particular instance of the Lord's judgments against haughty rebels. In the next two portions the fifth verses deal with lying and vanity, and pride is one of the most common forms of those evils.

22. Remove from me reproach and contempt. These are painful things to tender minds. David could bear them for righteousness' sake, but they were a heavy yoke, and he longed to be free from them. To be slandered, and then to be despised in consequence of the vile accusation, is a grievous affliction. The one who says, "I care nothing for my reputation" is not wise, for in Solomon's esteem "a good name is better than precious ointment." The best way to deal with slander is to pray about it: God will either remove it, or remove the sting from it. Our own attempts at clearing ourselves are usually failures. Be quiet and let your Advocate plead your cause.

For I have kept thy testimonies. Innocence may justly ask to be cleared from reproach. If there be truth in the charges alleged against us what can we urge with God? If, however, we are wrongfully accused, our appeal cannot be refused. If through fear of reproach we forsake the divine testimony we shall deserve the coward's doom; our safety lies in sticking close to the true and to the right. God will keep those who keep his testimonies. A good conscience is the best security for a good name; reproach will not abide with those who abide with Christ, neither will contempt remain upon those who remain faithful to the ways of the Lord.

This verse stands as a parallel both in sense and position to verse 6, and it has the catchword of **testimonies,** by which it chimes with verse 14.

23. Princes also did sit and speak against me. They saw in David a greatness which they envied, and therefore they abused him. On their thrones they might have found something better to consider and speak about, but they turned the seat of judgment into the seat of the scorner. To be spoken ill of by a great man is a great discouragement to most people, but the psalmist bore it with holy calmness. Many of the lordly ones were his enemies, and made it their business to speak ill of him; yet he survived all their attempts upon him.

But thy servant did meditate in thy statutes. This was brave indeed. He was God's servant, and therefore he attended to his Master's business and felt sure his Master would defend him. The rabble of princes were not worth five minutes' thought, if those five minutes had to be taken from holy meditation. It is very beautiful to see the two sittings: the princes sitting to reproach David, and David sitting with his God and his Bible, answering his traducers by never answering them at all. Those who feed upon the Word grow strong and peaceful, and are by God's grace hidden from the strife of tongues.

Note that in the close of the former octave he had said, "I will meditate," and here he shows how he had redeemed his promise, even under great provocation to forget it. It is a praiseworthy thing when the resolve of our happy hours is duly carried out in our seasons of affliction.

24. Thy testimonies also are my delight and my counselors. They were not only themes for meditation, but **also** sources of delight and means of guidance. While his enemies took counsel with each other, the holy man took counsel with the testimonies of God. The words of the Lord serve us for many purposes; in our sorrows they are our delight, and in our difficulties they are our guide; we derive joy from them and discover wisdom in them. When we follow their counsel it must not be with reluctance but with delight. This is the safest way of dealing with those who plot for our ruin; let us give more heed to the true testimonies of the Lord than to the false witness of our foes.

In verse 16 David said, "I will delight in thy statutes," and here he says, "they **are my delight**": thus resolutions formed in God's strength come to fruit, and spiritual desires ripen into actual attainments.

25–32. Here, it seems to me, we have the psalmist in trouble bewailing the bondage to earthly things in which he finds his mind to be held. His soul cleaves to the dust, melts for heaviness, and cries for enlargement from its spiritual prison. In these verses we shall see the influence of the divine word upon a heart which laments its downward tendencies, and is filled with mourning because of its deadening surroundings. The Word of the Lord arouses prayer (verses 25–29), confirms choice (verse 30), and inspires renewed resolve (verse 32): it is in all tribulation of body or mind the surest source of help.

25. My soul cleaveth unto the dust. He means in part that he was full of sorrow; for mourners in the east cast dust on their heads, and sat in ashes, and the psalmist felt as if these signs of woe were glued to him, and his very soul was made to cleave to them because of his powerlessness to rise above his grief. Does he not also mean that he felt ready to die? Did he not feel his life absorbed and fast held by the grave's mold, half choked by the death-dust? It may not be straining the language if we conceive that he also felt and bemoaned his earthly-mindedness and spiritual deadness. There was a tendency in his soul to cling to earth which he greatly bewailed. Whatever was the cause of his complaint, it was no surface evil, but an affair of the inmost spirit; his **soul** cleaved to the dust; and it was a continuous and powerful tendency. But what a mercy that the good man could feel and deplore whatever there was of evil in the cleaving! Many are of the earth, and never lament it; only the heaven-born and heaven-soaring spirit pines at the thought of being fastened to this world and bird-limed by its sorrows or its pleasures.

Quicken thou me according to thy word. More life is the cure for all our ailments. Only the Lord can give it. He can bestow it at once, and do it according to his Word, without departing from the usual course of his grace, as we see it mapped out in the Scriptures. It is well to know what to pray for; David seeks quickening: one would have thought that he would have asked for comfort of upraising, but he knew that these would come out of increased life, and therefore he sought that blessing which is the root of the rest. When a person is depressed in spirit, weak, and bent towards the ground, the main thing is to increase his stamina and put more life into him. The phrase **according to thy**

word means "according to thy revealed way of quickening thy saints." The Word of God shows us that he who first made us must keep us alive, and it tells us of the Spirit of God who through the ordinances pours fresh life into our souls. Perhaps David remembered the word of the Lord in Deuteronomy 32:39, where Jehovah claims both to kill and to make alive, and he beseeches the Lord to exercise that life-giving power.

Note how this first verse of the 4th octave tallies with the first of the third (verse 17) – "that I may live."

26. I have declared my ways. Open confession is good for the soul. Nothing brings more ease and more life to a man than a frank acknowledgment of the evil which has caused the sorrow and the lethargy. Such a declaration proves that the man knows his own condition and is no longer blinded by pride. Our confessions are not meant to make God know our sins, but to make us know them. **And thou heardest me.** His confession had been accepted; it was not lost labor; God had drawn near to him in it. We ought never to go from a duty till we have been accepted in it. Pardon follows upon penitent confession, and David felt that he had obtained it.

Teach me thy statutes. Being truly sorry for his fault, and having obtained full forgiveness, he is anxious to avoid offending again, and hence he begs to be taught obedience. Justified people always long to be sanctified. When God forgives our sins, we are all the more fearful of sinning again. Mercy, which pardons transgression, sets us longing for grace which prevents transgression. We may boldly ask for more when God has given us much; he who has washed out the past stain will not refuse that which will preserve us from present and future defilement. This cry for teaching is frequent in the psalm; in verse 12 it followed a sight of God, and here it follows from a sight of self.

27. Make me to understand the way of thy precepts. Give me a deep insight into the practical meaning of thy Word; let me get a clear idea of the tone and tenor of thy law. Blind obedience has but small beauty; God would have us follow him with our eyes open. To obey the letter of the Word is all that the ignorant can hope for; if we wish to keep God's precepts in their spirit we must come to an understanding of them, and that can be gained nowhere but at the Lord's hands. The psalmist is not anxious to understand the prophecies, but the precepts, and he is not concerned about the subtleties of the law, but the commonplaces and everyday rules of it.

So shall I talk of thy wondrous works. It is ill talking of what we do not understand. We must be taught of God till we understand, and then we may hope to communicate our knowledge to others with a hope of profiting them. Talk without intelligence is mere talk, and idle talk. When our heart has been opened to understand, our lips should be opened to impart knowledge; and we may hope to be taught ourselves when we feel in our hearts a willingness to teach the way of the Lord to those among whom we dwell.

Thy wondrous works. We see that the clearest understanding does not cause us to cease from wondering at the ways and works of God. Much of the wonder in the world is born of ignorance, but holy wonder is the child of understanding. When a man understands the way of the divine precepts he never talks of his own works. Some in this place read "meditate" or "muse" instead of **talk**; if we read the passage in this sense, we take it to mean that in proportion as David understood the Word of God he would meditate upon it and more. The thoughtless care not to know the inner meaning of the Scriptures, while those who know them best strive after a greater familiarity with them.

Observe the third verse of the last eight (verse 19), and see how the sense is akin to this. There he was a stranger in the earth, and here he prays to know his way; there, too, he prayed that the Word might not be hid from himself, and here he promises that he will not hide it from others.

28. My soul melteth for heaviness. He was dissolving away in tears. Heaviness of heart is a killing thing, and when it abounds it threatens to turn life into a long death. There is one good point in this downcast state, for it is better to be melted with grief than to be hardened by impenitence.

Strengthen thou me according to thy word. His hope in this state of depression lies not in himself but in his God. He asks for nothing more than to be dealt with after the recorded manner of the Lord of mercy. Grace can enable us to bear the constant fret of an abiding sorrow; it can give the believer the garment of praise for the spirit of heaviness. Let us always resort to prayer in our despondent times, for it is the surest and shortest way out of the depths. In that prayer let us plead nothing but the Word of God; for there is no plea like a promise, no argument like a word from our covenant God.

29. Remove from me the way of lying. This is the way of sin, error, idolatry, folly, self-righteousness, formalism, hypocrisy. David cannot endure to have it near him. He desired to be true and in the truth, but he feared that a measure of falsehood would cling to him unless the Lord took it away, and therefore he earnestly cried for its removal. False motives may at times sway us, and we may fall into mistaken notions of our own spiritual condition before God, which erroneous conceits may be kept up by a natural prejudice in our own favor, and so we may be confirmed in a delusion, and abide in our error unless grace comes to the rescue.

And grant me thy law graciously. David wishes to have the law opened up to his understanding, engraved upon his heart, and carried out in his life. If the law be not in our hearts the lie will enter. David would seem to have remembered those times when, according to the eastern fashion, he had practiced deceit for his own preservation, and he saw that he had been weak and erring upon that point; therefore he was bowed down in spirit and begged to be quickened and delivered from transgressing in that manner any more. Holy people cannot review their sins without tears, nor weep over them without intreating to be saved from further offending. There is an evident opposition between falsehood and the gracious power of God's law. The only way to expel the lie is to accept the truth. Grace and truth are ever linked together, and a belief of the doctrines of grace is a grand preservative from deadly error.

In the fifth of the preceding octave (verse 21) David cries out against pride, and here against lying. These are much the same thing. Is not pride the greatest of all lies?

30. I have chosen the way of truth. People do not drop into the right way by chance; they must choose it, and continue to choose it, or they will soon wander from it. There is a doctrinal way of truth which we ought to choose, rejecting every dogma of human devising; there is a ceremonial way of truth, detesting all the forms which apostate churches have invented; and then there is a practical way of truth, the way of holiness, to which we must adhere whatever may be our temptation to forsake it.

Thy judgments have I laid before me. What he had chosen he kept in mind, laying it out before his mind's eye. People do not become holy by a careless wish; there must be study, consideration, deliberation, and earnest inquiry. The commands of God must be set before us as the mark to aim at, the model to work by, the road to walk in. If we put God's judgments into the background we shall soon find ourselves departing from them.

Here again the sixth stanzas of the third and fourth octaves ring out a similar note.

31. I have stuck unto thy testimonies, or "I have cleaved," for the word is the same as in verse 25. He has kept fast hold of the divine Word. This was his comfort, and his faith stuck to it, his love and his obedience held on to it, his heart and his mind abode in meditation upon it. His choice was so heartily and deliberately made that he stuck to it for life. It is pleasant to look back upon past perseverance and to expect grace to continue equally steadfast in the future. He who has enabled us to stick to him will surely stick to us.

O LORD, put me not to shame. This would happen if God's promises were unfulfilled, and if the heart of God's servant was allowed to fail. This we have no reason to fear, since the Lord is faithful to his Word. But it might also happen through the believer's acting in an inconsistent manner, as David had himself once done, when he fell into the way of lying, and pretended to be a madman. If we are not true to our profession we may be left to reap the fruit of our folly, and that will be the bitter thing called **shame.** A believer ought never to be ashamed, but act the part of a brave person who has done nothing to be ashamed of in believing his God, and does not mean to adopt a craven tone in the presence of the Lord's enemies. If we beseech the Lord not to put us to shame, surely we ought not ourselves to be ashamed without cause.

The prayer of this verse is found in the parallel verse of the next section (verse 39): "Turn away my reproach which I fear." A brave heart is more wounded by shame than by any weapon which a soldier's hand can wield.

32. I will run the way of thy commandments. With energy, promptness, and zeal he would perform the will of God, but he needed more life and liberty from the hand of God. **When thou shalt enlarge my heart.** Let the affections be aroused and eagerly set on divine things, and our actions will be full of force, swiftness, and delight. God must work in us first, and then we shall will and do according to his good pleasure. He must change the heart, and enlarge the heart, and then the course of life will be gracious, sincere, happy, and earnest; so we must attribute all to the free favor of our God. We must run, for grace is not an overwhelming force which compels unwilling minds to move contrary to their will: our running is the spontaneous leaping forward of a mind which has been set free by the hand of God, and delights to show its freedom by its bounding speed.

What a change from verse 25 to the present, from cleaving to the dust to running in the way. It is the excellence of holy sorrow that it works in us the quickening for which we seek, and then we show the sincerity of our grief and the reality of our revival by being zealous in the ways of the Lord.

For the third time an octave closes with **I will.** The **I wills** of the psalms are right worthy of being each one the subject of study and discourse.

Note how the heart has been spoken of up to this point; there are many more allusions further on, and these all go to show what heart-work David's religion was.

33–40. A sense of dependence and a consciousness of extreme need pervade this section, which is all made up of prayer and plea. The former eight verses trembled with a sense of sin, quivering with a childlike sense of weakness and folly, which caused the man of God to cry out for the help by which alone his soul could be preserved from falling back into sin.

33. Teach me, LORD, the way of thy statutes. Alas for those who will never be taught. They dote upon their own wisdom; but their folly is apparent to all who rightly judge. The psalmist will have the Lord for his teacher, for he feels that his heart will not learn of any less effectual instructor. A sense of great slowness to learn drives us to seek a great teacher. The holy man would not only learn the **statues** but the **way** of them, the daily use of them. The very desire to learn this way is in itself an assurance that we shall be taught therein, for he who made us long to learn will be sure to gratify the desire.

And I shall keep it unto the end. Those who are taught of God never forget their lessons, but those who commence without the Lord's teaching soon forget what they learn, and start aside from the way upon which they professed to have entered. No one may boast that he will hold on his way in his own strength, for that must depend on the continual teaching of the Lord. It is a great comfort to know that it is the way with God to keep the feet of his saints, yet we are to watch as if our keeping of the way depended wholly on ourselves; for, according to this verse, our perseverance rests not on any force or compulsion, but on the teaching of the Lord, and no one can teach someone who refuses to learn. The **end** of which David speaks is the end of life, or the fullness of obedience. He trusted in grace to make him faithful to the utmost. As Christ loves us to the end, so must we serve him to the end. The end of divine teaching is that we may persevere to the end.

The portions of eight show a relationship still. Verse 17 has a prayer for life, that he may keep the Word; verse 25 cries for more life, according to that Word; and now comes a prayer for teaching, that he may keep the way of God's statutes. If a keen eye is turned upon these verses a closer affinity will be discerned.

34. Give me understanding, and I shall keep thy law. This is the same prayer enlarged, or rather it is a supplement which intensifies it. He not only needs teachings, but the power to learn: he requires not only to understand, but to obtain an **understanding.** How low has sin brought us, for we even lack the faculty to understand spiritual things. Will God in very deed give us understanding? This is a miracle of grace. It will, however, never be wrought upon us till we know our need of it; and we shall not even discover that need till God gives us a measure of understanding to perceive it. We are in a state of complicated ruin, from which nothing but manifold grace can deliver us. We are not to seek this blessing that we may be famous for wisdom, but that we may be abundant in our love to the law of God. The Gospel gives us grace to keep the law; there is no way of reaching to holiness but by accepting the gift of God. If God gives, we keep; but we never keep the law in order to obtain grace. The sure result of regeneration, or the bestowal of understanding, is a devout reverence for the law and a resolute keeping of it in the heart. The Spirit of God makes us to know the Lord and to understand somewhat of his love, wisdom, holiness, and majesty; and the result is that we honor the law and yield our hearts to the obedience of the faith.

Yea, I shall observe it with my whole heart. The understanding operates upon the affections; it convinces the heart of the beauty of the law, so that the soul loves it with all its powers; and then it reveals the majesty of the Lawgiver, and the whole nature bows before his supreme will. An enlightened judgment heals the divisions of the heart, and bends the united affections to a strict and watchful observance of the one rule of life. He alone obeys God who can say, "My Lord, I would serve thee, and do it with all my heart"; and none can truly say this till they have received as a free grant the inward illumination of the Holy Spirit.

Observe the parallel of verses 2 and 10 where the **whole heart** is spoken of in reference to seeking, and in verse 58 in pleading for mercy; these are all second verses in their octaves. The frequent repetition of this phrase shows the importance of undivided love. The heart is never one with God till it is one within itself.

35. Thou hast made me to love the way; now make me to move in it. This is the cry of a child that longs to walk, but is too feeble; of a pilgrim who is exhausted. We shall not go into the narrow path till we are made to do so by the Maker's own power. O thou who didst once make me, I pray thee make me again: thou hast made me to know; now make me to go. The psalmist does not ask the Lord to do for him what he ought to do for himself: he wishes himself to **go** or tread in the path of the command. Grace does not treat us as stones, to be dragged, but as creatures endowed with life, reason, will, and active powers, who are willing and able to do of themselves if once made to do so. The holiness we seek after is not a forced compliance with command, by the indulgence of a whole-hearted passion for goodness, such as shall conform our life to the will of the Lord. Where the heart already finds its joy the feet are sure to follow.

Note that the corresponding verse in the former eight (verse 35) was "Make me to understand," and here we have "make me to go." A clear understanding is a great assistance towards practical action.

36. Incline my heart unto thy testimonies. It may be that David felt a wandering desire, an inordinate leaning of his soul to worldly gain; possibly it even intruded into his most devout meditations, and at once he cried out for more grace. The only way to cure a wrong leaning is to have the soul bent in the opposite direction. Holiness of heart is the cure for covetousness. What a blessing it is that we may ask the Lord even for an inclination. Our wills are free and yet, without violating their liberty, grace can incline us in the right direction. This can be done by enlightening the understanding as to the excellence of obedience, by strengthening our habits of virtue and by many other ways. If any one duty is irksome to us it behooves us to offer this prayer with special reference thereto: we are to love all the Lord's testimonies, and if we fail in any one point we must pay double attention to it. The leaning of the heart is the way in which the life will lean; happy shall we be when we feel habitually inclined to all that is good.

And not to covetousness. This is the inclination of nature; it dethrones God; it is selfishness and sordid greed, a degrading, groveling, hardening, deadening sin, which withers everything around it that is lovely and Christlike. He who is covetous is of the race of Judas, and will in all probability turn out to be himself a son of perdition. The crime is common, but very few will confess it.

37. Turn away mine eyes from beholding iniquity. He had prayed about his heart; if the eyes do not see, perhaps the heart may not desire. The prayer is not so much that the eyes shall be shut as turned away, for we need to have them open, but directed to right objects. It is a proof of the sense of weakness felt by the psalmist and of his entire dependence upon God that he even asks to have his eyes turned for him; he meant not to make himself passive, but he intended to set forth his own utter helplessness apart from the grace of God.

For fear he should forget himself and gaze with a lingering longing upon forbidden objects, he intreats the Lord speedily to make him turn away his eyes, hurrying him off from so dangerous a parley with iniquity.

And quicken thou me in thy way. Give me so much life that dead vanity may have no power over me. Enable me to travel so swiftly on the road to heaven that I may not stop long enough within sight of vanity to be fascinated thereby. The prayer indicates our greatest need – more life in our obedience. If we would be full of life as to the things of God we must keep ourselves apart from sin and folly, or the eyes will soon captivate the mind, and, like Samson, who could slay his thousands, we may ourselves be overcome through the lusts which enter by the eye.

38. Stablish thy word unto thy servant. Make me sure of thy sure Word. If we possess the spirit of service, and yet are troubled with skeptical thoughts, we cannot do better than pray to be established in the truth. Times will arise when every doctrine and promise seems to be shaken, and our mind gets no rest: then we must appeal to God for establishment in the faith. Practical holiness is a great help towards doctrinal certainty: if we are God's servants he will confirm his Word in our experience. Atheism in the heart is a horrible plague to a God-fearing man; it brings more torment with it than can well be described; and nothing but a visitation of grace can settle the soul after it has been violently assailed thereby. Vanity or falsehood is bad for the eyes, but it is even worse when it defiles the understanding and casts a doubt upon the Word of the living God.

Who is devoted to thy fear, or simply "to thy fear." That is, make good thy Word to godly fear wherever it exists; strengthen the whole body of reverent people. Or, again, it may mean, "Stablish thy Word to thy fear," namely, that people may be led to fear thee, since a sure faith in the divine promise is the fountain and foundation of godly fear. People will never worship a God in whom they do not believe. We cannot look for the fulfillment of promises in our experience unless we live under the influence of holy watchfulness and prayerful energy. We shall never be rooted and grounded in our belief unless we daily practice what we profess to believe. Full assurance is the reward of obedience.

39. Turn away my reproach which I fear. He feared just reproach, trembling lest he should cause the enemy to blaspheme through any glaring inconsistency. We ought to fear this, and watch that we may avoid it. Persecution in the form of calumny may also be prayed against, for it is perhaps the sorest of trials to sensitive minds. We shall be kept from lies if we keep from lies.

For thy judgments are good. Therefore he is anxious that none may speak evil of the ways of God through hearing an ill report about himself. We mourn when we are slandered, because the shame is cast rather upon our religion than ourselves. If men would be content to attribute evil *to us*, and go no further, we might bear it, for we are evil; but our sorrow is that they cast a slur upon the Word and character of God. When people rail at God's government of the world it is our duty and privilege to stand up for him, and openly to declare before him, **thy judgments are good**; and we should do the same when they assail the Bible, the Gospel, the law, or the name of our Lord Jesus Christ. But we must take heed that they can bring no truthful accusation against us, or our testimony will be so much wasted breath.

This prayer against reproach is parallel to verse 31, and in general to many other of the seventh verses in the octaves, which usually imply opposition from without and a sacred satisfaction within.

40. Behold, I have longed after thy precepts. He can at least claim sincerity. He is deeply bowed down by a sense of his weakness and need of grace; but he does desire to be in all things conformed to the divine will. Where our longings are, there are we in the sight of God. If we have not attained perfection, it is something to have hungered after it. He who has given us to desire will also grant us to obtain. The precepts are grievous to the ungodly, and therefore when we are so changed as to long for them we have clear evidence of conversion, and we may safely conclude that he who has begun the good work will carry it on. **Quicken me in thy righteousness.** Give me more life wherewith to follow thy righteous law; or give me more life because thou hast promised to hear prayer, and it is according to thy righteousness to keep thy word. We need quickening every hour of the day, for we are so sadly apt to become slow and languid in the ways of God. It is the Holy Spirit who can pour new life into us; let us not cease crying to him. Let the life we already possess show itself by longing for more.

The last verses of the octaves have generally exhibited an onward look of resolve, hope, and prayer. Here past fruits of grace are made the plea for further blessing.

41–48. In these verses holy fear is apparent and prominent. The man of God trembles lest in any way or degree the Lord should remove his favor from him. The eight verses are one continued pleading for the abiding of grace in his soul, and it is supported by such holy arguments as would only suggest themselves to a spirit burning with love to God.

41. Let thy mercies come also unto me, O Lord. He desires mercy as well as teaching, for he was guilty as well as ignorant. He needed much mercy and varied mercy, hence the request is in the plural. He needed mercy from God rather than mercy from man, and so he asks for **thy mercies.** The way sometimes seemed blocked, and therefore he begs that the mercies may have their way cleared by God, and may **come** to him. It may be that under a sense of unworthiness the writer feared lest mercy should be given to others and not to himself.

Even thy salvation. This is the sum and crown of all mercies – deliverance from all evil, both now and forever. Here is the first mention of salvation in the psalm, and it is joined with mercy; salvation is styled **thy salvation,** thus ascribing it wholly to the Lord. What a mass of mercies are heaped together in the one salvation of our Lord Jesus! It includes the mercies which spare us before our conversion, and lead up to it. Then comes calling mercy, regenerating mercy, converting mercy, justifying mercy, pardoning mercy. Nor can we excluded from complete salvation any of those many mercies which are needed to conduct the believer safe to glory. Salvation is an aggregate of mercies incalculable in number, priceless in value, incessant in application, eternal in endurance. To the God of our mercies be glory, world without end.

According to thy word. The way of salvation is described in the Word, salvation itself is promised in the Word, and its inward manifestation is wrought by the Word. David loved the Scriptures, but he was not satisfied to read the Word: he longed to experience its inner sense.

Note that in verse 33 the psalmist prayed to be taught to keep God's Word, and here he begs the Lord to keep his Word. In the first case he longed to come to the God of mercies, and here he would have the Lord's mercies come to him; there he sought grace to persevere in faith, and here he seeks the end of his faith, namely the salvation of his soul.

42. So shall I have wherewith to answer him that reproacheth me. When God, by granting us salvation, gives to our prayers an answer of peace, we are ready at once to answer the objections of the unbeliever, the quibbles of the skeptical, and the sneers of the contemptuous. Revilers should be answered, and hence we may expect the Lord to save his people in order that a weapon may be put into their hands with which to rout his adversaries.

For I trust in thy word. His faith was seen by his being trustful while under trial, and he pleads it as a reason why he should be helped to beat back reproaches by a happy experience. Faith is our argument when we seek mercies and salvation, faith in the Lord who has spoken to us in his Word. Whoever can truly make this declaration has received power to become a child of God, and so to be the heir of unnumbered mercies. If any reproach us for trusting in God, we reply to them with arguments the most conclusive when we show that God has kept his promises, heard our prayers and supplied our needs. Even the most skeptical are forced to bow before the logic of facts.

In this second verse of this eight the psalmist makes a confession of faith, and a declaration of his belief and experience. He does the same in the corresponding verses of the sections which follow.

43. And take not the word of truth utterly out of my mouth. Do not prevent my pleading for thee by leaving me without deliverance; for how could I continue to proclaim thy word if I found it fail me? Such would seem to be the meaning. The Word of truth cannot be a joy to our mouths unless we have an experience of it in our lives, and it may be wise for us to be silent if we cannot support our testimonies by the verdict of our consciousness. This prayer may also refer to other modes by which we may be disabled from speaking in the name of the Lord: as, for instance, by our falling into open sin, by our becoming depressed and despairing, by our laboring under sickness or mental aberration, by our finding no door of utterance, or meeting with no willing audience.

For I have hoped in thy judgments. He had expected God to appear and vindicate his cause, so he might speak with confidence concerning his faithfulness. What God says in the Scriptures he actually performs in his government; we may therefore look for him to show himself strong in the behalf of his own threatenings and promises, and we shall not look in vain.

God's ministers are sometimes silenced through the sins of their people, and it becomes them to plead against such a judgment.

In the close of this verse there is a declaration of what the psalmist had done in reference to the Word of the Lord, and in this the thirds of the octaves are often alike (see verses 35, 43, 51, 67, 83, 99, etc.).

44. So shall I keep thy law continually for ever and ever. Nothing more effectually binds a man to the way of the Lord than an experience of the truth of his Word, embodied in the form of mercies and deliverances. Not only does the Lord's faithfulness open our mouths against his adversaries, but it also knits our hearts to his fear, and makes our union with him more and more intense. Great mercies lead us to an inexpressible gratitude. God's grace alone can enable us to keep his commandments without break and without end; eternal love must grant us eternal life, and out of this will come everlasting obedience. There is no other way to ensure our perseverance in holiness but by the Word of truth abiding in us; so David prayed it might abide with him. The verse begins with **So,** as did verse 42. When God grants his salvation we are *so* favored that we silence our enemy and glorify our best friend.

David prayed that the word of truth might not be taken out of his mouth, and so would he keep God's law: that is to say, by public testimony as well as by personal life he would fulfill the divine will, and confirm the bonds which bound him to the Lord forever. Undoubtedly the grace which enables us to bear witness with the mouth is a great help to ourselves as well as to others: we feel that the vows of the Lord are upon us, and that we cannot run back.

45. The Spirit of holiness is a free Spirit; he sets people at liberty and enables them to resist every effort to bring them under subjection. The more we seek after the perfection of our obedience, the more shall we enjoy complete emancipation from every form of spiritual slavery.

The verse is united to verse 44, for it begins with the word **And.** It mentions another of the benefits expected from the coming of mercies from God: liberty. He says **I will walk,** indicating his daily progress through life; **at liberty,** as one who is out of prison, unimpeded by adversaries, unencumbered with burdens, unshackled, allowed a wide range, and roaming without fear. Such liberty would be dangerous if a man were seeking himself or his own lusts; but when the one object sought after is the will of God, there can be no need to restrain the searcher. He said he would keep the law, but here he speaks of seeking it. Does he not mean that he will obey what he knows, and endeavor to know more? Is not this the way to the highest form of liberty – to be always laboring to know the mind of God and to be conformed to it? Those who *keep* the law are sure to **seek** it, and bestir themselves to keep it more and more.

46. He is free from fear of the greatest, proudest, and most tyrannical people. David was called to stand before kings when he was an exile; and afterwards, when he was himself a monarch, he knew the tendency of people to sacrifice their religion to pomp and statecraft; but it was his resolve to do nothing of the kind. He would sanctify politics, and make cabinets know that the Lord alone is governor among the nations. As a king he would speak to kings concerning the King of kings. He says, **I will speak**: prudence might have suggested that his life and conduct would be enough, and that it would be better not to touch upon religion in the presence of royal personages who worshiped other gods, and claimed to be right in so doing. He had already most fittingly preceded this resolve by the declaration, "I will walk," but he does not make his personal conduct an excuse for sinful silence, for he adds, **I will speak**. David claimed religious liberty, and took care to use it, for he spoke out what he believed, even when he was in the highest company. In what he said he took care to keep to God's own Word, for he says, **I will speak of *thy testimonies***. No theme is like this, and there is no way of handling that theme like keeping close to the Book, and using its thought and language. The great hindrance to our speaking upon holy topics in all companies is shame, but the psalmist will **not be ashamed**; there is nothing to be ashamed of, and yet many are as quiet as the dead for fear some creature like themselves should be offended. When God gives grace, cowardice soon vanishes.

47. Next to liberty and courage comes delight. When we have done our duty, we find a great reward in it. If David had not spoken for his Master before kings, he would have been afraid to think of the law which he had neglected; but after speaking up for his Lord he feels a sweet serenity of heart when musing upon the word. Obey the command and you will love it. After speaking of the law the psalmist retired to meditate upon it; he discoursed and then he delighted; he preached and then repaired to his study to renew his strength by feeding yet again upon the precious truth. The verse is in the future, and hence it sets forth not only what David had done but what he would do. He knew that grace would keep him in the same condition of heart towards the precepts of the Lord, so that he would throughout his whole life take a supreme delight in holiness. Here for the first time love is expressly spoken of. It is here coupled with delight, and in verse 165 with "great peace." See also verses 47, 97, 113, 119, 127, 140, 159, 163, 165, 167.

48. My hands also will I lift up unto thy commandments, which I have loved.

He will stretch out towards perfection as far as he can, hoping to reach it one day; when his hands hang down he will cheer himself out of languor by the prospect of glorifying God by obedience; and he will give solemn sign of his hearty assent and consent to all that his God commands. The phrase "lift up my hands" is very full of meaning. Again he declares his love, for a true heart loves to express itself. It was natural that he should reach out towards a law which he delighted in, just as a child holds out its hands to receive a gift which it longs for. When such a lovely object as holiness is set before us, we are bound to rise towards it with our whole nature, and till that is fully accomplished we should at least lift up our hands in prayer towards it. Where holy hands and holy hearts go, the whole man will one day follow.

And I will meditate in thy statutes. He can never have enough of meditation upon the mind of God. The prayer of verse 41 is already fulfilled in the person who is struggling upward and studying deeply. The whole of this verse may be viewed not only as a determination of David's mind, but as a result which he knew would follow from the Lord's sending him his mercies and his salvation. When mercy comes down, our hands will be lifted up; happy is the person who stands with hands uplifted both to receive the blessing and to obey the precept; he will not wait upon the Lord in vain.

49–56. These verses deal with the comfort of the Word. They begin by seeking the main consolation, namely the Lord's fulfillment of his promise, and then show how the Word sustains us under affliction and makes us so impervious to ridicule that we are moved by the harsh conduct of the wicked rather to horror of their sin than to any submission to their temptations. We are then shown how the Scripture furnishes songs for pilgrims, and memories for night-watchers; and the psalm concludes by the general statement that the whole of this happiness and comfort arises out of keeping the statutes of the Lord.

49. Remember the word unto thy servant. He asks for no new promise, but to have the old Word fulfilled. He is grateful that he has received so good a Word; he embraces it with all his heart, and now intreats the Lord to deal with him according to it. He does not say, "remember my service to thee," but "thy Word to me." The words of masters to servants are not always such that servants wish their lords to remember them, for they usually observe the faults and failings of the work done, inasmuch as it does not tally with the word of command. But we who serve the best of masters are not anxious to have one of his words fall to the ground, since the Lord will so kindly remember his word of command as to give us grace wherewith we may obey, and he will couple with it a remembrance of his word of promise, so that our hearts will be comforted. The psalmist does not fear a failure in the Lord's memory, but he makes use of the promise as a plea, and this is the form in which he speaks after the manner of men when they plead with one another. When the Lord remembers the sins of his servant, and brings them before his conscience, the penitent cries, Lord, remember thy word of pardon, and therefore remember my sins and iniquities no more. There is a world of meaning in that word **remember,** as it is addressed to God; it is used in Scripture in the tenderest sense, and suits the sorrowing and the depressed. In the present instance the prayer is as personal as the "Remember me" of the thief, for its essence lies in the words **unto thy servant.** It would be all in vain for us if the promise were remembered to all others if it did not come true to ourselves; but there is no fear, for the Lord has never forgotten a single promise to a single believer.

Upon which thou hast caused me to hope. God, having given grace to hope in the promise, would surely never disappoint that hope. He cannot have caused us to hope without cause. If we hope upon his Word we have a sure basis: our gracious Lord would never mock us by exciting false hope. The verse is the prayer of love fearing to be forgotten, of humility conscious of insignificance and anxious not to be overlooked, of penitence trembling lest the evil of its sin should overshadow the promise, of eager desire longing for the blessing, and of holy confidence which feels that all that is wanted is comprehended in the Word. Let but the Lord remember his promise, and the promised act is as good as done.

50. Thy Word is my comfort, or the fact that thy words has brought quickening to me is my comfort. Or he means that the hope which God had given him was his comfort, for God had quickened him thereby. Whatever may be the exact sense, it is clear that the psalmist had affliction peculiar to himself – **my affliction** – that he had comfort in it specially his own – **my comfort** – and that he knew what the comfort was, and where it came from – **this is my comfort.** The man whose hope comes from God feels the life-giving power of the Word of the Lord. Comfort in affliction is like a lamp in a dark place. Some are unable to find comfort at such times, but it is not so with believers, for their Saviour has said to them, "I will not leave you comfortless." God's Word frequently comforts us by increasing the force of our inner life – **thy word hath quickened me.** Often the near way to consolation is sanctification and invigoration. If we cannot clear away the fog, it may be better to rise to a higher level, and so to get above it. Troubles which weigh us down while we are half dead become mere trifles when we are full of life. Thus have we often been raised in spirit by quickening grace, and the same thing will happen again, for the Comforter is still with us, the Consolation of Israel ever lives, and the very God of peace is evermore our Father. On looking back upon our past life there is one ground of comfort as to our state – the Word of God has made us alive, and kept us so. We were dead, but we are dead no longer. From this we gladly infer that if the Lord had meant to destroy he would not have quickened us. If we were only hypocrites worthy of derision, he would not have revived us by his grace. An experience of quickening is a fountain of good cheer.

See how this verse is turned into a prayer in verse 107. Experience teaches us how to pray, and furnishes arguments in prayer.

51. The proud have had me greatly in derision. The proud never love gracious people, and as long as they fear them they veil their fear under a pretended contempt. In this case their hatred revealed itself in ridicule loud and long. They made sport of David because he was God's servant. People who are short of wit can generally provoke a broad grin by jesting at a saint. Conceited sinners make footballs of the godly; hatred of sin sets their tongues wagging at long-faced puritanism and strait-laced hypocrisy. If David was greatly derided, we may not expect to escape the scorn of the ungodly. It is the nature of the son of the bondwoman to mock the child of the promise.

Yet have I not declined from thy law. The deriders laughed, but they did not win. The godly man, so far from turning aside from the right way, did not even slacken his pace, or in any sense fall off from his holy habits. Many would have declined, many have declined, but David did not do so. It is paying too much honor to fools to yield half a point to them. Their unhallowed mirth will not harm us if we pay no attention to it.

From verse 61 we note that David was not overcome by the spoiling of his goods any more than by these cruel mockings. See also verse 157, where the multitude of persecutors and enemies were baffled in their attempts to make him decline from God's ways.

52. When we see no present display of the divine power it is wise to fall back upon the records of former ages, since they are just as available as if the transactions were of yesterday, seeing the Lord is always the same. As the histories of the olden times are full of divine interpositions it is well to be thoroughly acquainted with them. Moreover, if we are advanced in years we have the providences of our early days to review, and these should by no means be forgotten or left out of our thoughts. The argument is good and solid: he who has shown himself strong on behalf of his believing people is the immutable God, and therefore we may expect deliverance at his hands. The grinning of the proud will not trouble us when we remember how the Lord dealt with their predecessors. While in our own hearts we humbly drink of the mercy of God in quietude, we are not without comfort in seasons of turmoil and derision, for then we resort to God's justice, and remember how he scoffs at the scoffers (Psalm 2:4).

When he was greatly derided the psalmist did not sit down in despair, but rallied his spirits. He knew that comfort is needful for strength in service, and for the endurance of persecution, and therefore he comforted himself. In doing this he resorted not so much to the sweet as to the stern side of the Lord's dealings, and dwelt upon his judgments. Even the terrible things of God are cheering to believers. They know that nothing is more to the advantage of all God's creatures than to be ruled by a strong hand which will deal out justice. The righteous have no fear of the ruler's sword, which is only a

203

terror to evil-doers. When the godly are unjustly treated, they find comfort in the fact that there is a Judge of all the earth who will avenge his own elect, and redress the ills of these disordered times.

53. He was horrified at their action, at the pride which led them to it, and at the punishment which would be sure to fall upon them for it. When he thought upon the ancient judgments of God he was filled with terror at the fate of the godless; as well he might be. Their laughter had not distressed him, but he was distressed by a foresight of their overthrow. He saw them utterly turning away from the law of God, and he was astonished at their wickedness.

See verses 106 and 158, and note the tenderness which combined with all this. Those who are the firmest believers in the eternal punishment of the wicked are the most grieved at their doom. It is no proof of tenderness to shut one's eyes to the awful doom of the ungodly. Compassion is far better shown in trying to save sinners than in trying to make things pleasant all round.

54. David knew that he was not at home in this world, but a pilgrim through it, seeking a better country. He did not, however, sigh over this, but sang about it. Happy is the heart which finds its joy in the commands of God, and makes obedience its recreation. When religion is set to music it goes well. When we sing in the ways of the Lord it shows that our hearts are in them.

Note how in the sixth verses of their respective octaves we often find resolves to bless God, or records of testimony. In verse 46 it is "I will speak," and in verse 62 "I will give thanks," while here he speaks of songs.

55. I have remembered thy name, O LORD, in the night. When others slept I woke to think of thee, thy person, thy actions, thy covenant, **thy name,** under which last term he comprehends the divine character as far as it is revealed. He was so earnest after the living God that he woke up at dead of night to think upon him. It is well when our memory furnishes us with consolation, so that we can say with the psalmist: Having early been taught to know thee, I had only to remember the lessons of thy grace, and my heart was comforted. This verse shows not only that the man of God had remembered, but that he still remembered the Lord his God. We are to hallow the name of God, and we cannot do so if it slips from our memory.

And have kept thy law. He found sanctification through meditation; by the thoughts of the night he ruled the actions of the day. Are your thoughts in the dark full of light, because full of God? Is his name the natural subject of your evening reflections? Then it will give a tone to your morning and noonday hours. Or do you give your whole mind to the fleeting cares and pleasures of this world? If so, it is little wonder that you do not live as you ought to do. No one is holy by chance. If we do not think of Jehovah secretly we shall not obey him openly.

56. He had this comfort, this remembrance of God, this power to sing, this courage to face the enemy, this hope in the promise, because he had earnestly observed the commands of God, and striven to walk in them. We are not rewarded for our works, but there is a reward *in* them. Many a comfort is obtainable only by careful living: we can surely say of such consolations, "This I had because I kept thy precepts." How can we defy ridicule if we are living inconsistently? It may be that David means that he had been enabled to keep the law because he had attended to the separate precept: he had taken the commands in detail, and so had reached to holiness of life. Or, by keeping certain of the precepts he had gained spiritual strength to keep others: for God gives more grace to those who have some measure of it, and those who improve their talents will find themselves improving.

Here we have an apt conclusion to this section of the psalm, for this verse is a strong argument for the prayer with which the section commenced. The sweet singer had evidence of having kept God's precepts, and therefore he could the more properly beg the Lord to keep his promises.

57–64. In this section the psalmist seems to take firm hold upon God himself; appropriating him (verse 57), crying out for him (verse 58), returning to him (verse 59), solacing himself in him (verses 61–62), associating with his people (verse 63), and sighing for personal experience of his goodness (verse 64). Note how the first verse of this octave is linked to the last of the former one, of which indeed it is an expanded repetition.

57. Thou art my portion, O LORD. A broken sentence. The translators have mended it by insertions, but perhaps it had been better to have left it alone, and then it would have appeared as an exclamation: "My portion, O Lord!" The poet is lost in wonder while he sees that the great and glorious God is all his own! Well might he be so, for there is no possession like Jehovah himself. The form of the sentence expresses joyous recognition and appropriation. David here rejoices as one who seizes his share of the spoil; he chooses the Lord to be his part of the treasure. Like the Levites, he took the Lord to be his portion, and left other matters to those who coveted them. This is a large and lasting heritage, for it includes all, and more than all, and it outlasts all; and yet no one chooses it for himself until God has chosen and renewed him. Our author here addresses his joyful utterance directly to God whom he boldly calls his own. With much else to choose from, for he was a king, and a man of great resources, he deliberately turns from all the treasures of the world, and declares that the Lord is his portion.

I have said that I would keep thy words. We cannot always look back with comfort upon what we have said, but in this instance David had spoken wisely and well. He had declared his choice: he preferred the Word of God to the wealth of worldlings. It was his firm resolve to keep – that is, treasure up and observe – the words of his God, and as he had aforetime solemnly expressed it in the presence of the Lord himself, so here he confesses the obligation of his former vow. He was confident as to his interest in God, and therefore he was resolute in his obedience to him. Full assurance is a powerful source of holiness. The very words of God are to be stored up, for whether they relate to doctrine, promise, or precept, they are most precious. When the heart is determined to keep these words, and has registered its purpose in the court of heaven, it is prepared for all the temptations and trials that may befall it; for, with God as its heritage, it is always in good care.

58. I intreated thy favor with my whole heart. A fully assured possession of God does not set aside prayer, but rather urges us to it. Seeking God's presence is the idea conveyed by the marginal reading, "thy face," and this is true to the Hebrew. The presence of God is the highest form of his favor, and therefore it is the most urgent desire of gracious souls: the light of his countenance gives us a preview of heaven. Oh that we always enjoyed it! The good man intreated God's smile as one who begged for his life, and the entire strength of his desire went with the intreaty. Such eager pleadings are sure of success; that which comes form our heart will certainly go to God's heart.

Be merciful unto me according to thy word. He has intreated favor, and the form in which he most needs it is that of mercy, for he is more a sinner than anything else. He asks nothing beyond the promise; he only begs for such mercy as the word reveals. And what more could he want or wish for? God has revealed such an infinity of mercy in his Word that it would be impossible to conceive of more. See how the psalmist dwells upon his favor and mercy; he feels his own unworthiness. He remains a suppliant, though he knows that he has all things in his God. The confidence of faith makes us bold in prayer, but it never teaches us to live without prayer, or justifies us in being other than humble beggars at mercy's gate.

59. While studying the Word he was led to study his own life, and this caused a mighty revolution. Consideration is the commencement of conversion: first we think and then we turn. There will be no repenting until there is deep, earnest thought. Many people are averse to thought of any kind, and as to thought upon their ways, they cannot endure it, for their ways will not bear thinking of. David's ways had not been all that he could have wished them to be, but he did not end with idle lamentations, he set about a practical amendment; he turned and returned; he sought the testimonies of the Lord, and hastened to enjoy once more the conscious favor of his heavenly Friend. Action without thought is folly, and thought without action is sloth. He had intreated for renewed fellowship, and now he proved the genuineness of his desire by renewed obedience. If we are in the dark, and mourn an absent God, our wisest method will be not so much to think upon our sorrows as upon our ways: though we cannot turn the course of providence, we can turn the way of our walking, and this will soon mend matters. If we can get our feet right as to holy walking, we shall soon get our hearts right as to happy living. God will turn to his saints when they turn to him; he has already favored them with the light of his face when they begin to think and turn.

60. Delay in sin is increase of sin. A holy alacrity in service is much to be cultivated. It is wrought in us by the Spirit of God, and the preceding verses describe the method of it: we are made to perceive and mourn our errors, we are led to return to the right path, and then we are eager to make up for lost time by dashing forward to fulfill the precept. Many are zealous to obey custom and society, and yet they are slack in serving God.

61. The bands of the wicked have robbed me. Aforetime they derided him, and now they have defrauded him. Much of this opposition came from their being banded together: people will dare to do in company what they durst not have thought of alone.

But I have not forgotten thy law. This was well. Neither his sense of injustice, nor his sorrow at his losses, nor his attempts at defense diverted him from the ways of God. He would not do wrong to prevent the suffering of wrong, nor do ill to avenge ill. He was ready to forgive and forget the injuries done him, for his heart was taken up with the Word of God. Some read this passage, "The bands of the wicked environ me." They shut up every avenue of escape, but the man of God had his protector with him; a clear conscience relied upon the promise, and a brave resolve stuck to the precept. Some people are barely gracious among the circle of their friends, but this man was holy amid a ring of foes.

62. He was not afraid of the robbers; he rose, not to watch his house, but to praise his God. Midnight is the hour for burglars, and there were bands of them around David, but they did not occupy his thoughts; these were all up and away with the Lord his God. He thought not of thieves, but of **thanks**; not of what *they* would steal, but of what *he* would give to his God. A thankful heart is such a blessing that it drives out fear and makes room for praise. Thanksgiving turns night into day, and consecrates all hours to the worship of God. The psalmist did not lie in bed and praise; it would have been no sin to give thanks without rising, but to **rise** and give thanks is a happy combination. **At midnight** he would be unobserved and undisturbed; it was his own time which he saved from his sleep, and so he would be free from the charge of sacrificing public duties to private devotions. The **righteous** doings of the great Judge gladdened the heart of this godly man. His **judgments** are the terrible side of God, but they have no terror to the righteous; they admire them, and adore the Lord for them: they rise at night to bless God that he will avenge his own elect. Some hate the very notion of divine justice, and in this they are wide as poles asunder from this man of God. Doubtless in the expression **thy righteous judgments** David refers also to the written judgments of God upon various points of moral conduct; indeed, all the divine precepts may be viewed in that light; they are all of them the legal decisions of the supreme Arbiter of right and wrong. He could not find time enough by day to study the words of divine wisdom, or to bless God for them, and so he gave up his sleep that he might tell out his gratitude for such a law and such a Lawgiver.

This verse is an advance upon the sense of verse 52, and contains in addition the essence of verse 55.

63. I am a companion of all them that fear thee. The last verse said, "I will," and this says **I am.** We can hardly hope to be right in the future unless we are right now. David was a king, and yet he consorted with **all** who feared the Lord, whether they were obscure or famous, poor or rich. He did not select a few specially eminent saints and leave ordinary believers alone. He looked for inward godly fear, but he also expected to see outward piety in those whom he admitted to his society; hence he adds, **and of them that keep thy precepts.** David was known to be on the godly side; the men of Belial hated him for this, and no doubt despised him for keeping such unfashionable company as that of humble men and women who were strait-laced and religious; but the man of God is by no means ashamed of his associates. Those who love the saints on earth will be numbered with them in heaven.

There is a measure of parallelism between this seventh of its octave and the seventh verses 71 and 79; but the similarities which were so manifest in earlier verses are now becoming dim. As the sense deepens, the artificial form of expression is less regarded.

64. The earth, O Lord, is full of thy mercy. David had been exiled, but he had never been driven beyond the range of mercy, for he found the world to be everywhere filled with it. It is little wonder that, since he knew the Lord to be his portion, he hoped to obtain a measure of this mercy for himself, and so was encouraged to pray, **teach me thy statutes.** Surely he who fills the universe with his grace will grant such a request as this to his own child.

The first verse of this eight is fragrant with full assurance and strong resolve, and this last verse overflows with a sense of the divine fullness, and of the psalmist's personal dependence. This is an illustration of the fact that full assurance neither damps prayer nor hinders humility. It creates lowliness and suggests supplication. Those who have resolved to obey are the most eager to be taught. Whoever does not care to be instructed of the Lord has never honestly resolved to be holy.

65–72. In this ninth section the verses are the witness of experience, testifying to the goodness of God, the graciousness of his dealings, and the preciousness of his Word. Especially the psalmist proclaims the excellent use of adversity, and the goodness of God in afflicting him.

65. This is the summary of his life, and assuredly it is the sum of ours. The psalmist must speak his gratitude in the presence of Jehovah, his God. From the universal goodness of God in nature, in verse 64, it is an easy and pleasant step to a confession of the Lord's uniform goodness to ourselves personally. It is something that God has **dealt** at all with such undeserving beings as we are, and it is far more that he has dealt **well** with us, and so wondrously well. He promised to do so, and he has done it according to his Word. It is very precious to see the Word of the Lord fulfilled in our happy experience; it endears the Scripture to us, and makes us love the Lord of the Scripture. Our unbelief is repented of now that we see the mercy of the Lord to us, and his faithfulness to his Word; henceforth we are bound to display a firmer faith both in God and in his promise. It is to a very unworthy and incapable **servant** that he has acted thus blessedly; does not this cause us to delight in his service more and more? We lose ourselves in adoring thanksgiving, and find ourselves again in careful thanks-living.

66. Teach me good judgment and knowledge. Again he begs for teaching, as in verse 64, and again he uses God's mercy as an argument. Since God had dealt well with him, he is encouraged to pray for judgment to appreciate the Lord's goodness. Good judgment is the form of goodness which the godly man most needs and most desires, and it is one which the Lord is most ready to bestow. From want of knowledge David had misjudged the chastening hand of the Heavenly Father, and therefore he now asks to be better instructed, since he perceives the injustice which he had done to the Lord by his hasty conclusions. We are not able to judge, for our knowledge is so sadly inaccurate and imperfect; if the Lord teaches us knowledge we shall attain to good judgment, but not otherwise. The Holy Spirit alone can fill us with light.

For I have believed thy commandments. His heart was right, and therefore he hoped his head would be made right. He had faith, and therefore he hoped to receive wisdom. If in looking back upon our mistakes and ignorances we can yet see that we heartily loved the precepts of the divine will, we have good reason to hope that we are Christ's disciples, and that he will teach us and develop in us good judgment and sound knowledge. One who has learned discernment by experience, and has thus become someone of sound judgment, is a valuable member of a church, and the means of much edification to others. Let all who would be greatly useful offer the prayer of this verse.

67. Before I was afflicted I went astray. Partly, perhaps, through the absence of trial. If any of us remember a time in which we had no trouble, we also probably recollect that then grace was low, and temptation was strong. It may be that some believer cries, "Oh that it were with me as in those summer days before I was afflicted." Such a sigh is most unwise, and arises from a carnal love of ease: the spiritual man who prizes growth in grace will bless God that those dangerous days are over, and that if the weather be more stormy it is also more healthy.

But now have I kept thy word. Grace is that in the heart which profits by its chastening. It is of no use to plow barren soil. When there is no spiritual life affliction works no spiritual benefit; but where the heart is sound trouble awakens conscience, wandering is confessed, the soul becomes again obedient to the command, and continues to be so. In the psalmist's case the medicine of affliction worked a change – **but**; an immediate change – **now**; a lasting change – **have I**; an inward change – **have I kept**; a change Godward – **thy word**.

68. Thou art good, and doest good. Even in affliction God is good, and does good. This is the confession of experience. God is essential goodness in himself, and in every attribute of his nature he is good in the fullest sense of the term. His acts are according to his nature. God is not latent and inactive goodness; he is actively beneficent. It is well to worship the Lord as the psalmist here does by describing him. Facts about God are the best praise of God. All the glory we can give to God is to reflect his own glory upon himself. We believe in his goodness, and so honor him by our faith; we admire that goodness, and so glorify him by our love; we declare that goodness, and so magnify him by our testimony.

Teach me thy statutes. The man of God delighted to learn; he ascribed this to the goodness of the Lord, and hoped that for the same reason he would be allowed to remain in the school and learn on till he could perfectly practice every lesson. He knew the sad result of breaking those statutes, and by a painful experience he had been led back to the way of righteousness; and therefore he begged that he might be taught a perfect knowledge of the law, and a complete conformity to it.

In verse 12, which is the fourth verse of the second section, we have much the same sense as in this fourth verse.

69. The proud have forged a lie against me. They first derided him (verse 51), then defrauded him (verse 61), and now they have defamed him. To injure his character they resorted to falsehood, for they could find nothing against him if they spoke the truth. Proud people are usually the bitterest opponents of the righteous: they are envious of their good fame and are eager to ruin it. Slander is a cheap and handy weapon if the object is the destruction of a gracious reputation. It is painful to the last degree to hear unscrupulous people hammering away at the devil's anvil forging a new calumny; the only help against it is the sweet promise, "No weapon that is formed against thee shall prosper, and every tongue that riseth against thee in judgment thou shalt condemn."

But I will keep thy precepts with my whole heart. My one anxiety will be to mind my own business and stick to the commandments of the Lord. If we keep the precepts, the precepts will keep us in the day of contumely and slander. David renews his resolve – **I will keep**; he takes a new look at the commands, and sees them to be really the Lord's – **thy precepts**; and he arouses his entire nature to the work – **with my whole heart**. When slanders rouse us to more resolute and careful obedience they work our lasting good. If we try to answer lies by our words we may be beaten in the battle; but a holy life is an unanswerable refutation of all calumnies.

70. Their heart is as fat as grease. Their hearts, through sensual indulgence, have grown coarse and groveling; but thou hast saved me from such a fate through thy chastening hand. The proud grow fat through carnal luxuries, and this makes them prouder still. The fat in such people is killing the life in them. Living on the fat of the land, their nature is subdued to that which they have fed upon; the muscle of their nature has gone to softness and grease.

But I delight in thy law. How much better is it to joy in the law of the Lord than to joy in sensual indulgences! This makes the heart healthy, and keeps the mind lowly. No one who loves holiness has the slightest cause to envy the prosperity of the worldling. Delight in the law elevates and ennobles, while carnal pleasure clogs the intellect and degrades the affections. David had his relishes and dainties, his festivals and delights, and all these he found in doing the will of the Lord his God. When law becomes delight, obedience is bliss. Holiness in the heart causes the soul to eat the fat of the land. To have the law for our delight will breed in our hearts the very opposite of the effects of pride; deadness, sensuality, and obstinacy will be cured, and we shall become teachable, sensitive, and spiritual.

71. It is good for me that I have been afflicted. Even though the affliction came from bad men, it was overruled for good ends. It was not good to the proud to be prosperous, for their hearts grew sensual and insensible; but affliction was good for the psalmist. A thousand benefits have come to us through our pains and griefs, and among the rest is this – that we have thus been schooled in the law. **That I might learn thy statutes.** These we have come to know and to keep by feeling the smart of the rod. We prayed the Lord to teach us (verse 66), and now we see how he has already been doing it. We have been kept from the ignorance of the greasy-hearted by our trials, and this, if there were nothing else, is just cause for constant gratitude. To be larded by prosperity is not good for the proud; but for the truth to be learned by adversity is good for the humble. Very little is to be learned without affliction. There is no royal road to learning the royal statutes; God's commands are best read by eyes wet with tears.

72. The law of thy mouth. It comes from God's own mouth with freshness and power to our souls. Things written are as dried herbs; but speech has a liveliness and dew about it. We do well to look upon the Word of the Lord as though it were newly spoken into our ear. The same lips which spoke us into existence have spoken the law by which we are to govern that existence. Well may we prize beyond all price that which comes from such a source.

Is better unto me than thousands of gold and silver. This is the verdict of a man who owned his thousands, and could judge by actual experience the value of money and the value of truth. He speaks of great riches, and then he sets the Word of God before it all, as better *to him*, even if others did not think it better to them. Gold and silver may be stolen from us, but not the Word; these are useless in the hour of death, but the Word of the promise is most dear.

See how this portion of the psalm is flavored with goodness. God's dealings are good (verse 65), holy judgment is good (verse 66), affliction is good (verse 67), God is good (verse 68), and here the law is not only good, but better than the best of treasures. Lord, make us good, through thy good Word.

73–80. We have now come to the tenth portion; its subject would seem to be personal experience and its attractive influence upon others. The prophet is in deep sorrow, but looks to be delivered and made a blessing. Endeavoring to teach, the psalmist first seeks to be taught (verse 73), persuades himself that he will be well received (verse 74), and rehearses the testimony which he intends to bear (verse 75). He prays for more experience (verses 76–77), for the baffling of the proud (verse 78), for the gathering together of the godly to him (verse 79), and for himself again that he may be fully equiped for his witness-bearing and may be sustained in it (verse 80). This is the anxious yet hopeful cry of one who is heavily afflicted by cruel adversaries, and therefore makes his appeal to God as his only friend.

73. Thy hands have made me and fashioned me. It is profitable to remember our creation; it is pleasant to see that the divine hand has had much to do with us, for it never moves apart from the divine thought. It excites reverence, gratitude, and affection towards God when we view him as our Maker, putting forth the careful skill and power of his hands in our forming and fashioning. He took a personal interest in us, making us with his own hands; he was doubly thoughtful, for he is represented as making and molding us. In both giving existence and arranging existence he manifested love and wisdom; and therefore we find reasons for praise, confidence, and expectation in our being and well-being. **Give me understanding, that I may learn thy commandments.** As thou hast made me, teach me. Here is the vessel which thou hast fashioned; Lord, fill it. The plea is an enlargement of the cry, "Forsake not the work of thy hands." Without understanding the divine law and rendering obedience to it we are imperfect and useless; but we may reasonably hope that the great Potter will complete his work and give the finishing touch to it by imparting to it sacred knowledge and holy practice. We pray that we may not be left without a spiritual judgment. Only those who are taught of God can be holy. We often speak of gifted people; but they have the best gifts to whom God has given a sanctified understanding wherewith to know and prize the ways of the Lord. David's prayer is not for the sake of speculative knowledge and curiosity: he desires an enlightened judgment that he may learn God's commandments, and so become obedient and holy. No one has by nature an understanding capable of compassing so wide a field, and hence the prayer, as if to say, I can learn other things with the mind I have, but thy law is so pure, perfect, spiritual, and sublime that I need to have my mind enlarged before I can become proficient in it. We need a new creation, and who can grant us that but the Creator himself?

74. When someone obtains grace for himself he becomes a blessing to others, especially if that grace has made him of sound understanding and holy knowledge. God-fearing people are encouraged when they meet with experienced believers. When the hopes of one believer are fulfilled his companions are cheered and established, and led to hope also. It is good to see someone whose witness is that the Lord is true. We do not only meet to share each other's burdens, but to partake in each other's joys, and some people contribute largely to the stock of mutual gladness. Despondent spirits spread the infection of depression, and hence few are glad to see them, while those whose hopes are grounded upon God's Word carry sunshine in their faces, and are welcomed by their fellows.

75. I know, O LORD, that thy judgments are right. He who would learn most must be thankful for what he already knows, and be willing to confess it to the glory of God. The psalmist had been sorely tried, but he had continued to hope in God under his trial, and now he avows his conviction that he had been justly and wisely chastened. Saints are sure about the rightness of their troubles, even when they cannot see the intent of them. It made the godly glad to hear David say, **And that thou in faithfulness hast afflicted me.** Because love required severity, therefore the Lord exercised it. It was not because God was unfaithful that the believer found himself in a sore strait, but for just the opposite reason. Our Heavenly Father will not let his children sin without rebuke; his love is too intense for that.

76. Having confessed the righteousness of the Lord, he now appeals to his mercy, and while he does not ask that the rod may be removed, he earnestly begs for comfort under it. Righteousness and faithfulness afford us no consolation if we cannot also taste of mercy, and, blessed be God, this is promised us in the Word, and therefore we may expect it. The words **merciful kindness** express exactly what we need in affliction: mercy to forgive the sin, and kindness to sustain under the sorrow. Notwithstanding our faults we are still his servants, and we serve a compassionate Master. Some read the last clause, "according to thy saying unto thy servant": some special saying of the Lord was remembered and pleaded: can we not remember some such "faithful saying," and make it the groundwork of our petitioning? That phrase, **according to thy word,** shows the motive for mercy and the manner of mercy. Our prayers are according to the mind of God when they are according to the Word of God.

77. Let thy tender mercies come unto me, that I may live. He was so hard pressed that he was at death's door if God did not succor him. He needed not only mercy, but **mercies,** and these must be of a very gracious and considerate kind, even **tender mercies,** for he was sore with his wounds. These gentle favors must be of the Lord's giving, for nothing less would suffice; and they must **come** all the way to the sufferer's heart, for he was not able to journey after them. When tender mercy comes to us we do not merely exist but live; we know not what life is till we know God.

For thy law is my delight. He is no mean believer who rejoices in the law even when its broken precepts cause him to suffer. To delight in the Word when it rebukes us is proof that we are profiting under it. If we still delight in the law of God he cannot let us die; he must and will cast a tender look upon us and comfort our hearts.

78. Let the proud be ashamed. He begged that the judgments of God might no longer fall upon himself, but upon his cruel adversaries. God will not let those who hope in his word to be put to shame, for he reserves that reward for haughty spirits.

For they dealt perversely with me without a cause. Their malice was wanton; he had not provoked them. They had to bend his actions out of their true shape before they could assail his character. The psalmist felt a burning sense of injustice, and appealed to the righteous Lord to take his part and clothe his false accusers with shame. Sometimes he mentions the proud, and sometimes the wicked, but he always means the same people; the words are interchangeable.

But I will meditate in thy precepts. He would leave the proud in God's hands, and give himself up to holy studies and contemplations. To obey the divine precepts we need to know them, and think much of them. The proud are not worth a thought; the worst injury they can do us is to take us away from our devotions; let us baffle them by keeping all the closer to our God when they are most malicious in their onslaughts.

In a similar position to this we have met with the proud in other octaves, and shall meet them yet again. They are evidently a great plague to the psalmist, but he rises above them.

79. Perhaps the tongue of slander had alienated some of the godly, and probably the actual faults of David had grieved many more. He begs God to turn to him, and then to turn his people towards him. Those who are right with God are also anxious to be right with his children. David craved the love and sympathy of the gracious of all grades – those who were beginners in grace, and those who were mature in piety – **those that fear thee,** and **those that have known thy testimonies.** David was the leader of the godly party in the nation, and it wounded him to the heart when he perceived that those who feared God were not as glad to see him as they had been. He did not bluster and say that if they could do without *him* he could very well do without *them*; but he so deeply felt the value of their sympathy that he made it a matter of prayer that the Lord would turn their hearts to him again. Those who are dear to God, and are instructed in his word, should be very precious in our eyes, and we should do our utmost to be on good terms with them.

David has two descriptions for the saints: they are Godfearing and Godknowing. They possess both devotion and instruction; they have both the spirit and the science of true religion. We know some believers who are gracious, but not intelligent; we also know certain who have all head and no

214

heart. When fearing and knowing walk hand in hand they cause people to be thoroughly furnished unto every good work.

80. If the heart be sound in obedience to God, all is well, or will be well. If we be not sound before God, our name for piety is an empty sound. Only sincerity and truth will endure in the evil day. Whoever is right at heart has no reason for shame, and never will have any; hypocrites ought to be ashamed now, and they will one day be put to shame without end; their hearts are rotten, and their names will rot. This verse is a variation of the prayer of verse 73; there he sought sound understanding, here he goes deeper and begs for a sound heart. Those who have learned their own frailty by sad experience are led to dive beneath the surface and cry to the Lord for truth in the inward parts.

81–88. The psalmist's enemies have brought him to the lowest condition of anguish and depression; yet he is faithful to the law and trustful in his God. This octave is the midnight of the psalm, and very dark and black it is. Stars, however, shine out, and the last verse gives promise of the dawn. The strain will after this become more cheerful; but meanwhile it should minister comfort to us to see so eminent a servant of God so hard used by the ungodly: evidently in our own persecutions no strange thing has happened unto us.

81. My soul fainteth for thy salvation. He wished for no deliverance but that which came from God: his one desire was for **thy salvation.** But for that divine deliverance he was eager to the last degree – up to the full measure of his strength, yea, and beyond it till he fainted. So strong was his desire that it produced prostration of spirit. He grew weary with waiting, faint with watching, sick with urgent need. Thus the sincerity and the eagerness of his desires were proved. Nothing else could satisfy him but deliverance wrought out by the hand of God. **But I hope in thy word.** Therefore he felt that salvation would come, for God cannot break his promise, nor disappoint the hope which his own Word has excited: the fulfillment of his Word is near when our hope is firm and our desire fervent. Hope alone can keep the soul from fainting by using the smelling-bottle of the promise. Ye hope does not quench desire for a speedy answer to prayer; it increases our importunity, for it both stimulates ardor and sustains the heart under delays. To faint for salvation, and to be kept from utterly failing by the hope of it, is the frequent experience of the Christian. Hope sustains when desire exhausts. While the grace of desire throws us down, the grace of hope lifts us up again.

82. His eyes gave out with eager gazing for the kind appearance of the Lord, while his heart in weariness cried out for speedy comfort. To read the Word till eyes can no longer see is but a small thing compared with watching for the fulfillment of the promise till the inner eyes of expectancy begin to grow dim with hope deferred. We may not set times to God, yet we may urge our suit with importunity, and make fervent inquiry as to why the promise tarries. David's question is, **When wilt thou comfort me?** This experience of

215

waiting and fainting is well known by full-grown saints, and it teaches them many precious lessons which they would never learn by any other means. The body rises into sympathy with the soul, both heart and flesh cry out for the living God, and even the eyes find a tongue. Eyes can speak eloquently, and can sometimes say more than tongues. A humble eye lifted up to heaven in silent prayer may flash such flame as shall melt the bolts which bar the entrance of vocal prayer, and so heaven shall be taken by storm with the artillery of tears. Blessed are the eyes that are strained in looking after God. The eyes of the Lord will see to it that such eyes do not actually fail. How much better to watch for the Lord with aching eyes than to have them sparkling at the glitter of vanity.

83. For I am become like a bottle in the smoke. The skins used for containing wine, when emptied, were hung up in the tent, and when the place reeked with smoke the skins grew black and sooty, and in the heat they became wrinkled and worn. The psalmist's face through sorrow had become dark and dismal, furrowed and lined; indeed, his whole body had so sympathized with his sorrowing mind as to have lost its natural moisture, and to have become like a skin dried and tanned. His character had been smoked with slander, and his mind parched with persecution; he was half afraid that he would become useless and incapable through so much mental suffering, and that people would look on him as an old worn-out skin bottle, which could hold nothing and answer no purpose.

Yet do I not forget thy statutes. Here is the patience of the saints and the victory of faith. Blackened the man of God might be by falsehood, but the truth was in him, and he never gave it up. He was faithful to his King when he seemed deserted and left to the vilest uses. The promises came to his mind, and, what was a still better evidence of his loyalty, the statutes were there too: he stuck to his duties as well as to his comforts. The worst circumstances cannot destroy the true believer's hold upon his God. Grace is a living power which survives that which would suffocate all other forms of existence. A man may be reduced to skin and bone, and all his comfort may be dried out of him, and yet he may hold fast his integrity and glorify his God. It is, however, no marvel that in such a case the eyes which are tormented with the smoke cry out for the Lord's delivering hand, and the heart heated and faint longs for the divine salvation.

84. How many are the days of thy servant? I cannot hope to live long in such a condition. Perhaps the psalmist means that his days seemed too many when they were spent in such distress. He half wished that they were ended. It cannot be the Lord's mind that his own servant should always be treated so unjustly; there must be an end to it; when would it be?

When wilt thou execute judgment on them that persecute me? He had placed his case in the Lord's hands, and he prayed that sentence might be given and put into execution. He desired nothing but justice, that his character might be cleared and his persecutors silenced. He knew that God would certainly avenge his own elect, but the day of rescue tarried, the hours dragged heavily along, and the persecuted one cried day and night for deliverance.

85. David's foes went laboriously and cunningly to work to ruin him: they **digged pits**; not one, but many. Whereas they ought to have been ashamed of such meanness, they were conscious of no shame, but on the contrary were proud of their cleverness, proud of setting a trap for a godly man. **Which are not after thy law.** Neither the men nor their pits were according to the divine law: they were cruel and crafty deceivers, and their pits were contrary to the command which bids us love our neighbor. If people would keep to the statutes of the Lord, they would lift the fallen out of the pit, or fill up the pit so that none might stumble into it; but they would never spend a moment in working injury to others. When, however, they become proud, they are sure to despise others; and for this reason they seek to circumvent them, that they may afterwards hold them up to ridicule. It was well for David that his enemies were God's enemies, and that their attacks upon him had no sanction from the Lord. While he kept to the law of the Lord he was safe.

86. All thy commandments are faithful. He had no fault to find with God's law, even though he had fallen into sad trouble through obedience to it. Whatever the command might cost him it was worth it; he felt that God's way might be rough, but it was right; it might make him enemies, but still it was his best friend. He believed that in the end God's command would turn out to his own profit, and that he would be no loser by obeying it.

They persecute me wrongfully. The fault lay with his persecutors, and neither with his God nor with himself. He had done no injury to anyone, nor acted otherwise than according to truth and justice; therefore he confidently appeals to his God, and cries, **Help thou me.** Help was needed that the persecuted one might avoid the snare, might bear up under reproach, and might act so prudently as to baffle his foes. God's help is our hope. Whoever may hurt us, it matters not so long as the Lord helps us; for if indeed the Lord help us, none can really hurt us. Many a time have these words been groaned out by troubled saints, for they are such as suit a thousand conditions of need, pain, distress, weakness, and sin. "Help, Lord," will be a fitting prayer for youth and age, for labor and suffering, for life and death. No other help is sufficient, but God's help is all-sufficient, and we cast ourselves upon it without fear.

87. They had almost consumed me upon earth. Evidently he had fallen under their power to a large extent, and they had so used that power that he was well-nigh consumed. He was almost gone from off the earth; but almost is not altogether. The lions are chained: they can rage no further than our God permits. The psalmist perceives the limit of their power: they could only touch his earthly life and earthly goods. He had an eternal portion which they could not even nibble at. **But I forsook not thy precepts.** Nothing could drive him from obeying the Lord. If we stick to the precepts we shall be rescued by the promises. If ill-usage could have driven the oppressed saint from the way of right the purpose of the wicked would have been answered, and we should have heard no more of David. If we are resolved to die sooner than forsake the Lord, we may depend upon it that we shall not die, but shall live to see the overthrow of them that hate us.

88. Quicken me after thy lovingkindness. Most wise, most blessed prayer! If we are revived in our own personal piety we shall be out of reach of our assailants. Our best protection from tempters and persecutors is more life. Lovingkindness itself cannot do us greater service than by making us to have life more abundantly. When we are quickened we are able to bear affliction, to baffle cunning, and to conquer sin. We look to the lovingkindness of God as the source of spiritual revival, and we intreat the Lord to quicken us, not according to our deserts, but after the boundless energy of his grace. **So shall I keep the testimony of thy mouth.** If quickened by the Holy Spirit we shall be sure to exhibit a holy character. We shall be faithful to sound doctrine when the Spirit visits us and makes us faithful. We ought greatly to admire the spiritual prudence of the psalmist, who does not so much pray for freedom from trial as for renewed life that he may be supported under it. David prayed for a sound heart in the closing verse of the last octave, and here he seeks a revived heart; this is going to the root of the matter, by seeking that which is the most needful of all things.

89. After tossing about on a sea of trouble the psalmist here leaps to shore and stands upon a rock. Jehovah's word is not fickle or uncertain. In the former section David's soul fainted, but here the good man looks out of self and perceives that the Lord fainteth not, neither is weary, neither is there any failure in his Word. When we are tired with gazing upon the shifting scene of this life, the thought of the immutable promise fills our mouth with singing. God's purposes, promises, and precepts are all settled. Covenant settlements will not be removed, however unsettled people's thoughts may become; let us therefore settle it in our minds that we abide in the faith of our Jehovah as long as we have any being.

90. Thy faithfulness is unto all generations. This is an additional glory: God is not affected by the lapse of ages; he is not only faithful to one man throughout his lifetime, but to his children's children after him, and to all generations so long as they keep his covenant and remember his commandments to do them. He who succored his servants thousands of years ago still shows himself strong on the behalf of all them that trust him. **Thou hast established the earth, and it abideth.** Nature is governed by fixed laws; the globe keeps its course by divine command; all things are marshaled in their appointed order. There is an analogy between the Word of God and the works of God, and specially in this, that they are both of them constant, fixed, and unchangeable. God's

Word which established the world is the same as that which he has embodied in the Scriptures; when we see the world keeping its place and all its laws abiding the same, we have herein assurance that the Lord will be faithful to his covenant, and will not allow the faith of his people to be put to shame.

91. They continue this day according to thine ordinances. Because the Lord has bid the universe abide, therefore it stands, and all its laws continue to operate with precision and power. The Word which spoke all things into existence has supported them until now, and still supports them both in being and in well-being. **For all are thy servants.** Created by the Word they obey that Word, thus answering the purpose of their existence. Shall we wish to be free of the Lord's sway and become lords unto ourselves? If we were so, we should be dreadful exceptions to a law which secures the well-being of the universe. Rather let us serve more perfectly as our lives are continued.

92. That Word which has preserved the heavens and the earth also preserves the people of God in their time of trial. We should have felt ready to lie down and die of our griefs if the spiritual comforts of God's Word had not uplifted us; but by their sustaining influence we have been borne above all the depressions and despairs which naturally grow out of severe affliction. Some of us can set our seal to this statement. In our darkest seasons nothing has kept us from desperation but the promise of the Lord; at times nothing has stood between us and self-destruction save faith in the eternal Word of God. When worn with pain until the brain has become dazed and the reason well-nigh extinguished, a sweet text has whispered to us its heart-cheering assurance, and our poor struggling mind has reposed upon the bosom of God. That which was our delight in prosperity has been our light in adversity; that which in the day kept us from presuming has in the night kept us from perishing.

93. When we have felt the quickening power of a precept we can never forget it. It seems singular that the man of God should ascribe quickening to the precepts, and yet it lies in them and in all the words of the Lord alike. When the Lord raised the dead he addressed to them the word of command. He said, "Lazarus, come forth," or, "Maid, arise." We need not fear to address Gospel precepts to dead sinners, since by them the Spirit gives them life. The psalmist does not say that the precepts quickened him, but that the Lord quickened him by their means. Yet he prized the instruments of the blessing, and resolved never to forget them. He had already remembered them when he likened himself to a bottle in the smoke, and now he feels that whether in the smoke or in the fire the memory of the Lord's precepts will never depart from him.

94. I am thine, save me. A comprehensive prayer with a prevailing argument. Consecration is a good plea for preservation. If we are conscious that we are the Lord's we may be confident that he will save us. We are the Lord's by creation, election, redemption, surrender, and acceptance; and hence our firm hope and assured belief that he will save us. A man will surely save his own child: Lord, save *me*. The need of salvation is better seen by the Lord's people than by any others; they know that only God can save them, and that no merit can be found in themselves. **For I have sought thy precepts.** He might not have attained to all the holiness which he desired, but he had studiously aimed at being obedient to the Lord, and hence he begged to be saved even to the end. Someone may be seeking the doctrines and the promises, and yet be unrenewed in heart; but to seek the precepts is a sure sign of grace; no one ever heard of a rebel or a hypocrite seeking the precepts. When the Lord sets us seeking he will not refuse us the saving. He who seeks holiness is already saved: if we have sought the Lord we may be sure that the Lord has sought us, and will certainly save us.

95. They were like wild beasts crouching by the way, or highwaymen waylaying a defenseless traveler; but the psalmist went on his way without considering them, for he was considering something better, namely, the witness or testimony which God has borne. If the wicked cannot destroy us today they will wait for further opportunities; they will have to wait much longer yet, for if we are so unmoved that we do not even give them a thought their hope of destroying us must be a very poor one. Note the double waiting – the patience of the wicked who watch long and carefully for an opportunity to destroy the godly, and then the patience of the saint who will not quit his meditations, even to quiet his foes. See how the serpent's seed lie in wait, but the chosen of the Lord take no more notice of them than if they had no existence.

96. I have seen an end of all perfection. He had seen its limit, for it went but a little way; he had seen its evaporation under the trials of life, its detection under the searching glance of truth, its exposure by the confession of the penitent. Perfect people, in the absolute sense of the word, live only in a perfect world. Some see no end to their own perfection, but this is because they are perfectly blind. The experienced believer has seen an end of all perfection in himself, in his brethren, in the best people's best works. It would be well if some who profess to be perfect could even see the beginning of perfection, for we fear they cannot have begun aright, or they would not talk so exceedingly proudly. **But thy commandment is exceeding broad.** When the breadth of the law is known the notion of perfection in the flesh vanishes: that law touches every act, word, and thought, and is of such a spiritual nature that it judges the motives, desires, and emotions of the soul. It reveals a perfection which convicts us for shortcomings as well as for transgressions, and does not allow us to make up for deficiencies in one direction by special carefulness in others. The divine ideal of holiness is far too broad for us to hope to cover all its wide arena, and yet it is no broader than it ought to be. Who would wish to have an imperfect law? Its perfection is its glory; but it is the death of all glorying in our own perfection. Only in Jesus do we see it fully embodied. The law is in all respects a perfect code; each separate precept of it is far-reaching in its hallowed meaning, and the whole ten cover all, and leave no space wherein to please our passions. We may well adore the infinity of divine holiness, and then measure ourselves by its standard, and bow before the Lord in all lowliness, acknowledging how far we fall short of it.

97. O how I love thy law! He loves so much that he must express his love, and in making the attempt he perceives that it is inexpressible. We obey the law out of love, and even when it chides us for disobedience we love it none the less. **It is my meditation all the day.** He meditated on God's Word because he loved it, and then loved it the more because he meditated in it. In his worldly business he still kept his mind saturated with the law of the Lord. Familiarity with the Word of God breeds affection, and affection seeks yet greater familiarity. When **thy law** and **my meditation** are together all the day, the day grows holy, devout, and happy, and the heart lives with God.

98. Thou through thy commandments hast made me wiser than mine enemies. The commands were his book, but God was his teacher. The letter can make us knowing, but only the divine Spirit can make us wise. Wisdom is knowledge put to practical use. Wisdom comes to us through obedience (John 7:17). We learn not only from promise, and doctrine, and sacred history; from the commandments we gather the most practical wisdom, and that which enables us best to cope with our adversaries. A holy life is the highest wisdom and the surest defense. By uprightness we shall baffle fraud, by simple truth vanquish deep-laid scheming, and by open candor defeat slander.

For they are ever with me. He was always studying or obeying the commandments; they were his choice and constant companions. If we wish to become proficient we must be indefatigable. If we keep the wise law ever near us we shall become wise, and when our adversaries assail us we shall be prepared for them with that ready wit which lies in having the Word of God at our fingers' ends. As a soldier in battle must never lay aside his shield, so must we never have the Word of God out of our minds.

99. I have more understanding than all my teachers. Our teachers are not always to be trusted. If our teachers should be in all things sound and safe, they will be glad for us to excel them, and they will be ever ready to own that the teaching of the Lord is better than any teaching which they can give us. Disciples of Christ who sit at his feet are often better skilled in divine things than doctors of divinity. **For thy testimonies are my meditation.** This is the best mode of acquiring understanding. We may hear the wisest teachers and remain fools, but if we meditate upon the sacred Word we must become wise. David does not hesitate to speak the truth in this place concerning himself, for he is quite innocent of self-consciousness. In speaking of his understanding he means to extol the law and the Lord, and not himself. There is not a grain of boasting in these bold expressions, but only a sincere childlike desire to set forth the excellence of the Lord's Word.

100. He had been taught to observe in heart and life the precepts of the Lord, and this was more than the most venerable sinner had ever learned, more than the philosopher of antiquity had so much as aspired to know. The oldest of all is the best of all, and what is that but the word of the Ancient of Days.

101. There is no treasuring up the holy Word unless there is a casting out of all unholiness. David had zealously watched his steps and put a check upon his conduct. No one evil way could entice him, for he knew that if he went astray in one road he had practically left the way of righteousness. Sin avoided that obedience may be perfected is the essence of this verse; or it may be that the psalmist would teach us that there is no real reverence for the book where there is not carefulness to avoid every transgression of its precepts.

102. What we learn from the Lord we never forget. We follow his way when he teaches us; we do not depart from holiness. If we begin to depart a little we can never tell where we shall end. The Lord brings us to persevere in holiness by abstinence from the beginning of sin; but whatever be the method he is the worker of our perseverance, and to him be all the glory.

103. How sweet are thy words unto my taste! He had not only heard the words of God, but fed upon them: they affected his palate as well as his ear. God's words are many and varied, and the whole of them make up what we call "the word"; David loved them each one, individually, and the whole of them as a whole. Oh for a deep love to all that the Lord has revealed, whatever form it may take.

Yea, sweeter than honey to my mouth. When he did not only eat but also speak the Word, by instructing others, he felt an increased delight in it. When the psalmist fed on it he found it sweet; but when he bore witness of it, it became sweeter still. It must be sweet to our taste when we think of it, or it will not be sweet to our mouth when we talk of it.

104. Through thy precepts I get understanding. God's direction is our instruction. Obedience to the divine will begets wisdom of mind and action. As God's way it is always best; those who follow it are sure to be justified by the result. If the Lawgiver were foolish his law would be the same, and obedience to such a law would involve us in a thousand mistakes; but as the reverse is the case, we may count ourselves happy to have such a wise, prudent, and beneficial law to be the rule of our lives. We are wise if we obey, and we grow wise by obeying!

Therefore I hate every false way. Because he had understanding, and because of the divine precepts, he detested sin and falsehood. Every sin is a falsehood; we commit sin because we believe a lie, and in the end the flattering evil turns a liar to us and we find ourselves betrayed. True hearts are not indifferent about falsehood; they grow warm in indignation. The way of self-will, of self-righteousness, of worldliness, of pride, of unbelief, of hypocrisy – these are all false ways, and therefore not only to be shunned, but to be abhorred.

This final verse of the section marks a great advance in character, and shows that the man of God is growing stronger, bolder, and happier than aforetime. He has been taught of the Lord, so that he discerns between the precious and the vile, and while he loves the truth fervently he hates falsehood intensely. May all of us reach this state of discrimination and determination, so that we may greatly glorify God.

105. Thy word is a lamp unto my feet. We are often called to go out into the darkness; let us never venture without the light-giving Word. Each of us should use the Word of God personally, practically, and habitually, to see the way and what lies in it. Having no fixed lamps in eastern towns, in old time each passenger carried a lantern with him that he might not fall into the open sewer, or stumble over the heaps of excrement which defiled the road. This is a true picture of our path through this dark world. One of the most practical benefits of Holy Writ is guidance in the acts of daily life: it is not sent to astound us with its brilliance, but to guide us by its instruction. It is true the head needs illumination, but even more the feet need direction, else head and feet may both fall into a ditch. **And a light unto my path.** Whoever walks in darkness is sure, sooner or later, to stumble, while the one who walks by the light of day, or by the lamp of night, does not stumble but keeps upright. Ignorance is painful upon practical subjects; it breeds indecision and suspense, and these are uncomfortable: the Word of God, by imparting heavenly knowledge, leads to decision, and when that is followed by determined resolution, as in this case, it brings with it great restfulness of heart. This verse converses with God in adoring and yet familiar tones. Have we not something of like tenor to address to our Heavenly Father?

Note how like verse 1 this is, and the first verse of other octaves.

106. Under the influence of the clear light of knowledge he had firmly made up his mind, and solemnly declared his resolve in the sight of God. Perhaps mistrusting his own fickle mind, he had pledged himself in sacred form to abide faithful to the determination and decisions of his God. Whatever path might open before him, he was sworn to follow that only upon which the lamp of the Word was shining. The Scriptures are God's judgments, or verdicts, upon great moral questions; these are all righteous, and hence righteous people should be resolved to keep them at all hazards. Will not every believer own that he is under bonds to the redeeming Lord to follow his example, and keep his words? Yes, the vows of the Lord are upon us, especially upon such as have made profession of discipleship, have been baptized into the thrice-holy name, have eaten of the consecrated memorials, and have spoken in the name of the Lord Jesus. We are enlisted, and sworn in, and are bound to be loyal soldiers all through the war. Thus having taken the Word into our hearts by a firm resolve to obey it, we have a lamp within our souls as well as in the

Book, and our course will be light unto the end.

107. I am afflicted very much. Our service of the Lord does not screen us from trial, but rather secures it for us. The psalmist was a consecrated man, and yet a chastened man; nor were his chastisements light, for it seemed as if the more he was obedient the more he was afflicted. He evidently felt the rod to be cutting deep, and this he pleads before the Lord. He speaks not by way of grumbling but by way of pleading; from the very much affliction he argues for very much quickening.

Quicken me, O LORD, according unto thy word. This is the best remedy for tribulation; the soul is raised above the thought of present distress, and is filled with that holy joy which attends all vigorous spiritual life, and so the affliction grows light. Jehovah alone can quicken: he has life in himself, and therefore can communicate it readily; he can give us life at any moment, even at this present instant; for it is of the nature of quickening to be quick in its operation. The Lord has promised, prepared, and provided this blessing of renewed life for all his waiting servants: it is a covenant blessing, and it is as obtainable as it is needful. Frequently the affliction is made the means of the quickening, just as the stirring of a fire promotes the heat of the flame. In their affliction some desire death; let us pray for life. Our forebodings under trial are often very gloomy; let us intreat the Lord to deal with us, not according to our fears, but according to his own Word. David had but few promises to quote, and probably these were in his own psalms, yet he pleads the Word of the Lord; how much more should we do so, since to us so many holy men have spoken by the Spirit of the Lord in that wonderful library which is now our Bible. Seeing we have more promises, let us offer more prayers.

108. Accept, I beseech thee, the freewill offerings of my mouth, O LORD. The living praise the living God, and therefore the quickened one presents his sacrifice. He offers prayer, praise, confession, and testimony; these, presented with his voice in the presence of an audience, were the tribute of his mouth unto Jehovah. He trembles lest these should be so ill uttered as to displease the Lord, and therefore he implores acceptance. He pleads that the homage of his mouth was cheerfully and spontaneously rendered; all his utterances were freewill offerings. There can be no value in extorted confessions: God's revenues are not derived from forced taxation, but from freewill donation. There can be no acceptance where there is no willingness; there is no work of free grace where there is no fruit of free will. Acceptance is a favor to be sought from the Lord with all earnestness, for without it our offerings are worse than useless. What a wonder of grace that the Lord will accept anything from such unworthy ones as we are!

And teach me thy judgments. When we render unto the Lord our best, we become all the more concerned to do better. After quickening we need teaching: life without light, or zeal without knowledge, would be but half a blessing.

These repeated cries for teaching show the humility of the man of God, and also discover to us our own need of similar instruction. Our judgment needs educating till it knows, agrees with, and acts upon the judgments of the Lord. Those judgments are not always so clear as to be seen at once; we need to be taught in them till we admire their wisdom and adore their goodness as soon as ever we perceive them.

109. My soul is continually in my hand. He lived in the midst of danger. He had to be always fighting for existence – hiding in caves, or contending in battles. This is a very uncomfortable and trying state of affairs, and men are apt to think any expedient justifiable by which they can end such a condition, but David did not turn aside to find safety in sin, for he says, **Yet do I not forget thy law.** No danger of body should make us endanger our souls by forgetting that which is right. Trouble makes many a man forget his duty, and it would have had the same effect upon the psalmist if he had not obtained quickening (verse 107) and teaching (verse 108). In his memory of the Lord's law lay his safety; he was certain not to be forgotten of God, for God was not forgotten of him. It is a special proof of grace when nothing can drive truth our of our thoughts, or holiness out of our lives. If we remember the law even when death stares us in the face, we may be well assured that the Lord is remembering us.

110. The wicked have laid a snare for me. Spiritual life is the scene of constant danger: the believer lives with his life in his hand, and all seem plotting to take it from him, by cunning if they cannot by violence. We shall not find it an easy thing to live the life of the faithful. Wicked spirits and wicked people will leave no stone unturned for our destruction. When we know that we are thus assailed, we are too apt to become timorous, and rush upon some hasty device for deliverance, not without sin in the endeavor; but David calmly kept his way: **Yet I erred not from thy precepts.** He was not snared, for he kept his eyes open, and kept near his God. He was not entrapped and robbed, for he followed the King's highway of holiness, where God secures safety to every traveler. He did not err from the right, and he was not deterred from following it, because he referred to the Lord for guidance, and obtained it. If we err from the precepts, we part with the promises; if we get away from God's presence, we wander into the wilds where the fowlers freely spread their nets.

111. Thy testimonies have I taken as an heritage for ever. He chose them, and what is more he laid hold upon them, taking them into possession and enjoyment. If we might have our desire, we would desire to keep the commands of God perfectly. Sometimes, like Israel, we have to take our heritage by hard fighting, but always it has to be taken by a decided choice of the heart and grip of the will. What God gives we must take. **For they are the rejoicing of my heart.** The gladness which had come to him through the Word of the Lord had caused him to make an unalterable choice of it. That which rejoices the heart is sure to be chosen and treasured. It is not the head-knowledge but the heart-experience which brings the joy.

In this verse, which is the seventh of its octave, we have reached the same sweetness as in the last seventh (verse 103). How good a thing it is when experience ripens into joy, passing up through sorrow, prayer, conflict, hope, desire, and holy content into rejoicing! Joy fixes the spirit.

112. He was not half inclined to virtue, but heartily inclined to it. His whole heart was bent on practical, persevering godliness. He was resolved to keep the statutes of the Lord with all his heart, throughout all his time, without erring or ending. He made it his end to keep the law unto the end, and that without end. He had by prayer, and meditation, and resolution made his whole being lean towards God's commands; or as we should say in other words, the grace of God had inclined him to incline his heart in a sanctified direction. Many are inclined to preach, but the psalmist was inclined to practice; many are inclined to perform ceremonies, but he was inclined to perform statutes; many are inclined to obey occasionally, but David would obey always; and, alas, many are inclined for temporary religion, but this godly man was bound for eternity, and would perform the statutes of his Lord and King to the end. Lord, send us such a heavenly inclination of heart as this: then shall we show that thou hast quickened us and taught us. To this end create in us a clean heart, and daily renew a right spirit within us, for only so shall we incline in the right direction.

113. In this paragraph the psalmist deals with thoughts and things and persons which are the opposite of God's holy thoughts and ways. He is evidently in great fear of the powers of darkness, and of their allies, and his whole soul is stirred up to stand against them with a determined opposition. Just as he began the octave in verse 97 with "Oh, how I love thy law," so here he begins with a declaration of hatred against that which breaks the law. He did not glory in his thoughts; and that which was called "thought" in his day was a thing which he detested. Some of our thoughts are especially vain in the sense of vainglory, pride, conceit, and self-trust; others in the sense of bringing disappointment, such as fond ambition, sinful dreaming, and confidence in man; others in the sense of emptiness and frivolity; and too many of our thoughts are vain in the sense of being sinful, evil, and foolish. The psalmist looks upon them with a hate as true as was the love with which he clung to the pure thoughts of God.

The last octave was practical, this is thoughtful; there the man of God attended to his feet, and here to his heart: the emotions of the soul are as important as the acts of the life, for they are the fountain and spring from which the actions proceed. When we love the law it becomes a law of love, and we cling to it with out whole heart.

114. Thou art my hiding place and my shield. To his God he ran for shelter from vain thoughts; there he hid himself away from their tormenting intrusions, and in solemn silence of the soul he found God to be his hiding-place. When called into the world, if he could not be alone with God as his hiding-place, he could have the Lord with him as his shield, and by this means he could ward off the attacks of wicked suggestions. This verse testifies to what the writer knew of his own personal knowledge: he could not fight with his own thoughts, or escape from them, till he flew to his God, and then he found deliverance. He does not speak of God's Word as his double defense, but he ascribes that to God himself. When we are beset by very spiritual assaults, such as those which arise out of vain thoughts, we shall do well to fly to our Lord and cast ourselves upon his real presence. **I hope in thy word.** He had tried and proved it: he looked for protection from all danger, and preservation from all temptation to him who had hitherto been the tower of his defense on former occasions. It is easy to exercise hope where we have experienced help. Sometimes when gloomy thoughts afflict us, the only thing we can do is to hope, and happily the Word of God always sets before us objects of hope and reasons for hope, so that it becomes the very sphere and support of hope, and thus tiresome thoughts are overcome. Amid fret and worry a hope of heaven is an effectual balm.

115. Depart from me, ye evildoers. Those who make a conscience of their thoughts are not likely to tolerate evil company. If we fly to God from vain thoughts, much more shall we avoid vain people. Kings are all too apt to be surrounded by a class of people who flatter them, and at the same time take liberty to break the laws of God: David purged his palace of such parasites. Herein he anticipated the sentence of the last great day, when the Son of David will say, "Depart from me, ye workers of iniquity." We cannot thus send all malefactors out of our houses, but it will often become a duty to do so where there is right and reason for it. We are bound at all hazards to keep ourselves clear of such companions as come to us by our own choice if we have any reason to believe that their character is vicious. Those who say unto God, "Depart from us" ought to hear the immediate echo of their words from the mouths of God's children.

For I will keep the commandments of my God. Since he found it hard to keep the commandments in the company of the ungodly, he gave them their marching orders. The word **God** only occurs in this one place in all this lengthened psalm, and then it is attended by the personal word **my.** Because Jehovah is our God we resolve to obey him, and to chase out of our sight those who would hinder us in his service. It is a grand thing for the mind to be steadfastly fixed in the holy determination, "I will keep thy commandments."

116. Uphold me according unto thy word, that I may live. It was so necessary that the Lord should hold up his servant, that he could not even live without it. Our soul would die if the Lord did not continually sustain it, and every grace which makes spiritual life to be truly life would decay if he withdrew his upholding hand. It is a sweet comfort that this great necessity of upholding is provided for in the Word, and we have not to ask for it as for an uncovenanted mercy, but simply to plead for the fulfillment of a promise. He who has given us eternal life has in the gift secured to us all that is essential thereto, and as gracious upholding is one of the necessary things we may be sure that we shall have it. **And let me not be ashamed of my hope.** In verse 114 he had spoken of his hope as founded on the Word, and now he begs for the fulfillment of that Word that his hope might be justified in the sight of all. We may be ashamed of our thoughts, and our words, and our deeds, for they spring from ourselves; but we never shall be ashamed of our hope, for that springs from the Lord our God. Such is the frailty of our nature that unless we are continually upheld by grace, we shall fall so foully as to be ashamed of ourselves, and ashamed of all those glorious hopes which are now the crown and glory of our life. The man of God had uttered the most positive resolves, but he felt that he could not trust in his own solemn determination. It was not wrong to make resolutions, but it will be useless to do so unless we salt them well with believing cries to God. David meant to keep the law of the Lord, but he first needed the Lord of the law to keep him.

117. Hold thou me up. As a nurse holds up a little child. **And I shall be safe.** Unless thou hold me up I shall be falling about like an infant that is weak upon its knees. We are saved by past grace, but we are not safe unless we receive present grace. The psalmist had vowed to keep the Lord's commands, but here he pleads with the Lord to keep him. Our version reads the word **uphold** (verse 116), and then **hold up**; and truly we need this blessing in every shape in which it can come, for in all manner of ways our adversaries seek to cast us down. To be safe is a happy condition; there is only one door to it, and that is to be held up by God himself; thank God, that door is open to the least among us. **And I will have respect unto thy statutes continually.** In obedience is safety; in being held up is obedience. No man will outwardly keep to the Lord's statutes for long together unless he has an inward respect for them, and this will never be unless the hand of the Lord perpetually upholds the heart in holy love. Perseverance to the end, obedience continually, comes only through the divine power; we start aside as a deceitful bow unless we are kept right by him that first gave us grace. Happy is the man who realizes this verse in his life: upheld through his whole life in a course of unswerving integrity, he becomes a safe and trusted man, and maintains a sacred delicacy of conscience which is unknown to others. He feels a tender respect for the statutes of the Lord, which keeps him clear of inconsistencies and conformities to the world that are so common among others, and hence he is a pillar in the house of the Lord.

118. Thou hast trodden down all them that err from thy statutes. They are thrown down and then trodden down, for they choose to go down into the wandering ways of sin. Sooner of later God will set his foot on those who turn their foot from his commands: it has always been so, and it always will be so. If the salt has lost its savor, what is it fit for but to be trodden under foot?

For their deceit is falsehood. They call it far-seeing policy, but it is absolute falsehood, and it will be treated as such. Ordinary people call it clever diplomacy, but the man of God calls a spade a spade, and declares it to be falsehood, for he knows that it is so in the sight of God. People who err from the right road invent pretty excuses with which to deceive themselves and others, and so quiet their consciences and maintain their credits; but their mask of falsehood is too transparent. God treads down falsehoods. How horrified must those be who have spent all their lives in contriving a confectionery religion, and then see it all trodden upon by God as a sham which he cannot endure!

119. Thou puttest away all the wicked of the earth like dross. He does not trifle with them, or handle them with kid gloves. No, he judges them to be the scum of the earth, and he puts them away from his church, and at last away from himself. They looked like precious metal, they were intimately mixed up with it, they were laid up in the same heap, but the Lord is a refiner, and every day he removes some of the wicked from among his people, either by making a shameful discovery of their hypocrisy or by consuming them from off the earth. As the metal is the better for losing its alloy, so is the church better for having the wicked removed. These wicked ones are **of the earth,** and they have no right to be with those who are not of the world; the Lord perceives them to be out of place and injurious, and therefore he puts them away, **all** of them. The process will one day be perfect; no dross will be spared, no gold will be left impure. Where shall we be when that great work is finished?

Therefore I love thy testimonies. Even the severities of the Lord excite the love of his people. If he allowed people to sin with impunity, he would not be so fully the object of our loving admiration.

120. My flesh trembleth for fear of thee. Such was his awe in the presence of the Judge of all the earth that he did quake. Even the grosser part of his being, his flesh, felt a solemn dread at the thought of offending one so good and great, who would so effectually sever the wicked from among the just. **And I am afraid of thy judgments.** We may well cry for cleansed thoughts, and hearts, and ways, lest his judgments should light on us. When we see the great Refiner separating the precious from the vile, we may well feel a godly fear, lest we should be put away by him, and left to be trodden under his feet.

Love in the previous verse is quite consistent with fear in this verse: the fear which has torments is cast out, but not the filial fear which leads to reverence and obedience.

121. I have done judgment and justice. This was a great thing for an eastern ruler to say at any time, for these despots mostly cared more for gain than justice. Some of them would not even do judgment at all, preferring their pleasures to their duties; and many more of them sold their judgments to the highest bidders by taking bribes, or regarding the persons of men. Some rulers gave neither judgment nor justice, others gave judgment with justice, but David gave judgment and justice, and saw that his sentences were carried out. He could claim before the Lord that he had dealt out even-handed justice, and was doing so still. On this fact he founded a plea with which he backed the prayer: **Leave me not to mine oppressors.** He who, as far as his power goes, has been doing right, may hope to be delivered from his superiors when attempts are made by them to do him wrong. Nor is this kind of pleading to be censured as self-righteous: when we are dealing with God as to our shortcomings, we use a very different tone from that with which we face the censures of our fellow-men; when they are in the question, and we are guiltless towards them, we are justified in pleading our innocence.

122. Be surety for thy servant for good. Answer for me. Do not leave thy poor servant to die by the hand of his enemy and thine. Take up my interests and weave them with thine own, and stand for me. As my Master, undertake thy servant's cause, and represent me before the faces of haughty people till they see what an august ally I have in the Lord my God.

Let not the proud oppress me. When the proud see that thou art my advocate they will hide their heads. We should have been crushed beneath our proud adversary the devil if our Lord Jesus had not stood between us and the accuser, and become a surety for us. It is by his suretyship that we escape like a bird from the snare of the fowler. What a blessing to be able to leave our matters in our Surety's hands, knowing that all will be well, since he has an answer for every accuser, a rebuke for every reviler.

Good people dread oppression, and they send up their cries to heaven for deliverance; nor shall they cry in vain, for the Lord will undertake the cause of his servants, and fight their battles against the proud.

123. Mine eyes fail for thy salvation. He wept, waited, and watched for God's saving hand, and these exercises tried the eyes of his faith till they were almost ready to give out. He looked to God alone, he looked eagerly, he looked long. The mercy is that if our eyes fail, God does not fail, nor do *his* eyes fail. Eyes are tender things, and so are our faith, hope and expectancy: the Lord will not try them above what they are able to bear. **And for the word of thy righteousness**: a word that would silence the unrighteous words of his oppressors. His eyes as well as his ears waited for the Lord's word: he looked to see the divine word come forth as a fiat for his deliverance. He was waiting for the verdict of righteousness itself. How happy are we if we have righteousness on our side; for then that which is the sinners' terror is our hope, that which the proud dread is our expectation and desire. David left his reputation entirely in the Lord's hand.

124. Deal with thy servant according unto thy mercy. Here he recollects himself: although before men he was clear, before the Lord he felt that he must appeal to mercy. We feel safest here. Our heart has more rest in the cry, "God be merciful to me," than in appealing to justice. A master should clear the character of his servant if he be falsely accused, and rescue him from those who would oppress him; and, moreover, the master should show mercy to a servant, even if he deal severely with a stranger. The Lord does not spurn his servants, but communes with them in a tender and merciful way. **And teach me thy statutes.** This will be one way of dealing with us in mercy. We may expect a master to teach his own servant the meaning of his own orders. Yet since our ignorance arises from our own sinful stupidity, it is great mercy on God's part that he condescends to instruct us in his commands.

125. I am thy servant. We who rejoice that we are sons of God are by no means the less delighted to be his servants. Did not the firstborn Son assume the servant's form and fulfill the servant's labor to the full? What higher honor can the younger brethren desire than to be made like the Heir of all things?

Give me understanding, that I may know thy testimonies. In the previous verse he sought teaching; but here he goes much further, and craves for understanding. We are to confess ourselves fools, and then our Lord will make us wise, as well as give us knowledge. The best understanding is that which enables us to render perfect obedience and to exhibit intelligent faith, and it is this which David desires. Some would rather not know these things; they prefer to be at ease in the dark than possess the light which leads to repentance and diligence.

The psalmist does not pray for understanding through acquiring knowledge, but begs of the Lord first that he may have the gracious gift of understanding, and then may obtain the desired instruction. All that we know before we have understanding is apt to spoil us and breed vanity in us; but if there be first an understanding heart, then the stores of knowledge enrich the soul, and bring neither sin nor sorrow therewith. Moreover, this gift of understanding acts also in the form of discernment, and thus the good man is preserved from hoarding up that which is false and dangerous: he knows what are and what are not the testimonies of the Lord.

126. David was a servant, and therefore it was always his time to work: but being oppressed by the sight of man's ungodly behavior, he feels that his Master's hand is wanted, and therefore he appeals to him to work against the working of evil. People make void the law of God by denying it to be his law, by promulgating commands and doctrines in opposition to it, by setting up tradition in its place, or by utterly disregarding and scorning the authority of the Lawgiver. Then sin becomes fashionable, and a holy walk is regarded as a contemptible puritanism; vice is styled pleasure. Then the saints sigh for the presence and power of their God: Oh for another Pentecost with all its wonders, to reveal the energy of God to gainsayers, and make them see that there is a God in Israel! Man's extremity, whether of need or sin, is God's opportunity. When the earth was without form and void, the Spirit came and moved upon the face of the waters; should he not come when society is returning to a like chaos? When Israel in Egypt was reduced to the lowest point, and it seemed that the covenant would be void, then Moses appeared and wrought mighty miracles; so, too, when the church of God is trampled down, and her message is derided, we may expect to see the hand of the Lord stretched out for the revival of religion, the defense of the truth, and the glorifying of the divine name. The Lord can work either by judgments which hurl down the ramparts of the foe, or by revivals which build up the walls of his own Jerusalem. How heartily may we pray the Lord to raise up new evangelists, to quicken those we already have, to set his whole church on fire, and to bring the world to his feet. God's work is ever honorable and glorious; as for our work, it is as nothing apart from him.

127. As it was God's time to work, so it was David's time to love. So far from being swayed by the example of evil people, so as to join them in slighting the Scriptures, he was the rather led into a more vehement love of them. As he saw the commandments slighted by the ungodly, his heart was in sympathy with God, and he felt a burning affection for his holy precepts. It is the mark of a true believer that he does not depend upon others for his religion, but drinks water out of his own well, which springs up even when the cisterns of the earth are all dried. Wealth brings with it so many conveniences that people naturally esteem it, and God's laws are more enriching, and bring with them more comfort than all the choicest treasures. The psalmist could not boast that he always kept the commands, but he could declare that he loved them.

128. Therefore I esteem all thy precepts concerning all things to be right. Because the ungodly found fault with the precepts of God, therefore David was all the more sure of their being right. The censure of the wicked is a certificate of merit; that which they sanction we may justly suspect, but that which they abominate we may ardently admire. The good person's delight in God's law is unreserved.

And I hate every false way. Love of truth begat hatred of falsehood. This godly man was a good lover or a good hater, but he was never a waverer. The fact that such large multitudes follow the broad road had no influence upon this holy man, except to make him more determined to avoid every form of error and sin. May the Holy Spirit so rule in our hearts that our affections may be in the same decided condition towards the precepts of the word.

129. Thy testimonies are wonderful. Full of wonderful revelations, commands, and promises. Wonderful in their nature, as being free from all error, and bearing within themselves overwhelming self-evidence of their truth; wonderful in their effects as instructing, elevating, strengthening, and comforting the soul. Jesus the eternal Word is called Wonderful, and all the uttered words of God are wonderful in their degree. Those who know them best wonder at them most. It is wonderful that God should have borne testimony at all to sinful men, and more wonderful still that his testimony should be of such a character, so clear, so full, so gracious, so mighty. **Therefore doth my soul keep them.** Their wonderful character so impressed itself upon his mind that he kept them in his memory; their wonderful excellence so charmed his heart that he kept them in his life. Some people wonder at the words of God, and use them for their speculation; but David was always practical, and the more he wondered the more he obeyed. Note that his religion was soul work; not with head and hand alone did he keep the testimonies, but his soul, his truest and most real self, held fast to them.

130. **The entrance of thy words giveth light.** No sooner do they gain admission into the soul than they enlighten it: what light may be expected from their prolonged indwelling! Their very entrance floods the mind with instruction, for they are so full, so clear; but, on the other hand, there must be such an **entrance,** or there will be no illumination. The mere hearing of the Word with the external ear is of small value by itself, but when the words of God enter into the chambers of the heart, then light is scattered on all sides. The Word finds no entrance into some minds because they are blocked up with self-conceit, or prejudice, or indifference; but where due attention is given, divine illumination must surely follow upon a knowledge of the mind of God. Oh that thy words, like the beams of the sun, may enter through the window of my understanding, and dispel the darkness of my mind! **It giveth understanding unto the simple.** The sincere and candid are the true disciples of the Word. To such it gives not only knowledge, but understanding. These simple-hearted ones are frequently despised, and their simplicity has another meaning infused into it, so as to be made the theme of ridicule; but what matters it? Those whom the world dubs as fools are among the truly wise if they are taught of God. What a divine power rests in the Word of God, since it not only bestows light, but gives that very mental eye by which the light is received – **It giveth understanding.** Hence the value of the words of God to the simple, who cannot receive mysterious truth unless their minds are aided to see it and prepared to grasp it.

131. **I opened my mouth, and panted.** So animated was his desire that he looked into the animal world to find a picture of it. He was filled with an intense longing, and was not ashamed to describe it by a most expressive, natural, and yet singular symbol. Like a stag that has been hunted in the chase, and is hard pressed, and therefore pants for breath, so did the psalmist pant for the entrance of God's Word into his soul. Nothing else could content him. All that the world could yield him left him still panting. **For I longed for thy commandments.** Longed to know them, longed to obey them, longed to be conformed to their spirit, longed to teach them to others. He was a servant of God, and his industrious mind longed to receive orders; he was a learner in the school of grace, and his eager spirit longed to be taught of the Lord.

132. Look thou upon me. A godly person cannot long be without prayer. During the previous verses he had been expressing his love to God's Word, but here he is upon his knees again. He besought the Lord to let his condition and his unexpressed longings plead for him. He desires to be known of God, and daily observed by him. He wishes also to be favored with the divine smile which is included in the Word – **look. And be merciful unto me.** Christ's look at Peter was a look of mercy, and all the looks of the Heavenly Father are of the same kind. If he looked in stern justice his eyes would not endure us, but looking in mercy he spares and blesses us. If God looks and sees us panting, he will not fail to be merciful to us. **As thou usest to do unto those that love thy name.** Look on me as thou lookest on those who love thee; be merciful to me as thou art accustomed to be towards those who truly serve thee. David would not have the Lord deal either better or worse with him than he was accustomed to deal with his saints – worse would not save him, better could not be.

133. Order my steps in thy word. This is one of the Lord's customary mercies to his chosen – "He keepeth the feet of his saints." By his grace he enables us to put our feet step by step in the very place which his Word ordains. This does not stop short of perfect holiness, neither will the believer's desires be satisfied with anything beneath that blessed consummation. **And let not any iniquity have dominion over me.** This is the negative side of the blessing. We ask to do all that is right, and to fall under the power of nothing that is wrong. Believers pant for perfect liberty from the power of evil, and being conscious that they cannot obtain it of themselves, they cry unto God for it.

134. Deliver me from the oppression of man. David had tasted all the bitterness of this great evil. It had made him an exile from his country, and banished him from the sanctuary of the Lord: therefore he pleads to be saved from it. It is said that oppression makes a wise man mad, and no doubt it has made many a righteous man sinful. Oppression is in itself wicked, and it drives people to wickedness. We little know how much of our virtue is due to our liberty; if we had been in bonds under haughty tyrants we might have yielded to them, and instead of being confessors we might now have been apostates. He who taught us to pray, "Lead us not into temptation," will sanction this prayer, which is of much the same tenor, since to be oppressed is to be tempted. **So will I keep thy statutes.** When the stress of oppression was taken off he would go his own way, and that way would be the way of the Lord. Although we ought not to yield to the threatenings of men, yet many do so; the wife is sometimes compelled by the oppression of her husband to act against her conscience; children and servants, and even whole nations have been brought into the same difficulty. Their sins will be largely laid at the oppressor's door, and it usually pleases God ere long to overthrow those powers and dominions which compel people to do evil. The worst of it is that some people, when the pressure is taken off from them, follow after unrighteousness of their own accord. These give evidence of being sinners in nature. As for the righteous, it happens to them as it did to the apostles of old – "Being let go, they went to their own company." When saints are freed from the tyrant they joyfully pay homage to their King.

135. Make thy face to shine upon thy servant. Oppressors frown, but do thou smile. Shine upon me, and all will be bright. The psalmist again declares that he is God's servant, and he seeks for no favor from others, but only from his own Lord and Master. **And teach me thy statutes.** This is the favor which he considers to be the shining of the face of God upon him. If the Lord will be exceeding gracious, and make him his favorite, he will ask no higher blessing than still to be taught the royal statutes. The most favored believer needs teaching; even when he walks in the light of God's countenance he has still to be taught the divine statutes or he will transgress.

136. He wept in sympathy with God to see the holy law despised and broken. He wept in pity for the people who were thus drawing down upon themselves the fiery wrath of God. In his torrents of woe he became like the Lord Jesus, who beheld the city, and wept over it; and like Jehovah himself, who has no pleasure in the death of someone who dies, but that they should turn unto him and live. The experience of this verse indicates a great advance upon anything we have had before: the psalm and the psalmist are both growing. That man is a ripe believer who sorrows because of the sins of others. In verse 120 his flesh trembled at the presence of God, and here it seems to melt and flow away in floods of tears. None are so affected by heavenly things as those who are much in the study of the Word, and are thereby taught the truth and essence of things. Carnal people are afraid of brute force, and weep over losses and crosses; but spiritual people feel a holy fear of the Lord himself, and most of all lament when they see dishonor cast upon his holy name.

137–144. This passage deals with the perfect righteousness of Jehovah and his Word, and expresses the struggles of a holy soul in reference to that righteousness. The initial letter with which every verse commences sounds like the Hebrew word for righteousness.

137. Righteous art thou, O Lord. The psalmist has not often used the name of Jehovah in this vast composition. The whole psalm shows him to have been a deeply religious man, thoroughly familiar with the things of God; and such people never use the holy name of God carelessly, nor do they even use it at all frequently in comparison with the thoughtless and ungodly. Familiarity begets reverence in this case. Here he uses the sacred name in worship. He praises God by ascribing to him perfect righteousness. God is always right, and he is always actively right, that is, righteous. **And upright are thy judgments.** Here he extols God's Word, or recorded judgments, as being right, just as their Author is righteous. When we are most sorely afflicted, and cannot see the reason for the dispensation, we may fall back upon this most sure and certain fact, that God is righteous, and his dealings with us are righteous too. It should be our glory to sing this brave confession when all things around us appear to suggest the contrary.

138. All that which God has testified in his Word is right and truthful. It is righteous, and may be relied upon for the present; it is faithful, and may be trusted in for the future. Not only the precepts but the promises also are commanded of the Lord, and so are all the teachings of Scripture. It is not left to our choice whether we will accept them or not; they are issued by royal command, and are not to be questioned. They are the essence of justice and the soul of truth.

Very faithful. What a mercy that we have a God to deal with who is scrupulously faithful, true to all the items and details of his promises, punctual, steadfast. Well may we risk all upon a Word which is "ever faithful, ever sure."

139. In the last two verses David spoke concerning his God and his law; here he speaks of himself. His zeal was like a fire burning within his soul. The sight of man's forgetfulness of God acted as a fierce blast to excite the fire to a more vehement flame, and it blazed until it was ready to consume him. David could not bear that people should forget God's words. The ungodly were David's enemies because they hated him for his godliness and because he abhorred them for their ungodliness. These people had gone so far in iniquity that they not only violated and neglected the commands of God, but they appeared actually to have forgotten them. David burned with indignation. How dare they trample on sacred things!

140. Thy word is very pure. It is truth distilled, holiness in its quintessence. In the Word of God there is no admixture of error or sin. It is pure in its sense, pure in its language, pure in its spirit, pure in its influence, and all this to the very highest degree – **very** pure. **Therefore thy servant loveth it,** which is a proof that he himself was pure in heart. His heart was knit to the Word because of its glorious holiness and truth. He admired it, delighted in it, sought to practice it, and longed to come under its purifying power.

141. That fault of forgetfulness which he condemned in others (verse 139) could not be charged upon himself. His enemies regarded him as a man without power or ability, and therefore looked down upon him. He appears to accept the situation and humbly take the lowest room, but he carries God's Word with him. How many a man has been driven to do some ill action in order to reply to the contempt of his enemies: to make himself conspicuous he has either spoken or acted in a manner which he could not justify. The beauty of the psalmist's piety was that it was calm and well-balanced, and as he was not carried away by flattery, so was he not overcome by shame. If small, he the more jealously attended to the smaller duties; and if despised, he was the more in earnest to keep the despised commandments of God.

142. Thy righteousness is an everlasting righteousness. Having in a previous verse ascribed righteousness to God, he now goes on to declare that that righteousness is unchanging and endures from age to age. This is the joy and glory of the saints, that what God is he always will be, and his mode of procedure towards the sons of men is immutable: having kept his promise, and dealt out justice among his people, he will do so world without end. Both the righteousness and the unrighteousness of men come to an end, but the righteousness of God is without end. **And thy law is the truth.** As God is love, so his law is the truth, the very essence of truth, truth applied to ethics, truth in action, truth upon the judgment-seat. We hear great disputes about, "What is truth?" The holy Scriptures are the only answer to that question. They are not only true, but the truth itself. We may not say of them that they contain the truth, but that they are the truth: **thy law is the truth.** There is nothing false about the law or preceptive part of Scripture. Those who are obedient thereto will find that they are walking in a way consistent with fact, while those who act contrary thereto are walking in a vain show.

143. Trouble and anguish have taken hold on me. This affliction may have arisen from his circumstances, or from the cruelty of his enemies, or from his own internal conflicts, but certain it is that he was the subject of much distress, a distress which apprehended him, and carried him away a captive to its power. His griefs, like fierce dogs, had taken hold upon him; he felt their teeth. He had double trouble: trouble without and anguish within. **Yet thy commandments are my delights.** Thus he became a riddle; troubled, and yet delighted. The child of God can understand this enigma, for well he knows that while he is cast down on account of what he sees within himself he is all the more lifted up by what he sees in the Word. He is delighted with the commandments, although he is troubled because he cannot perfectly obey them. He finds abundant light in the commandments, and by the influence of that light he discovers and mourns over his own darkness.

144. The righteousness of thy testimonies is everlasting. First he had said that God's testimonies were righteous, then that they were everlasting, and now that their righteousness is everlasting. Thus he gives us a larger and more detailed account of the Word of God the longer he is engaged in writing upon it. Long as the earth stands, long as there is a single intelligent creature in the universe, it will be confessed that God's plans of mercy are in all respects marvelous proofs of his love of justice: even though he may be gracious Jehovah will not be unjust. **Give me understanding, and I shall live.** To live without understanding is not to live human life, but to be dead while we live. Only as we know and apprehend the things of God can we be said to enter into life. The more the Lord teaches us to admire the eternal righteousness of his Word, and the more he quickens us to the love of such rightness, the happier and the better we shall be. As we love life, and seek many days that we may see good, it behoves us to seek immortality in the everlasting Word, and to seek good in that renewal of our entire nature which begins with the enlightenment of the understanding and passes on to the regeneration of the entire person. Here is our need of the Holy Spirit, the Lord and giver of life, and the guide of all the quickened ones, who will lead us into all truth.

145–152. This section is given up to memories of prayer. The psalmist describes the time and the manner of his devotions, and pleads with God for deliverance from his troubles. He who has been with God in the closet will find God with him in the furnace. If we have cried we shall be answered. Delayed answers may drive us to importunity; but we need not fear the ultimate result, since God's promises are not uncertain, but are "founded for ever." The whole passage shows us how he prayed (verse 145); what he prayed for (verse 146); when he prayed (verse 147); how long he prayed (verse 148); what he pleaded (verse 149); what happened (verse 150); how he was rescued (verse 151); what was his witness as to the whole matter (verse 152).

145. I cried with my whole heart. His prayer was a sincere, plaintive, painful, natural utterance, as of a creature in pain. We cannot tell whether at all times he used his voice when he thus cried; but we are informed of something which is of much greater consequence, he cried with his heart. Heart-cries are the essence of prayer. He mentions the unity of his heart: his whole soul pleaded with God, his entire affections, his united desires all went out towards the living God. It is well when we can say as much as this of our prayers: it is to be feared that many never cried to God with their whole heart in all their lives. There may be no beauty of elocution about such prayers, no length of expression, no depth of doctrine, nor accuracy of diction; but if the whole heart be in them they will find their way to the heart of God. **Hear me, O Lord.** He desires of Jehovah that his cries may not die upon the air, but that God may have respect to them. True supplicants are not satisfied with the exercise itself; they have an end and object in praying, and they look out for it. If God does not hear prayer we pray in vain. The term "hear" is often used in Scripture to express attention and consideration. In one sense God hears every sound that is made on earth, and every desire of every heart; but David meant much more; he desired a kindly, sympathetic hearing, such as a physician gives to his patient when he tells him his pitiful story. He asked that the Lord would draw near, and listen with friendly ear to the voice of his complaint, with the view of pitying him and helping him. Observe that his whole-hearted prayer goes to the Lord alone; he has no second hope or help. **I will keep thy statutes.** He could not expect the Lord to hear him if he did not hear the Lord; neither would it be true that he prayed with his whole heart unless it was manifest that he labored with all his might to be obedient to the divine will. His object in seeking deliverance was that he might be free to fulfill his religion and carry out every ordinance of the Lord. He would be a free man that he might be at liberty to serve the Lord. Note well that a holy resolution goes well with an importunate supplication: David is determined to be holy. He will not willfully neglect or violate any one of the divine laws.

146. I cried unto thee. Again he mentions that his prayer was to God alone. He prayed vehemently, and very often; it had become one of the greatest facts of his life that he cried unto God. **Save me.** This was his prayer: very short, but very full. He needed saving, none but the Lord could save him, to him he cried, "Save me" from the dangers which surround me, from the enemies that pursue me, from the temptations which beset me, from the sins which accuse me. He did not multiply words, and people never do when they are in down-right earnest. He did not multiply objects, and people seldom do when they are intent upon the one thing needful: "save me" was his one and only prayer. **And I shall keep thy testimonies.** This was his great object in desiring salvation, that he might be able to continue in a blameless life of obedience to God, that he might be able to believe the witness of God, and also to become himself a witness for God. It is a great thing when people seek salvation for so high an end. He did not ask to be delivered that he might sin with impunity; his cry was to be delivered from sin itself. He had vowed to keep the statutes or laws; here he resolves to keep the testimonies or doctrines, and so to be sound of head as well as clean of hand. Salvation brings all these good things in its train. David had no idea of a salvation which would allow him to live in sin, or abide in error: he knew right well that there is no saving a man while he abides in disobedience and ignorance.

147. I prevented the dawning of the morning, and cried. He was up before the sun, and began his pleadings. This is the third time that he mentions that he **cried.** His supplications had become so frequent, fervent, and intense that he might hardly be said to be doing anything else from morning to night but crying unto his God. So strong was his desire after salvation that he could not rest in his bed; so eagerly did he seek it that at the first possible moment he was on his knees. **I hoped in thy word.** Hope is a very powerful means of strengthening us in prayer. Who would pray if he had no hope that God would hear him? Who would not pray when he has a good hope of a blessed issue to his entreaties? His hoped was fixed upon God's Word, and this is a sure anchorage, because God is true, and in no case has he ever run back from his promise, or altered the thing that has gone forth from his mouth. He who is diligent in prayer will never be destitute of hope. Observe that as the early bird gets the worm, so the early prayer is soon refreshed with hope.

148. Mine eyes prevent the night watches. Or rather, "the watches." Before the watchman cried the hour, he was crying to God. He did not need to be informed as to how the hours were flying, for every hour his heart was flying towards heaven. He began the day with prayer, and he continued in prayer through the watches of the day, and the watches of the night. Specially, however, at night did he keep his eyes open, and drive away sleep, that he might maintain communion with his God. He worshiped on from watch to watch as travelers journey from stage to stage. **That I might meditate in thy word.** This had become meat and drink to him. Meditation was the food of his hope, and the solace of his sorrow: the one theme upon which his thoughts ran was that blessed **word** which he continually mentions, and in which his heart rejoices. He preferred study to slumber; and he learned to forego his necessary sleep for much more necessary devotion. It is instructive to find meditation so constantly connected with fervent prayer: it is the fuel which sustains the flame. How rare an article is it in these days.

149. Hear my voice according to thy lovingkindness. People find it very helpful to use their voices in prayer; it is difficult long to maintain the intensity of devotion unless we hear ourselves speak; hence David at length broke through his silence, arose from his quiet meditations, and began crying with voice as well as heart unto the Lord his God. Note that he does not plead his own deservings; he takes the free-grace way, **according to thy lovingkindness.** When God hears prayer according to his lovingkindness he overlooks all the imperfections of the prayer, he forgets the sinfulness of the offerer, and in pitying love he grants the desire though the suppliant be unworthy. It is according to God's lovingkindness to answer speedily, to answer frequently, to answer exceeding abundantly above all that we ask or even think. Kindness has much in it that is most precious, but lovingkindness is doubly dear. **O LORD, quicken me according to thy judgment.** He first cried, "Save me"; then, "Hear me"; and now, **Quicken me.** This is often the very best way of delivering us from trouble – to give us more life that we may escape from death; and to add more strength to that life that we may not be overloaded with its burdens. He asks to receive quickening according to God's judgment, that is, in such a way as should be consistent with infinite wisdom and prudence. God's methods of communicating greater vigor to our spiritual life are exceedingly wise; it would probably be in vain for us to attempt to understand them; and it will be our wisdom to wish to receive grace, not according to our notion of how it should come to us, but according to God's heavenly method of bestowing it. It is his prerogative to make alive as well as to kill, and that sovereign act is best left to his infallible judgment. Has he not already given us to have life more and more abundantly?

150. They draw nigh that follow after mischief. He could hear their footfalls close behind him. He points them out to God, and intreats the Lord to fix his eyes upon them, and deal with them to their confusion. They were already upon him, and he was almost in their grip, and therefore he cries the more earnestly. **They are far from thy law.** Before these men could become persecutors of David they were obliged to get away from the restraints of God's law. Those who keep God's law neither do harm to themselves nor to others. Sin is the greatest mischief in the world. When we know that our enemies are

God's enemies, and ours because they are his, we may well take comfort.

151. Thou art near, O Lord. Near as the enemy might be, God was nearer: this is one of the choicest comforts of the persecuted child of God. The Lord is near to hear our cries, and to speedily afford us succor. He is near to chase away our enemies, and to give us rest and peace. **And all thy commandments are truth.** God neither commands a lie, nor lies in his commands. Virtue is truth in action, and this is what God commands. Sin is falsehood in action, and this is what God forbids. If all God's commands are truth, then the true person will be glad to keep near to them, and therein will find the true God near. This sentence will be the persecuted man's protection from the false hearts that seek to do him mischief: God is near and God is true, therefore his people are safe. If at any time we fall into danger through keeping the commands of God we need not suppose that we have acted unwisely: we may, on the contrary, be quite sure that we are in the right way; for God's precepts are right and true. It is for this very reason that wicked men assail us: they hate the truth, and therefore hate those who do the truth. Their opposition may be our consolation, while God's presence upon our side is our glory and delight.

152. It is a very blessed thing to be so early taught of God that we know substantial doctrines even from our youth. Those who think that David was a young man when he wrote this psalm will find it rather difficult to reconcile this verse with the theory; it is much more probable that he was now grown gray, and was looking back upon what he had known long before. He knew at the very first that the doctrines of God's Word were settled before the world began, that they had never altered, and never could by any possibility be altered. He had begun by building on a rock, by seeing that God's testimonies were **founded,** that is, grounded, laid as foundations, settled and established, and that with a view to all the ages that should come, during all the changes that should intervene. It was because David knew this that he had such confidence in prayer, and was so importunate in it. It was because of this that David learned to hope: a man cannot have much expectation from a changing friend, but he may well have confidence in a God who cannot change. It was because of this that he delighted in being near the Lord, for it is a most blessed thing to keep up close intercourse with a Friend who never varies. Let those who choose follow at the heels of the modern school and look for fresh light to break forth which will put the old light out of countenance; we are satisfied with the truth which is old as the hills and as fixed as the great mountains. Let "cultured intellects" invent another God, more gentle and effeminate than the God of Abraham; we are well content to worship Jehovah, who is eternally the same. Things everlastingly established are the joy of established saints. Bubbles please children, but grown adults prize those things which are solid and substantial, which will bear the test of the ages.

153–160. In this section the psalmist seems to draw still nearer to God in prayer, and to state his case and to invoke the divine help with more boldness and expectation. It is a pleading passage, and the key-word of it is **Consider**. With much boldness he pleads his intimate union with the Lord's cause as a reason why he should be aided. The special aid that he seeks is personal quickening, for which he cries to the Lord again and again.

153. Consider mine affliction, and deliver me. The writer has a good case, though it be a grievous one, and he is ready, indeed anxious, to submit it to the divine arbitration. His manner is that of one who feels safe at the throne. Yet there is no impatience: he does not ask for hasty action, but for consideration. In effect he cries, "Look into my grief, and see whether I do not need to be delivered. From my sorrowful condition judge as to the proper method and time for my rescue." The psalmist desires two things blended: first, a full consideration of his sorrow; secondly, deliverance; and, then, that this deliverance should come with a consideration of his affliction. The words **mine affliction** seem to portion off a special spot of woe as the writer's own inheritance: he possesses it as no one else had ever done, and he begs the Lord to have that special spot under his eye, just as a farmer looking over all his fields may yet take double care of a certain selected plot. His prayer is eminently practical, for he seeks to be delivered; that is, brought out of the trouble and preserved from sustaining any serious damage by it. Men consider and do nothing, but such is never the case with our God. **For I do not forget thy law.** His affliction was not sufficient, with all its bitterness, to drive out of his mind the memory of God's law; nor could it lead him to act contrary to the divine command. He forgot prosperity, but he did not forget obedience. If we are kept faithful to God's law we may be sure that God will remain faithful to his promise. If we do not forget his law the Lord will not forget us. He will not long leave that person in trouble whose only fear in trouble is lest he should leave the way of right.

154. Plead my cause, and deliver me. In the last verse he had prayed, "Deliver me," and here he specifies one method in which that deliverance might be vouchsafed, namely, by the advocacy of his cause. In providence the Lord has many ways of clearing the slandered of the accusations brought against them. He can make it manifest to all that they have been belied, and in this way he can practically plead their cause. He can, moreover, raise up friends for the godly who will leave no stone unturned till their characters are cleared; or he can smite their falsehood, and thus the righteous will be delivered without the striking of a blow. Alexander reads it, "Strive my strife, and redeem me" – that is, stand in my stead, bear my burden, fight my fight, pay my price, and bring me out to liberty. When we feel ourselves dumb before the foe, here is a prayer made to our hand. What a comfort that if we sin we have an advocate, and if we do *not* sin the same pleader is engaged on our side. **Quicken me.** As the soul is the center of everything, so to be quickened is the central blessing. It means more love, more grace, more faith, more courage, more strength, and if we get these we can hold up our heads before our adversaries. God alone can give this quickening; but to the Lord and giver of life the work is easy enough, and he delights to perform it. **According to thy word.** David had found such a blessing among the promised things, or at least he perceived that it was according to the general tenor of God's Word that tried believers should be quickened and brought up again from the dust of the earth; therefore he pleads the Word, and desires the Lord to act to him according to the usual run of that Word. What a mighty plea is this.

155. Salvation is far from the wicked. By their perseverance in evil they have almost put themselves out of the pale of hope. They talk about being saved, but they cannot have known anything of it or they would not remain wicked. Every step they have taken in the path of evil has removed them further from the kingdom of grace: they go from one degree of hardness to another till their hearts become as stone. When they fall into trouble it will be irremediable. Yet they talk big, as if they either needed no salvation or could save themselves whenever their fancy turned that way. **For they seek not thy statutes.** They do not endeavor to be obedient, but quite the reverse; they seek themselves, they seek evil, and therefore they never find the way of peace and righteousness. When men have broken the statutes of the Lord their wisest course is by repentance to seek forgiveness, and by faith to seek salvation: then salvation is near them, so near them that they will not miss it; but when the wicked continue to seek after mischief, salvation is set further and further from them. Salvation and God's statutes go together: those who are saved by the King of grace love the statutes of the King of glory.

156. This verse is exceedingly like verse 149, and yet it is no vain repetition. In the first case he mentions prayer, but leaves the method of its accomplishment with the wisdom or judgment of God, while here he pleads to be quickened by judgments rather than to be left to spiritual lethargy. We may take it for granted that an inspired author is never so short of thought as to be obliged to repeat himself: where we think we have the same idea in this psalm we are misled by our neglect of careful study. **Great are thy tender mercies, O LORD.** Here the psalmist pleads the largeness of God's mercy, the immensity of his tender love; he speaks of **mercies** – many, tender, great; and with the glorious Jehovah he makes this a plea for his one leading prayer, the prayer for quickening. Quickening is a great and tender mercy; and it is many mercies in one. Shall one so greatly good permit his servant to die? **Quicken me according to thy judgments.** A measure of awakening comes with the judgments of God; they are startling and arousing; and hence the believer's quickening thereby. David would have every severe stroke sanctified to his benefit, as well as every tender mercy. The first clause of this verse may mean "Many," or "manifold are thy compassions, O Jehovah." This he remembers in connection with the "many persecutors" of whom he will speak in the next verse. By all these many mercies he pleads for enlivening grace.

157. Many are my persecutors and mine enemies. Those who actually assail me, or who secretly abhor me, are many. He sets this over against the many tender mercies of God. It seems a strange thing that a truly godly man, as David was, should have many enemies; but it is inevitable. The disciple cannot be loved where his Master is hated. **Yet do I not decline from thy testimonies.** He did not deviate from the truth of God, but proceeded in the straight way, however many adversaries might endeavor to block up his path. Some people have been led astray by one enemy, but here is a saint who held on his way in the teeth of many persecutors. There is enough in the testimonies of God to recompense us for pushing forward against all the hosts that may combine against us. So long as they cannot drive or draw us into a spiritual decline our foes have done us no great harm, and they have accomplished nothing by their malice. Faithfulness to the truth is victory over our enemies.

158. I beheld the transgressors. I saw the traitors; I understood their character, their object, their way, and their end. I could not help seeing them, for they pushed themselves into my way. As I was obliged to see them I fixed my eyes on them, to learn what I could from them. **And was grieved.** I was sick of them, disgusted with them, I could not endure them. I found no pleasure in them; they were a sad sight to me, however fine their clothing or witty their chattering. **Because they kept not thy word.** My grief was occasioned more by their sin against God than by their enmity against myself. Thy Word is so precious to me that those who will not keep it move me to indignation; I cannot keep the company of those who keep not God's Word.

159. Consider, or see, **how I love thy precepts.** He loved the precepts of God unspeakably, so as to be grieved with those who did not love them. This is a sure test: many there are who have a warm side towards the promises, but as for the precepts, they cannot endure them. The psalmist so loved everything that was good and excellent that he loved all God had commanded. The precepts are all of them wise and holy; therefore the man of God loved them extremely, loved to know them, to think of them, to proclaim them, and principally to practice them. He asked the Lord to remember and consider this, not upon the ground of merit, but that it should serve as an answer to the slanderous accusations which at this time were the great sting of his sorrow. **Quicken me, O LORD, according to thy lovingkindness.** He prays again the third time, using the same words. We may understand that David felt ready to faint under their incessant malice. What he wanted was revival, restoration, renewal; therefore he pleaded for more life. O thou who didst quicken me when I was dead, quicken me again that I may not return to the dead! Quicken me that I may outlive the blows of my enemies, the faintness of my faith, and the swooning of my sorrow. This time he says, **according to thy lovingkindness.**

This is his ultimate argument. When he had fallen into great sin this was his plea, "Have mercy upon me, O God, according to thy lovingkindness," and now that he is in great trouble he flies to the same effectual reasoning. Because God is love he will give us life; because he is kind he will again kindle the heavenly flame within us.

160. The sweet singer finishes up this section in the same way as the last by dwelling upon the sureness of the truth of God: note the likeness between verses 144, 152, and 160. **Thy word is true.** Whatever the transgressors may say, God is true, and his Word is true. The ungodly are false, but God's Word is true. They charge us with being false, but our solace is that God's true Word will clear us. **From the beginning.** God's Word has been true from the first moment in which it was spoken, true throughout the whole of history, true to us from the instant in which we believed it, true to us before we were true to it. Some read it, "Thy word is true from the head"; true as a whole, from top to bottom. Experience had taught David this lesson, and experience is teaching us the same. **And every one of thy righteous judgments endureth for ever.** That which thou hast decided remains irreversible in every case. There is not one single mistake either in the Word of God or in the providential dealings of God. God's justice endures forever. This is a cheering thought, but there is a much sweeter one, which of old was the song of the priests in the temple; let it be ours: "His mercy endureth for ever."

161. Princes have persecuted me without a cause. Such people ought to have known better; they should have had sympathy with one of their own rank. Moreover, if honor be banished from all other breasts it should remain in the bosom of kings, and honor forbids the persecution of the innocent. Princes are appointed to protect the innocent and avenge the oppressed, and it is a shame when they themselves become the assailants of the righteous. It was a sad case when the man of God found himself attacked by the judges of the earth, for eminent position added weight and venom to their enmity. It was well that the sufferer could truthfully assert that this persecution was without cause. He had not broken their laws, he had not injured them, he had not even desired to see them injured, he had not been an advocate of rebellion or anarchy, he had neither openly nor secretly opposed their power, and therefore, while this made their oppression the more inexcusable, it took away a part of its sting. **But my heart standeth in awe of thy word.** He might have been overcome by awe of the princes had it not been that a greater fear drove out the less, and he was swayed by awe of God's Word. We are not likely to be disheartened by persecution, or driven by it into sin, if the Word of God continually has supreme power over our minds.

162. I rejoice at thy word, as one that findeth great spoil. His awe did not prevent his joy; his fear of God was not the kind which perfect love casts out, but the sort which it nourishes. He compares his joy to that of one who has been long in battle, and has at last won the victory and is dividing the spoil. This usually falls to the lot of princes, and though David was not one with them in their persecutions, yet he had his victories, and his spoil was equal to their greatest gains. The profits made in searching the Scriptures were greater than the trophies of war. We too have to fight for divine truth; every doctrine costs us a battle, but when we gain a full understanding of it by personal struggles it becomes doubly precious to us. In these days godly people have a full share of battling for the Word of God; may we have for our spoil a firmer hold upon the priceless Word. Perhaps, however, the psalmist may have rejoiced as one who comes upon hidden treasure for which he had not fought, in which case we find the analogy in the man of God who, while reading the Bible, makes grand and blessed discoveries of the grace of God laid up for him – discoveries which surprise him, for he looked not to find such a prize. Whether we come by the truth as finders or as warriors fighting for it, the heavenly treasure should be equally dear to us.

163. I hate and abhor lying. A double expression for an inexpressible loathing. Falsehood in doctrine, in life, or in speech, falsehood in any form or shape, had become utterly detestable to the psalmist. He does not, however, alone refer to falsehood in conversation; he evidently intends perversity in faith and teaching. He set down all opposition to the God of truth as lying, and then he turned his whole soul against it in the intensest form of indignation. Godly men should detest false doctrine even as they abhor a lie. **But thy law do I love,** because it is all truth. His love was as ardent as his hate. Both love and hate are contagious, and when they are sanctified the wider their influence the better.

164. He labored perfectly to praise his perfect God, and therefore fulfilled the perfect number of songs. Seven may also intend frequency. Frequently he lifted up his heart in thanksgiving to God for his divine teaching in the Word, and for his divine actions in providence. With his voice he extolled the righteousness of the Judge of all the earth. As often as ever he thought of God's ways, a song leaped to his lips. At the sight of the oppressive princes, and at the hearing of the abounding falsehood around him, he felt all the more bound to adore and magnify God, who in all things is truth and righteousness. When others rob us of our praise it should be a caution to us not to fall into the same conduct towards our God, who is so much more worthy of honor. If we praise God when we are persecuted, our music will be all the sweeter to him because of our constancy in suffering. If we keep clear of all lying, our song will be the more acceptable because it comes out of pure lips. If we never flatter other people we shall be in the better condition for honoring the Lord. Do we praise God seven times a day? Do we praise him once in seven days?

165. Great peace have they which love thy law. This verse deals not with those who perfectly keep the law (for where should such people be found?), but with those who love it, whose hearts and hands are made to square with its precepts and demands. They are ever striving with all their hearts to walk in obedience to the law, and though they are often persecuted they have **great peace**; for they have learned the secret of the reconciling blood, they have felt the power of the comforting Spirit, and they stand before the Father accepted. They have many troubles, and are likely to be persecuted by the proud, but their usual condition is that of deep calm – a peace too great for this little world to break. **And nothing shall offend them,** or, "shall really injure them." Offenses must come, but these lovers of the law are peacemakers, and so they neither give nor take offense. That peace which is founded upon conformity to God's will is a living and lasting one, worth writing of with enthusiasm, as the psalmist does here.

166. Here we have salvation by grace, and the fruits thereof. All David's hope was fixed upon God; he looked to him alone for salvation; and then he endeavored most earnestly to fulfill the commands of the law. Those who place least reliance upon good works are very frequently those who have the most of them; that same divine teaching which delivers us from confidence in our own doings leads us to abound in every good work to the glory of God. In times of trouble there are two things to be done; the first is to hope in God, and the second is to do that which is right. The first without the second would be mere presumption: the second without the first mere formalism. It is well if in looking back we can claim to have acted in the way which is commanded of the Lord. If we have acted rightly toward God we are sure that he will act kindly with us.

167. My soul hath kept thy testimonies. My outward life has kept thy precepts, and my inward life – my soul – has kept thy testimonies. God has borne testimony to many sacred truths, and these we hold fast as for life itself. The gracious man stores up the truth of God within his heart as a treasure exceedingly dear and precious – he keeps it. His secret soul, his inmost self, becomes the guardian of these divine teachings which are his sole authority in soul matters. **And I love them exceedingly.** This was why he kept them, and having kept them this was the result of the keeping. He did not merely store up revealed truth by way of duty, but because of a deep, unutterable affection for it. He felt that he could sooner die than give up any part of the revelation of God. The more we store our minds with heavenly truth, the more deeply shall we be in love with it: the more we see the exceeding riches of the Bible, the more will our love exceed measure, and exceed expression.

168. I have kept thy precepts and thy testimonies. Both the practical and the doctrinal parts of God's Word he had stored up, and preserved, and followed. It is a blessed thing to see the two forms of the divine Word, equally known, equally valued, equally confessed: there should be no picking and choosing as to the mind of God. We know those who endeavor to be careful as to the precepts, but who seem to think that the doctrines of the Gospel are mere matters of opinion, which they may shape for themselves. This is not a perfect condition of things. We have known others again who are very rigid as to the doctrines, and painfully lax with reference to the precepts. This also is far from right. When the two are **kept** with equal earnestness, then we have perfection. **For all my ways are before thee.** Probably he means to say that this was the motive of his endeavoring to be right both in head and heart, because he knew that God saw him, and under the sense of the divine presence he was afraid to err. Or else he is thus appealing to God to bear witness to the truth of what he has said. In either case it is no small consolation to feel that our Heavenly Father knows all about us, and that if princes speak against us, and worldlings fill their mouths with cruel lies, yet he can vindicate us, for there is nothing secret or hidden from him.

We are struck with the contrast between this verse, which is the last of its octave, and verse 176, which is similarly placed in the next octave. This is a protest of innocence, "I have kept thy precepts," and that a confession of sin, "I have gone astray like a lost sheep." Both were sincere, both accurate. Experience makes many a paradox plain, and this is one. Before God we may be clear of open fault and yet at the same time mourn over a thousand heart-wanderings which need his restoring hand.

169–176. The psalmist is approaching the end of the psalm, and his petitions gather force and fervency; he seems to break into the inner circle of divine fellowship, and to come even to the feet of the great God whose help he is imploring. This nearness creates the most lowly view of himself, and leads him to close the psalm upon his face in deepest self-humiliation, begging to be sought out like a lost sheep.

169. Let my cry come near before thee, O Lord. He is tremblingly afraid lest he should not be heard. He is conscious that his prayer is nothing better than the cry of a poor child, or the groan of a wounded beast. He dreads lest it should be shut out from the ear of the Most High, but he very boldly prays that it may come before God, that it may be looked upon with his acceptance. He wants the Lord's attention to his prayer to be very close and considerate. He uses a figure of speech and personifies his prayer. It is to Jehovah that this prayer is expressed with trembling earnestness; our translators, filled with holy reverence, translate the word **O Lord.** We crave audience of none else, for we have confidence in none beside. **Give me understanding according to thy word.** This is the prayer about which the psalmist is so exceedingly anxious. With all his gettings he would get understanding, and whatever he misses he is resolved not to miss this priceless boon. He desires spiritual light and understanding as it is promised in God's Word, as it proceeds from God's Word, and as it produces obedience to God's Word. He pleads as though he had no understanding whatever of his own, and asks to have it given to him. In truth, he had an understanding according to human judgment, but what he sought was an understanding according to God's Word, which is quite another thing. To understand spiritual things is the gift of God. To have a judgment enlightened by heavenly light and conformed to divine truth is a privilege which only grace can give. Many a man who is accounted wise after the manner of this world is a fool according to the Word of the Lord. May we be among those happy children who will all be taught of the Lord.

170. Let my supplication come before thee. It is the same entreaty with a slight change of words. He humbly calls his cry a **supplication**, a sort of beggar's petition; and again he asks for audience – let it come. Other believers are heard – let my prayer come before thee. **Deliver me according to thy word.** Rid me of mine adversaries, clear me of my slanderers, preserve me from my tempters, and bring me up out of all my afflictions, even as thy Word has led me to expect thou wilt do. It is for this that he seeks understanding. His enemies would succeed through his folly, if they succeeded at all; but if he exercised a sound discretion they would be baffled, and he would escape from them. The Lord in answer to prayer frequently delivers his children by making them wise as serpents as well as harmless as doves.

171. He will not always be pleading for himself; he will rise above all selfishness, and render thanks for the benefit received. He promises to praise God when he has obtained practical instruction in the life of godliness: this is something to praise for; no blessing is more precious. The best possible praise is that which proceeds from people who honor God, not only with their lips, but in their lives. We learn the music of heaven in the school of holy living. David would not only be grateful in silence, but he would express that gratitude in appropriate terms.

172. My tongue shall speak of thy word. When he had done singing he began preaching. When the tongue speaks of God's Word it has a most fruitful subject. People will gather to listen to such talk, and they will treasure it up in their hearts. The worst of it is that for the most part we are full of our own words, and speak but little of God's Word. Oh, that we could come to the same resolve as this godly man; then should we break through our sinful silence; we should no more be cowardly and half-hearted, but should be true witnesses for Jesus. It is not only of God's works that we are to speak, but of his Word. We may extol its truth, its wisdom, its preciousness, its grace, its power; and then we may tell of all it has revealed, all it has promised, all it has commanded, all it has effected. **For all thy commandments are righteousness.** David seems to have been mainly enamored of the preceptive part of the Word of God, and concerning the precepts his chief delight lay in its purity and excellence. When a man can speak this from his heart, his heart is indeed a temple of the Holy Spirit. He had said (verse 138), "Thy testimonies are righteous," but here he declares that they are righteousness itself. The law of God is not only the standard of right, but it is the essence of righteousness. This the psalmist affirms of each and every one of the precepts.

173. Let thine hand help me. Give me practical succor. Do not entrust me to my friends or thy friends, but put thine own hand to the work. Thy hand has both skill and power, readiness and force: display all these qualities on my behalf. I am willing to do the utmost that I am able to do; but what I need is thine help, and this is so urgently required that if I have it not I shall sink. Do not refuse thy succor. Great as thy hand is, let it light on me, even me. The prayer reminds us of Peter walking on the sea and beginning to sink; he, too, cried, "Lord, help me," and the hand of his Master was stretched out for his rescue. **For I have chosen thy precepts.** We may fitly ask help from God's hand when we have dedicated our own hand to the obedience of the faith. His mind was made up. In preference to all earthly rules and ways, in preference even to his own will, he had chosen to be obedient to the divine commands. Will not God help such a man in holy work and sacred service? Assuredly he will. If grace has given us a heart with which to will, it will also give us the hand with which to perform. Whenever, under the constraints of a divine call, we are engaged in any high and lofty enterprise, and feel it to be too much for our strength, we may always invoke the right hand of God in words like these.

174. I have longed for thy salvation, O LORD. He knew God's salvation, and yet he longed for it; that is to say, he had experienced a share of it, and he was therefore led to expect something yet higher and more complete. There is a salvation yet to come, when we shall be clean delivered from the body of this death, set free from all the turmoil and trouble of this mortal life, raised above the temptations and assaults of Satan, and brought near unto our God, to be like him and with him forever and ever. **And thy law is my delight.** The first clause tells us what the saint longs for, and this informs us what is his present satisfaction. God's law, contained in the Ten Commandments, gives joy to believers. God's law, that is, the entire Bible, is a well-spring of consolation and enjoyment to all who receive it. Though we have not yet reached the fullness of our salvation, yet we find in God's Word so much concerning a present salvation that we are even now delighted.

175. Let my soul live. Fill it full of life, preserve it from wandering into the ways of death, give it to enjoy the indwelling of the Holy Spirit, let it live to the fullness of life. **And it shall praise thee.** The more it lives, the more it will praise, and when it lives in perfection it will praise thee in perfection. Spiritual life is prayer and praise. **And let thy judgments help me.** While I read the record of what thou hast done, in terror or in love, let me be quickened and developed. While I see thy hand actually at work upon me, and upon others, chastening sin, and smiling upon righteousness, let me be helped both to live aright and to praise thee.

176. This is the finale: **I have gone astray like a lost sheep** – often, willfully, wantonly, and even hopelessly, but for thine interposing grace. Before I was afflicted, and before thou hadst fully taught me thy statutes, I went astray from the practical precepts, from the instructive doctrines, and from the heavenly experiences which thou hadst set before me. I lost my road, and I lost myself. Even now I am apt to wander, and, in fact, have roamed already; therefore, Lord, restore me. **Seek thy servant.** He was not like a dog, that somehow or other can find its way back; but he was like a lost sheep, which goes further and further away from home; yet still he was a sheep, and the Lord's sheep, his property, and precious in his sight, and therefore he hoped to be sought in order to be restored. However far he might have wandered he was still not only a sheep, but God's "servant," and therefore he desired to be in his Master's house again, and once more honored with commissions for his Lord. Had he been only a lost sheep he would not have prayed to be sought; but being also a "servant" he had the power to pray. He cries, **Seek thy servant,** and he hoped to be not only sought, but forgiven, accepted, and taken into work again by his gracious Master.

Notice this confession; many times in the psalm David has defended his own innocence against foul-mouthed accusers, but when he comes into the presence of the Lord his God he is ready enough to confess his transgressions. Here he sums up, not only his past, but even his present life, under the image of a sheep which has broken from its pasture, forsaken the flock, left the shepherd, and brought itself into the wild wilderness, where it has become as a lost thing. The sheep bleats, and David prays, **Seek thy servant.** His argument is a forcible one – **for I do not forget thy commandments.** I know the right, I approve and admire the right; what is more, I love the right, and long for it. I cannot be satisfied to continue in sin, I must be restored to the ways of righteousness. I have a home-sickness after my God, I pine after the ways of peace; I do not and I cannot forget thy commandments, nor cease to know that I am always happiest and safest when I scrupulously obey them and find all my joy in doing so. Now, if the grace of God enables us to maintain in our hearts the loving memory of God's commandments it will surely yet restore us to practical holiness. We cannot be utterly lost if our heart is still with God. If we be gone astray in many respects, yet still, if we be true in our soul's inmost desires, we shall be found again, and fully restored. Yet, let us remember the first verse of the psalm while reading the last: the major blessedness lies not in being restored from wandering, but in being upheld in a blameless way even to the end. Be it ours to keep the crown of the causeway, never leaving the King's Highway for By-path Meadow, or any other flowery path of sin. May the Lord uphold us even to the end. Yet even then we shall not be able to boast with the Pharisee, but shall still pray with the publican, "God be merciful to me a sinner," and with the psalmist, **Seek thy servant.**

Psalm 120

1. In my distress. Slander occasions distress of the most grievous kind. Those who have felt the edge of a cruel tongue know assuredly that it is sharper than the sword. Calumny rouses our indignation by a sense of injustice, and yet we find ourselves helpless to fight with the evil, or to act in our own defense. We could ward off the strokes of a cutlass, but we have no shield against a liar's tongue. We do not know who was the father of the falsehood, nor where it was born, nor where it has gone, nor how to follow it, nor how to stay its withering influence. We are perplexed, and know not which way to turn. Like the plague of flies in Egypt, it baffles opposition, and few can stand before it. Detraction touches us in the tenderest point, cuts to the quick, and leaves a venom behind which it is difficult to extract. In all ways it is a sore distress to come under the power of slander. Silence to man and prayer to God are the best cures for the evil of slander.

I cried unto the LORD (or Jehovah). The wisest course that he could follow. It is of little use to appeal to our fellows on the matter of slander, for the more we stir in it the more it spreads; it is of no avail to appeal to the honor of the slanderers, for they have none, and the most piteous demands for justice will only increase their malignity and encourage them to issue fresh insult. To whom should children cry but to their father? Does not some good come even out of that vile thing, falsehood, when it drives us to our knees and to our God? **And he heard me.** The psalmist remembered and recorded this instance of prayer-hearing, for it had evidently much affected him. When we are slandered it is a joy that the Lord knows us, and cannot be made to doubt our uprightness: he will not hear the lie against us, but he will hear our prayer against the lie.

If Psalms 120–134 were sung at the ascent of the ark to Mount Zion, and then afterwards by the pilgrims to Jerusalem at the annual festivals and at the return from Babylon, we shall find in the life of David a reason for this being made the first of them. Did not this servant of God meet with Doeg the Edomite when he inquired of the oracle by Abiathar, and did not that wretched creature belie him and betray him to Saul? This made a very painful and permanent impression upon David's memory, and therefore in commencing the ark-journey he poured out his lament before the Lord. The poet, like the preacher, may find it to his advantage to begin low, for then he has the more room to rise: the next psalm is a full octave above the present mournful hymn. Whenever we are abused it may console us to see that we are not alone in our misery: we are traversing a road upon which David left his footprints.

2. Deliver my soul, O LORD, from lying lips. It will need divine power to save a man from these deadly instruments. Lips are soft, but when they are **lying** lips they suck away the life of character and are as murderous as razors. Lips should never be red with the blood of honest people's reputes, nor salved with malicious falsehoods. The soul, the life of the man, is endangered by lying lips. The faculty of speech becomes a curse when it is degraded into a mean weapon for smiting people behind their backs. We need to be delivered from slander by the Lord's restraint upon wicked tongues, or else to be delivered out of it by having our good name cleared from the liar's calumny. **And from a deceitful tongue.** This is rather worse than downright falsehood. Those who fawn and flatter, and all the while have enmity in their hearts, are horrible beings; they are the offspring of the devil, and he works in them after his own deceptive nature. It should be a warning to liars and deceivers when they see that all good people pray against them, and that even bad people are afraid of them. From gossips, talebearers, writers of anonymous letters, forgers of newspaper paragraphs, and all sorts of lie-mongers, good Lord deliver us!

3. What shall be given unto thee? It ought to be something great to make it worthwhile to work in so foul an atmosphere and to ruin one's soul. The liar will have no welcome recompense: he will meet with his deserts; but what will they be? What punishment can equal his crime? The psalmist seems lost to suggest a fitting punishment.

Or what shall be done unto thee, thou false tongue? The law of retaliation can hardly meet the case, since the slanderer is too black to be blackened. He fights with weapons which true men cannot touch. What will God do with lying tongues? He has uttered his most terrible threats against them, and he will terribly execute them in due time.

4. Sharp arrows of the mighty. Swift, sure, and sharp will be the judgment. Nor will one form of judgment suffice to avenge this complicated sin. The slanderer will feel woes comparable to **coals of juniper,** which are quick in flaming, fierce in blazing, and long in burning. Juniper coals long retain their heat, but hell burneth ever, and the deceitful tongue may not deceive itself with the hope of escape from the fire which it has kindled. What a crime is this to which the Almighty allots a doom so dreadful! Let us hate it with perfect hatred. It is better to be the victim of slander than to be the author of it. The shafts of calumny will miss the mark, but not so the arrows of God: the coals of malice will cool, but not the fire of justice. Shun slander as you would avoid hell.

5. Gracious people are vexed with the conversation of the wicked. Our poet felt himself to be as ill-at-ease among lying neighbors as if he had lived among savages. He had some hope from the fact that he was only a sojourner in Mesech; but as years rolled on the time dragged heavily, and he feared that he might call himself a dweller in Kedar. The wandering tribes to whom he refers were constantly at war with one another; it was their habit to travel armed to the teeth; they were a kind of plundering gypsies, with their hand against every man and every man's hand against them; and to these he compared the false-hearted ones who had assailed his character. Those who defame the righteous are worse than cannibals; for savages only eat men after they are dead, but these wretches eat them up alive.

6. Too long had he been an exile among such barbarians. A peacemaker is a blessing, but a peace-hater is a curse. To lodge with such for a night is dangerous, but to dwell with them is horrible. The verse may apply to any one of the psalmist's detractors: he had seen enough of him and pined to quit such company. Perhaps the sweet singer did not at first detect the nature of the man, for he was a deceiver; and when he did discover him he found himself unable to shake him off, and so was compelled to abide with him. Thoughts of Doeg, Saul, Ahithophel, and the sons of Zeruiah come to our mind – these last, not as enemies, but as hot-blooded soldiers who were often too strong for David. What a change for the man of God from the quietude of the sheepfold to the turmoil of court and the tumult of combat! How he must have longed to lay aside his scepter and resume his crook. He felt the time of his dwelling with quarrelsome spirits to be long, too long; and he only endured it because, as the Prayer-book version has it, he was "constrained" so to abide.

7. I am for peace. Properly, "I am peace"; desirous of peace, peaceful, forbearing – in fact, peace itself. **But when I speak, they are for war.** My kindest words appear to provoke them, and they are as daggers drawn at once. Nothing pleases them; if I am silent they count me morose, and if I open my mouth they cavil and controvert. Let those who dwell with such pugilistic company console themselves with the remembrance that both David and David's Lord endured the same trial. It is the lot of the saints to find foes even in their own households. Others besides David dwelt in the place of dragons. Others besides Daniel have been cast into a den of lions. Meanwhile, let those who are in quiet resting-places and peaceful habitations be greatly grateful for such ease. God has given us this tranquillity. Be it ours never to inflict upon others that from which we have been screened ourselves.

Psalm 121

1. It is wise to look to the strong for strength. Dwellers in valleys are subject to many disorders for which there is no cure but a sojourn in the uplands, and it is well when they shake off their lethargy and resolve upon a climb. Down below they are the prey of marauders, and to escape from them the surest method is to fly to the strongholds upon the mountains. Often before the actual ascent the sick and plundered people looked towards the hills and longed to be upon their summits. The holy man who here sings looked away from the slanderers by whom he was tormented to the Lord who saw all from the high places, and was ready to pour down succor for his injured servant. Help comes to saints only from above; they look elsewhere in vain. Let us lift up our eyes with hope, expectancy, desire, and confidence. Satan will endeavor to keep our eyes upon our sorrows that we may be disquieted and discouraged; be it ours firmly to resolve that we will look out and look up, for there is good cheer for the eyes, and they that lift up their eyes to the eternal hills will soon have their hearts lifted up also. The purposes of God; the divine attributes; the immutable promises; the covenant, ordered in all things and sure; the providence, predestination, and proved faithfulness of the Lord – these are the hills to which we must lift up our eyes, for from these our help must come. It is our resolve that we will not be bandaged and blindfolded, but will lift up our eyes.

Or is the text in the interrogative? Does he ask, "Shall I lift up mine eyes to the hills?" Does he feel that the highest places of the earth can afford him no shelter? Or does he renounce the idea of recruits hastening to his standard from the hardy mountaineers? Does he again inquire, "Whence cometh my help?" If so, the next verse answers the question, and shows whence all help must come.

2. What we need is help – help powerful, efficient, constant: we need a very present help in trouble. What a mercy that we have it in our God. Our hope is in Jehovah, for our help comes from him. Help is on the road, and will not fail to reach us in due time, for he who sends it to us was never known to be too late. Jehovah who created all things is equal to every emergency; heaven and earth are at the disposal of him who made them, therefore let us be very joyful in our infinite helper. He will sooner destroy heaven and earth than permit his people to be destroyed, and the perpetual hills themselves will bow rather than he fail whose ways are everlasting. We are bound to look beyond heaven and earth to him who made them both; it is vain to trust the creatures: it is wise to trust the Creator.

3. He will not suffer thy foot to be moved. Though the paths of life are dangerous and difficult, yet we shall stand fast, for Jehovah will not permit our feet to slide; and if he will not suffer it we shall not suffer it. If our feet will be thus kept we may be sure that our head and heart will be preserved also. In the original the words express a wish or prayer – "May he not suffer thy foot to be moved." Promised preservation should be the subject of perpetual prayer; and we may pray believingly, for those who have God for their keeper will be safe from all the perils of the way. Among the hills and ravines of Palestine the literal keeping of the feet is a great mercy; but in the slippery ways of a tried and afflicted life, the boon of upholding is of priceless value, for a single false step might cause us a fall fraught with awful danger. To stand erect and pursue the even tenor of our way is a blessing which only God can give, which is worthy of the divine hand, and worthy also of perennial gratitude. Our feet will move in progress, but they will not be moved to their overthrow. **He that keepeth thee will not slumber** – or "thy keeper will not slumber." We should not stand a moment if our keeper were to sleep; we need him by day and by night; not a single step can be safely taken except under his guardian eye. This is a choice stanza in a pilgrim song. God is the convoy and bodyguard of his saints. When dangers are awake around us we are safe, for our Preserver is awake also, and will not permit us to be taken unawares. No fatigue or exhaustion can cast our God into sleep; his watchful eyes are never closed.

4. The consoling truth must be repeated: it is too rich to be dismissed in a single line. It were well if we always imitated the sweet singer, and would dwell a little upon a choice doctrine, sucking the honey from it. What a glorious title is in the Hebrew – "the Keeper of Israel" – and how delightful to think that no form of unconsciousness ever steals over him, neither the deep slumber nor the lighter sleep. He will never let the house be broken up by the silent thief; he is ever on the watch, and speedily perceives every intruder. This is a subject of wonder, a theme for attentive consideration; therefore the word **Behold** is set up as a waymark. Israel fell asleep, but his God was awake. Jacob had neither walls, nor curtains, nor bodyguard around him; but the Lord was in that place though Jacob knew it not, and therefore the defenseless man was safe as in a castle. In after days he mentioned God under this enchanting name – "The God that led me all my life long": perhaps David alludes to that passage in this expression. The word **keepeth** is also full of meaning: he keeps us as a rich man keeps his treasures, as a captain keep s a city with a garrison, as a royal guard keeps his monarch's head. If the former verse is in strict accuracy a prayer, this is the answer to it. In verse 3 the Lord is spoken of as the personal keeper of one individual, and here of all those who are in his chosen nation, described as Israel: mercy to one saint is the pledge of blessing to them all. Happy are the pilgrims to whom this psalm is a safe-conduct; they may journey all the way to the celestial city without fear.

5. The LORD is thy keeper. Here the preserving One, who had been spoken of by pronouns in the two previous verses, is distinctly named – Jehovah is thy keeper. Here is a glorious person – Jehovah, assuming a gracious office and fulfilling it in person – Jehovah is thy **keeper,** in behalf of a favored individual – **thy,** and a firm assurance of revelation that it is even so at this hour – Jehovah **is** thy keeper. We may journey through the valley of the shadow of death and fear no evil. **The LORD is thy shade upon thy right hand.** A shade gives protection from burning heat and glaring light. We cannot bear too much blessing; even divine goodness, which is a right-hand disposition, must be toned down and shaded to suit our infirmity, and this the Lord will do for us. God is as near us as our shadow, and we are as safe as angels.

6. Doubtless there are dangers of the light and of the dark, but in both and from both we shall be preserved – literally from excessive heat and from baneful chills; mystically from any injurious effects which might follow from doctrine; spiritually from the evils of prosperity and adversity; eternally from the strain of overpowering glory and from the pressure of terrible events, such as judgment. Day and night make up all time: thus the ever-present protection never ceases. All evil may be ranked as under the sun or the moon, and if neither of these can smite us we are indeed secure. God has not made a new sun or a fresh moon for his chosen; they exist under the same outward circumstances as others, but the power to **smite** is in their case removed from temporal agencies; saints are enriched, and not injured, by the powers which govern the earth's condition; to them has the Lord given "the precious things brought forth by the sun, and the precious things brought forth by the moon," while at the same moment he has removed from them all bale and curse of heat or damp, of glare or chill.

7. The LORD shall preserve thee from all evil. It is a great pity that our admirable translation did not keep the word "keep" all through the psalm, for all along it is one. God not only keeps his own in all evil times but from evil influences and operations, indeed from evils themselves. The wings of Jehovah amply guard his own from evils great and small, temporary and eternal. There is a most delightful double personality in this verse: Jehovah keeps the believer, not by agents, but by himself; and the person protected is definitely pointed out by the word **thee** – it is not our estate or name which is shielded, but the proper person. To make this even more intensely real and personal another sentence is added, **The LORD shall preserve thee from all evil: he shall preserve thy soul,** or Jehovah will keep thy soul. Soulkeeping is the soul of keeping. If the soul be kept all is kept. Our soul is kept from the dominion of sin, the infection of error, the crush of despondency, the puffing up of pride; kept from the world, the flesh, and the devil; kept for holier and greater things; kept in the love of God; kept unto the eternal kingdom and glory. What can harm a soul that is kept of the Lord?

8. When we go out in the morning to labor, and come home at eventide to rest, Jehovah will keep us. When we go out in youth to begin life, and come in at the end to die, we shall experience the same keeping. Our exits and our entrances are under one protection. Three times have we the phrase, "Jehovah shall keep," as if the sacred Trinity thus sealed the word to make it sure: ought not all our fears to be slain by such a threefold flight of arrows? This keeping is eternal, continuing from this time forth forevermore. The whole church is thus assured of everlasting security: the final perseverance of the saints is thus ensured, and the glorious immortality of believers is guaranteed. Under the aegis of such a promise we may go on pilgrimage without trembling, and venture into battle without dread. None are so safe as those whom God keeps, none so much in danger as the self-secure. To goings out and comings in belong particular dangers, since every change of position turns a fresh quarter to the foe, and it is for these weak points that an especial security is provided: Jehovah will keep the door when it opens and closes, and this he will perseveringly continue to do so long as there is left a single person who trusts in him, as long as a danger survives, and in fact as long as time endures. Glory be unto the Keeper of Israel, who is endeared to us under that title, since our growing sense of weakness makes us feel more deeply than ever our need of being kept.

Psalm 122

1. Good children are pleased to go home, and glad to hear their brothers and sisters call them thither. David's heart was in the worship of God, and he was delighted when he found others inviting him to go where his desires had already gone: it helps the ardor of the most ardent case to hear others inviting them to a holy duty. The word was not "go," it was **let us go**; hence the ear of the psalmist found a double joy in it. He was glad *for the sake of others*: glad that they wished to go themselves, glad that they had the courage and liberality to invite others. He knew that it would do them good; nothing better can happen to us than to love the place where God's honor dwells. But David was glad *for his own sake*: he loved the invitation to the holy place, he delighted in being called to go to worship in company, and, moreover, he rejoiced that good people thought enough of him to extend their invitation to him. Some people would have been offended, and would have said, "Mind your own business; let my religion alone"; but not so King David, though he had more dignity than any of us, and less need to be reminded of his duty. He was glad to go into the house of the Lord, glad to go in holy company, glad to find good men and women willing to have him in their society. He may have been sad before, but this happy suggestion cheered him up. He pricked up his ears at the very mention of his Father's house. Is it so with us? Are we glad when others invite us to public worship, or to church fellowship? Then we shall be glad when the spirits above call us to the house of the Lord not made with hands, eternal in the heavens. We love our Lord, and therefore we love his house, and pangs of strong desire are upon us that we may soon reach the eternal abode of his glory. An aged saint, when dying, cheered herself with this evidence of grace, for she cried, "I have loved the habitation of thy house, and the place where thine honor dwelleth," and therefore she begged that she might join the holy congregation of those who forever behold the King in his beauty. Our gladness at the bare thought of being in God's house is detective as to our character, and prophetic of our being one day happy in the Father's house on high. In prospect of the Lord's day, and all its hallowed associations, our soul rejoices. How well, also, may it refer to the church! We are happy when we see numerous bands ready to unite themselves with the people of God. The pastor is specially glad when many come forward and ask of him assistance in entering into fellowship with the church. No language is more cheering to him than the humble request, "Let us go into the house of the Lord."

2. Our feet shall stand within thy gates, O Jerusalem, or, better, "our feet are standing." The words imply present and joyous standing within the walls of the city of peace; or perhaps the pilgrims felt so sure of getting there that they antedated the joy, and spoke as if they were already there, though they were as yet only on the road. If we are within the church we may well triumph in the fact. Outside the gates all is danger, and one day all will be destruction; but within the gates all is safety, seclusion, serenity, salvation, and glory. The gates are opened that we may pass in, and they are only shut that our enemies may not follow us. The Lord loveth the gates of Zion, and so do we when we are enclosed within them. What a choice favor, to be a citizen of the New Jerusalem! Why are *we* so greatly favored? Many feet are running the downward road, or kicking against the pricks, or held by snares, or sliding to an awful fall; but our feet, through grace divine, are standing – an honorable posture – **within thy gates, O Jerusalem** – an honorable position, and there shall they stand forever – an honorable future.

3. David saw in vision the city built; no more a waste, or a mere collection of tents, or a city upon paper, commenced but not completed. God's mercy to the Israelite nation allowed peace and plenty, sufficient for the uprise and perfecting of its capital: that city flourished in happy times, even as the church is only built up when all the people of God are prospering. Thanks be to God, the Lord by his glorious appearing has built up Zion. Furthermore, it is not erected as a set of booths, or a conglomeration of hovels, but as a city, substantial, architectural, designed, arranged, and defended. The church is a permanent and important institution, founded on a Rock, built with art, and arranged with wisdom. In a church one of the most delightful conditions is the compactness of unity: "one Lord, one faith, one baptism." A church should be one in creed and one in heart, one in testimony and one in service, one in aspiration and one in sympathy. They greatly injure our Jerusalem who would build dividing walls within her; she needs compacting, not dividing. There is no joy in going up to a church which is rent with internal dissension: the gladness of holy people is aroused by the adhesiveness of love, the unity of life; it would be their sadness if they saw the church to be a house divided against itself. Some bodies of Christians appear to be periodically blown to fragments, and no gracious person is glad to be in the way when the explosions take place: thither the tribes do not go up, for strife and contention are not attractive forces.

4. Whither the tribes go up, the tribes of the LORD. When there is unity within, there will be gatherings from without: the tribes go up to a compact center. Note that Israel was one people, but yet it was in a sense divided by the mere surface distinction of tribes; and this may be a lesson to us that all Christendom is essentially one, though from various causes we are divided into tribes. Let us as much as possible sink the tribal individuality in the national unity, so that the church may be many waves, but one sea; many branches, but one tree; many members, but one body. The tribes were all the Lord's. Oh that all the regiments of the Christian army may be all and equally the Lord's own, alike chosen, redeemed, accepted, and upheld by Jehovah. **Unto the testimony of Israel.** They went up to the holy city to hear and to bear testimony. Everything in the Temple was a testimony unto the Lord, and the annual journeys of the tribes to the hallowed shrine partook of the same testifying character, for these journeys were Israel's open avowal that Jehovah was their God, and that he was the one only living and true God. When we assemble on the Sabbath a large part of our business is giving out and receiving testimony: we are God's witnesses. **To give thanks unto the name of the LORD.** Another part of our delightful duty is to praise the Lord. Sacred praise is a chief design of the assembling of ourselves together. All Israel had been fed by the fruit of the field, and they went up to give thanks unto the name of their great Husbandman: we, too, have countless mercies, and it becomes us unitedly in our solemn gatherings to magnify the name of our loving Lord. Testimony should be mingled with thanks, and thanks with testimony, for in combination they bless both God and man, and tend to spread themselves over the hearts of our companions, who, seeing our joyful gratitude, are the more inclined to hearken to our witness-bearing.

5. For there are set thrones of judgment. If discontented with the petty judgments of their village lords, the people could bring their hard matters to the royal seat, and the beloved King would be sure to decide aright; for the judgment-thrones were **the thrones of the house of David.** We who come to the church and its public worship are charmed to come to the throne of God, and to the throne of the reigning Saviour. To a true saint the throne is never more amiable than in its judicial capacity; the righteous love judgment, and are glad that right will be rewarded and iniquity punished. The throne of judgment is not removed, but firmly **set,** and there it will remain till the work of justice is accomplished, and truth and right are set on the throne with their King. Happy people to be under so glorious a rule.

6. Pray for the peace of Jerusalem. Peace was her name; pray that her condition may verify her title. That sacred shrine stood in the center of an area of peace: well might Israel pray that such peace should be continued. In a church peace is to be desired, expected, promoted, and enjoyed. If we may not say, "Peace at any price," yet we may certainly cry, "Peace at the highest price." In a church one of the main ingredients is internal peace: strife, suspicion, party-spirit, division – these are deadly things. Those who break the peace of the church should be our daily prayer, and in so praying we shall bring down peace upon ourselves, for the psalmist goes on to say, **They shall prosper that**

love thee, or perhaps we may read it as a prayer, "May they have peace that love thee." Prosperity of soul is already enjoyed by those who take a deep interest in the church and the cause of God: they are people of peace, and find peace in their holy endeavors: God's people pray for them, and God himself delights in them. Prosperity of worldly condition often comes to the lovers of the church if they are able to bear it: many a time the house of Obed-edom is blessed because of the ark of the Lord. Because the Egyptian midwives feared the Lord, therefore the Lord made them houses. No one will ever be a permanent loser by the house of the Lord: in peace of heart alone, if in nothing else, we find recompense enough for all that we can do in promoting the interests of Zion.

7. **Peace be within thy walls.** See how the poet personifies the church, and speaks to it: his heart is with Zion, and therefore his conversation runs in that direction. A second time is the sweet favor of peace earnestly sought after: "There is none like it, give it me." Walls were needed to keep out the foe, but it was asked of the Lord that those walls might prove sufficient for her security. May the munitions of rock so securely defend the city of God that no intruder may ever enter within her inclosure. May her ramparts repose in safety. **And prosperity within thy palaces,** or "Repose within thy palaces." Peace is prosperity; there can be no prosperity which is not based on peace, nor can there long be peace if prosperity be gone, for decline of grace breeds decay of love. We wish for the church rest from internal dissension and external assault: war is not her element (Acts 9:31). Our Jerusalem is a city of palaces: kings dwell within her walls, and God himself is there. The smallest church is worthy of higher honor than the greatest confederacies of nobles. For the sake of all the saintly spirits which inhabit the city of God we may well entreat for her the boons of lasting peace and abounding prosperity.

8. It is to the advantage of all Israel that there should be peace in Jerusalem. It is for the good of every Christian, indeed of every person, that there should be peace and prosperity in the church. By a flourishing church our children, our neighbors, our fellow-countrymen are likely to be blest. Moreover, we cannot but pray for a cause with which our dearest relatives and choicest friends are associated.

9. He prays for Jerusalem because of Zion. How the church salts and savors all around it. The presence of Jehovah, our God, endears to us every place wherein he reveals his glory. Well may we seek her good within whose walls dwells God who alone is good. We are to live for God's cause, and to be ready to die for it. First we love it (verse 6) and then we labor for it: we see its good, and then seek its good. If we can do nothing else we can intercede for it. Our covenant relation to Jehovah as our God binds us to pray for his people – they are **the house of the LORD our God.** If we honor our God we desire the prosperity of the church which he has chosen for his indwelling.

Psalm 123

1. Unto thee lift I up mine eyes. It is good to have someone to look up to. The psalmist looked so high that he could look no higher. Not to the hills, but to the God of the hills he looked. He believed in a personal God, and knew nothing of that modern pantheism which is nothing more than atheism wearing a figleaf. The uplifted eyes naturally and instinctively represent the state of heart which fixes desire, hope, confidence, and expectation upon the Lord. God is everywhere, and yet it is most natural to think of him as being above us. **O thou that dwellest in the heavens** just sets forth the unsophisticated idea of a child of God in distress: God is, God is in heaven, God resides in one place, and God is evermore the same; therefore will I look to him. When we cannot look to any helper on a level with us it is greatly wise to look above us; in fact, if we have a thousand helpers, our eyes should still be toward the Lord. The higher the Lord is, the better for our faith, since that height represents power, glory, and excellence, and these will be all engaged on our behalf. We ought to be very thankful for spiritual eyes; the blind men of this world, however much of human learning they may possess, cannot behold our God, for in heavenly matters they are devoid of sight. Yet we must use our eyes with resolution, for they will not go upward to the Lord of themselves, but they incline to look downward, or inward, or anywhere but to the Lord: let it be our firm resolve that the heavenward glance shall not be lacking. If we cannot see God, at least we will look towards him. God is in heaven as a king in his palace; he is there revealed, adored, and glorified; thence he looks down on the world and sends succors to his saints as their needs demand; hence we look up, even when our sorrow is so great that he permits us to lift up our eyes to his glorious high throne; moreover, he invites and even commands us so to do. When we are looking to the Lord in hope, it is well to tell him so in prayer: the psalmist uses his voice as well as his eye. We need not speak in prayer; a glance of the eye will do it all. Still it is helpful to the heart to use the tongue, and we do well to address ourselves in words and sentences to the God who hears his people. It is no small joy that our God is always at home: he is not on a journey, like Baal, but he dwells in the heavens. Let us think no hour of the day inopportune for waiting upon the Lord, no watch of the night too dark for us to look to him.

2. Behold. See, O Lord, how we look to thee, and in thy mercy look on us. This **Behold** has, however, a call to us to observe and consider. Whenever saints of God have waited upon the Lord their example has been worthy of earnest consideration. Sanctification is a miracle of grace; therefore let us behold it. For God to have wrought in us the spirit of service is a great marvel, and as such let everyone turn aside and see this great sight. **As the eyes of servants** (or slaves) **look unto the hand of their masters.** Orientals speak less than we do, and prefer to direct their slaves by movements of their hands; hence, the domestic must fix his eyes on his master, or he might miss a sign, and so fail to obey it: just so, the sanctified person lifts his eyes unto God, and endeavors to learn the divine will from every one of the signs which the Lord is pleased to use. Creation, providence, grace; these are all motions of Jehovah's hand, and from each of them a portion of our duty is to be learned; therefore should we carefully study them, to discover the divine will. **And as the eyes of a maiden unto the hand of her mistress.** This second comparison may be used because Eastern women are even more thorough than the men in the training of their servants. **Even so our eyes wait upon the LORD our God.** Believers desire to be attentive to each and all of the directions of the Lord; even those which concern apparently little things are not little to us, for we know that even for idle words we shall be called to account, and we are anxious to give that account with joy, and not with grief. True saints, like obedient servants, look continuously, for there is never a time when they are off duty. Upon the Lord they look expectantly, looking for supply, succor, and safety from his hands, waiting that he may have mercy upon them. They have no other confidence, and they learn to look submissively, waiting patiently for the Lord, seeking both in activity and suffering to glorify his name. When they are smitten with the rod they turn their eyes imploringly to the hand which chastens, hoping that mercy will soon abate the rigor of the affliction. Though we are sons, have we learned the full obedience of servants? Have we surrendered self, and bowed our will before the heavenly Majesty? Do we desire in all things to be at the Lord's disposal? If so, happy are we.

Observe the covenant name, "Jehovah our God": it is sweet to wait upon a covenant God. Because of that covenant he will show mercy to us; but we may have to wait for it. **Until that he have mercy upon us.** God has his time and season, and we must wait **until** it comes. For the trial of our faith our blessed Lord may for a while delay, but in the end the vision will be fulfilled. Mercy is that which we need, that which we look for, that which our Lord will manifest to us. Even those who look to the Lord, with that holy look which is here described, still need mercy, and as they cannot claim it by right they wait for it till sovereign grace chooses to vouchsafe it. Blessed are those servants whom their Master finds so doing. Waiting upon the Lord is a posture suitable both for earth and heaven; it is, indeed, in every place the right and fitting condition for a servant of the Lord. Nor may we leave the posture so long as we are by grace dwellers in the realms of mercy. It is a great mercy to be enabled to wait for mercy.

3. Have mercy upon us, O LORD, have mercy upon us. He hangs upon the word **mercy,** and embodies it in a vehement prayer: the very word seems to hold him, and he harps upon it. It is well for us to pray about everything, and turn everything into prayer; and especially when we are reminded of a great necessity we should catch at it as a keynote, and pitch our tune to it. Note that he has left the first person singular for the plural. All the saints need mercy; they all seek it; they shall all have it; therefore we pray, have mercy upon *us*.

For we are exceedingly filled with contempt, and this is an acid which eats into the soul. **Contempt** is bitterness; the person who feels it may well cry for mercy to God. **Filled** with contempt, as if the bitter wine had been poured in till it was up to the brim. This had become the chief thought of their minds, the peculiar sorrow of their hearts. Excluding all other feelings, a sense of scorn monopolized the soul and made it unutterably wretched. Another word is added – **exceedingly** filled. Filled to running over. A little contempt they could bear, but now they were satiated with it, and weary of it. Nothing is more wounding, embittering, festering than disdain. When our companions make little of us we are far too apt to make little of ourselves and of the consolations prepared for us. Oh to be filled with communion, and then contempt will run off from us, and never be able to fill us with its biting vinegar.

4. Our soul is exceedingly filled with the scorning of those that are at ease. Knowing no troubles of their own, the easy ones grow cruel and deride the people of the Lord. Having the godly already in secret contempt, they show it by openly scorning them. Those who do this are not the poor, the humble, the troubled, but those who have a merry life of it, and are self-content. They are easy in heart through a deadened conscience. They are easy as to any anxiety to improve, for their conceit of themselves is boundless. Such people take things easily, and therefore they scorn the holy carefulness of those who watch the hand of the Lord. Place someone perfectly at ease and he derides the godly, and becomes himself proud in heart and conduct. **And with the contempt of the proud.** The proud think so much of themselves that they must think all the less of those who are better than themselves. Pride is both contemptible and contemptuous. The contempt of the great ones of the earth is especially acrid. Great hearts have been broken, and brave spirits have been withered beneath the accursed power of falsehood and the horrible blight of contempt. Our divine Lord was despised and rejected of men, yet he ceased not from his perfect service till he was exalted to dwell in the heavens. Let us bear our share of this evil which still rages, and let us firmly believe that the contempt of the ungodly will turn to our honor in the world to come: even now it serves as a certificate that we are not of this world.

Psalm 124

1. The opening sentence is abrupt, and remains a fragment. By such a commencement attention was aroused as well as feeling expressed. The many words in italics in our Authorized Version will show the reader that the translators did their best to patch up the passage, which, perhaps, had better have been left in its broken grandeur, and it would then have run thus:

Had it not been Jehovah! He was for us, oh let Israel say!
Had it not been Jehovah! He who was for us when men rose against us.

The glorious Lord became our ally; he took our part, and entered into treaty with us. If Jehovah were not our protector where should we be? Nothing but his power and wisdom could have guarded us from the cunning and malice of our adversaries; therefore, let all his people say so, and openly give him the honor of his preserving goodness. Here are two ifs, and yet there is no if in the matter. The Lord was on our side, and is still our defender, and will be so forever. We are far too slow in declaring our gratitude, hence the exclamation which should be rendered, "O let Israel say." We grumble without being stirred up to it, but our thanksgiving needs a spur, and it is well when some warm-hearted friend bids us say what we feel. Imagine what would have happened if the Lord had left us, and then see what has happened because he has been faithful to us.

2. When the whole race of men seemed set upon stamping out the house of Israel, what must have happened if the covenant Lord had not interposed? When they combined to assault our quietude and safety, what would we have done if the Lord had not also arisen? There is no doubt as to our deliverer; we cannot ascribe our salvation to any second cause, for it would not have been equal to the emergency; nothing less than omnipotence and omniscience could have wrought our rescue. We set every other claimant on one side, and rejoice because the Lord was on our side.

3. They were so eager for our destruction that they would have made only one morsel of us, and have swallowed us up alive and whole in a single instant. The fury of the enemies of the church is raised to the highest pitch; nothing will content them but the total annihilation of God's chosen. Their wrath is like a fire which is kindled, and has taken such firm hold upon the fuel that there is no quenching it. Anger is never more fiery than when the people of God are its objects. Sparks become flames, and the furnace is heated seven times hotter when God's elect are to be thrust into the blaze. The cruel world would make a full end of the godly were it not that Jehovah bars the way. When the Lord appears, the consuming fire cannot destroy; it is only because the Lord liveth that his people are alive.

4. **Then the waters had overwhelmed us.** Rising irresistibly, like the Nile, the flood of opposition would soon have rolled over our heads. We should have looked in vain for escape. **The stream had gone over our soul.** The rushing torrent would have drowned our soul, our hope, our life. In the great water-floods of persecution and affliction who can help but Jehovah? We have

experienced seasons in which the combined forces of earth and hell must have made an end of us had not omnipotent grace interfered for our rescue.

5. Then the proud waters had gone over our soul. The figure represents the waves as proud, and so they seem to be when they overleap the bulwarks of a frail ship, and threaten every moment to sink her. The opposition of men is usually embittered by a haughty scorn which derides all our godly efforts as mere fanaticism or obstinate ignorance. In all the persecutions of the church a cruel contempt has largely mingled with the oppression, and this is overpowering to the soul. Had not God been with us our disdainful enemies would have made nothing of us, and dashed over us as a mountain torrent sweeps down the side of a hill, driving everything before it. Not only would our goods and possessions have been carried off, but our soul, our courage, our hope would have been borne away by the impetuous assault, and buried beneath the insults of our antagonists. Let us pause here, and as we see what might have been, let us adore the guardian power which has kept us in the flood, and yet above the flood. In our hours of dire peril we must have perished had not our Preserver prevailed for our safe keeping.

6. He compares the adversaries of Israel to wild beasts who desired to make the godly their prey. Their teeth are prepared to tear, and they regard the godly as their victims. The Lord is heartily praised for not permitting his servants to be devoured when they were between the jaws of the raging ones. It implies that none can harm us till the Lord permits: and that our loving Lord will never do. The verse reads like a merely negative blessing, but no boon can be more positively precious. He has given us to his Son Jesus, and he will never give us to our enemies.

7. Our soul is escaped as a bird out of the snare of the fowlers. Fowlers have many methods of taking small birds, and Satan has many methods of entrapping souls. Some are decoyed by evil companions, other are enticed by the love of dainties; hunger drives many into the trap, and fright impels numbers to fly into the net. The birds see not the snare so as to avoid it, and they cannot break it so as to escape from it. Happy is the bird that hath a deliverer strong, and mighty, and ready in the moment of peril; happier still is the soul over which the Lord watches day and night to pluck its feet out of the net. What joy there is in this song, **Our soul is escaped.** Escaped from our natural slavery; escaped from the guilt, the degradation, the habit, the dominion of sin; escaped from the vain deceits and fascinations of Satan; escaped from all that can destroy. What a miraculous escape that we who are so easily misled should not have been permitted to die by the dread fowler's hand. The Lord has heard the prayer which he taught us to pray, and he has delivered us from evil. **The snare is broken, and we are escaped.** The song is worth repeating. The snare may be false doctrine, pride, lust, or temptation or despair; what a high favor it is to have it broken before our eyes, so that it has no more power over us.

We see not the mercy while we are in the snare; perhaps we are so foolish as to deplore the breaking of the Satanic charm; the gratitude comes when the escape is seen, and when we perceive what we have escaped from, and by what hand we have been set free. Then our Lord has a song from our mouths and hearts.

8. Our help for the future, our ground of confidence in all trials present and to come. **Is in the name of the LORD.** Jehovah's revealed character is our foundation of confidence; his person is our sure fountain of strength. **Who made heaven and earth.** Our Creator is our preserver. He is immensely great in his creating work; he has not fashioned a few little things alone, but all heaven and the whole round earth are the works of his hands. When we worship the Creator let us increase our trust in our Comforter. Did he create all that we see, and can he not preserve us from evils which we cannot see? He has rendered us help in the moment of jeopardy. He will to the end break every snare. He made heaven for us, and he will keep us for heaven; he made the earth, and he will succor us upon it until the hour comes for our departure. Every work of his hand preaches to us the duty and the delight of reposing upon him only.

Psalm 125

1. They that trust in the LORD shall be as mount Zion. The emphasis lies upon the object of their trust, namely, Jehovah the Lord. What a privilege to be allowed to repose in God! How condescending is Jehovah to become the confidence of his people! To trust elsewhere is vanity; and the more implicit such misplaced trust becomes the more bitter will be the ensuing disappointment; but to trust in the living God is sanctified common sense which needs no excuse; its result will be its best vindication. There is no conceivable reason why we should not trust in Jehovah, and there is every possible argument for so doing; but, apart from all argument, the end will prove the wisdom of the confidence. The result of faith is not occasional and accidental; its blessing comes, not to some who trust, but to all who trust in the Lord. Trusters in Jehovah will be as fixed, firm, and stable as the mount where David dwelt, and where the ark abode. To move Mount Zion was impossible: the mere supposition was absurd. **Which cannot be removed, but abideth for ever.** Zion was the image of eternal steadfastness – this hill which, according to the Hebrew, "sits to eternity," neither bowing down nor moving to and fro. Thus doth the trusting worshiper of Jehovah enjoy a restfulness which is the mirror of tranquillity; his hope is sure. As the Lord as sitteth as King forever, so do his people sit enthroned in perfect peace when their trust in him is firm. We are, we have been, we shall be as steadfast as the hill of God. Zion cannot be removed, and does not move; so the people of God can neither be moved by force from without or fickleness from within.

2. The hill of Zion is the type of the believer's constancy, and the surrounding mountains are made emblems of the all-surrounding presence of the Lord. The mountains around the holy city, though they do not make a circular wall, are nevertheless set like sentinels to guard her gates. God does not enclose his people within ramparts and bulwarks, making their city to be a prison; but yet he so orders the arrangements of his providence that his saints are as safe as if they dwelt behind the strongest fortifications. It is not said that Jehovah's power or wisdom defends believers, but he himself is round about them: they have his personality for their protection, his Godhead for their guard. We are here taught that the Lord's people are those who trust him, for they are thus described in the first verses: the line of faith is the line of grace; those who trust in the Lord are chosen of the Lord. The two verses together prove the eternal safety of the saints: they must be able to abide where God has placed them, and God must forever protect them from all evil.

3. For the rod of the wicked shall not rest upon the lot of the righteous. The people of God are not to expect immunity from trial because the Lord surrounds them, for they may feel the power and persecution of the ungodly. The graceless often bear rule and wield the rod; and when they do so they are pretty sure to make it fall heavily upon the Lord's believing people, so that the godly cry out by reason of their oppressors. Egypt's rod was exceeding heavy upon Israel, but the time came for it to be broken. God has set a limit to the woes of his chosen: the rod may light on their portion, but it shall not *rest* upon it. The saints abide forever, but their troubles will not.

Lest the righteous put forth their hands unto iniquity. The tendency of oppression is to drive the best people into some hasty deed for self-deliverance or vengeance. Therefore the Lord puts a limit to the tyranny of the wicked. He ordained that an Israelite who deserved punishment should not be beaten without measure: forty stripes save one was the appointed limit. We may therefore expect that he will set a bound to the suffering of the innocent, and will not allow them to be pushed to the uttermost extreme.

It seems that even the righteous are in peril of sinning in evil days, and that it is not the will of the Lord that they should yield to the stress of the times in order to escape from suffering. The power and influence of the wicked when they are uppermost are used to lead or drive the righteous astray; but the godly must not accept this as an excuse, and yield to the evil pressure; far rather must they resist with all their might till it pleases God to stay the violence of the persecutor, and give his children rest. This the Lord here promises to do in due time.

4. Do good, O LORD, unto those that be good, and to them that are upright in their hearts. To be good at all we must be good at heart. Those who trust in the Lord are good, for faith is the root of righteousness, and the evidence of uprightness. Faith in God is a good and upright thing, and its influence makes the rest of the person good and upright. To such God will do good: the prayer of the text is but another form of promise, for that which the Lord prompts us to ask he virtually promises to give. Jehovah will take off evil from his people, and in the place thereof will enrich them with all manner of good. Meanwhile it is for us to pray that it may be well with all the upright who are now among men.

5. **As for such as turn aside unto their crooked ways, the LORD shall lead them forth with the workers of iniquity.** Two kinds of people are always to be found, the upright and those of crooked ways. How sad that those who once walked in the right way should turn aside from it! Observe the course of the false-hearted: first, they look out for crooked ways; next, they choose them and make them *their* **crooked ways**; and then they turn aside into them. They never intend to go back unto perdition, but only to make a curve and drop into the right road again. These people are neither upright in heart, nor good, nor trusters in Jehovah, and therefore the Lord will deal otherwise with them than his own people: when execution day comes these hypocrites and time-servers will be led out to the same gallows as the openly wicked.

But peace shall be upon Israel. In fact the execution of the deceivers will tend to give the true Israel peace. When God is smiting the unfaithful not a blow will fall upon the faithful. The chosen of the Lord will not only be like Salem, but they will have *salem,* or peace. Like a prince, Israel has prevailed with God, and therefore he need not fear the face of man; his wrestlings are over, the blessing of peace has been pronounced upon him. He who has peace with God may enjoy peace concerning all things.

Psalm 126

1. Being in trouble, the gracious pilgrims remember for their comfort times of national woe which were succeeded by remarkable deliverances. Then sorrow was gone like a dream, and the joy which followed was so great that it seemed too good to be true, and they feared that it must be the vision of an idle brain. So sudden and so overwhelming was their joy that they felt like people in a trance. It was not the freedom of an individual which the Lord in mercy had wrought, but of all Zion, of the whole nation; and this was reason enough for overflowing gladness. Let us look to the prison-houses from which we have been set free. At our conversion what a turning again of captivity we experienced. Since then, from multiplied troubles, from depression of spirit, from miserable backsliding, from grievous doubt, we have been emancipated, and we are not able to describe the bliss which followed each emancipation. This

verse will have a higher fulfillment in the day of the final overthrow of the powers of darkness when the Lord comes forth for the salvation and glorification of his redeemed. Then in a fuller sense than even at Pentecost our old men will see visions, and our young men will dream dreams: all things will be so wonderful, so far beyond all expectation, that those who behold them will ask themselves whether it be not all a dream. The past is ever a sure preview of the future; we shall again and again find ourselves amazed at the wonderful goodness of the Lord. Let our hearts gratefully remember the former lovingkindnesses of the Lord: we were sadly low, sorely distressed, and completely past hope, but when Jehovah appeared he did not merely lift us out of despondency, he raised us into wondering happiness. He turns exile into ecstasy, and banishment into bliss.

2. Then was our mouth filled with laughter, and our tongue with singing. So full were they of joy that they could not contain themselves. They must express their joy and yet they could not find expression for it. Irrepressible mirth could do no other than laugh, for speech was far too dull a thing for it. The mercy was so unexpected, so amazing, so singular that they could not do less than laugh; and they laughed much, so that their mouths were full of it, and that because their hearts were full too. When at last the tongue could move articulately, it could not be content simply to talk, but it must sing; and sing heartily too, for it was full of singing. God's *when* is our *then*. At the moment when he turns our captivity, the heart turns from its sorrow; when he fills us with grace we are filled with gratitude.

Then said they among the heathen, The LORD hath done great things for them. The heathen heard the songs of Israel, and the better sort among them soon guessed the cause of their joy. Jehovah was known to be their God, and to him the other nations ascribed the emancipation of his people, reckoning it to be no small thing which the Lord had thus done; for those who carried away the nations had never in any other instance restored a people to their ancient dwelling-place. These foreigners were no dreamers; though they were only lookers-on, and not partakers in the surprising mercy, they plainly saw what had been done, and rightly ascribed it to the great Giver of all good. It is a blessed thing when saints set sinners talking about the lovingkindness of the Lord, and it is equally blessed when the saints who are hidden away in the world hear of what the Lord has done for his church, and themselves resolve to come out from their captivity and unite with the Lord's people.

3. The LORD hath done great things for us; whereof we are glad. They did not deny the statement which reflected so much glory upon Jehovah; with exultation they admitted and repeated the statement of Jehovah's notable dealings with them. To themselves they appropriated the joyful assertion; they said, **The LORD hath done great things *for us,*** and they declared their gladness at the fact. It is a poor modesty which is ashamed to own its joy in the Lord. Call it rather a robbery of God. There is so little of happiness abroad that if we possess a full share of it we ought not to hide our light under a bushel, but let it shine on all that are in the house. Let us avow our joy, and the reason of it, stating the **whereof** as well as the fact. None are so happy as those who are newly turned and returned from captivity; none can more promptly and satisfactorily give a reason for the gladness that is in them. The Lord himself has blessed us, blessed us greatly, blessed us individually, blessed us assuredly; and because of this we sing unto his name. I heard one say the other day in prayer, "whereof we desire to be glad." Strange dilution and defilement of Scriptural language! Surely if God has done great things for us we are glad, and cannot be otherwise. No doubt such language is meant to be lowly, but in truth it is loathsome.

4. Turn again our captivity, O LORD. Remembering the former joy of a past rescue they cry to Jehovah for a repetition of it. When we pray for the turning of our captivity, it is wise to recall former instances thereof: nothing strengthens faith more effectually than the memory of a previous experience. The text shows us how wise it is to resort anew to the Lord who in former times has been so good to us. Where else should we go but to him who has done such great things for us? Who can turn again our captivity but he who turned it before?

As the streams in the south. Even as the Lord sends floods down the dry beds of southern torrents after long droughts, so can he fill our wasted and wearied spirits with floods of holy delight. This the Lord can do for any of us, and he can do it at once, for nothing is too hard for the Lord. Do not let us forget the past, but in the presence of our present difficulty let us resort unto the Lord, and beseech him to do that for us which we cannot possibly do for ourselves – that which no other power can perform on our behalf. Israel did return from the captivity in Babylon. Suddenly and plenteously the people filled again the temple courts.

5. They that sow in tears shall reap in joy. Hence, present distress must not be viewed as if it would last forever: it is not the end, by any means, but only a means to the end. Sorrow is our sowing; rejoicing will be our reaping. Workers, waiters, and weepers, in due season they *shall* reap. It is not every sowing which is thus insured against all danger, and guaranteed a harvest; but the promise specially belongs to sowing **in tears.** When someone's heart is so stirred that he weeps over the sins of others, he is elect to usefulness. Winners of souls are first weepers for souls. As there is no birth without travail, so is there no spiritual harvest without painful tillage. When our own hearts are broken with grief at man's transgression we shall break other people's hearts; tears of earnestness beget tears of repentance.

6. He. The general assurance is applied to each one in particular. That which is spoken in the previous verse in the plural – "they" – is here repeated in the singular – **he.** He leaves his couch to go forth into the frosty air and tread the heavy soil; and as he goes he weeps because of past failures, or because the ground is so sterile, or the weather so unseasonable, or his corn so scarce, and his enemies so plentiful and so eager to rob him of his reward. You will gather sheaves from your sowing. This is a figurative description of that which was literally described in the first three verses. It is the turning of the worker's captivity, when, instead of seed buried beneath black earth, he sees the waving crops inviting him to a golden harvest. It is somewhat singular to find this promise of fruitfulness in close contact with return from captivity; and yet it is so in our own experience, for when our own soul is revived the souls of others are blessed by our labors. If any of us, having been once lonesome and lingering captives, have now returned home, and have become longing and laboring sowers, may the Lord, who has already delivered us, soon transform us into glad-hearted reapers, and to him shall be praise forever and ever. Amen.

Psalm 127

1. Except the LORD build the house, they labor in vain that build it. The word **vain** is the keynote here, and we hear it ring out clearly three times. People desiring to build know that they must labor, and accordingly they put forth all their skill and strength; but let them remember that if Jehovah is not with them their designs will prove failures. So was it with the Babel builders; they said, "Go to, let us build us a city and a tower"; and the Lord returned their words, saying, "Go to, let us go down and there confound their language." In vain they toiled, for the Lord's face was against them. When Solomon resolved to build a house for the Lord, matters were very different, for all things united under God to aid him in his great undertaking: even the heathen were at his beck and call that he might erect a temple for the Lord his God. In the same manner God blessed him in the erection of his own palace; for this verse evidently refers to all sorts of house-building. Without God we are nothing. Great houses have been erected by ambitious men; but like the baseless fabric of a vision they have passed away, and scarce a stone remains to tell where once they stood.

Except the LORD keep the city, the watchman waketh but in vain. Note that the psalmist does not bid the builder cease from laboring, nor suggest that watchmen should neglect their duty, nor that people should show their trust in God by doing nothing; he supposes that they will do all that they can and assures them that all creature effort will be in vain unless the Creator puts forth his power.

In Scriptural phrase a dispensation or system is called a house. Moses was faithful as a servant over all his house; and as long as the Lord was with that house it stood and prospered; but when he left it, the builders of it became foolish and their labor was lost. They sought to maintain the walls of Judaism, but sought in vain: they watched around every ceremony and tradition, but their care was idle. Of every church, and every system of religious thought, this is equally true: unless the Lord is in it, and is honored by it, the whole structure must sooner or later fall in hopeless ruin.

2. It is vain for you to rise up early, to sit up late, to eat the bread of sorrows. We are bound to be diligent, for this the Lord blesses; we ought not to be anxious, for that dishonors the Lord, and can never secure his favor. Some deny themselves needful rest. They threaten to brings themselves into the sleep of death by neglect of the sleep which refreshes life. They stint themselves in their meals, they eat the commonest kind of food, and the smallest possible quantity of it, and what they do swallow is washed down with the salty tears of grief, for they fear that daily bread will fail them. Hard earned is their food, scantily rationed, and scarcely ever sweetened, but perpetually smeared with sorrow; and all because they have no faith in God, and find no joy except in hoarding up the gold which is their only trust. Not thus, not thus, would the Lord have his children live. He would have them, as princes of the race, lead a happy and restful life.

For so he giveth his beloved sleep. Through faith the Lord makes his chosen ones to rest in him in happy freedom from care. The text may mean that God gives blessings to his beloved in sleep, just as he gave Solomon the desire of his heart while he slept. The meaning is much the same: those whom the Lord loves are delivered from the fret and fume of life. God is sure to give the best thing to his beloved, and we here see that he gives them sleep – a laying aside of care, a forgetfulness of need, a quiet leaving of matters with God: this kind of sleep is better than riches and honor. Note how Jesus slept amid the hurly-burly of a storm at sea. He knew that he was in his Father's hands.

3. Lo, children are an heritage of the LORD. This points to another mode of building up a house, namely, by leaving descendants to keep our name and family alive upon the earth. Without this what is a man's purpose in accumulating wealth? Yet in this matter a man is powerless without the Lord.

And the fruit of the womb is his reward, or a reward from God. He gives children, not as a penalty nor as a burden, but as a favor. They are a token for good if men know how to receive them, and educate them. Where society is rightly ordered children are regarded, not as an incumbrance, but as an inheritance; and they are received, not with regret, but as a reward. With all the straits of limited incomes, our best possessions are our own dear offspring, for whom we bless God every day.

4. As arrows are in the hand of a mighty man; so are children of the youth.

Children born to men in their early days, by God's blessing become the comfort of their riper years. A man of war is glad of weapons which may fly where he cannot; good sons are their father's arrows speeding to hit the mark which their sires aim at. What wonders a good man can accomplish if he has affectionate children to second his desires, and lend themselves to his designs! To this end we must have our children in hand while they are yet children, or they are never likely to be so when they are grown up; and we must try to point them and straighten them, so as to make arrows of them in their youth, lest they should prove crooked and unserviceable in after life. Let the Lord favor us with loyal, obedient, affectionate offspring, and we shall find in them our best helpers. We shall see them shot forth into life to our comfort and delight, if we take care from the very beginning that they are directed to the right point.

5. Happy is the man that hath his quiver full of them. Those who have no children bewail the fact. The writer of this comment gives it as his own observation that he has seen the most frequent unhappiness in marriages which are unfruitful; that he has himself been most grateful for two of the best of sons; but as they have both grown up, and he has no child at home, he has without a tinge of grumbling, or even wishing that he were otherwise circumstanced, felt that it might have been a blessing to have had a more numerous family. He therefore heartily agrees with the psalmist's verdict herein expressed. A quiver may be small and yet full; and then the blessing is obtained. In any case we may be sure that a man's life consists not in the abundance of children that he possesses.

They shall not be ashamed, but they shall speak with the enemies in the gate. They can meet foes both in law and in fight. Nobody cares to meddle with a man who can gather a clan of brave sons about him. Does not the Lord Jesus thus triumph in his offspring? Looked at literally, this favor comes of the Lord: without his will there would be no children to build up the house, and without his grace there would be no good children to be their parents' strength. If this must be left with the Lord, let us leave every other thing in the same hands. He will undertake for us and prosper our trustful endeavors, and we shall enjoy a tranquil life, and prove ourselves to be our Lord's beloved by the calm and quiet of our spirit. We need not doubt that if God gives us children as a reward he will also send us the food and raiment which he knows they need.

He who is the father of a host of spiritual children is unquestionably happy. He can answer all opponents by pointing to souls who have been saved by his means. Converts are emphatically the heritage of the Lord, and the reward of the preacher's soul-travail. By these, under the power of the Holy Spirit, the city of the church is built up and watched, and the Lord has the glory of it.

Psalm 128

1. Blessed is every one that feareth the LORD. The last psalm ended with a blessing – for the word there translated "happy" is the same as that which is here rendered "blessed"; thus the two songs are joined by a catchword. There is also in them a close community of subject. The fear of God is the cornerstone of all blessedness. We must reverence the ever-blessed God before we can be blessed ourselves. Some think that this life is an evil, an infliction, a thing upon which rests a curse; but it is not so; the God-fearing person has a present blessing. It is not true that it would be to him "something better not to be." He is even here a joint-heir with Jesus Christ, whose heritage is not misery, but joy. This is true of every one of the God-fearing, of all conditions, in all ages: each one and every one is blessed. Their blessedness may not always be seen by carnal reason, but it is always a fact, for God himself declares that it is so. Let us cultivate that holy filial fear of Jehovah which is the essence of all true religion – the fear of reverence, of dread to offend, of eagerness to please, and of entire submission and obedience.

That walketh in his ways. The religious life, which God declares to be blessed, must be practical as well as emotional. It is idle to talk of fearing the Lord if we act like those who have no care whether there be a God or no.

2. For thou shalt eat the labor of thine hands. The general doctrine of the first verse here receives a personal application: note the change to the second person: *thou* shalt eat . . . This is the portion of God's saints – to work and to find a reward in so doing. God is the God of laborers. We are not to leave our worldly callings because the Lord has called us by grace; we are not promised a blessing upon romantic idleness or unreasonable dreaming, but upon hard work and honest industry. He will give us daily bread, but it must be made our own by labor. All kinds of labor are here included; for if one toils by the sweat of his brow, and another does so by the sweat of his brain, there is no difference in the blessing; save that it is generally more healthy to work with the body than with the mind only. Without God it would be vain to labor; but when we are laborers together with God a promise is set before us. The promise is that labor will be fruitful, and that he who performs it will himself enjoy the recompense of it. It is a grievous ill for a man to slave his life away and receive no fair remuneration for his toil. Some never enjoy their labor, for they give themselves no time for rest. Eagerness to get takes from them the ability to enjoy. Surely, if it is worthwhile to labor, it is worthwhile to eat of that labor. **Happy shalt thou be,** or, **Oh, thy happinesses.** Heaped up happinesses in the plural belong to that man who fears the Lord. **And it shall be well with thee,** or, **good for thee.** In walking in God's ways we shall be under his protection, provision, and approval; danger and destruction will be far from us: all things will work our good. In God's view it would not be a blessed thing for us to live without exertion, nor to eat the unearned bread of dependence: the happiest state on earth is one in which we have something to do, strength to do it, and a fair return for what we have done. This, with the divine blessing, is all that we ought to desire.

3. Thy wife. To reach the full of earthly felicity a man must not be alone. A helpmeet was needed in Paradise, and assuredly she is not less necessary out of it. He that finds a wife finds a good thing. It is not every man that feareth the Lord who has a wife; but if he has, she will share in his blessedness and increase it.

Shall be as a fruitful vine. To complete domestic bliss children are sent as the lawful fruit of marriage. Good wives are also fruitful in kindness, thrift, helpfulness, and affection: if they bear no children, they are by no means barren if they yield us the wine of consolation and the clusters of comfort. **By the sides of thine house.** She is a fruitful vine, and a faithful housekeeper. It is her husband's house, and she is her husband's; as the text puts it, **thy wife** and **thine house** – but by her loving care her husband is made so happy that he is glad to own her as an equal proprietor with himself, for he is hers, and the house is hers too.

Thy children like olive plants round about thy table. The psalmist never intended to suggest the idea of olive plants round a table, but of young people springing up around their parents, just as olive plants surround the fine, well-rooted tree. The figure is very striking, and would be sure to present itself to the mind of every observer in the olive country. How beautiful to see the gnarled olive, still bearing abundant fruit, surrounded with a little band of sturdy successors, any one of which would be able to take its place should the central olive be blown down, or removed in any other way. The notion of a table in a bower may suit a cockney in a tea-garden, but would never occur to an oriental poet; it is not the olive plants, but the children, that are round about the table. Moreover, note that it is not olive *branches*, but **plants** – a very different thing. Our children gather around our table to be fed, and this involves expenses: how much better is this than to see them pining upon beds of sickness, unable to come for their meals! What a blessing to have sufficient to put upon the table! Let us for this benefit praise the bounty of the Lord. The wife is busy all over the house, but the youngsters are busiest at meal-times; and if the blessing of the Lord rest upon the family, no sight can be more delightful. Here we have the vine and the olive blended – joy from the fruitful wife, and solid comfort from the growing family; these are the choicest products earth can yield: our families are gardens of the Lord.

4. Behold, that thus shall the man be blessed that feareth the Lord. It is not to be inferred that all blessed men are married, and are fathers, but that this is the way in which the Lord favors godly people who are placed in domestic life. He makes their relationships happy and profitable. In this fashion does

Jehovah bless God-fearing households, for he is the God of all the families of Israel. Family blessedness comes from the Lord, and is a part of his plan for the preservation of a godly race, and for the maintenance of his worship in the land. To the Lord alone we must look for it. The possession of riches will not insure it; the choice of a healthy and beautiful bride will not insure it; the birth of numerous comely children will not insure it: there must be the blessing of God, the influence of piety, the result of holy living.

5. The LORD shall bless thee out of Zion. A spiritual blessing will be received by the gracious man, and this will crown all his temporal mercies. He is one among the many who make up God's inheritance; his tent is part and parcel of the encampment around the tabernacle; and therefore when the benediction is pronounced at the center it will radiate to him in his place. Zion was the center of blessing, and to it the people looked when they sought for mercy: from the altar of sacrifice, from the mercy-seat, from the Shekinah-light, indeed from Jehovah himself the blessing will come to each one of his holy people. **And thou shalt see the good of Jerusalem all the days of thy life.** He will have a patriot's joy as well as a patriarch's peace. God will give him to see his country prosper, and its metropolitan city flourish. This favor is to be permanent throughout the good man's life, and that life is to be a long one, for he is to see his sons' sons. Many a time does true religion bring such blessings to men; and when these good things are denied them, they have a greater reward as a compensation.

6. Yea, thou shalt see thy children's children. He rejoices in the belief that other homes will be built up wherein altars to the glory of God will smoke with the morning and evening sacrifice. This promise implies long life rendered happy by its being continued in our offspring. It is one token of the immortality of man that he derives joy from extending his life in the lives of his descendants.

And peace upon Israel. We count it our own prosperity for the chosen of the Lord to find rest and quiet. Jacob knew little of peace; but yet the Lord delivered him out of all his tribulations, and brought him to a place of rest in Goshen, and afterwards to sleep with his fathers in the cave of Machpelah. His glorious Seed was grievously afflicted and at last crucified; but he has risen to eternal peace, and in his peace we dwell. Israel's spiritual descendants share his conditions, but there remains a rest for them also, and they will have peace from the God of peace. Israel was a praying petitioner in the days of his wrestling, but he became a prevailing prince, and therein his soul found peace.

Psalm 129

1. In Israel's present hour of trial she may remember her former afflictions and speak of them for her comfort, drawing from them the assurance that he who has been with her for so long will not desert her in the end. The song begins abruptly. The poet has been musing, and the fire burns, therefore speaks he with his tongue: he cannot help it, he feels that he must speak, and therefore **may . . . now say** what he has to say. The trials of the church have been repeated again and again, times beyond all count: the same afflictions are fulfilled in us as in our fathers. Jacob of old found his days full of trouble; each Israelite is often harassed; and Israel as a whole has proceeded from tribulation to tribulation. **Many a time,** Israel says, because she could not say how many times. She speaks of her assailants as **they,** because it would be impossible to write or even to know all their names. They had straitened, harassed, and fought against her from the earliest days of her history – from her **youth** – and they had continued their assaults right on without ceasing. Persecution is the heirloom of the church, and the ensign of the elect. Israel among the nations was special, and this brought against her many restless foes, who could never be easy unless they were warring against the people of God. When in Canaan, at the first, the chosen household was often severely tried; in Egypt it was heavily oppressed; in the wilderness it was fiercely assailed; and in the promised land it was often surrounded by deadly enemies. It was something for the afflicted nation that it survived to **say,** "Many a time have they afflicted me." The affliction begins early – **from my youth** – and it continued late. The earliest years of Israel and of the church of God were spent in trial. Babes in grace are cradled in opposition. No sooner is the man-child born than the dragon is after it. "It is," however, "good for a man that he bear the yoke in his youth," and he will see it to be so when in after days he tells the tale.

2. **Many a time have they afflicted me from my youth.** Israel repeats her statement of her repeated afflictions. The fact was uppermost in her thoughts, and she could not help soliloquizing upon it again and again. These repetitions are after the manner of poetry: thus she makes a sonnet out of her sorrows, music out of her miseries. **Yet they have not prevailed against me.** We seem to hear the beat of timbrels and the clash of cymbals here: the foe is derided; his malice has failed. That **yet** breaks in like the blast of trumpets, or the roll of kettledrums. "Cast down, but not destroyed," is the shout of a victor. Israel has wrestled, and has overcome in the struggle. Who wonders? If Israel overcame the angel of the covenant, what man or devil shall vanquish him? The fight was oft renewed and long protracted: the champion severely felt the conflict, and was at times fearful of the issue; but at length he takes breath, and cries, **Yet they have not prevailed against me.** The enemy has **many a time** had his opportunity and his advantage, but not so much as once has he gained the victory.

3. **The plowers plowed upon my back.** The scourgers tore the flesh as plowmen furrow a field. The people were maltreated like a criminal given over to cruel whips; the back of the nation was scored and furrowed by oppression. It is a grand piece of imagery condensed into few words. A writer says the

metaphor is muddled, but he is mistaken: there are several figures, like wheel within wheel, but there is not confusion. The afflicted nation was, as it were, lashed by her adversaries so cruelly that each blow left a long red mark, or perhaps a bleeding wound, upon her back and shoulders, comparable to a furrow which tears up the ground from one end of the field to the other. Many a heart has been in like case, smitten and sore wounded by them that use the scourge of the tongue; so smitten that their whole character has been cut up and scored by calumny. The true church has in every age had fellowship with her Lord under his cruel flagellations: his sufferings were a prophecy of what she would be called hereafter to endure, and the foreshadowing has been fulfilled. Zion had in this sense been plowed as a field.

They made long their furrows. As if delighting in cruel labor. They missed not an inch, but went from end to end of the field, meaning to make thorough work of their congenial engagement. Those who laid on the scourge did it with a thoroughness which showed how hearty was their hate. Assuredly the enemies of Christ's church never spare pains to inflict the utmost injury: they never do the work of the devil deceitfully, or hold back their hand from blood. They smite so as to plow into the man; they plow the quivering flesh as if it were clods of clay; they plow deep and long with countless furrows, until they leave no portion of the church unfurrowed or unassailed. Well did Latimer say that there was no busier plowman in all the world than the devil: whoever makes short furrows, he does not. Whoever balks and shirks, he is thorough in all that he does. He and his children plow like practiced plowmen, but they prefer to carry on their pernicious work upon the saints behind their backs, for they are as cowardly as they are cruel.

4. **The Lord is righteous.** Whatever men may be, Jehovah remains just, and will therefore keep covenant with his people and deal out justice to their oppressors. Here is the hinge of the condition: this makes the turning point of Israel's distress. The Lord bears with the long furrows of the wicked, but he will surely make them cease from their plowing before he has done with them. **He hath cut asunder the cords of the wicked.** The rope which binds the oxen to the plow is cut; the cord which bound the victim is broken; the bond which held the enemies in cruel unity has snapped. As in Psalm 114:7 we read, "the snare is broken; we are escaped," so here the breaking of the enemies' instrument of oppression is Israel's release. Sooner or later a righteous God will interpose, and when he does so, his action will be most effectual; he does not unfasten, but cuts asunder, the harness which the ungodly use in their labor of hate. Never has God used a nation to chastise his Israel without destroying that nation when the chastisement has come to a close: he hates those who hurt his people even though he permits that hate to triumph for a while for his own purpose.

5. If this be an imprecation, let it stand, for our heart says "Amen" to it. It

is but justice that those who hate, harass, and hurt the good should be brought to naught. Those who confound right and wrong ought to be confounded, and those who turn back from God ought to be turned back. Loyal subjects wish ill to those who plot against their king. We desire their welfare as people, their downfall as traitors. Let their conspiracies be confounded, their policies turned back. How can we wish prosperity to those who would destroy that which is dearest to our hearts? This present age is so flippant that if a man loves the Saviour he is styled a fanatic, and if he hates the powers of evil he is named a bigot. The church of God is so useful, so beautiful, so innocent of harm, so fraught with good, that those who do her wrong are wronging all mankind and deserve to be treated as the enemies of the human race.

6. Grass on the housetop is soon up and soon down. It sprouts in the heat, finds enough nutriment to send up a green blade, and then it dies away before it reaches maturity, because it has neither earth nor moisture sufficient for its proper development. Before it grows up it dies; it needs not to be plucked up, for it hastens to decay of itself. Such is and such ought to be the lot of the enemies of God's people. The height of their position, as it hastens their progress, also hurries their doom. Had they been lower in station they had perhaps been longer in being. Persecutors are all sound and fury, flash and flame; but they speedily vanish – more speedily than is common to mankind. Grass in the field withers, but not so speedily as grass on the housetops. Grass on the housetop is a nonentity in the world: the house is not impoverished when the last blade is dried up; just so, the opposers of Christ pass away, and none lament them. Evil carries the seeds of dissolution within itself. So let it be.

7. When with his sickle the farmer would cut down the tufts, he found nothing to lay hold upon: the grass promised fairly enough, but there was no fulfillment, there was nothing to cut or to carry, nothing for the hand to grasp, nothing for the lap to gather. Eastern people carry their corn in their bosoms, but in this case there was nothing to bear home. Thus do the wicked come to nothing. By God's just appointment they prove a disappointment. Their fire ends in smoke; their verdure turns to vanity; their flourishing is but a form of withering. No one profits by them; least of all are they profitable to themselves. Their aim is bad, their work is worse, their end is worst of all.

8. In harvest times men bless each other in the name of the Lord; but there is nothing in the course and conduct of the ungodly man to suggest the giving or receiving of a benediction. Upon a survey of the sinner's life from beginning to end, we feel more inclined to weep than to rejoice, and we feel bound rather to wish him failure than success. We dare not use pious expressions as mere compliments, and hence we dare not wish Godspeed to evil men lest we be partakers of their evil deeds. It would be infamous to compromise the name of the righteous Jehovah by pronouncing his blessing upon unrighteous deeds.

See how the ungodly are roughly plowed by their adversaries, and yet a harvest comes of it which endures and produces blessing; the ungodly, though they flourish for a while and enjoy a complete immunity, dwelling as they think quite above the reach of harm, are found in a short time to have gone their way and to have left no trace behind. Lord, number me with thy saints. Let me share their grief if I may also partake of their glory. Thus would I make this psalm my own, and magnify thy name, because thine afflicted ones are not destroyed, and thy persecuted ones are not forsaken.

Psalm 130

1. This is the psalmist's statement and plea: he had never ceased to pray even when brought into the lowest state. The depths usually silence all they engulf, but they could not close the mouth of this servant of the Lord; on the contrary, it was in the abyss itself that he cried unto Jehovah. Beneath the floods prayer lived and struggled; above the roar of the billows rose the cry of faith. It little matters where we are if we can pray; but prayer is never more real and acceptable than when it rises out of the worst places. Deep places beget deep devotion. Depths of earnestness are stirred by depths of tribulation. The more distressed we are, the more excellent is the faith which trusts bravely in the Lord, and therefore appeals to him, and to him alone. Good men may be in the depths of temporal and spiritual trouble, but good men in such cases look only to their God, and they stir themselves up to be more instant and earnest in prayer than at other times. The depth of their distress moves the depths of their being; and from the bottom of their hearts an exceeding great and bitter cry rises unto the one living and true God. David had often been in the deep, and as often had he pleaded with Jehovah, his God, in whose hand are all deep places. He prayed, and remembered that he had prayed, and pleaded that he had prayed; hoping ere long to receive an answer. It would be dreadful to look back on trouble and feel forced to own that we did not cry unto the Lord in it; but it is most comforting to know that whatever we did not do, or could not do, yet we did pray, even in our worst times. He that prays in the depth will not sink out of his depth, but will soon sing in the heights.

2. **Lord, hear my voice.** It is all we ask; but nothing less will content us. If the Lord will but hear us we will leave it to his superior wisdom to decide whether he will answer us or no. It is better for our prayer to be heard than answered. If the Lord were to make an absolute promise to answer all our requests it might be rather a curse than a blessing, for it would be casting the responsibility of our lives upon ourselves, and we should be placed in a very anxious position; but now the Lord hears our desires, and that is enough; we only wish him to grant them if his infinite wisdom sees that it would be for our good and for his glory. Note that the psalmist spoke audibly in prayer: this is not at all

needful, but it is exceedingly helpful, for the use of the voice assists the thoughts. Still, there is a voice in silent supplication, a voice in our weeping, a voice in that sorrow which cannot find a tongue; that voice the Lord will hear if its cry is meant for his ear. **Let thine ears be attentive to the voice of my supplication.** The psalmist's cry is a beggar's petition; he begs the great King and Lord to lend an ear to it. He has supplicated many times, but always with one voice, or for one purpose; and he begs to be noticed in the one matter which he has pressed with so much importunity. He would have the King hearken, consider, remember, and weigh his request. He is confused, and his prayer may therefore be broken, and difficult to understand; he begs therefore that his Lord will give the more earnest and compassionate heed to the voice of his many and painful pleadings. When we have already prayed over our troubles it is well to pray over our prayers. If we can find no more words, let us intreat the Lord to hear those petitions which we have already presented. If we have faithfully obeyed the precept by praying without ceasing, we may be confident that the Lord will faithfully fulfill the promise by helping us without fail. Though the psalmist was under a painful sense of sin, and so was in the depth, his faith pleaded in the teeth of conscious unworthiness; for well he knew that the Lord's keeping his promise depends upon his own character and not upon that of his erring creatures.

3. If Jah, the all-seeing, should in strict justice call every person to account for every want of conformity to righteousness, where would any one of us be? Truly, he does record all our transgressions; but as yet he does not act upon the record, but lays it aside till another day. If people were to be judged upon no system but that of works, who among us could answer for himself at the Lord's bar, and hope to stand clear and accepted? This verse shows that the psalmist was under a sense of sin, and felt it imperative upon him not only to cry as a suppliant but to confess as a sinner. Here he owns that he cannot stand before the great King in his own righteousness, and he is so struck with a sense of the holiness of God, and the rectitude of the law that he is convinced that no one of mortal race can answer for himself before a Judge so perfect, concerning a law so divine. Well does he cry, **O Lord, who shall stand?** None can do so: there is none that does good, no, not one. Iniquities are matters which are not according to equity: what a multitude we have of these! Jehovah, who sees all, and is also our *Adonai*, or Lord, will assuredly bring us into judgment concerning those thoughts, and words, and works which are not in exact conformity to his law. Were it not for the Lord Jesus, could we hope to stand? Dare we meet him in the dread day of account on the footing of law and equity? What a mercy it is that we need not do so, for the next verse sets forth another way of acceptance to which we flee.

4. But there is forgiveness with thee. Blessed **but**. Free, full, sovereign pardon is in the hand of the great King: it is his prerogative to forgive, and he delights to exercise it. Because his nature is mercy, and because he has provided a sacrifice for sin, therefore forgiveness is with him for all that come to him confessing their sins. The power of pardon is permanently resident with God: he has forgiveness ready to his hand at this instant. **That thou mayest be feared.** This is the fruitful root of piety. None fear the Lord like those who have experienced his forgiving love. Gratitude for pardon produces far more fear and reverence of God than all the dread which is inspired by punishment. If the Lord were to exact justice upon all, there would be none left to fear him; if all were under apprehension of his deserved wrath, despair would harden them against fearing him: it is grace which leads the way to a holy regard of God, and a fear of grieving him.

5. I wait for the Lord, my soul doth wait. Expecting him to come to me in love, I quietly wait for his appearing; I wait *upon* him in service, and **for** him in faith. For God I wait and for him only: if he will manifest himself I shall have nothing more to wait for; but until he appears for my help I must wait on, hoping even in the depths. This waiting of mine is no mere formal act; my very soul is in it – **my soul doth wait.** If the Lord Jehovah makes us wait, let us do so with our whole hearts, for blessed are all they that wait for him. He is worth waiting for. The waiting itself is beneficial to us: it tries faith, exercises patience, trains submission, and endears the blessing when it comes. The Lord's people have always been a waiting people: they waited for the First Advent, and now they wait for the Second. They waited for a sense of pardon, and now they **wait** for perfect sanctification. They waited in the depths, and they are not now wearied with waiting in a happier condition. They have cried and they do wait; probably their past prayer sustains their present practice.

And in his word do I hope. This is the source, strength, and sweetness of waiting. Those who do not hope cannot wait; but if we hope for that we see not, then do we with patience wait for it. God's Word is a true Word, but at times it tarries; if ours is true faith it will wait the Lord's time. A Word from the Lord is as bread to the soul of the believer; and, refreshed thereby, it holds out through the night of sorrow expecting the dawn of deliverance and delight. Waiting, we study the Word, believe the Word, hope in the Word, and live on the Word; and all because it is *his word,* the Word of him who never speaks in vain. Jehovah's Word is a firm ground for a waiting soul to rest upon.

6. My soul waiteth for the Lord more than they that watch for the morning. Men who guard a city, and women who wait by the sick, long for daylight. Worshipers tarrying for the morning sacrifice, the kindling of the incense and the lighting of the lamps, mingle fervent prayers with their holy vigils, and pine for the hour when the lamp will smoke upon the altar. David, however, waited more than these, waited longer, waited more longingly, waited more expectantly. He was not afraid of the great Adonai before whom none can stand in their own righteousness, for he had put on the righteousness of faith, and therefore longed for gracious audience with the Holy One. God was no more dreaded by him than light is dreaded by those engaged in a lawful calling. He pined and yearned after his God.

I say, more than they that watch for the morning. The figure was not strong enough, though one can hardly think of anything more vigorous: he felt that his own eagerness was unique. Oh to be thus hungry and thirsty after God! Our version spoils the abruptness of the language; the original runs thus – "My soul for the Lord more than those watching for the morning – watching for the morning." This is a fine poetical repeat. We long for the favor of the Lord more than weary sentinels long for the morning light which will release them from their tedious watch. Indeed this is true. He that has once rejoiced in communion with God is sore tried by the hidings of his face, and grows faint with strong desire for the Lord's appearing.

7. Let Israel hope in the LORD. Or, "Hope thou, Israel, in Jehovah." Jehovah is Israel's God; therefore, let Israel hope in him. What one Israelite does he wishes all Israel to do. That man has a just right to exhort others who is himself setting the example. Israel of old waited upon Jehovah and wrestled all the night long, and at last he went his way succored by the Hope of Israel: the like will happen to all his offspring. God has great things in store for his people; they ought to have large expectations. **For with the LORD there is mercy.** This is in his very nature, and by the light of nature it may be seen. But we have also the light of grace, and therefore we see still more his mercy. With us there is sin; but hope is ours, because with the Lord is mercy. Let us look out of self and its poverty to Jehovah and his riches of mercy. **And with him is plenteous redemption.** He can and will redeem all his people out of their many and great troubles; indeed, their redemption is already wrought out and laid up with him, so that he can at any time give his waiting ones the full benefit thereof. The attribute of mercy, and the fact of redemption, are two most sufficient reasons for hoping in Jehovah; and the fact that there is mercy or deliverance elsewhere should effectually wean the soul from all idolatry. Are not these deep things of God a grand comfort for those who are crying out of the depths? Is it not better to be in the deeps with David, hoping in God's mercy, than up on the mountainside, boasting in our own fancied righteousness?

8. Our iniquities are our worst dangers: if saved from these, we are saved altogether; but there is no salvation from them except by redemption. What a blessing that this is here promised in terms which remove it out of the region of question: the Lord will certainly redeem his believing people from all their sins. Well may the redemption be plenteous since it concerns all Israel and all iniquities! Truly, our psalm has ascended to a great height in this verse: this is no cry out of the depths, but a chorale in the heights. Redemption is the top of covenant blessings. Is not this a clear prophecy of the coming of our Lord Jesus the first time? And may we not now regard it as the promise of his second and more glorious coming for the redemption of the body? For this out soul waits; our heart and our flesh cry out for it with joyful expectation.

Psalm 131

1. LORD, my heart is not haughty. The psalm deals with the Lord, and it is a solitary colloquy with him, not a discourse before other people. We have a sufficient audience when we speak with the Lord, and we may say to him many things which were not proper for the ears of other people. The holy man makes his appeal to Jehovah, who alone knows the heart: we should be slow to do this upon any matter, for the Lord is not to be trifled with; and when any-one ventures on such an appeal he should be sure of his case. He begins with his heart, for that is the center of our nature, and if pride be there it defiles everything. It is a grand thing for a man to know his own heart so as to be able to speak before the Lord about it. It is beyond all things deceitful and desper-ately wicked; who can know it, unless taught by the Spirit of God? It is a still greater thing if, upon searching himself thoroughly, a man can solemnly pro-test unto the Omniscient One that his heart is not haughty: that is to say, neither proud in his opinion of himself, contemptuous to others, nor self-righteous before the Lord; neither boastful of the past, proud of the present, nor ambitious for the future. **Nor mine eyes lofty.** What the heart desires, the eyes look for. Where the desires run, the glances usually follow. This holy man felt that he did not seek after elevated places where he might gratify his self-esteem, neither did he look down upon others as being his inferiors. A proud look the Lord hates; and in this all people are agreed with him; even the proud themselves hate haughtiness in the gestures of others. Lofty eyes are so generally hateful that haughty men have been known to avoid the manner natural to the proud in order to escape the ill-will of their fellows. The pride which apes humility always takes care to cast its eyes downward, since every-one's consciousness tells him that contemptuous glances are the sure ensigns of a boastful spirit.

Neither do I exercise myself in great matters. As a private man he did not usurp the power of the king or devise plots against him: he minded his own business, and left others to mind theirs. As a thoughtful man he did not pry into things unrevealed; he was not speculative, self-conceited or opinionated. As a secular person he did not thrust himself into the priesthood as Saul had done before him, and as Uzziah did after him. It is well so to exercise ourselves unto godliness that we know our true sphere, and diligently keep to it. Many through wishing to be great have failed to be good: they were not content to adorn the lowly stations which the Lord appointed them, and so they have rushed at grandeur and power, and found destruction where they looked for honor. **Or in things too high for me.** High things may suit others who are of greater stature, and yet they may be quite unfit for us. We do well to know our own size. Such is the vanity of many that if a work be within their range they despise it, and think it beneath them: the only service which they are willing to undertake is that to which they have never been called, and for which they are by no means qualified. What a haughty heart must he have who will not serve God at all unless he may be trusted with five talents at the least! His looks are indeed lofty who disdains to be a light among his poor friends and neighbors here below, but demands to be created a star of the first magnitude to shine among the upper ranks, and to be admired by gazing crowds. It is just on God's part that those who wish to be everything should end in being nothing. It is a righteous retribution from God when every matter turns out to be too high for the man who exercised himself in things too high for him.

2. Surely I have behaved and quieted myself. The original bears somewhat of the form of an oath, and therefore our translators exhibited great judgment in introducing the word **surely**; it is not a literal version, but it correctly gives the meaning. The psalmist had been upon his best behavior, and had smoothed down the roughnesses of his self-will; by holy effort he had mastered his own spirit, so that towards God he was not rebellious, even as towards man he was not haughty. It is no easy thing to quiet yourself: sooner may a man calm the sea, or rule the wind, or tame a tiger, than quiet himself. We are clamorous, uneasy, petulant; and nothing but grace can make us quiet under afflictions, irritations, and disappointments. **As a child that is weaned of his mother.** Eastern people put off the time of weaning far later than we do, and we may conclude that the process grows none the easier by being postponed. At last there must be an end to the suckling period, and then a battle begins: the child is denied his comfort, and therefore frets and worries, flies into tantrums, or sinks into sulks. It is facing its first great sorrow, and it is in sore distress. Yet time brings not only alleviations, but the ending of the conflict; the boy ere long is quite content to find his nourishment at the table with his brothers, and he feels no lingering wish to return to those dear fountains from which he once sustained his life. He is no longer angry with his mother, but buries his head in that very bosom after which he pined so grievously: he is weaned **of** his mother rather than *from* her.

To the weaned child his mother is his comfort though she has denied him comfort. It is a blessed mark of growth out of spiritual infancy when we can forego the joys which once appeared to be essential, and can find our solace in him who denies them to us: then we behave manfully, and every childish complaint is hushed. If the Lord removes our dearest delight we bow to his will without a grumbling thought; in fact, we find a delight in giving up our delight. This is no spontaneous fruit of nature, but a well-tended product of divine grace: it grows out of humility and lowliness, and it is the stem upon which peace blooms as a fair flower. **My soul is even as a weaned child**; or it may be read, "as a weaned child on me my soul," as if his soul leaned upon him in mute submission, neither boasting nor complaining. It is not every child of God who arrives at this weanedness speedily. Some are sucklings when they ought to be fathers; others are hard to wean, and cry, and fight, and rage against their Heavenly Father's discipline. When we think ourselves safely through the weaning, we sadly discover that the old appetites are rather wounded than slain, and we begin crying again for the breasts which we had given up. It is easy to begin shouting before we are out of the wood, and no doubt hundreds have sung this psalm long before they have understood it. Blessed are those afflictions which subdue our affections, which wean us from all self-sufficiency, which educate us into Christian manliness, which teach us to love God not merely when he comforts us, but even when he tries us. Well might the sacred poet repeat his figure of the weaned child; it is doubly desirable and difficult of attainment. Such weanedness from self springs from the gentle humility declared in the former verse, and partly accounts for its existence. If pride is gone, submission will be sure to follow; and, on the other hand, if pride is to be driven out, self must also be vanquished.

3. See how lovingly a man who is weaned from self thinks of others! David thinks of his people, and loses himself in his care for Israel. How he prizes the grace of hope! He has given up the things which are seen, and therefore he values the treasures which are not seen except by the eyes of hope. There is room for the largest hope when self is gone, ground for eternal hope when transient things no longer hold the mastery of our spirits. This verse is the lesson of experience: a man of God who had been taught to renounce the world and live upon the Lord alone, here exhorts all his friends and companions to do the same. He found it a blessed thing to live by hope, and therefore he would have all his kinsmen do the same. Let all the nation hope, let all their hope be in Jehovah, let them at once begin hoping **from henceforth,** and let them continue hoping **forever.** Weaning takes the child out of a temporary condition into a state in which he will continue for the rest of his life: to rise above the world is to enter upon a heavenly existence which can never end. When we cease to hanker for the world we begin hoping in the Lord.

Psalm 132

1. With David the covenant was made, and therefore his name is pleaded on behalf of his descendants, and the people who would be blessed by his dynasty. Jehovah, who changes not, will never forget one of his servants, or fail to keep his covenant; yet for this thing he is to be intreated. That which we are assured the Lord will do must, nevertheless, be made a matter of prayer.

The request is that the Lord would **remember**, and this is a word full of meaning. We know that the Lord remembered Noah, and assuaged the flood; he remembered Abraham, and sent Lot out of Sodom; he remembered Rachel, and Hannah, and gave them children; he remembered his mercy to the house of Israel, and delivered his people. The plea is urged with God that he would bless the family of David for the sake of their progenitor; how much stronger is our master-argument in prayer that God would deal well with us for Jesus' sake! David had no personal merit; the plea is based upon the covenant graciously made with him; but Jesus has deserts which are his own, and of boundless merit – these we may urge without hesitation. When the Lord was angry with the reigning prince, the people cried, **Lord, remember David**; and when they needed any special blessing, again they sang it. This was good pleading, but it was not so good as ours, which runs, "Lord, remember *Jesus*, and all his afflictions."

The **afflictions** of David here meant were those which came upon him as a godly man in his endeavors to maintain the worship of Jehovah, and to provide for its decent and suitable celebration. There was always an ungodly party in the nation, and these persons were never slow to slander, hinder, and molest the servant of the Lord. Whatever were David's faults, he kept true to the one, only, living, and true God; ad for this he was a speckled bird among monarchs. Since he zealously delighted in the worship of Jehovah, his God, he was despised and ridiculed by those who could not understand his enthusiasm. God will never forget what his people suffer for his sake. No doubt innumerable blessings descend upon families and nations through the godly lives and patient sufferings of the saints. We cannot be saved by the merits of others, but beyond all question we are benefited by their virtues (see Hebrews 6:10). Under the New Testament dispensation, as well as under the Old, there is a full reward for the righteous. That reward frequently comes upon their descendants rather than upon themselves; they sow, and their successors reap. We may at this day pray, Lord, remember the martyrs and confessors of our race, who suffered for thy name's sake, and bless our people and nation with Gospel grace for our fathers' sakes.

2. Moved by intense devotion, David expressed his resolve in the form of a solemn vow, which was sealed with an oath. The fewer of such vows the better under a dispensation whose great Representative has said, "Swear not at all." Perhaps even in this case it had been wiser to have left the pious resolve in the hands of God in the form of a prayer, for the vow was not actually fulfilled as intended, since the Lord forbade David to build him a temple. We had better not swear to do anything before we know the Lord's mind about it, and then we shall not need to swear. The instance of David's vow shows that vows are allowable, but it does not prove that they are desirable. Probably David went too far in his words, and it is well that the Lord did not hold him to the letter of his bond, but accepted the will for the deed, and the meaning of his promise instead of the literal sense of it. David imitated Jacob, that great maker of vows at Bethel, and upon him rested the blessing pronounced on Jacob by Isaac, "God Almighty bless thee" (Genesis 28:3), which was remembered by the patriarch on his death-bed, when he spoke of "the mighty God of Jacob." God is mighty to hear us, and to help us in performing our vow. We should be full of awe at the idea of making any promise to the mighty God: to dare to trifle with him would be grievous indeed. It is observable that affliction led both David and Jacob into covenant dealings with the Lord: many vows are made in anguish of soul. We may also remark that, if the votive obligations of David are to be remembered of the Lord, much more are the suretyship engagements of the Lord Jesus before the mind of the great Lord, to whom our soul turns in the hour of our distress.

Jehovah was the God of Jacob, the same God evermore; he had this for his attribute, that he is mighty – mighty to succor his Jacobs who put their trust in him, though their afflictions be many. He is, moreover, especially the Mighty One of his people; he is the God of Jacob in a sense in which he is not the God of unbelievers.

3. Our translators give the meaning, though not the literal form, of David's vow, which ran thus: "If I go" – "If I go up," etc. This was an elliptical form of imprecation, implying more than it expressed, and having therefore about it a mystery which made it all the more solemn. David would not take his ease in his house, nor his rest in his bed, till he had determined upon a place for the worship of Jehovah. The ark had been neglected, the Tabernacle had fallen into disrespect; he would find the ark, and build for it a suitable house; he felt that he could not take pleasure in his own palace till this was done. David meant well, but he spoke more than he could carry out. His language was hyperbolical and the Lord knew what he meant: zeal does not always measure its terms, for it is not thoughtful of human criticisms, but is carried away with love to the Lord, who reads the hearts of his people. David would not think himself housed till he had built a house for the Lord, nor would he reckon himself rested till he had said, "Arise, O Lord, into thy rest." Alas, we have many around us who will never carry their care for the Lord's worship too far! No fear of their being indiscreet! They are housed and bedded, and as for the Lord, his people may meet in a barn, or never meet at all, it will be all the same to them. Observe that Jacob in his vow spoke of the stone being God's house, and David's vow also deals with a house for God.

4. He could not enjoy sleep till he had done his best to provide a place for the ark. It is a strong expression, and it is not to be coolly discussed by us. Remember that the man was all on fire, and he was writing poetry also, and therefore his language is not that which we should employ in cold blood. Everybody can see what he means, and how intensely he means it. Oh that many more were seized with sleeplessness because the house of the Lord lies waste! They can slumber fast enough, and not even disturb themselves with a dream, though the cause of God should be brought to the lowest ebb by their covetousness. What is to become of those who have no care about divine things, and never give a thought to the claims of their God?

5. He resolved to find a place where Jehovah would allow his worship to be celebrated, a house where God would fix the symbol of his presence, and commune with his people. At that time, in all David's land, there was no proper place for that ark whereon the Lord had placed the mercy-seat, where prayer could be offered, and where the manifested glory shone forth. All things had fallen into decay, and the outward forms of public worship were too much disregarded; hence the King resolves to be first and foremost in establishing a better order of things.

Yet one cannot help remembering that the holy resolve of David gave to a place and a house much more importance than the Lord himself ever attached to such matters. This is indicated in Nathan's message from the Lord to the king, in 2 Samuel 7:5–7. Stephen in his inspired speech puts the matter plainly (Acts 7:47–48). It is a striking fact that true religion never flourished more in Israel than before the temple was built, and that from the day of the erection of that magnificent house the spirit of godliness declined. Good people may have on their hearts matters which seem to them of chief importance, and it may be acceptable to God that they should seek to carry them out; and yet in his infinite wisdom he may judge it best to prevent their executing their designs. God does not measure his people's actions by their wisdom, or want of wisdom, but by the sincere desire for his glory which has led up to them. David's resolution, though he was not allowed to fulfill it, brought a blessing upon him: the Lord promised to build the house of David, because he had desired to build the house of the Lord. Moreover, the King was allowed to prepare the treasure for the erection of the glorious edifice which was built by his son and successor. The Lord shows the acceptance of what we desire to do by permitting us to do something else which his infinite mind judges to be fitter for us, and more honorable to himself.

6. Meanwhile, where was the habitation of God among men? He was wont to shine forth from between the cherubim, but where was the ark? It was like a hidden thing, a stranger in its own land. **Lo, we heard of it at Ephratah.** Rumors came that it was somewhere in the land of Ephraim, in a temporary lodging; rather an object of dread than of delight. Is it not wonderful that so renowned a symbol of the presence of God should be lingering in neglect – a neglect so great that it was remarkable that we should have heard of its whereabouts at all? When a man begins to think upon God and his service it is comforting that the Gospel is heard of. Considering the opposition which it has encountered it is marvelous that it should be heard of, and heard of in a place remote from the central city; but yet we are sorrowful that it is only in connection with some poor despised place that we do hear of it.

David instituted a search for the ark. It had to be hunted for high and low; and at last at Kirjath-jearim, the forest-city, he came upon it. How often do souls find Christ and his salvation in out-of-the-way places! What matters where we meet with him so long as we do behold him, and find life in him? That is a blessed Eureka which is embedded in our text – **we found it.** The matter began with hearing, led on to a search, and concluded in a joyful find. **We found it in the fields of the wood.** Alas that there should be no room for the Lord in the palaces of kings, so that he must take to the woods. If Christ be in a wood he will yet be found of those who seek for him. He is as near in the rustic home, embowered among the trees, as in the open streets of the city; he will answer prayer offered from the heart of the black forest where the lone traveler seems out of all hope of hearing. The text presents us with an instance of one whose heart was set upon finding the place where God would meet with him; this made him quick of hearing, and so the cheering news soon reached him. The tidings renewed his ardor, and led him to stick at no difficulties in his search; and so it came to pass that, where he could hardly have expected it, he lighted upon the treasure which he so much prized.

7. **We will go into his tabernacles.** Having found the place where he dwells we will hasten thereto. He has many dwellings in the various courts of his house, and each of these will receive the reverence due: in each the priest will offer for us the appointed service; and our hearts will go where our bodied may not enter. David is not alone; he is represented as having sought for the ark with others, for so the word **we** implies; and now they are glad to attend him in his pilgrimage to the chosen shrine, saying "*We* found it . . . *we* will go." Because these are the Lord's courts we will resort to them. **We will worship at his footstool.** The best ordered earthly house can be no more than the footstool of so great a King. His ark can only reveal the glories of his feet, according to the promise that he will make the place of his feet glorious: yet thither will we hasten with joy, in glad companionship, and there we will adore him. Where Jehovah is, there shall he be worshiped. It is well not only to go to the Lord's house, but to **worship** there: we do but profane his tabernacles if we enter them for any other purpose.

Before leaving this verse let us note the ascent of this psalm of degrees – "we heard . . . we found . . . we will go . . . we will worship."

8–11. In these three verses we see the finders of the ark removing it to its appointed place, using a formula somewhat like that used by Moses when he said, "Rise up, Lord," and again, "Return, O Lord, unto the many thousands of Israel."

8. The ark had been long upon the move, and no fit place had been found for it in Canaan, but now devout men have prepared a temple, and they sing.

They hoped that now the covenant symbol had found a permanent abode – a rest, and they trusted that Jehovah would now abide with it forever. Vain would it be for the ark to be settled if the Lord did not continue with it, and perpetually shine forth from between the cherubim. Unless the Lord rests with us, there is no rest for us; unless the ark of his strength abides with us we are ourselves without strength. The ark of the covenant is here mentioned by a name which it well deserved, for in its captivity it smote its captors, and broke their gods, and when it was brought back it guarded its own honor by the death of those who dared to treat it with disrespect. The power of God was thus connected with the sacred chest. Reverently, therefore, did Solomon pray concerning its as he besought the living God to consecrate the temple by his presence. It is the Lord and the covenant, or rather say the covenant Jehovah whose presence we desire in our assemblies, and this presence is the strength of his people. Oh that the Lord would indeed abide in all the churches, and cause his power to be revealed in Zion.

9. Let thy priests be clothed with righteousness. No garment is so resplendent as that of a holy character. In this glorious robe our great High Priest is evermore arrayed, and he would have all his people adorned in the same manner. Then only are priests fit to appear before the Lord, and to minister for the profit of the people, when their lives are dignified with goodness. They must ever remember that they are God's priests, and should therefore wear the livery of their Lord, which is holiness: they are not only to have righteousness, but to be clothed with it, so that upon every part of them righteousness will be conspicuous. Whoever looks upon God's servants should see holiness if they see nothing else. Now, this righteousness of the ministers of the temple is prayed for in connection with the presence of the Lord; and this instructs us that holiness is only to be found among those who commune with God, and only comes to them through his visitation of their spirits. God will dwell among a holy people; and where God is, the people become holy.

And let thy saints shout for joy. Holiness and happiness go together; where the one is found, the other ought never to be far away. Holy persons have a right to great and demonstrative joy: they may shout because of it. Since they are saints, and thy saints, and thou hast come to dwell with them, O Lord, thou hast made it their duty to rejoice, and to let others know of their joy. The sentence, while it may read as a permit, is also a precept: saints are commanded to rejoice in the Lord. Happy religion makes it a duty to be glad! Where righteousness is the clothing, joy may well be the occupation.

10. King Solomon was praying, and here the people pray for him that his face may not be turned away, or that he may not be refused an audience. It is a dreadful thing to have our face turned away from God, or to have his face turned away from us. If we are anointed of the Spirit the Lord will look upon us with favor. Specially is this true of him who represents us, and is on our behalf the Christ – the truly anointed of the Lord. Jesus is both our David and God's anointed; in him is found in fullness that which David received in measure. For his sake all those who are anointed in him are accepted. God blessed Solomon and succeeding kings, for David's sake; and he will bless us for Jesus' sake. The Son of the Highest took upon himself the form of a **servant**, to be anointed for us, and to go in before the mercy-seat to plead on our behalf. The psalm sings of the ark, and it may well remind us of the going in of the anointed priest within the veil: all depended upon his acceptance, and therefore well do the people pray, "Turn not away the face of thine anointed."

Thus, in these three verses, we have a prayer for the temple, the ark, the priests, the Levites, the people, and the king: in each petition there is a fullness of meaning well worthy of careful thought. We cannot plead too much in detail; the fault of most prayers is their indefiniteness. In God's house and worship everything needs a blessing, and every person connected therewith needs it continually. As David vowed and prayed when he was minded to consecrate the ark, so now the prayer is continued when the temple is consecrated, and the Lord deigns to fill it with his glory. We shall never have done praying till we have done needing.

11. Here was come to a grand covenant pleading of the kind which is always prevalent with the Lord. **The Lord hath sworn in truth unto David.** We cannot urge anything with God which is equal to his own word and oath. Jehovah swears that our faith may have strong confidence in it: he cannot forswear himself. He swears **in truth**, for he means every word that he utters; people may be perjured, but none will be so profane as to imagine this of the God of truth. By Nathan this covenant of Jehovah was conveyed to David, and there was no delusion in it. **He will not turn from it.** Jehovah is not a changeable being. He never turns from his purpose, much less from his promise solemnly ratified by oath. What a rock they stand upon who have an immutable oath of God for their foundation! We know that this covenant was really made with Christ, the spiritual descendant of David, for Peter quotes it at Pentecost. Christ therefore sits on a sure throne forever and ever, seeing that he has kept the covenant, and through him the blessing comes upon Zion, whose poor are blessed in him. **Of the fruit of thy body will I set upon thy throne.** Jesus sprang from the race of David, as the Evangelists are careful to record; he was "of the house and lineage of David"; at this day he is the King of the Jews, and the Lord has also given him the heathen for his inheritance. He must reign, and of his kingdom there shall be no end. God himself has set him on the throne, and no rebellion of men or devils can shake his dominion. The honor of Jehovah is concerned in his reign, and therefore it is never in danger, for the Lord will not let his oath be dishonored.

12. If thy children will keep my covenant and my testimony that I shall teach them. There is a condition to the covenant so far as it concerned kings of

David's line before the coming of Jesus, who has fulfilled that condition, and made the covenant indefeasible henceforth and forever as to himself and the spiritual offspring in him. Considered as it related to temporal things it was no small blessing for David's dynasty to be secured the throne upon good behavior. These monarchs held their crowns from God upon the terms of loyalty to their superior Sovereign, the Lord who had elevated them to their high position. They were to be faithful to the covenant by obedience to the divine law, and by belief of divine truth. They were to accept Jehovah as their Lord and their Teacher, regarding him in both relations as in covenant with them. How gladly they ought to render intelligent obedience! What a proper, righteous, and needful stipulation for God to make that they should be true to him when the reward was the promise, **Their children shall also sit upon thy throne for evermore.** If they sit at his feet God will make them sit on a throne; if they keep the covenant they shall keep the crown from generation to generation.

The kingdom of Judah might have stood to this day had its kings been faithful to the Lord. No internal revolt or external attack could have overthrown the royal house of David: it fell by its own sin, and by nothing else. The Lord was continually provoked, but he was amazingly longsuffering, for long after seceding Israel had gone into captivity, Judah still remained. Miracles of mercy were shown to her. Divine patience exceeded all limits, for the Lord's regard for David was exceeding great. The princes of David's house seemed set on ruining themselves, and nothing could save them; justice waited long, but it was bound at last to unsheathe the sword and strike. Still, if in the letter man's breach of promise caused the covenant to fail, yet in spirit and essence the Lord has been true to it, for Jesus reigns, and holds the throne forever. David's descendant is still royal, for he was the progenitor according to the flesh of him who is King of kings and Lord of lords.

This verse shows the need of family piety. Parents must see to it that their children know the fear of the Lord, and they must beg the Lord himself to teach them his truth. We have no hereditary right to the divine favor: the Lord keeps up his friendship to families from generation to generation, for he is loath to leave the descendants of his servants, and never does so except under grievous and long-continued provocation. As believers, we are all in a measure under some such covenant as the line of David: certain of us can look backward for four generations of saintly ancestors, and we are now glad to look forward and to see our children, and our children's children, walking in the truth. Yet we know that grace does not run in the blood, and we are filled with holy fear lest in any of our seed there should be an evil heart of unbelief in departing from the living God.

13. For the LORD hath chosen Zion. It was no more than any other Canaanite town till God chose it, David captured it, Solomon built it, and the Lord dwelt in it. So was the church a mere Jebusite stronghold till grace chose it, conquered it, rebuilt it, and dwelt in it. Jehovah has chosen his people, and hence they are his people. He has chosen the church, and hence it is what it is. Thus in the covenant David and Zion, Christ and his people, go together. David is for Zion, and Zion for David: the interests of Christ and his people are mutual. **He hath desired it for his habitation.** David's question is answered. The Lord has spoken: the site of the temple is fixed: the place of the divine manifestation is determined. Indwelling follows upon election, and arises out of it: Zion is chosen, chosen for a habitation of God. The desire of God to dwell among the people whom he has chosen for himself is very gracious and yet very natural: his love will not rest apart from those upon whom he has placed it. God desires to abide with those he has loved with an everlasting love; and we do not wonder that it should be so, for we also desire the company of our beloved ones. It is a double marvel that the Lord should choose and desire such poor creatures as we are: the indwelling of the Holy Ghost in believers is a wonder of grace parallel to the incarnation of the Son of God. God in the church is the wonder of heaven, the miracle of eternity, the glory of infinite love.

14. This is my rest for ever. Oh, glorious words! It is God himself who here speaks. Think of rest for God! A Sabbath for the Eternal and a place of abiding for the Infinite. He calls Zion **my rest.** Here his love remains and displays itself with delight. And this **for ever.** He will not seek another place of repose, nor grow weary of his saints. In Christ the heart of Deity is filled with content, and for his sake he is satisfied with his people, and will be so world without end. These august words declare a distinctive choice – **his** and no other; a certain choice – **this** which is well known to me; a present choice – **this** which is here at this moment. God has made his election of old, he has not changed it, and he never will repent of it: his church was his rest and **is** his rest still. As he will not turn from his oath, so he will never turn from his choice. Oh that we may enter into *his* rest, may be part and parcel of his church, and yield by our loving faith a delight to the mind of him who takes pleasure in them that fear him, in them that hope in his mercy. **Here I will dwell; for I have desired it.** Again are we filled with wonder that he who fills all things should dwell in Zion – should dwell with them; he desires them. He is already in Zion, for he says **here,** as one upon the spot. Not only will he occasionally come to his church, but he will dwell in it, as his fixed abode. He cared not for the magnificence of Solomon's temple, but he determined that at the mercy-seat he would be found by suppliants, and that thence he would shine forth in brightness of grace among the favored nation. All this, however, was but a type of the spiritual house of which Jesus is foundation and cornerstone, upon which all the living stones are builded together for an habitation of God through the Spirit. Oh, the sweetness of the thought that God *desires* to dwell in his people and rest among them! Surely if it be his desire he will cause it to be so. If the desire of the righteous is granted, much more shall the desire of the righteous God be accomplished. This is the joy of our souls, for surely we shall rest in God, and certainly our desire is to dwell in him. This also is the end of our fears for the church of God, for if the Lord dwell in her, she shall not be moved; if the Lord desire her, the devil cannot destroy her.

15. I will abundantly bless her provision. It must be so. How can we be without a blessing when the Lord is among us? We live upon his Word, we are clothed by his charity, we are armed by his power: all sorts of provision are in him, and how can we be otherwise than blessed? The provision is to be **abundantly** blessed; then it will be abundant and blessed. Daily provision, royal provision, satisfying provision, overflowingly joyful provision the church shall receive; and the divine benediction will cause us to receive it with faith, to feed upon it by experience, to grow upon it by sanctification, to be strengthened by it to labor, cheered by it to patience, and built up by it to perfection. **I will satisfy her poor with bread.** The citizens of Zion are poor in themselves, poor in spirit, and often poor in pocket, but their hearts and souls will dwell in such abundance that they will neither need more nor desire more. Satisfaction is the crown of experience. Where God rests his people will be satisfied. They are to be satisfied with what the Lord himself calls **bread,** and we may be sure that he knows what is really bread for souls. He will not give us a stone. The Lord's poor will have that which will suit their palate, remove their hunger, fill their desire, build up their frame, and perfect their growth. The bread of earth is "the bread that perisheth," but the bread of God endureth to life eternal. In the church where God rests his people shall not starve; the Lord would never rest if they did. He did not take rest for six days till he had prepared the world for the first man to live in; he would not stay his hand till all things were ready; therefore, we may be sure if the Lord rests it is because "it is finished," and the Lord has prepared of his goodness for the poor. Where God finds his desire his people will find theirs; if he is satisfied, they will be.

Taking the two clauses together, we see that nothing but an abundant blessing in the church will satisfy the Lord's poor people: they are naked and miserable till that comes. All the provision that Solomon himself could make would not have satisfied the saints of his day: they looked higher, and longed for the Lord's own boundless blessing, and hungered for the bread which came down from heaven. Blessed be the Lord, for we see in this verse two of the **I will**s of God to rest upon, and nothing could be a better support to our faith.

16. More is promised than was prayed for. See how the ninth verse asks for the priests to be clad in righteousness, and the answer is, **I will also clothe her priests with salvation.** God is wont to do exceeding abundantly, above all that we ask or even think. Righteousness is but one feature of blessing; salvation is the whole of it. What cloth of gold is this! What more than regal array! Garments of salvation! Not every priest shall be thus clothed, but only **her** priests, those who truly belong to Zion, by faith which is in Christ Jesus, who has made them priests unto God. These are clothed by the Lord himself, and none can clothe as he does. If even the grass of the field is so clothed by the Creator as to outvie Solomon in all his glory, how must his own children be clad? Truly he shall be admired in his saints; the liveries of his servants will be the wonder of heaven. **And her saints shall shout aloud for joy.** Again we have a golden answer to a silver prayer. The psalmist would have the "saints shout for joy." "That they shall do," says the Lord, "and **aloud** too"; they will be exceedingly full of delight; their songs and shouts will be so hearty that they will sound as the noise of many waters, and as great thunders. These joyful ones are not, however, the mimic saints of superstition, but **her** saints, saints of the Most High, "sanctified in Christ Jesus." These shall be so abundantly blessed and so satisfied and so appareled that they cannot do otherwise than shout to show their astonishment, their triumph, their gratitude, their exultation, their enthusiasm, their joy in the Lord. Zion has no dumb saints. The sight of God at rest among his chosen is enough to make the most silent shout. If the morning stars sang together when the earth and heavens were made, much more will all the sons of God shout for joy when the new heavens and the new earth are finished, and the New Jerusalem comes down out of heaven from God, prepared as a bride for her husband. Meanwhile, even now the dwelling of the Lord among us is a perennial fountain of sparkling delight to all holy minds. This shouting for joy is guaranteed to Zion's holy ones: God says they **shall** shout aloud, and depend upon it they will: who shall stop them of this glorying? The Lord has said by his Spirit, "let them shout," and then he has promised that "they shall shout aloud": who is he that will make them hold their peace? The Bridegroom is with them, and will the children of the bride-chamber fast? No, indeed, we rejoice, and will rejoice.

17. There will I make the horn of David to bud. In Zion David's dynasty will develop power and glory. The growth of the horns of stags is the natural fact from which we conceive the expression to be borrowed. As the stag is made noble and strong by the development of his horns, so the house of David will advance from strength to strength. This was to be by the work of the Lord – **there will I make** – and therefore it would be sure and solid growth. When God makes us to bud none can cause us to fade. When David's descendants left the Lord and the worship of his house, they declined, for it was only through the Lord, and in connection with his worship, that their horn would bud. **I have ordained a lamp for mine anointed.** David's name was to be illustrious, and brilliant as a lamp; it was to continue shining like a lamp in the sanctuary; it was thus to be a comfort to the people, and an enlightenment to the nations. God would not let the light of David go out by the extinction of his race: his holy ordinances had decreed that the house of his servant should remain in the midst of Israel. What a lamp is our Lord Jesus! A light to lighten the Gentiles, and the glory of his people Israel. As the anointed – the true Christ – he shall be the light of heaven itself. Oh for grace to receive our illumination and our consolation from Jesus Christ alone.

18. His enemies will I clothe with shame. They will be utterly defeated, they will loathe their evil design, they will be despised for having hated the Ever Blessed One. Their shame they will be unable to hide: it will cover them. God will array them in it forever, and it will be their convict dress to all eternity. **But upon himself shall his crown flourish.** Green will be his laurels of victory. He will win and wear the crown of honor, and his inherited diadem will increase in splendor. Is it not so to this hour with Jesus? His kingdom cannot fail; his imperial glories cannot fade. It is **himself** that we delight to honor; it is to himself that the honor comes, and upon himself that it flourishes. If others snatch at his crown their traitorous aims are defeated; but he in his own person reigns with ever-growing splendor.

Psalm 133

1. Behold. It is a wonder seldom seen, therefore behold it! It may be seen, for it is the characteristic of real saints – therefore fail not to inspect it! It is well worthy of admiration; pause and gaze upon it! It will charm you into imitation, therefore note it well! God looks on with approval, therefore consider it with attention. **How good and how pleasant it is for brethren to dwell together in unity!** No one can tell the exceeding excellence of such a condition; and so the psalmist uses the word **how** twice. He does not attempt to measure either the good or the pleasure, but invited us to behold for ourselves. The combination of the two adjectives **good** and **pleasant** is more remarkable than the conjunction of two stars of the first magnitude. Everyone loves pleasant things, and yet it frequently happens that the pleasure is evil; but here the condition is as good as it is pleasant, as pleasant as it is good, for the same **how** is set before each qualifying word.

For **brethren** according to the flesh to dwell together is not always wise; for experience teaches that they are better a little apart, and it is shameful for them to dwell together in disunion. They had much better part in peace like Abraham and Lot, than dwell together in envy like Joseph's brothers. When brethren can and do dwell together **in unity,** then is their communion worthy to be gazed upon and sung of in holy psalmody. Such sights ought often to be seen among those who are near of kin, for they are brethren, and therefore should be united in heart and aim; they dwell together, and it is for their mutual comfort that there should be no strife; and yet how many families are rent by fierce feuds, and exhibit a spectacle which is neither good nor pleasant!

As to brethren in spirit, they ought to dwell together in church fellowship, and in that fellowship one essential matter is unity. We can dispense with uniformity if we possess unity: oneness of life, truth, and way; oneness in Christ Jesus; oneness of object and spirit – these we must have, or our assemblies will be synagogues of contention rather than churches of Christ. The closer the unity the better, for the more of the good and the pleasant there will be. Since we are imperfect beings, somewhat of the evil and the unpleasant is sure to intrude; but this will readily be neutralized and easily ejected by the true love of the saints, if it really exists. Christian unity is good in itself, good for ourselves, good for the brethren, good for our converts, good for the outside world, and for certain it is pleasant, for a loving heart must have pleasure and give pleasure in associating with others of like nature. A church united for years in earnest service of the Lord is a well of goodness and joy to all those who dwell round about it.

2. It is like the precious ointment upon the head. In order that we may the better behold brotherly unity David gives us a resemblance, so that as in a glass we may perceive its blessedness. It has a *sweet perfume* about it, comparable to that precious ointment with which the first high priest was anointed at his ordination. It is a *holy thing,* and so again is like the oil of consecration which was to be used only in the Lord's service. What a sacred thing must brotherly love be when it can be likened to an oil which must never be poured on anyone but on the Lord's high priest alone! It is a *diffusive* thing: being poured on his head the fragrant oil flowed down upon Aaron's head, and thence dropped upon his garments till the utmost hem was anointed therewith; and just so does brotherly love extend its benign power and bless all who are beneath its influence. Hearty concord brings a benediction upon all concerned; its goodness and pleasure are shared in by the lowliest members of the household, even the servants are the better and the happier because of the lovely unity among the members of the family. *It has a special use*; for as by the anointing oil Aaron was set apart for the special service of Jehovah, so those who dwell in love are the better fitted to glorify God in his church. The Lord is not likely to use for his glory those who are devoid of love; they lack the anointing needful to make them priests unto the Lord. **That ran down upon the beard, even Aaron's beard.** This is a chief point of comparison, that as the oil did not remain confined to the place where it first fell, but flowed down the high priest's hair and bedewed his beard, just so brotherly love descending from the head distills and descends, anointing as it runs, and perfuming all it lights upon. **That went down to the skirts of his garments.** Once set in motion it would not cease from flowing. The sacred unguent could not be restrained; it flowed over his holy robes. Just so does brotherly love not only flow over the hearts upon which it was first poured out, and descend to those who are an inferior part of the mystical body of Christ, but it runs where it is not sought for, asking neither leave nor license to make its way. Christian affection knows no limits of parish, nation, sect, or age. Is the man a believer in Christ? Then he is in the one body, and I must yield him an abiding love. Is he one of the poorest, one of the least spiritual, one of the least lovable? Then he is as the skirts of the garment, and my heart's love must fall even upon him. Brotherly love comes from the head, but falls to the feet. It **ran down** and it **went down**: love for the brethren is not puffed up, but is lowly and meek. Oil would not anoint if it did not flow down; neither would brotherly love diffuse its blessing if it did not descend.

3. As the dew of Hermon, and as the dew that descended upon the mountains of Zion. From the loftier mountains the moisture appears to be wafted to the lesser hills: the dews of Hermon fall on Zion. The Alpine Lebanon ministers to the minor elevation of the city of David; and so does brotherly love descend from the higher to the lower, refreshing and enlivening in its course. Holy concord is as dew, mysteriously blessed, full of life and growth for all plants of grace. It brings with it so much benediction that it is as no common dew, but as that of Hermon which is specially copious, and far-reaching. The proper rendering is, "As the dew of Hermon that descended upon the mountains of Zion," and this tallies with the figure which has been already used. **For there the Lord commanded the blessing, even life for evermore.** That is, In Zion, or better still, in the place where brotherly love abounds. Where love reigns God reigns. Where love wishes blessing, there God commands the blessing. God has but to command, and it is done. He is so pleased to see his dear children happy in one another that he fails not to make them happy in himself. He gives especially his best blessing of eternal life, for love is life; dwelling together in love we have begun the enjoyments of eternity, and these shall not be taken from us. Let us love forevermore, and we shall live forevermore. This makes Christian brotherhood so good and pleasant; it has Jehovah's blessing resting upon it.

Oh for more of this rare virtue! Not the love which comes and goes, but that which dwells; not that spirit which separates and secludes, but that which dwells together; not that mind which is all for debate and difference, but that which dwells together in unity. Never shall we know the full power of the anointing till we are of one heart and of one spirit; never will the sacred dew of the Spirit descend in all its fullness till we are perfectly joined together in the same mind; never will the covenanted and commanded blessing come forth from the Lord our God till once again we have "one Lord, one faith, one baptism." Lord, lead us into this most precious spiritual unity, for thy Son's sake.

Psalm 134

1. Behold. By this call the pilgrims bespeak the attention of the nightwatch. The retiring pilgrims stir up the holy brotherhood of those who are appointed to keep the watch of the house of the Lord. Let them look around them upon the holy place, and everywhere **behold** reasons for sacred praise. Let them look above them at night and magnify him that made heaven and earth, and lighted the one with stars and the other with his love. Let them see to it that their hallelujahs never come to an end. Their departing brethren arouse them with the shrill cry of **Behold!** – see, take care, be on the watch, diligently mind your work, and incessantly adore and bless Jehovah's name.

Bless ye the LORD. Think well of Jehovah, and speak well of him. Adore him with reverence, draw near to him with love, delight in him with exultation. Be not content with praise, such as all his works render to him; but, as his saints, see that you **bless** him. He blesses you: therefore, be zealous to bless him. The word "bless" is the characteristic word of the psalm. The first two verses stir us up to bless Jehovah, and in the last verse Jehovah's blessing is invoked upon the people. Oh to abound in blessing! May "blessed" and "blessing" be the two words which describe our lives. Let others flatter their fellows, or bless their stars, or praise themselves; as for us, we will bless Jehovah, from whom all blessings flow. **All ye servants of the LORD.** It is your office to bless him; take care that you lead the way therein. Servants should speak well of their masters. Not one of you should serve him as of compulsion, but all should bless him while you serve him; bless him for permitting you to serve him, fitting you to serve him, and accepting your service. To be a servant of Jehovah is an incalculable honor, a blessing beyond all estimate. To be a servant in his temple, a domestic in his house, is even more a delight and a glory: if those who are ever with the Lord, and dwell in his own temple, do not bless the Lord, who will? **Which by night stand in the house of the LORD.** We can well understand how the holy pilgrims half envied those consecrated ones who guarded the temple, and attended to the necessary offices thereof through the hours of night. To the silence and solemnity of night there was added the awful glory of the place where Jehovah had ordained that his worship should be celebrated; blessed were the priests and Levites who were ordained to a service so sublime. That these should bless the Lord throughout their nightly vigils was most fitting: the people would have them mark this, and never fail in the duty. They were not to move about like so many machines, but to put their hearts into all their duties, and worship spiritually in the whole course of their duty. It would be well to watch, but better still to be "watching unto prayer" and praise.

When night settles down on a church the Lord has his watchers and holy ones still guarding his truth, and these must not be discouraged, but must bless the Lord even when the darkest hours draw on. Be it ours to cheer them, and lay upon them this charge – to bless the Lord at all times, and let his praise be continually in their mouths.

2. Lift up your hands in the sanctuary. In the holy place they must be busy, full of strength, wide-awake, energetic, and moved with holy ardor. Hands, heart, and every other part of their manhood must be upraised, elevated, and consecrated to the adoring service of the Lord. As the angels praise God day without night, so must the angels of the churches be instant in season and out of season. **And bless the LORD.** This is their main business. They are to bless men by their teaching, but they must yet more bless Jehovah with their worship. Too often people look at public worship only from the side of its usefulness to the people; but the other matter is of even higher importance: we must see to it that the Lord God is adored, extolled, and had in reverence. For a second time the word **bless** is used, and applied to Jehovah. Bless the Lord, O my soul, and let every other soul bless him. There will be no drowsiness about even midnight devotion if the heart is set upon blessing God in Christ Jesus, which is the Gospel equivalent of God **in the sanctuary.**

3. This last verse is the answer from the temple to the pilgrims preparing to depart as the day breaks. It is the ancient blessing of the high priest condensed, and poured forth upon each individual pilgrim. **The LORD that made heaven and earth bless thee out of Zion.** You are scattering and going to your homes one by one; may the benediction come upon you one by one. You have been up to Jehovah's city and temple at his bidding; return each one with such a benediction as only he can give – divine, infinite, effectual, eternal. You are not going away from Jehovah's works or glories, for he made the heaven above you and the earth on which you dwell. He is your Creator, and he can bless you with untold mercies; he can create joy and peace in your hearts, and make for you a new heaven and a new earth. May the Maker of all things make you to abound in blessings.

The benediction comes from the City of the Great King, from his appointed ministers, by virtue of his covenant, and so it is said to be **out of Zion.** To this day the Lord blesses each one of his people through his church, his Gospel, and the ordinances of his house. It is in communion with the saints that we receive untold blessings. May each one of us obtain yet more of the blessing which cometh from the Lord alone. Zion cannot bless us; the holiest ministers can only wish us a blessing; but Jehovah can and will bless each one of his waiting people. So may it be at this good hour. Do we desire it? Let us then bless the Lord ourselves. Let us do it a second time. Then we may confidently hope that the third time we think of blessing we shall find ourselves conscious receivers of it from the Ever-blessed One.

Psalm 135

1. **Praise ye the LORD,** or, "Hallelujah." Let those who are themselves full of holy praise labor to excite the like spirit in others. It is not enough for us to praise God ourselves; we are quite unequal to such a work; let us call in all our

friends and neighbors, and if they have been slack in service, let us stir them up to it with loving exhortations. **Praise ye the name of the LORD.** Let his character be extolled by you, and let all that he has revealed concerning himself be the subject of your song, for this is truly his **name.** Especially let his holy and incommunicable name of "Jehovah" be the object of your adoration. By that name he sets forth his self-existence, and his immutability; let these arouse your praises of his Godhead. Think of him with love, admire him with heartiness, and then extol him with ardor. Do not only magnify the Lord because he is God; but study his character and his doings, and thus render intelligent, appreciative praise. **Praise him, O ye servants of the LORD.** If others are silent, you must not be; you must be the first to celebrate his praises. You are **servants,** and this is part of your service; his **name** is named upon you, therefore celebrate his name with praises; you know what a blessed Master he is, therefore speak well of him. Those who shun his service are sure to neglect his praise; but as grace has made you his own personal servants, let your hearts make you his court musicians. Here we see the servant of the Lord arousing his fellow-servants by three times calling upon them to praise. Are we, then, so slow in such a sweet employ? Or is it that when we do our utmost it is all too little for such a Lord? Both are true. We do not praise enough; we cannot praise too much. We ought to be always at it, answering to the command here given – Praise, Praise, Praise. Let the Three-in-one have the praises of our spirit, soul, and body. For the past, the present, and the future, let us render three-fold hallelujahs.

2. You are highly favored; you are the domestics of the palace, nearest to the Father of the heavenly family, privileged to find your home in his house; therefore you must, beyond all others, abound in thanksgiving. You **stand,** or abide, in the temple; you are constant occupants of its various courts; and therefore from you we expect unceasing praise. Should not ministers be celebrated for celebrating the praises of Jehovah? Should not church officers and church members excel all others in the excellent duty of adoration? Should not all of every degree who wait even in his outer courts unite in his worship? Ought not the least and feeblest of his people to proclaim his praises, in company with those who live nearest to him? Is it not a proper thing to remind them of their obligations? Is not the psalmist wise when he does so in this case and in many others? Those who can call Jehovah *our* **God** are highly blessed, and therefore should abound in the work of blessing him. Perhaps this is the sweetest word in these two verses, signifying possession, communion in possession, assurance of possession, delight in possession. Oh the unutterable joy of calling God our own!

3. **Praise the LORD.** Do it again; continue to do it; do it better and more heartily; do it in growing numbers; do it at once. There are good reasons for praising the Lord, and among the first is this – **for the LORD is good.** He is so

good that there is none good in the same sense or degree. He is so good that all good is found in him, flows from him, and is rewarded by him. The word God is brief for good; and truly God is the essence of goodness. Should not his goodness be well spoken of? **Sing praises unto his name; for it is pleasant.** The adjective may apply to the singing and to the name – they are both pleasant. The vocal expression of praise by sacred song is one of our greatest delights. We were created for this purpose, and hence it is a joy to us. It is a charming duty to praise the lovely name of our God. All pleasure is to be found in the joyful worship of Jehovah; all joys are in his sacred name as perfumes lie slumbering in a garden of flowers. The mind expands, the soul is lifted up, the heart warms, the whole being is filled with delight when we are engaged in singing the high praises of our Father, Redeemer, Comforter. When in any occupation goodness and pleasure unite, we do well to follow it up without stint: yet it is to be feared that few of us sing to the Lord at all in proportion as we talk to other people.

4. For the LORD hath chosen Jacob unto himself. Should not the sons of Jacob praise him who has so singularly favored them? Election is one of the most forcible arguments for adoring love. "Jacob have I loved," said Jehovah, and he gave no reason for his love except that he chose to love. Jacob had then done neither good nor evil, yet thus the Lord determined, and thus he spoke. If it be said that the choice was made upon foresight of Jacob's character, it is, perhaps, even more remarkable, for there was little enough about Jacob that could deserve special choice. No, it was sovereign grace which dictated the choice. But it was not a choice whose main result was the personal welfare of Jacob's descendants: the nation was chosen by God **unto himself,** to answer the divine ends and purposes in blessing all mankind. Jacob's race was chosen to be the Lord's own, the mirrors of his mercy. Chosen they were, but mainly for this end, that they might be a special people, set apart unto the service of the Lord.

And Israel for his peculiar treasure. God's choice exalts; for here the name is changed from Jacob, the supplanter, to Israel, the prince. The love of God gives a new name and imparts a new value, for the comparison to a royal treasure is a most honorable one. As kings have a special regalia, and a selection of the rarest jewels, so the Lord deigns to reckon his chosen nation as his wealth, his delight, his glory. What an honor to the spiritual Israel that they are all this to the Lord! We are a people near and dear unto him, precious and honorable in his sight. How can we refuse our loudest, heartiest, sweetest music?

5. The greatness of God is as much a reason for adoration as his goodness, when we are once reconciled to him. God is great positively, great comparatively, and great superlatively – **above all gods.** Of this the psalmist had an assured personal persuasion. He says positively, **I know.** It is knowledge worth possessing. He knew by observation, inspiration, and realization; he was no agnostic, he was certain and clear upon the matter. He not only knows the greatness of Jehovah, but that as the Adonai, or Ruler, **our Lord** is infinitely superior to all the imaginary deities of the heathen, and to all great ones besides. Many have thought to worship Jehovah, and other gods with him; but this holy man tolerated no such notion. Others have thought to combine their religion with obedience to the unrighteous laws of tyrannical princes; this, also, the sweet singer of Israel denounced; for he regarded the living God as altogether above all people, who as magistrates and princes have been called gods. Observe here the fourth of the five **for**s. Verses 3, 4, 5, and 14 contain reasons for praise, each set forth with **for**.

6. His will is carried out throughout all space. The King's warrant runs in every portion of the universe. The heathen divided the great domain; but Jupiter does not rule in heaven, nor Neptune on the sea, nor Pluto in the lower regions; Jehovah rules over all. His decree is not defeated, his purpose is not frustrated: in no one point is his good pleasure set aside. The word **whatsoever** is of the widest range and includes all things, and the four words of place which are mentioned comprehend all space; therefore the declaration of the text knows neither limit nor exception. Jehovah works his will: he pleases to do, and he performs the deed. None can stay his hand. How contrary even to those Christian conceptions of God which subordinate him to human will, and make his eternal purposes the football of human caprice. Our theology teaches us no such degrading notions of the Eternal as that he can be baffled by man.

7. He causeth the vapors to ascend from the ends of the earth. Here we are taught the power of God in creation. The process of evaporation is passed by unnoticed by the many, because they see it going on all around them; the usual ceases to be wonderful to the thoughtless, but it remains a marvel to the instructed. When we consider upon what an immense scale evaporation is continually going on, and how needful it is for the existence of all life, we may well admire the wisdom and the power which are displayed therein. All around us from every point of the horizon the vapor rises, condenses into clouds, and ultimately descends as rain. Whence the vapors originally ascended from which our showers are formed it would be impossible to tell; most probably the main part of them comes from the tropical regions, and other remote places at **the ends of the earth.** It is the Lord who causes them to rise, and not a mere law. What is law without a force at the back of it? **He maketh lightnings for the rain.** There is an intimate connection between lightning and rain, and this would seem to be more apparent in Palestine than even with ourselves, for we constantly read of thunderstorms in that country as attending heavy downpours of rain. Lightning is not to be regarded as a lawless force, but as a part of that wonderful machinery by which the earth is kept in a fit condition: a force as much under the control of God as any other, a force most essential to our existence. The ever-changing waters, rains, winds, and electric currents circulate as if they were the lifeblood and vital spirits of the universe. **He bringeth the wind out of his treasuries.** This great force which seems left to its own wild will is really under the supreme and careful government of the Lord. As a monarch is specially master of the contents of his own treasure, so is our God the Lord of the tempest and hurricane; and as princes do not spend their treasure without taking note and count of it, so the Lord does not permit the wind to be wasted, or squandered without purpose. Everything in the material world is under the immediate direction and control of the Lord of all. It is well for us that it is so: one bandit force wandering through the Lord's domains defying his control would cast fear and trembling over all the provinces of providence. Let us praise Jehovah for the power and wisdom with which he rules clouds, and lightnings, and winds, and all other mighty and mysterious agencies.

8. This deadly smiting was an act of justice against Egypt, and of love to Israel. But what a blow it was! All the firstborn slain in a moment! How it must have horrified the nation, and cowed the boldest enemies of Israel! Beasts because of their relationship to man as domestic animals are in many ways made to suffer with him. The firstborn of beasts must die as well as the firstborn of their owners, for the blow was meant to astound and overwhelm, and it accomplished its purpose. The firstborn of God had been sorely smitten, and were set free by the Lord's meting out to their oppressors the like treatment.

9. The Lord is still seen by the psalmist as sending judgments upon rebellious people; he keeps before us the personal action of God. Even in plagues God is to be seen, as truly as in mercies. The plagues were not only terrible wonders which astounded people, but forcible tokens or signs by which they were instructed. No doubt the plagues were aimed at the various deities of the Egyptians, and were a grand exposure of their impotence: each one had its own special significance. The judgments of the Lord were no side blows, they struck the nation at the heart; he sent these bolts **into the midst of thee, O Egypt!** These marvels happened in the center of the proud and exclusive nation of Egypt, which thought itself far superior to other lands; and many of these plagues touched the nation in points upon which it prided itself. The psalmist addresses that haughty nation, saying, **O Egypt,** as though reminding it of the lessons which it had been taught by the Lord's right hand. Imperious Pharaoh had been the ringleader in defying Jehovah, and he was made personally to smart for it; nor did his flattering courtiers escape; upon each one of them the scourge fell heavily. God's servants are far better off than Pharaoh's servants: those who stand in the courts of Jehovah are delivered, but the courtiers of Pharaoh are smitten, all of them, for they were all partakers in his evil deeds. The Lord is to be praised for thus rescuing his own people.

10. The nations of Canaan joined in the desperate resistance offered by their monarchs, and so they were smitten, while their kings, ringleaders of the fight, were slain. Those who resist the divine purpose will find it hard to kick against the pricks. The greatness of the nations and the might of the kings availed nothing against the Lord. He is prepared to mete out vengeance to those who oppose his designs: those who dream of him as too tender to come to blows have mistaken the God of Israel. He intended to bless the world through his chosen people, and he would not be turned from his purpose: cost what it might, he would preserve the candle of truth which he had lighted, even though the blood of nations should be spilt in its defense. The wars against the Canaanite races were a price paid for the setting up of a nation which was to preserve for the whole world the lively oracles of God.

11. Sihon king of the Amorites, and Og king of Bashan. These two kings were the first to oppose, and they were among the most notable of the adversaries; their being smitten is therefore a special object of song for loyal Israelites. The enmity of these two kings was wanton and unprovoked, and hence their overthrow was the more welcome to Israel. Sihon had been victorious in his war with Moab, and thought to make short work with Israel, but he was speedily overthrown; Og was of the race of the giants, and by his huge size inspired the tribes with dread; but they were encouraged by the previous overthrow of Sihon, and soon the giant king fell beneath their sword. **And all the kingdoms of Canaan.** Many were these petty principalities, and some of them were populous and valiant; but they all fell beneath the conquering hand of Joshua, for the Lord was with him. Just so all the foes of the Lord's believing people in these days will be put to the rout: Satan and the world will be overthrown, and all the hosts of sin will be destroyed, for our greater Joshua leads forth our armies, conquering and to conquer.

In this verse we have the details of matters which were mentioned in the bulk in the previous stanza: it is well when we have sung of mercies in the gross to consider them one by one, and give to each individual blessing a share in our song. It is well to preserve abundant memorials of the Lord's deliverance, so that we not only sing of mighty kings as a class, but also of distinct persons.

12. Jehovah is Lord Paramount, and permits people to hold their lands upon lease, terminable at his pleasure. The nations of Canaan had become loathsome with abominable vices, and they were condemned by the great Judge of all the earth to be cut off from the face of the country which they defiled. The twelve tribes were charged to act as their executioners, and as their fee they were to receive Canaan as a possession. Of old the Lord had given this land to Abraham and his descendants by a covenant of salt, but he allowed the Amorites and other tribes to sojourn in it till their iniquity was full, and then he bade his people come and take their own out of the holders' hands. Canaan was their heritage because he had long before given it to them by promise. The Lord's chosen still have a heritage from which none can keep them back. Covenant blessings of inestimable value are secured to them. Their heritage comes by gift, though they have to fight for it. Often does it happen when they slay a sin or conquer a difficulty that they are enriched by the spoil: to them even evils work for good, and trials ensure triumphs. No enemy will prevail so as to really injure them, for they will find a heritage where once they were opposed by "all the kingdoms of Canaan."

13. Thy name, O LORD, endureth for ever. God's name is eternal, and will never be changed. His character is immutable; his fame and honor also will remain to all eternity. There will always be life in the name of Jesus, and sweetness and consolation. Those upon whom the Lord's name is named in verity and truth will be preserved by it, and kept from all evil, world without end. Jehovah is a name which will outlive the ages, and retain the fullness of its glory and might forever. **And thy memorial, O LORD, throughout all generations.** Never shall people forget thee, O Lord. The ordinances of thine house will keep thee in men's memories, and thine everlasting Gospel and the grace which goes therewith will be abiding remembrancers of thee. Grateful hearts will forever beat to thy praise, and enlightened minds will continue to marvel at all thy wondrous works. Human memorials decay, but the memorial of the Lord abides evermore. This verse must be construed in its connection, and it teaches us that the honor and glory gained by the Lord in the overthrow of the mighty kings would never die out. Israel for long ages reaped the benefit of the prestige which the divine victories had brought to the nation. Moreover, the Lord in thus keeping his covenant which he made with Abraham, when he promised to give the land to his descendants, was making it clear that his memorial contained in promises and covenant would never be out of his sight. His name endures in all its truthfulness, for those who occupied Israel's land were driven out that the true heirs might dwell therein in peace.

14. For the LORD will judge his people. He will exercise personal discipline over them, and not leave it to their foes to maltreat them at pleasure. When the correction is ended he will arise and avenge them of their oppressors, who for a while were used by him as his rod. He may seem to forget his people, but it is not so; he will undertake their cause and deliver them. The judges of Israel were also her deliverers, and such is the Lord of hosts: in this sense – as ruling, preserving, and delivering his chosen – Jehovah will judge his people. **And he will repent himself concerning his servants.** When he has smitten them, and they lie low before him, he will pity them as a father pitieth his children, for he does not afflict willingly. The psalm speaks after a human manner: the nearest description is that he repents the evil which he inflicted upon them. He acts as if he had changed his mind and regretted smiting them. It goes to the heart of God to see his beloved ones oppressed by their enemies: though they deserve all they suffer, and more than all, yet the Lord cannot see them smart without a pang. It is remarkable that the nations by which God has afflicted Israel have all been destroyed as if the tender Father hated the instruments of his children's correction. The chosen nation is here called, first, **his people,** and then **his servants**: as his people he judges them, as his servants he finds comfort in them, for so the word may be read. He is most tender to them when he sees their service; hence the Scripture says, "I will spare them, as a man spareth his own son that serveth him."

Now we come to the psalmist's denunciation of idols, which follows most naturally upon his celebration of the one only living and true God.

15. Their essential material is dead metal, their attributes are but the qualities of senseless substances, and what of form and fashion they exhibit they derive from the skill and labor of those who worship them. It is the height of insanity to worship metallic manufactures. Though silver and gold are useful to us when we rightly employ them, there is nothing about them which can entitle them to reverence and worship. If we did not know the sorrowful fact to be indisputable, it would seem to be impossible that intelligent beings could bow down before substances which they must themselves refine and fashion. One would think it less absurd to worship one's own hands than to adore that which those hands have made.

16. They have mouths. For their makers fashioned them like themselves. An opening is made where the mouth should be, and yet it is no mouth, for they eat not, **they speak not.** They cannot communicate with their worshipers; they are dumb as death. If they cannot even speak, they are not even so worthy of worship as our children at school. When our philosophical teachers deny that God has made any verbal revelation of himself they also confess that their god is dumb.

Eyes have they, but they see not. Who would adore a blind man – how can the heathen be so mad as to bow themselves before a blind image? The eyes of idols have frequently been very costly; diamonds have been used for that purpose; but of what avail is the expense, since they see nothing? The worshiper is certainly physically in advance of his god, and yet mentally he is on a level with it; for assuredly his foolish heart is darkened, or he would not so absurdly play the fool.

17. They have ears, and very large ones, too, if we remember certain of the Hindu idols. **But they hear not.** Useless are their ears; in fact, they are mere counterfeits and deceits. Ears which men make are always deaf: the secret of hearing is wrapped up with the mystery of life, and both are in the unsearchable mind of the Lord. **Neither is there any breath in their mouths.** They are dead; no sign of life is perceptible; and breathing, which is of the essence of animal life, they never knew. Shall a man waste his breath in crying to an idol which has no breath?

18. They that make them are like unto them. They are as blockish, as sense-less, as stupid as the gods they have made, and, like them, they are the objects of divine abhorrence, and will be broken in pieces in due time. **So is every one that trusteth in them.** The idol-worshipers are as bad as the idol-makers; for if there were none to worship, there would be no market for the degrading manufacture. Idolaters are spiritually dead, they are the mere images of men, their best being is gone, they are not what they seem. Their mouths do not really pray, their eyes see not the truth, their ears hear not the voice of the Lord, and the life of God is not in them. Those who believe in their own inventions in religion betray great folly, and an utter absence of the quickening Spirit. Gracious people can see the absurdity of forsaking the true God and setting up rivals in his place; but those who perpetrate this crime think not so: on the contrary, they pride themselves upon their great wisdom, and boast of "advanced light" and "modern culture." Others there are who believe in a baptismal regeneration which does not renew the nature, and they make members of Christ and children of God who have none of the spirit of Christ, or the signs of adoption. May we be saved from such mimicry of divine work lest we also become like our idols.

19. Bless the LORD, O house of Israel. All of you, in all your tribes, praise the one Jehovah. Each tribe, from Reuben to Benjamin, has its own special cause for blessing the Lord, and the nation as a whole has substantial reasons for pouring out benedictions upon his name. Those whom God has named the **house of Israel,** a family of prevailing princes, ought to show their loyalty by thankfully bowing before their sovereign Lord. **Bless the LORD, O house of Aaron.** These were elected to high office and permitted to draw very near to the divine presence; therefore they beyond all others were bound to bless the Lord. Those who are favored to be leaders in the church should be foremost in adoration. In God's house the house of Aaron should feel bound to speak well of his name before all the house of Israel.

20. Bless the LORD, O house of Levi. These helped the priests in other things; let them aid them in this also. The house of Israel comprehends all the chosen people; then we come down to the smaller but more central ring of the house of Aaron, and now we widen out to the whole tribe of Levi. Let reverence and adoration spread from person to person until the whole lump of humanity is leavened. The house of Levi had choice reasons for blessing God: read the Levite story and see. Remember that the whole of the Levites were set apart for holy service, and supported by the tribes allotted to them; therefore they were in honor bound above all others to worship Jehovah with cheerfulness.

Ye that fear the LORD, bless the LORD. These are the choicer spirits, the truly spiritual: they are not the Lord's in name only, but in heart and spirit. The Father seeks such to worship him. If Aaron and Levi both forget and fail, these will not. It may be that this verse in intended to bring in God-fearing men who were not included under Israel, Aaron, and Levi. They were Gentile proselytes, and this verse opens the door and bids them enter. Those who fear God need not wait for any other qualification for the priesthood with Aaron, and in the service of the Lord with Levi. Filial fear, such as saints feel towards the Lord, does not hinder their praise; it is indeed the main source and fountain of their adoration.

21. Blessed be the Lord out of Zion, which dwelleth at Jerusalem. Let him be most praised at home. Where he blesses most, let him be blessed most. Let the beloved mount of Zion and the chosen city of Jerusalem echo his praises. He remains among his people: he is their dwelling-place, and they are his dwelling-place: let this intimate communion insure intense gratitude on the part of his chosen. The temple of holy solemnities which is Christ, and the city of the Great King, which is the church, may fitly be regarded as the headquarters of Jehovah, the God of Israel. **Praise ye the Lord.** Hallelujah. Amen, and amen.

Psalm 136

1. O give thanks unto the Lord. The exhortation is intensely earnest: the psalmist pleads with the Lord's people to **give thanks,** three times repeated. Thanks are the least that we can offer, and these we ought freely to give. The inspired writer calls us to praise Jehovah for all his goodness to us, and all the greatness of his power in blessing his chosen. We thank our parents; let us praise our Heavenly Father. We are grateful to our benefactors; let us give thanks unto the Giver of all good. **For he is good.** Essentially he is goodness itself, practically all that he does is good, relatively he is good to his creatures. Let us thank him that we have seen, proved, and tasted that he is good. He is good beyond all others; indeed, he alone is good in the highest sense; he is the source of all good, the good of all good, the sustainer of good, the perfecter of good, and the rewarder of good. For this he serves the constant gratitude of his people. **For his mercy endureth for ever.** We shall have this repeated in every verse of the song, but not once too often.

2. O give thanks unto the God of gods. If there be powers in heaven or on earth worthy of the name of gods he is the God of them; from him their dominion comes, their authority is derived from him, and their very existence is dependent upon his will. Moreover, for the moment assuming that the deities of the heathen were gods, yet none of them could be compared with our Elohim, who is infinitely beyond what they are fabled to be. Jehovah is our God, to be worshiped and adored, and he is worthy of our reverence to the highest degree. If the heathen cultivate their gods with zeal, how much more intently should we seek the glory of the God of gods – the only true and real God. Foolish persons have gathered from this verse that the Israelites believed in the existence of many gods, at the same time believing that their Jehovah was the chief among them; but this is an absurd inference, since gods who have a God over them cannot possibly be gods themselves. The words are to be understood after the usual manner of human speech, in which things are often spoken of not as they really are, but as they profess to be. God as God is worthy of our warmest thanks, **for his mercy endureth for ever.** Imagine supreme Godhead without everlasting mercy! It would then have been as fruitful a source of terror as it is now a fountain of thanksgiving. Let the Highest be praised in the highest style, for right well do his nature and his acts deserve the gratitude of all his creatures.

3. O give thanks to the Lord of lords. There are lords many, but Jehovah is the Lord of them. All lordship is vested in the Eternal. He makes and administers law, he rules and governs mind and matter, he possesses in himself all sovereignty and power. All lords in the plural are summed up in this Lord in the singular: he is more lordly than all emperors and kings condensed into one. For this we may well be thankful, for we know the superior Sovereign will rectify the abuses of the underlings who now lord it over mankind. He will call these lords to his bar, and reckon with them for every oppression and injustice. He is as truly the Lord of lords as he is Lord over the meanest of the land, and he rules with a strict impartiality, for which every just man should give heartiest thanks. **For his mercy endureth for ever.** Yes, he mingles mercy with his justice, and reigns for the benefit of his subjects. He pities the sorrowful, protects the helpless, provides for the needy, and pardons the guilty from generation to generation, never wearying of his grace, "because he delighteth in mercy." Let us arouse ourselves to laud our glorious Lord!

4. To him who alone doeth great wonders. Jehovah is the great Wonderworker. None can be likened unto him, the Creator and Worker of true marvels, compared with which all other remarkable things are as child's play. His works are all great in wonder even when they are not great in size; in fact, in the minute objects of the microscope we behold as great wonders as even the telescope can reveal. All the works of his unrivaled skill are wrought by him alone and unaided, and to him, therefore, must be undivided honor. None of the gods or the lords helped Jehovah in creation, or in the redemption of his people: his own right hand and his holy arm have wrought for him these great deeds. What have the gods of the heathen done? If the question be settled by doings, Jehovah is indeed **alone.** Even when the Lord uses people as his instruments, yet the wonder of the work is his alone; therefore let us not trust in people, or idolize them, or tremble before them. Praise is to be rendered to Jehovah, **for his mercy endureth for ever.** The mercy of the wonder is the wonder of the mercy; and the enduring nature of that mercy is the central wonder of that wonder. The Lord causes us often to sit down in amazement as we see what his mercy has wrought and prepared for us.

5. To him that by wisdom made the heavens. His goodness appears in creating the upper regions. He set his wisdom to the task of fashioning a firmament, or an atmosphere suitable for a world upon which mortals should dwell. What a mass of wisdom lies hidden in this one creating act! The discoveries of our keenest observers have never searched out all the evidences of design which are crowded together in this work of God's hands. The lives of plants, animals, and men are dependent upon the fashioning of our heavens: had the skies been other than they are we had not been here to praise God. Divine foresight planned the air and the clouds, with a view to the human race. **For his mercy endureth for ever.** The psalmist's details of mercy begin in the loftiest regions, and gradually descend from the heavens to "our low estate" (verse 23); and this is an ascent, for mercy becomes greater as its objects become less worthy. Mercy is far-reaching, long-enduring, all-encompassing. Nothing is too high for its reach, as nothing is beneath its stoop.

6. To him that stretched out the earth above the waters. Lifting it up from the mingled mass, the dank morass, the bottomless bog, of mixed land and sea, and so fitting it to be the abode of humanity. Who but the Lord could have wrought this marvel? Few even think of the divine wisdom and power which performed all this of old; yet, if a continent can be proved to have risen or fallen an inch within historic memory, the fact is recorded in the transactions of learned societies, and discussed at every gathering of philosophers. **For his mercy endureth for ever,** as is seen in the original upheaval and perpetual upstanding of the habitable land, so that no deluge drowns the race. By his strength he sets fast the mountains and consolidates the land upon which we sojourn.

7. To him that made great lights. This also is a creating miracle worthy of our loudest thanks. What could people have done without light? Though they had the heavens above them, and dry land to move upon, yet what could they see, and where could they go without light? Thanks be to the Lord, who has not consigned us to darkness. In great mercy he has not left us to an uncertain, indistinct light, floating about fitfully, and without order; but he has concentrated light upon two grand luminaries, which, as far as we are concerned, are to us **great lights.** The psalmist is making a song for common people, not for your critical experts, and so he sings of the sun and moon as they appear to us. **For his mercy endureth for ever.** Mercy gleams in every ray of light, and it is most clearly seen in the arrangement by which it is distributed with order and regularity from the sun and moon.

8. The sun to rule by day. We cannot be too specific in our praises; after mentioning great lights, we may sing of each of them, and yet not outwear our theme. The influences of the sun are too many for us to enumerate them all, but untold benefits come to all order of beings by its light, warmth, and other operations. Whenever we sit in the sunshine, our gratitude should be kindled.

The sun is a great ruler, and his government is pure beneficence, because by God's mercy it is moderated to our feebleness; let all who rule take lessons from the sun which rules to bless. By day we may well give thanks, for God gives cheer. The sun rules because God rules; it is not the sun which we should worship, but the Creator of the sun. **For his mercy endureth for ever.** Day unto day utters speech concerning the mercy of the Lord; every sunbeam is a mercy, for it falls on undeserving sinners who else would sit in doleful darkness, and find earth a hell.

9. The moon and stars to rule by night. No hour is left without rule. Blessed be God, he leaves us never to the doom of anarchy. The rule is one of light and benediction. The moon with her charming changes, and the stars in their fixed spheres, gladden the night. The sun is enough alone; but when he is gone a numerous band cannot suffice to give more than a humble imitation of his radiance. Jesus, the Sun of Righteousness, alone, can do more for us than all his servants put together. He makes our day. When he is hidden, it is night, and remains night, even though our human comforters shine at their full. **For his mercy endureth for ever.** Let our thanks be as many as the stars, and let our lives reflect the goodness of the Lord, just as the moon reflects the light of the sun.

10. We have heard of the glory of the world's creation; we are now to praise the Lord for the creation of his favored nation by their Exodus from Egypt. Because the monarch of Egypt stood in the way of the Lord's gracious purposes it became needful for the Lord to deal with him in justice; but the great design was mercy to Israel, and through Israel mercy to succeeding ages, to all the world. **To him that smote Egypt in their firstborn.** The last and greatest of the plagues struck all Egypt to the heart. The sorrow and the terror which it caused throughout the nation it is hardly possible to exaggerate. From king to slave each one was wounded in the tenderest point. The joy and hope of every household was struck down in one moment, and each family had its own wailing. The former blows had missed their aim compared with the last; but that **smote Egypt.** Justice lingered, but it struck home at last. **For his mercy endureth for ever.** Yes, even to the extremity of vengeance upon a whole nation the Lord's mercy to his people endured. He is slow to anger, and judgment is his strange work; but when mercy to people demands severe punishments he will not hold back his hand from the needful surgery. What were all the firstborn of Egypt compared with those divine purposes of mercy to all generations which were wrapped up in the deliverance of the elect people? Let us even when the Lord's judgments are abroad in the earth continue to sing of his unfailing grace.

11. And brought out Israel from among them. Scattered as the tribes were up and down the country, and apparently held in a grasp which would never be relaxed, the Lord wrought their deliverance, and severed them from their idolatrous task-masters. None of them remained in bondage. The Lord brought them all out; brought them out at the very hour when his promise was due; brought them out despite their being mingled among the Egyptians; brought them out never to return. Unto his name let us give thanks for this further proof of his favor to the chosen ones, **For his mercy endureth for ever.** Once the Israelites did not care to go out, but preferred to bear the ills they had rather than risk they knew not what; but the Lord's mercy endured that test also, and ceased not to stir up the nest till the birds were glad to take to their wings. He turned the land of plenty into a house of bondage, and the persecuted nation was glad to escape from slavery. The unfailing mercy of the Lord is gloriously seen in his separating his elect from the world. He brings out his redeemed, and they are henceforth a people who show forth his praise.

12. With a strong hand, and with a stretched out arm. Not only the matter but the manner of the Lord's mighty acts should be the cause of our praise. We ought to bless the Lord for adverbs as well as adjectives. In the Exodus the great power and glory of Jehovah were seen. He dashed in pieces the enemy with his right hand. He led forth his people in no mean or clandestine manner. Egypt was glad when they departed. God worked with great display of force, and with exceeding majesty; he stretched out his arm like a workman intent on his labor; he lifted up his hand as one who is not ashamed to be seen. Even thus was it in the deliverance of each one of us from the thralldom of sin. **For his mercy endureth for ever.** Therefore his power is put forth for the rescue of his own. If one plague will not set them free there shall be ten; but free they shall all be at the appointed hour; not one Israelite shall remain under Pharaoh's power. God will not only use his hand but his arm – his extraordinary power will be put to work sooner than his purpose of mercy fail.

13. To him which divided the Red sea into parts. He made a road across the sea-bottom, causing the divided waters to stand like walls on either side. People deny miracles, but, granted that there is a God, they become easy of belief. Since it requires me to be an atheist that I may logically reject miracles, I prefer the far smaller difficulty of believing in the infinite power of God. He who causes the waters of the sea ordinarily to remain as one mass can with equal readiness divide them. He who can throw a stone in one direction can with the same force throw it another way: the Lord can do precisely what he wills, and he wills to do anything which is for the deliverance of his people. **For his mercy endureth for ever,** and therefore it endures through the sea as well as over the dry land. He will do a new thing to keep his old promise. His way is in the sea, and he will make a way for his people in the same pathless region.

14. And made Israel to pass through the midst of it. He gave the people courage to follow the predestined tack through the yawning abyss, which might well have terrified a veteran host. It needed no little generalship to conduct so vast and motley a company along a way so novel and apparently so dangerous. He made them to pass by the untrodden road; he led them down into the deep and up again on the further shore in perfect order, keeping their enemies back by the thick darkness of the cloudy pillar. Herein is the glory of God set forth, as all his people see it in their own deliverance from sin. By faith we also give up all reliance upon works and trust ourselves to pass by a way which we have not known, even by the way of reliance upon the atoning blood: thus are we effectually sundered from the Egypt of our former estate, and our sins themselves are drowned. The people marched dry shod through the heart of the sea. Hallelujah! **For his mercy endureth for ever.** Mercy cleared the road, mercy cheered the host, mercy led them down, and mercy brought them up again. Even to the depth of the sea mercy reaches – there is no end to it, no obstacle in the way of it, no danger to believers in it, while Jehovah is all around.

15. But overthrew Pharaoh and his host in the Red sea. Here comes the thunder-clap. Though we hear them sounding peal upon peal, yet the judgments of the Lord were only loud-mouthed mercies speaking confusion to the foe, that the chosen might tremble before him no longer. The king and his warriors were alike overwhelmed; broken was the power and conquered was the pride of Egypt. Jehovah had vanquished the enemy. None are too great for the Lord to subdue, none are too high for the Lord to abase. The enemy in his fury drove after Israel into the sea, but there his wrath found a terrible recompense beneath the waves. **For his mercy endureth for ever.** Mercy continued to protect its children, and therefore called in the aid of justice to fulfill the capital sentence on their foes. Taken red-handed, in the very act of rebellion against their sovereign Lord, the audacious adversaries met the fate which they had themselves invited. Sin is self-damnation. The finally impenitent, however terrible their doom, will not be witnesses against mercy; but rather this shall aggravate their misery, that they went on in defiance of mercy, and would not yield themselves to him whose mercy endureth forever.

16. To him which led his people through the wilderness. He led them into it, and therefore he was pledged to lead them through it. They were "his people," and yet they must go into the wilderness, and the wilderness must remain as barren as ever it was; but in the end they must come out of it into the promised land. God's dealing are mysterious, but they must be right, simply because they are his. The people knew nothing of the way, but they were led; they were a vast host, yet they were all led; there were neither roads nor tracks, but being led by unerring wisdom they never lost their way. He who brought them out of Egypt also led them through the wilderness. By Moses, and Aaron, and Jethro, and the pillar of cloud he led them. What a multitude of mercies are comprehended in the conduct of such an enormous host through a region wherein there was no provision even for single travelers; yet the Lord by his infinite power and wisdom conducted a whole nation for forty years through a desert land, and their feet did not swell, neither did their garments wax old in all the journey. **For his mercy endureth for ever.** Their conduct in the wilderness tested his mercy most severely, but it bore the strain; many a time he forgave them; and though he smote them for their transgressions, yet he waited to be gracious and speedily turned to them in compassion. *Their* faithfulness soon failed, but *his* did not: the fiery, cloudy pillar which never ceased to lead the nation was the visible proof of his immutable love.

17. To him which smote great kings. Within sight of their inheritance Israel had to face powerful enemies. Kings judged to be great because of the armies at their back blocked their road. This difficulty soon disappeared, for the Lord smote their adversaries, and a single stroke sufficed for their destruction. He who had subdued the really mighty ruler of Egypt made short work of these petty sovereigns, great though they were in the esteem of neighboring princes. **For his mercy endureth for ever.** Mercy, which had brought the chosen tribes so far, would not be balked by the opposition of boastful foes. The Lord who smote Pharaoh at the beginning of the wilderness march, smote Sihon and Og at the close of it. How could these kings hope to succeed when even mercy itself was in arms against them?

18. And slew famous kings. What good was their fame to them? As they opposed God they became infamous rather than famous. Their deaths made the Lord's fame to increase among the nations while their fame ended in disgraceful defeat. **For his mercy endureth for ever.** Israelite patriots felt that they could never have too much of this music; God had protected their nation, and they chanted his praises with unwearied iteration.

19. Sihon king of the Amorites. Let the name be mentioned that the mercy may be the better remembered. Sihon smote Moab, but he could not smite Israel, for the Lord smote *him.* He was valiant and powerful, so as to be both great and famous; but as he willfully refused to give a peaceful passage to the Israelites, and fought again them in malice, there was no choice for it but to let him run into that destruction which he courted. His fall was speedy and final, and the chosen people were so struck with it that they sung of his overthrow in their national songs. **For his mercy endureth for ever.** His mercy is no respecter of persons, and neither the greatness nor the fame of Sihon could protect him after he had dared to attack Israel. The Lord will not forsake his people because Sihon blusters.

20. And Og the king of Bashan. He was of the race of giants, but he was routed like a pygmy when he entered the battles with Israel's God. The Lord's people were called upon to fight against him, but it was God who won the victory. The fastnesses of Bashan were no defense against Jehovah. Og was soon ousted from his stronghold when the captain of the Lord's host led the war against him. Glory be to the divine conqueror, **for his mercy endureth for ever.** If Sihon could not turn the Lord from his purpose we may be sure that Og could not. He who delivers us out of one trouble will rescue us out of another, and fulfill all the good pleasure of his grace in us.

21. And gave their land for an heritage. As the Lord of the whole earth he transferred his estate from one tenant to another. The land did not become the property of the Israelites by their own sword and bow, but by a grant from the throne. This was the great end which all along had been aimed at from Egypt to Jordan. He who brought his people out also brought them in. He who had promised the land to the descendants of Abraham also saw to it that the deed of gift did not remain a dead letter. Both our temporal and our spiritual estates come to us by royal charter. What God gives us is ours by the best of titles. Inheritance by God's gift is a tenure which even Satan cannot dispute. **For his mercy endureth for ever.** Faithful love endures without end, and secures its own end.

22. Even an heritage unto Israel his servant. Repetitions are effective in poetry, and the more so if there be some little variation in them, bringing out into fuller light some point which else had not been noticed. The lands of the heathen kings were given to **Israel,** the name by which the chosen people are here mentioned for the third time in the psalm, with the addition of the words **his servant.** The leasehold of Canaan to Israel after the flesh was made dependent upon suit and service rendered to the Lord-of-the-manor by whom the lease was granted. It was a country worth singing about, richly justifying the two stanzas devoted to it. The division of the country by lot, and the laws by which the portions of ground were reserved to the owners and their descendants for a perpetual inheritance, were fit subjects for song. Had other nations enjoyed land-laws which insured to every family a plot of ground for cultivation, much of the present discontent would never have arisen, beggary would soon have become uncommon, and poverty itself would have been rare. **For his mercy endureth for ever.** Yes, mercy fights for the land, mercy divides the spoil among its favored ones, and mercy secures each man in his inheritance.

23. Who remembered us in our low state. Personal mercies awake the sweetest song. Our prayer is, "Lord remember me," and this is our encouragement – he has remembered us. For the Lord even to think of us is a wealth of mercy. Ours was a sorry estate – an estate of bankruptcy and mendicancy. Israel rested in its heritage, but we were still in bondage, groaning in captivity: the Lord seemed to have forgotten us, and left us in our sorrow; but it was not so for long: he turned again in his compassion, bethinking himself of his afflicted children. Our state was once so low as to be at hell's mouth; since then it has been low in poverty, sinfully low in faith, and love, and every other grace; and yet the Lord has not forgotten us as a dead thing out of mind, but he has tenderly remembered us still. We thought ourselves too small and too worthless for his memory to burden itself about us, yet he remembered us. **For his mercy endureth for ever.** Yes, this is one of the best proofs of the immutability of his mercy, for if he could have changed towards any, it would certainly have been towards us who have brought ourselves low, kept ourselves low, and prepared ourselves to sink yet lower. It is memorable mercy to remember us in our low estate: in our highest joys we will exalt Jehovah's name, since of this we are sure – he will not now desert us.

24. And hath redeemed us from our enemies. Israel's enemies brought the people low; but the Lord intervened, and turned the tables by a great redemption. The expression implies that they had become like slaves, and were not set free without price and power, for they needed to be **redeemed.** In our case the redemption which is in Christ Jesus is an eminent reason for giving thanks unto the Lord. Sin is our enemy, and we are redeemed from it by the atoning blood; Satan is our enemy, and we are redeemed from him by the Redeemer's power; the world is our enemy, and we are redeemed from it by the Holy Spirit. We are ransomed; let us enjoy our liberty. Christ has wrought our redemption; let us praise his name. **For his mercy endureth for ever.** Even to redemption by the death of his Son did divine mercy stretch itself. What more can be desired? What more can be imagined? Many waters could not quench love, neither could the floods drown it.

25. Who giveth food to all flesh. Common providence, which cares for all living things, deserves our devoutest thanks. If we think of heavenly food, by which all saints are supplied, our praises rise to a still greater height; but meanwhile the universal goodness of God in feeding all his creatures is as worthy of praise as his special favors to the elect nation. Because the Lord feeds all life therefore we expect him to take special care of his own family. **For his mercy endureth for ever.** Reaching downward even to beasts and reptiles, it is a boundless mercy, which knows no limit because of the meanness of its object.

26. O give thanks unto the God of heaven. The title is full of honor. The Lord is God in the highest realms, and among celestial beings. His throne is set in glory, above all, out of reach of foes, in the place of universal oversight. He who feeds ravens and sparrows is yet the glorious God of the highest realms. Angels count it their glory to proclaim his glory in every heavenly street. See herein the greatness of his nature, the depth of his condescension, and the range of his love. Mark the one sole cause of his bounty – **For his mercy endureth for ever.** He has done all things from this motive; and because his mercy never ceases, he will continue to multiply deeds of love world without end. Let us with all our powers of heart and tongue give thanks unto the holy name of Jehovah forever and ever.

Psalm 137

1. By the rivers of Babylon, there we sat down. Water-courses were abundant in Babylon, wherein were not only natural streams but artificial canals; it was some slight comfort to be out of the crowd, and to have a little breathing room, and therefore they sat down, as if to rest a while and solace themselves in their sorrow. In little groups they sat down and made common lamentation, mingling their memories and their tears. The rivers were well enough, but, alas, they were the rivers of Babylon, and the ground whereon the sons of Israel sat was foreign soil, and therefore they wept. Those who came to interrupt their quiet were citizens of the destroying city, and their company was not desired. Everything reminded Israel of her banishment from the holy city, her servitude beneath the shadow of the temple of Bel, her helplessness under a cruel enemy; and therefore her sons and daughters sat down in sorrow.

Yea, we wept, when we remembered Zion. Nothing else could have subdued their brave spirits; but the remembrance of the temple of their God, the palace of their king, and the centre of their national life quite broke them down. Destruction had swept down all their delights. They did not weep when they remembered the cruelties of Babylon; the memory of fierce oppression dried their tears and made their hearts burn with wrath; but when the beloved city of their solemnities came into their minds they could not refrain from floods of tears. So do true believers mourn when they see the church despoiled, and find themselves unable to succor her: we could bear anything better than this. In our times the Babylon of error ravages the city of God, and the hearts of the faithful are grievously wounded as they see truth fallen in the streets, and unbelief rampant among the professed servants of the Lord. Be it ours to weep in secret for the hurt of our Zion: it is the least thing we can do; ours also to sit down and deeply consider what is to be done. Be it ours, in any case, to keep upon our mind and heart the memory of the church of God which is so dear to us. The frivolous may forget, but Zion is graven on our hearts, and her prosperity is our chief desire.

2. The drooping branches appeared to weep as we did, and so we gave to them our instruments of music; the willows could as well make melody as we, for we had no mind for music. In the midst of the willows, or in midst of the rivers, or in the midst of Babylon, it matters little which, they hung their harps. Sad indeed is the child of sorrow when he grows weary of his harp, from which in better days he had been able to draw sweet solaces. Music has charms to give unquiet spirits rest; but when the heart is sorely sad it only mocks the grief which flies to it. People put away their instruments of mirth when a heavy cloud darkens their souls.

3. For there they that carried us away captive required of us a song. What cruelty to make a people sigh, and then require them to sing! It is indeed "woe to the conquered" when they are forced to sing to increase the triumph of their conquerors. **And they that wasted us required of us mirth.** The captives must not only sing but smile, and add merriment to their music. This was wormwood and gall to the true lovers of God and his chosen land. **Saying, Sing us one of the songs of Zion.** Nothing would serve their turn but a holy hymn, and a tune sacred to the worship of Jehovah. Nothing will content the Babylonian mockers but one of Israel's psalms when in her happiest days she sang unto the Lord whose mercy endureth forever: this would make rare fun for their persecutors, who would deride their worship and ridicule their faith in Jehovah. In this demand there was an insult to their God as well as a mockery of themselves, and this made it the more intensely cruel. These wanton persecutors had followed the captives into their retirement, and had remarked upon their sorrowful appearance, and **there** and then they bade the mourners make mirth for them.

4. How shall they sing at all? Sing Jehovah's song among the uncircumcised? With one voice they refuse, but the refusal is humbly worded by being put in the form of a question. If the men of Babylon were wicked enough to suggest the defiling of holy things for the gratification of curiosity, or for the creation of amusement, the men of Zion had not so hardened their hearts as to be willing to please them at such a fearful cost. There are many things which the ungodly could do, and think nothing of the doing thereof, which the gracious cannot venture upon. The question "How can I?" or **How shall we?** comes of a tender conscience and an inability to sin which is greatly to be cultivated.

5. To sing Zion's songs for the pleasure of Zion's foes would be to forget the Holy City. Each Jew declares for himself that he will not do this; for the pronoun alters from "we" to **I**. Individually the captives pledge themselves to fidelity to Jerusalem, and each one asserts that he had sooner forget the art which drew music from his harp-strings than use it for Babel's delight.

6. **If I do not remember thee, let my tongue cleave to the roof of my mouth.** Thus the singers imprecate eternal silence upon their mouths if they forget Jerusalem to gratify Babylon. **If I prefer not Jerusalem above my chief joy.** The sacred city must ever be first in their thoughts, the queen of their souls; they had sooner be dumb than dishonor her sacred hymns, and give occasion to the oppressor to ridicule her worship. If such the attachment of a banished Jew to his native land, how much more should we love the church of God. How jealous should we be of her honor, how zealous for her prosperity. Never let us find jests in the words of Scripture, or make amusement out of holy things, lest we be guilty of forgetting the Lord and his cause. It is to be feared that many tongues have lost all power to charm the congregations of the saints because they have forgotten the Gospel, and God has forgotten *them*.

7. **Remember, O LORD, the children of Edom in the day of Jerusalem.** The case is left in Jehovah's hands. He is a God of recompenses, and will deal out justice with impartiality. The Edomites ought to have been friendly with the Israelites, from kinship; but there was a deep hatred and cruel spite displayed by them. The elder loved not to serve the younger, and so when Jacob's day of tribulation came, Esau was ready to take advantage of it. The captive Israelites, being moved by grief to lodge their plaints with God, also added a prayer for

his visitation of the nation which meanly sided with their enemies, and even urged the invaders to more than their usual cruelty. **Who said, Rase it, rase it, even to the foundation thereof.** They wished to see the last of Jerusalem and the Jewish state; they would have no stone left standing; they desired to see a clean sweep of temple, palace, wall, and habitation. It is horrible for neighbors to be enemies, worse for them to show their enmity in times of great affliction, worst of all for neighbors to egg others on to malicious deeds. Those are responsible for other people's sins who would use them as the tool of their own enmity. It is a shame for people to incite the wicked to deeds which they are not able to perform themselves. The Chaldeans were ferocious enough without being excited to greater fury; but Edom's hate was insatiable. Those deserve to be remembered by vengeance who in evil times do not remember mercy; how much more those who take advantage of calamities to wreak revenge upon sufferers. When Jerusalem's day of restoration comes Edom will be remembered and wiped out of existence.

8. O daughter of Babylon, who art to be destroyed. Or the destroyer: let us accept the word either way, or both ways: the destroyer would be destroyed, and the psalmist in vision saw her as already destroyed. It is usual to speak of a city as a virgin daughter. Babylon was in her prime and beauty, but she was already doomed for her crimes. **Happy shall he be that rewardeth thee as thou hast served us.** The avenger would be fulfilling an honorable calling in overthrowing a power so brutal, so inhuman. Assyrian and Chaldean armies had been boastfully brutal in their conquests; it was meet that their conduct should be measured back into their own hearts. No awards of punishment can be more unanswerable than those which closely follow the law of retaliation, even to the letter. Babylon must fall, as she caused Jerusalem to fall; and her sack and slaughter must be such as she appointed for other cities. The patriot-poet sitting sorrowfully in his exile finds a solace in the prospect of the overthrow of the empress city which holds him in bondage, and he accounts Cyrus right happy to be ordained to such a righteous work. The whole earth would bless the conqueror for ridding the nations of a tyrant. Future generations would call him blessed for enabling people to breathe again, and for once more making liberty possible upon the earth.

We may rest assured that every unrighteous power is doomed to destruction, and that from the throne of God justice will be measured out to all whose law is force, whose rule is selfishness, and whose policy is oppression. Happy is the one who will help in the overthrow of the spiritual Babylon, which, despite its riches and power, is **to be destroyed.**

9. Fierce was the heart of the Jew who had seen his beloved city the scene of such terrific butchery. His heart pronounced a like sentence upon Babylon. She should be scourged with her own whip of wire. The desire for righteous retribution is rather the spirit of the law than of the Gospel; and yet in moments of righteous wrath the old fire will burn; and while justice survives in the human heart it will not lack for fuel among the various tyrannies which still survive. We shall be wise to view this passage as a prophecy. History informs us that it was literally fulfilled: the Babylonian people in their terror agreed to destroy their own offspring, and men thought themselves happy when they had put their own wives and children to the sword. Horrible as was the whole transaction, it is a thing to be glad of if we take a broad view of the world's welfare; for Babylon, the gigantic robber, had for many a year slaughtered nations without mercy, and her fall was the rising of many people to a freer and safer state. The murder of innocent infants can never be sufficiently deplored, but it was an incident of ancient warfare which the Babylonians had not omitted in their massacres, and therefore they were not spared it themselves. The revenges of providence may be slow, but they are ever sure; neither can they be received with regret by those who see God's righteous hand in them. A feeling of universal love is admirable, but it must not be divorced from a keen sense of justice.

The captives in Babylon did not make music, but they poured forth their righteous maledictions, and these were far more than they desire, to their own confusion: they will have little enough to make mirth for them, and more than enough to fill them with misery. The execrations of good men are terrible things, for they are not lightly uttered, and they are heard in heaven. But will despots crush virtue beneath their iron heel and never be punished?

Psalm 138

1. I will praise thee with my whole heart. His mind is so taken up with God that he does not mention his name: to him there is no other God, and Jehovah is so intimately known that the psalmist, in addressing him, no more thinks of mentioning his name than we should do if we were speaking to a father or a friend. He is resolved to praise the Lord with the whole force of his life, with his **whole heart.** He would not act because of the opinions of others, but in the presence of the opponents of the living God he would be as hearty in worship as if all were friends and would cheerfully unite with him. If others do not praise the Lord, there is all the more reason why we should do so with eagerness. We need a broken heart to mourn our own sins, but a whole heart to praise the Lord's perfections. **Before the gods will I sing praise unto thee.** The psalmist will not for a moment suspend his songs because there are images before him, and their foolish worshipers might not approve of his music. I believe David referred to the false gods of the neighboring nations, and the deities of the surviving Canaanites. In these days when new religions are daily thought up, it is well to know how to act. Controversy is apt to advertise the heresy; the very best method is to go on personally worshiping the Lord with unvarying zeal. Do they deny the divinity of our Lord? Let us the more fervently adore him. Do they despise the atonement? Let us the more constantly proclaim it. Praising and singing are our armor against the idolatries of heresy, our comfort under the depression caused by insolent attacks upon the truth, and our weapons for defending the Gospel. Faith, when displayed in cheerful courage, has about it a sacred contagion.

2. **I will worship toward thy holy temple,** or the place of God's dwelling, where the ark abode. He would worship God in God's own way. The Jew looked to the temple; we are to look to Jesus, the living temple. **And praise thy name for thy lovingkindness and for thy truth.** Praise would be the main part of David's worship, the **name** or character of God the great object of his song, and the special point of his praise the grace and truth which shone so conspicuously in that name. The person of Jesus is the temple of the Godhead, and therein we behold the glory of the Father, "full of grace and truth." It is upon these two points that the name of Jehovah is at this time assailed – his grace and his truth. He is said to be too stern, too terrible, and therefore "modern thought" set up an effeminate deity of its own making. True believers hear the thunder of his justice, and yet they do not doubt his lovingkindness. But not only do people attack the lovingkindness of God, but the truth of God is at this time assailed on all sides; some doubt the truth of the inspired histories, others challenge the doctrines, many sneer at the prophecies; the Word of the Lord is treated as the writing of impostors, and only worthy to be carped at. **For thou hast magnified thy word above all thy name.** The name of the Lord in nature is not so easily read as in the Scriptures, which are a revelation in human language, treating of human need, and of a Saviour who appeared in human nature to redeem humanity. Heaven and earth will pass away, but the divine Word will not pass away. It is his Word which creates, sustains, quickens, enlightens, and comforts. As a word of command it is supreme; and in the person of the incarnate Word it is set above all the works of God's hands.

3. **In the day when I cried thou answeredst me.** No one doubts the power of prayer after he has received an answer of peace to his supplication. It is the distinguishing mark of the true and living God that he hears the pleadings of his people and answers them. What answer can there be to a cry – to a mere inarticulate wail of grief? Our Heavenly Father is able to interpret tears, and cries, and he replies to their inner sense. The answer came to David in the same **day** as the cry ascended: so speedily does prayer rise to heaven, so quickly does mercy return to earth. This also is our defense against modern heresies: we cannot forsake the Lord, for he has heard our prayers.

And strengthened me with strength in my soul. This was a true answer to his prayer. If the burden was not removed, yet strength was given wherewith to bear it. It may not be best for us that the trial should come to an end; it may be far more to our advantage that by its pressure we should learn patience. Strength imparted to the soul means courage, fortitude, assurance, heroism. The man having been strengthened for one emergency remains vigorous for life, and is prepared for all future labors and sufferings; unless, indeed, he throw away his force by unbelief, or pride, or some other sin.

4. Kings have usually small care to hear the Word of the Lord; but David feels assured that if they do hear it they will feel its power. Brighter days are coming, in which rulers will become hearers and worshipers. The way of conversion for kings is the same as for ourselves: faith to them also comes by hearing, and hearing by the Word of God. Happy are those who can cause the Word of the Lord to penetrate palaces; the occupants of thrones are usually the last to know the joyful sounds of the Gospel. David, the king, cared for kings' souls, and it will be wise for each of us to look first after those of our own order.

5. **Yea, they shall sing in the ways of the LORD.** Here is a double wonder – kings in God's ways, and kings singing there. The difficulty is to bring the great ones of the earth into ways so little attractive to the carnal mind. **For great is the glory of the LORD.** Kings will be stirred by a sight of it to obey and adore. David, under a sense of Jehovah's glory, exclaimed, "I will sing" (verse 1), and here he represents the kings as doing the same thing.

6. **Though the LORD be high.** In greatness, dignity, and power, Jehovah is higher than the highest, even the loftiest soarings of imagination. **Yet hath he respect unto the lowly.** He views them with pleasure, thinks of them with care, listens to their prayers, and protects them from evil. Because they think little of themselves he thinks much of them. **But the proud he knoweth afar off.** He does not need to come near them to discover their utter vanity. He will keep them at arm's length in this life, and shut them up in hell in the next.

7. **Though I walk in the midst of trouble, thou wilt revive me.** God is with me, and will give me new life. When we are somewhat in trouble it is bad enough, but it is worse to traverse its **midst**: yet in such a case the believer makes progress, for he walks; he keeps to a quiet pace, for he does no more than **walk**; his God is near to pour fresh life into him. If our God be away at any other time, yet he is pledged to be with us in trying hours. He is in a blessed condition who can confidently use the language of David – **thou wilt revive me.** How often has the Lord quickened us by our sorrows! Are they not his readiest means of exciting to fullness of energy the holy life which dwells within us? **Thou shalt stretch forth thine hand against the wrath of mine enemies, and thy right hand shall save me.** This is the fact which would revive fainting David. Our foes fall when the Lord comes to deal with them; he makes short work of the enemies of his people – with one **hand** he routs them. God's right hand cannot forget its cunning; Jerusalem is his chief joy, and he will defend his own elect.

325

8. The Lord will perfect that which concerneth me. All my interests are safe in Jehovah's hands. God is concerned in all that concerns his servants. He will see to it that none of their precious things fail of completion. **Thy mercy, O Lord, endureth for ever.** The first clause of the verse is the assurance of faith, and this second one reaches to the full assurance of understanding. God's work will abide in us to perfection because God's mercy towards us thus abides. **Forsake not the works of thine own hands.** Our confidence encourages us to pray all the more. If there be anything good in us, it is the work of God's own hands; will he leave it? It would be a sheer waste of effort. He who has gone so far will surely persevere with us to the end. Our hope for the final perseverance of the believer lies in the final perseverance of the believer's God. If the Lord begins to build, and does not finish, it will not be to his honor. He will have a desire to finish the work of his hands, for he knows what it has cost him already, and he will not throw away a vessel upon which he has expended so much labor and skill. Therefore we praise him with our whole heart, even in the presence of those who set up another God and another Gospel.

Psalm 139

1. He invokes in adoration Jehovah, the all-knowing God, and he proceeds to adore him by proclaiming one of his especial attributes. If we would praise God aright we must draw the matter of our praise from himself – **thou hast.** The Lord knows all things as a matter of course, and not by any effort on his part. He knows us as thoroughly as if he had examined us minutely, and had pried into the most secret corners of our being. Note how the psalmist makes his knowledge personal: he does not say, "O God, thou knowest all things," but, **thou . . . hast known me.** It is wisdom to lay truth home to ourselves.

2. Thou knowest my downsitting and mine uprising. *Me* thou knowest, and all that comes of me. My most common and casual acts, my most needful and necessary movements, are noted by thee, and thou knowest the inward thoughts which regulate them. Whether I sink in lowly self-renunciation, or ascend in pride, thou seest the motions of my mind, as well as those of my body. Sitting down to consider, or rising up to act, we are still seen, known, and read by our Lord. **Thou understandest my thought afar off.** Before it is my own it is foreknown and comprehended by thee. Though as yet I be not myself cognizant of the shape my thought is assuming, yet thou perceivest its nature, its source, its drift, its result.

3. Thou compassest my path and my lying down. My running and my resting are alike within thine observation. I may leave thy path, but thou never leavest mine. I may sleep and forget thee, but thou dost never slumber, nor fall into oblivion concerning thy creature. The original signifies not only surrounding, but winnowing and sifting. The Lord judges our active life and our quiet life; he marks that in them which is good and also that which is evil. **And art acquainted with all my ways.** Nothing is concealed from thee, nor misunderstood by thee. This should fill us with awe, so that we sin not; with courage, so that we fear not; with delight, so that we mourn not.

4. Divine knowledge is perfect, since not a single word is unknown, not even an unspoken word, and each one is **altogether** or wholly known. What hope of concealment can remain when the speech with which too many conceal their thoughts is itself transparent before the Lord?

5. Thou hast beset me behind and before. As though we were caught in an ambush, or besieged by an army, we are surrounded by the Lord. Behind us there is God recording our sins, or in grace blotting out the remembrance of them; and before us there is God foreknowing all our deeds, and providing for all our wants. Lest we should imagine that the surrounding presence is yet a distant one, it is added, **And laid thine hand upon me.** The prisoner marches along surrounded by a guard, and gripped by an officer. God is very near; we are wholly in his power; from that power there is no escape. It is not said that God *will* thus beset us and arrest us, but it is done – **Thou hast beset me.** Shall we not alter the figure, and say that our Heavenly Father has folded his arms around us, and caressed us with his hand?

6. Such knowledge is too wonderful for me. I cannot grasp it. I can hardly endure to think of it. The theme overwhelms me. I am amazed and astounded at it. Such knowledge not only surpasses my comprehension, but even my imagination. **It is high, I cannot attain unto it.** This truth seems to be always above me, even when I soar in spiritual thought. Is it not so with every attribute of God? Can we attain any idea of his power, his wisdom, his holiness? Our mind has no line with which to measure the Infinite.

7–12. Here omnipresence is the theme – a truth to which omniscience naturally leads.

7. Whither shall I go from thy Spirit? Not that the psalmist wished to avoid the power of the divine life. Note that the writer makes the matter personal to himself – **Whither shall *I* go?** Jehovah is omnipresent *to me.* **Or whither shall I flee from thy presence?** No answer comes. From the sight of God he cannot be hidden, but that is not all – from the immediate, actual, constant presence of God he cannot be withdrawn. This makes it dreadful to sin, for we commit treason at the very foot of his throne. His mind is in our mind, himself within ourselves. His Spirit is over our spirit; our presence is ever in his presence.

8. If I ascend up into heaven thou art there. Jehovah is in the heavenly place, upon his throne. Note the abrupt words: "Thou, there." **If I make my bed in hell, behold, thou art there.** Descending into the lowest imaginable depths among the dead, there we should find the Lord. "Thou!" says the psalmist, as if he felt that God was the one great Existence in all places. A **behold** is added, since it seems more a wonder to meet with God in hell than in heaven. Of course the presence of God produces very different effects in these places, but it is unquestionably in each; the bliss of one, the terror of the other.

9. Light flies with inconceivable rapidity, but its speed would utterly fail if employed in flying from the Lord. Were we to break into oceans unknown to chart and map, yet there we should find the Lord already present. He who saves to the uttermost would be with us in the uttermost parts of the sea.

10. Even there shall thy hand lead me. We could only fly from God by his own power. The Lord would be leading, covering, preserving, sustaining us even when we were fugitives from him. **And thy right hand shall hold me.** Both the hands of God are with his own servants to sustain them, and against rebels to overthrow them; and in this respect it matters not to what realms they resort, the active energy of God is around them still.

11. If I say, Surely the darkness shall cover me. Dense darkness may oppress me, but it cannot shut me out from thee, or thee from me. Thou art present with me whatever the hour, and being present thou discoverest all that I think, or feel, or do. **Even the night shall be light about me.** Let us think of this if ever we are tempted to take license from the dark. Note well how David keeps his song in the first person; let us mind that we do the same as we cry with Hagar, "Thou God seest *me*."

12. Yea, beyond all denial. **The darkness hideth not from thee.** It veils nothing. It hides from people, but not from God. **But the night shineth as the day** – quite as clearly manifesting all that is done. **The darkness and the light are both alike to thee.** This sentence seems to sum up all that went before. The ungodly are still duped by their groveling notions of God, and inquire, "How does God know?" They must fancy that he is as limited in his powers of observation as they are, and yet if they would but consider for a moment they would conclude that he who could not see in the dark could not be God, and he who is not present everywhere could not be the Almighty Creator. The Great Spirit comprehends within himself all time and space, and yet he is infinitely greater than these, or aught else that he has made.

13. For thou hast possessed my reins. Thou art the owner of my inmost parts and passions: not the indweller and observer only, but the acknowledged Lord and possessor of my most secret self. The word **reins** signifies the kidneys, which by the Hebrews were supposed to be the seat of the desires and longings; but perhaps it indicates here the most hidden and vital portions of the person; this God not only inspects and visits, but it is his own. **Thou hast covered me in my mother's womb.** There I lay hidden – covered by thee. Before I could know thee, or aught else, thou hadst a care for me, and didst hide me away as a treasure till thou didst see fit to bring me to the light.

14. I will praise thee. A good resolve, and one which he was even now carrying out. Those who wish to praise have subjects for adoration ready to hand. We too seldom remember our creation, and all the skill and kindness bestowed upon our frame. **For I am fearfully and wonderfully made.** The science of anatomy was quite unknown to the psalmist, and yet he had seen enough to arouse his admiration of the work and his reverence for the Worker. **Marvelous are thy works.** These parts of my frame are all **thy** works; and though they be close under my own eye, yet are they wonderful to the last degree. They are within my own self, yet beyond my understanding. We need not go to the ends of the earth for marvels; they abound in our own bodies. **And that my soul knoweth right well.** He was no doubter – his soul knew. Those know of a truth who first know the Lord, and then know all things in him. He was made to know the marvelous nature of God's work with assurance and accuracy, for he had found by experience that the Lord is a master-worker, performing inimitable wonders when accomplishing his kind designs. What shall we not say of that new birth which is even more mysterious than the first, and exhibits even more the love and wisdom of the Lord?

15. My substance was not hid from thee. The substantial part of my being was before thine all-seeing eye. The essential materials of my being before they were arranged were all within the range of thine eye. They were hidden from all human knowledge, but not from thee. **When I was made in secret.** Most beautifully is here described the formation of our being before the time of our birth. Much of the formation of our inner man still proceeds in secret; hence the more of solitude the better for us. The true church also is being fashioned in secret, so that none may cry, "Lo, here!" or "Lo, there!" as if that which is visible could ever be identical with the invisibly growing body of Christ. **And curiously wrought in the lowest parts of the earth.** "Embroidered with great skill" is an accurate poetical description of the creation of veins, sinews, muscles, nerves, etc. Cannot he who made us wondrously when we were not, still carry on his work of power till he has perfected us, though we feel unable to aid in the process, and are lying in great sorrow and self-loathing, as though cast into the lowest parts of the earth?

16. Thine eyes did see my substance, yet being unperfect. While the vessel was upon the wheel the Potter saw it all. **And in thy book all my members were written, which in continuance were fashioned, when as yet there was none of them.** An architect draws his plans, and makes out his specifications; just so did the great Maker of our frame write down all our members in the book of his purposes. That we have eyes, and ears, and hands, and feet, is all due to the wise and gracious purpose of heaven: it was so ordered in the secret decree by which all things are as they are. God's purposes concern our limbs and faculties. Their form, and shape, and everything about them were appointed of God long before they had any existence. God saw us when we could not be seen, and he wrote about us when there was nothing of us to write about. When as yet there were none of our members in existence, all those members were before the eye of God in the sketch-book of his foreknowledge and predestination.

This verse is an exceedingly difficult one to translate, but we do not think that any of the proposed amendments are better than the rendering afforded us by the Authorized Version. The large number of words in italics will warn the English reader that the sense is hard to come at, and difficult to express, and that it would be unwise to found any doctrine upon the English words; happily there is no temptation to do so.

The great truth expressed in these lines has by many been referred to the formation of the mystical body of our Lord Jesus. Of course, what is true of man, as man, is emphatically true of Him who is the representative man. The great Lord knows who belong to Christ; his eye perceives the chosen members who will yet be made one with the living person of the mystical Christ. He sees their substance, unperfect though they be.

17. How precious also are thy thoughts unto me, O God! He is not alarmed at the fact that God knows all about him; on the contrary, he is comforted, and even feels himself to be enriched. That God should think upon him is the believer's treasure and pleasure. It is a joy worth worlds that the Lord should think upon us who are so poor and needy: it is a joy which fills our whole nature to think upon God, returning love for love, thought for thought, after our poor fashion. **How great is the sum of them!** Thoughts of our pardon, renewal, upholding, supplying, educating, perfecting, and a thousand more kinds perpetually well up in the mind of the Most High. What a contrast is this to the notion of a world without a thinking, personal God! Conceive of a grim providence of machinery – a fatherhood of law! Such philosophy is hard and cold. But a God always thinking of us makes a happy world, a rich life, a heavenly hereafter.

18. If I should count them, they are more in number than the sand. The task of counting God's thoughts of love would be never-ending. This is not hyperbole, but the solid fact of inspired statement: God thinks upon us infinitely; there is a limit to the act of creation, but not to the might of divine love. **When I am awake, I am still with thee.** Thy thoughts of love are so many that my mind never gets away from them; they surround me at all hours. I go to my bed, and God is my last thought; and when I wake I find my mind still hovering about his palace-gates: God is ever with me, and I am ever with him. If during sleep my mind dreams, it only wanders upon holy ground. The psalmist does not say, "When I awake I return to thee," but, **I am still with thee,** as if his meditations were continuous, and his communion unbroken.

19. Surely thou wilt slay the wicked, O God. Thou hast seen all their transgressions, which indeed have been done in thy presence. If the eye of God is grieved with the presence of evil, it is but natural to expect that he will remove the offending object. God who sees all evil will slay all evil. Such is his love of holiness, and hatred of wrong, that he will carry on war to the death with those whose hearts and lives are wicked. God will not always let his creation be defiled by the presence of wickedness. **Depart from me therefore, ye bloody men.** Men who delight in cruelty and war are not fit companions for those who walk with God. David chases them from his court, for he is weary of those of whom God is weary. We tremble in the society of the ungodly lest their doom should fall upon them suddenly, and we should see them dead at our feet. We do not wish to have our place of fellowship turned into a gallows of execution.

20. **For they speak against thee wickedly.** Why should I bear their company when their talk sickens me? When people speak against God they will be sure to speak against us, if they find it serve their turn; hence godless people are not the stuff out of which true friends can ever be made. God gave these people their tongues, and they turn them against their Benefactor, from sheer malice. **And thine enemies take thy name in vain.** To insult Jehovah's glorious name is their amusement. How can God do other than slay them? How can we do other than withdraw from association with them? We ought not to wonder that people slander and deride us, for they do the same with the Most High.

21. **Do not I hate them, O Lord, that hate thee?** He hated only those who hated good. Of this hatred he is not ashamed, but sets it forth as a virtue. To love everyone with benevolence is a duty, but to love any wicked person with complacency would be a crime. To hate someone for his own sake, or for any evil done to us, would be wrong; but to hate someone because he is the foe of all goodness and the enemy of all righteousness is an obligation. The more we love God the more indignant shall we grow with those who refuse him their affection. **And am not I grieved with those that rise up against thee?** He appeals to heaven that he took no pleasure in those who rebelled against the Lord, but was made to mourn by a sight of their ill behavior.

22. **I hate them with perfect hatred.** He is as wholehearted in his hate of wickedness as in his love of goodness. **I count them mine enemies.** They may have done him no ill, but if they are opposed to God, to his laws, and to the great principles of truth and righteousness, David proclaims war against them. Wickedness excludes people from the communion of the just.

23. **Search me, O God, and know my heart.** He is sure that even by such an investigation there will be found in him no complicity with the wicked. We may each one desire such searching, for it would be a terrible calamity to us for sin to remain in our hearts unknown and undiscovered. **Try me, and know my thoughts.** Read not alone the desires of my heart, but the fugitive thoughts of my head. What a mercy that there is one being who can know us to perfection! He is graciously inclined towards us, and is willing to bend his omniscience to serve the end of our sanctification. Let us pray as David did, and let us be as honest as he. We cannot hide our sin: salvation lies the other way, in a plain discovery of evil, and an effectual severance from it.

24. **And see if there be any wicked thing in me.** See whether there be in my

heart, or in my life, any evil habit unknown to myself. If there be such an evil way, take me from it, take it from me. No matter how dear the wrong may have become, nor how deeply prejudiced I may have been in its favor, be pleased to deliver me therefrom altogether, effectually, and at once, that I may tolerate nothing which is contrary to thy mind. As I hate the wicked in their way, so would I hate every wicked way in myself. **And lead me in the way everlasting.** If thou hast introduced me already to the good old way, be pleased to keep me in it, and conduct me further and further along it. It is a way which thou hast set up of old, it is based upon everlasting principles, and it is the way in which immortal spirits will gladly run forever. Conduct me into it, O Lord, and conduct me throughout the whole length of it.

Psalm 140

1. Deliver me, O LORD, from the evil man. It reads like a clause of the Lord's prayer, "Deliver us from evil." David does not so much plead against an individual as against the species. We shall not find an unregenerate person who is not in some sense evil, and yet all are not alike evil. It is well for us that our enemies are evil: it would be a horrible thing to have the good against us. When **the evil man** bestirs himself against the godly he is as terrible a being as a serpent, or even a devil. The persecuted turn to God in prayer. We cannot of ourselves baffle the enemy, but the Lord knows how to deliver his saints. **Preserve me from the violent man.** "The evil man" soon develops into the **violent man.** Our Lord was surrounded by those who thirsted for his blood. We may not, therefore, hope to pass through the world without enemies, but we may hope to be delivered out of their hands, and preserved from their rage, so that no real harm will come of their malignity.

    2. Which imagine mischiefs in their heart. They cannot be happy unless they are plotting and planning, conspiring and contriving. They seem to have but one heart, for they are completely agreed in their malice. One piece of mischief is not enough for them. What they cannot actually do they nevertheless like to think over. When the imagination gloats over doing harm to others, it is a sure sign that the entire nature is far gone in wickedness. **Continually are they gathered together for war.** They are a committee of opposition in permanent session; they are a standing army always ready for the fray. It is hard dealing with persons who are only in their element when they are at daggers drawn with you. Such a case calls for prayer, and prayer calls on God.

    3. They have sharpened their tongues like a serpent. The rapid motion of a viper's tongue gives you the idea of its sharpening it; even thus do the malicious move their tongues at such a rate that one might suppose them to be in the very act of wearing them to a point, or rubbing them to a keen edge. It was a common notion that serpents inserted their poison by their tongues, and the poets used the idea as a poetical expression, although it is certain that the serpent wounds by his fangs and not by his tongue. We are not to suppose that all authors who used such language were mistaken in their natural history any more than a writer can be charged with ignorance of astronomy because he speaks of the sun's traveling from east to west. **Adders' poison is under their lips.** The deadliest of all venom is the slander of the unscrupulous. Our text, however, must not be confined in its reference to some few individuals, for in the inspired epistle to the Romans it is quoted as being true of us all. The old serpent has not only inoculated us with his venom, but he has caused us to be ourselves producers of the like poison: it lies under our lips, ready for us, and, alas, it is all too freely used when we grow angry, and desire to take vengeance upon any who have caused us vexation. It is sadly wonderful what hard things even good people will say when provoked. O Lord, take the poison-bags away, and cause our lips to drop nothing but honey. **Selah.** This is heavy work. Go up, go up, my heart! Sink not too low. Fall not into the lowest key. Lift up thyself to God.

4. Keep me, O LORD, from the hands of the wicked. To fall into their hands would be a calamity indeed. David in his most pitiable plight chose to fall into the hand of a chastising God rather than to be left in the power of men. The Lord by providence and grace can keep us out of the power of the wicked. He alone can do this, for neither our own watchfulness nor the faithfulness of friends can secure us against the serpentine assaults of the foe. **Preserve me from the violent man.** He will strike anyhow, use any weapon, smite from any quarter: he is so furious that he is reckless of his own life if he may accomplish his detestable design. Lord, preserve us by thine omnipotence when men attack us with their violence. **Who have purposed to overthrow my goings.** They resolve to turn the good man from his resolve; they would defeat his designs, injure his integrity, and blast his character. Their own goings are wicked, and therefore they hate those of the righteous, seeing they are a standing rebuke to them. This is a formidable argument to use in prayer with God: he is the patron of holiness, and when the pure lives of his people are in danger, he may be expected to interpose. Never let the pious forget to pray, for this is a weapon against which the most determined enemy cannot stand.

5. The proud have hid a snare for me. Their victim may be taken like a poor hare who is killed without warning – killed in the usual run, by a snare which it could not see. **And cords.** With these they pull the net together and bind their captive. **They have spread a net by the wayside.** Where it will be near their prey; where the slightest divergence from the path will bring the victim into it. Birds are taken in nets, and men are taken by deceit. **They have set gins for me.** Those who avoid the snare and the net may yet be caught in a trap, and accordingly traps are placed in all likely places. If a godly man can be cajoled, or bribed, or cowed, or made angry, the wicked will make the attempt. Ready are they to twist his words, misread his intentions, and misdirect his efforts. **Selah.** The harp needs tuning after such a strain, and the heart needs lifting towards God.

6. I said unto the LORD, Thou art my God. He was assured that Jehovah was his God, he expressed that assurance, and he expressed it before Jehovah himself. Often the less we say to our foes, and the more we say to our best Friend, the better it will fare with us. David rejoiced in the fact that he had already said that Jehovah was his God: he was content to have committed himself, he had no wish to draw back. The Lord was David's own by deliberate choice, to which he again sets his seal with delight. **Hear the voice of my supplications, O LORD.** Since thou art mine, I pray thee, hear my cries. So long as the Lord doth but hear us we are content. The more we consider his greatness and our insignificance, his wisdom and our folly, the more shall we be filled with praise when the Lord attends unto our cry.

7. In the day of the clash of arms, or of the putting on of armor (as some read it), the glorious Lord had been his constant Protector. He had obtained a deliverance in which the strength of the Omnipotent was clearly to be seen. This is a grand utterance of praise, a gracious ground of comfort, a prevalent argument in prayer. He that has covered our head before will not now desert us. Wherefore let us fight a good fight, and fear no deadly wound.

8. Grant not, O LORD, the desires of the wicked. They can do not more than thou dost permit. Assuredly the Lord Jehovah will be no accomplice with the malevolent; their desires will never be his desires; if they thirst for blood he will not gratify their cruelty. **Further not his wicked device.** They are so united as to be like one man in their wishes; but do not hear their prayers. The Lord may allow success to attend the policy of the wicked for a time for wise reasons unknown to us, but we are permitted to pray that it be not so. **Lest they exult themselves.** If successful, the wicked are sure to grow proud, and insult the righteous over whom they have triumphed. If God seems to favor them they grow too high for this world, and their heads strike against the heavens. Let us hope that the Lord will not let this be. **Selah.** Here let us exalt our thoughts and praises high over the heads of self-exalting sinners.

9. To the Lord who had covered his head amid the din of arms the psalmist appeals against his foes, that their heads may be covered in quite another sense – covered with the reward of their own malice. The poet represents his adversaries as so united as to have but one head. The law of retaliation often brings down upon the violent the evil which they planned for others. When a person's lips vent curses they will probably, like chickens, come home to roost.

David's words may be read in the future as a prophecy, but in this verse at any rate there is no need to do so in order to soften their tone. It is so just that the mischief which people plot and the slander which they speak should recoil upon themselves that every righteous person must desire it: he who does not desire it may wish to be considered humane and Christlike, but the chances are that he has a sneaking agreement with the wicked, or is deficient in a manly sense of right and wrong. We suspect that some of our excessively soft-spoken critics only need to be put into David's place, and they would become a vast deal more bitter than he ever was.

10. Let burning coals fall upon them. Then will they know that the scattering of the firebrands is not the sport they thought it to be. **Let them be cast into the fire.** They have kindled the flames of strife, and it is fair that they should be cast therein. **Into the deep pits, that they rise not up again.** They made those ditches for the godly, and it is meet that they should themselves fall into them and never escape. When a righteous man falls he rises again, but when the wicked goes down "he falls like Lucifer, never to hope again."

11. Let not an evil speaker be established in the earth. For that would be an established plague, a perpetual curse. God will not allow the specious orators of falsehood to retain the power they temporarily obtain by their deceitful speaking. They may become prominent, but they cannot become permanent. All evil bears the element of decay within itself; for what is it but corruption? **Evil shall hunt the violent man to overthrow him.** He hunted the good, and now his own evil will hunt him. He tried to overthrow the goings of the righteous, and now his own unrighteousness will prove his overthrow.

12. All through the psalm the writer is bravely confident, and speaks of things about which he had no doubt. The slandered saint knew Jehovah's care for the afflicted, for he had received actual proofs of it himself. "I will maintain it" is the motto of the great Defender of the rights of the needy. Many talk as if the poor had no rights worth noticing, but they will sooner or later find out their mistake when the Judge of all the earth begins to plead with them.

13. Surely the righteous shall give thanks unto thy name. As surely as God will slay the wicked he will save the oppressed, and fill their hearts and mouths with praises. Whoever else may be silent, the righteous will give thanks; and whatever they may suffer, it will end in their living through the trial, and magnifying the Lord for his delivering grace. **The upright shall dwell in thy presence.** Thus shall they give thanks in the truest and fullest manner. Their living and walking with their God will be their practical form of gratitude. How high have we climbed in this psalm – from being hunted by the evil man to dwelling in the divine presence; so does faith upraise the saint from the lowest depths to heights of peaceful repose. Well might the song be studded with Selahs, or uplifters.

Psalm 141

1. LORD, I cry unto thee. My prayer is painful and feeble, and worthy only to be called a cry; but it is a cry unto Jehovah, and this ennobles it. Others trust to themselves, but I cry unto thee. The weapon of all-prayer is one which the believer may always carry with him, and use in every time of need. **Make haste unto me.** When we are sorely pressed we may with holy importunity quicken the movements of mercy. In many cases, if help should come late, it would come too late, and we are permitted to pray against such a calamity. **Give ear unto my voice, when I cry unto thee.** There is a voice to the great Father in every cry, and groan, and tear of his children; he can understand what they mean when they are quite unable to express it. It troubles the spirit of the saints when they fear that no favorable ear is turned to their cries. When prayer is our only refuge, we are deeply distressed at the bare idea of failing therein.

2. **Let my prayer be set forth before thee as incense.** As incense is carefully prepared, kindled with holy fire, and devoutly presented unto God, so let my prayer be. We are not to look upon prayer as easy work requiring no thought; it needs to be **set forth**; what is more, it must be set forth before the Lord, by a sense of his presence and a holy reverence for his name: neither may we regard all supplication as certain of divine acceptance; it needs to be set forth before the Lord **as incense,** concerning the offering of which there were rules to be observed, otherwise it would be rejected of God. **And the lifting up of my hands as the evening sacrifice.** Prayer is sometimes presented without words by the very motions of our bodies: bended knees and lifted hands are the tokens of earnest, expectant prayer. Certainly work, or the lifting up of the hands in labor, is prayer if it be done in dependence upon God and for his glory; there may be a hand-prayer as well as a heart-prayer. Holy hope, the lifting up of hands that hang down, is also a kind of worship. The psalmist would have his humble cries and prayers to be as much regarded of the Lord as the appointed morning and evening sacrifices of the holy places. After all, the spiritual is in the Lord's esteem higher than the ceremonial.

So far we have a prayer about prayer; we have a distinct supplication in the two following verses.

3. **Set a watch, O LORD, before my mouth.** That mouth had been used in prayer; it would be a pity it should ever be defiled with untruth, or pride, or wrath; yet so it will become unless carefully watched, for these intruders are ever lurking about the door. When the Lord becomes the guard of our mouth the whole person is well garrisoned. **Keep the door of my lips.** In times of persecution we are especially liable to speak hastily, or evasively, and therefore we should be specially anxious to be preserved in that direction from every form of sin. We are ennobled by being door-keepers for the Lord, and yet he deigns to be a door-keeper for us.

4. **Incline not my heart to any evil thing.** This is equivalent to the petition, "Lead us not into temptation." Oh that nothing may arise in providence which would excite our desires in a wrong direction. **To practise wicked works with men that work iniquity.** The way the heart inclines, the life soon tends.

Alas, there is great power in company; hence the fear that we may practice wicked works when we are with wicked workers. We must endeavor not to be with them lest we sin with them. It is apt to increase unto a high degree of ungodliness when the backslider runs the downward path with a whole horde of sinners around him. It is an aggravation of sin rather than an excuse for it to say that it is our custom and our habit. It is God's practice to punish all who make a practise of iniquity. Good men are horrified at the thought of sinning as others do; the fear of it drives them to their knees. **And let me not eat of their dainties.** If we work with them we shall soon eat with them. The trap is baited that we may be captured and become meat for their malice. If we would not sin with people we had better not sit with them.

5. Let the righteous smite me; it shall be a kindness. He would rather be smitten by the righteous than feasted by the wicked. When the ungodly smile upon us their flattery is cruel; when the righteous smite us their faithfulness is kind. Fools resent reproof; the wise endeavor to profit by it. **And let him reprove me; it shall be an excellent oil, which shall not break my head.** Oil breaks no heads, and rebuke does no one any harm. My friend must love me well if he will tell me of my faults. **For yet my prayer also shall be in their calamities.** Gracious people never grow wrathful with candid friends so as to harbor an ill-feeling against them. Wisely grateful souls are greatly concerned to see their instructors in trouble. They do not merely pray for them, but they so closely and heartily sympathize that their prayers are **in their calamities,** down in the dungeon with them.

6. This is a verse of which the meaning seems far to seek. Does it refer to the righteous among the Israelites? We think so. David surely means that when their leaders fell never to rise again, they would then turn to him and take delight in listening to his voice. And so they did: the death of Saul made all the best of the nation look to the son of Jesse as the Lord's anointed; his words became sweet to them. They smote him when he erred, but they recognized his excellencies. He, on his part, bore no resentment, but loved them for their honesty. He would come to their rescue when their former leaders were slain; and his words of courageous hopefulness would be sweet in their ears.

7. David's case seemed hopeless: the cause of God in Israel was as a dead thing. **Our bones are scattered at the grave's mouth.** David himself was like one of these dried bones, and the rest of the godly were in much the same condition. **As when one cutteth and cleaveth wood upon the earth.** They were like wood divided and thrown apart. Leaving out the word **wood,** which is supplied by the translators, the figure relates to cleaving upon the earth, which probably means plowing, but may signify any other form of chopping and splitting, such as felling a forest, tearing up bushes, or otherwise causing confusion and division. How often have good people thought thus of the cause of God! Wherever they have looked, death, division, and destruction have stared them in the face. Scattered at the grave's mouth! We have seen churches in such a state, and have been heart-broken. What a mercy that there is always a place above the earth to which we can look! There lives One who will give a resurrection to his cause, and a reunion to his divided people.

8. But mine eyes are unto thee, O GOD the Lord. He looked upward and considered the promise rather than the external providence; and he expected from God rather than from men. He did not shut his eyes in indifference or despair, neither did he turn them to the creature in vain confidence, but he gave his eyes to his God, and saw nothing to fear. **In thee is my trust.** Not alone in thine attributes or in thy promises, but in thyself. **Leave not my soul destitute,** as it would be if the Lord did not remember and fulfill his promise. To be destitute in circumstances is bad, but to be destitute in soul is far worse; to be left of God would be destruction.

9. Keep me from the snares which they have laid for me. He asked in verse 3 that the door of his mouth might be kept; but his prayer now grows into **Keep me.** He seems more troubled about covert temptation than open attacks. Brave men do not dread battle, but they hate secret plots. We cannot endure to be entrapped like unsuspecting animals; therefore we cry to God for protection. **And the gins of the workers of iniquity.** These evil workers sought to catch David in his speech or acts. Nobody could preserve David but the Omniscient and Omnicompetent One: he also will preserve us.

10. It may not be a Christian prayer, but it is a very just one. Do we not all wish the innocent to be delivered, and the guilty to reap the result of their own malice? Of course we do, if we are just. There can be no wrong in desiring that to happen in our own case which we wish for all good people. Yet there is a more excellent way.

Psalm 142

1. I cried unto the LORD with my voice. It was a cry of such anguish that he remembers it long after. In the loneliness of the cave he could use his voice as much as he pleased; and therefore he made its gloomy vaults echo with his appeals to heaven. **With my voice unto the LORD did I make my supplications.** He dwells upon the fact that he spoke aloud in prayer. It is well when our supplications are such that we find pleasure in looking back upon them. He that is cheered by the memory of his prayers will pray again. He did not go round about to men, but ran straight forward to Jehovah. He first poured out his natural longings – **I cried**; and then he gathered up all his wits and arranged his thoughts. An impromptu cry and a preconceived supplication must alike ascend towards the one prayer-hearing God, and he will accept each of them with equal readiness. No doubt the psalmist was glad of the prayers of others, but he was not content to remain silent himself. Everything is in the first person. It is good to pray in the plural – "Our Father" – but in times of trouble we shall feel forced to change our note into "Let his cup pass from *me.*"

2. I poured out my complaint before him. He could not keep it in, but he took care *where* he poured his complaint. If he poured it out before man he might only receive contempt from the proud, hard-heartedness from the careless, or pretended sympathy from the false; and therefore he resolved upon an outpouring before God alone, since *he* would pity and relieve. The word is scarcely **complaint,** but even if it be so we may learn from this text that our complaint must never be of a kind that we dare not bring before God. We may complain *to* God, but not *of* God. **I showed before him my trouble.** He exhibited his griefs to one who could assuage them. This verse is parallel with the first; David first pours out his complaint, letting it flow in a natural, spontaneous manner, and then he makes a more elaborate show of his affliction. Praying men pray better as they proceed. Note that we do not show our trouble before the Lord that *he* may see *it,* but that *we* may see *him.* It is for *our* relief, and not for his information that we make plain statements concerning our woes: it does us much good to set out our sorrow in order, for much of it vanishes in the process, like a ghost which will not abide the light of day; and the rest loses much of its terror, because the veil of mystery is removed by a clear and deliberate stating of the trying facts. Pour out your thoughts and you will see what they are; show your trouble and the extent of it will be known to you: let all be done before the Lord, for in comparison with his great majesty of love the trouble will seem to be as nothing.

3. When my spirit was overwhelmed within me, then thou knewest my path. The bravest spirit is sometimes sorely put to it. A heavy fog settles down upon the mind, and the man seems drowned and smothered in it; covered with a cloud, crushed with a load, confused with difficulties, conquered by impossibilities. David was a hero, and yet his spirit sank: he could smite a giant down, but he could not keep himself up. He did not know his own path, nor feel able to bear his own burden. Observe his comfort: he looked away from his own condition to the ever-observant, all-knowing God; all was known to his heavenly Friend. Truly it is well for us to know that God knows what we do not know. We lose our heads, but God never closes his eyes; our judgments lose their balance, but the eternal mind is always clear.

In the way wherein I walked have they privily laid a snare for me. This the Lord knew at the time, and gave his servant warning of it. Looking back, the sweet singer is rejoiced that he had so gracious a Guardian, who kept him from unseen dangers. Nothing is hidden from God; no secret snare can hurt the person who dwells in the secret place of the Most High, for he will abide under the shadow of the Almighty. The use of concealed traps is disgraceful to our enemies, but they care little to what tricks they resort for their evil purposes.

Wicked people must find some exercise for their malice, and therefore when they dare not openly assail they will privately ensnare. They watch the gracious man to see where his haunt is, and there they set their trap; but they do it with great caution, avoiding all observation, lest their victim being forewarned should escape. This is a great trial, but the Lord is greater still, and makes us to walk safely in the midst of danger, for he knows us and our enemies, our way and the snare which is laid in it. Blessed be his name.

4. I looked upon my right hand, and beheld, but there was no man that would know me. He did not miss a friend for want of looking for him, nor for want of looking in a likely place. Surely some helper would be found in the place of honor; someone would stand at his right hand to undertake his defense. He looked steadily, and saw all that could be seen, for he **beheld**; but his anxious gaze was not met by an answering smile. Strange to say, all were strange to David. He had known many, but none would know him. When a person is in ill odor it is wonderful how weak the memories of his former friends become; they quite forget, they refuse to know. This is a dire calamity. It is better to be opposed by foes than to be forsaken by friends. When friends look for us they affect to have known us from our birth, but when we look for friends it is wonderful how little we can make them remember. The fact is that in times of desertion it is not true that no man did know us, but no man **would** know us. Their ignorance is willful. **Refuge failed me.** Where in happier days I found a ready harbor I now discovered none at all. My refuge gave me a refusal. **No man cared for my soul.** Whether I lived or died was no concern of anybody's. I was cast out as an outcast. No soul cared for my soul. I dwelt in no-man's-land, where none cared to have me, and none cared about me. This is an ill plight – no place to lay our head, and no head willing to find us a place. How pleased were his enemies to see the friend of God without a friend! How sad was he to be utterly deserted in his utmost need! Can we not picture David in the cave, complaining that even the cave was not a refuge for him, for Saul had come even there? Hopeless was his looking out; we shall soon see him looking up.

5. I cried unto thee, O LORD. As man would not regard him, David was driven to Jehovah, his God. Was not this a gain made out of a loss – wealth gained by a failure? Anything which leads us to cry unto God is a blessing to us. This is the second time that in this short psalm we find the same record: the saintly man is evidently glad to remember his cry and its results. Here is a bitter cry which comes from an outcast in wretched lodgings, forgotten by those who should have helped him. **I said, Thou art my refuge and my portion in the land of the living.** There is a sort of progressive repetition all through this sacred song; he **cried** first, but he **said** afterwards: his cry was bitter, but his saying was sweet; his cry was sharp and short, but his saying was fresh and full. It gives a believer great pleasure to remember his own believing speeches: he may well desire to bury his unbelieving grumbling in oblivion, but the triumphs of grace in working in him a living faith he will not dream of forgetting. What a grand confession of faith was this! David spoke to God, and of God – *thou art my refuge*. Not "thou hast provided me a refuge," but "thou thyself art my refuge." He fled to God alone. He not only believed this, but said it, and practiced it. David, when banished from his portion in the promised land, and cut off from the portion of goods which he by right inherited, found his portion in God; indeed, God *was* his portion. This was so not only in reference to a future date, but here among living people. It is sometimes easier to believe in a portion in heaven than in a portion upon earth: we could die more easily than live; at least, we think so. But there is no living in the land of the living like living upon the living God. For the man of God to say these things in his dire distress was a grand attainment. It is easy to prate bravely when we dwell at ease, but to speak confidently in affliction is quite another matter. It is something to have Jehovah for our refuge, but it is everything to have him for our portion. If David had not *cried* he would not have *said*; and if the Lord had not been his *refuge* he would never have been his *portion*. The lower step is as needful as the higher; but it is not necessary always to stop on the first rung of the ladder.

6. Attend unto my cry. People of God look upon prayer as a reality, and they are not content without having an audience with God; moreover, they have such confidence in the Lord's condescending grace that they hope he will even attend to that poor broken prayer which can only be described as a cry. **For I am brought very low,** and therefore all the prayer I can raise is a mournful cry. This is his argument with God: he is reduced to such a sad condition that if he be not rescued he will be ruined. Gracious people may not only be low, but very low; and this should not be a reason for their doubting the efficacy of their prayers, but rather a plea with the Lord why they should have special attention. **Deliver me from my persecutors.** If he did not get out of their hands, they would soon kill him out of hand, and as he could not himself effect an escape, he cried to God, **Deliver me. For they are stronger than I.** As he before found a plea in his sadness, so now in his feebleness: Saul and his courtiers were in power, and could command the aid of all who sought royal favor; but poor David was in the cave. Saul was a monarch, and David a fugitive; Saul had all the forms of law on his side, while David was an outlaw: so that the prayer before us comes from the weak, who proverbially go to the wall – a good place to go to if they turn their faces to it in prayer, as Hezekiah did in his sickness. The Lord is wont to take the side of the oppressed, and to show his power by baffling tyrants; David's supplication was therefore sure to speed. In these sentences we see how explicitly the man of God described his case in his private communings with his Lord: in real earnest he poured out his complaint before him, and showed before him his trouble.

7. Bring my soul out of prison, that I may praise thy name. That God may be glorified is another notable plea for a suppliant. Escaped prisoners are sure to speak well of those who give them liberty. Soul-emancipation is the noblest form of liberation, and call s for the loudest praise: he who is delivered from the dungeons of despair is sure to magnify the name of the Lord. We are in such a prison that only God himself can bring us out of it, and when he does so he will put a new song into our mouths. The cave was not half such a dungeon to David's body as persecution and temptation made for his soul. To be exiled from the godly is worse than imprisonment; hence David makes it one point of his release that he would be restored to church fellowship – **The righteous shall compass me about.** Saints gather around a child of God when his Father smiles upon him; they come to hear his joyful testimony, to rejoice with him, and to have their own faith encouraged. All the true believers in the twelve tribes were glad to have their own faith encouraged. All the true believers in the twelve tribes were glad to rally to David's banner when the Lord enlarged his spirit; they glorified God for him and with him and through him. They congratulated him, consorted with him, crowned him, and championed him. This was a sweet experience for righteous David, who had for a while come under the censure of the upright. He bore their smiting with patience, and now he welcomes their sanction with gratitude. **For thou shalt deal bountifully with me.** God's bountiful dealing is sure to bring with it the sympathy and alliance of all the favorites of the great King. What a change from looking for a friend and finding none to this enthusiastic concourse of allies around the man after God's own heart! When we can begin a psalm with crying, we may hope to close it with singing. The voice of prayer soon awakens praise.

Psalm 143

1. Hear my prayer, O Lord, give ear to my supplications. In the preceding psalm he began by declaring that he had cried unto the Lord; here he begs to be favorably regarded by Jehovah, whose memorial is that he heareth prayer. He knew that Jehovah did hear prayer, and therefore he intreated him to hear his supplication, however feeble and broken it might be. In two forms he implores the one blessing of gracious audience: **hear** and **give ear.** Gracious people are so eager to be heard in prayer that they double their intreaties for that boon. The psalmist desires to be heard and to be considered; hence he cries, **hear,** and then **give ear.** Our case is difficult, and we plead for special attention. It is probable that David wished his suit against his adversaries to be heard by the righteous Judge, confident that if he had a hearing in the matter whereof he was slanderously accused, he would be triumphantly acquitted. Yet he prefers to turn it all into a petition; hence he cries rather **hear my prayer**

than **hear my suit.** Indeed David is especially earnest that he himself, and the whole of his life, may not become the subject of trial, for in that event he could not hope for acquital. Observe that he offered so much pleading that his life became one continual **prayer**; but that petitioning was so varied in form that it broke out in many **supplications.**

In thy faithfulness answer me, and in thy righteousness. Saints desire to be answered as well as heard: they long to find the Lord faithful to his promise and righteous in defending the cause of justice. It is a happy thing when we dare appeal even to righteousness for our deliverance; and thus we can do upon Gospel principles, for "if we confess our sins he is faithful and just to forgive us our sins." Even the sterner attributes of God are upon the side of the one who humbly trusts, and turns his trust into prayer. It is a sign of our safety when our interests and those of righteousness are blended. With God's faithfulness and righteousness upon our side we are guarded on the right hand and on the left. These are active attributes, and fully equal to the answering of any prayer which it would be right to answer. Requests which do not appeal to either of these attributes it would not be for the glory of God to hear, for they must contain desires for things unpromised, and unrighteous.

2. And enter not into judgment with thy servant. He had intreated for audience at the mercy-seat, but he has no wish to appear before the judgment-seat. Though clear before men, he could not claim innocence before God. He knew himself to be the Lord's servant, yet he did not claim perfection, or plead merit, for even as a servant he was unprofitable. **For in thy sight shall no man living be justified.** None can stand before God upon the footing of the law. In this verse David told out the doctrine of universal condemnation by the law long before Paul had taken his pen to write the same truth. To this day it stands true: no man living may dare to present himself for trial before the throne of the great King on the footing of the law. This foolish age has produced specimens of a pride so rank that people have dared to claim perfection in the flesh; but these boasters are no exception to the rule here laid down: they are but human, and poor specimens of humanity. When their lives are examined they are frequently found to be more faulty than the humble penitents before whom they vaunt their superiority.

3. For the enemy hath persecuted my soul. The attack was upon the soul or life of the psalmist: our adversaries mean us the worst possible evil; their attacks are no child's play; they hunt for the precious life. **He hath smitten my life down to the ground.** The existence of David was made bitter by the cruelty of his enemy; he was as one who was hurled down and made to lie upon the ground, where he could be trampled on by his assailant. Slander has a very depressing effect upon the spirits; it is a blow which overthrows the mind as though it were knocked down with the fist. **He hath made me to dwell in darkness, as those that have been long dead.** The enemy was not content with

343

bringing his life to the ground – he would lay him lower still, even in the grave; and lower than that, if possible, for the enemy would shut up the saint in the darkness of hell if he could. David was driven by Saul's animosity to haunt caverns, like an unquiet ghost; he wandered out by night, and lay hid by day like an uneasy spirit which had long been denied the repose of the grave. Good men began to forget him, as though he had been long dead. Poor David! He was qualified to bless the house of the living, but he was driven to consort with the dead! Such may be our case, and yet we may be very dear to the Lord. One thing is certain: the Lord who permits us to dwell in darkness among the dead will surely bring us into the light, to dwell with those who enjoy life eternal.

4. David was no Stoic; he felt his banishment, and smarted under the cruel assaults which were made upon his character. He felt perplexed and over-turned, lonely and afflicted. He was a man of thought and feeling, and suffered both in spirit and in heart from the undeserved and unprovoked hostility of his persecutors. Moreover, he labored under the sense of fearful loneliness; he was for a while forsaken of God, and his soul was exceeding heavy, even unto death. Such words our Lord Jesus might have used: in this the Head is like the members, and the members are as the Head.

5. I remember the days of old. When we see nothing new which can cheer us, let us think upon old things. We once had merry days, days of deliverance, and joy and thanksgiving; why not again? Jehovah rescued his people in the ages which lie back, centuries ago; why should he not do the like again? We ourselves have a rich past to look back upon; we have many memories, sacred memories, satisfactory memories, and these are as flowers for the bees of faith to visit, from whence they may make honey for present use. **I meditate on all thy works.** When my own works reproach me, thy works refresh me. If at the first view the deeds of the Lord do not encourage us, let us think them over again, ruminating and considering the histories of divine providence. We ought to take a wide and large view of *all* God's works, for as a whole they work together for good, and in each part they are worthy of reverent study. **I muse on the work of thy hands.** This he had done even in his most trying hours. Creation had been the book in which he read of the wisdom and goodness of the Lord. He repeats his perusal of the page of nature, and counts it a balm for his wounds, a cordial for his cares, to see what the Lord has made by his skillfull hands. When the work of our own hand grieves us, let us look to the work of God's hands. Memory, meditation, and musing are here set together as the three graces, ministering grace to a mind depressed and likely to be dis-eased. As David with his harp played away the evil spirit from Saul, so does he here chase away gloom from his own soul by holy communion with God.

6. I stretch forth my hands unto thee. He was eager for his God. His thoughts of God kindled in him burning desires, and these led to energetic expressions of his inward longings. As a prisoner whose feet are bound extends his hands in supplication when there is hope of liberty, so does David. **My soul thirsteth after thee, as a thirsty land.** As the soil cracks, and yawns, and thus opens its mouth in dumb pleadings, so did the psalmist's soul break with longings. No heavenly shower had refreshed him from the sanctuary: banished from the means of grace, his soul felt parched and dry, and he cried out, "My soul to thee"; nothing would content him but the presence of his God. Not alone did he extend his hands, but his heart was stretched out towards the Lord. He was athirst for the Lord. If he could but feel the presence of his God he would no longer be overwhelmed or dwell in darkness; everything would turn to peace and joy. **Selah.** It was time to pause, for the supplication had risen to agony point. Both harp-strings and heart-strings were strained, and needed a little rest to get them right again for the second half of the song.

7. **Hear me speedily, O Lord: my spirit faileth.** If long delayed, the deliverance would come too late. The afflicted suppliant faints, and is ready to die. His life is ebbing out; each moment is of importance; it will soon be all over with him. No argument for speed can be more powerful than this. Who will not run to help a suppliant when his life is in jeopardy? Mercy has wings to its heels when misery is in extremity. God will not fail when our spirit fails, but the rather he will hasten his course and come to us on the wings of the wind. **Hide not thy face from me, lest I be like unto them that go down into the pit.** Communion with God is so dear to a true heart that the withdrawal of it makes the person feel ready to die and perish utterly. God's withdrawals reduce the heart to despair, and take away all strength from the mind. Moreover, his absence enables adversaries to work their will without restraint; and thus, in a second way, the persecuted one is likely to perish. If we have God's countenance we live, but if he turns his back upon us we die. When the Lord looks with favor upon our efforts we prosper, but if he refuses to countenance them we labor in vain.

8. **Cause me to hear thy lovingkindness in the morning; for in thee do I trust.** Lord, my sorrow makes me deaf: **cause me to hear.** There is but one voice that can cheer me: cause me to hear **thy lovingkindness.** That music I desire to hear at once – cause me to hear it **in the morning,** at first dawning hour. A sense of divine love is to the soul both dawn and dew; the end of the night of weeping, the beginning of the morning of joy. Only God can take away from our weary ears the din of our care, and charm them with the sweet notes of his love. Our plea with the Lord is our faith: if we are relying upon him, he cannot disappoint us: **in thee do I trust** is a sound and solid argument with God. He who made the ear will cause us to hear; he who is love itself will bring his lovingkindness before our minds. **Cause me to know the way wherein I should walk; for I lift up my soul unto thee.** The Great First Cause must cause us to hear and to know. Spiritual senses are dependent upon God, and heavenly knowledge

345

comes from him alone. To know the way we ought to take is exceedingly needful, for how can we be exact in obedience to a law with which we are not acquainted? If we know not the way, how shall we keep in it? The psalmist lifts up his soul: the soul that trusts will rise. We will not allow our hope to sink, but we will strive to get up and rise out of our daily griefs. This is wise. When David was in any difficulty as to his way he lifted his soul towards God himself, and then he knew that he could not go very far wrong. If the soul will not rise of itself we must lift it up unto God. This is good argument in prayer: surely the God to whom we endeavor to lift our soul will condescend to show us what he would have us to do. Let us attend to David's example, and when our heart is low, endeavor to lift it up to the Lord himself.

9. **Deliver me, O LORD, from mine enemies.** Many foes beset us, we cannot overcome them, we cannot even escape from them; but Jehovah can and will rescue us if we pray to him. The weapon of all-prayer will stand us in better stead than sword and shield. **I flee unto thee to hide me.** This was a good result from his persecutions. That which makes us flee to our God may be an ill wind, but it blows us good. There is no cowardice in such flight, but much holy courage. God can hide us out of reach of harm, and even out of sight of it. He is our hiding-place; Jesus has made himself the refuge of his people: the sooner, and the more entirely, we flee to him the better for us. Beneath the crimson canopy of our Lord's atonement believers are completely hidden; let us abide there and be at rest. In verse 7 our poet cried, "Hide not thy face," and here he prays, "Hide me." Note also how often he uses the words **unto thee**; he is after his God; he must travel in that direction by some means, even though he may seem to be beating a retreat; his whole being longs to be near the Lord. Is it possible that such thirstings for God will be left unsupplied?

10. **Teach me to do thy will.** How childlike – **teach me!** How practical – teach me **to do!** How undivided in obedience – to do **thy will!** To do all of it, let it be what it may. This is the best form of instruction, for its source is God, its object is holiness, its spirit is that of hearty loyalty. The man is hidden in the Lord, and spends his peaceful life in learning the will of his Preserver. A heart cannot long be desolate which is thus docile. **For thou art my God.** Who else can teach me as thou canst? Who else will care to do it but my God? Thou hast given me thyself; thou wilt surely give me thy teaching. If I have thee, may I not ask to have thy perfect mind? When the heart can sincerely call Jehovah **my God,** the understanding is ready to learn of him, the will is prepared to obey him, the whole man is eager to please him. **Thy spirit is good.** God is all spirit and all good. His essence is goodness, kindness, holiness: it is his nature to do good, and what greater good can he do to us than to hear such a prayer as that which follows – **Lead me into the land of uprightness?** David desires to be among the godly, in a land of another sort from that which had cast him out. He sighed for the upland meadows of grace, the table-lands of peace, the

346

fertile plains of communion. He could not reach them of himself; he must be led there. God, who is good, can best conduct us to the godly land. There is no inheritance like a portion in the land of promise, the land of precept, the land of perfectness. He who teaches us must put us into a baby's harness, and guide and conduct us to his own dwelling-place in the country of holiness. The way is long, and steep, and he who goes without a divine leader will faint on the journey; but with Jehovah to lead, it is delightful to follow, and there is neither stumbling nor wandering.

11. Quicken me, O LORD, for thy name's sake. Oh for more life as well as more light! Teaching and leading call for invigoration, or we shall be dull scholars and slow pilgrims. Jehovah, the Lord and giver of life, is the only one from whom life can come to renew and revive us; hence, the prayer is to him only. Perchance a servant might teach and lead, but only the Master can enliven. We are often near to death, and hence each one may fitly cry, **Quicken me.** But what is there in us which we can plead as a reason for such a favor? Nothing, literally nothing. We must beg it for his name's sake. He must quicken us because he is the living God, the loving God, the Lord who delighteth in mercy. What blessed arguments lie clustered together in his glorious name! We need never cease praying for want of acceptable pleas; and we may always fall back upon the one before us – **thy name's sake.** It will render the name of Jehovah the more glorious in human eyes if he creates a high degree of spiritual life in his servants; and this is a reason for his doing so, which we may urge with much confidence.

For thy righteousness' sake bring my soul out of trouble. Let people see that thou art on the side of the right, and that thou wilt not allow the wicked to ride rough-shod over those who trust in thee. Thou hast promised to succor thy people; thou art not unrighteous to forget their work of faith; thou art, on the contrary, righteous in answering sincere prayer, and in comforting thy people. David was heavily afflicted. Not only was there trouble in his soul, but his soul was in trouble; plunged in it as in a sea, shut up in it as in a prison. God could bring him out of it, and especially he could at once lift up his soul or spirit out of the ditch. We may be sure that trouble was soon over when the Lord heard such supplications.

12. And of thy mercy cut off mine enemies, and destroy all them that afflict my soul. He believes that it will be so, and thus prophesies the event; for the words may be read as a declaration, and it is better so to understand them. We could not **pray** just so with our Christian light; but under Old Testament arrangements the spirit of it was congruous to the law. It is a petition which justice sanctions, but the spirit of love is not at home in presenting it. *We,* as Christians, turn the petition to spiritual use only. Yet David was of so generous a mind, and dealt so tenderly with Saul, that he could hardly have meant all that his words are made in our version to say. **For I am thy servant;** and therefore I hope that my Master will protect me in his service, and grant me victory while I fight his battles. It is a warrior's prayer, and smells of the dust and smoke of battle. It was heard, and therefore it was not asking amiss. Still there is a more excellent way.

Psalm 144

1. Blessed be the LORD my strength. He bursts at once into a loud note of praise. When the heart is in a right state it must praise God. We ought not to receive strength to resist evil, to defend truth, and to conquer error without knowing who gave it to us, and rendering to him the glory. God is full of power, and he becomes the power of those who trust him. It may be read "My Rock," but this hardly so well consorts with the following words: **Which teacheth my hands to war, and my fingers to fight.** The word "rock" is the Hebrew way of expressing strength. If we have strength we are not much the better unless we have skill also. Untrained force is often an injury to the possessor, and even becomes a danger to those round about, and therefore the psalmist blesses the Lord as much for teaching as for strength. Let us also bless Jehovah if he has in anything made us efficient. The instruction mentioned was not so much of the brain as of the hands and fingers. People with little scholastic education should be grateful for deftness and skill in their handicrafts. To a fighting man the education of the hands is of far more value than mere book-learning. People are too apt to fancy that a worker's efficiency is to be ascribed to himself, but this is a popular fallacy. A clergyman may be supposed to be taught of God, but people do not allow this to be true of weavers or workers in brass; yet these callings are specially mentioned in the Bible as having been taught to holy women and earnest men when the tabernacle was set up. All wisdom and skill are from the Lord. David was eminently successful in his battles; he does not trace this to his good generalship or valor, but to his being taught and strengthened for the war. If the Lord deigns to have a hand in such unspiritual work as fighting, surely he will help us to proclaim the Gospel and win souls.

Jehovah is now his strength, and is still teaching him; we ought to make a point of presenting praise while yet the blessing is on the wing. The verse is also preeminently practical. Some of us who are grievously tormented with rheumatism might cry, "Blessed be the Lord, my Comforter, who teaches my knees to bear in patience, and my feet to endure in resignation." Others who are on the look-out to help young converts might say, "Blessed be God who teaches my eyes to see wounded souls, and my lips to cheer them." David has his own especial help from God, and praises him accordingly. This tends to make the harmony of heaven perfect when all the singers take their parts; if we all followed the same score, the music would not be so full and rich.

2. My goodness, and my fortress. The word for **goodness** signifies "mercy." It is all of mercy that God is any of the other good things to us, so that this is a highly comprehensive title. So is he himself also our **fortress** and safe abode: we cannot be driven out, or starved out, for our fortress is prepared for a siege. **My high tower, and my deliverer.** As from a lofty watch-tower the believer, trusting in the Lord, looks down upon his enemies. He is out of bow-shot; he dwells on high. Jehovah is our Deliverer as well. These different figures set forth the varied benefits which come to us from our Lord. He is every good thing which we can need for this world or the next. He not only places us out of harm's way full often, but when we must be exposed, he comes to our rescue. **My shield, and he in whom I trust.** The believer opposes the Lord to the blows of the enemy, and finds himself secure. **Who subdueth my people under me.** People who rule others should thank God if they succeed in the task. The victories of peace are as much worthy of joyful gratitude as the victories of war. Leaders in the Christian church cannot maintain their position except as the Lord preserves to them the mighty influence which insures obedience and evokes enthusiastic loyalty. For every particle of influence for good which we may possess let us magnify the name of the Lord.

3. LORD, what is man, that thou takest knowledge of him! The psalmist turns from the glorious all-sufficiency of God to the insignificance and nothingness of man. Man is too feeble and too fickle to be relied upon. The psalmist's wonder is that God should stoop to know him. God knows his people with a tender intimacy, a constant, careful observation: he foreknew them in love, he knows them by care, he will know them in acceptance at last.

Or the son of man, that thou makest account of him! The son of man is a weaker being still – so the original word implies. He is not so much man as God made him, but man as his mother bore him. The Lord thinks much of man, and in connection with redeeming love makes a great figure of him: this can be believed, but it cannot be explained. It is meet for us to be humble and to distrust ourselves, but all this should make us the more grateful to the Lord, who knows man better than we do, and yet communes with him, and even dwells in him. If God makes account of man it is not for us to despise our own kind.

4. Man is like to vanity. He is actually vain, and resembles a puff, a bubble. Yet he is not vanity, but only **like** it. He is not so substantial as that unreal thing. **His days are as a shadow that passeth away.** He is short-lived; his life is only like to a shadow, which is a vague resemblance, an absence of something rather than in itself an existence. Human life is not only as a shade, but as a shade which is about to depart. It is a mere mirage. How is it that the Eternal should make so much of mortal man, who begins to die as soon as he begins to live?

5. Bow thy heavens, O LORD, and come down. The Lord has often done this, and never more fully than when in Bethlehem the Word was made flesh and dwelt among us. He never refuses to come down to defend his chosen ones. **Touch the mountains, and they shall smoke.** It was so when the Lord appeared on Sinai. If Jehovah appeared, nothing could stand before him; all mortal power which is opposed to the Lord must end in smoke.

6. **Cast forth lightning, and scatter them.** The artillery of heaven soon puts the enemy to flight: a single bolt sets the armies running hither and thither in utter rout. **Shoot out thine arrows, and destroy them.** It was no common faith which led the poet-king to expect the Lord to use his thunderbolts on behalf of a single member of that race which he had just now described as "like to vanity." A believer in God may without presumption expect the Almighty Lord to use on his behalf all the stores of his wisdom and power. When we have once mastered the greater difficulty of the Lord's taking any interest in us, it is but a small thing that we should expect him to exert his great power on our behalf.

7. **Send thine hand from above.** Let thy long and strong arm be stretched out till thine hand seizes my foes, and delivers me from them. **Rid me, and deliver me out of great waters.** Make a Moses of me – one drawn out of the waters. My foes pour in upon me like torrents; they threaten to overwhelm me. save me from their force and fury; take them from me, and me from them. **From the hand of strange children.** From foreigners of every race, people strange to me and thee, who therefore must work evil to me, and rebellion against thyself. Those against whom he pleaded were out of covenant with God; they were Philistines and Edomites, or else people of his own nation of black heart and traitorous spirit. Oh to be delivered from deceptive lips and false hearts! No wonder these words are repeated, for they are the frequent cry of many a tried child of God – **Rid me and deliver me.** The devil's children are strange to us: we can never agree with them, and we are despised by them. O Lord, deliver us from the evil one, and from all who are of his race.

8. **Whose mouth speaketh vanity.** They cannot be depended upon; their solemn declarations are as light as the foam of the sea. Of all people deceivers and liars are among the most disgusting to true hearts. **And their right hand is a right hand of falsehood.** They act as falsely as they speak. It is a dreadful thing when a person's expertness dwells more in lies than in truth.

9. **I will sing a new song unto thee, O God.** Weary of the false, I will adore the true. Fired with fresh enthusiasm, my gratitude will make a new channel for itself. I will sing as others have done; but it will be a new song, such as no others have sung. I will extol none but the Lord, from whom my deliverance has come. **Upon a psaltery and an instrument of ten strings will I sing praises unto thee.** His hand should aid his tongue, not as in the case of the wicked, co-operating in deceit, but his hand would unite with his mouth in truthful praise. Music dropped naturally into place in the "worldly sanctuary," but after all it can do no more than represent praise, and assist our expression of it;

the real praise is in the heart. When artistic skill takes a higher place than hearty singing, it is time that instruments were banished from public worship; but when they are subordinate to the song, as here, it is not for us to prohibit them, or condemn those who use them. The private worshiper, singing his solo unto the Lord, has often found it helpful to accompany himself on some familiar instrument, and David says, "*I* will sing praise unto thee," that is, not so much in the company of others as by himself alone.

10. It is he that giveth salvation unto kings. Those whom the Lord sets up he will keep up. Kings, from their conspicuous position, are exposed to special danger, and when their lives and their thrones are preserved to them they should give the Lord the glory of it. David had by his valor wrought salvation for Israel, but he lays his laurels at the feet of his Lord. **Who delivereth David his servant from the hurtful sword.** He traces his escape from death to the delivering hand of God. Note, he speaks in the present tense, for this was an act which covered his whole life. He styles himself the Lord's **servant**, accepting this as the highest title he had attained or desired.

11. He begs deliverance from him who is ever delivering him. **Rid me, and deliver me from the hand of strange children.** This is the refrain of the song, the burden of the prayer. **Whose mouth speaketh vanity, and their right hand is a hand of falsehood.** Those who are surrounded by such serpents know not how to deal with them, and the only available method seems to be prayer to God for a riddance and deliverance. David in verse 7, according to the original, had sought the help of both the Lord's hands; his deceitful enemies, with remarkable unanimity, were with one mouth and one hand seeking his destruction.

12–15. Riddance from the wicked and the gracious presence of the Lord are sought with a special eye to the peace and prosperity which will follow thereupon. The sparing of David's life would mean the peace and happiness of a whole nation. We can scarcely judge how much of happiness may hang upon the Lord's favor to one person.

12. God's blessing works wonders for a people. **That our sons may be as plants grown up in their youth.** What the young men are the older men will be. If in their opening manhood they are dwarfed, they will never get over it. But when we see them developed in holiness, what joy we have of them! **That our daughters may be as corner stones, polished after the similitude of a palace.** Daughters unite families as cornerstones join walls together, and they adorn them as polished stones garnish the structure into which they are built.

13. That our garners may be full, affording all manner of store. Where there are happy households, there must be plentiful provision for them, for famine brings misery where love abounds. When all the fruits of the earth are plentiful, the fruits of our lips should be joyful worship and thanksgiving. **That our sheep may bring forth thousands and ten thousands in our streets,** or rather in the open places, the fields, and sheep-walks where lambs should be born. A teeming increase is here described. Food and clothing come from the flock, and both are of first consideration.

14. That our oxen may be strong to labor, so that the plowing and cartage of the farm may be duly performed, and the farmer's work accomplished without unduly taking the cattle, or working them cruelly. **That there be no breaking in, nor going out;** no marauders, no forced emigration, no burglaries, no evictions. **That there be no complaining in our streets;** no secret dissatisfaction, no public riot; no fainting from poverty, no clamor for rights denied, nor concerning wrongs unredressed. This has been the condition of our own country, and if it should now be changed, who can wonder, for our ingratitude well deserves to be deprived of blessings which it has despised.

These verses may with a little accommodation be applied to a prosperous church, where the converts are growing and beautiful, the Gospel stores abundant, and the spiritual increase most cheering. The ministers and workers are in full vigor, and the people are happy and united.

15. Happy is that people, that is in such a case. Temporal blessings are not trifles, for the miss of them would be a dire calamity. It is a great happiness to belong to a people so highly favored. **Yea, happy is that people, whose God is the LORD.** This comes in as an explanation of their prosperity. Under the Old Testament Israel had present earthly rewards for obedience. This sentence is also a sort of correction of all that had gone before, as if the poet would say, all these temporal gifts are a part of happiness, but still the heart and soul of happiness lies in the people being right with God, and having a full possession of him. Those who worship the happy God become a happy people. Then if we have not temporal mercies literally we have something better.

Happy was the nation which David ruled: happy in its king, its families, its prosperity, and in the possession of peace; but yet more in enjoying true religion and worshiping Jehovah.

Psalm 145

1. I will extol thee, my God, O king. David as God's king adores God as his King. When we cannot express all our praise just now, it is wise to register our resolution to continue in the blessed work – **I will extol thee.** See David's pronoun **my,** and his allegiance – the title **king. And I will bless thy name for ever and ever.** David determined that his praise should rise to blessing, should intelligently spend itself upon the name or character of God, and should be continued world without end. To **bless** God is to praise him with a personal affection for him, and a wishing well to him: this is growingly easy exercise as we advance in experience and grow in grace.

2. Every day will I bless thee. Whatever the character of the day, or of my circumstances during that day, I will continue to glorify God. We should see abundant cause in each day for rendering special blessing to the Lord. Our love to God is not a matter of holy days: every day is alike holy to holy people. David says, **I will bless *thee***: we do not only admire the Lord's words and works, but himself. **And I will praise thy name for ever and ever.** He said he would bless that name, and now he vows to praise it; he will extol the Lord in every sense and way. Four times he says *I will*: praise is not to be discharged by proxy; there must be your very self in it, or there is nothing in it.

3. **Great is the LORD, and greatly to be praised.** Worship should be great praise for a great God. Praise may be said to be great when the song contains great matter, when the hearts producing it are intensely fervent, and when large numbers unite in the great acclaim. **And his greatness is unsearchable.** Song should be founded upon search; hymns composed without thought are of no worth. Yet when we meditate most, and search most studiously, we shall still find ourselves surrounded with unknowable wonders, which will baffle all attempts to sing them worthily. The best adoration of the Unsearchable is to own him to be so. He is past finding out, and therefore his deserved praise is still above and beyond all that we can render to him.

4. **One generation shall praise thy works to another.** There will be a tradition of praise: people will instruct their descendants in this hallowed exercise. Let us see to it that we praise God before our children, and never make them think that his service is an unhappy one. **And shall declare thy mighty acts.** The generations together will make up an extraordinary history. Each generation will contribute its chapter, and all the generations together will compose a volume of matchless character. All glory be unto him who remains the same Lord throughout all generations.

5. **I will speak of the glorious honor of thy majesty.** David cannot give over the worship of God into the hands of others, even though all generations should undertake to perpetuate it: he must have his own individual share in it, and so he says, **I will speak.** He multiplies the terms by which he would extol Jehovah. **And of thy wondrous works.** All the works of God among men are Godlike, but certain of them are specially calculated to create surprise. His work of grace is wondrous above all. This specially, and all the rest proportionately, should be spoken of by holy people, by experienced people, and by people who have the ability to speak with power. Let it be the delight of each one of us according to our position to speak lovingly of our Lord.

6. **And men shall speak of the might of thy terrible acts.** Under mercies people may be dumb, but concerning miseries they raise a great outcry. While they are thus occupied with "fearsome facts," David would look at these affairs in another light, and sing another tune. **And I will declare thy greatness.** Those acts which were terrible deeds to most people were mighty deeds, or "greatnesses," to our poet. It is the occupation of every true believer to tell of

353

the great doings of his great God. We are personally to make a declaration of what we have seen and known. We are even bound in deep solemnity of manner to warn people of the Lord's greatness in his terrible acts of justice: thus will they be admonished to abstain from provoking him.

7. They shall abundantly utter the memory of thy great goodness. The Lord's redeemed people having been filled with his great goodness will retain the happy recollection of it, and it will be their delight to speak with one another of God's dealings with them, and to compare notes of their experiences. There is no scarcity of matter, and it is not meet that the goodness of the living God should be buried in the grave of ingratitude. **And shall sing of thy righteousness.** They will say and then sing of that righteousness which is the sinner's terror, which even good people mention with deep solemnity. Righteousness received by Gospel light is in reality the secret foundation of the believer's hope. Since Jesus died as our Substitute, righteousness requires and secures the salvation of all the redeemed. Modern thinkers would expunge the idea of righteousness from their notion of God, but converted people would not. Even a rebel may rejoice in mercy, which he looks upon as laxity, but a loyal subject rejoices that God is so just that not even to save his own elect would he consent to violate the righteousness of his moral government.

8. The LORD is gracious. Was it not in some such terms that the Lord revealed himself to Moses? His words and ways, his promises and gifts, his plans and purposes all manifest his grace, or free favor. **And full of compassion.** If the Lord be full of compassion there is no room in him for forgetfulness or harshness. **Slow to anger.** Even those who refuse his grace yet share in longsuffering. When people do not repent, but on the contrary go from bad to worse, he is still averse to let his wrath flame forth against them. **And of great mercy.** This is his attitude towards the guilty. When people at last repent, they find pardon awaiting them.

9. The LORD is good to all. Not even his fiercest enemy can deny this, since the very existence of the lips that slander him is a proof that it is slander. He allows his enemies to live, he even supplies them with food, and smooths their way with many comforts; for them the sun shines as brightly as if they were saints, and the rain waters their fields as plentifully as if they were perfect. Is not this goodness to all? **And his tender mercies are over all his works.** Kindness is a law of God's universe: the world was planned for happiness; even now that sin has so sadly marred God's handiwork, and introduced elements which were not from the beginning, the Lord has so arranged matters that the fall is broken, the curse is met by an antidote, and the inevitable pain is softened with mitigations. Even in this sin-stricken world, under its disordered economy, there are abundant traces of a hand skillful to soothe distress and heal disease. That which makes life bearable is the tenderness of the great Father. Man's body was framed for a joyful activity, and a peaceful enjoyment of God. Jehovah has in great consideration laid up in the world cures for our ailments, and helps for our feebleness, and if many of these have been long in their discovery, it is because it was more for man's benefit to find them out himself than to have them labeled and placed in order before his eyes. Jehovah has never taken delight in the ills of his creatures, but has sought their good.

The duty of kindness to animals may logically be argued from this verse. Should not the children of God be like their Father in kindness?

10. All thy works shall praise thee, O LORD. There is a something about every creature which redounds to the honor of God. The skill, kindness, and power manifested in the formation of each living thing is in itself to the praise of God, and when observed by an intelligent mind the Lord is honored thereby. **And all thy saints shall bless thee.** They wish well to God; they would make him more blessed, if such a thing were possible. If we praise Jehovah because of his works around us, we must go on to bless him for his works within us.

11. They shall speak of the glory of thy kingdom. Those who bless God from their hearts rejoice to see him enthroned, glorified, and magnified in power. No subject is more profitable for humility, obedience, hope, and joy than that of the reigning power of the Lord our God. His works praise him, but they cannot crown him: this remains for holy hands and hearts. **And talk of thy power.** All power comes from God. Apart from him the laws of nature would be inoperative. His power is the one source of force – mechanical, vital, mental, spiritual. Who can calculate the reserve forces of the Infinite? How, then, can his kingdom fail?

12. To make known to the sons of men his mighty acts. Few reckon such knowledge to be an essential part of education. As the state cannot teach these holy histories the people of God must do it themselves. The saints are the religious instructors of the race; they ought to be not only the historians of the past, but the bards of the present, whose duty it is to keep the sons of men in memory of the great deeds which the Lord did in the days of their fathers and in the old time before them. **And the glorious majesty of his kingdom.** How shall we make this known? Let us first labor to know it ourselves, and then make it a frequent subject of discourse; so shall people know it from us, the Holy Spirit attending our word.

13. Thy kingdom is an everlasting kingdom. His meditation has brought him near to God, and God near to him: he speaks to him in adoration, changing the pronoun from "his" to **thy.** He sees the great King, and prostrates himself before him. The Lord's kingdom is without beginning, without break, without bound, and without end. None can overthrow his power, or break away from his rule. Herein is rest for faith. **And thy dominion endureth throughout all generations.** Men come and go like shadows, but God reigns eternally.

These three verses are a reverent hymn concerning the kingdom of God.

They will be best appreciated by those who are in that kingdom in the fullest sense, and are most truly loyal to the Lord.

14–16. In these verses Jehovah is adored for his gracious providence; we see how he rules his kingdom and provides for his subjects.

14. The LORD upholdeth all that fall. Read this in connection with verse 13, and admire the unexpected contrast. He who reigns in glorious majesty lifts and holds up those who are apt to fall. The form of the verb shows that he is always doing this. The fallen of our race are shunned by us, and it is especial tenderness on the Lord's part that he looks upon those who are the chief of sinners and the least regarded among mankind. The falling ones among us are too apt to be pushed down by the strong. The Lord loves to reverse things.

And raiseth up all those that be bowed down. Many are despondent, and cannot lift up their heads in courage, or their hearts with comfort; but these he cheers. Some are bent with their daily load, and these he strengthens. The two **all**s should not be overlooked: the Lord has a kindly heart towards the whole company of the afflicted.

15. The eyes of all wait upon thee. They have learned to look to thee: it has become their nature to turn to thee for all they want. As children look to a father for all they need, so do the creatures look to God. **And thou givest them their meat in due season.** The Lord is feeding the hungry all around us, giving food to all creatures, and to ourselves among them. Observe the punctuality of the Lord in giving food at meal-time – in the season when it is due. This he does for all, and each living thing has its own season, so that the Lord is feeding his great flock during every moment of time.

16. God has suitable supplies at hand, and these he gives till inward satisfaction is produced, and the creature sighs no longer. In spiritual things, when God has raised a desire, he always gratifies it; hence the longing is prophetic of the blessing. In no case is the desire of the living thing excited to produce distress, but in order that it may seek and find satisfaction.

These verses refer to natural providence; but they may equally well apply to the stores of grace, since the same God is king in both spheres. If we will but wait upon the Lord for pardon, renewing, or whatever else we need, we shall not wait in vain. The hand of grace is never closed while the sinner lives.

17–21. In these verses we behold our God in the realm of his free grace dealing well with his believing people.

17. The LORD is righteous in all his ways, and holy in all his works. His ways and works are both worthy to be praised. Jehovah cannot be unjust or impure. In the salvation of his people he is as righteous and holy as in any other of his ways and works: he has not manifested mercy at the expense of justice.

18. The LORD is nigh unto all them that call upon him. Not only near by his omnipresence, but near to sympathize and favor. He does not leave praying people, and people who confess his name, to battle with the world alone, but he is ever at their side. This favor is not for a few of those who invoke him; but for each one of the pious company. **All** who place themselves beneath the shield of his glorious name by calling themselves by it, and calling upon it in supplication, will find him a very present help in trouble. **To all that call upon him in truth.** There are many whose formal prayers and false professions will never bring them into communion with the Lord. To pray in truth, we must have a true heart, and the truth in our heart; and then we must be humble, for pride is a falsehood; and be earnest, or else prayer is a lie. A God of truth cannot be nigh to the spirit of hypocrisy; neither can he be far from a sincere spirit, since it is his work, and he forsakes not the work of his own hands.

19. **He will fulfill the desire of them that fear him.** That is, those who reverence his name and his law. Inasmuch as they have respect unto his will, he will have respect unto their will. They will have their way, for they have his way in their hearts. A holy heart only desires what a holy God can give, and so its desire is filled full out of the fullness of the Lord. **He also will hear their cry, and will save them.** He will listen to their piteous cry, and then send salvation from every ill. This he will do himself personally; he will not trust them to angels or saints.

20. **The Lord preserveth all them that love him.** They keep him in their love, and he keeps them by his love. See how these favored ones have advanced from fearing the Lord and crying to him, to loving him; and in that love they are secure from all danger. **But all the wicked will he destroy.** Wickedness is an offense to all holy beings, and therefore those who are determined to continue in it must be weeded out. As good sanitary laws remove all creators of pest and plague, so does the moral government of God mark every evil thing for destruction.

21. **My mouth shall speak the praise of the Lord.** Whatever others may speak upon, my topic is fixed once for all: I will speak of the praise of Jehovah. I am doing it, and I will do it as long as I breathe. **And let all flesh bless his holy name for ever and ever.** No one need think that he will be rejected when he comes with his personal note of praise; all are permitted, invited, and exhorted to magnify the Lord. Specially should his holiness be adored: this is the crown, and in a certain sense the sum, of all his attributes. Once let the song begin and there will be no end to it.

Psalm 146

1. **Praise ye the Lord,** or, "Hallelujah." With holy awe let us pronounce the word, and by it summon ourselves and all others to adore the God of the whole earth. People need to be called to praise; it is important that they should praise; and there are many reasons why they should do it at once.

Praise the LORD, O my soul. He would be the leader of the choir which he had summoned. It is a poor business if we exhort others, and do not stir up our own soul. If my voice should be of the poorer sort, and somewhat lacking in melody, yet my soul shall accomplish my resolve to magnify the Lord.

2. While I live will I praise the LORD. I cannot tell how long or short my life may be; but every hour of it shall be given to the praises of my God. As our life is the gift of God's mercy, it should be used for his glory. **I will sing praises unto my God while I have any being.** When I am no longer in being on earth, I hope to have a higher being in heaven, and there I will not only praise, but *sing* praises, for the glorious Jehovah is my God, my own God by covenant, and by blood relationship in Christ Jesus. I have no being apart from God; therefore I will not attempt to enjoy my being other than by singing to his honor.

3. Put not your trust in princes. If David be the author this warning comes from a prince. In any case it comes from the Spirit of the living God. People are always far too apt to depend upon the great ones of earth, and forget the Great One above; and this habit is the fruitful source of disappointment. Princes are only men, and men with greater needs than others; why, then, should we look to them for aid? They are in greater danger, are burdened with greater cares, and are more likely to be misled than other people; therefore, it is folly to select them for our confidence. So live as to deserve *their* trust, but do not burden them with your trust. **Nor in the son of man, in whom there is no help.** Man is a helpless creature without God; therefore, look not for help in that direction. All men are like the few who are made into princes – they are more in appearance than in reality, more in promising than in performing, more apt to help themselves than to help others. How many have turned away heart-sick from men on whom they once relied! Never was this the case with a believer in the Lord!

4. His breath goeth forth, he returneth to his earth. There is a spirit in man, and when that goes the man goes. The spirit returns to God who gave it, and the flesh to the dust out of which it was fashioned. This is a poor creature to trust in.

In that very day his thoughts perish. Whatever he may have proposed to do, the proposal ends in smoke; and our trusts have perished, for their thoughts have perished. Is this a being to be relied upon?

5. Happy is he that hath the God of Jacob for his help. He has happiness indeed: the true and the real delight is with him. The God of Jacob is the God of the covenant, the God of wrestling prayer, the God of the tried believer; he is the only living and true God, who led the tribes of Jacob out of Egypt, and through the wilderness. The Lord never dies, neither do his thoughts perish; his purpose of mercy, like himself, endures throughout all generations. Hallelujah! **Whose hope is in the LORD his God.** He is happy in help for the present and in hope for the future who has placed all his confidence in Jehovah, who is his God by a covenant of salt. Happy is he when others are despairing! Happiest shall he be in that very hour when others are discovering the depths of agony. We have here a statement which we have personally tried and proved: resting in the Lord, we know a happiness which is beyond description, beyond comparison, beyond conception. Unless Jehovah be his God no one can find confidence in the fact that he was Jacob's God; but when by faith we know the Lord to be ours, then we are "rich to all the intents of bliss."

6. Which made heaven, and earth, the sea, and all that therein is. He who made heaven can make a heaven for us, and make us fit for heaven. He who made the earth can preserve us while we are on earth, and help us to make good use of it while we sojourn upon it. He who made the sea and all its mysteries can steer us across the pathless deeps of a troubled life, and make it a way for his redeemed to pass over. This God who still makes the world by keeping it in existence is assuredly able to keep us to his eternal kingdom and glory. The making of the worlds is the standing proof of the power and wisdom of that great God in whom we trust. It is our joy that he not only made heaven, but the sea; not only things which are bright and blessed, but things which are deep and dark. Concerning all our circumstances, we may say that the Lord is there. In storms and hurricanes the Lord reigneth as truly as in that great calm which rules the firmament above. **Which keepeth truth forever.** This is a second and most forcible justification of our trust: the Lord will never permit his promise to fail. He is true to his own nature, true to the relationships which he has assumed, true to his covenant, true to his Word, true to his Son. He keeps true, and is the keeper of all that is true.

7. Which executeth judgment for the oppressed. He is a swift and impartial administrator of justice. He is never a respecter of persons. He is the friend of the down-trodden, the champion of the helpless. **Which giveth food to the hungry.** All food comes from God; but when we are reduced to hunger, and providence supplies our necessity, we are especially struck with the fact. Let every hungry person lay hold on this statement, and plead it before the mercy-seat, whether he suffer bodily hunger or heart hunger. **The LORD looseth the prisoners.** The Lord brought Israel from the house of bondage. Jesus is the Emancipator, spiritually, providentially, and nationally. As faith in Jehovah becomes common, freedom will advance in every form; especially will mental, moral, and spiritual bonds be loosed, and the slaves of error, sin, and death will be set free. Well may the loosened ones be loudest in the song!

8. The LORD openeth the eyes of the blind. Jesus did this very frequently, and hereby proved himself to be Jehovah. How often is the mental eye closed in moral night! And who can remove this dreary effect of the fall but the Almighty God? This miracle of grace he has performed in myriads of cases, and it is in each case a theme for loftiest praise. **The LORD raiseth them that are bowed down.** This also Jesus did literally. Jehovah consoles the bereaved, cheers the defeated, solaces the despondent, comforts the despairing. Let those who are bowed to the ground appeal to him, and he will speedily upraise them. **The LORD loveth the righteous.** He gives to them the love of content, communion, and reward. Loved ones, you must never pause from his praise whose infinite love has made you what you are!

9. **The LORD preserveth the strangers.** Many monarchs hunted aliens down, or transported them from place to place, or left them as outlaws unworthy of human rights; but Jehovah made special laws for their shelter within his domain. **He relieveth the fatherless and widow.** These excite his compassion, and he shows it in a practical way by upraising them from their forlorn condition. The Mosaic law made provision for these destitute persons. **But the way of the wicked he turneth upside down.** The wicked man's way is in itself a turning of things upside down, and the Lord makes it so to him providentially: everything goes wrong with him who goes wrong.

10. **The LORD shall reign for ever.** Jehovah is king, and his kingdom can never come to an end. Neither does he die, nor abdicate, nor lose his crown by force. **Even thy God, O Zion, unto all generations.** The God of his worshiping people is he who in every age will reign. There will always be a Zion; Zion will always have Jehovah for her king, for her he will always prove himself to be reigning in great power. What should we do in the presence of so great a King, but enter into his courts with praise, and pay to him our joyful homage? **Praise ye the LORD.** Do we not also say, "Hallelujah"?

Psalm 147

1. **Praise ye the LORD,** or Hallelujah. The flow of the broad river of the Book of Psalms ends in a cataract of praise. Jehovah and happy praise should ever be associated in the mind of a believer. **Praise ye the LORD.** Such an exhortation may fitly be addressed to all those who owe anything to the favor of God; and which of us does not? **For it is good to sing praises unto our God.** It is good because it is right, acceptable with God, beneficial to ourselves, and stimulating to our fellows. Singing in the heart is good, but singing with heart and voice is better, for it allows others to join with us. **For it is pleasant; and praise is comely.** It is refreshing to the truly refined mind, and it is agreeable to the eye of the pure in heart: it is delightful both to hear and to see a whole assembly praising the Lord. Let each reader feel that he and his family ought to constitute a choir for the daily praises of the Lord.

2. **The LORD doth build up Jerusalem.** His grace, wisdom, and power are all seen in the formation and establishment of the chosen seat of his worship; once a city with material walls, but now a church composed of spiritual stones. **He gathereth together the outcasts of Israel,** and thus he repairs the

waste places, and causes the former desolations to be inhabited. This may relate to Nehemiah, but there is not reason why it should not with equal fitness be referred to David, who was once an outcast but became the means of building up Jerusalem. Spiritually we see the hand of God in the edification of the church, and in the ingathering of sinners. What are people under conviction of sin but outcasts from God, from holiness, from heaven, and even from hope? Who could make citizens of them in Christ Jesus save the Lord our God? This deed of love he is constantly performing. Therefore let the song begin at Jerusalem our home, and let every living stone in the spiritual city echo the strain; for it is the Lord who has brought again his banished ones, and builded them together in Zion.

3. He healeth the broken in heart, and bindeth up their wounds. This the Holy Spirit mentions as a part of the glory of God, and a reason for our declaring his praise: the Lord is not only a Builder, but a Healer; he restores broken hearts as well as broken walls. Few will associate with the despondent, but Jehovah chooses their company, and abides with them till he has healed them by his comforts. The Lord is still healing and binding, as the original has it.

4. He telleth the number of the stars. None but he can count the mighty host, but as he made them and sustains them he can number them. To Jehovah stars are as mere coins which the merchant counts as he puts them in his bag. **He calleth them all by their names.** He gives to each its appropriate title, because he knows its constitution and nature. They are perfectly obedient, as soldiers to a captain who calls their names, and allots them their stations. He who acts a surgeon's part with wounded hearts marshals the heavenly host.

5. Great is our Lord. None can describe his majesty, or reckon up the number of his excellencies. **And of great power.** Doing as he wills, and willing to do mighty deeds. His acts reveal something of his might, but the mass of his power is hidden, for all things are possible with God. **His understanding is infinite.** He is infinite in existence, in power, and in knowledge, as these three phrases plainly teach us. This is he who so tenderly nurses sick souls, and waits to be gracious to sinful people. Let him be extolled because of each of his attributes.

6. He reverses the evil order of things. The Lord loves those who are reverent to himself, humble in their own eyes, and gentle to their fellows: these he lifts up to hope, to peace, to power, to eternal honor. Proud men are, in their own esteem, high enough already; only those who are low will care to be lifted up, and only such will Jehovah upraise. As for the wicked, they must come down from their seats of vain glory. God is accustomed to overthrow such.

7–11. In this paragraph the contrast announced in the former section is enlarged upon as it is seen in nature and in providence.

7. Sing unto the LORD with thanksgiving. Or rather, "respond to Jehovah." He speaks to us in his works; let us answer him with our thanks. Jehovah is ever engaged in giving; let us respond with thanksgiving. **Sing praise upon the harp unto our God.** Blend music with song. Under a dispensation of ritual the use of music was most commendable, and suitable for the great congregation. He is **our** God, and this fact is one choice joy of the song. We have chosen him because he has chosen us. He is **our** God in covenant relationship forever, and to him be praise in every possible form.

8. Who covereth the heaven with clouds. Clouds are not caused by accident; the great Artist's hand thus covers the canvas of the heavens. **Who prepareth rain for the earth.** The Lord prepares clouds with a view to rain, and rain with an eye to the fields below. **Who maketh grass to grow upon the mountains.** By the shower he produces vegetation where the hand of man is all unknown.

9. He giveth to the beast his food. By causing the grass to grow on the hills the Lord feeds the cattle. Too often people treat their cattle with cruelty, but the Lord himself feeds them. **And to the young ravens which cry.** These wild creatures, which seems to be of no use to man, are they therefore worthless? By no means; they fill their place in the economy of nature. He who feeds the sons of the raven will surely nourish the sons of God!

10. He delighteth not in the strength of the horse. He cares as much for helpless birds in the nest as for the war-horse in the pride of its power. **He taketh not pleasure in the legs of a man.** These are the athlete's glory, but God has no pleasure in them. Not the capacities of the creature, but rather its weakness and necessity win the regard of our God. Monarchs trust in their cavalry and infantry; but physical or material greatness and power are of no account with Jehovah; he has respect to other and more precious qualities. Men who boast in the valor of gigantic might will not find themselves the favorites of God, who is a spirit and delights most in spiritual things. The expression of the text may be viewed as including all creature power, even of a mental or moral kind. God does not take pleasure in us because of our attainments, or potentialities: he respects character rather than capacity.

11. The Lord taketh pleasure in them that fear him, in those that hope in his mercy. While the bodily powers give no content to God, spiritual qualities are his delight. It is a striking thought that God should not only be at peace with some kinds of people, but even find a solace and a joy in their company. Some of them are the least in his family, who have never risen beyond hoping and fearing. Others are more fully developed, but still they exhibit a blended character composed of fear and hope: they fear God with holy awe and filial reverence, and they also hope for forgiveness and blessedness because of the divine mercy. As a father takes pleasure in his own children, so does the Lord solace himself in his own beloved ones, whose marks of new birth are fear and hope. They fear, for they are sinners; they hope, for God is merciful. Is there not rich cause for praise in the special feature of the divine character?

12. The city of peace should be the city of praise. Note that we are to praise the Lord in our own houses in Jerusalem as well as in his own house in Zion.

13. For he hath strengthened the bars of thy gates. Her fortifications were finished, even to her bolts and bars. Oh that our churches were thus preserved from all false doctrine and unholy living! This must be the Lord's doing, and where he has wrought it his name is greatly to be praised. Modern libertines would tear down all gates and abolish all bars; but so do not we, because of the fear of the Lord. **He hath blessed thy children within thee.** Internal happiness is as truly the Lord's gift as external security. It would little avail to fortify a wretched, starving city; but when the walls are strengthened, it is a still greater joy to see that the inhabitants are blessed with all good gifts. How much our churches need a present and abiding benediction.

14. He maketh peace in thy borders. Even to the boundaries quiet extends; no enemies are wrangling with the borderers. "When a man's ways please the Lord he maketh even his enemies to be at peace with him." Considering the different constitutions, conditions, tastes, and opinions of people, it is a work of God when in large churches unbroken peace is found year after year; and it is an equal wonder if worldlings, instead of persecuting the godly, treat them with marked respect. **And filleth thee with the finest of the wheat.** It is a great reason for thanksgiving when people's wants are so supplied that they are filled: it takes much to fill some people: perhaps none are ever filled but the inhabitants of Zion. Gospel truth is the finest of the wheat, and those are indeed blessed who are content to be filled therewith, and are not hungering after the husks of the world.

15. He sendeth forth his commandment upon earth. From his church his word goes forth. **His word runneth very swiftly.** His purposes of love are speedily accomplished. The Lord can deliver his people right speedily, or send them supplies immediately from his courts above. God's commands in nature and providence are fiats and all things rush to put them into effect. The expressions in the text are so distinctly in the present that they are meant to teach us the present mission and efficiency of the Word of the Lord, and thus to prompt us to present praise.

16. Here follow instances of the power of God upon the elements. **He giveth snow like wool.** Snow falls softly, covers universally, and clothes warmly, like fleecy wool. The most evident resemblance lies in the fleecy whiteness, but many other likenesses are to be seen by the observant eye. It is wise to see God in winter and in distress as well as in summer and prosperity. **He scattereth the hoarfrost like ashes.** Let us praise the Lord who condescends to wing each flake of snow and scatter each particle of rime. Ours is no absent or inactive deity: he works all things, and is everywhere at home.

17. He casteth forth his ice like morsels. Such are the crumbs of hail which he casts forth, or the crusts of ice which he creates upon the waters. The two expressions indicate a very real presence of God in the phenomena of nature. **Who can stand before his cold?** None can resist the utmost rigors of cold any more than they can bear the vehemence of heat. God's withdrawals of light are a darkness that may be felt, and his withdrawals of heat are a cold which is absolutely omnipotent. It is ours to submit to deprivations with patience, seeing the cold is *his* cold. That which God sends, whether it be heat or cold, no one can defy with impunity.

18. He sendeth out his word, and melteth them. When the frost is sharpest, and the ice is hardest, the Lord intervenes. The phenomena of winter are not so abundant in Palestine as with us, yet they are witnessed sufficiently to cause the devout to bless God for the return of spring. **He causeth his wind to blow, and the waters flow.** The Lord is the great first cause of everything; even the fickle, wandering winds are caused by him. Simple but effectual are the methods of Jehovah in the natural world; equally so are those which he employs in the spiritual kingdom; for the breath of his Holy Spirit breathes upon frozen hearts, and streams of penitence and love gush forth at once.

Observe how in these two sentences the word and the wind go together in nature. They attend each other in grace; the Gospel and the Holy Spirit cooperate in salvation. The truth which the Spirit breathes into prophets and apostles he breathes into dead souls, and they are quickened into spiritual life.

19. He who is the Creator is also the Revealer. We are to praise the Lord above all things for his manifesting himself to us as he does not unto the world. Whatever part of his mind he discloses to us, whether it be a word of instruction, a statute of direction, or a judgment of government, we are bound to bless the Lord for it. He who causes summer to come in the place of winter has also removed the coldness and death from our hearts by the power of his word, and this is abundant cause for singing unto his name. By knowledge of the Lord, Jacob is ennobled into Israel; let him who is made a prevailing prince in prayer be also a chief musician in praise. Why were the elect people so especially favored if they did not, above all others, tell forth the glory of their God?

20. He hath not dealt so with any nation. Israel had clear and exclusive knowledge of God, while others were left in ignorance. Election is the loudest call for grateful adoration. **And as for his judgments, they have not known them;** or, "and judgments they had not known them," as if not knowing the laws of God, they might be looked upon as having no laws at all worth mentioning. The nations were covered with darkness, and only Israel sat in the light. This was sovereign grace in its fullest noontide of power. **Praise ye the Lord.** When we mentioned electing, distinguishing love, our praise can rise no higher, and therefore we close with one more hallelujah.

Psalm 148

1. Praise ye the LORD. Whoever you may be that hear this word, you are invited, intreated, commanded to magnify Jehovah. Assuredly he has made you, and, if for nothing else, you are bound, upon the ground of creatureship, to adore your Maker. **Praise ye the LORD from the heavens.** Since you are nearest to the High and Lofty One, be sure to lead the song. Angels, cherubim and seraphim, and all others who dwell in the precincts of his courts, praise Jehovah. Keep not your worship to yourselves, but let it fall like a golden shower from the heavens on people beneath. **Praise him in the heights.** God is not only to be praised *from* the heights, but *in* them: the adoration is to be perfected in the heavens from which it takes its rise. No place is too high for the praises of the Most High. See how the psalmist trumpets out the word **Praise.** It sounds forth some nine times in the first five verses of this song. Praise not his servants nor his works, but praise *him.*

2. Praise ye him, all his angels. Living intelligences, perfect in character and in bliss, lift up your loudest music to your Lord. Cease not, you messengers of Jehovah, to sound forth his praise while you move at his bidding. **Praise ye him, all his hosts.** This includes angelic armies, but groups with them all the heavenly bodies. Though they be inanimate, the stars, clouds, the lightnings, have their ways of praising Jehovah. The countless armies are all **his** by creation, and preservation, and consequent obligation. Both these sentences claim unanimity of praise from those in the upper regions who are called upon to commence the strain – *all* his angels, *all* his hosts. That same hearty oneness must pervade the whole orchestra of praising ones; hence, further on we read of all starts of light, all deeps, all hills, all cedars, and all people. How well the concert begins when all angels, and all the heavenly host, strike the first joyful notes! In that concert our souls would at once take their part.

3. The sun and moon, as joint rulers of day and night, are paired in praise: the one is the complement of the other, and so they are closely associated in the summons to worship. There is a perpetual adoration of the Lord in the skies: it varies with night and day, but it ever continues while sun and moon endure. There is ever a lamp burning before the high altar of the Lord. Nor are the greater luminaries allowed to drown with their floods of light the glory of the lesser brilliants, for all the stars are bidden to the banquet of praise. Their light is praise in a visible form. Light is song glittering before the eye instead of resounding in the ear. Christians without light rob the Lord of his glory. However small our beam, we must not hide it: if we cannot be sun or moon we must aim to be one of the **stars of light,** and our every twinkling must be to the honor of our Lord.

4. Praise him, ye heavens of heavens. By these means are meant those regions which are heavens to those who dwell in our heavens; or those most heavenly of abodes where the most choice spirits dwell. As the highest of the highest, so the best of the best are to praise the Lord. There can be none so great and high as to be above praising Jehovah. **And ye waters that be above the heavens.** Let the clouds roll up the volumes of adoration. Let the sea above roar at the presence of Jehovah, the God of Israel. There is something of mystery about these supposed reservoirs of water; but let them be what they may, they shall give glory to the Lord our God. Let the most unknown and perplexing phenomena take up their parts in the universal praise.

5. The Maker should have honor from his works; they should tell forth *his* character by *their* praise; and thus they should praise his **name** – by which his character is intended. The name of Jehovah is written legibly upon his works, so that his power, wisdom, goodness, and other attributes are therein made manifest to thoughtful people, and thus his name is praised. The highest praise of God is to declare what he is. We can invent nothing which would magnify the Lord: we can never extol him better than by repeating his name, or describing his character. The Lord is to be extolled as creating all things that exist, and as doing so by the simple agency of his word. He created by a command; what a power is this! Well may he expect those to praise him who owe their being to him. Evolution may be atheistic, but the doctrine of creation logically demands worship; and hence, as the tree is known by its fruit, it proves itself to be true. Those who were created by command are under command to adore their Creator. The voice which said, "Let them be," now says, "Let them praise."

6. **He hath also stablished them for ever and ever.** The continued existence of celestial beings is due to the supporting might of Jehovah, and to that alone. They do not fail because the Lord does not fail them. Without his will these things cannot alter; he has impressed upon them laws which only he himself can change. Therefore ought the Lord to be praised because he is Preserver as well as Creator, Ruler as well as Maker. **He hath made a decree which shall not pass.** The heavenly bodies are ruled by Jehovah's decree: they cannot pass his limit, or trespass against his law. His rule and ordination can never be changed except by himself, and in this sense his decree **shall not pass.** Moreover, the highest and most wonderful of creatures are perfectly obedient to the statutes of the great King, and thus his decree is not passed over. This submission to law is praise. His almighty power upholds all things in their spheres, securing the march of stars and the flight of seraphs; and thus the music of the upper regions is never marred by discord, nor interrupted by destruction. The eternal hymn is forever chanted; even the solemn silence of the spheres is a perpetual psalm.

7. **Praise the Lord from the earth.** The song descends to our abode, and so comes nearer home to us. We who are "bodies terrestrial" are to pour out our portion of praise. Jehovah is to be praised not only *in* the earth from *from* the

earth, as if the adoration ran over from this planet into the general accumulation of worship. In the first verse the song was "from the heavens"; here it is "from the earth": songs coming down from heaven are to blend with those going up from earth. The **earth** here meant is our entire globe of land and water. **Ye dragons, and all deeps.** It would be idle to inquire what special sea-monsters are here meant; but we believe all of them are intended, and the places where they abide are indicated by **all deeps.** Terrible beasts or fishes, whether they roam the earth or swim the seas, are bidden to the feast of praise.

8. Fire and hail. Lightning and hailstones go together. In the plagues of Egypt they cooperated in making Jehovah known in all the terrors of his power. Fire and ice-morsels are a contrast in nature, but they are combined in magnifying the Lord. **Snow, and vapors.** Offsprings of cold, or creations of heat, are to be equally consecrated to his praise. **Stormy wind fulfilling his word.** Though rushing with incalculable fury, the storm-wind is still under law, and moves in assigned order, to carry out the designs of God. It is a grand orchestra which contains such wind-instruments as these!

9. Mountains, and all hills. Towering steeps and swelling knolls alike declare their Creator. **All hills** are to be consecrated: we have no longer Ebal and Gerizim, the hill of the curse and the hill of the blessing, but all are to rejoice in the name of the Lord. **Fruitful trees, and all cedars.** Fruit trees and forest trees are equally full of benevolent design, and alike subserve some purpose of love; therefore for all and by all let the great Designer be praised. Varieties in the landscape are produced by the rising and falling of the soil, and by the many kinds of trees which adorn the land: yet all, and all alike, glorify their one Lord. When the trees clap their hands in the wind, or their leaves rustle, they sing out unto the Lord.

10. Beasts, and all cattle. Animals fierce or tame; wild beats and domestic cattle; let all these show forth the praises of Jehovah. Those are worse than beasts who do not praise our God. **Creeping things, and flying fowl.** The multitudes that throng the earth and the air; insects of every form and birds of every wing are called upon to join the universal worship. No one can become familiar with insect and bird life without feeling that they constitute a wonderful chapter in the history of divine worship. The minute insect marvelously proclaims the Lord's handiwork: when placed under the microscope it tells a wondrous tale. So, too, the bird which soars aloft displays in its adaptation for an aerial life an amount of skill which our balloonists have in vain attempted to emulate. True devotion not only hears the praises of God in the sweet song of feathered minstrels, but even discovers it in the croaking from the marsh, or in the buzz of "the blue fly which singeth in the window-pane." More base than reptiles, more insignificant than insects, are songless people.

11. Now the poet has reached our own race, and very justly he would have rulers and subjects, chieftains and magistrates, unite in worshiping the sovereign Lord of all. Monarchs must not disdain to sing, nor must their people refrain from uniting with them. Those who lead in battle and those who decide in courts must neither of them allow their vocations to keep them from reverently adoring the Chief and Judge of all. All people, and all judges, must praise the Lord of all. Let us pray that the song of the psalmist may be realized in fact.

12. Both sexes and all ages are summoned to the blessed service of song. Those who usually make merry together are to be devoutly joyful together; those who make up the ends of families, that is to say, the elders and the juveniles, should make the Lord their one and only end. Old men should by their experience teach children to praise; and children by their cheerfulness should excite old men to song. None can be dispensed with: all parts of creation must take their parts in devotion.

13. Let them praise the name of the LORD. All that is contained in the name or character of Jehovah is worthy of praise, and all the objects of his creating care will be too few to set it forth in its completeness. **For his name alone is excellent.** It alone deserves to be exalted in praise, for alone it is exalted in worth. There is none like unto the Lord, none that for a moment can be compared unto him. His unique name should have a monopoly of praise. **His glory is above the earth and heaven**; it is therefore alone because it surpasses all others.

14. He also exalteth the horn of his people. He has made them strong, famous, and victorious. His goodness to all his creatures does not prevent his having a special favor to his chosen nation: he is good to all, but he is God to his people. He lifts up the down-trodden, but he in an especial manner lifts up his people. When they are brought low he raises up a horn for them by sending them a deliverer; when they are in conflict he gives them courage and strength, so that they lift up their horn amid the fray; and when all is peaceful around them, he fills their horn with plenty, and they lift it up with delight. **The praise of all his saints.** He is their glory: to him they render praise; and he by his mercy to them evermore gives them further reasons for praise, and higher motives for adoration. He lifts up their horn, and they lift up his praise. He is their God, and they are his saints; he makes them blessed, and they bless him in return. **Even the children of Israel.** The Lord knows them that are his. He knows the name of him with whom he made a covenant, and how he came by that name, and who his children are, and where they are. All nations are bidden in verse 11 to praise the Lord; but here the call is especially addressed to his elect people, who know him beyond all others. Those who are children of privilege should be children of praise. **A people near unto him,** near by kin and by care. This is true even more emphatically of the spiritual Israel. This nearness should prompt us to perpetual adoration. The Lord's elect are the children of his love, and therefore they are bound beyond all others to be filled with reverence for him, and delight in him. **Praise ye the LORD.**

Psalm 149

1. Praise ye the LORD. Specially you, chosen people, whom he has made to be his saints. With renewed zeal and fresh delight lift up your song unto Jehovah. **Sing unto the LORD a new song.** Sing, for it is the fittest method for expressing reverent praise. Sing a hymn newly composed, for you have now a new knowledge of God. He is ever new in his manifestations; his mercies are new every morning; his deliverances are new in every night of sorrow; let your gratitude and thanksgivings be new also. It is well to repeat the old; it is more useful to invent the new. Our singing should be **unto the LORD**; the songs we sing should be of him and to him, "for of him, and to him, and through him are all things." Among our novelties there should be new songs; alas, people are fonder of making new complaints than new psalms. Our new songs should be devised in Jehovah's honor; indeed all our newest thoughts should run towards him. Never can we find a nobler subject for a song than the Lord, nor one more full of fresh matter for a new song, nor one which we are personally so much bound to sing as a new song "unto the Lord." **And his praise in the congregation of saints.** God is in the midst of saints, and because of this we may well long to be among them. They are so full of his praise that we feel at home among them when we are ourselves full of praise. The sanctuary is the house of praise as well as the house of prayer. All saints praise God: they would not be saints if they did not. Personal praise is sweet unto God, but congregated praise has a multiplicity of sweetnesses in it. Saints do not gather to amuse themselves with music, nor to extol one another, but to sing his praise whose saints they are. A congregation of saints is heaven upon earth. Yet at times even saintly conclaves need to be stirred up to thanksgiving; for saints may be sad and apprehensive, and then their spirits require to be stimulated to happier worship.

2. Let Israel rejoice in him that made him. Here is that new creation which calls for the new song. It was Jehovah who made Israel to be Israel, and the tribes to become a great nation: therefore let the Founder of the nation be had in perpetual honor. Joy and rejoicing are evidently to be the special characteristics of the new song. The religion of the dead in sin is more apt to chant dirges than to sing hallelujahs; but when we are made new in the spirit of our minds we rejoice in him that made us. **Let the children of Zion be joyful in their King.** Those who had seen the tribes formed into a settled kingdom as well as into a united nation should rejoice. Israel is the nation, Zion is the capital of the kingdom: Israel rejoices in her Maker, Zion in her King. In the case of our God we who believe in him are as glad of his government as we are of his creation: his reign is as truly the making of us as was his divine power. The children of Israel are happy to be made a people; the children of Zion are equally happy to be ruled as a people. In every way our God is the source of joy to us:

this verse issues a permit to our joy; it lays an injunction upon us to be glad in the Lord.

3. Let them repeat the triumph of the Red Sea, which was ever the typical glory of Israel. Miriam led the daughters of Israel in the dance when the Lord had triumphed gloriously. The sacred dance of devout joy is no example, nor even excuse, for frivolous dances, much less for lewd ones. Who could help dancing when Egypt was vanquished, and the tribes were free? Every mode of expressing delight was bound to be employed on so memorable an occasion. Dancing, singing, and playing on instruments were all called into requisition, and most fitly so. There are unusual seasons which call for unusual expressions of joy. When the Lord saves a soul its holy joy overflows, and it cannot find channels enough for its exceeding gratitude: if the man does not leap, or play, or sing, at any rate he praises God, and wishes for a thousand tongues with which to magnify his Saviour. Who would wish it to be otherwise? Young converts are not to be restrained in their joy. Let them sing and dance while they can. How can they mourn now that their Bridegroom is with them? Let us give the utmost liberty to joy. Let us never attempt its suppression, but issue in the terms of this verse a double license for exultation. If any ought to be glad it is the children of Zion; rejoicing is more fit for Israel than for any other people: it is their own folly and fault that they are not oftener brimming with joy in God, for the very thought of him is delight.

4. For the LORD taketh pleasure in his people. Therefore they should take pleasure in him. If our joy be pleasing to him let us make it full. What condescension is this on Jehovah's part, to notice, to love, and to delight in his chosen! Surely there is nothing in our persons, or our actions, which could cause pleasure to the Ever-blessed One, were it not that he condescends to people of low estate. The thought of the Lord's taking pleasure in us is a mine of joy never to be exhausted. **He will beautify the meek with salvation.** They are humble, and feel their need of salvation; he is gracious, and bestows it upon them. They lament their deformity, and he puts a beauty upon them of the choicest sort. He saves them by sanctifying them, and thus they wear the beauty of holiness, and the beauty of a joy which springs out of full salvation. He makes his people meek, and then makes the meek beautiful. Herein is grand argument for worshiping the Lord with the utmost exultation: he who takes such a pleasure in us must be approached with exceeding joy.

God takes pleasure in all his children as Jacob loved all his sons; but the meek are his Josephs, and upon these he puts the coat of many colors, beautifying them with peace, content, joy, holiness, and influence. A meek and quiet spirit is called "an ornament," and certainly it is "the beauty of holiness." When God himself beautifies someone, that person becomes beautiful indeed and beautiful forever.

The verse may be read, "He shall beautify the meek with salvation," or "He shall beautify the afflicted with deliverance," or "He shall beautify the meek with victory"; each of these readings gives a new shade of meaning, well worthy of quiet consideration and joyful adoration.

5. Let the saints be joyful in glory. God has honored them, and put a rare glory upon them; therefore let them exult therein. Shall those to whom God is their glory be cast down and troubled? No, let their joy proclaim their honorable estate. **Let them sing aloud upon their beds.** Their exultation should express itself in shouts and songs, for it is not a feeling of which they have any need to be ashamed. Even in their quietest retreats let them burst into song; when no one hears them, let them sing aloud unto God. If confined by sickness let them joy in God. In the night watches let them not lie awake and weep, but like nightingales let them charm the midnight hours. Their shouts are not now for the battlefield, but for the places of their rest: they can peacefully lie down and yet enjoy the victory with which the Lord has beautified them. Without fighting, faith wins and sings the victory. What a blessing to have our beds made into thrones, and our retirements turned into triumphs!

6. It seems they are not always on their beds, but are ready for deeds of prowess. When called to fight, the meek are very hard to overcome; they are just as steady in conflict as they are steadfast in patience. Besides, their way of fighting is of an extraordinary sort, for they sing to God but keep their swords in their hands. They can do two things at a time: if they do not wield the trowel and the sword, at least they sing and strike. In this Israel was not an example, but a type: we will not copy the chosen people in making literal war, but we will fulfill the emblem by carrying on spiritual war. We praise God and contend with our corruptions; we sing joyfully and war earnestly with evil of every kind. Our weapons are not carnal, but they are mighty. The Word of God is all edge; whichever way we turn it, it strikes deadly blows at falsehood and wickedness. If we do not praise we shall grow sad in our song. The verse indicates a happy blending of chorister and crusader.

Note how each thing in the believer is emphatic: if he sings, it is high praises, and praises deep down in his throat, as the original has it; and if he fights, the sword is two-edged. The living God imparts vigorous life to those who trust him: people both hear them and feel them. Quiet is their spirit, but in that very quietude abides the thunder of an irresistible force. When godly people give battle to the powers of evil each conflict is high praise unto the God of goodness. Even the tumult of our holy war is a part of the music of our lives.

7. Israel when they came into Canaan fulfilled the righteous sentence of the Lord upon guilty nations. At this hour, under the gentler dispensation of grace, we wrestle not with flesh and blood; yet is our warfare none the less stern, and our victory none the less sure. All evil will eventually be overthrown: the Lord will display his justice against evildoers, and in that warfare his servants will play their parts. The saints will judge the world. Both the conflict and the victory at the end of it will cause glory to God, and honor to his holy ones.

8. Thus are the greatest enemies of Jehovah and his people reduced to shame, rendered helpless, and themselves punished. This was Israel's boast in actual fact; it is ours spiritually. The chief powers of evil will be restrained and ultimately destroyed. Those who made captives of the godly will themselves be made captive. The powers of evil cannot bind *our* King, but by his power *their* king will be bound with a great chain, and shut up in the bottomless pit, that he may at length be trodden under the feet of saints.

9. To execute upon them the judgment written. Israel as a nation had this to do, and did it, and then they rejoiced in the God who gave success to their arms. *We* praise our God after another fashion; we are not executioners of justice, but heralds of mercy. It would be a sad thing for anyone to misuse this text: lest any warlike believer should be led to do so, we would remind them that the execution must not go beyond the sentence and warrant; and we have received no warrant of execution against our fellow-men. Christians have no commission of vengeance; it is theirs to execute the command of mercy, and that alone. **This honor have all his saints.** All the godly shared in the triumphs of the Lord when he smote Israel's foes. *We* have like honor, but it is shown in victories of another sort. All the holy ones are sent upon errands by their holy Lord. The honors described in this psalm are common to all the family of grace; and such service as the Lord appoints is to be undertaken by every one of them, without exception. The Lord honors all his chosen here, and he will glorify them all hereafter: this rule is without exception. Surely in this we have the best argument for glorifying the Lord, wherefore we close our new song with another Hallelujah, **Praise ye the LORD.**

Psalm 150

1. Praise ye the LORD. Hallelujah! The exhortation is to all things in earth or in heaven. Should they not all declare the glory of him for whose glory they are, and were created? Jehovah, the one God, should be the one object of adoration. To give the least particle of his honor to another is shameful treason; to refuse to render it to him is heartless robbery. **Praise God in his sanctuary.** Praise El, or "the strong one," in his holy place. See how power is mentioned with holiness in this change of names. Praise begins at home. "In God's own house pronounce his praise." The holy place should be filled with praise, just as of old the high priest filled the Holy of Holies with the smoke of sweet-smelling incense. In his church below and in his courts above hallelujahs should be continually presented. In the person of Jesus God finds a holy dwelling or sanctuary, and there he is greatly to be praised. He may also be said to dwell in holiness, for all his ways are right and good; for this we ought to extol him with heart and voice. Whenever we assemble for holy purposes our main work should be to present praises unto the Lord our God. **Praise him in the firmament of his power.** It is a blessed thing that in our God holiness and power are united. Power without righteousness would be too weak for usefulness; but put the two together in an infinite degree and we have God. What an expanse we have in the boundless firmament of divine power! Let it all be filled with praise. Let the heavens, so great and strong, echo with the praise of the thrice holy Jehovah, while the sanctuaries of earth magnify the Almighty.

2. **Praise him for his mighty acts.** Here is a reason for praise. In these deeds of power we see himself. These doings of his omnipotence are always on behalf of truth and righteousness. His works of creation, providence, and redemption all call for praise; they are his acts, and his acts of might; therefore let him be praised for them. **Praise him according to his excellent greatness.** His being is unlimited, and his praise should correspond therewith. He possesses a multitude or a plenitude of greatness, and therefore he should be greatly praised. There is nothing little about God, and there is nothing great apart from him. If we were always careful to make our worship fit and appropriate for our great Lord how much better should we sing! How much more reverently should we adore! Such excellent deeds should have excellent praise.

3. **Praise him with the sound of the trumpet.** With the loudest, clearest note call the people together. Make everyone know that we are not ashamed to worship. Summon them with unmistakable sound to bow before their God. The sound of trumpet is associated with the grandest and most solemn events, such as the giving of the law, the proclamation of Jubilee, the coronation of Jewish kings, and the raging of war. It is to be thought of in reference to the coming of our Lord in his second advent and the raising of the dead. If we cannot give voice to this martial instrument, at least let our reference to the coming of our Lord in his second advent and the raising of praise be as decided and bold as if we could give a blast upon the horn. Let us never sound a trumpet before us to our own honor, but reserve all our trumpeting for God's glory. When the people have been gathered by blast of trumpet, then proceed to **praise him with the psaltery and harp.** Stringed instruments are to be used as well as those which are rendered vocal by wind. Dulcet notes are to be consecrated as well as more startling sounds. The Gospel meaning is that all powers and faculties should praise the Lord – all sorts of persons, under all circumstances, and with differing constitutions, should do honor unto the Lord of all. If there be any virtue, if there by any talent, if there be any influence, let all be consecrated to the service of the universal Benefactor. Harp and lyre – the choicest, the sweetest – must be all our Lord's.

4. **Praise him with the timbrel and dance.** Associated with the deliverance at the Red Sea, this form of worship set forth the most jubilant and exultant of

worship. The hands and the feet were both employed, and the entire body moved in sympathy with the members. Are there not periods of life when we feel so glad that we would dance for joy? Let not such exhilaration be spent upon common themes, but let the name of God stir us to ecstasy. There is enough in our holy faith to create and to justify the utmost degree of rapturous delight. If people are dull in the worship of the Lord our God they are not acting consistently with the character of their religion. **Praise him with stringed instruments and organs.** We have here the three kinds of musical instruments: timbrels, which are struck, and strings, and pipes: all may be sanctified to highest uses. Many people, many minds, and these as different as strings and pipes; but there is only one God, and that one God all should worship. The word translated **organs** signifies pipe – a simpler form of wind instrument than the more modern and more elaborate organ. Doubtless many a pious shepherd has poured out gracious pastorals from a reed or oaten pipe, and so has magnified his God.

5. Let the clash of the loudest music be the Lord's: let the joyful clang of the loftiest notes be all for him. Praise has beaten the timbrel, swept the harp, and sounded the trumpet, and now for a last effort, awakening the most heavy of slumberers, and startling the most indifferent of onlookers, she dashes together the disks of brass, and with sounds both loud and high proclaims the glories of the Lord.

6. Let everything that hath breath praise the LORD. "Let all breath praise him": that is to say, all living things. He gave them breath – let them breathe his praise. His name is in the Hebrew composed rather of breathings than of letters, to show that all breath comes from him: therefore let it be used for him. Join, all living things, in the eternal song. Least or greatest, withhold not your praises. What a day will it be when all things in all places unite to glorify the one only living and true God! This will be the final triumph of the church of God.

Praise ye the LORD. Once more, Hallelujah! Thus is the psalm rounded with the note of praise; and thus is the Book of Psalms ended by a glowing word of adoration. Hallelujah!